Oliver K. Olson

MATTHIAS FLACIUS AND THE SURVIVAL OF LUTHER'S REFORM

Second Edition with Corrections

Lutheran Press · Minneapolis 2011

Matthias Flacius. Portrait by Nicolas Haublin. Herzog August Bibliothek.

CERTO STATUUNT

POST OBITUM SANCTISSIMI ORGANI D. MARTINI LUTHERI

QUI SE TAM EXCELSO ANIMO AC FORTITER

FURORIBUS DIABOLI COMPLURIBUS OPPONERET

ATQUE IPSE FECIT HACTENUS ET ADHUC FACIT

POSTHABITIS FAMA, OPIBUS, FORTUNISQUE OMNIBUS

FUISSE NEMINEM

Printed by Lutheran Press
Minneapolis, MN 55432
© 2011 by Lutheran Press
All rights reserved.
Printed in the United States of America.

Originally appearing as Vol. 20, Wolfenbütteler Abhandlungen
zur Renaissanceforschung 2002

Licensed edition with permission from Herzog August Bibliothek
Wolfenbüttel
(c) Herzog August Bibliothek Wolfenbüttel 2009

ISBN-13:   978-0-9845351-0-1

Library of Congress Control Number: 2011923556

·

General Editor, Paul Strawn
Technical Editor, Scott Krieger
Cover Revision, Roxanne Nelson

CONTENTS

PART THREE. MAGDEBURG

ABBREVIATIONS

ADB	*Allgemeine Deutsche Biographie.* Leipzig 1875–1912. Reprint, Berlin, 1968.
ARG	Archiv für Reformationsgeschichte/Archive for Reformation History
Bibl 1896-1893	Viktor Bibl. "Der Briefwechsel zwischen Flacius und Nidbruck. Aus den Handschriften 9737 b, i und k aus der k.u.k. Hofbibliothek in Wien." JGGPO XVII(1896) 1–24; XVIII (1897) 201–238; XIX (1898) 96–110; XX (1899) 83–116.
Bericht 1559.	Matthias Flacius. *Bericht von etlichen Artikeln der christlichen Lehr und von seinem Leben, und endlich auch von den Adiaphorischen Handlungen, wider die falschen Geticht der Adiaphoristen.* [Jena: Thomas Rebart] 1559.
Bindseil	Heinrich Ernst Bindseil. *Philippi Melanchthonis epistolae, iudicia, consilia, testimonia aliorumque ad eum epistolae quae in Corpore Reformatorum desiderantur.* Halle Saxonum: Gustav Schwetschke, 1874. Reprint, Hildesheim and New York: Olds, 1975
BSELK	*Die Bekenntnisschriften der evangelisch-lutherischen Kirche.* 6. ed. Göttingen, 1967.
Catalogus 1556, 1562	Matthias Flacius. *Catalogus Testium Veritatis, qui ante nostram aetatem reclamarunt Papae.* Basel: Oporinus, 1556. *Catalogus Testium Veritatis, qui ante nostram aetatem Pontifici Romano, eiusque erroribus clamarunt; iam denuo longe quam antea, & emendatior & auctorior editus.* Strassburg: Paul Messerschmidt, 1562.
Clemen KS	Otto Clemen. *Kleine Schriften zur Reformations Geschichte,* 1897–1944. 8 vols. ed. by Ernst Koch. Leipzig: Zentralantiquariat der DDR, 1982ff.
Cod. Guelf.	Codex Guelferbytanus, Herzog August Bibliothek Wolfenbüttel
CR	*Corpus Reformatorum*
CS	*Corpus Schwenckfeldianorum*
DB	*Dänische Bibliothec oder Sammlung von Alten und Neuen Gelehrten Sachen aus Dännemark.* Copenhagen and Leipzig.
FS	*Fortgesetzte Sammlung von Alten und Neuen Theologischen Sachen.*
HAB	Herzog August Bibliothek Wolfenbüttel
JGGPO	*Jahrbuch der Gesellschaft für die Geschichte der Protestantismus in Oesterreich.*
LW	*Luther's Works* (American Edition) ed. by Jaroslav Pelikan et al. 55 vols. St. Louis: Concordia, 1958–1976.
MBW	*Melanchthons Briefwechsel.* Stuttgart-Bad Cannstatt: Froman-Holzboog, 1977–

MGH	*Monumenta Germaniae Historica*
PG	*Patrologia Graeca*
PL	*Patrologia Latina.*
PKMS	*Politische Korrespondenz des Herzogs und Kurfürsten Moritz von Sachsen.* Johannes Herrmann and Günther Wartenburg, eds. [Abhandlungen der Sächsischen Akademie der Wissenschaften zu Leipzig, Philologisch-historische Klasse Bd. 72 IV Bd. 16. Mai–8.Januar 1551]. Berlin: Akademie Verlag, 1551.
RE2,3	*Realencyclopädie für protestantische Theologie und Kirche.* 2nd and 3rd editions.
Sammlung	*Sammlung von Alten und Neuen*
Tappert	*The Book of Concord. The Confessions of the Evangelical Lutheran Church.* Theodore Tappert, ed. Philadelphia: Fortress Press, 1958.
TSK	*Theologische Studien und Kritiken*
UN	*Unschuldige Nachrichten*
WA	*Weimarer Ausgabe. (D. Martin Luthers Werke, Kritische Gesamtausgabe).* Weimar, 1883 ff.
WAB	*WA, Reihe Briefwechsel.* Weimar 1906–1961
ZKG	*Zeitschrift für Kirchengeschichte*

INTRODUCTION

In 1547 Emperor Charles V won his war against the Germans and began "teaching them Spanish." Followed by priests to reconsecrate churches, his troops grimly set about transforming the Holy Roman Empire into a universal Hapsburg monarchy. Luther's reform was consigned to history.

Then, unexpectedly, princely rebels reversed the political verdict of the war, and the Reformation was saved. The credit is sometimes given alone to the leader of the rebellion, Elector Maurice of Saxony. "It is to him almost exclusively that thanks should be given for the public recognition of Protestantism in the empire."[1] But Maurice, known to his subjects as the "Judas of Meißen," was an opportunist Renaissance prince, hardly hampered by religious conviction. Weighing the political realities, he had concluded that the threat from the imperial government was less dangerous than the threat of sedition by restive Saxon Lutherans. Inciting the dissatisfaction, and therefore moving Maurice to action, was a young Croat, Matthias Flacius, "totally fire and flame." "If Luther's work was saved in those days," wrote Gustav Kawerau, "it was in a special way due to Flacius."[2]

This book is an account of how he did it. It follows him to 1557, when the Reformation could no longer be halted by unity-minded princes. The generous notes are meant to ease future Flacian studies. *Sub conditione Jacobi*, a second volume will follow: *Matthias Flacius and the Struggle for the Freedom of the Church.*

It is also a book about what he wrote. When the military and political basis for the Evangelical church – which he had done so much to lay – was secured, Flacius chose two tasks. First, preparing a church history and, second, providing assistance to interpreters of the Bible. For completing the one, he is remembered as the Father of Church History; for completing the other, he is remembered as the Father of Hermeneutics, of both the theological and philosophical varieties.

He conceived and planned the folio volumes of the Magdeburg Centuries, the first comprehensive church history since Eusebius' in the fourth century. Together with his *Catalogus Testium Veritatis*, it replaced the fanciful lives of the saints with accurate documentation, using primary sources. "He is the true founder," wrote Marc Fumaroli, "of the critical history of the Middle Ages."[3] "Protestant historiography was occasioned by the Interim," wrote Adolf von Harnack, "and Flacius is the Father."[4] "English Church History, too," testifies Eduard Fueter, "has to thank the Magdeburg theologian for its foundation."[5]

1 Wilhelm Maurenbrecher. "Kurfürst Moritz von Sachsen." *Studien und Skizzen zur Geschichte der Reformation.* Leipzig: Wilhelm Grunow, 1874. 140.
2 "Matthias Flacius." RE3, VI, 83.
3 "Aux origines de la conaissance historique du Moyen Age: Humanisme, Réforme et Gallicanisme au XVIe Siècle." *XVII Siècle* CXIV– CXV (1977). 8.
4 *Lehrbuch der Dogmengeschichte*, 3. Aufl. Freiburg and Leipzig: J. C. B. Mohr (Paul Siebeck) I, 1894. 28n.
5 *Geschichte der Neueren Historiographie.* Munich and Berlin: R. Oldenbourg, 1936. 254.

6 Donald R. Kelley. "The Theory of History." *Cambridge History of Renaissance Philosophy.* Cambridge: Cambridge University Press, 1988. 755.

7 *Renaissance Humanism. Foundations, Form and Legacy.* Philadelphia: University of Pennsylvania Press, 1988. 286.

8 Bernhard Bischoff. "Über mittelalterliche Handschriften in Wolfen-büttel." Paul Raabe (ed.). *400 Jahre Bibliothek zu Wolfenbüttel. Reden-Vorträge-Berichte aus dem Festjahr 1972.* Frankfurt am Main: Vittorio Klostermann, 1973. 97.

9 Wolfgang Milde. "The Library at Wolfenbüttel from 1550 to 1618." *The Modern Language Review* LXVI (1971). 104.

10 Heinrich Schneider. *Beiträge zur Geschichte der Universitätsbibliothek Helmstedt.* Helmstedt: J. C. Schmidt, 1934. 34.

11 Ronald Diener. "The Magdeburg Centuries: A Bibliothecal and Historiographical Analysis." Diss., Harvard Divinity School, 1978. 359.

12 Deborah K. Shuger. *Sacred Rhetoric. The Christian Style in the English Renaissance.* Princeton: Princeton University Press, 1988. 169.

13 Kurt Hannemann. "Der Humanist Georg Fabricius in Meissen, das Luthermonotessaron in Wittenberg und Leipzig und der Heliand-praefatiokodex aus Naumburg a. d. Saale." *Filologia Germanica* XII (1774). 78.

14 Adolf Herte. "Matthias Flacius." *Lexikon für Theologie und Kirche,* 2nd. ed. Freiburg: Herder, 1932. IV, col. 27.

15 "Flacius – Radikale Theologie." *Matthias Flacius Illyricus, 1575-1975.* Regensburg: Lassleben, 1975. 40.

16 Gustav Frank. Review of Wilhelm Preger, *Matthias Flacius Illyricus und seine Zeit.* 2 vols. (Erlangen: Theodor Bläsing, 1859–1861). *Protestantische Kirchenzeitung für das Evangelische Deutschland* XXVI (1859). 772.

For interpreters of Holy Scripture he prepared the *Clavis Scripturae Sacrae,* known to generations of grateful pastors as "the golden key." It was by writing the *Clavis* that he invented a new academic discipline. "Flacius also laid down the rules – indeed, founded the modern tradition – of historical hermeneutics, later celebrated and carried on by Schleiermacher, Dilthey and Gadamer."[6]

Albert Rabil, Jr. reports that Flacius left behind "work of such scholarly and humanist breadth as surpassed the frontiers of purely religious activity."[7] His part in rescuing the medieval heritage has often been recognized. "He rescued much from libraries which would in the meanwhile have been ruined"[8]; he also assembled "the most significant collection of printed and hand-written texts to be found in the hands of any private individual in the Germany of that time"[9]; Flacius' own collection of books and manuscripts "can hardly be overestimated"[10]; he was "one of the brightest and strongest bibliophiles of all time."[11]

Deborah Shuger calls his *Clavis Scripturae Sacrae* the fullest statement of an anti-Ciceronian "grand style" of sacred rhetoric.[12] He had a hand in the development of secular political theory, ecclesiastical polity – even the English novel. According to Kurt Hannemann, he was the equal of humanist Beatus Rhenanus[13]. One standard lexicon calls him "one of the greatest scholars of his time."[14] Since the German idiom permits comparing men to diamonds, Jörg Baur was able to say of Flacius that "history does not offer humanity too many figures of an equal number of carats."[15]

His polemical writings, meanwhile, in the second Reformation generation, served the church doctrinally as a "principle of stability."[16] As a theologian, one source ranks Flacius "directly beside Erasmus and Melanchthon"[17]; Ignaz von Döllinger thought him superior to most theologians of his time, Melanchthon included.[18] If Luther's theological legacy was saved after the Reformer's death from creative rivals, that, too, in a special way was due to Flacius.

In Croatia, where the Counter-Reformation destroyed the memory of the Reformation, Flacius was recalled to mind by the 1938 monograph, – the first of three biographies– by Mijo Mirković,[19] who had discovered his countryman while studying economics in Berlin. Flacius would have been pleased that Mirković succeeded in making his publications required reading in their common native land.

> Flacius' work, also in more recent times, must be counted among those obligatory texts of Croatian *Geistesgeschichte,* through which the self-understanding of the Croatian people as a cultural community is constituted, interpreted, and thereby further developed.[20]

The passionate theologian would have been less pleased that, with the exception of a dissertation by Ante Bilokapić,[21] his countrymen's interest in him[22] is secular. It began with Mirković, who saw history from a Marxist perspective, in which religious palaver masks more important economic and historical forces. Since for Mircović, servility toward Rome was a profound evil in Croatian history, international Communism presented an opportunity for his countrymen like that once offered by international Lutheranism:

> The essential thing was whether the Croats would accept and appropriate the progressive and modern ideas which were in the world, and from them to create their own culture. Everything depended on it, as it also did then.[23]

After the Communist takeover, now in agreement with the reigning ideology, and with state support, Mirković published another edition of his biography, in which Flacius was made to play a part in the new "scientific socialist" interpretation of the Croatian past. He subjected Flacius' theological positions, which he considered static, conservative, and counter-revolutionary, to correction on the basis of Marxist "historical principle," "historical perspective," "independence of scientific cognition," and "the positive dialectical influence on science."[24] For him, Wittenberg was a metaphor for Moscow, Croatian Protestantism a metaphor for leftist liberalism, and Flacius a cultural revolutionary. Writing a biography of Flacius was a way of recommending Marxism.

Mirković admired Flacius because he "followed wherever truth drove him" – ubi iacet veritas.[25] Flacius' responsibility, of course, was the same as for any other Christian teachers: to distinguish the Christian faith from what it is not. That in carrying out that responsibility he incited controversies that many of his contemporaries did not appreciate, can be laid to his ability to detect subtle threats to the Christian faith that others missed.

The late Arthur Carl Piepkorn of Concordia Seminary, St. Louis, once observed to me that Flacius had been a regrettable role-model for American seminarians – as a nay-sayer. If Piepkorn's reproach has merit, it is because his students had read Gerhard Friedrich Bente's narrative about Flacius' steadfastness in his survey of the period leading to the 1577 Formula of Concord.[26] As an introduction to a large volume, Bente's essay was necessarily summary. Perhaps a more detailed narrative can introduce evidence that Flacius is not a satisfactory model for the narrow-minded.

> ... the relentless combatant as a theologian did not aim to break with education and culture. As a radical he aimed not for isolation, but the rooting of theological work in language and history. Right theology and barbarism cancel each other out.[27]

In Austria, to all appearances, the Counter-Reformation won a complete victory. Flacius' "great achievement," however, according to Willy Hoppe, "could not be shaken essentially even by the great Jesuits."[28] Evidence of the solid foundations he laid there is supplied by Bishop Oskar Sakrausky.

> Today, nothing more is known about his importance for Protestantism in Styria, Carinthia and Carniola. But still, there are connections that cannot be denied between the congregations of the latter sixteenth century influenced by Flacius and their revival after 150 years of clandestine existence. After the publication of the Tolerance Patent in 1871, precisely there in Inner Austria, where such congregations existed at the end of the sixteenth century, suddenly whole congregations appeared, and arose to light out of the underground.[29]

17 Johannes Ficker and Otto Winckelmann. *Handschriftenproben des sechzehnten Jahrhunderts*. Straßburg: Karl J. Tübner, 1905. II, Nr. 95.

18 Johann Joseph Ignaz von Döllinger. *Die Reformation, ihre innere Entwicklung und ihre Wirkungen im Umfange des Lutherischen Bekenntnisses*. Arnheim: Josue Witz, I, 1853. 407; II, 1854. 233.

19 *Flacius*. Zagreb: Hrvatska naklada, 1938. Followed by *Matija Vlačić*. Belgrade: Nolit, 1957, and *Matija Vlačić-Ilirik*. Zagreb: Jugoslavenske Akademije Znanosti i Umjetnosti, 1960.

20 Franjo Zenko. "Flacius-Rezeption in Kroatien als ideologisierende Vermittlung mit dem gegenwärtigen Leben." Josip Matešić (ed.). *Matthias Flacius Illyricus – Leben & Werk. Internationales Symposium, Mannheim, Februar 1991*. Munich: Südosteuropa-Gesellschaft, 1993. 171.

21 *Attivitá letteraria di Mattia Flacio Illirico* (Pars dissertationis, Antonianum). Rome, 1981; discussing recent Flacius research, Zenko, 175, sees a return to a theological interpretation, part of a post-Marxist re-interpretation.

22 Editor Josip Bratulić included a bibliography in his edition of Mirković's work, *Matija Vlačić-Ilirik*. I. Pula, Rijeka: 1980. 21 f.

23 Mirković, quoted by Zenko. 160, 165.

24 Ibid. 168 f.

25 Mijo Mirković. *Matija Vlačić-Ilirik*. Zagreb: Jugoslavenske Akademije Znanosti i Umjetnosti, 1960. 256.

26 *Triglot Concordia: The Symbolical Books of the Ev. Lutheran Church*. St. Louis: Concordia, 1921. Historical introduction.

27 J. Baur. Op. cit. 43.

28 "Matthias Flacius." *Biographisches Wörterbuch zur deutschen Geschichte*. Munich: R. Oldenbourg, 1952. 44.

29 Oskar Sakrausky. "Theologische Strömungen in der reformatorischen Literatur der Slowenen und Kroaten." *Abhandlungen über die*

Slowenische Reformation. Munich: Rudolf Trofenik, 1968. 151.

30 Ernst Fedderson. "Philippismus und Luthertum in Dänemark und Schleswig-Holstein." Otto Scheel (ed.). *Festschrift für Hans von Schubert* [ARG Texte und Untersuchungen. Ergänzungsband V]. Leipzig: M. Heinsius Nachfolger, Eger & Sievers, 1929. 92–114.

31 J. Baur. 40.

32 *Speners Kritik am landesherrlichen Kirchenregiment und ihre Vorgeschichte*. Witten: Luther Verlag, 1971. 60 f.

33 "Matthias Flacius Illyricus." *Gestalten der Kirchengeschichte* VI. Stuttgart et al.: Kohlhammer, 1981. 280.

34 *Luther in den Wandlungen seiner Kirche*. Gießen: Töpelmann, 1907. 3.

35 "Matthias Flacius Illyricus." *Lutherische Kirchen in der Welt: Jahrbuch des Martin Luther Bundes* XXII (1975). 12.

36 "Science, Academic Research and the Church." *Origins* XII, Nr. 23 (18th November 1982). 369.

37 "Johannes Paul II.: Vorblick auf das Jubiläumsjahr 2000." *Herder-Korrespondenz* XLVIII (1994). 604.

In contrast, in Schleswig-Holstein, where Melanchthon's party, the Philippists, triumphed and Flacius' party had no influence, the church largely succumbed to rationalism.[30]

At an academic conference in 1975 that honored Flacius as one who attempted to found a university at Regensburg, Jörg Baur observed that discovering Flacius is to take leave of "the legend of a passive Lutheranism, submissive to the state."[31] Bishop Martin Kruse of Berlin writes that Flacius and his colleagues "... made visible in extreme clarity the problems involved in the rule of the church by the government" and "in the circle of the Gnesio-Lutherans its answers have kept alive the suspicion of a church government carried on by absolutist government."[32] Peter Barton considers them a saving remnant.

> That the increasingly depraved Evangelical state-churches of middle and North Germany did not completely lose their credibility in view of government-true mediating theologians and scheming politicians they owed in large part to Flacius and his followers, who were ready to practice church discipline on the secular authority.[33]

Those who call Flacius rigid tend to be the same ones who think of the Reformation as a solely German movement. "Luther," Horst Stephan observed, "was a German to such a degree that almost only the German Evangelical Church could accept him inwardly and grow up on him."[34] But Flacius, a candidate for the title of the successor of Luther, and the most important theological influence on the 1577 Formula of Concord, was noticeably not German. He practiced Italian manners, was mimicked for speaking German with a foreign accent, and was reviled for being *undeutsch*. He thus qualified himself to represent those of us from other parts of the world who revere Luther as a Father of the Church, but are indifferent to the hearty ethnic traits that endear him to Germans.

Max Tratz suggested a corrective: Flacius' life must be understood against the background of his Southern homeland.[35] His steely determination, the alarums he sounded in the North were a counterpoint to the grim thunder in the South. I have attempted, therefore, to take into account his reaction to the Counter-Reformation and the Inquisition in Venice and Istria.

Some murkier periods of history could perhaps conveniently be forgotten for the sake of harmony. But consider the words of Pope John Paul II, who favors remembering. In 1982 at the University of Madrid he admitted that "... moments like that of the Inquisition produced tensions, errors and excesses – facts which the church today evaluates in the objective light of history..."[36] He now hopes that the celebrations of the year 2000 will be "an especially auspicious and providential opportunity" for his church to face the "dark side of its history,"[37] and that Protestants will forgive the "errors and excesses." Genuine rapprochement, of course, cannot take place without a clear knowledge of the past. In order to deal with the current pope's appeals for forgiveness one must know for what forgiveness is being sought.

No biography of Matthias Flacius can be written without investigation of that "dark side." The frequently-expressed opinion that he was mad or irrational is not tenable if one considers his context among the "excesses" of the Counter-Reformation, among them the judicial murder of his mother's cousin.

Having taught among friends at a Jesuit university for more than a decade, I am pleased to pass on a 1975 judgment by Bishop Hermann Dietzfelbinger at the University of Regensburg, who expressed satisfaction that many of the difficulties which divided his Lutherans and the Roman Catholics in Bavaria had been eased. Cautioning that Flacius' controversies are not exact models for contemporary action, he nevertheless recommended that contemporaries study Flacius' life:

> Evangelical Christians and Catholic Christians are not called to account separately for their understanding of the truth. It is precisely in this sense that we as Christendom as a whole, as Catholic and Evangelical Christians, learn something today from Matthias Flacius, something which H.U. von Balthasar once called "action in an emergency": "whoever wants to be sure of his faith and remain in it can do no better than to confess it freely and openly, even when it brings on trouble."[38]

"A Flacian," wrote Nicolaus Selnecker in 1570, "is someone who slanders and condemns Wittenberg and Leipzig."[39] In other words, a partisan. The impression has persisted. Centuries later and degrees calmer, however, Isaak August Dorner noticed that "the decisive factor" in the controversies was "not a conscious partisanship but a concern for the matter itself."[40] I have heeded Peter Barton's observation that to use partisan terms for Flacius and his friends – consistent, gnesio,[41] high, observant, radical, rigid, rigorist, strict, or ultra – is inappropriate in discussing the period before 1560.[42] Whether Flacians were properly thought of as a party after that date is a question that must be left for a second volume.

A summary treatment of such a formidable figure would not do him justice. This study, accordingly, took on large proportions, in spite of my reluctant decision to turn away from great drifts of manuscript Flaciana. I have taken into account some of the more than one hundred printed books and pamphlets lacking in Wilhelm Preger's bibliography. And it seemed worthwhile – to make up for centuries of neglect – to investigate some of his historical influence and the fate of some of the manuscripts he rescued.

More time would have permitted sleuthing to establish the identity of more shadowy people, possible Flacian pseudonymns: Publius Aesquilus, Blasius Arg, Johannes Freyesleben, Carolus Azaraias Gotburgensis, Theodor Henetus, Petrus Henius, Johan Hermann, Petrus Hoppius, Christian Lauterwar, Johannes N., P. Oppius, Petrus Pan (Peter Pan!), Andreas Petri, Hermann Primatus, L. Rhodius, M. Rhodius, M. Theophilus, Johannes Waremundus, Johannes Tullius, and Janus Zymaius all turn out to be Matthias Flacius. The mysterious Peter Arbiter, according to the *Gesamtkatalog der preussischen Bibliotheken*,[43] was Flacius as well, but August Salig reports that he was Pastor at Münchewumburg.[44] Antonius Abbas was not Flacius, but Anton Otto of Nordhausen,[45] and in spite of suspicion,

38 "Matthias Flacius – Ein Zeuge Evangelischer Wahrheit." *Matthias Flacius Illyricus, 1575–1975.* Regensburg: Lassleben, 1975. 16 f.

39 *Christliche unnd notwendige verantwortung auff der Flaccianer Lesterung, so sie auff sein und etliche andere unschüldige Personen in jhren verdechtigen Actis des Colloquij zu Aldenburg, unverschembter weise ausgesprenget haben. Item, Kurtze Antwort auff des Celestini schmehcharten.* Leipzig: Jacob Berwaldt, 1570. D ij r.

40 *Geschichte der protestantischen Theologie*, 2nd printing. Munich: J. G. Cotta, 1867. 335. *History of Protestant Theology.* Edinburgh: T. and T. Clark, 1871. 343.

41 The origin of the term is discussed by Otto Ritschl. *Dogmengeschichte des Protestantismus* II. Leipzig: Hinrichs, 1912. 326n.; W. H. Neuser. *Luther und Melanchthon: Einheit im Gegensatz.* Munich: Christian Kaiser Verlag, 1961. 9.

42 *Um Luthers Erbe. Studien und Texte zur Spätreformation. Tilemann Heshusius (1527–1559).* Witten: Luther Verlag, 1972. 10.

43 VI, 43.

44 Christian Salig. *Vollständige Historie der Augspurgischen Confeßion und derselben Apologie* III. Halle: Rengerische Buchhandlung, 1735. 245, 248.

45 Johannes Seehawer. *Zur Lehre vom Brauch des Gesetzes und zur Geschichte des späteren Antinomismus.* Rostock: Carl Bolet, 1887. 28.

46 Georg Biundo. *Kaspar Aquila. Ein Kämpfer für das Evangelium, in Schwaben und in der Pfalz, in Sachsen und Thüringen.* Grünstadt/Pfalz: Verlag des Vereins für Pfälzische Kirchengeschichte, 1963. 81n. mistakenly makes Aleman and Cunrad pseudonymns of Flacius.

47 *Beiträge zur Entstehungsgeschichte der Magdeburger Centurien.* Niesse: Graveur G. Neumann, 1877. 69.

48 "Der Plan der Magdeburger Zenturien und ihre ungedruckte Reformationsgeschichte." Diss., Heidelberg, 1960.

49 Op. cit.

50 Heinz Scheible. *Die Entstehung der Magdeburger Zenturien.* Gütersloh: Gütersloher Verlagshaus Gerd Mohn, 1966. 11 f.; Theodor Gottlieb. "Zwei Schriften über die Magdeburger Centuriatores." [Review] *Göttingische Gelehrte Anzeigen* CLXIV (1902). 448; Peter Fraenkel. *Testimonia Patrum: The Function of the Patristic Argument in the Theology of Philip Melanchthon.* Geneva: Droz, 1961. 266n.

51 Karl Schottenloher. "Handschriftenschätze zu Regensburg im Dienste der Zenturiatoren (1554–1562)." *Zentralblatt für Bibliothekswesen* XXXIV (1917). 80 ff.

52 "Eine verlorene Handschrift der Schriften Bernos von Reichenau in den Magdeburger Centurien." *ZKG* LIII (1934). To medieval specialists he recommends Flacius' *Kollektaneen*, especially Cod. Guelf. Helmst. 807, 808, 820, 1010. 419.

53 Review of Heinz Scheible, *Die Entstehung der Magdeburger Zenturien. Bibliothèque d'humanisme et renaissance* XXIX (1967). 268.

54 Max Tratz. Review of Rudolf Keller, *Der Schlüssel zur Schrift. Zeitschrift für Bayerische Kirchengeschichte* LIV (1985). 243.

55 Günter Moldaenke. *Schriftverständnis und Schriftdeutung im Zeitalter der Reformation. Teil I: Matthias Flacius Illyricus.* Stuttgart: W. Kohlhammer, 1936. 3; J. Baur, 3.

Christian Aleman and Christof Cunrad turn out to be Basilius Monner.[46] But who were Dominus Aquinas, Sigismundus Cephalus, Johannes Cassius, Marco Civile, Civilius, Rhodius, Sartzelemigurck and Senjanin?

Johann Wilhelm Schulte's hope that Flacius' correspondence with Caspar von Nidbruck would appear in print[47] was realized when Victor Bibl published part of it in the *Jahrbuch der Gesellschaft für die Geschichte des Protestantismus in Österreich* from 1896 to 1898. Schulte's call for "a comprehensive description of his activity" was realized in part by Heinz Scheible, who investigated the planning,[48] and by Ronald Diener, who described the execution of the history project.[49] I would like to add my voice here to theirs who have called for investigation of the sources of Flacius' historical publications[50] and of his celebrated library.[51] Practicable is Arno Duch's suggestion about the the Centuries project: "It would by no means be a superfluous enterprise to put together a register of the texts used."[52] The same can be said not only for the sources of the *Catalogus Testium Veritatis* and his other lesser-known collations. Peter Fraenkel comments:

> We would take this opportunity to say once more that, though research on sources may be slow and painstaking work, it would seem to us to be one of the best means of understanding such sciences of the past as were largely, if not entirely, conceived with the use of sources: theology, history, and, of course, theological history.[53]

In view of Flacius' historical importance, modern editions of his major publications are overdue.[54] Günter Moldaenke suggests the project as a fitting sequel to the *Corpus Reformatorum.*[55]

At the celebrated Herzog August library in Wolfenbüttel, Flacius has a unique place. The founding document of the library, the 1572 *Liberey-Ordnung*, was written in part to protect its collection against depredations of the dread *culter flacianus*, a wholly imaginary knife, responsible for damage to books that Flacius is "supposed to have done." It is a pleasant irony, then, that for four centuries the precautions put in place by the *Ordnung* have protected Flacius' own books, papers and manuscripts. Pleasant, too, was the opportunity to examine them during the library's metamorphosis into an international research institution. I am indebted to Director Paul Raabe, and to the gracious and unbureaucratic Sabine Solf, who have assisted my investigation in many ways. The *civitas academia augusta*, the international community they created, made possible useful exchanges, not least with Hans-Heinrich Solf (†), who after retiring as *conseiller* at the Council of Europe, enjoyed presiding at the readers' after-lunch coffee. Kim Veltman was very helpful to me while he was putting together his *Linear Perspective and the Visual Dimensions of Science and Art* [Studies on Leonardo da Vinci I, Munich: Deutscher Kunstverlag, 1986] across the corridor, although his Italian died just when my Italian was born.

My doctoral advisor, Bishop Georg Kretschmar, now in St. Petersburg, then at Hamburg, altered my life by introducing me to Flacius. I am pleased to thank him here in print. The supportive words of George Williams of Harvard Divinity School, gratefully acknowledged here, were crucial at the beginning of this project. Valuable also along the way has been the expertise of Fedja Anzelewski of the *Kupferstichkabinett, Staatliche Museen Preussischer Kulturbesitz,* Berlin; paleographic assistance by Reinhard Aulich of Wertheim/Main; the advice of Charles Béné, University of Grenoble; Josip Bratulić, University of Zagreb; Vladimir Deutsch, Pastor of the Evangelical-Lutheran congregation in Zagreb, the host to a Matthias Flacius Seminar; and that of Ronald Diener; *Burgvogt* Bodo von der Dollen of the Marksburg on the Rhine; Christian Eisenberg of the Braunschweig *Predigerseminar*; Joseph Freedman of Illinois Wesleyan University; Thomas A. Fudge of Warner Pacific College, Portland, Oregon; Marquette Graduate student Andjelco Galić for finding material in Croatia; Pastor Lowell Green of Buffalo; William Hammer (†) of Carleton College; Hans Christoph von Hase of Kassel; doctoral candidate Thomas Haye of the University of Göttingen; Felix Hecht of the *Stadtbibliothek,* Dessau; *Stadtchronist* Alfred Heidelmayer of the *Kulturhistorisches Museum,* Magdeburg; Christoph Kampmann of the University of Bayreuth; Rudolf Keller of Erlangen; Eva Holland, editor of the Moses Mendelssohn edition; Robert Kolb of Concordia Seminary, St. Louis, for two decades of discussion on the Late Reformation; Armin Kunz, art critic of the *Neue Zürcher Zeitung;* Janusz Mallek of the University of Thorun, Poland; *Superintendent* Joachim Massner of Osnabrück; D. Andrew Penny of the King's University College, Edmonton; Luther Peterson of the State University of New York at Oswego; Edo Pivcević of the University of Bristol; Edward Roesner and Steven Immel of New York University; *Oberkirchenrat* Konrad von Rabenau of Berlin; Adalbert Roth of Rome; Werner Schade of the *Anhaltische Gemäldegalerie Georgium,* Dessau; Loris Storlese of the *Schuola Normale Superiore,* Pisa; doctoral candidates Paul Strawn at Marburg and Jonathan Strom at Rostock; *Diakon* Max Tratz of Ocksenfurt; Tullio and Marija Vorano of the National Museum in Labin, Croatia; and Günther Wartenberg of the University of Leipzig.

I have profited from the assistance of Joan Sommer and others of library staff at Marquette University, and the staffs of many other libraries, including the Huntington, Newberry and Folger collections. My thanks are also due to the Center for Reformation Research, St. Louis, to Paul Jackson and Jeffrey Oschwald at Concordia Seminary at Fort Wayne, and to Terry Dinovo of the Lutheran Brotherhood Library, St. Paul. I am indebted to Martin Boghardt, Manfred Neugebauer, and others from the staff of the Herzog August Library at Wolfenbüttel, especially Ulrich Kopp, expert at classifying sixteenth-century books and formidable squash partner. The maps were prepared by Nick Schroeder of the Graphics Department, Instructional Media Center, Marquette University. I am grateful to Pamela Schwandt for correction the manuscript, for editorial supervision by Oswald Schönberg, who has overseen many distinguished Wolfenbüttel publications, and to Library Director Helwig Schmidt-Glintzer for accepting this volume for the series, *Wolfenbütteler Abhandlungen zur Renaissanceforschung.*

56 Ficker and Winckelmann, Nr. 91.

57 *Matthias Flacius Illyicus und seine Zeit.* Erlangen: Theodor Blaesing, 1569–61. v.

My thanks go also to the National Endowment for the Humanities for a research grant at the Newberry Library in Chicago and for a travel grant; to the Aid Association for Lutherans for supporting Croatian language study at the Yale Summer Language Institute; to Marquette University for travel funds; to the *Freunde der Bibliothek* at Wolfenbüttel for study grants; to the Volkswagen Foundation and the State of Lower Saxony, first, for a two-year research fellowship at Wolfenbüttel, and, later, for an extended Standing Invitation.

The Latin laudation on page five was prepared by the clergy of Strassburg, before political calculus added them to Flacius' opponents.[56] The German words below are those of Wilhelm Preger of Munich, written when he finished his first Flacius volume one hundred and thirty-six years ago. I share their admiration, his hope: "Möge auch diese Arbeit nach ihrem Maße der Kirche des Herrn dienlich sein."[57]

Oliver K. Olson

The Feast of St. Matthias, Apostle
February 24th, 1995

PART ONE: VENICE

I am bound to them [the Doge and the Senate of Venice] not only by the common law of love ... but also with that special bond observed for many generations by my ancestors from Alvone in Istria (also called Albona by ancient writers) under their rule, between the river Arsia and the Flanatic gulf; where I, too, was born and educated and until today have many relatives, brothers and sisters. – Flacius

Ever since, long ago, Venice ruled the sunny walled town of Labin, southeast of Trieste, a bas-relief lion on the wall has stood guard over number seven Ulica Guiseppina Martinuzzi. The venerable house is worth a visit by those who travel to Trieste or to the Adriatic resort of Opatija. Part of the Old Town, latterly become an artists' colony, it has been transformed into a museum to honor the nineteenth-century communist, Giuseppina Martinuzzi, and Baldo Lupetino. According to Cardinal Cervini, Lupetino was *il piu gran Luterano del mundo*;[1] he was also a victim of the Inquisition. But as a verse indicates, *Matthia Flacio, Risveli Patriotici Carmen*, written by Martinuzzi herself and painted on the wall, the house is mainly a memorial for Labin's greatest son, Matthias Flacius.

The present façade dates from the eighteenth century. But, according to the brochure from the *turističko društvo*, it is the very house in which Matthias Flacius was born on March 3, 1520 – the year justification by faith was first preached in Venice by the Franciscan, Andrea da Ferrara, on the Campo San Stefano and in the church of San Marco.[2] According to Eberhard Gothein, Flacius was "the last creative head among the Reformers, unsurpassed in talent, zeal, purity and inflexibility." Gothein tempered his praise by adding that he was "a homeless half-barbarian, whose lack of moderation shattered his own party."[3] Matthias Murko, sometime professor at Graz, Prague and Leipzig, countered, "... at least the 'half barbarian' would have to be qualified ... neither Austrian nor Venetian Istria was especially backward in the culture of the higher levels, and Flacius came from patrician stock on both his father's and his mother's sides."[4] Murko, too, needs a bit of correcting. Flacius' father, Andreas Vlačić, albeit well-to-do, was plebian.[5] Flacius' blue blood came from his mother, daughter of the nobleman, Bartholomaeus Luciani,[6] who died giving him birth.[7]

The book of German heroes by Heinrich Pantlin, his friend of student days, treats him as an honorary German because "since his youth he lived among Germans and published several books in that language, and adorned Germany with his constancy and erudition ..."[8] On the basis of the radical, *Vlah*, in his surname, Ermano Nacinovich thinks (happy thought!) that the rescuer of the German Reformation had Rumanian blood and a

1 Gottfried Buschbell. *Reformation und Inquisition in Italien um die Mitte des XVI. Jahrhunderts.* Paderborn: Ferdinand Schöningh, 1910. 289 f.

2 Philip M. J. McNair. "The Reformation of the Sixteenth Century in Renaissance Italy." *Religion and Humanism.* Ed. Keith Robbins. Oxford:Basil Blackwell, 1981. 154.

3 "Der letzte schöpferische Kopf unter den Reformatoren ... unübertroffen an Talent, Fleiß, Reinheit und Unbeugsamkeit des Charakters, freilich zugleich ein heimatloser Halbbarbar, dessen Maßlosigkeit die eigene Partei gerüttelte..." "Die kulturellen Grundlagen der Gegenreformation." *Internationale Wochenschrift für Wissenschaft, Kunst und Technik* I (1907). 588.

4 *Die Bedeutung der Reformation und Gegenreformation für das geistige Leben der Südslaven.* Prague: Česka Grafica and Heidelberg: Winter, 1927. 503, cf. 122. Jean-François Gilmont, "Flacius Illyricus" in *Dictionnaire d'Histoire et de Géographie Ecclésiastique* 17, col. 311, is mistaken about his having "poor parents."

5 "On je bio plebejac." Mirković 1960. 149; 1980, I, 231.

6 "Seine Mutter stammte aus edlem Geschlecht, sie war die Tochter eines adligen herrn Bartholomaeus Lucianus, wohl italienischer Herkunft." Eduard Böhl. *Beiträge zur Geschichte der Reformation in Österreich.* Jena: Gustav Fischer, 1902. 40.

7 Kaspar Ulenberg. "Vita et res gestae Matthiae Flacii Illyrici, ab Ortu ad Obitum usque." *Historia de vita, moribus, rebus gestis, studiis ac de-*

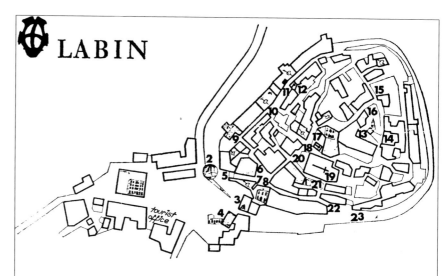

Map of Labin, Labin Tourist Board

1. THE OLD COAT OF ARMS OF THE TOWN LABIN
2. THE ROUND BASTION
3. THE HOUSE OF THE COAL MINERS FEDERATION
4. THE TOWN LODGE
5. THE GATE OF THE TOWN
6. THE TOWN PALACE
7. RENAISANCE PALACE
8. THE OLD THEATRE
9. THE BAROQUE FACADE OF THE FAMILY FRANKOVIĆ HOUSE
10. THE PALACE »NEGRI«
11. THE MANZINI-HOUSE
12. THE CLASSICISTIC CHAPEL
13. THE CHURCH TOWER FROM THE XVII C1
14. ROMANIQUE FACADE
15. STYLISTIC FACADE
16. ROMANIQUE PORTAL — XIV CT.
17. BAROQUE PALACE-MUSEUM
18. THE BAROQUE CHAPEL
19. THE PARISH CHURCHE
20. RENAISSANCE PALACE
21. OLD FORTIFICATIONS — XIII CT.
22. THE »USKOK« DOOR (Uskok = rebels against the Venetians)
23. PROMENADE AROUND THE OLD TOWN
    THE LABIN-ATELIEURS

nique morte praedicantium Lutheranorum etc. Cologne: Bernardus Gualterus, 1622. 372.

8 Heinrich Pantaleon. *Prosopographie heroum atque Illustrium Virorum Totius Germaniae* III. Basel: Nicolaus Brylinger, 1566. 438.

9 Ermano Nacinovich (Istriano) "I Vlacich sono di probabile origine rumena, se si pone mente alla radice del nome (vlah) e il fatto che, tanto nel territorio colonie disperse de questa stirpe." *Flacio: Studio Biografico Storico.* Fiume [Rijeka]: Emidio Mohovich, 1886. 3n. The British Library copy carries the author's dedication to W. E. Gladstone. On the Vlasi, cf. Dominik Mandić. "Postanak Vlaha Nova Povijesna Istraživanja." *Rasprave i Prilozi iz Stare Hrvatske Povijesti.* Rome: Hrvatski Povijesni Institut, 1963. 515–517, and John van Antwerp Fine. *The Late Medieval Balkans. A Critical Survey from the Sixth to the Late Twelfth Century.* Ann Arbor: University of Michigan Press, 1983. passim.

10 Miroslav Bertoša. "Etnički Sastav Pučanstva Labina u nopoviod XVI. Stoljeću." *Istra* VIII (1975). 43.

11 Op. cit. 1960. 7; 1980. I, 30.

12 *Beweisung das nicht die unsere Christi, sonder die papistische Religion, new und auffrürisch, und ein ursach alles unglücks sey.* Magdeburg: Christian Rödinger, 1553.

13 Heinrich Reusch. *Die Indices Librorum Prohibitorum des sechzehnten Jahrhunderts.* Tübingen, 1886. Reprint, Nieuwkoop: de Graaf, 1961. 273, 503.

14 "... das nicht das Wort Flacius, wie es die Adversarij verdrisslich gnug anziehen, auch also von uns odiose lautend, gesetz werde," he wrote to the publisher, "Velim enim non secundum adversariorum morem tam absolute et quasi invidiose poni Flacij vocabulum." *Der Briefwechsel des M. Cyriacus Spangenberg. Briefe von 1550–1584.* Heinrich Rembe (ed.). I. Dresden: Heinrich J. Naumann, 1877. 66.

remote origin in the semi-gypsy Dacian tribe of the Vlasi.[9] Since at the time Istrian names were often italianized, an Italian name is no proof, but the blood of the Lucianis may have made him part Italian, and thus typical of Labin's racial mix – one quarter Italian and three-quarters Croatian.[10] Mirković, who also calls attention to his subject's mastery of the local Chacavian dialect, concluded that his descent was Croatian.[11]

Later in life, his Christian name seemed to him a portent of his replacing the perfidious Melanchthon. His *Clavis Scripturae Sacrae, Demonstrationes Evidentissimae XXX, Glossa Compendaria, Refutatio Invectivae Bruni, Solida*

Labin, Croatia. Courtesy of Tullio Vorano, National Museum, Labin.

The Frankovic House in Labin, Croatia. Courtesy of Julio Vorano.

Refutatio Vanissimorum Sophistarum, and *De Translatione Imperii*, were all dated on St. Matthias' Day, February 24. In the introduction to his *Beweisung, das nicht die unsere Christi, sonder die papistische religion new und auffrürisch*, as well, he explained that it was "the day of Matthias, who was chosen by the Holy Spirit for the apostolic office (*Acts of the Apostles* 1.15–26) instead of the niggard Judas, betrayer of Christ."[12]

Getting his surname right has proved to be difficult. When they denounced him as a "prohibited author, first class," compilers of the Index of Prohibited Books added innacuracy to their high-handedness by spelling his name "Flaccus" or "Flavius."[13] So bitter did the theological wars become eventually that even choosing to use the name, "Flacius," became a sign of hostility; his loyal friend, Cyriacus Spangenberg, made it a point to instruct his publisher to use instead the cognomen, "Illyricus."[14] But although they used the name his Philippist opponents adopted,[15] older French encyclopedias made no mistake when they called him "Francowitz."[16] On a Wittenberg salary receipt, for example, he used that name himself.[17]

Vlačić or Francowitz? A document issued at Flacius' request and marked with the seal of San Marco by the Podesta of Labin to answer those who called him a Jew and a bastard, sets the matter straight: he had two surnames, Vlačić (Vlacich or, latinized, Flacius) and Francowitz (Fran-

15 Johann Balthasar Ritter. *M. Matthiae Flacii, Illyrici, Ehemahls berümt- und gelährten Theologi in Teutschland Leben und Tod: Aus theils bekant – theils unbekannten Urkunden, Schrifften und Brieffen anderer und seiner selbst, zur Erläuterung der Kirchen-Historie des XVI. Seculi mit sonderbarem Fleiß beschrieben von Johann Balthasar Ritter. 2. vermehret und verbesserte Auflage.* Frankfurt and Leipzig: Joh. Conrad Maximilian Ziegler, 1725. 5n.

16 "Flacii nomen ego ex certis authoribus cognovi esse tale: Matthias Francowitzius, cognomentio Flacius, gente Illyricus, patria Albonensis." Paul Colomiés. *Bibliothèque Choisie.* La Rochelle: Pierre Savouret, 1682. 15. Jean Pierre Niceron. *Memoires pour servir à l'histoire des hommes illustres dans la république des lettres.* Tome XXIV. Paris: Briasson, 1733. 2: "Le véritable nom de famille était Francowitz." Niceron's source is Abraham Bucholzer. *Index Chronologicus cura secunda Gottfridi Bucholzeri ... locupletus ... et ad finem 1589 continuatus.* Görlitz: J. Ramba, 1599. 831, who insists that Frankowitz is "verum & integrum ipsius nomen."

17 Walter Friedensburg. "Die Anstellung des Flacius Illyricus an der

Universität Wittenberg." ARG, XI (1914). 307n.

18 *Demonstrationes evidentissimae doctrinae de essentia imaginis Dei et Diaboli, iustitiaeque ac iniustitiae originalis una cum testimoniis veterum ac recentium theologorum etc.* Basel: Peter Perna, 1570. 324–326. "Literae Testimoniales Baltheris Trivisani de Nativitate Matthiae Flacii." UN, 1733. 696–698.

19 Mirković, 1960. 7 f.; 1980. I, 31 f.

20 We know their names from the publication of Celia Vlačić's will by Tomaso Luciani. *Matthia Flacio Istriano de Albona, Notizie e documenti.* Pula: G. Seraschen, 1896. 15 ff.

21 Pietro Stancovich. "Matthia Francovich." *Biografia degli Uomini Distinti dell' Istria* I. Trieste: Gio Marenigh, 1828. 110; Mirković, 1960. 18. 1980. I, 47.

22 Cf. Mate Krizman. "O Nekim izvorima Vlačićeve Jezikoslovne Naobrazbe." [On some sources of Flacius' linguistic education]. *Istra* XIV (1976). 16–34.

23 *De voce et re fidei, quod que sola fide iustificemur, contra pharisaicum hypocritarum fermentum, liber.* Basel: Johannes Oporinus, 1555. Ab v f.

24 *De sectis, dissensionibus, contradictionibus et confusionibus doctrinae, religionis, scriptorum & doctorum Pontificorum Liber.* Basel: Paul Queck, 1565. 17.

25 *Ein kurtzer Bericht vom Interim, darauß man leichtlich kan die leer und Geist desselbigen Buchs erkennen, durch Theodorum Henetum allen fromen Christen zu dieser zeit nützlich unnd tröstlich.* [Magdeburg: Michael Lotter] 1548. Preger. 1859. 59. O. Ritschl, II. 354n takes "Henetus" to mean "Wend" or "Slav."

26 Veljko Gortan and Vladimir Vratović. "The Basic Characteristics of Croatian Latinity." *Humanistica Lovaniensis* XX (1971). 40.

27 Zenko. 170.

28 *Gründliche Verlegung aller schedlichen Schwermereyen des Stenckfelds*

kowich).[18] Edo Pivcević, professor at Bristol, suggests that the alternative surname is based on the charming Croatian custom of giving nicknames to families. Mirković's guess is that when Flacius' great-grandfather or grandfather married a Francowitz, he moved into the Francowitz household and accepted a second surname without abandoning the first.[19]

Matija had two brothers, Franjo and Jakov, and three sisters, Celia, Dominica, and Martina, all older than he was.[20] When one strolls through the pleasant streets of Labin's Old Town, one can imagine a small Matija playing on the gentle stages which lead up to St. Just's and St. Mary's churches, sitting on the hill nearby, watching white ships on the turquoise Adriatic, or peering from a window into the valley far below, frightened when his brothers warned that someday the valley would be filled with fearful Turks.

For a while he probably descended the hill to the Franciscan monastery established in 1434 in the valley by the Lupetini and Luciani clans.[21] Otherwise, it is difficult to explain where he mastered the Cyrillic and Glagolitic scripts, then a monopoly of nationalist Slavic priests. One would like to know more about his early language training, since later as professor at Jena, he was the mentor of several of the linguists of the "literary springtime" of south Slavic languages that distinguished the Reformation movement.[22] He himself reports only that his elementary education was overseen by his father, Andreas, and that was interrupted for a while when he was twelve by his father's death.

Judge Lucian Luciani, his uncle, was appointed his guardian. From Luciani and his other uncles, who had supported Venice's military campaigns, he learned to be a Venetian patriot.[23] He talks about his "special bond" to Venice,[24] and in one of his first publications he calls himself "Henetus," the Greek word for Venetian.[25] When he grew older he was assigned a tutor, Franciscus Ascerius of Milan, presumably one of the men who made Capo d'Istria, Prian and Labin centers of humanistic learning.[26]

One of the obvious faults of Mirković's biography is the exaggerated contrast he makes between Vlačić's pure Slavic background, to which he attributes his virtues, and the decadent German world of his later life.

> Mirković made an effort to explain Flacius' "protestant spirit" in a dogmatic scientific fashion, that is, basically and exclusively through Vlačić's origin, the milieu of Labin, his family connections, his schooling and the formation of his personality in Labin and Venice up to his nineteenth year, that is, to his arrival in Germany. Such a scientific-naturalistic interpretation is in contradiction to the fact that Flacius the theologian witnesses his Christian-theological self-understanding through his own life and work. That is shown by the fact that after his conversion to true Christian faith brought about – as he says – by the grace of God, he makes little reference to his previous natural life – something which remains incomprehensible to Mirković.[27]

Long before he came under the influence of Martin Luther, Vlačić wrote, he had become a Christian believer by reading the Bible.[28] "Even before I learned Luther's doctrine," he testified, "I felt in myself the peace of conscience and the joy in the Holy Spirit, loved the religion and the Holy Scripture and often with my whole heart wished to contribute something in theology, so that I could advance in the Holy Scripture and serve the church of Christ some time and then be able to return to the Lord."[29] Perhaps it was Ascerius who introduced him to the Bible. It was his tutelage, at any rate, that prepared him for advanced education. At sixteen, Matija was sent off to school in Venice, a night and a day distant by sea.

A RENAISSANCE TRADE

> Venice, which used to be truly Christian, is very much poisoned by the Lutheran plague. – Cardinal Jacobo Sadoleto

> Already Christ has begun to penetrate in Italy, but I would like Him to enter in glory and openly, and I believe Venice will be the door. – Capuchin General Bernardino Ochino

The school on the Rialto reserved for young aristocrats of Venice was medieval and aristotelian. But the *other* school, near the piazza of San Marco,[1] was not so old-fashioned, and reflected the "almost unbelievable burst of enthusiasm for classical languages"[2] in early sixteenth-century Venice. In 1536, Matija Vlačić was enrolled at that other one, the school of San Marco. It was shaped by the man, than whom "no other publisher has made such a staggering contribution to the human spirit,"[3] Aldus Manutius. That he founded the Aldine press in 1490 to produce editions of ancient Greek and Latin classics is well-known. Less well-known is Aldus' "prominent but unnoticed position ... in the most important parts of early sixteenth-century education."[4] With his friends of the New Academy, he developed a specialized curriculum to serve the dreams of the Venetian High Renaissance. Unlike the high-born boys on the Rialto, then, and – ominously – far differently from his contemporaries in Germany, young Vlačić was trained as an editor of classical manuscripts.

> Partnership in the Venetian patriciate secured to this group a powerful voice when questions of schools and of intellectual life had to be decided by the government. Obviously this group had an interest in having in the school of San Marco lecturers who might co-operate in the enterprises of Aldus and of other printers and who would be able to train future editors of Greek and Roman texts. Material considerations probably were also involved in making the *Pregadi* [members of the city council] amenable to the urgings of this group: book production and printing shops represented a valuable economic asset. Thus, the men who gravitated toward the Aldine Academy must probably be considered the moving force in shifting the tasks of the lecturers at the school of San Marco from rhetoric and humanities to Greek and Latin philology.[5]

There he became familiar with the printing business,[6] and was caught up in his life-long passion, finding and publishing manuscripts. The two famous Venetians were not unlike. Aldus was intensely interested in

zur Unterricht und warnung der einfeltiger Christen. [Nuremberg: Johann vom Berg and Ulrich Newberg, 1557]. T v iiij r.

29 *Entschuldigung, geschrieben an die Universitet zu Wittenberg, der Mittelding halben.* [Magdeburg: Christian Rödinger], 1549. [D iiij v].

1 *"juxta forum B. Marci."* Melchior Adam. *Vitae Germanorum theologorum qui superiori seculo Ecclesiam Christi voce scriptisque propagarunt et propugnarunt congestae ad annum 1618 deductae.* Heidelberg: Jona Rosa, 1620. 472.

2 Martin Lowry. *The World of Aldus Manutius: Business and Scholarship in Renaissance Venice.* [Ithaca, New York]: Cornell University Press, 1979. 187.

3 Alan G. Thomas. *Great Books and Book Collectors.* London: Weidenfeld and Nicolson, 1975. 39.

4 Martin Lowry. "The 'New Academy' of Aldus Manutius: A Renaissance Dream." *Bulletin of the John Rylands Library* LVIII (1975/76). 408.

5 Felix Gilbert. "Biondo, Sabellico, and the Beginnings of Venetian Official Historiography." John Gordon Rowe and W. H. Stockdale (eds.). *Florilegium Historiale: Historical Essays Presented to Wallace K. Ferguson.* Toronto: University of Toronto Press [1971]. 285. Fernando Lepori. "La Scuola di Rialto dalla Fondazione alla metà del Cinquecento." *Storia Della Cultura Veneta* 3/II. Vicenza: Neri Possa Editore, 1980. Bruno Nardi contrasts the two schools, *Saggi sulla Cultura Veneta del Quattro e Cinquecento a cura di Paulo Muzzantini.* Padua: Editrice Antenore, 1971. 51.

6 Andreas Burckhardt. *Johannes Basilius Herold: Kaiser und Reich im protestantischen Schrifttum des Basler*

Buchdruckes um die Mitte des sech-zehnten Jahrhunderts. Basel and Stuttgart: Helbing & Lichtenhahn, 1967. 32.

7 Margaret Oliphant. *The Makers of Venice*. London and New York: AMS Press, 1972. 407.

8 *Aristotelous Hapanta. Aristotelis Opera*. Basel: J. Bebel and M. Isen-grin, 1550. [A v].

9 *Der Text der Aristotelischen Rhetorik: Prolegomena zu einer Kritischen Ausgabe*. Berlin and New York: de Gruyter, 1971. 102.

10 Lowry, *World*. 75.

11 "It must be regarded as certain that Aldus never gained direct access to the Greek codies bequeathed to Venice by Cardinal Bessarion." Ibid. 301. According to Marino Zorzi, it is possible that he did consult them to illuminate ob-scure passages. *La Libreria di San Marco: Libri, Lettori, Società nella Venezia dei Dogi*. Milan: Arnoldo Mondadori, 1987. 93.

12 Martin Sicherl. "Handschriftliche Vorlagen der Editio Princeps des Aristoteles." *Abhandlungen der Akademie Mainz. Geistes- und sozial-wissenschaftliche Reihe* VIII (1976). 67; Lowry, *World*. 234 ff.

13 Lotte Labowsky. *Bessarion's Library and the Biblioteca Marciana: Six early inventories*. Rome: Edizioni dei Storia e Letteratura, 1979. 75.

14 Gigliola Fragnito. "Cultura uma-nistica e riforma religiosa: il 'De of-ficio Boni viri ac Probi Episcopi' di Gasparo Contarini." *Studi Venezia-ni* XI (1969). 83.

15 Rudolf Keller. "Flacius und Eras-mus." *Der Schlüssel zur Schrift. Die Lehre vom Wort Gottes bei Mat-thias Flacius Illyricus*. Hannover: Lutherisches Verlagshaus, 1984. 172–176.

16 Thomas F. Mayer. *Thomas Starkey and the Commonweal: Humanist Politics and Religion in the Reign of Henry VIII*. Cambridge et al.: Cam-bridge University Press, 1989. 55.

17 Pio Paschini. *Pier Paolo Vergerio il giovane e la sua Apostasia: un Epi-*

Hebrew; Vlačić became a professor of Hebrew. Aldus was a bookseller; Vlačić was a bookseller. Aldus was an avid collector of manuscripts; Vlačić was an avid collector of manuscripts. It is not too much to say that Aldus Manutius was a role model: if for the word, "ancient," one substi-tutes "medieval," what was said about the one can be said about the other:

> It is difficult to form an idea of the passion with which he devoted himself to a repro-duction of the great works of ancient literature. If he heard of the existence anywhere of a manuscript unpublished, or which could throw light upon an existing text, he never rested till he had it in his possession. He did not shrink from long journeys, great expenditures, applications of all kinds ...[7]

Vlačić also caught the Aldine vision of producing an accurate text of Aristotle. The editor's preface to the 1550 Basel edition of Aristotle testifies that in several of the works, Vlačić improved the tradition of the Venetian edition of 1495–1498, one reason to dismiss the charge of his later critics that he was ignorant of Aristotle. "Mendacium esse testan-tur meae Emendationes eius, quas in impressione Aristotelis Basiliensis Anno 1550 sequuti sunt." *Necessario Detensio contra famosam Chartam titulo Witebergensium Scholasticorum editam*. Jena: [Christian Rhodius], 1558 Bij f.

> Matthias Flacius Illyricus, a man not so renowned as distinguished in doctrine and in Greek, especially in Aristotle, and endowed with acute judgment, shared with us his comments on the *Ars Dicendi* [Rhetoric], the *Moralia*, and the books *De Mundo* and *Virtutes*. He did such a diligent work in his comments, that it showed me that he is someone able to make judgments on such a matter.[8]

A recent investigator, Rudolf Kassel, who gives him credit for "the few successful emendations" of the text of the *Rhetoric*,[9] agrees with the judgment of the Basel editor.

The question arises, which Vlačić's better sources were. It is not im-probable that he learned that the "colossal enterprise,"[10] the *editio princeps* of Aristotle's works at the Aldine press, had not taken into account the fabled manuscripts willed to the city by Cardinal Bessarion in 1468.[11] Since 1469 they had been stored in the *sala novissima* of the Doge's pal-ace.[12] During Vlačić's school days, however, just before the construction of the Marciana library, they were in a temporary depository, the chapel of St. Zeno at the San Marco church, and thus more easily available.[13] It is possible, then, that his improvements to the Aldine text were based on the Bessarion manuscripts. Vlačić's teacher, Egnazio (Giovanni Battista di Cippeli 1473–1553), as a public official, would have had access to the collection, and could have arranged their use by a favored pupil.

Egnazio was a close associate of Aldus, who considered him a "polyhis-tor maximus," of humanists Willibald Pirkheimer, Pietro Bembo, Cardinal Gasparo Contarini,[14] and of Erasmus of Rotterdam, whence, perhaps, Vlačić's respect for Erasmus.[15] Among Egnazio's other students were Paolo Manuzio[16] and the bishop of Capo d'Istria, Papal legate and Lutheran convert, Pier Paolo Vergerius.[17] Despite his student load – he had 500 students in 1520[18] – Egnazio demonstrated "skill in meeting the needs of students and teachers in the form of indices, annotations, translations from the Greek and the like."[19] From Erasmus' report of a visit to his classroom, we learn that he entertained his students by interspersing his Latin lectures with stories in Italian.[20]

Egnazio's essay, "On the Origin of the Turks" in *De Caesaribus libri III*, a protest against tyranny in church and state, for which he was praised as the "Venetian Valerius Maximus,"[21] influenced Erasmus' historical writing.[22] Did he influence Vlačić's historical writing as well?[23] His *On Examples of Illustrious Men of the City of Venice and of Other Peoples*,[24] according to Lester Libby, was "disorganized and repetitive, lacking in any broad main themes to bind the various examples into a unity..." On the other hand, he did "reflect a coherent view of Venetian history, a conception which is fundamental with the ideas of Mocenigo and Contarini."[25] Vlačić may also have been influenced by his teacher's known hostility toward Pope Paul III and to Emperor Charles V, who threatened reprisal for a panegyric he had written in honor of the king of France, "To Francis, the First of His Name."[26] Whatever the quality of his publications, however, Egnazio qualifies as a historian. A certain suspicion, then, is in order when one reads that Vlačić was "historicamente autodidacta" or that he found his way "tout seul."[27]

Vlačić wrote little about his teacher, perhaps because Egnatio, suspected of having embraced *Lutheranismo*, was vulnerable to the Inquisition.[28] It is useful, then, to quote the following from Thomas Mayer about Egnatio's influence on his famous pupil.

> The political views expressed in Egnazio's *De caesaribus libri III* resembled Gabriele's and Cardano's, or what Hans Baron has called the "new Guelphism" of the later fifteenth century which rested on opposition to tyrants in both church and secular world, beginning with Caesar. John Libby calls Egnazio's outlook "traditional" rather than republican, and faults him for failing to understand "the significance of the Venetian struggle with despotic Milan," but this may give Egnazio too little credit for his forthright stand against tyranny in *De caesaribus* and condemn him by a standard which would have found most other humanists wanting, too. Egnazio's later religion continued to fit the Evangelical mold. In 1536 his library held the best book on ancient councils which an ally of Contarini's could find, and near the end of his life he sheltered the fugitive Vergerio, even though Egnazio claimed to have thrown Vergerio out when he realized the bishop was no longer a *buono cattolico*. Vergerio may have been Egnazio's student and he certainly trained the evangelically-inclined Paolo Manuzio and the Gnesio-Lutheran Matthias Flaccius [sic] Illyricus.[29]

Wolfenbüttel librarian Otto von Heinemann questioned the breadth of Vlačić's non-historical interests.

> Nevertheless, it remains striking that among the manuscripts of the Flacian legacy, there are also a number that have nothing to do with the Church-historical works he was preparing, and others, about which it cannot be assumed that they were purchased from their original owners or even given as gifts. To the former belong the manuscripts by classical authors, to the latter, those which were used for services in the cloisters and churches ...[30]

sodio delle lotte religiose nel Cinquecento. Rome: Scuola tipografica Pio X, 1925. 6.

18 Girolamo Tiraboschi. *Storia della Letteratura Italiana* VII. Milan: Società Tipografica dei Classici Italiani, 1824. 2187.

19 James Bruce Ross. "Venetian Schools and Teachers, Fourteenth to Early Sixteenth Century: A Survey and a Study of Giovanni Battista Egnazio." *Renaissance Quarterly* XXIX (1976). 552.

20 *Opus Epistolarum Desiderii Erasmi Roterodami* 12. P. S. Allen and H. W. Garrod (eds.). Oxford: Clarendon Press, 1938. 413.

21 Karl Christ. "Zur Geschichte der griechischen Handschriften der Palatina." *Zentralblatt für Bibliothekswesen* XXXVI (1919). 22.

22 A. G. Weiler. "The Turkish Argument and Christian Piety in Desiderius Erasmus' 'Consultatio de Bello Turcis Inferendo' (1530)." J. Sperna Weiland and W. Th. M. Frijhoff. *Erasmus of Rotterdam: The Man and the Scholar.* Leiden et al.: E. J. Brill, 1988. 31 ff.

23 The question is asked by Sándor Balla. "Značenje Flaciusove Povijesti Kršćanstva (Magdeburgske Centurije)." *Susreti* III (1971). 52.

24 *De Exemplis Illustrium Virorum Venetae Civitatis atque Aliarum Gentium.* Venice: Tridentinus, 1554.

25 Lester J. Libby, Jr. "Venetian History and Political Thought After 1509." *Studies in the Renaissance* XX. New York: Renaissance Society of America, 1973. 33. Felix Gilbert. op. cit. 285, mentions a Venetian trend "toward clarification of the causal connection between historical events." A bibliography of Egnazio's publications in Ambroise Firmin-Didot. *Alde Manuce et l'Hellénisme à Venise.* Paris: Typographie d'Ambroise Firmin-Didot, 1875. 451 f.

26 *Ad Franciscum huius Nominis Primum, De eius in Italiam ... Adventu, deque clarissima ex Helvetiis Panegyricus.* Mediolani, 1515.

27 Jose L. de Orella y Unzue. *Respuestas Católicas a Las Centurias de Magdeburgo (1559–1588)*. Madrid: Fundacion Universitaria Espanola. Seminaro "Suarez," 1976. 17. Pontien Polman. *L'Elément historique dans la controverse religieuse du XVIe siècle*. Gembloux: J. Duculot, 1932. 214.

28 Mirković 1960, 29; 1980. I, 61.

29 T. Mayer. *Politics*. 54 f.

30 Otto von Heinemann. *Die Herzogliche Bibliothek zu Wolfenbüttel, 1550–1893*, 2. Aufl. Wolfenbüttel: Zwissler, 1894. 23 f.

31 Milde. "Library". 108.

32 "Extat quoque dialogus Pyladis & Orestis, sub nomine Petrarchae, non omnino indoctus aut illepidus: in quo disputatur, Romam modis omnibus fugiendam esse, tanquam quandam latronum speluncam, & malorum fontem ac primatiam officinam. Credo sane Petrarchae non esse: sed tamen certe est hominis haud quaquam insciti: & ante annos circiter 50. editus in publicum est, seu impressus." *Catalogus*. 1562. 508. Cf. Paul Piur. *Petrarcas "Buch Ohne Namen" und die Päpstliche Kurie: ein Beitrag zur Geistesge-schichte der frühen Renaissance*. Halle/Saale: Max Niemeyer, 1925. xii, 108n.

33 Adolf Schmitthenner. "Dante in der konfessionellen Politik des sechzehnten und siebzehnten Jahrhunderts." *Die Grenzboten* LXIII (1904). Nr. 2. 91.

34 Pantaleon. 439. Caspar Heldelin. *Eine Christliche predigt uber der Leiche des Ehrnwürdigen und hoch-gelerten Herrn, M. Matthiae Flacij Illyrici*. [Oberursel: Nicolaus Henricus], 1575. G r.

35 *De Sectis*. 38.

36 *Clavis Scripturae Sacrae*. Jena: Samuel Krebs, 1674. II, 753.

Wolfgang Milde, director of the Department of Manuscripts, and the current guardian of much of Vlačić's legacy, echoes his predecessor:

> Even today it strikes one as singular that there should be amongst his manuscripts some which have no connexion with the works of ecclesiastical history in preparation (such as those of classical authors), as well as others which cannot be assumed to have been sold or given away by their original owners (such as liturgical texts essential for church and monastic services).[31]

That Vlačić had interests beyond history, however, is not difficult to establish. He knew Petrarch well enough, for instance, to dispute (correctly) his authorship of the *Dialogus inter Pyladem et Orestem*.[32] At a time when it had been forgotten even in Italy, he could quote Dante's *Convivio* from memory and – a theme to which we will return – make his *De Monarchia* available to the learned world.[33] With regard to his collection of liturgical materials, it needs no demonstration that at a time when monasteries were being dissolved, and when the invention of printing made manuscripts dispensable, such materials were not difficult to obtain. No argument therefore based on his presumed sole interest in church history can be convincing.

Vlačić told his classmate, Heinrich Pantlin, that he had often gone to church in Venice, and heard not only the mass, but also the canonical hours (*publicas psalmodias adiuvaret*).[34] He was put off, however, by the cults of San Fantin, San Rocco, the miracle-working icon of San Maria dei Miracoli, the religious charlatans he had seen on the streets. He ridiculed the jugglers and mimes on the Piazza San Marco and the Rialto and the woman paid to mislead the gullible by pointing at a picture, shouting that St. Mary was shedding tears: "La madonna pianze!"

He was particularly critical of the inscriptions on the cathedral church. Years later, he remembered:

> Under the four gilded horses on the portico of the splendid St. Marco church, in the sumptuous picture commonly called "Musaica," are depicted four evangelists, each with a verse, by which they are to be invoked or compelled. To St. Matthew, the first, the invocation is attached: "Holy Matthew, wash away all evil of mind." To St. John, the last, this invocation: "Lead us, Virgin John, to where you abide without end."

> By these prayers the dead saints are clearly represented not only as mediators, but also as veritable and omnipotent gods. For what greater and better can anyone ask from the eternal God than purification of mind, righteousness, eternal life, or the kingdom of heaven?[35]

He remembered that "In Italy, shouting and quarreling monks profess Aristotle's metaphysics instead of the Word of God and the Pauline Epistles."[36] Because the Reformation had made a deep impression there, the monks he described were probably not from the Franciscan houses. The Franciscan Provincial, Baldo Lupetino, a cousin of Vlačić's mother, ruled several Franciscan monasteries besides his own, San Francesco della Vigna. That monastery was built on the very spot, they say, where St. Mark landed, and the words of the angel were heard – "Peace to Thee,

Mark My Evangelist." They were very words remembered on Venice's coat-of-arms on the wall of the Francowitz house in Labin, "Pace a te Marco Evangelista mio."

Matija liked dining at the refectory at San Francesco, where the food was cooked by a woman from Istria. Perhaps it was while he was enjoying Istrian cooking that he first heard about the new publication, *Massoreth Ha-Massoreth*, by the Jewish humanist, Elias Levita.[37] It was Levita's argument that he attempted to refute in his Master's thesis. Another dinner

37 *The Massoreth Ha-Massoreth of Elias Levita.* Christian David Ginsburg (ed.). London: Longmanns, Green, Reader & Dyer, 1867.

The Piazza of San Marco in the Sixteenth Century. From Francanzio di Monalboddo. *Paesi nuovamenti ritrovanti.* Venice, 1517. Young Matthias school was near the Piazza

38 Paolo Piccolomini (ed.). "Due lettere inedite di Bernardino Ochino." *Archivio della società romana di storia patria* XXVIII (1905). 207.

39 John Martin. *Venice's Hidden Enemies. Italian Heretics in a Renaissance City.* Berkeley, Los Angeles and London: University of California Press, 1993. 25.

40 Antonio Santosuosso. "The Moderate Inquisition: Giovanni Della Casa's Venetian Nunciature, 1554– 1559." *Studi Veneziani* N. S. II (1978). 152.

41 Ibid. 28n.

42 Pio Paschini. *Eresia e riforma cattolica al confine orientale dell' Italia.* Rome: Lateranum, 1951. 24.

43 Jules Bonet. "La Reforme à Venise: Les Martyres." *Bulletin Historique et Littéraire. Societé de l'Histoire du Protestantisme Français* (1870/1871). 156.

44 Martin. 5.

45 *De Sectis.* 41.

46 Clyde Manschreck is mistaken that Flacius was "trained for the Roman Catholic priesthood." "A Critical Examination and Appraisal of the Adiaphoristic Controversy in the Life of Philip Melanchthon." Diss., Yale University, 1948. 5.

47 Martin. x.

48 Werner Elert. *Morphologie des Luthertums* III. Munich: C. H. Beck, 1958. 191.

table topic may have been the bizarre cosmic feminism of Guillaume Postel (1547–1549), chaplain of the hospital of San Giovanni e Paolo. It is probable, in fact, since at the time, Madre Zuana, the woman Postel declared the "Venetian Virgin," and Mother of the World, was under the spiritual direction of one of Lupetino's monks.

Already, according to Capuchin general Bernardino Ochino, "Christ has begun to penetrate in Italy, but I would like Him to enter in glory and openly, and I believe Venice will be the door."[38] Paul III saw it in another way. The Reformation, he warned, had infected "persons of every order."[39] Cardinal Jacobo Sadoleto sounded the same warning: "Today the city of Venice, which used to be truly Christian is very much poisoned by the Lutheran plague, so that it has taken over the minds of those who govern, of those who write, or any order of persons, in such a way that the neighboring lands of Lombardy, which are afflicted with the same malady, boast to have Venice as a companion, or better still, as a source."[40]

At the moment, the Reform movement was *contagiosissima*,[41] and had lept over the Carinthian border from Witteburg (now Pisono) on one side, and over the sea from Venice on the other side. Trieste was affected, and according to a report of nuncio Girolamo Aleandro to the curia in 1534, the city of Pirano as well.[42] The church in Vlačić's homeland was on the way to being completely reformed. "Istria, one says, is converting entirely to Lutheranism because of the efforts of the bishop of Capo d'Istria. Already no one invokes St. Roch any more against the pest, nor St. Anthony against measles; the cult of the saints has been abandoned."[43] Delio Cantimori reported that the Italian Reformation was not especially influenced by Luther.[44] One exception, however, according to Cardinal Cesarini, was Baldo Lupetino, who had become *il pui gran Luterano del Mundo.*

Vlačić called him "my preceptor of truth."[45] He confided to him that he wanted to study theology. No one studied theology except monks, he explained, and he was therefore willing to enter a Franciscan house at Bologna or Padua and to surrender half of his inheritance. After a few weeks Lupetino decided to show him several of his Lutheran books. Instead of becoming a Franciscan,[46] his new mentor advised him to study in the North, in Wittenberg, where Martin Luther "had brought the gospel to honor again." And thus, just in time, Vlačić escaped the Inquisition.

During his last year in school, in spite of the papal decree against Protestants arranged by the Patriarch, and despite an agreement between Emperor Charles V and Pope Clement VII to stamp out Protestantism in Venice and the neighboring cities, whole libraries of books by Luther from the Frankfurt Book Fair were sold in the city. But pope and Emperor prevailed. Their hapless victims have been forgotten. Whole communities would soon vanish in the storm, as once Pompeii had vanished. They "quite deliberately left little imprint on the historical memory."[47] Evidence that they even existed remains chiefly in the place names – Cherso, Arbe, Pago, Sebenica, Spalato, Curzola, Cattaro – in the records of the Inquisition.[48]

The storm would be most disastrous in Venice. "Throughout the Venetian territory the inquisitorial plague prevailed; but the secrecy of that tribunal, and the contempt of Italian historians toward heretics, hide their names, and we have only the general statement of foreign writers that their brethren of the Venetian republic everywhere suffered bonds, poverty, and death."[49] Unable to survive the assault, the Lutheran community of Venice, too, vanished, and the "greatest Lutheran in the world" was silenced. But not before they had passed the torch to a formidable young man.

49 William H. Rule. *Martyrs of the Reformation.* London: John Mason, 1851. 18.

THE WAY NORTH

... having put aside all other matters, he passed the time in reading, hearing and writing, and was an example to other students in our academy by his diligence and integrity of life. – Heinrich Pantlin

Interested in the Italian influence on German literature, someone calculated that when he joined a company of traders headed north in 1539, the slight nineteen-year-old Matija Vlačić tucked a copy of the *Divine Comedy* of Dante Alighieri into his travel bag.[1] Into his purse he could drop very little, since his brothers Franjo and Jacov had refused the finances. They were not adverse to his joining the Franciscans, but they opposed the new adventure.

When he reached Augsburg, the northern terminal of the trade route, he was received by Bonifacius Wolfhardt (Lykosthenes), pastor of St. Anne's church and a prominent Zwinglian. Wolfhardt advised him to continue on to Basel, the city of Erasmus.[2] Probably because he called himself Frankowitz at registration at Basel, he was officially enrolled as "Matheus de Franciscis of Albona of the diocese of Pola in Illyria, under Venetian rule, pauper."[3]

At Basel, young Vlačić concentrated on Hebrew under Sebastian Münster.[4] He became the recognized leader of a small group of gifted students, who admired his Italian manners – the Frankfurter Johannes Cellarius, later counsellor in Königstein; Johannes Reifstein of Stolberg, later created poet laureate by Emperor Maximilian II; and Michael Barisius, later a physician in Mühlhausen. He brought "unrest and movement" into the life of another member of the circle, Heinrich Pantlin (Pantaleon),[5] later a Basel physician and writer. Preparing his Book of German Heroes, Pantlin recalled that Vlačić was "very eager to learn the Hebrew and Greek languages, especially sacred readings, so that having put aside all other

1 Schmitthenner. 91.
2 Heldelin. T ij v.
3 Hans Georg Wackernagel. *Die Matrikel der Universität Basel* II. Basel: Verlag der Universitätsbibliothek, 1956. 22. A photographic reproduction of the entry appears in Mirković, 1960, plate 2.
4 Moldaenke. 180.
5 Hans Buscher. *Heinrich Pantaleon und sein Heldenbuch.* Basel: Helbing & Lichtenhahn, 1946. 5, 42.

6 Pantaleon. 439.

7 Josip Talanga. "Paralimpomena dialectices des Matthias Flacius Illyricus." Josip Matešić (ed.). *Matthias Flacius Illyricus – Leben & Werk. Internationales Symposium. Mannheim, February 1991.* Munich: Südosteuropa-Gesellschaft, 1993. 116 f.

8 Heldelin. T iij r.

9 *L'Elément.* 213.

10 C. W. T. Davies. "A Bibliography of John Bale." *Oxford Bibliographical Society. Proceedings and Papers* V. Oxford: Oxford University Press, 1940. 203.

11 F. J. Levy. *Tudor Historical Thought.* San Marino, California: The Huntington Library, 1967. 104.

12 On the relationship of Bale and Flacius, cf. Manfred Edwin Welti. *Der Basler Buchdruck und Britannien.* Basel: Helbing and Lichtenhahn, 1964. 95 f., 205; Thomas Haye. "Der 'Catalogus Testium Veritiatis' des Matthias Flacius Illyricus – zur Auswahl, Verarbeitung und Kritischen Bewertung seiner Quellen." Unpublished paper, Seminar für Lateinische Philologie des Mittelalters, University of Göttingen, 1960. 62 f.; Idem. "Der Catalogus testium veritatis des Matthias Flacius Illyricus – eine Einführung in die Literatur des Mittelalters?" ARG LXXXIII (1992). 45.

13 Lee Piepho. "Mantuan's Ecologues in the English Reformation." *Sixteenth Century Journal* XXV (1994). 626 f.; *Catalogus Testium Veritatis.* 1562. 568 f.

matters, he passed the time in reading, hearing and writing, and was an example to other students in our academy by his diligence and integrity of life."[6]

They all had been taken into the home of Professor Simon Grynaeus, intimate friend and successor of Erasmus of Rotterdam. From him, Vlačić learned the basic elements of philosophy[7] and Reformation thought. The boys had reason to be impressed with their mentor; in 1527 he had discovered the five lost books of Livy, and his lectures on the Epistle to the Romans were being compared favorably with those of Philipp Melanchthon.

Vlačić became acquainted with the publisher, Johannes Oporinus, whose lectures on Greek and Hebrew he heard,[8] and with Conrad Gessner, pioneer of bibliography. In the judgment of Pontien Polman, he was little influenced by the historical writing being done at the university.[9]

Young Vlačić may indeed have been an influence on the history writing of others. In his article in the Book of German Heroes, Pantlin volunteers that he was an influence on his *Chronographiae Ecclesiae*, but without saying when the influence took place. It may have resulted from enthusiastic descriptions by the twenty-year old about the workshop of Aldus Manutius. His influence on another Marian exile, John Bale, is also understandable. Bale, remembered as the most influential author in England during the reign of Edward VI, was "the first real scholar in the history of English studies."[10] We know that they influenced John Foxe's "Book of Martyrs" in common.

> What Foxe did was to take the grand scheme evolved by John Bale and develop it into a fully articulated church history. In doing so, he absorbed his master's work, as he absorbed the products of Flacius Illyricus and his school. Foxe had no choice: if he wanted to forge an armory as well as a history and to put the whole into some form of order, then these were the writers from whom to borrow. But Foxe did more than play the jackdaw. He searched for his own sources, and while he learned something about historical criticism from the Germans and as much from Valla and the humanists, he knew how to apply the knowledge. His best pieces of critical writing have to do with English history, where he had no models. The emphasis on sources presumably came from Flacius, though Bale had published some. It was Foxe who showed men how to use them.[11]

A former Carmelite from the remote North, Bale would have been open to stimulation from the South. Because of the influence on history of the two extraordinary men, in England and on the continent, respectively, one would like to know more about the details of how they worked together.[12] One modest recent discovery was that together they were responsible for the popularity in England of Baptista Mantuanus ("the Mantuan"), whose Ecologues, cited earlier by Luther in "Against the Roman Papacy" and by Flacius in his *Catalogus*,[13] became part of the curriculum in English grammar schools. F. J. Levy thinks that Vlačić convinced him of the importance of using primary sources.

> Thus, when one comes to examine Bale's career on the continent, it is best to recollect

that one reason for the high respect in which he was held was his ability to help the German church historians, working under the direction of Matthias Flacius, with vast quantities of bibliographical information. Whereas Flacius did not publish his own bibliography, the *Catalogus,* until 1556, Bale had prepared its British equivalent years earlier. Moreover, the evident similarity of Flacius' view of the course of church history to Bale's is as likely to be due to Bale's influence on the Germans as the other way about.

The much greater prominence of the Magdeburg Centuries has obscured the fact that Flacius was less historically minded than Bale. To suggest that Bale's writings were the model for Flacius would probably be an exaggeration: there is certainly no proof. It is certain, however, that the peculiarities of henrician apologetics forced their authors into a historical mold and that, under the influence of Tyndal and Barnes, Bale applied the techniques of history to theological polemics. Unlike his predecessors, however, Bale was a historian before he was a theologian, and that he would have picked up the historical hints in Luther's writing was only to be expected. What Bale probably learned from Flacius and his associates was the value of printing the relevant documents *in extenso.*[14]

Leslie Fairfield is sceptical. "Bale's thought had taken shape a decade before Flacius' historical works began to appear."[15] According to Andreas Burkhardt, however, Vlačić met Bale "early,"[16] perhaps as early as 1540, when the twenty-year-old Vlačić studied in Basel, the year that Thomas Cromwell fell from royal grace in England and Bale fled to the continent.

That same year, Vlačić removed to the University of Tübingen, where he found congenial lodging with Matija Grbać, professor of Greek and Ethics and translator of Hesiod and Aeschylus into Latin, and a fellow native of Istria. Grbać, who thought of his homeland in humanist fashion, as the Roman province of Illyria, called himself "Matthias Garbitius Illyricus."

Librarians have to contend with three men named "Matthias Illyricus." One early clarification of the name was written by a glossator at the Grbać entry in the Wittenberg record of awards of master's degrees. That Matthias Illyricus was not Matthias Flacius Illyricus – "not that apostate cuckoo."[17] When he adopted the style, "Matthias Flacius Illyricus," Matija Vlačić could have been imitating Professor Peter Gucetić of the Sorbonne and Louvain, known as "Doctor Illyricus;"[18] it is more likely that his model was Grbać.[19]

Young Matthias was also on friendly terms with Ludwig Grempius of the law faculty, and with Johann Forster, an avid follower of Luther.[20] Despite twenty years' difference in age, he won the friendship of Professor Leonhart Fuchs, whose name persists in the name of the drooping primrose, fuchsia, and its color. Fuchs, it is interesting to note, was the godfather of Jakob Andreae, Flacius' formidable last opponent, but his devotion to Luther, the excuse for his dismissal from Ingolstadt, bound him to Flacius his whole life.[21] Fuchs is remembered primarily as the Father of Botany, as the teacher of Vesalius, and for giving the name, digitalis, to the foxglove plant. It is possible that his ground-breaking work, *Methodus seu Ratio,* the first printed system of medicine,[22] influenced Flacius' writings

14 Op. cit. 95 f.

15 *John Bale. Mythmaker for the English Reformation.* West Lafayette, Indiana: Purdue University Press, 1976. 218 f. Fairfield may not have taken into account that Flacius began publishing collections of original sources in 1548.

16 Op. cit. 21. Cf. Theodor Vetter. *Englische Flüchtlinge in Zürich während der ersten Hälfte des 16. Jahrhunderts.* Zürich: Druck des Art. Institut O. Füssli, 1893. 16 f.; Jesse W. Harris. *John Bale: A Study in the Minor Lite-rature of the Reformation.* Urbana: The University of Illinois Press, 1940. 32; *Martin Steinmann. Johannes Oporinus.* Basel and Stuttgart: Helbing & Lichtenhahn, 1967. 69n.

17 Julius Köstlin. *Die Baccalauri und Magistri der Wittenberger Philosophischen Fakultät 1518–1537.* Halle: Max Niemeyer, 188. 22n.; "Zwei Briefe von Tübinger Universitätsprofessoren an Melanchthon." Clemen KS VI, 400. In the course of the defamatory campaign against him, the epithet, "cuckoo," was standard. On the confusion of the names, Ritter. 24.

18 Rabil. 273.

19 Erwin Wedel. "Matthias Flacius Illyricus, ein bedeutender kroatischer Humanist." *Matthias Flacius Illyricus.* 1525–1575. Regensburg: Lassleben, 1. 1975. 25.

20 Christiana Frank. "Untersuchungen zum Catalogus testium veritatis des Matthias Flacius Illyricus." Diss., Tübingen, 1990. 13.

21 Eberhard Stübler. *Leonhart Fuchs Leben und Werk.* Munich: Verlag der Münchner Drucke, 1928. 175.

22 William P. D. Wrightman. "Quid sit Methodus? 'Method' in Sixteenth Century Medical Teaching and Discovery." *Journal of the History of Medicine* XIX (1964). 360, 364.

23 Ritter. 15; Heinrich Heppe. *Geschichte des deutschen Protestantismus in den Jahren 1555– 1581* III. Marburg: R. G. Elwer'scher Druck und Verlag, 1853. 383; Georg Matthias König. *Bibliotheca vetus atque nova.* Altdorf: Heinrich Meyer, 1687. 321.

on scholarly method. There has also been speculation that Flacius' well-known assertion that sin is man's substance, was influenced by Fuchs' "unphilosophical" statement that human illness is man's substance – that *morbum esse substantiam.*[23]

Another of his acquaintances was Professor Joachim Camerarius, who later, as Melanchthon's biographer and apologist, disparaged him. At the moment, however, Camerarius was well-disposed, and wrote him a warm letter of recommendation to Melanchthon. Travelling through Regensburg at the time of the imperial religious colloqium, Flacius finally found his way to Luther's university.

PART TWO: WITTENBERG

The Pope Strikes

AN ARISTOTLE HOUSE

It is false to say that without Aristotle one cannot become a theologian. The opposite is true: no one can become a theologian unless he be without Aristotle ... The whole of Aristotle is to theology as darkness is to light. – Luther

... it is of highest importance to the state that Aristotle is retained and stands out in the schools and is handled by students. For without this author one can retain neither pure philosophy, nor even any proper way of teaching and learning. – Melanchthon

Was Flacius a "born fighter"? Erich Beyreuther wanted to know.[1] Was he the "born polemicist" that Arno Duch called him?[2] Was there "something rigid," Karl Brandi asked, "in the personality or the nationality of this Illyricus from Istria?"[3] From the distance of four and one-half centuries it is difficult to make judgments about his personality. It is doubtful, however, whether he would have succeeded at bringing together the specialist team that produced the Magdeburg Centuries, and, later, at commanding the loyalty that held together the formidable Flacian party without certain winning personality traits.

In his student days he won not a few friends, among them Paul Eber,[4] Sicilian landowner Hieronymus Othitz, and Imre Eschehy (Eszeki), also called Emerius Zigerius, (Zsiger). Eschehy testified to his friendship in a letter in which he reported on the tolerance of a Muslim government. After leaving Wittenberg he had become pastor of a congregation of five hundred in Tolna, 120 miles from Budapest in Turkish-occupied Hungary, where he is still honored as the founder of a school modelled on the Wittenberg academy.[5] He reported having convinced several priests to accept the Reformation and surviving a murder plot. Offered a bribe to kill him, the local Pasha investigated and – unlike Charles V! – decreed that the Evangelical faith be tolerated. Flacius published the letter as a rebuke of the Christian emperor and his murderous campaign against Protestants.[6]

Another friend was the nobleman Sebastian von Zedlitz, to whose castle, at Neukirch an der Katzbach, Luther had dispatched the first evangelical clergyman in Silesia, Melchior Hoffmann. Sebastian's grandfather, Sigismund, was an eye-witness to the burning alive of John Huss at the council of Constance. George von Zedlitz, Sebastian's father, had sent two men to ask Luther whether he was the swan that Huss (Czech: "goose") had promised would succeed him. Sebastian later lent his weight to Flacius' struggle against the heresiarch, Caspar von Schwenckfeld. When Flacius

1 "Flacius, der geborene Kämpfer und von einem wütenden Enthusiasmus erfüllt." Erich Beyreuther. "Die Kirche in der Neuzeit." *Geschichte Thüringens* IV. Hans Patze and Walter Schlesinger (eds.). Cologne and Vienna: Böhlau, 1972. 3.

2 Op. cit. 417.

3 "Lag etwas Starres in Persönlichkeit oder Volkstum dieses Illyriers aus Istrien?" *Gegenreformation und Religionskriege.* Leipzig: Quelle & Meyer, 1930. 67.

4 Heldelin. T iij r.

5 On Eschehy's school, Kathona Géza. *Fejezetek a torok hódoltsági reformáció történetéböl.* [Contribution to the History of the Reformation in the Territory under Turkish Occupation] Budapest, 1964. 19–22.

6 *Eine Schrifft eines fromen Predigers aus der Türkey an Illyricum geschrieben. Darinnen angezeigt wird, wie es dort mit der Kirche und dem Evangelio zugehet.* Magdeburg: Michael Lotter, 1550.

7 Heldelin. X ij r.

8 *Entschuldigung ... an die Universitet.* H r–H v.

9 "non prius uxorem nebulo fugitivus habebat, hic igitur coniunx illi, curante Philippo, contigit." Georg Sabinus. *Carmen de Natalibus, parentibus, Vita, Moribus, Rebus Gestis Flacii Illyrici.* 1558. C ij. "data ei uxor." Jocham Camerarius. *D. Philippi Melanchthonis Ortu, Totius Vitae Curri-cula et Morte ... Narratio.* Leipzig: Ernest Vögelin, 1566. 286.

10 *Entschuldigung ... an die Universitet.* [H r], J iij v.

11 Epistola apologetica ad quandam pastorem [Bugenhagen]. *Omnia latina scripta hactenus sparsim contra Adiaphorica fraudes & errores aedita, et quaedam prius non excusa, catalogum versa pagina indicabit. Omnia correcta et aucta.* Magdeburg: Michael Lotter, 1550. [M viij v].

12 CR, VIII, 840.

13 "Fuit mihi dulcis et amicitia et familiaritas cum Illyrico." Ibid. 798.

14 J. Döllinger. II, 243.

15 Carolus Eduardus Förstemann. *Album Academiae Vitebergensis* I. Leipzig: Carolus Tauchnitius, 1841. 191. The odd name is the reason G. Plitt could not find his name in the register. RE 2, IV, 563. It was not because his name had been erased, as Plitt thought. The "Matthias Illyricus" registered on p. 191 of the *Album* is Matthias *Garbitius* Illyricus.

16 *Entschuldigung ... an die Universitet.* E v.

17 *Von der Einigkeit derer, so für und wider die Adiaphora in vergangenen Jaren gestritten haben, christlicher einfeltiger bericht, sehr nützlich zu lesen.* [Oberursel: Nicolaus Henricus] 1556. A iiiij r.

18 Sachiko Kusukawa. "Providence Made Visible: The Creation and Establishment of Lutheran Natural Philosophy." Diss., Cambridge University, 1991. Ch. 2.

was under attack, he offered him permanent refuge, and when he died he built a hospital to honor him.

Flacius enjoyed the friendship of Melanchthon himself, the *Praeceptor Germaniae*, than whom no other German professor has ever been so famous. He found lodging in Melanchthon's big house on the main street, and with his help found employment. He served three years as *Korrepetitor* with him, and Melanchthon arranged that he serve as language tutor to Paul Eber, Johann Mathesius, Johann Aurifaber and Friedrich Staphylus – to list the best-known.[7] When Melanchthon was considering going to the Council of Trent, Flacius offered to act as his *famulus* in spite of the danger.[8] Melanchthon eventually even found him a bride.[9] "I honestly have loved you," Flacius wrote to the Preceptor," more than any other."[10]

> I have often said it in the sight of God and among good friends, and with these words: would that I or someone like me, unlearned, paltry little man of no authority would be doing these things, and not such a man as this. Surely, less evil would follow in the church. Indeed, I often [was willing] to be accursed in his place.[11]

For his part, Melanchthon called him "an old friend who truly loved you."[12] "Between myself and Illyricus", he recalled, "there was sweet friendship and intimacy."[13]

His opponents later chose to express their hostility by calling him "Meister Matz" and "Lyrx."[14] If we had more evidence, however, we might discover that some of his impressive collection of nicknames – Mattes, Mats, Mats Flax, Matz, Matzs Unflat, Flach, Flachen, Fleze, Flicksflax, Lyric, Lirix, Lyrx, and Lyricus – were a sign of fondness. (His name, "Matheus Watzer," in the Wittenberg matriculation record,[15] is probably only evidence of a foreigner's bad pronunciation.)

Flacius himself hoped he would be judged on his behavior during the years before the provocations of the Counter-Reformation and the fissures within the Evangelical camp. "I have been careful to be calm and quiet," he wrote about those years, "and have caused no aversion either in the school or in the churches, or even considered causing it, as many know and must give witness."[16] "No one can rightly reproach me, either before the adiaphoristic matter at Wittenberg, or thereafter anywhere, nor during my time in Germany, now almost sixteen years, of having been especially or for a long time quarrelsome or angry at anyone, except about religion. That may well be an indication of my nature and personality, and demonstrate that I am not a quarrelsome and disputatious person."[17]

A decade earlier, the University of Wittenberg had faced a crisis. New students were not enrolling in large numbers. From 1523 to 1533 no doctoral degrees were awarded, and in the years 1527 to 1929 enrollment sank to a low level partly because of the Wittenberg disturbances. In those days, partly under the threat of popular unrest,[18] Melanchthon began to change his attitude toward philosophy. Another reason was the impossibility of building a university on a biblical foundation. Luther, who called Aristotle "the worst enemy of grace," had campaigned for eliminating

Aristotelian philosophy from the curriculum. But as Melanchthon saw it now, the Pauline-Augustinian doctrine of salvation was too narrow a basis for a university curriculum,[19] and he began to think of reconstructing it.

> As the Pauline-Augustinian doctrine of salvation failed, because it believed it could dispense with speculation and thought it is enough to present dogma in a purely irrational fashion, and as the whole educational system in Protestant lands suffered the greatest misfortune, then in Melanchthon the humanist awakened with faith in the power of reason, with the love for classical antiquity and the conviction of the worth of studies for conducting one's life and morality.[20]

"The more he freed himself inwardly from the basic thoughts of Luther, the stronger appeared the kernels, and they grew to patterns of independent structures."[21] The curriculum had to be reconstructed, he concluded, on another, a philosophical, basis. The philosophical system chosen had to offer a common foundation for various disciplines of the university: ethics, political science, and physics. "I need a learned philosophy," he explained, "not those jestings, under which there is no substance."[22] He found the Epicureans godless, the Stoics fatalistic, Plato and the Neoplatonists vague and the middle Scholastics sceptical. For a while he tried Pliny as the text for his lectures on natural philosophy.[23] Rejecting the alternatives he chose the peripatetic, Aristotle. "There is no better contriver of method," he concluded, "than Aristotle,"[24] and even called himself a "homo peri-pateticus."[25] "I have said that one certain kind of philosophy should be chosen, that which has the fewest sophistries and maintains a proper method: that is the teaching of Aristotle."[26]

Luther had said, "It is false to say that without Aristotle one cannot become a theologian. The opposite is true: no one can become a theologian unless he be without Aristotle ..."[27] Now Melanchthon was saying something quite different: "without this author one can retain neither pure philosophy, nor even any proper way of teaching and learning.[28]

> Whereas heretofore, at most, the formal structure of the logic, rhetoric and poetic was used, Melanchthon now addressed himself to the contents, published the pertinent writings, explained them and on their basis also wrote his own books. Thus in the framework of Protestant doctrine he developed an ethic, a psychology and a physics. The doctrines of the pagans which did not correspond to dogma were either explained away or excused with a reference to their pagan origin. In any case, no insuperable obstacle to using Aristotle in instruction was seen any more.[29]

He gave the new philosophical basis systematic form in his 1532 *Philosophiae Moralis Epitome*. "After I lectured on Aristotle's Ethics," he explained, "I added this commentary, in which I followed not only Aristotle's ideas, but also his method."[30] In 1536 Aristotelian philosophy was officially made the basis of instruction. The curriculum at Wittenberg, according to Sachiko Kusukawa, underwent a "Lutheran reformulation," in which it was structured to fit the distinction between law and gospel. "Luther the theologian attacked scholastic philosophy which was a hindrance to his theology; Melanchthon the Greek teacher, teaching in the arts faculty,

19 Peter Petersen. *Geschichte der aristotelischen Philosophie im protestantischen Deutschland.* Leipzig: Felix Meiner, 1921. 40.
20 Ibid. 40.
21 Siegfried Wollgast. *Zur Philosophie in Deutschland von der Reformation bis zur Aufklärung.* Berlin: Akademie-Verlag, 1982. 454.
22 CR, XI, 282.
23 Charles G. Nauert, Jr. "Humanists, Scientist and Pliny: Changing Approaches to a Classical Author." *American Historical Review* LXXXIV (1979). 80.
24 CR, XVI, 423.
25 CR, III, 383.
26 CR, XI, 282.
27 WA, I, 226; LW, 31.12.
28 CR, II, 956.
29 Max Wundt. *Die Geschichte der Philosophie an der Universität Jena.* Jena: Gustav Fischer, 1932. 7.
30 CR, III, 361.
31 Op. cit. 44, 46.

32 Max Frischeisen-Köhler and Willy Moog. *Die Philosophie der Neuzeit bis zum Ende des XVIII. Jahrhunderts* III. 13. Aufl. Basel: Benno Schwabe, 1953. 101.

33 Op. cit. 9.

34 Preger. I, 34 f.

35 *Gesammelte Aufsätze*. Leipzig and Berlin: Tuebner, 1924–1936. II, 186.

36 CR, XI, 281.

37 See the section, "A Catalog of Witnesses," below.

38 Gustav Milchsack. "Faustbuch und Faustsage." *Gesammelte Aufsätze über Buchkunst und Buchdruck, Doppeldrucke, Faustsage, sowie über neue Handschriften von Tischreden Luthers und Dicta Melanchthonis.* Wolfen-büttel: In Kommission bei Julius Zwißlers Verlag, 1922. 133 f.

39 See the section, "Who Wrote the Centuries?" below.

40 Georg Mentz. *Johann Friedrich der Großmütige (1503–1534)* III. Jena: Gustav Fischer, 1908. 295.

41 *Gründliche verlegung aller Sophisterey, so Juncker Issleb, D. Interim, Morus, Pfeffinger, D. Geitz in seinem gründlichen bericht und ihre gesellen, die andere Adiaphoristen, das Leipzische Interim zu beschönen, gebrauchen.* [Magdeburg: Christian Rödinger, 1551]. [H iiij v.].

42 "Law and Gospel: The Importance of Philosophy at Reformation Wittenberg." *History of Universities* XI. Oxford: Oxford University Press, 1992. 44.

43 Quoted in Lynn Thorndike. *A History of Magic and Experimental Science* V. London and New York: Columbia University Press, 1941. 378.

44 Georg Hoffmann. "Luther und Melanchthon. Melanchthons Stellung in der Theologie des Luthertums." *Zeitschrift für Systematische Theologie* XV (1938). 105.

45 Hans Christoph von Hase. *Die Gestalt der Kirche Luthers. Der casus confessionis im Kampf des Matthias Flacius gegen das Interim von 1548.* Göttingen: Vandenhoeck & Ruprecht, 1940. 92.

found a new meaning for philosophy in support of Luther's cause."[31]

Other commentators have not been as positive. One standard history of philosophy calls his the first step toward the theology of the Enlightenment.[32] Siegfried Wollgast argued that by sanctioning Aristotle's metaphysics, which he grossly underestimated, Melanchthon introduced into German thought the seed of agnosticism.[33] Wilhelm Preger made Melanchthon responsible for a new scholasticism in the sixteenth century, rationalism and pantheism in the eighteenth, and a "free, personal principle" in the nineteenth.[34] Wilhelm Dilthey wondered "whether the whole natural theology, which the English Deists and the German rationalists preached in the nineteenth century, is not already present in Melanchthon? It would take only the omission of the myth of the fall into sin and the use St. Paul makes of it, and the natural theology would be there; not a kernel of it, a beginning, but totally ready and armed, complete and whole."[35]

"Philosophy is necessary not only for the sake of method," Melanchthon wrote, "but many things must be accepted into theology from physics."[36] He was tampering not just with the method, but also the *content* of theology. Was Melanchthon thus making a pact with satan? It is just possible that in his *Catalogus Testium Veritatis*, Flacius had served up the medieval materials for the original legend of Faust, who had sold his soul to the devil.[37] One plausible hypothesis is that Melanchthon was not only the model for the original Faust, but also for Mephistopheles.

> It is this Mephistopheles-Melanchthon who, boasting of his "free will," entices the Faust-Melanchthon to presumption and defection from the Lutheran faith, produces a Catholic remorse that does not relieve the Faust-Melanchthon's harrowing doubt about his justification, because through the threats he clings to his catholicizing tendency; he taunts him and at last kills him in a frightful way (*rabies theologorum*). And it is this Mephistopheles-Melanchthon who wills to initiate Melanchthon into the knowledge of the elements, and fobs him off with a childish jumble of medieval-superstitious nature contemplation and theology into hell, up to heaven and over the whole world.[38]

Elector Johann Friedrich had predicted that under Melanchthon's influence the University of Wittenberg would become a "sophistic school of scoundrels" (*sophistische Bubenschule*). In the introduction of the third tome of the Magdeburg Centuries, Flacius' associates[39] express their anger at the new intellectual climate at Luther's university. The Elector's prediction had come true.

> Those people now had no more taste for anything except what is taken from this philosophy. So one no more hears, marks, and learns the Holy Scripture at all, but it is relegated again to a corner … If anyone objects, the whole gang of these heathen philosophers immediately cries out that one is rejecting all arts, and that barbarism is returning. If one reminds these heathens that such means should be used sparingly and for elucidation, the cry goes up, "Great is Diana!" … a shameful eclipse of divine truth.[40]

The critical young Flacius, bent on perfecting his Greek with Viet Örtel (Winsheimius), avoided the lectures of Johan Bugenhagen and Georg Major,[41] but listened intently to Melanchthon's lectures. Honored as the *Praeceptor Germaniae*, he was an extremely effective teacher. How concisely, how purely, they were saying, how well he spoke and taught! How famous was his succinct, pure and elegant way of learning and teaching – the *succinctum, purum et elegans genus dicendi et docendi Philippicum*! "It is striking," observes Kusukawa, "how most students and lecturers disputed and wrote about philosophy in virtually the same way Melanchthon did."[42] "...all who were true disciples of Melanchthon employed a very similar style and form of oration in speaking and writing, molded and turned out in imitation of their most erudite preceptor."[43]

Matthias Flacius was no exception. "... if one opens a work of Flacius," Georg Hoffmann observed, "the *Clavis Scripturae Sacrae*, for example, one meets an unmistakable pupil of Melanchthon. The scholarly *minutiae*, the methodical care, the development of proofs and citations – these and many other formal, but also partly substantial traits, betray the theological school of Melanchthon."[44] His understanding of political organization came from Melanchthon;[45] his psychology from Melanchthon's essay, *On the Soul*.[46] It was Melanchthon, too, who stimulated his striving for doctrinal orthodoxy.[47]

Even if one credits the speculations of various commentators about who may have influenced Flacius' historical publications – John Bale, Flavio Biondo, Johannes Cochläus,[48] Egnazio, John Huss, Wolfgang Lazius, Heinrich Pantlin – the structure of his historical work, the chain of tradition, the succession of ages of the church, the point at which corruption began and how it gained ground, came from Melanchthon.[49] Friedrich Lauchert sees the roots of Flacius' historical viewpoint in Melanchthon's *Didymi Faventini adversus Thomam Placentinum Oratio pro Martino Luthero, Theologo.*[50]

Should Flacius, already as a student, have had doubts about his famous teacher? It would have been expecting too much, since Luther was in his declining days, and was already a distant figure. In 1546 Melanchthon made the famous announcement, "Ach, obiit auriga et currus Israel qui rexit Ecclesiam in hac ultima senecta mundi": "The waggoner and chariot of Israel, has died, who guided the church in this last age of the world."[51] In those days there was little doubt about a *Consensus Lutheri et Melanchthoni*. Melanchthon himself insisted on it. "... with regard to predestination, the consent of the will, the necessity of our obedience and mortal sin," he wrote in 1537, "I say many things less rudely [than Luther]. In all these points I know that Luther basically thinks the same, but those lacking insight are too fond of some of his exaggerated expressions, not seeing in which context they belong."[52] There are still many scholars who insist that Luther and Melanchthon agreed on doctrine.[53]

Others, however, deny such a consensus. The well-known fact that Luther never broke with Melanchthon,[54] is less convincing evidence than a careful comparison of their writings. When Albrecht Ritschl made such a comparison, he found differences. *In hoc*, he found, referring to the all-important doctrine of justification, *magister non tenetur*.[55]

46 Lauri Haikola. *Gesetz und Evangelium bei Matthias Flacius Illyricus. Eine Untersuchung zur lutherischen Theologie vor der Konkordienformel.* Lund: CWK Gleerup, 1952. 59.

47 Albrecht Ritschl. "Die Entstehung der Lutherischen Kirche." ZKG, I (1877). 100.

48 Karl Schottenloher. *Pfalzgraf Ottheinrich und das Buch: Ein Beitrag zur Geschichte der Evangelischen Publizistik, mit Anhang: Das Reformationsschrifftum in der Palatina.* Münster: Aschendorff, 1927. 157n.

49 Scheible. "Plan" 209 f.; John N. King. *English Reformation Literature: The Tudor Origins of the Protestant Tradition.* Princeton: Princeton University Press, 1982. 60; Cf. Fraenckel. *Testimonium Patrum.* 264. Idem, Review of Scheible, Op. cit. 167.

50 *Die italienischen literarischen Gegner Luthers.* Freiburg im Breisgau: Herder, 1802; Nieuwkoop: de Graaf, 1972. 193n; CR, I, 286–358.

51 CR, VI, 59.

52 CR, III, 383.

53 "Any differences were simply reflections of personality, the stormy Luther, the thoughtful Melanchthon." Gustav Mix. "Luther und Melan-chthon in ihrer gegenseitigen Beurteilung." *Theologische Studien und Kritiken* I (1901). 520.

54 Wilhelm Mangold "Luther und Melanchthon." *Theologische Arbeiten aus dem rheinischen wissenschaftlichen Predigerverein* VII. 48; Eduard Schwartz. "Flaciana und die Sy-node der Vögel." *Zeitschrift für die unirte ev. Kirche* XIII (1853). 229.

55 *A Critical History of the Doctrine of Justification and Reconciliation.* Edinburgh: Edmonston and Douglas, 1872. 175.

56 "According to my view, knowledge of religion is to be taken from the Holy Scripture; about civil usages, I want to know Cicero." CR, XI, 88.

57 Frischeisen-Köhler and Moog. 101.

58 Hans-Georg Geyer. "Welt und Mensch. Zur Frage des Aristotelismus bei Melanchthon." Diss., Bonn, 1959. 11.

59 Wilhelm Maurer. "Melanchthon als Humanist." Walter Elliger, ed. *Philipp Melanchthon. Forschungsbeiträge zur 400. Wiederkehr seines Todestages dargeboten in Wittenberg. 1960.* Götttingen: Vandenhoeck und Ruprecht, 1961. 128.

60 Haikola. *Gesetz und Evangelium.* 33.

61 Ibid. 37.

62 "... the most central concepts of the theology of Flacius are derived from aristotelian metaphysics." Ibid. 13 f. According to David Loefgren, Haikola had an eye more for the differences between Luther and the later Lutheran tradition than for the continuities. "Verschiedene Tendenzen in der neueren Lutherforschung." *Kerygma und Dogma* V (1959). 153. Cf. Lauri Haikola. "Melanchthons und Luthers Lehre von der Rechtfertigung: ein Vergleich" in Vilmos Vajta, ed. *Luther und Melanchthon.* Göttingen: Vandenhoeck und Ruprecht, 1961. 89.

63 "It is obvious that he himself did not represent aristotelian philosophy; which one he represented, on the contrary, is less evident ... it is none other than platonism." Lutz Geldsetzer. "Matthias Flacius Illyricus und die wissenschaftliche Begründung der protestantischen Theologie." Josip Matešić, ed. *Matthias Flacius Illyricus – Leben und Werk. Internationales Symposium, Mannheim, Februar 1991.* Munich: Südosteuropa-Gesellschaft, 1993. 209 f.

64 *Gesammelte Schriften* II, 162 f.

65 Ibid. 105.

66 Hans Emil Weber. *Reformation, Orthodoxie und Rationalismus.* Gütersloh: C. Bertelsman, 1937. I/1, 121; O. Ritschl. II, 405.

67 Albrecht Ritschl. *Theologie und Metaphysik.* Bonn: Adolph Marcus, 1881. 55.

68 A. Ritschl. "Entstehung". 55.

69 Wollgast. 9.

Influenced by the Stoics, by Cicero,[56] Galen,[57] Quintilian,[58] Ficino and Pico,[59] Melanchthon was a philosophical eclectic.[60] Flacius, too, was a philosophical eclectic,[61] a safe adjective, at least until it is decided whether his thought was was essentially (1) aristotelian,[62] or (2) platonist.[63]

Wilhelm Dilthey observed about Melanchthon that "under his hand all questions became simple and plain."[64] For those who sat in his lecture-hall, Georg Hoffmann writes, Melanchthon's pedagogy was a "transformer," by which "the high-tension of Luther's thought about faith was re-formed on the lowest, non-dangerous tension, for purposes of theological home-use, whereby a certain loss of current must be accepted." "We have to do with very consequential doctrinal deviations which seriously endangered the purity of the concern of the Reformation. To stay with the metaphor, with damage to the wires, which can put the whole provision of current into question." "So much were the young people who sat at Luther's feet under the influence of his colleague's teaching methods," he continues, naming one of the complexities of Luther research, "that when they were reproducing what they had heard from Luther, involuntarily very familiar scholastic expressions from Melanchthon's lecture flowed into their pens."[65]

About Flacius' relationship to Melanchthon, it can be said that to a large extent *magister tenetur*: "like master, like student." In his early years he accepted Melanchthon's teaching (which he later emphatically denied) that good works are the *sine qua non* of salvation.[66] Even after years of theological warfare, Flacius was unable to shake off the influence of his famous teacher.[67] The 1577 Formula of Concord, largely a triumph of Flacius over Melanchthon, nevertheless reveals Melanchthon's continuing influence.

> ... the principal opponent of Melanchthon, Flacius, who is, all things considered, demonstrably the victor, was a special pupil of Melanchthon, and was hardly free from the characteristic influence of that teacher during the same time that loyalty to Luther and his historical work drove him to the struggle against him.[68]

Melanchthon's "pure peripatetic doctrine" eventually came to dominate all the Protestant universities of Germany through his admirers, Joachim Camerarius at Leipzig, Jakobus Schegk at Tübingen, David Chytraeus at Rostock, Victorin Strigel at Jena, Jacob Martini at Wittenberg and Phillip Scherbius at Helmstedt. So pervasive was the new philosophical influence that it spread to preparatory schools, which for that reason were called "Aristotle Houses."[69]

Aldus Manutius and his friends had excluded Aristotle at their school as old-fashioned; Luther had excluded Aristotle from his as a heathen. But the old pagan was not to be avoided. Once, Luther likened his relationship to theology as darkness to light. But now, the Philosopher was firmly in charge of the turf from which he had been expelled. When the odd name, "Matheus Watzer," was entered in the matriculation record at Wittenberg, it was the signal that Matthias Flacius had been taken into an Aristotle House.

I am not an untested Christian, which Doctor Luther especially wanted to have in a theologian. – Flacius

I learned more through my own temptations and study than through his [Melanchthon's] lectures. – Flacius

Luther's best years, Flacius observed, were behind him. "Behold, this is our old, venerable Father in Christ," he wrote, "the faithful man of God and true Elijah, who as an undismayed hero has fought, confidently and happily against the Antichrist, all kinds of heresies and Baalites. Today or tomorrow our Lord God will take him from here."[1] But on Sundays, the Reformer could still be seen in person, striding with head erect into St. Mary's church to preach. Standing in the courtyard, Flacius was carried back to Venice, to the *Riva degli Schiavoni*: Martin Luther was a war galley moving through the lagoon, sails unfurled, headed for combat.[2]

Curious about the early history of the reform, he searched out one of Luther's fellow Augustinians, who told him about life in the Black Cloister and certified that Luther's conduct there had been upright.[3] Someone else told him about a Franciscan prior named Fleck, and he repeated the story. Despite the rule of silence, when Fleck read the 95 theses he laughed out loud in the refectory of the Franciscan monastery of Steinlausigk near Bitterfeld, and shouted to the monks, "Ha, ha, ha, he is come, with whom you will have to do!" He wrote a letter to Luther, asking him to persevere.[4]

For some time Flacius had been battling depression and was no longer able to study. Accustomed to the bright skies of the Adriatic he cannot have been unaffected by Wittenberg's leaden clouds. The name of his native Albona, he explained to young Pantlin in Basel, meant "from the white sun" – *ab albedine soli*.[5] Nor could he have been unaffected by his brothers' disapproval of his going North. But he understood his malady as theological – an acute consciousness of the evil in the world, the tyranny of Satan, the power of sin, the evil of the Old Adam, the fury of unconverted men against God, of predestination, of God's damnation. He was seeing the world, comments the Croatian philosopher, Vladimir Filipović, as it really is.[6] He remembered asking "my God, why hast thou forsaken me?" and considered suicide.

His distress lasted longer than it should have, he decided later, because he had remained silent. His deliverance began with asking for help. "Toward the end of my third year in Wittenberg," he wrote, "when I was living at the home of Dr. Friedrich Backofen, then deacon, when the evil had become so bad that I was certain I would die, he noticed that because of inner confusion I could not work. He pressed me until I admitted what was wrong. Buoying me up with promise and with prayer, he arranged that Dr. Pomeranus [Johann Bugenhagen] bring me to Martin Luther."[7] Luther

1 *Etliche greiffliche gewisse unnd scheinbarliche warzeichen, daraus ein jeder wie geringes verstands er auch sey, Wo er nur zu erforschung der warheit geneigt ist, vermerken kan, das die Lehre der Evangelischen des Herrn Christi Lehre selbst ist, und das der papisten Lehr falsch, gottlos, vom Antichrist erfunden ist.* Magdeburg: Christian Rödinger, (1549). Aij v; (1550). A iij r.

2 "Saepe cum picae erecta fronte in templum vadentem intuitus sum, eiusque actiones plane ipso Elia dignas perpendi, visus mihi sum Venetam illam longe maximam nauim (quam illi Galeonem vocant) omnibus velis vento instatis contra hostes pergentem cernere." *De Voce et Re Fide.* 1555. 49 f.

3 *Etliche greiffliche ... warzeichen.* 1550. Aij v, G r.

4 *Catalogus.* 1556. 1008, 1562. 573; Hans Preuss. *Luther der Prophet.* Gütersloh: Bertelsmann, 1933. 30.

5 Pantaleon. III, 438.

6 "Aktuelni Vlačić". *Dometi* [Rijeka] VIII (1970). Unpaginated.

7 *Entschuldigung ... an die Universitet.* E r.

8 *Ein rechter lesteriger Rabsakes brieff, geschrieben von einem Bischoff an einen Christlichen Fürsten, in welchem er ihn vermanet das er sol von der erkanten warheit Christi zu dem Antichrist abfallen ...* [Magdeburg: Christian Rödinger] 1549. A ij r. A recent article on the genre: Meinrad Limbeck. "Die Klage – eine verschwundene Gebetsgattung". *Theologische Quartalschrift* CLVII (1977). 16.

9 *Entschuldigung ... an die Universitet.* D r, E v.

10 Op. cit. II, 484.

11 J. Baur. 41.

12 *Christliche Anfechtung - Schul.* Nuremberg: Johann Andreae Etners, 1669. 240 ff.

13 *Seelen-Schatz.* III. Teil, Leipzig: Andreas Zeidler, 1698. 528. Cf. Ritter. 20.

treated him sympathetically, not as someone rejected, but as someone being tempted. He comforted him with his own experience and that of others, and encouraged him to pray prayers of complaint, on the model of the psalter. "It makes no difference that He knows it anyway," Luther told him. "He wants to have it so."[8] At St. Mary's church intercessory prayer was said for the distressed student, and "the evil decreased from day to day and at year's end I was well."

The lasting result of his spiritual struggles was that his theological thought was not mere abstract speculation, but was built on a religious base. "I tell you all this," Flacius wrote afterwards, "so that you do not think I have learned the teaching of the gospel only from reading or leisurely thought, but through my own experience, and that I am not an untested Christian, which Doctor Martin Luther especially wanted to have in a theologian."[9] Otto Ritschl observed:

> Indeed, it was in Flacius, who here again first achieved the most energetic work, that the religious motif of this direction of thought emerges in its clearest form. For it was he who revolved the question of imputed justification from the abstract sphere of speculation, into which it was ever again in danger of getting lost, and placed it wholly into the concrete life of personal piety. He taught that the situation, known to every believer from his own experience, in which the practice of the justification became concrete, was the prayer for divine forgiveness of sin.[10]

The pain and deliverance of his religious experience, comments Jörg Baur, made him a "radical theologian." His thought went "to the roots," because a thought process was at work in it that draws the thinker himself into the matter. "In this theology, the theologian puts himself into the game without reservation, even the consequences in his daily life. Truth is never abstract; it is always united with its witnesses..."

> Here, not only a new aspect for the understanding of the period between Luther and Orthodoxy is offered to us; rather, we come upon an essential element of the modern world: Christian subjectivity of the immediate individual before God: Luther, Flacius, Pascal, Hamann, Kierkegaard. It certainly does not mean that Flacius himself depicts himself as "romantic," or, with Descartes, makes himself the original source of certainty. For him, the undisputed unity of personal life is not for the self-realization of his own identity. It is received alone in the working-over of the foreign, in constant hearing of the Word, in taking pains with biblical interpretation, in the trust of the heart that looks away from itself to the coming of Christ, who is for me the Other. *Certitudo* needs *doctrina*, and is constituted by doctrine; just as certainly it is not achieved without experience.[11]

To avoid falling again into despair, he resolved to speak the truth – and here is another clue for understanding his career – "rather than carry around the worm which gnaws on my heart because of a bad conscience, and bring God's wrath down upon me."

Flacius' story took on a kind of classical status in the literature of pastoral care. It was cited in *The Christian School of Temptation* by Solomon Glass,[12] who advised his readers to reveal their conflicts openly rather than bottling them up, and in *The Treasure of the Soul* by the electoral Saxon court preacher, Christian Scriver.[13] The same story was central to his historical rehabilitation in the last century. After centuries of obloquy, a more positive estimation of Flacius began to be heard, which can be traced to the interest in Berlin in evidence of religious subjectivity. In an 1844 lecture, the beginning of modern Flacius studies, August Twesten, who, like his predecessor, Friedrich Schleiermacher, was interested in religious experience, emphasized Flacius' internal crisis. His religious torment and the release, he wrote, was the "key to his whole life."[14]

Flacius' religious experience and his consequent concern for the troubled conscience,[15] was not dissimilar to Luther's own, and they helped him to understand Luther. "For all that he was able to enter into the thought-world of Luther's view, his structure and coherent order," Otto Ritschl observed about Melanchthon, "he was not able sympathetically to reproduce the depths and rich background of experience and feeling of Luther's theology."[16] "I learned more through my own temptations and study," Fla-cius reported, "than through his [Melanchthon's] lectures."[17] "I have experienced more what it means to struggle and fight with the devil, sin and a bad conscience," he wrote about himself, reacting to their theological speculation, "than Dr. Major and Maximus [Melanchthon?]."[18]

Although he had several interviews with him,[19] Flacius was never a part of Luther's inner circle. Christiana Frank dismisses the possibility that Luther ever considered him his chief spiritual heir.[20] It is worth noting, however, that Kaspar Ulenberg – known for consulting contemporary sources – does give him that honor. Luther, he wrote, acknowledged him as "a man of his own spirit," as a man he held "in high honor," and it was Flacius on whom after his death he could hang his hopes for his reform.[21]

THE PAPAL INQUISITION CLOSE UP

Non ricantare, anzi cantare! – Baldo Lupetino

"We Excommunicate ... all heretics," Pope Paul III made it known in the Holy Thursday reading of the bull, *Coena Domini*,[1] "the Kathareni, the Patareni ... who are followers of the godless and abominable heresies of Martin Luther, condemned by Leo X, and all who favour or protect him in any way, and all who read or distribute the writings of the said Martin." But the religious negotiations with the Evangelicals at Regensburg had broken down, and the said Martin was making inroads into Italy. He had deeply influenced the Franciscan order, and among the Capuchins, the General himself, Bernardino Ochino, the most influential preacher in the country. So powerful was the movement that the cities of Lucca and Modena were at the point of accepting the Reformation officially.

14 *Matthias Flacius Illyricus, eine Vorlesung. Mit autobiographischen Beilagen und einer Abhandlung über Melanchthons Verhalten zum Interim von Hermann Rössel.* Berlin: G. Bethge, 1844. 6.

15 Haikola. *Gesetz und Evangelium.* 311 f. Cf. 313 ff.

16 Op. cit. II, 117 f. Cf. 227 f.: "Denn vermöge blosser Anempfindung an die gleichartigen Erfahrungen Luthers wäre er doch wohl kaum fähig gewesen, diese Lehre immer wieder mit dem größten Nachdruck als eine Hauptsache in der christlichen Theologie zu verteten."

17 *Gründliche Verlegung . . . Iss leb.* [H iiij v].

18 *Eine kurtze Antwort auff das lange Comment D. Geiz von Guten Werken.* Magdeburg: Christian Rödinger, [1553]. B v.

19 Heldelin. T iiij v.

20 Op. cit. 235.

21 "Lutherus interim, qui ob perturbatam Ecclesiae pacem publicam, hoc genus daemonum terriculamentis frequentitius agitabatur, Flacium in his angoribus quoquo pacto censuit fovendum, eumque ut a fide dignis familiaribus Lutheri audire memini, tamquam genii sui hominem, illum [Flacium] summo loco habuisse, hunc fore ominatus, in quem se vita functo spes inclinata recumberet." Op. cit. 376 f.

1 On the history of the bull, Myroslav Hroch and Anna Skybova. *Ecclesia Militans. Inquisition im Zeitalter der Gegenreformation.* Leipzig: Edition Leipzig, 1985. 66–68.

2 Carl Mirbt. *Quellen zur Geschichte des Papsttums und des römischen Katholizismus* I. 6. Aufl. Tübingen: J. C. B. Mohr (Paul Siebeck), 1967. 537. English translation: B. J. Kidd (ed.). *Documents Illustrative of the Continental Reformation.* Oxford: Clarendon Press, 1911. 346–350.

3 Leopold von Ranke. *The Popes of Rome.* Vol. I. London: John Murray, 1866. 141.

4 George Kenneth Brown. *Italy and the Reformation to 1563.* New York: Russel and Russel, 1971. 138.

5 Emilio Comba. "Baldo Lupetina". *Revista Christiana* III (1875). 7.

6 Text in Georg Theodor Strobel. *Miscellaneen Literarischen Inhalts* I. Nuremberg: Martin Jakob Bauer, 1778. 200–218.

7 Theodor Kolde. *Analecta Lutherana.* Gotha: Friedrich Andreas Perthes, 1883. 390.

8 Strobel. *Miscellaneen* I. 202. Cf. Idem. "Von der Evangelischen Gemeinde in Venedig." *Neue Beiträge zu Litteratur* IV, Stück 2. 1793. 10.

9 Theodor Elze. *Geschichte der Protestantischen Bewegungen und der deutschen evangelischen Gemeinde in Venedig.* Florence: Im Selbstverlag des Herausgebers und in Commission bei B. Coppini, 1941. 20n.

What was to be done? The pope held urgent consultations with the Cardinal of Toledo, Jesuit general Ignatius Loyola, and Cardinal Pietro Caraffa. They determined to reinstitute the papal inquisition. Now they would not follow the practice of the earlier, milder, Italian tradition, but rather that of the successful Spanish Inquisition. On July 21, 1542, Paul III accordingly issued the bull, *Licet ab Initio*, which set the new rules in place, to preserve "the integrity of Christ's tunic" by impoverishing, imprisoning and executing.[2]

> It appointed six cardinals, among whom Caraffa and Toledo were the first, as commissaries of the Holy See, general and universal inquisitors in affairs of faith on either side the Alps. It conferred on them the right of delegating similar powers to ecclesiastics wherever they thought fit; also the sole right of deciding on appeals against their acts, and of proceeding without the intervention of the regular ecclesiastical courts. Every individual without exception, without regard to any rank or dignity whatsoever, was declared subject to their jurisdiction; they had power to imprison the suspected, and to punish the guilty with death and confiscation of goods. Only one limitation was imposed on them. They had full power to punish, but the pope reserved to himself the right of pardoning heretics whom they convicted. They were thus to contrive and to execute whatever could tend to suppress the errors that had broken out in the Christian community, and to pluck them up by the very roots.[3]

An early victim was Matthias Flacius' mentor, Franciscan Provincial Baldo Lupetino. According to report, Lupetino preached that God had not predestined some to hell, that prayers were of no avail for the souls of the dead, that purgatory did not exist, and that indulgences were useless – pope and priest received them solely for extracting money – that Christ saved men by his own merits, that Sunday prayer must be addressed to God alone, and that the church had no right to require fasting.[4] So convincingly did he preach one day in the fateful year of 1542 in the cathedral church on the island of Cherzo (now Cres), just off the coast of Istria, that he won over the congregation. "The town was turned upside down, and only a little was required to make the whole place heretic."[5] One listener was not convinced, a monk named Iacopo Curzula, who denounced him to the Inquisition. Arrested by an agent of the papal nuncio in November, on the basis of the new law, Lupetino was carried away to Venice and locked in prison.

The following summer Matthias Flacius made his way from Wittenberg across the Alps to help his mentor. He was fortified with a letter to Doge Pietro Lando asking for his release, signed by the chieftains of the Smalcaldic League, the princes of Hesse and Electoral Saxony.[6] It qualified him to appear in person before the Signory of Venice.[7] According to Georg Theodor Strobel, "without doubt"[8] Flacius himself had arranged for the letter – no small feat for a twenty-three-year old foreign student.

When he arrived at the Signory, officials had no idea where Baldo was being held. No stranger to the streets and canals of the *serenissima*, Flacius went on a search himself. He found Lupetino and a cellmate, Pietro Speziali, formerly rector of a school in Cittadella, in a prison not far from the Arsenal, near the church of San Giovanni in Bragora.[9] Speziali was sick;

their cell was just above water level.[10] When Flacius reported to the Signory three days later, there were bureaucratic difficulties. The letter he had delivered had not been dated properly and, as the efficient Venetian diplomatic service knew, for a long time Elector Johann Friedrich and Landgrave Philipp had not been at the same place. How, then, could they have signed the letter on the same day? It was written, furthermore, on behalf of all the Protestants in Venice. Why, then, did it mention only Lupetino? And why had Flacius appeared without a proper letter of accreditation? It was all very regrettable, of course, but the government was powerless to act. Lupetino's fate was in the hands of the Inquisition.

On Luther's behalf, Flacius delivered another letter to the Evangelical community, led by Baldassare Altieri, secretary to the English ambassador, agent for the Smalcaldic League, and the overseer of Evangelical congregations also in Vicenza and Treviso. In the letter, an answer to Altieri's appeal for help from the German princes, Luther called Flacius "a man well-known to me and of great faith."[11] It was a happy reunion. Young Vlačić had been part of the community during his schooldays, as one can gather from the congregation's reply, which called him intelligent, learned beyond his years, and "our Matthias."[12]

Before returning to Wittenberg, Flacius went shopping for books for resale, the earliest evidence of his trade as bookseller.[13]

Upon his return, he reported his experiences to Luther,[14] not omitting mention of the dissension in Venice caused by Zwingli.[15] But his efforts had been in vain. In August 1543 Baldo was fined a hundred ducats payable to the treasury of the Arsenal and sentenced to prison for life. His distress was felt keenly by the Germans. From time to time, Wolf Herwart of Augsburg[16] and Johann Baier, agent for the businessmen of the *Fondaceo Tedeschi*, brought him money. Even though the heresiarch, Caspar von Schwenckfeld, considered it necessary to write a refutation of Baldo's Sixteen Articles of Faith, he, too, sent him money and urged his friends to do the same. He even sent instructions on how to smuggle food to his cell.[17] Whether or not he relied on Schwenckfeld's instructions, Jeronimus Fröschel Moser of Salzburg arranged with a local woman to do such smuggling.

The significant result of the long journey was not to liberate Lupetino as he had hoped, but Flacius' own experience of the papal Inquisition at close range. When one considers that the early years of his activity in Germany were coterminus with the years of Lupetino's imprisonment, one begins to understand his motivation. In the prison by the Arsenal, he had witnessed the cruelty of the Inquisition, and had been in the presence of an authentic martyr.

How could he forget? "Do not recant," Fra Baldo had said, "but sing!" They were words for remembering persecuted believers, for lamenting the lost reform in Italy. Words, too, for firing a passion to resist in the North, where resistance was still possible: "non ricantare, anzi cantare!"[18]

10 Eduard von Kausler and Theodor Schott (eds.). *Briefwechsel zwischen Christoph, Herzog von Württemberg und Petrus Paulus Vergerius.* Stuttgart: Litterarischer Verein, 1875. 82.

11 "homo notissimus et magnae fidei vel supra aetatem." WAB, 10, 328.

12 "tametsi Matthias noster satis prudenter vel supra aetatem ..." WAB, 10, 379.

13 "Venetiis emerat codices ad usum scholae," according to Melanchthon in a letter recommending Flacius to the Braunschweig Superintendent Medler, "nunc istic vendere cupit, qua in re eum adiuvare poteris." CR, VI, 286.

14 The report of F. Petri that on the return journey to Germany Flacius accompanied Francesco Patrizi to Ingolstadt has been disproved by Cesare Vasoli. "A proposito di Francesco Patrizi, Gian Giorgio Patrizi, Baldo Lupatino e Flacio Illirico. Alcune Precisioni." *L'Umanesimo in Istria a cura di Vittore Branca e Sante Graciotti.* Florence: Olschki, 1983. 47.

15 WAB, 10, 681.

16 Heldelin. T ij v.

17 CS, XII, 34 f. Schwenckfeld wrote a commentary on Baldo's confession. CS, XI, 488 f., 493 ff.

18 Mirković. 1960, 489.

1 WAB, 10, 461.
2 Friedensburg. "Anstellung". 304.
3 Ibid. 306.
4 Walter Friedensburg. *Geschichte der Universität Wittenberg.* Halle: Max Niemeyer, 1917. 232. The rivalry between Brück and Melanchthon for university leadership seems to have played no part in the matter. WAB, 10, 457 ff.
5 Friedensburg. "Anstellung". 309.

A PROFESSORSHIP OF HEBREW

> The Hebrew language is profitable not only for investigating the sounder and more genuine sense of the Old Testament, but also of the New, for it is full of hebraisms, not only in individual words, and phrases, but also in whole sentences. By no means can it [the New Testament] be studied adequately without this language. – Flacius

> There is no doubt that God, with the holy angels and all the company of heaven, are eagerly delighted by our language study. – Flacius

Hebraists, Luther observed, tend to be more rabbinical than Christian. For the newly vacant professorship of Hebrew he cautiously recommended Electoral Librarian Lucas Edenberger, former tutor to the Elector's brother. "Who knows the others, who have arrived recently and not yet proved themselves?"[1] Walter Friedensburg wondered whether, when Luther referred to those "who have arrived recently," he had Flacius in mind."[2] If so, he had forgotten that in his letter to Venice he had certified that Flacius was "well-known to me."

The professorship and the one hundred florin salary was divided between Theodor Fabritius and Edenberger. In a memorandum of December 20, Flacius was listed as candidate, but he was "not as eminent a person" as Theodor Fabritius; he was, in fact, "as good as nameless."[3] Since he could also keep his forty florin salary, Edenberger agreed. But Fabritius found the pay too low and resigned; the half-time job went to Flacius. Flacius, too, felt the stricture, and importuned Chancellor Gregor Brück "almost daily" for a raise. When he was consulted about the matter, out of deference to Edenberger, Melanchthon did nothing.[4]

The choice was finally made by the students themselves. When the chancellor saw them gathering around Flacius outside church on Sunday wanting answers to questions about their language study, he concluded that someone who enjoyed such obvious confidence among students would make a good professor. After Melanchthon certified that he was competent in Latin, Greek, Hebrew, and in the liberal arts, Brück recommended him to the Elector. Such an appointment would be disadvantageous for Edenberger, of course. But otherwise the university might lose a promising teacher; there was a new vacancy for a Hebrew specialist at Leipzig. The most important consideration was the good of the university, and he recommended prompt action.

> What especially moves me to write this is that in the church I saw how the fine young fellows gathered around the said Illyricus on feast days with Hebrew books that they are reading. When they have need, they ask him. He cheerfully gives them information and instruction. I can conclude that he would be very useful to the students because he is young, learned, and, as a foreigner, poor. The students would feel less shyness about consulting him at any time than an old one, as Master Lucas is.[5]

The Elector took heed. To soften the blow for Edenberger, Flacius volunteered to deduct twenty florins a year from his salary to be given to him for two years. And thus, at twenty-four, without faculty participation, as he would point out later,[6] Flacius was appointed a Wittenberg professor.

Enrollment rose in 1544; the eight hundred and sixteen students set a record for German universities.[7] Although at times he had to endure lecturing in an obscure classroom near the wine cellar,[8] when he began drawing the full 100 florins, he had the highest salary in the philosophical faculty.

Having arrived professionally, he could afford to marry. His bride was Elizabeth Faustus, the daughter of Pastor Michael Faustus of Dabrun.[9] Among the guests at his wedding – in one of his last public appearances – was Martin Luther.[10]

Eight days after Luther's funeral, Flacius was awarded the degree of Master of Philosophy and swore an oath to defend the evangelical faith.[11] A decade and a half later, when every possible reproach was being made against him, it was spread around that he had made a mistake in his oral examination by failing to diagram correctly a syllogism from Aristotle's *Prior Analytics*, Chapter Four, Book One.[12] The Wittenberger critics neglected to add that among the thirty-nine candidates who took the Master's Degree examination that year, including Olavus Petri, later Archbishop of Uppsala, who ranked nineteenth, Flacius ranked first.[13]

Modern students of logic may elect to analyze syllogisms by means of a Venn diagram or an Euler circle, but Flacius was expected to draw a triangle. "In the examination thirteen years ago," he had to explain, "Philipp asked me to draw three terms of a syllogism in the first figure on the table. Trained by a simpleton, I drew them connected by a vertical line. He then exclaimed that I was not an Aristotelian, and asked me to draw a line perpendicular to the middle, making the conclusion the hypotenuse – the line underlying the right angle of the middle term." That was the monstrous lapse, he observed wryly, that was worth bringing up against him after so many years.[14]

Since no student had been present at his examination, obviously one of his examiners had violated the pledge to secrecy. It was not Caspar Cruciger, who had since died. The rule of academic confidence, then, was breached by Erasmus Reinhold, by Johannes Stolz, or by Philipp Melanchthon.

A more appropriate basis for reproach would have been Flacius' master's thesis, *That Holy Scripture was Written Completely from the Beginning, Not Only with Consonants, but Also With Vowel-Points.*[15] It was written against the humanistic Rabbi, Elias Levita, who, as noted above, lived in Venice during Flacius' school days there, and whose *Massoreth Ha-Massoreth* ("Fettering the Tradition"), was published in that city in 1538. He argued that the vowel points in the Hebrew text were not part of the original text. Luther (correctly) agreed with Levita: "At the time of St. Jerome, the points did not as yet exist, and the whole Bible was read without them. I submit that it is the modern Hebrews who affixed them, in order to give a proper sense and meaning to the Hebrew language."[16]

6 *Apologia auff zwo unchristliche Schrifften Justi Menij. Darinnen von den grewlichen Verfelschungen der Adiaphoristerey und Maioristerey allerley nützlichs angezeigt wird.* Jena: Christian Rödinger der Ältere Erben, 1558. E r; On the dating, Moldaenke. 133n.

7 Hans Volz. *Die Frequenz der deutschen Universitäten in der Reformationszeit.* [Deutscher Kulturatlas III]. Ed. Gerhard Lüdtke and Lutz Mackensen. Berlin and Leipzig: Walter de Gruyter, 1928–1937. III, card 43a, cf. 223a.

8 G. Frank. Review of Preger. 774.

9 Friedrich Gottlieb Kettner. *Clericus Magdeburgensis, Clerus Ulrico-Levinianus.* Magdeburg, 1728. 235 ff.

10 *Von der Einigkeit* [A vij v].

11 Köstlin. *Baccalaurei.* 1888. 18: "Decano Johanne Stolzio Vitaebergensi decretus est gradus Magisterii philosophici his quorum subscripta sunt nomina die 25. Februarii anno 1546. 1. Matth. Illyricus professor hebraeae linguae."

12 *Scholasticorum Vitteb. Epistolae. Editae contra Flacium.* Wittenberg: Georg Rhau Erben, 1558. A iij v.

13 Köstlin. 1538–1546, 1894. 18. *Necessaria Defensio contra famosam chartam titulo, Wittebergensium scholasticorum editam.* Jena: Christian Rödinger der Ältere, 1558. Biij r.

14 Ibid. Aij–A iij.

15 Quod sacra Scriptura integre, non tantum consonantibus, sed et inde ab initio scripta fuerint, scriptum, olim in promotione, ut moris est praeceptoribus exhibitum. It is appended to the *Regulae et tractatus quidam de sermone sacrarum literarum, ad genuinam multorum difficulium locorum explicationem perutiles.* Magdeburg: Michael Lotter, 1551, and appears in Part Two of the *Clavis Scripturae Sacrae.* Cf. Keller. 111 f., 158 f.

16 WA, 44, 683; LW, 8, 141 ff.; Ginsburg. 45–48. Walter Köhler gives a short summary of the discussion in

his *Dogmengeschichte*. Zürich: Max Niehaus, 1951. 132.

17 "Regulae cognoscendi sacras literas," *Clavis* II, Tractate 1, paragraph 3.

18 *Hilfsbuch zum Studium der Dogmatik. Die Dogmatik der Reformatoren und der altevangelischen Lehrer quellenmässig belegt und verdeutscht.* 4th ed. Berlin: de Gruyter, 1964. 314.

19 Op. cit. 177. cf. 112, 158 f.

20 J. Baur. 40.

21 *Clavis* II. 666.

22 "Adhortatio ad Studium Linguae Hebraeae". *Clavis* II. 651–667. According to Günter Moldaenke the lecture was delivered either at Wittenberg or Jena. Op. cit. 179n.

"Will not the whole of the Scriptures be unclear for us," Flacius asked on the other hand, "if the church permits the devil to set forth this hypothesis?"[17] Emanuel Hirsch cited the statement in his doctrinal handbook to demonstrate that Flacius was the first to teach verbal inspiration of the Bible.[18] More recently, Rudolf Keller has shown that as a mature scholar, he abandoned that view. "He does not clearly reject his master's thesis, but it is very clear that he no longer understands it in the same way, in spite of its being reproduced in the *Clavis*."[19] Flacius' defense of verbal inspiration, thus, can be ascribed to youthful enthusiasm.

The best Hebraist of the second third of the sixteenth century,[20] Flacius on occasion could lecture like a humanist. "What else can one expect from despising languages," he asked his students, "than bottomless ignorance, obscuring of true religion and of all good arts, indeed, the return of the old and of a still much more vexing barbarism and darkness?"[21] But unlike most humanists, he urged students to advance beyond Latin and Greek to Hebrew. In his lecture, "Exhortation to the Study of the Hebrew Language,"[22] he explained that Hebrew was the original language, given by

With his "Golden Key" Flacius founded the discipline of hermeneutics

God in creation, the mother of all languages.[23] Other languages express an angry god – *deus iratus*. But Hebrew is the language of the God well-pleased and propitiated – *deus placatus ac propitius*. "Just as one wants to see one's best friend face-to-face, without a translator, it is a joy to experience God's living Word directly. "There is no doubt that God, with the holy angels and all the company of heaven, are eagerly delighted by our language study."[24]

He was scornful of the contemporary dictionaries that defined biblical words on the basis of their use in the Greek classics. "What, pray, more pernicious inversion of the sense of Holy Scripture could be invented, than that the meaning of the more important words, or matters, rather, as sin, righteousness, justification, faith, grace, flesh, spirit, and the like, are introduced into holy scripture, and thus turned upside down?"[25] That insight was the basic idea of his 1567 *Clavis Scripturae Sacrae*, which came to be prized by generations of pastors as "the golden key," and with which he founded the discipline of hermeneutics. Part two was a collection of essays on interpretation; part one, a biblical dictionary that explained Greek words on the basis of their Hebrew background. He called it his "book of hebraisms."[26]

Although today his notion about Hebrew as the "mother of all languages" strikes one as quaint, his insight about the relationship between the two languages he was teaching does not. Günter Moldaenke commented:

> It seems to me that here we have to do with ... the most important insight, one which determined the outline of the *Clavis* [*Scripturae Sacrae*, 1567] · itself, as well as at the same time the biblical hermeneutic places the New as well as the Old Testament under the decisive viewpoint of the "hebraisms" and addresses them both, beginning with Hebraistic: example and challenge.[27]

As Melanchton's student, Flacius emphasized that *although the writers of the New Testament wrote in Greek, they were thinking in Hebrew.*

23 *Clavis* II. 652. He cites Pliny, Herodotus and St. Jerome. He may also have been influenced by Dante's *De Vulgari Eloquentia*, who took up a theme of Eunomius and Gregory of Nyssa, or by his *Paradiso*. 26, 124 ff.
24 *Clavis* II. 666.
25 *Clavis* II. 2.
26 Ibid. "Initio huius Secunda Patris [sic] Hebraismorum ..."
27 Op. cit. 184.

1 Martin. 31.

2 *Galateo*. Tr. Konrad Eisenbichler and Kenneth Bartlett. Toronto: Dovehouse Editions, 1985. 37.

3 Alan Cowell. "Pope Bids Church See Old Errors." *New York Times.* November 15, 1994.

4 Antonio Santosuosso. "Giovanni della Casa and the Galateo. On Life and Success in the Late Renaissance." *Renaissance and Reformation* XI (1975). 1.

5 "Intorno a talune opere di Monsignor Giovanni Della Casa." *Tra due crisi: L'Italia del Rinascimento.* Turin: Einaudi, 1971. 170.

6 "So kam es, daß die päpstliche Politik die Unterdrückung abweichender religiöser Bekenntnisse streckenweise im Interesse der Erhaltung des sozialen Status quo unterstützte." Stefan Oswald. *Die Inquisition, die Lebenden und die Toten. Venedigs deutsche Protestanten.* Sigmaringen: Jan Thorbecke Verlag, 1989. 23. "The chief opponent of the German Protestants was the papal nuntius." Ibid. 13.

7 J.-M. De Bujanda (ed.). *Index de Venise 1549: Venise et Milan, 1554.* Sherbrooke, Quebec: Centre d'Etudes de la Renaissance; Geneva: Droz, 1987.

8 John Bale. *Scriptorum Illustrium Maioris Brytanniae quam nunc Angliam et Scotiam vocant: Catalogus* I. Basel: Johannes Oporinus, 1557. 682. "Il Casa ammetterà di aver avuto delle esperienze pederastiche ..." Antonio Santosuosso. *Vita di Giovanni Della Casa.* Rome: Bulzoni, 1979, 49. Thomas Naogeorgus published "In Joannem Del'la Casa, Archiepiscopum Beneventanum, Sodomiae patronum, Satyra." *Regnum Papisticum* [Basel: Oporinus, 1559]. 175–197. Della Casa's homosexuality was also the theme of Gilles Menagé *Anti-Baillet ou*

To what purpose do we fatigue ourselves, if those, O noble Venice, Queen of the Adriatic, if those who preach to you the truth are to be thrown into prison, thrust into cells and leaded with chains and fetters?" – Bernardino Ochino

"It is not proper to rub one's teeth with one's napkin," according to Archbishop Giovanni Della Casa, papal legate to Venice, "and even less with one's finger, for these are unsightly acts ..." The Archbishop knew whereof he spoke; he moved on the loftiest social level, on terms of the strictest intimacy with the house of Caraffa. In Italian society, advising one's prince was a "privilege gained ... only through the rigorous cultivation of certain social graces and the strict observance of the rules and genteel rituals of the court."[1] It is not a polite habit, he advised the ambitious, "to carry a toothpick in one's mouth when getting up from the table ..." The prudent words come from his *Galateo*, a manual on etiquette that has seen 140 editions, most recently in 1985 in Toronto.[2]

A recent papal statement regrets the "aquiescence given, especially in certain centuries, to intolerance and violence in the service of truth" in the Inquisition.[3] But the Venetian Inquisition can hardly have been about "the service of truth," since Archbishop Della Casa was religiously indifferent. He "had no religious beliefs to back his claim as enforcer of conformity."[4] Instead, his efforts were in the service of the Italian upper class. According to Ruggerio Romano, Della Casa represented "a social group defending its privileges, its life, and its style of life."[5] The same accusation is made by Stefan Oswald: papal policy in Venice was directed toward preserving the social status quo.[6]

The arbiter of polite behavior who discouraged the use of toothpicks also had a murderous disdain of Lutherans. Social climbers could be held off by a baffling code of etiquette. The Protestant threat, however, required stronger measures. In 1548 he organized book-burnings on the piazza San Marco and the Rialto. In 1549, encouraged by Pope Paul III, he published an Index of Prohibited Books.[7] Since he also published dirty poetry, he was taken to task by the Bishop of Capo d'Istria, Pier Paolo Vergerio. "Aren't you ashamed, you wretched archbishop?" he wrote. "You dare come forth and damn holy books – you who have written poems in which you have extolled the most excrable evils of Sodom as a divine work?"[8] One of the verses by which the archbishop earned his reputation as pornographer was his *Capitolo del Forno* ("oven," a *double entendre* for vagina).[9] It is not available in English translation, but because by translating Della Casa's sonnets ("fourteeners"), the late Rudolf Gottfried made it possible to sample his style:

By day I used to search the woodlands through
For cave or rill, where griefs might sing and preen

Themselves in rhyme, and I on nights serene
Would lie awake with Love and Phoebus too;
Nor did I fear, Bernard, to climb with you
That secret mount where few men now have been.
But like the ocean's force which knows no mean
The mob's foul usages me also drew
And swept into a life of weeping sore
In which false honor's signs were held to be
Of worth, not laurel shades or fountains bright.
Now with reflections not from envy free,
I watch you climb that steep secluded height
Where no bold footstep signed the grass before.[10]

As long as the Smalcald League remained in power, Venice was reluctant to offend the evangelical princes. The defeat of the League ended Venice's cautious policy and, with it, the conspiratorial hope of Altieri and others of an insurrection that would restore "the ancient liberty of Italy" and make possible the introduction of the Reformation.[11] On the very day of the League's defeat, April 24, 1547, Doge Francesco Dona welcomed the "Holy Office," the *Sant' Uffizio*, to his city and appointed three Sages on Heresy – *Savii sull' eresia*, lay representatives of the Council of Ten, Nicolo Tiepolo, Francesco Contarini and Antonio Venier, to cooperate with the clerical members, the Patriarch, the Father Inquisitor, Marino da Venezia, and the papal legate, Della Casa.

One of Della Casa's victims was Baldo Lupetino's fellow prisoner, Francesco Spiera. Summoned before the Inquisition in June, 1548, Spiera admitted owning a Bible, translating the Lord's Prayer into Italian, having read modern books and doubting the existence of purgatory, since it implied that Christ's atonement was not complete. Worried, however, about his pregnant wife and eight children, he recanted. He told a crowd of two thousand in Citadella that he did, in fact, believe in purgatory, the invocation of saints, indulgences, free will, good works, and human merit. Then he was seized by convulsions that resisted treatment. By deliberately denying the faith of his heart, he lamented afterward, he had committed the sin against the Holy Spirit about which Jesus had warned: "all sins will be forgiven the sons of men, and whatever blasphemies they utter; but whoever blasphemes against the Holy Spirit never has forgiveness, but is guilty of an eternal sin" (Mark 3: 28 ff.). He felt within himself the sentence of eternal damnation.[12] Refusing food or medicine, he died December 27, 1548, in despair, not able even to utter the words of the Lord's Prayer. In a letter of 1554, Flacius warned Doge Franciscus Venerius and the Signory of Venice that they were in danger of sharing Spiera's condemnation.[13]

For Vergerio, Spiera's despair was a warning to abandon Nicodemism – secret Protestantism. For the sake of his soul's salvation, he knew he had to confess his faith openly. After a visit to Spiera, during which he quoted Luther and attempted vainly to console the dying man, he announced publicly his adherence to the Reformation.[14] Now a special target of the Inquisition, he fled Italy. One of his followers, a certain Calzano, not so fortu-

Critique du Livre de Mr. Baillet Inti-tulé Jugement des Savans II. The Hague: Estienne Foulque et Louis van Dole, 1688. 88–153. A list of authors who made accusations against Della Casa. 113–153.

9 Bibliographical reference in Antonio Santosuosso. "Books, Readers and Critics. The Case of Giovanni Della Casa, 1537–1575." *La Bibliofila* LXXIX (1977). 127.

10 Rime XXV. *Fifteen Fourteeners from Giovanni Della Casa.* Bloomington, Indiana: Edited and published by Rudolf B. Gottfried, 1979. My thanks to Mrs. Gottfried for copyright permission.

11 Martin. 48.

12 *Eine Erschreckliche Historia von einem, den die feinde des Evangelii inn welsch Land gezwungen haben, den erkanten Christum zuvorleugnen.* [Magdeburg: Michael Lotter] 1549. According to Jean François Gilmont. *Les Martyrologes Protestants du XVIe Siècle: Essai de Présentation Générale.* Diss., Louvain, 1966. 36. Gilmont lists other reports, *Martyrologes.* 33–42. Flacius' account is independent of Vergerio's, he reports, and probably based on the report of Matteo Gribaldi Mofa. The British Library catalog lists three reports in German and more than 35 in Latin, French, and English. Cf. "Anmerckungen über Franc. Spierae Verzweifflung." UN, 1702. 832–836; Lorenz Hein. *Die Reformation und ihr Weg in die Republik Venedig.* Venice: Centro di Meditazione Tra Oriente e Occidente; Florence: Leo S. Olschki Editione, 1977. 563. In a Hungarian account of Flacius' followers in Hungary, Sandor Payor reports a song on the same subject: "Flacianus lelkészek Magyarországban." *Theologiai Szalkap* XIV (1916). 2n.

13 In the prefatory letter to *Historia certaminum inter romanos episcopos et sextam carthaginensem synodum, Africanasque Ecclesias, de primatu seu potestate Papae bona fide ex au-*

thenticis monumentis collecta. Basel: [Johannes Oporinus], 1554.

14 Anne Jacobson Schutte. *Piero Paolo Vergerio: the Making of an Italian Reformer.* Geneva: Droz, 1977. 239–244.

15 Santosuoso. "Inquisition". 204; Martin. 54.

16 John Tedeschi. "Toward a Statistical Profile of the Italian Inquisition, Sixteenth to Eighteenth Centuries." John Tedeschi and William Monte (eds.). *The Prosecution of Heresy. Collected Studies on the Inquisition in Early Modern Italy.* Binghamton, N. Y.: Center for Medieval and Early Renaissance Studies, State University of New York, 1991. 105.

17 CS, XI, 487.

18 Oswald. 13.

19 Mirko Breyer. "O Istraninu Fra Baldu Lupetini (1502–1556)." *Istra* II (1972). In the offprint, 6.

20 *Corpus Iuris Canonici.* E. A. Friedberg (ed.). Leipzig: Bernhard Tauchnitz, 1881. II, 838: "Clericus, auctoritatem vel consilium directe vel indirecte homocidio practans, irregularis efficitur."

21 Bartolomeo Fontana. "Documenti Vaticani inediti Contro l'eresia lutherana in Italia." *Archivio della R. Società Romana di Storia Patria* XV (1892). 401.

22 G. Brown. 147.

nate, was arrested at Della Casa's order, dressed in yellow with a paper mitre on his head, officially degraded according to the newly-formulated ritual, and sentenced to two years of service as a galley slave. Antonio Santosuosso, for whom the inquisitor's activity in Venice was a "moderate Inquisition," calls for understanding. When Della Casa removed the tongues of one Calcagno (later decapitated) at Brescia and demanded the same treatment for Fra Angelico of Crema for the success of his sermons at the church of San Barnabà, the legate was not departing from the usual custom. Torture, the stake, and cutting out of tongues, Santosuosso explains, were normal proceedures. "The life of the common friar or a common man was not worth much, especially if the person was tainted with non-conformity."[15]

At the beginning of the Council of Trent, on December 13, 1545, the pope issued an edict demanding the surrender of all Reformation literature and the punishment of those who possessed it. Inquisition archives reveal 1,224 trials between 1547 and 1587, 717 of them for "Lutheranism."[16] Balthasare Altieri, appealing for the second time to Luther, begged him to arrange relief.[17] Altieri himself had to gather up his family and flee, penniless. Their fate is unkown.[18]

In 1547 Baldo was brought before the tribunal a second time, bearded now, emaciated and with an eye injury, the result of an attack by a fellow-prisoner. He was accused of fresh crimes – converting two fellow prisoners and publishing a religious book, *On the Knowledge of God.* Publishing a book was a great feat for a prisoner; he had the complicity of Jihajlo Katarić from Cres, manager of a pharmacy named "Three Angels."[19]

A certain awkwardness was presented to the Inquisition by the ancient inhibition, *ecclesia abhorret a sanguine*: the clergy was not allowed to shed human blood.[20] The temporary inconvenience, however, was removed in Rome, when in a 1547 letter to Della Casa, Pope Paul III suspended canon law.

> ... in addition to the other powers granted to you by Us, you may also freely advance against heretics beyond this even to blood and mutilation of members, and also to the sentences of ultimate punishment and degradation, and not be impeded by fear of incurring irregularity.[21]

Thus reassured, on October 27, 1547 the Holy Office ordered Baldo Lupetino beheaded between the pillars of the piazetta, his body to be burned and thrown into the sea "to the honor of Jesus Christ."[22]

Yet I will leave seven thousand in Israel,
All the knees that have not bowed to Baal,
and every mouth that has not kissed him.
– I Kings 19.18

His manuscript research has nothing more of the philological-antiquarian joy of discovery of the Renaissance, but is service to the church militant. – Arno Duch

In a treaty of July 28, 1546, the pope requested Emperor Charles "to rescue and protect the authority of the Tridentine council, the holy Christian faith, and the unity of the same with the sword and armed hand against the heretics."[1] Against that background, the pope's attempt to have Baldo Lupetino burned alive, so devastating to Flacius and his family, could not fail to invoke the image of "the man of lawlessness, the son of perdition" of II Thessalonians 2.4, who "takes his seat in the temple of God." In Wittenberg, Flacius reports, "I came to the realization that the doctrine of these churches is God's very own Word, and I have embraced it with my whole soul." "On the other hand," he went on, "I concluded that the pope is the real Antichrist, and, together with his errors, I have execrated and condemned the Pope as the Antichrist and his errors and abuses with my whole heart."[2]

August Twesten identified the experience of justification by faith under Luther's pastoral care as the key to Flacius' life.[3] By juxtaposing texts, however, Jesuit Joseph Niemöller, suggested that Flacius' main motivation was anti-papalism.

> Flacius himself related in greater detail what had happened to him. "I was now sure," he writes in relationship to the experience above [overcoming his spiritual crisis] "that the pope is in truth the antichrist, and I cursed and execrated his errors and abuses with my whole heart." "Here we have the key to his whole life," remarked Twesten on that theme of despair and its conclusion ... From then on hate against the Antichrist constituted the basic drive of his life and his whole existence, cursing the Antichrist the innermost activity of his heart.[4]

The misleading word here is "conclusion." The conclusion of his spiritual crisis, Flacius reports, was the certainty of justification. Following Niemöller, another Jesuit, James Brodrick, is still bolder.

> ... but he [Flacius] discovered on his own account the chief dogma of his creed and one that supplies they key to his whole life. "It is now my absolute conviction," he wrote at the time, "that the pope is, in very truth, the Antichrist."[5]

Neither takes account of the provocations which led to Flacius' conclusion – the activities Pope John Paul II regretted as "tensions, errors and excesses." Murder done to a member of the family does produce an understandable tension.

1 *Ehrendenkmal treuer Zeugen Christi* III. Zwickau: Johannes Hermann, 1879. 9.
2 *Entschuldigung ... an die Universitet.* E v.
3 Twesten. 6.
4 Joseph Niemöller. "Matthias Flacius und der Flacianische Geist in der älteren protestantischen Kirchenhistorie." *Zeitschrift für katholische Theologie* XII (1888). 78.
5 James Brodrick. *Peter Canisius, S. J. 1521–1597.* New York: Sheed and Ward, 1935. 676. Brodrick is also innacurate when on p. 678 he states that Flacius was driven from Magdeburg.

6 *Die Annalen der lateinischen Hym-nendichtung. Ein Handbuch* I. Berlin: Erich Schmidt Verlag, 1964. 281.

7 Op. cit. 418.

8 *Cantio de Papa Romanaque Ecclesia per Boemen Quendam ante annos circiter 100 composita, secundum ordinem alphabeti.* n. p. [1548].

9 Cod. Guelf. 1099 Helmstedt. Luther A. Dittmer. *Facsimile Reproduction of the Manuscript Wolfenbüttel 1099 Helmstadiensis (1206) W2 with an Introduction by Luther A. Dittmer.* Brooklyn: Institute of Mediaeval Music, 1960.

10 *Carmina vetusta ante trecentos annos scripta, quae deplorant inscitiam Evangelij, & taxant abusus ceremoniarum, ac quae ostendunt doctrinam huiu temporis non esse nouam. Fulsit enim semper & fulgebit in aliquibus vera Ecclesiae Doctrina.* Wittenberg: Georg Rhau, 1548.

11 *Repertorium Organorum Recentioris et Motetorum Vetastissimi Stili. 2. erweiterte Auflage herausgegeben von Luther A. Dittmer.* Bd. I, Abteilung I. Halle, 1910. 157 ff.

12 Ibid. 222–227.

13 *Pia quaedam vetustissimaque poemata, partim Antichristum eiusque spirituales filiolos insectantia, partim etiam Christum eiusque beneficium mira spiritus alacritate celebrantia.* Magdeburg: Michael Lotter, 1552.

14 Edward H. Roesner. "The Manuscript Wolfenbüttel, Herzog August Bibliothek, 628 Helmstadiensis: A Study of its Origins and of its Eleventh Fascicle." Diss., New York University, 1974. I, 15, 17; Idem. "The Origins of W1." *Journal of the American Musicological Society* XXIX (1976). 337–380. More on W1 in Friedrich Ludwig. "Über den Entstehungsort der grossen Notre-Dame-Handschriften." *Festschrift Guido Adler zum 75. Geburtstag.* Vienna and Leipzig: Universal-Edition A. G., 1930. 45–90; Rudolf Flotzinger. *Beobachtungen zur Notre-Dame Handschrift W1 und ihrem 11. Faszikel.* [Sonderdruck aus dem Anzeiger der phil.-hist. Klasse der

Was there a way for Flacius, with his limited resources, to resist the pope? Joseph Szöverffy, the musicologist, thought that the fact that "many tropes were collected, rescued and printed in the sixteenth century precisely by a champion of the Reformation, by Flacius Illyricus," was "a remarkable accident."[6] It was no accident. In the Aldine tradition, he would in any case have collected old documents. But new circumstances brought new motivation. "His manuscript research," noticed Arno Duch," no longer has the philological-antiquarian joy of discovery of the Renaissance, but is service for the church militant."[7] Although printing the texts of old parchments was not a powerful weapon, it was *something.*

A first protest, which he published complete with musical notation, was *A Song about the Pope and the Roman Church by a Certain Bohemian Composed a Hundred Years ago According to the Order of the Alphabet.*[8] A collection of medieval texts, all but one from a French manuscript dating from 1235 to 1250 A. D.[9] which he issued the same year,[10] packed more punch. The discovery of those *Carmina Vetusta*, as he called them, is equal in significance to the discovery of the *Carmina Burana* in the nineteenth century, and includes many of the same texts. Musicologists first learned about Flacius' manuscript from the classification made by Friedrich Ludwig in 1910. He called it "W2" for "Wolfenbüttel 2."[11] In an essay in the same volume, "The Latin Motet Texts published by Flacius,"[12] Ludwig gives Flacius high marks for concluding – at a time when nobody could read the music – that they had been sung "with extraordinary animation," *mira spiritus alacritate celebrantia.* They were words from the title of Flacius' next collection: *Certain Pious and Very Old Poems. In Part Censuring the Antichrist and His Little Spiritual Sons, and in Part Celebrating Christ and His Kindness, with Extraordinary Animation of Spirit.*[13]

Acquired too late[14] for use in his text collections[15] was a similar manuscript classified in Wolfenbüttel as Cod. Guelf. 628 Helmstedt, and by Ludwig as "W1."[16] It is famous for including the oldest version of the Notre-Dame repertory of the 12th and 13th centuries. As befits a Scots national treasure – it was found in Scotland – it has been reproduced photographically.[17] Together, "W1" and "W2" supply most of what is known about early polyphony, and qualify Flacius for an honored place in the history of music. They are supplemented by a third, Florence Codex Pluteus 19.2, called "F," which once belonged to Piero di Medici, and a fragment, 20 486, of the National Library in Madrid. With no other basis than the legend about a "culter flacianus,"[18] Ludwig makes Flacius responsible for missing leaves.

The middle sections of W1 and W2 furnish copies of the "Great Book of Organon," [organon = a form of early polyphony] produced by two teachers at the Cathedral of Notre Dame of Paris about 1200, Leonin and his successor, Perotin. It consists of sections for interpolation into Gregorian chant. The existence of the Great Book is attested by a letter from a student, "Anonymous IV."[19] Traces of the influence of the Great Book have been found from Scotland to Castile.

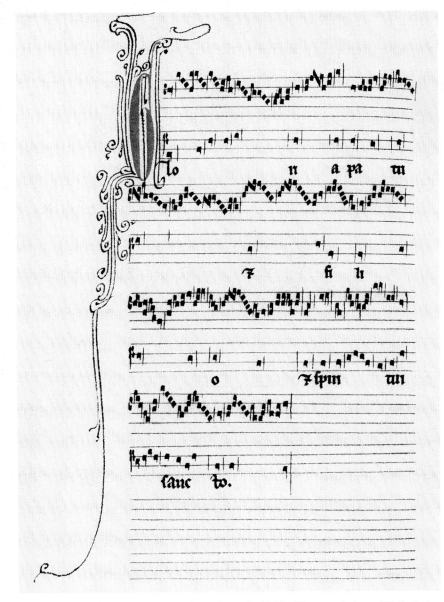

A page from Codex Guelf. 1099 Helmstedt (W2). Herzog August Bibliothek. Flacius guessed that the many notes expressed "animation"

österreichischen Akademie der Wissenschaften 105], 1968; Heinrich Husman. "The Origin and Destination of the Magnus Liber Organi." *The Musical Quarterly* XLIX (1963). 311–330.

15 A modern collection of texts from Flacius' manuscripts is Gustav Milchsack, *Hymni et Sequentia cum Compluris aliis et Latinis et Calicis necnon Theotiscis Carminibus medio aevo compositis Quae ex libris impressis et ex codicibus manuscriptis Saeculorum a IX usque ad XVI partim post M. Flacii Illyrici curas congessit variisque lectionibus illustravit, et nunc primum in lucem proditi, pars prior* [all]. Hallis Saxonum: Maximilian Niemaher, 1888.

16 Ibid. 7.

17 *An Old St. Andrews Music Book (Cod. Helmst. 628). Published in facsimile with an introduction by James H. Baxter.* London: Oxford University Press and Paris: H. Champion, 1931. Reprint, New York, 1973; Rebecca Baltzer. "Wolfenbüttel, Helmstedt 628 (St. Andrews MS)." *Dictionary of the Middle Ages* XII. 670–672.

18 Oliver K. Olson. "Der Bücherdieb Flacius. Geschichte eines Rufmords." *Wolfenbüttler Beiträge* IV (1981). 111–145.

19 Fritz Rechow. *Die Musiktraktate des Anonymus IV.* 2 vols. Wiesbaden: Steiner, 1967. Cf. Charles Edmond Henri de Coussemacher. *Scriptorum de Musica Medii Aevi Nova Series,* Vol. I. Paris, 1864. 342. Edward H. Roesner, "Magnus Liber Organi." *Dictionary of the Middle Ages.* Joseph R. Strayer, New York: Scribner, 1987. VIII, 42–45.

20 Ethel Thurston (ed.). *The Conductus Collections of ms Wolfenbüttel W1099.* Madison: A–R Editions, 1980.

Flacius' *Carmina Vetusta* texts, however, were taken not from the Great Book section, but from the other two sections – a collection of motets, and a collection of "conductus,"[20] choral compositions in a free, song-like style. The texts were often irreverent observations on various themes – feudal organization, survival, relationship with God, and the church. They have been translated into English, the careful work of G. A. Anderson. In his second volume, Anderson supplies the notation. It is thus possible for us to sing the ancient accusations: "In truth the unity that exists among the clergy," one of the texts reads, "is to be found as they indulge in license.

21 "In veritate comperi." *Carmina vetusta.* B r. Gordon Athol Anderson. *The Latin Compositions in Fascicules VII and VIII of the Notre Dame Manuscript Wolfenbüttel Helmstadt [sic] 1099 (1206). Part I: Critical Commentary, Translation of the Texts and Historical Observations.* Brooklyn: The Institute of Medieval Music [1968]. 119.

22 "Omni pene curie." *Carmina vetusta.* B r. Anderson. I, 91.

23 *Die Lyrik des Mittelalters: Eine Einführung.* Munich: C. H. Beck, 1973. 48. "Deduc Sion," which may be by Philipp the Chancellor, is No. 34 in the Carmina Burana collection: Alfons Hilka and Otto Schumann (eds.). *Carmina Burana I. Band: Text.* Heidelberg: Carl Winter, 1930. 56 f.

24 *Carmina vetusta.* A iij v.

25 Ibid. "A cave for buriers of the dead", (*vespilonum*, from *vespo*, corpse, and *vespilo*, corpse-bearer) appears in other manuscripts as "cave of robbers" (*vespillonum*, from *vispellio*, a class of thieves who robbed corpses of their grave-clothes). Cf. Hilka and Schumann. I, 57 and II, 52–53. Flacius refers to the verse again in *Etliche Greifliche … Warzeichen.* 1549. G iij r (edition of 1550 N iij v). *Catalogus.* 1562. 390.

26 Hilka and Schumann. II, 53.

27 *Catalogus.* 1556. 649; 1562. 390 c.

28 The suggestion of Mary Wolinski, then a graduate student in musicology at Brandeis University.

29 *Varia doctorum piorumque virorum de corrupto ecclesiae statu poemata ante nostram aetatem conscripta, ex quibus multa historicae quoque utiliter ac summa cum voluptate cognosci possunt.* Magdeburg: Michael Lotter, 1554. Unaware of Flacius' earlier efforts, Ernst Philip Goldschmidt mistakenly calls it "the first compilation of such poetry from early manuscripts to be printed." *Medieval Texts and Their First Appearance in Print.* London: Bibliographical Society, Oxford, 1943. 38.

Envy rules and truth is given a burial."[21] Or, "The church is being ruled by false judges. The negligent are governing almost the whole church, in whose power the career of justice and the judges make no distinction between the holy and the impious; nay, the impious are given a free hand; nor do they give any place for pardon without the promise of reward."[22]

Whatever the explanations of their origin, the verses served Flacius' critical purpose. His collection begins with a text, "Deduc Sion," according Peter Dronke, "a peal of thunder":[23]

> Vide devs vltionum
> Vide videns omnia,
> Quod spelunca vespillonum
> Facta est Ecclesia.
> Quod in templum Salomonis
> Venit princeps Babylonis,
> Et excelsum sibi thronum
> Posuit in medio,
> Sed arrepto gladio
> Scelus hoc ulciscere.
> Veni, iudex gentium
> Cathedras vendentium
> Columbas evertere.

> Look and see, O God of vengeance
> Look and see, you who see everything,
> That your church has been turned
> into a cave for buriers of the dead;
> That the prince of Babylon
> has entered the temple of Solomon
> and placed his proud throne in the center.
> Draw the sword and avenge this evil!
> Come, Judge of the nations,
> Overturn the seats of the pigeon vendors!

In his introduction, Flacius remembers a priest at Augsburg soliciting mass stipends. "If it doesn't help the dead," said the priest, "at least it helps us!"[24] The amused congregation chose to understand his plea as referring to the lucrative funeral business in the "caves for buriers of the dead."[25] Commenting on the mention of the "prince of Babylon," Ethel Thurston observes[26] that Nebuchadnezzar was never reported visiting the Jerusalem temple. It escaped her that in the biblical tradition, "Babylon" is sometimes a term for the opposition, and that the "proud throne" is that of the "son of perdition" of II Thessalonians – the Antichrist.

Besides W1 and W2, Flacius owned another manuscript of the same sort (now lost), about which he writes that "some [pieces] are monody, some in two, others in three voices; some are in Latin and some in French."[27] He is not referring to W2, because it has only one example of monody – unless he was misled by the consecutive notation, which could indeed have looked to him like monody.[28] Nor does he mean W1, which contains no French texts. He refers, then, to another text, which, had it survived, would also have been important for the history of early polyphony.

Another, expanded, collection was his 1554 *Various Poems of Learned and Pious Men on the Corrupt State of the Church*,[29] grouped around four themes – clergy, pope, Rome, monastics. For the new collection he used other sources besides W1.[30] According to Bale, "Ye shall fynde thereof muche also in ii other bokes lately set fourthe by me and Illyricus, the one is called Catalogus testium veritatis, the other beareth thys tyttle: Varia doctorum piorumque virorum. Antilogia Pape, wyll also correspounde to the same."[31] Honor McCusker doubts his statement,[32] and Leslie Fairfield thinks he is just boasting.[33] But there is ample evidence to demonstrate their collaboration.[34] The similarity of Flacius' title to Bale's "Very Old Poems on the Corrupt State of the Church,"[35] is not conclusive, of course, since Flacius could have borrowed his title from "On the Corrupt State of the Church" by Nicolas of Clémanges (ca. 1367–1437).[36] But the biography of Walter Mapes appears both in Flacius' 1556 *Catalogus Testium Veritatis*, and Bale's 1557 *Scriptorum illustrium Maioris Brytannie Catalogus*.[37]

The thirteenth-century verse, *Utar contra vitia* by Walter of Châtillon,[38] appears in Bale's *Catalogus* as well. It was popular as a rebel chant, and ranks as the *chef d'oeuvre* of irreverent medieval poetry.

> Utar contra vitia carmine rebelli
> Mel propunant alii, sel supponunt melli
> Pectus subeat ferreum daurati belli
> Et leonis spolium unuunt aselli.
>
> Against depravity I will employ a rebel song
> Others set forth honey, but mix the honey with venom
> And cover the skin of an ass with that of a lion.

The clever contrast of "caput mundi" and "nil capit mundum" in Stanza 4 gets lost in translation.

> Roma caput mundi est, sed nil capit mundum;
> quod pendet a capite, totum est immundum.
> trahit enim vitium primum in secundum,
> et de fundo redolet, quod est iuxta fundum.
>
> Rome is the head of the world, but receives nothing pure.
> Whatever has to do with this head is totally impure,
> For the first vice drags a second with it,
> and everything near the ground stinks like the ground.

Ernst Philip Goldschmidt wrote that Flacius included some "late and clumsy trash."[39] Perhaps he had in mind the couplet on Pope Alexander VI, who, Goldschmidt comments, was "as close to the prince of darkness as human beings are likely to come."

> Vendit Alexander claves, altaria, Christum.
> Emerat ipse prius, vendere iure potest.
>
> Alexander sells keys, altars, Christ.
> He is entitled to sell them,
> Because he purchased them himself.

30 On his sources, see Friedrich Ludwig. *Repertorium Organorum Recentioris et Motetorum Vetustissimi Stili. 2. erweiterte Aufl. hrsg. von Luther Ditmer, and I. Catalog Raisonée der Quellen. Abteilung I: Handschriften in Quadrat Notation*. Halle, 1910. 7 ff., 15 ff.; Karl Strecker. "Quellen des Flacius Illyricus." *Zeitschrift für deutsches Altertum und deutsche Literatur* LXVI (1929). 65–67; and Clemen KS, V, 193 f.

31 Bale to Archbishop Parker, reprinted in *Communications of the Cambridge Antiquarian Society* III. 1864– 1876. Cambridge: Cambridge Antiquarian Society, 1879. 164.

32 *John Bale. Dramatist and Antiquary*. Freeport, New York: Books for Libraries Press, 1971. 61n.

33 Op. cit. 151.

34 Goldschmidt. 144; Hilka and Schumann. I, 80–82; André Wilmart "Poèmes de Gautier de Châtillon" (Suite). *Revue Bénédictine* XLIX (1937). 333 n. f.; Davies. 222; Haye. 1990. 62–65; Bibl. 1897. 200; McCusker. 68 f.

35 *Rhithmi Vetustissimi de Corrupto Ecclesiae Statu*. Antwerp, 1546.

36 Schletstadt: Lazarus Schuerer, 1519. Text and French translation in A. Coville (ed.). *Le Traité de la Ruine de l'église de Nicolas de Clamages*. Paris: Droz, 1936; An entry on Clémanges in the *Catalogus*. 1562. 541–543.

37 Their inclusion of the Mapes biography suggested a theory of authorship that proved to be a hindrance to research. Oscar Hubatsch. *Die lateinischen Vagantenlieder des Mittelalters*. Osnabrück: Zeller, 1976. 13.

38 *Carmina Burana* No. 42. Hilka and Schumann. I, 76 ff.

39 Op. cit. 77.

40 *Varia ... poemata.* 1557. 388 f.

41 Ibid. 470.

42 Cf. Polycarp Leyser. *Historia poeta-rum et poematum medii aevi decem, post annum a nato Christo CCCC, seculorum: centum et amplius codicum.* Halle/Saale: Sumptu novi bibliopolii, 1721. 779.

43 *Reinhart Fuchs.* Berlin: Reimer, 1834. CLXXXV; *Varia ... poemata.* 199–214.

44 Ibid. 491. Jean-Barthélemy Hauréau. *Notice sur les Mélanges Poétiques d' Hildebert de Lavardin.* Paris: G. Pedone-Lauriel, 1882. 155.

45 *Varia ... poemata.* 418–454.

46 Edmond Farel. *Les Arts Poétiques du XVe et du XIIIe Siècle.* Geneva: Slatkine and Paris: Champion, 1982. 20 ff.; Goldschmidt. 77 f.

47 "Magister Heinrich der Poet in Würzburg und die römische Kurie." *Abhandlungen der bayerischen Aka-demie der Wissenschaften, Philosophisch-Historische Klasse* XXVII, March 1925. 1–528. Cf. 192.

48 *Les Poésies des Goliards.* Paris: Éditions Reider, 1931. 23, 25.

Or perhaps the verse against Pope Innocent VIII:

> Octo nocens pueros genuit, totidemque puellas
> Hunc merito poterit dicere Roma patrem.[40]

> Wickedly he begot eight boys, and as many girls.
> Hence Rome will rightly be able to call him father.

"An Old Song About Simony," may also qualify. Or,

> Ut bene pascatur monachus,
> nil amplius optat,
> superbo et insatiabili corde.
> Sic igitur sperant coelestia regna mereri?
> non sic impii, non sic.[41]

> With a proud and unsatiatable heart
> the monk wants nothing more
> than to be well-fed.
> Does he hope to merit the heavenly kingdom thus?
> Not so, impious ones, not so.

Flacius' collection popularized the verse, "Ad papam causa liquid obtinendi" of Walter of Châtillon, one of which appears in the Carmina Burana at number 247.[42] Jacob Grimm, who was fond of wicked stepmothers, creepy castles and evil forests, liked the fox in Flacius' collection who appears in it disguised as a monk, and thought it would have been very important, had it had survived complete. In his book on Reinhart Fuchs, Grimm also liked the *Poenitentionarius Lupi, Vulpis et Asini*, which he reprinted from Flacius' collection, a long satire by Pseudo-Ovid on immoral prelates.[43]

Another verse, number 53, *In vestimentis non est contritio cordis* – "contrition of heart is not to be found in vestments"– became proverbial.[44] "De Planctu ecclesiae," revised in Portugal and published in 1474 in Ulm and in 1507 in Lyon, reports a visit by the Spaniard, Alvarus Pelagius, to the papal court in Avignon in 1340. The thirteenth-century Book on the State of the Roman Curia[45] is variously attributed to Geoffrey of Vinsauf, and to Heinrich of Würzburg.[46] Flacius took it to be a satire; the Maurist historian, Jean Mabillon, seconded by Polykarp Leyser of Helmstedt, pronounced it a straightforward report. In a more recent study, Hermann Grauert says it is something between.[47]

Flacius and Bale were the first to publish the texts of the witty songs of the "goliards," minor clerics of the thirteenth century, who took advantage of their ecclesiastical freedom from taxation and military service – and their claim on society's charity – to lead a vagrant life. The term, "Golias," according to Walafrid Strabo, suggested the pride of the devil, and derives from the name of David's adversary, Goliath. Olga Dobiache-Rojdestvensky criticizes Flacius for falsifying the image of the goliards. According to her, they were not presented correctly until Polycarp Leyser published his *Historia Poetarum et Poematum Medii Aevi* at Halle in 1721.[48] Friedrich Heer, however, recognizes the verses as serious criticism. "Much of this," he wrote, "was admittedly the expression of a momentary mood of personal resentment; but it was also the far from negligible reflection of widespread responsible opinion, which found its spokesmen in a class of people who were not an 'estate' and had no chance of becoming one."[49]

Flacius did recognize the obvious fun. The goliards, he observed, sang *magna cum voluptate* – with high good humor. At the hour of matins, it appears, the goliards slept in; the *Regula beati Libertini Ordinis Nostri* forbade getting up.

> Ordo noster prohibet matutinas plane
> Si quis tunc surrexit, non est mentis sanae.[50]

> Our order distinctly prohibits matins.
> If anyone gets up then,
> he is not of sound mind.

The abbot, moreover, is required to carouse, the abbess to dance, the prior to drink and the monks to wear expensive clothes and to play at dice. "The goliard of the later days is Panurge at his ungentlemanly worst; but the original goliard, starved cat though he is, has more of Pantagruel than Panurge. His oracle is the oracle of the Holy Bottle, Trinq! Bacchus and Scachus are his gods, but he can sing, and the songs that he jigged out in taverns and alehouses, in monastic refectories after supper, at the tables of easy-going prelates, caught the ear of Europe."[51] In "The Apocalypse of Bishop Golias,"[52] the most celebrated and popular poem of the class, which Flacius also borrowed from Bale,[53] the "bishop" learns in a trance about the vices of his priests. The poet's indignation comes across in a sixteenth-century English translation.

> Divinis interest sacerdos turpiter
> divina celebrans, de vino iugiter
> qui Deo crapulam aspirat, aliter
> sacerdos, aliter dicendus presbyter.

> Full filthelie the priest dothe serve celebrate
> With voyce, and breathes on God his surfet's belchinge cheere;
> And hathe twoo Latin names, but not bothe of one rate
> Sacerdos is the one, the other's Presbiter.

And a little farther on,

> Abominabilis Deo vir sanguinum,
> plus mortem cupiens, quam vitam hominum:
> unam puerperam capacem seminum
> mallet, quam sedecim millia virginum.[54]

> Good dothe this bloudie man abhorre above all thinge,
> For he desires men deathe more than their life to save;
> A covettes more a whoore that may him children bringe,
> The eleven towsand virgins or maides for to have.[55]

49 *The Medieval World from 1100 to 1350.* New York and Washington: Praeger, 1969. 94.

50 *Varia ... Poemata.* 489.

51 Ibid. 489, 189. Helen Waddell. *The Wandering Scholars.* London: Constable, 1927. 170.

52 *Varia ... poemata.* 133–149. Karl Strecker. *Die Apokalypse des Golias.* Rome: W. Regensburg, 1928.

53 On page 380 Goldschmidt claimed Flacius' was the *editio princeps*, but corrected himself on page 144.

54 *Varia ... Poemata.* 143.

55 Thomas Wright. *The Latin Poems Commonly Attributed to Walter Mapes.* London: Printed for the Camden Society. John Bowyer Nichols and Son, 1841. xvii, 13, 277.

56 *Varia ... poemata.* 217–222. Commentary in Paul Klopsch. *Lateinische Lyrik des Mittelalters.* Stuttgart: Philipp Reclam, 1985. No. 90. Hilka and Schumann. I, 65–76; Cf. W. Holzmann. "Propter Sion non tacebo: Zur Erklärung von Carmina Burana No. 41." *Deutsches Archiv für Erforschung des Mittelalters* X (1953). 170–175.

57 Mark Pattison. *Isaac Casaubon 1559–1614.* Oxford: Clarendon Press, 1892. 322.

58 note 10.

59 *Carmina vetusta.* [B iij v]; G. Anderson. I, 55; II, 27.

The verse by Walter of Châtillon, number 41 in the Carmina Burana collection, is an attack on clerical avarice.

> Propter Syon non tacebo
> Sed ruinas Romae flebo
>   quousque justitia
> nobis rursus oriatur
> et ut lampas accedatur
>   justus in ecclesia.[56]

> For the sake of Zion I cannot remain silent
> but will weep over the ruin of Rome
> Until justice reappears for us
>   and, like a torch,
> the Just One shines forth in the church.

In his *Various Poems*, for the first time, Flacius deals with the theme of the church's catholicity. Corruption in the church (II Thessalonians 2), he concluded, was "not the mere rust of age which gathers about all human institutions. The Church was the work of God and time alone would not have marred and scarred its divine lineaments. Its degradation was the work of a special principle of evil, the mystery of iniquity, the visible embodiment of which was now enthroned on the seven hills."[57] The Reformers' coming to terms with "the mystery of iniquity" made it impossible to make the simple claim that whatever had been transmitted through the centuries was necessarily catholic. It made necessary a complex explanation of catholicity, beyond what had handed down from the past, or whatever had papal approval – *the chain of authentic tradition in the face of evil.*

Flacius explained catholicity by appropriating the Old Testament theme of the saving remnant: "Yet I will leave seven thousand in Israel, all the knees that have not bowed to Baal, and every mouth that has not kissed him" (I Kings, 19.18, compare Romans 11.4). The same theme, also the structure of the Magdeburg Centuries, is even clearer in the title of another collection, *Old Poems Written Three Hundred Years Ago, That Deplore the Ignorance of the Gospel, Censure the Misuse of Ceremonies and Show that the Doctrine of the Present Time is Not New. For in Some of them the True Doctrine Shines Through and Will Always Shine Through.*[58] "From these songs it is clear that at all times there have been seven thousand men, who did not bend their knees to Baal."

An example of the doctrine that "shines" is the beautiful *Doce nos hodie.*

> Doce nos hodie
> Viam prudentiae stabilem,
> Christe veritas,
> Et qui lucem habitas
> Immarcessibilem,
> Pelle gratia splendoris
> Noctis taedia.
> Fer remedia moeroris
> Gentibus intus gementibus.[59]

Teach us today
the firm way of wisdom,
O Christ, the truth;
And thou who dwellest in unfailing light,
Drive away the tedium of night,
And grant a remedy to the sadness
Among Thy groaning people.

"On Contempt of the World" by Bernard of Morval, which Flacius now prints for the first time,[60] expresses both the "mystery of iniquity" and "true doctrine shining through." H. C. Hoskier identifies the dark theme, *Hora novissima tempora pessima sunt, vigilemus*, in a hymn done into English by M. M. Neal.

The world is very evil;
the times are waxing late;
Be sober and keep vigil;
the judge is at the gate.

In the same poem, however, in lines 269 ff., one can recognize the luminous confidence of *Aurea, patria lactea, civi decora*, the basis of three English hymns, "Jerusalem the Golden," "For Thee, O Dear, Dear, Country," and "Brief Life is Here our Portion."

When Caspar von Nidbruck began discreetly to collaborate with Flacius on a new church history and learned Flacius was about to publish his *Old Poems*, he was alarmed. Ferdinand, the Emperor's brother and rival for the imperial throne, was becoming more aware of the Protestant sympathies of King Maximilian. Nidbruck's situation would be imperiled by such a publication, and he asked Flacius not to write his usual incendiary preface.

Wissenburg wrote that Oporinus will publish the collected ancient verses and some other things that I sent to him that you want to introduce with a preface. I certainly would like that such books can be bought without the front matter, so that they can make a better profit. Many people will be appalled by that, if they see your name on the front. It would be enough to have advanced and assisted the church! I am writing these things, not because I am jealous of your fame, but to advise you of this matter, which would perhaps produce some benefit. You, go ahead and do nothing; it will seem a good thing.

Nevertheless, in the work underway, be very, very careful that you do not make yourself suspect. That will happen if you are anxious to tell too much and if you add only those points that seem to serve your purpose. For as you know, in history writing, above all, reliability is required.[61]

Two hundred and fifty years later, when Emperor Josef II issued his Tolerance Patent, which granted religious freedom to Evangelical-Lutherans in Austria, Flacius' balance between abuses and catholic continuity struck the editor of a new edition of the *Carmina Vetusta* as ecumenical. "Soon, soon, the time will come," he wrote, "that no more will one hear about Catholics, Lutherans and Reformed, and we will all be called Christians and show ourselves as such."[62]

60 *Varia ... poemata*. 247–354. Gustav Kawerau. "Matthias Flacius." *The New Schaff-Herzog Encyclopedia of Religious Knowledge* IV, 323. Denying a reported 1483 Paris edition, H. C. Hoskier writes that the 1597 Bremen edition by Nathan Chytraeus was the first. *De Contemptu Mundi: A Bitter Satirical Poem of 3000 Lines upon the Morals of the XIIth Century by Bernard of Morval, Monk of Cluny*. London: Bernard Quartich, 1972. xvi. Other editions: PL, CLXXIV, 1307.

61 Bibl 1899. 111 f.

62 *Alte Gedichte gegen das Jahr 1250 geschrieben welche die Unwissenheit des Evangelii beweinen, den Misbrauch der Ceremonien tadeln und zeigen, dass die Lehre dieser Zeit der Reformation Lutheri nicht new sey. Ehedem von Matthias Flaccius [sic] Illyricus als ein Beitrag zur Reformationsgeschichte der neueren Zeit aus dem lateinischen prosaisch übersetzt, und hier und da umschrieben.* Mülhausen: Johann Daniel Müller, 1781. A ij v.

The Emperor Strikes

BRAUNSCHWEIG, REFUGE FROM THE IMPERIAL ARMY

[Flacius] excels that pentaglot, the Salaminian, Epiphanius, not only in knowledge of languages, but in knowledge of affairs. – Melanchthon

Hardly had Luther been decently buried when Charles V declared war on his followers, with assistance of troops and money from the pope. On November 6, 1546, Duke Maurice's troops advanced on Wittenberg, and the Elector closed the university. By happy chance a "higher school" was being organized in Braunschweig, and Flacius found refuge there in the Winter and Spring of 1546–47. He was recommended to Nicolas Medler, Pastor of St. Martin's Church and Superintendent in Braunschweig, by Melanchthon, who compared him to the fourth-century Metropolitan bishop of Salamis in Cyprus. Flacius, he wrote, "excels that pentaglot, the Salaminian, Epiphanius, not only in knowledge of languages, but in knowledge of affairs."[1] From May 3 to 10, in the company of Katharina Luther and Georg Major, Melanchthon honored the new school with a visit.

Had the plan not been opposed by the ducal family, and had Medler succeeded in using funds from the St. Blasius and St. Cyriakus foundations,[2] Medler's school – already in 1547 – would have become the University of Braunschweig (the present University was founded as the Collegium Carolinum in 1745). He combined the *prima* (senior) classes of two Latin schools, St. Martin's and St. Catherine's – and moved them to the newly-vacated Franciscan monastery. The vanished Franciscans are still remembered in the name of the adjoining church, "St. Ulrici-Brüdern."[3]

As a *schola major*, the new *Pädagogium zu den Brüdern* offered not only the subjects of the trivium and Latin, Greek and Hebrew, but also mathematics, astronomy and theology. The rector of St. Martin's school, Johannes Glandorp, later professor in Marburg, taught part-time and Medler's son-in-law, Johannes Streitberger, served as rector. The humanist city physician, Antonius Niger,[4] and Georg Curio taught Greek and physics. Students were expected to read not only Terence, Virgil, Cicero, Caesar, Suetonius, Sallust, Livy and Demosthenes, but also the Acts of the Apostles and the First Epistle of John in the original and the Psalter in Hebrew.[5] The erotic poems of Catullus and Ovid's *Amores* were excluded. A dispute arose whether to use pagan authors at all. Medler, whom Luther had considered one of his best students, defended them in his *System for Teaching Christian Youth in Particular Schools*.[6]

1 CR, VI, 286. Melanththon later thanks Medler for giving Flacius the position. CR, VI, 304.

2 Ernst E. Doell. *Die Kollegiatstifte St. Blasius und St. Cyriakus zu Braunschweig*. Braunschweig: Waisenhaus, 1967. 215.

3 Friedrich Koldewey. *Geschichte des Schulwesens im Herzogtum Braunschweig*. Wolfenbüttel: Julius Zwissler, 1891. 40 f. The [Franciscan] Brothers' church building was occupied later by the congregation of St. Ulrich's parish, hence the double name.

4 Gustav Bauch. "Das Leben des Humanisten Antonius Niger." *Zeitschrift des Vereins für Geschichte und Alterthum Schlesiens* XVI (1882). 204 ff.

5 "Gesetze und Lehrpläne des Pädagogiums im Brüdernkloster. 1547." *Schulordnung der Stadt Braunschweig*. Friedrich Koldewey (ed.). Berlin: A. Hofmann & Co., 1886. 73–81.

6 *Ratio instituendi Juventutem Christianum in Scholis particularibus*. Wittenberg, 1550.

A Vision of Three Merchants. Flacius. *Ein Wunderlich Geschicht.*
The talk of Braunschweig

7   CR, VII, 653. Cf. Thorndike. 399.
    The vision was reported also by Le-
    onhard Krenzheim in *Coniecturae.*
    Christliche vermutungen von
    künfftiger Zeit, Zutraut in Kirchen und
    Regimenten ... Sampt den Weissagun-
    gen des Hocherleuchten Cardinals Ni-
    colai Cusani. Liegnitz: Marcus Rul-
    lus, 1552. v ij v. Görlitz: Ambrosius
    Fritsch, 1582. [B vij v.] ff.

8   *Ein wunderlich gesicht newlich bey*
    Braunschweig am hiemel gesehen, be-
    schriben durch den hochgelerten hern
    Doctorem Nicolaum Medlerum super-
    attendenten zu Braunschweig. Wit-
    tenberg: Pankraz Kempf, 1549.
    Other publications of the same
    kind are described in *Zeichen am*
    Himmel. Flugblätter des 16. Jahrhun-
    derts. Nuremberg: Germanisches
    Nationalmuseum. Catalog 15,
    1982.

9   *Exhortatio ad liberalium artium stu-*
    dia, solidam erudiendae adolescentiae
    rationem complectens. Magdeburg:
    Michael Lotter, 1550.

10 Otto Clemen. "Sechs Briefe aus
    Braunschweig an Melanchthon."
    Zeitschrift der Gesellschaft für
    niedersächsische Kirchengeschich-
    te XLIII (1938). 112. Reprint, Cle-
    men. KS, VI, 264.

The talk of the town in Braunschweig in the summer of 1549 was an apparition reported by three merchants – a crucifixion, three rotating moons, a man with a sword threatening a weeping woman, flaming cities surrounded by camels, a fiery lion and a two-headed eagle, a likeness of Johann Friedrich, and God the father dandling Adam and Eve on his breast, which Melanchthon agreed was a portent of the Last Things. The camels signified devastation in Germany by the Turks.[7] Asked to investigate, Medler pronounced the merchants sane. Flacius reported it all in *A Miraculous Sight Recently Seen in Heaven near Braunschweig.*[8] He also wrote an introduction to Niger's Exhortation to Study Liberal Arts, published in Magdeburg.[9] In a letter to Melanchthon, Niger explained to Melanchthon that the introduction did not imply he had taken sides in their controversy.[10]

Despite promising beginnings at the school, however, complaints arose about mixing younger boys with older ones who were ill-prepared, about corporal punishment, about faculty dissension, about using tax money for an unproductive purpose, and about engaging teachers (like Flacius) from out of town. Medler made problems for himself by being tactless with the

11 Johann Andreas Fabricius. *Abriß einer allgemeinen Historie der Gelehrsamkeit* III. Leipzig: Wiedmann, 1754. 77. Johannes Martinus Schamelius. *Numburgum Literatum.* Leipzig: Lanckisch Erben, 1727. 34–36.

12 "... ibidemque docendo famam nominis sui latè disseminavit." Adam. 473.

13 Werner Spieß. *Geschichte der Stadt Braunschweig im Nachmittelalter* I. Braunschweig: Waisenhaus-Buchdruckerei und Verlag, 1966. 735.

14 *Etliche Greiffliche ... warzeichen.* 1549. E ij v – E iij v, D iiij v – D v r; 1550. [H iiij v] – J v; G iij r.

15 Spieß. 87.

Burgomaster and by his domestic difficulties. To make things worse, he had hired a clothmaker named Hase who had picked up a knowledge of Greek in Naples, and an apprentice joiner, Georg Schweitzberg, who had learned Hebrew from the Jews in Pressburg (Bratislava). They both departed, Hase under suspicion as a counterfeiter, Schweizburg complaining about the "head work".[11]

Flacius' lectures at the *Pädagogium* were well received, and contributed to his growing reputation.[12] At St. Andrew's church, he made use of a library that dated from 1309.[13] At St. Martin's he learned to know Pastor Ludolphus Petroselinus, who in 1547 had expelled an evil spirit from a young girl. Petroselinus told him that the Reformation itself was an exorcism – old stories about ghosts and poltergeists were disappearing.[14] Flacius, known to have influenced the opposition of other North German cities to the Augsburg Interim, may have had some influence on Medler, who, in stormy sessions of June 11 and July 14 of the year following, convinced the Braunschweig city council to reject the law.[15]

In Spring came the shattering news of the catastrophe at Mühlberg. The Emperor had defeated the princes of the Smalcald League. The two major protectors of the Reformation, Elector Johann Friedrich and Philipp of Hesse were taken into imperial custody. In the Fall, Matthias and Elizabeth, with Matthias Junior, who had come into the world in Braunschweig, returned to Wittenberg; the University was opening its doors once more.

WITTENBERG, REWARD FOR INFIDELITY

1 Hermann Gebhardt. *Thüringische Kirchengeschichte.* Zweite Hälfte: *Vom Beginn der Reformation bis zur neueren Zeit.* Gotha: Friedrich Andreas Pustet, 1881. 169.

2 Maurenbrecher. 144.

In Luther's lifetime and afterward, I rejected these Stoic and Manichaean follies. – Melanchthon

To the melody of "Lord, Keep Us Steadfast in Your Word," the faithful in Thuringia prayed for their prince, Johann Friedrich.

Ach, Herr, laß Dir befohlen sein
unsern Landesherrn,
den Diener Dein
In vestem Glauben ihn erhalt,
Und rett'ihn aus des Feinds Gewalt.[1]

Lord, we commend to Thee
The Lord of our land, thy servant.
Keep him in firm faith
And save him from the power of the enemy.

The enemy was Emperor Charles V, who had imprisoned Johann Friedrich and robbed him of his rank as Elector of the Holy Roman Empire. As a reward for helping him defeat the Lutheran princes, with papal encouragement,[2] he transferred the title to Duke Maurice of the other Saxony. For fighting against the Lutheran princes in the late war and for the theft of the electorate from his cousin, Maurice was reviled by his subjects as "the Judas of Meissen." And they said that Wittenberg University, which now belonged to Maurice, was a reward for infidelity.[3]

The Wittenberg faculty was loyal to the old prince – for a time. At Johann Friedrich's request, his counsellor, Franz Burchart, began to plan a school to replace the University of Wittenberg in the reduced territory that prince still ruled, "where God's word and languages might be taught, even though it could not be a university." As was to be expected, he consulted with Melanchthon. Where Melanchthon was, one heard, there was Wittenberg. As the site of the new institution the Praeceptor chose the city of Jena. "I would rather serve your princely grace in poverty," he assured the prince, "than in other places in riches."[4]

Empty words. Melanchthon listened to the soft words of the new elector, who needed him as symbol of legitimacy. Probably at the 1547 *Landtag*,[5] Maurice assured members of the Wittenberg faculty of his good intentions. Instead of a call to Jena, then, with Johann Bugenhagen and others, Melanchthon broke faith with Johann Friedrich, chose allegiance to the new elector, and returned to Wittenberg. Flacius was critical. "Some among them," he wrote about his colleagues, "are justly worthy of punishment, who, although they had promised other Christian princes their service, soon had forgotten their promise."[6]

Why did Melanchthon break faith?[7] Was he afraid to link his career to a political loser? Was it to please his wife?[8] Were his ties to Wittenberg too strong?[9] Was it to prevent the dissolution of the Wittenberg university?[10] Did he think that founding a new university was impossible?[11] Was it because Jena could not afford proper salaries for the whole Wittenberg faculty?[12] Or was it, as some people were saying, because Maurice caressed him with money (*demulcebat muneribus*)?

> The gifts of the new Elector Maurice soon uncovered the spirit and the passions of these toadies. Melanchthon promised the unfortunate Elector to sketch a plan of the new University of Jena. The Dukes of Saxony, the sons of this prince, called him to Weimar, and he hastened there. But as soon as he received letters from the court of Maurice, he suddenly forgot all the favors that Johann Friedrick had done for him. With one word, Melanchthon goes secretly back to Wittenberg, and by his flight he publicly dishonors these princes.[13]

Melanchthon may also have been wary of the Lutheran influence at Jena. Perhaps he would not be able to introduce his humanistic pedagogy in Jena. Perhaps "in another place without an academic tradition it would probably be much more difficult, in the presence of more decided and more determined Lutherans, whose service the sons of Johann Friedrich would hardly dispense with, to assert the predominant place that he had in Wittenberg, or to achieve it?"[14] The disappointed Ernestine chancellor, Franz Burchart, came to the conclusion centuries earlier. Although Flacius had not yet received a call to Jena, Melanchthon feared that he

3 Franz Xaver von Wegele. "Zwei ungedruckte Aktenstücke zur Geschichte der Universität Jena." *Zeitschrift des Vereins für Thüringische Geschichte* II (1856). 188.

4 CR, VI, 565.

5 Günther Wartenberg. "Nachwirkungen des Bauernkrieges in der albertinischen Politik unter Moritz von Sachsen (1547–1551)." *Jahrbuch für Regionalgeschichte* VII (1979). 246.

6 *Gründliche Verlegung des langen Comments der Adiaphoristen oder Verzelung irer Handlungen*. [Jena: Donat Richtenhan] 1560. B iiij r.

7 A discussion in Friedrich Schneider. "Melanchthons Entscheidung nach der Katastrophe von Mühlbert." *Festschrift der Universität Halle und Wittenberg*, 1952. 313–322; Manschreck. "Examination." 35 f., 38, 40–42.

8 Christmann. 154.

9 Georg Theodor Strobel. *Die Ehre Melanchthons gerettet wider die ungegründete Beschuldigungen herrn Prof. Hausens*. Altdorf: John Paul Meyer, 1775. 24.

10 Heinz Scheible. "Melanchthons Auseinandersetzung mit dem Reformkatholicismus." Rolf Decot (ed.). *Vermittlungsversuche auf dem Augsburger Reichstag*. 1530. Stuttgart: Franz Steiner Verlag, 1989. 76.

11 Curt Christmann. *Melanchthons Haltung im Schmalkaldischen Krieg*. Vaduz: Kras, 1965. 149.

12 Otto Vogt. "Melanchthon's und Bugenhagen's Stellung zum Interim und die Rechtfertigung des letztern in seinem Jonascommentar." *Jahrbuch für Protestantische Theologie* XIII (1887). 4.

13 Strobel. *Ehre*. 3 f. Cf. Karl Renatus Hausen. *Pragmatische Geschichte der Protestanten in Deutschland*. Halle: Curtius, 1767.

14 Ritschl. II, 335.

15 Hermann Weissenborn. *Melan-chthons Briefwechsel über die Gründung der Universität Jena und seine Berufung an dieselbe aus zum Theil noch ungedruckten Briefen.* Jena: I. G. Schreiber, 1848. 9.

16 *Admonitio M. Alberti Christiani ad primarium nostri temporis Ecebolum Eislebium scripta. Anno M.D. XLIX.* Magdeburg: Michael Lotter, 1550. Aiiiij r.

17 CR, XXI, 277.

18 Ibid. 87 f.

19 CR, XXIII, 15. Deriving Melan-chthon's "causes" from Aristotele's doctrine of four causes would not satisfy the critics who were con-cerned lest the common man understand the word in a Pelagian fashion.

20 G. Hoffmann. 125.

21 CR, IX, 766.

22 Karl Matthes. *Philipp Melanchthon, Leben und Wirken.* Altenburg: Julius Helbig, 1841. 168 f.

23 CR, XXI, 659.

24 Deus trahit, sed volentem trahit. CR, XXI, 376. From Chrysostom's gloss on John 6.44. "no man can come to me, except that the Father who sent me draws him." PG, 51, 143: "Id vero jam volo, vos id probe nosse, Deum nempe non vim in-ferre nolentibus, sed volentes tra-here. ideo nameque dicit: nemo venit ad me, nisi pater meus traxer-it eum. Quo vero trahit, volentem trahit, humique jacentem ac ma-num porrigentem." Cf. N. P. Wil-liams. *The Grace of God.* London: Longmans, Green and Co., 1930. 81.

25 CR, XXI, 915.

would be called eventually. "A chief reason for his declining may well be that Flacius is turning toward Jena: he fears the firm direction which Jena would take under Flacius' influence.[15]

In his early years at the University, 1519 to 1521, Melanchthon had made common cause with Luther. But no sooner had the elector been taken prisoner, Albert Christian reported, than Melanchthon announced he would no longer use the word, *sola*, as in *sola gratia*.[16] "The doctrine of the gospel," he had written in the first edition of his *Loci Communes*, "takes away free will."[17] "We can do nothing but sin ... since all things happen necessarily according to divine predestination, there is no freedom of our wills."[18] But now, influenced by Erasmus' *Hyperaspistes*, he had changed his mind, and opted for free will. "Necesse est in nobis," he wrote, "esse aliquam discriminis causam": in us, there is necessarily a cause for discrim-ination. It was the idea over which the controversy about "synergism" raged: that faith begins with an act of the will, an "assent to the Word of God."

Explaining the bondage of the will, Luther had explained that there was only once cause of conversion, "God's work in us, without us." But in the 1535 *Loci Communes* Melanchthon listed three – the word, the Holy Spirit, and the human will.[19] Now that Luther was dead, Melanchthon dis-tanced himself yet further from him. The 1548 edition of the *Loci Com-munes*, the first after the Reformer's death, is "a milestone on the path on which Melanchthon had taken back to Erasmus."[20] Luther's doctrine of the bound will, he decided, was stoic. "In Luther's lifetime and after," he wrote, "I rejected these Stoic and Manichaean follies."[21] Indeed, the old Elector had long suspected that Melanchthon had looked forward to Luther's death.[22]

Melanchthon now accepted Erasmus's notion of free will: "the ability to apply oneself to grace."[23] "God draws us," he wrote, quoting John Chry-sostom," "but draws him who wants to be drawn."[24] In his 1559 *Loci Com-munes* he has it both ways. The initiative is God's.

> It is rightly said that the cause of election is mercy in the will of God, who does not will the entire human race to perish, but on account of the Son gathers and preserves the Church. Paul intends this when he mentions the saying in Romans, Chapter 9: "I have compassion on whom I have compassion."

And it is man's.

> Nevertheless, in the matter of accepting, it is fitting that apprehension of the promise and recognition of Christ occur.[25]

Matthaeus Razeberger, "the fiercest Flacian," related an encounter at the Stone Gate in Wittenberg between Melanchthon and Chilian Goldstein. Melanchthon told him he could now teach what was not allowed while Luther was alive. "Herr Preceptor," Goldstein answered, "if you had any differences with Luther, you should have made it known while Luther was still alive. Now if you teach anything different from him, you will surely experience many who will speak against you." Melanchthon's face flushed and he turned away abruptly."[26]

The university reopened October 16, 1547. During the Fall semester Flacius lectured on biblical and aristotelian themes. He also taught Greek, without help, he noted, from Melanchthon.[27] The lecture notes on Flacius' Aristotle lectures taken by student George Tanner, the least legible of all the Flacian material, record that the lectures were interrupted in November when Maurice's troops approached the city.[28]

Flacius' new religious confidence was expressed in his "little book of Hebrew phrases," *A True and Useful Explanation of the Word, "Faith," and Certain Other Words, taken from Hebrew Sources,*[29] in which he explicated his argument that the New Testament should be interpreted on the basis of the Old, that behind the Greek words of the new Testament lay Hebrew forms of thought. The troublesome notion that God is the author of sin, for example, can be dealt with when one knows the language. His major subject was the word, "faith." In the Qual form, the Hebrew word, "amen," true, means "to be faithful." In the Hiphil form, however, he explained – correctly! – it means "to impart belief."

26 Neudecker. *Geschichte Ratzeberger's.* 186n.; The story is rejected by Georg Theodore Strobel in his edition of Ratzeberger's memoire: *D. Matthiae Ratzebergers Geheime Geschichte von den Chur- und Sächsischen Höfen und den Religions-Streitigkeiten seiner Zeit.* Altorf: Lorenz Schüpfel, 1774. 90 ff.; It was accepted by O. Ritschl. II, 332.

27 *Apologia auf ... Menij.* J iiij r.

28 "Hac privata Rhetoricorum Aristotelis praelectio postea exercitu ducis mauricii hostili, quem ad moenia Wittebergensia duxerat, interturbata est anno 1547 mense Nov. cum apud Jacob Mylich age." Schola in Aristotelis lib. 2 Posteriorum ex Matthiae Illyrici Praelectionis a Georgio Tannero Collecta. Vienna Nationalbibliothek, Ms. 10570; Gottlieb 464; Caught up in World War II, Moldaenke, who promised to investigate the Aristotle lectures, op. cit. 139n. was not able to do so.

29 *De vocabulo fidei et aliis quibusdam vocabulis. Explicatio vera & utilis, sumpta ex fontibus Ebraicis.* Wittenberg: Vitus Creucer, 1549. Analysis in Preger. I, 25–29.

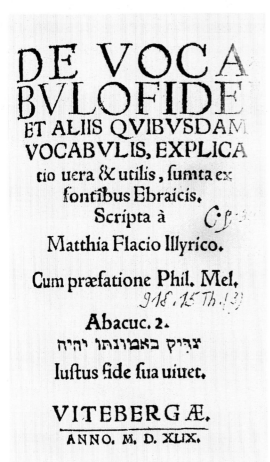

DE VOCA
BVLOFIDE
ET ALIIS QVIBVSDAM
VOCABVLIS, EXPLICA
tio uera & utilis, sumta ex
fontibus Ebraicis.
Scripta à
Matthia Flacio Illyrico.

Cum præfatione Phil. Mel.

Abacuc. 2.

צדיק באמונתו יהיה

Iustus fide sua uiuet.

VITEBERGÆ.
ANNO. M. D. XLIX.

30 *Widder die newe Reformation D. Pfef-fingers, des Meisnischen Thumbherrn.* Magdeburg: Christian Rödinger, 1550. [A iiij r].

31 CR, VII, 345–349.

32 *Testimonium.* 95.

33 "Entstehung." 95.

34 Primus Trubar. *Ta Pervi dejl Tiga Noviga Testamenta.* Tübingen: [Ulrich Morhart, 1557].

35 In the appendix to Primus Trubar [Philopatridus Illyricus]. *Catechismus in der Wendischen Sprach, sambt einer kürzen Ausslegung in gesang weiss. Item die Litanae und ein predig von rechten Glauben.* Sybernburgen: Jernei Skuryaniz [Tübingen: Ulrich Morhart, 1550]. Having escaped the wrath of the Bishop of Laibach, Trubar falsified the place of publication and the publisher. "Skuryaniz" is an old family name in Lower Carinthia. Theodor Elze. "Die slovenischen Protestantischen Katechismen des XVI. Jahrhunderts." JGGPO, XIV (1893). 83, 100.

36 *Katechismus, Edna malahna kniga, ukoi esu vele potribni i prudni nauki i Artikuli prave Krstianske Vere, skratkim istomačenem, Za mlade i priproste ljudi, I edna predika, od Kriposti i ploda prave karstianske vere, Krozi Stipana Istranina, spomoću dobrih Hrvatov, sad naiprvo istomačena.* Tübingen: Ulrich Morhart d. Ä. Witwe, 1561.

A True and useful Explanation was a great success, and well-received in Wittenberg.[30] It was honored by Melanchthon, who wrote a friendly preface dated March 2, 1549, addressed to the Archbishop of Canterbury.[31] In his preface, Melanchthon argued that the church was essentially a school – a notion Peter Fraenkel calls "the quintessence of antiquity,"[32] and which Albrecht Ritschl makes responsible for the later mistakes of Lutheran theology.[33] The "Little Book of Hebrew Phrases" was reprinted in 1554, 1555 and 1563, and appended to a translation of the New Testament into Slovenian in 1550 and 1557.[34] Since it appeared also in Primus Trubar's catechism,[35] the first book printed in Croatian (Glagolitic) script,[36] it earned a place in the "springtime" of Slavic literature.

> I am certain of this, and can explain it with good grounds, that in the first apostolic church the true and holy body and the salutary blood of Christ in the eucharist had the name and also the action called "mass," and that both the name and the action has been maintained in the church everywhere up until our time. – Michael Helding

During the 1547 "Armored" Diet, Michael Helding, coadjutor bishop of Mainz, preached a series of sermons in the cathedral at Augsburg. The city was still nine-tenths Lutheran; a significant part of his hearers was uncomprehending Spanish soldiers paid to listen.[1] In the presence of the emperor's brother, King Ferdinand, and high officials of the Empire, the bishop announced that the Roman liturgy had been transmitted from apostolic times to the present totally unchanged. He made the same absurd claim about the eucharistic prayer, or mass canon. "We know … that the canon has been preserved from the time of the apostles absolutely in all its parts (*gar nach alle wort*), and that all the words of the canon … are found in the books of those who lived and wrote a thousand years ago."[2]

Published by order of King Ferdinand and distributed as a concomitant text[3] to the Augsburg Interim, Helding's sermons acquired the force of law, and therefore must be understood as a great deal more significant than the simple "catechetical instruction" that Eric Feifel makes them.[4] The official directive read, "...the canon in the mass shall be interpreted and explained approximately in the way that the Mainz coadjutor bishop preached here..."[5]

The sermons were laid before Luther's imprisoned patron, Landgrave Philipp of Hesse, by Spanish theologian, Pedro Malvenda, who informed him that accepting them was the condition for his release from imperial captivity. He had a relatively easy task convincing him. Philipp was so anxious to get out of confinement, according to the English ambassador, that he "would fight, if the Emperor would bid him, with Turk, French, England, God and the Devil."[6] On January 13, 1549, the Landgrave announced his change of mind. Together with a point-by-point approval of the Interim, he sent copies of the sermons to the Lutheran Superintendents of Hesse asking for adoption of the Interim law and of Helding's liturgical notions. The Emperor's law, he informed them, agreed with the church fathers "in holy signs and ceremonies."[7]

The clergy in Hesse, where the Interim was unpopular, rejected their prince's appeal. Even though they might have to leave the country, they replied, the earth was the Lord's. If they had to leave the world, they comforted themselves with what Christ had said: "In my Father's house are many mansions."[8]

It is worth noticing that the thesis basic to the *Missarum Solemnia*, by Roman Catholic scholar, Joseph Andreas Jungmann, is that the mass and the eucharistic prayer are the result of long historical growth. "... built in,"

1   Salig. I, 564; "Der erwelte Bischoff zu Merseburgk Michel Sidonius predige fast alle sontage im thum quem Hispani non intelligentes summo ardore audiunt." Pflug. *Correspondance* III. Ed. Jacques V. Pollet. Leiden: E.J. Brill, 1977. 241.

2   *Von der Hailigsten Messe. Fünffzehn Predige zu Augspurg auff dem Reichsztag im Jar M. D. XLVIII gepredigt. Durch Micheln Bischoff zu Sidonien, Meintzischen Suffraganeen.* Ingolstadt: Alexander Weissenhorn, 1548. C r, N iij r. Further editions in Nikolaus Paulus. "Michael Helding, Ein Prediger und Bischof des 16. Jahrhunderts." *Der Katholik* LXXIV (1894). 422–424.

3   "Begleittext." Heribert Smolinsky. "Michael Helding." Erwin Iserloh (ed.). *Katholische Theologen der Reformationszeit* II. Münster: Aschendorff, 1985. 130. Cf. *Urkundliche Quellen zur hessischen Reformationsgeschichte.* III. (1547–1567), bearbeitet nach Walter Köhler, Walter Sohm, Theodor Suppel und Friedrich Wilhelm Schaffer von Günther Franz und Eckhart G. Franz. Marburg: N. G. Elwert Verlag, 1955. 33, 94, 11.

4   *Grundzüge einer Theologie des Gottesdienstes. Motive und Konzeption der Glaubensverkündigung Michael Heldings (1506–1561) als Ausdruck einer "Katholischen Reformation."* Freiburg et al.: Herder, 1960. 49.

5   Georg Pfeilschrifter (ed.). *Acta Reformationis Catholicae* V. Regensburg: Pustet, 1973. 242. On its implementation: Alis Knöpfler. *Die Kelchbewegung in Bayern unter Herzog Albrecht V.* Munich: E. Stahl Sen. (Julius Stahl), 1891. 143.

6   *The Whole Works of Roger Acham.* J. A. Giles (ed.). I. London: J. R. Smith, 1864. 244.

7   Fritz Hermann. *Das Interim in Hessen. Ein Beitrag zur Reformationsge-*

schichte. Marburg: N. G. Elwert'sche Verlagsbuchhandlung, 1888. 19 ff.; Pflug. *Correspondance* III. 123 ff.

8 Bernhard Bess. "Die Entwicklung der hessischen Kirche unter Philipp dem Grossmütigen." ZKG, XXXIII (1912). 334.

9 5. Aufl. Vienna, Freiburg, Basel: Herder, 1962. 3.

10 *De Sectis.* 109.

11 *Was die Evangelische Meß sey, Grundtliche und Christenliche Anzeigung unnd auß der Hayligen Geschrifft, unnd auß den alten heiligen Kirchenlerern.* Dillingen: Sebastian Mayer, 1555. Cf. Paulus. *Dominikaner.* 156, lists subequent editions.

12 Op. cit. 46.

13 *Eine freuntliche, demütige und andechtige erinnerung an das heilige Volck, und künigliche priesterthumb des Antichrists, von der besserung des heiligen Canons oder Stilmessen.* Magdeburg: Michael Lotter, 1550. A iij r.

14 Ibid. 165.

15 Ibid. 17.

16 *Refutatio Missae. Widerlegung des sophistischen Buchs des schwarzen Münchs von der Opfermess.* [Strassburg: Samuel Emmel?] 1557. [A iiij r].

17 *Publicum Ecclesiae Sacrum. Von der Warheit der Altkyrchischen Liturgy und Opferung, das ist, Catholischer Missen. Antwort Georgii Wicelii Orthodoxi, wider den Mathis Illyric, zu Magdeburg.* Cologne: Johan Quentel, 1551. A ij r.

18 *Brevis Censura impiarum aliquot concionium Illius Suffraganaei.* Copenhagen, 1548. Martin Schwarz Lausten. *Biskop Peder Palladius og Kirchen (1537–1560).* Copenhagen: Akademisk Forlag, 1987. 201–206, 312.

19 *The Works of John Jewel, Bishop of Salisbury.* John Ayre (ed.). Cambridge: Cambridge University Press, 1845–1850. III, 235, IV, 109.

20 *De Ficticio Missae Sacrificio Argumenta erronea Sophistarum Pontificiorum, cum Refutationibus eorundem.*

he writes, "have been the ideas about construction of many generations."[9] Jungmann's argument and his "genetic method" were anticipated by Flacius: "Sidon [Helding] maintained that the whole canon as now in use came from the apostles word-for-word, yet all the pontifical writers witness the contrary. In turn they ... recount who invented which part of the canon, which part of the mass."[10] In contrast to Flacius and Jungmann, Helding and Johann Fabri[11] must therefore be considered liturgical fundamentalists.

Feifel, reluctant to say that Helding's ideas were false, calls them "inadequate." "The historical sense," he explains, excusing Helding, "was precious little developed."[12] Flacius made the wry remark about Helding that *forte ignorantia excusat peccatum*: perhaps ignorance excuses sin.[13] Feifel does concede that Flacius demonstrated "clear proof of the impossibility of the apostolic institution of the liturgical form of the Roman mass,"[14] but he rejects the proof on the singular ground that Flacius had a tendency to slander.[15]

Flacius anticipated Helding's own reaction: "Shut your mouth, you Lutheran scoundrel. I know it quite otherwise. Or if you do not remain silent, according to our law you should die and be burned."[16] A similar tirade was hurled against Flacius by George Witzel. What else, Witzel asked, could one expect from the great desecrator, the "despicable Slav," who is destroying all saints, all sacraments, and the whole ancient service of God?

> Illyricus, you are a man who is not worthy that a pious Christian should answer your false, slanderous, seditious nonsense, public ravings and obvious lies. By rights, you should be cast away as a damned member of the common churches and as a cut-off, unsound vine, and be considered an outlaw, until punishment, which is ready for you because of your deserts.[17]

In Denmark, Petrus Palladius and Johann Machabaeus attacked Helding's sermons in their *Brief Censure of The Impious Sermons of That Suffragan.*[18] In England, Bishop John Jewel of Salisbury, quoting from Flacius' *De Sectis*, charged that "The Bishop of Sidon, in the late diet of the emperor holden at Augusta avounched openly that ye had your whole canon from the apostles of Christ, word by word, even as it is ... written in your mass books ... There is no toy so vain or so fabulous but ye are able by yur cunning to bring it lineally, either from Christ himself or from his apostles or from one or tother of the ancient fathers."[19] In Germany, as "Andreas Epitimus," Justus Jonas joined the controversy in *False Arguments on the Counterfeit Sacrifice of the Mass of the Sophist Pontifexes, with Refutations of the Same. True, Solid, and Manifest Arguments against the Sacrifice of the Papist Mass,*[20] and Bernhard Ziegler of Leipzig did the same in a *Disputation on the Sacrament of the Altar or the Lord's Supper and Mass.*[21] Flacius injected Luther's observation that proof the apostles did not write the canon can be derived from the canon text itself, and from the fact that the texts of the canon differed.

Because here there is no Holy Scripture and the canons are nowhere identical, one can recognize that it is a human regulation, not a divine one. Why, therefore, should one defend it so vigorously, as if it were the one eternal word of God, because men act thus outside and without the Holy Scripture, can err and fail. Whoever wants to read the canon may read it, so he will find the names of various saints who lived long after the time of the apostles.[22]

In *A Friendly, Humble and Devout Reminder of Matthias Flacius Illyricus to the Holy People and Royal Priesthood of the Antichrist on the Improvement of the Holy Canon or Silent Mass*, Flacius attacked the antiquity, and therefore, the authority of the canon/eucharistic prayer.

> ... your bishop of Sidon knows for certain that the whole canon has been in the church from the time of the apostles up to the present day, and therefore without any doubt was written by the apostles, the holy Virgin Mary, or by the Lord Christ himself ... But I would gladly like to know, whether the holy man, the bishop of Sidon, when he left the Holy Land Canaan for Germany, brought a copy of the Hebrew, Chaldean or Greek canon.[23]

He was mocking Helding's titular bishopric of Sidon in Lebanon. "He must be a very holy man, since he came from the most Holy Land, where even stones are holy."[24] "He is the spectral bishop [*Larvenbischof*] of Sidon, because he has sworn to go to Sidon, to care for the church of Christ there, but his whole life long he did not go, and had not even considered doing so."[25] Perhaps his clergy could speak Greek! It was highly improbable, however, that the apostles wrote the canon in Latin, since that language was not spoken in Syria.[26] Helding was insisting that not a word of the liturgy had been changed, and not a word should be changed – not a *dütlein*, not a *crüzlein*.

All that was necessary to confute Helding's claim, of course, was to produce authentic historical texts of the canon that were not identical with the contemporary text, something that as a collector of manuscripts Flacius was eminently well-equipped to do.

The primary sources he produced in succession were often accompanied by explanations that presupposed his notion of "gregorianism," the idea that the basic departure from the original mass occured at the time of the Gregorian reform, when the Western liturgy took a new direction – the "known fact that the Mass was first born about one thousand years ago at the time of Pope Gregory I."[27]

> ... that in his sermons he can so often bellow that his mass stood for fifteen hundred years, namely, from the apostolic age, and that his only sacrifice will remain until Antichrist removes it – because it is a known fact that the mass was first born about one thousand years ago at the time of Pope Gregory I [A. D. 598 – 604] and had even grown and changed in the four hundred years before that. The mass was not as ancient as Helding said it was.

> From Platina and other writers it is sufficiently apparent that one pope after another always added different ceremonies and rites to those existing earlier, and consequently that the greater part of church rite and the law of papal idolatry and abuse are clearly of human invention and are not especially old.

Argumenta vera, firma & perspicua, contra Sacrificium Missae Papisticae. Magdeburg: Christian Rhodium, 1550; Otto Clemen. "Andreas Epitimus = Hartmann Beyer?" KS, II, 338–342.

21 *De Sacramento altaris seu Coena Dominica et Missa Disputatio et Capita Proposita.* n. p. 1548.

22 *Bedencken Doctoris Martini Lutheri Auff dem Reichstage zu Augspurgk im xxx. yare gestellet.* [Magdeburg: Michael Lotter], 1548. B ij r.

23 Op. cit. B iij r.

24 *Widderlegung des Catechismi des larven Bischoffes von Sidon.* [Magdeburg: Michael Lotter] 1550. A ij r.

25 *Verlegung der Apologiae Sidonii, damit er seinen Catechismum verteidiget.* [Magdeburg: Christian Rödinger] 1553. A ij r.

26 *Eine freuntliche ... Erinnerung.* [A iv r], B iij r.

27 *Zwei Capitel Polydori Virgilii.* A ij r. Below, note 31. Cf. Cod. Guelf. 71a Helmst. 374 v.

28 Ibid. A ij r.

29 *Widderlegung der Predigten von der allerheiligsten Antichristischen Missa des frembden Bischoffs von Sydon, Meintzischen Weihbischoff.* Magdeburg: Christian Rödinger, 1550. Emanuel Hirsch found a certain similarity between Helding's explanation of Christ's eternal priesthood and the doctrine of Andreas Osiander. *Die Theologie des Andreas Osiander und ihre geschichtlichen Voraussetzungen.* Göttingen: Vandenhoeck & Ruprecht, 1919. 192.

30 Polydore Vergile Urbinatis. *Adagiorum Liber. Eiusdem de inuentionibus rerum libri octo.* Basel: Johann Froben, 1521.

31 *Zwei Capitel Polydori Virgili vom Namen und Stifftern der Meß, ausgangen zu einen anfang widder des Sidonij predigten. Daraus erscheinet, wie er in seinen predigten öffentlich leugt, da er sagt, das die gantze Christenheit von 1500. Jaren her die Pap. Meß allezeit eintrechtliglich gehalten habe. Und das der Canon in allen seinen stücken von der Apostel zeit her im brauch gewesen sei. Item, Widderlegung D. M. Luth. des grewels der Stillmesse, so man den Canon nennet.* Magdeburg: Christian Rödinger, 1550.

32 *Catalogus.* 1562. 50.

Yet the seducing hypocrites of Antichrist can continue their shameless cry: this is the Catholic, rightly Christian and apostolic religion! Those inexperienced in history suppose readily that they mean all papal abominations have been treasured since Christ's time and were established by him and his apostles.

From an earlier edition of the canon he produced an earlier version of the prayer, *Fiat commixtio et consecratio corpori et sanguinis domini nostri Iesu Christi accipientibus nobis in vitam aeternam.* At an earlier time the prayer had been longer:

> *Hac sacrosancta commixtio corporis et sanguinis domini nostri Iesu Christi fiat omnibus sumentibus salus mentis & corporis ad vitam aeternam capessendam praeparatio salutari.*

It followed that the text that the rigorists themselves were using was an altered text. Another petition, the *Communicantes*, following the names of Cosmas and Damian, Dionysius, Martin, Gregory, Augustine, Jerome, Benedict, Andreas, and Boniface were named.[28] In the petition, *libera nos quaesumus*, another manuscript adds, *Andreae nec non et beato Bonifacio marytre tuo, atque pontifice cum omnis*, etc." In still another manuscript, between the words, *omni Benedictione repleatur*, and *Memento etiam Domine famulorum* there was a prayer no longer in the canon.

The word, *etiam* (also) in the section, *memento etiam* ("be mindful, also") refers to something mentioned previously. But that something is not there. From William Durand's *Rationale Divinorum Officiorum* he supplied the missing prayer, *memento mei quaeso*, once part of the canon. The same prayer, he reported, was to be found in other older manuscripts.

Flacius commented on Helding's sermons in more detail in his *Confutation of the Sermons on the Most Holy and Antichristian Mass of the Foreign Bishop of Sidon*.[29] He appended excerpts from a work of Polydore Vergile (eventually placed on the Index), *The Invention of Things:*[30] *Two Chapters of Polydore Vergil on the Name and Institutors of the Mass. Published as a Beginning Against the Sermons of Sydonius, from Which it is Clear that He is Publicly Lying in Saying that All of Christendom for 1500 years Has Performed the Papal Mass at All Times, and that the Canon in All its Parts Has Been in Use Since the Time of the Apostles*,[31] to which he appended Luther's treatise on the eucharistic prayer.

Pursuing the "gregorianism" theme, he argued that the Gregorian Sacramentary was quite different from the contemporary practice, containing no sequences by Abbot Notker of St. Gall, no "minor canon," no ceremonial rubrics. After the Our Father there was a variant embolism.

> He [Pope Gregory I] says that the canon recited in the mass was put together by some scholastic. Thus it is clear how simple the apostolic mass was. On the other hand, it is clear that the apostles made use of the body of the Lord only for communion, and had no mass or sacrifice. For they never said, "I offer or sacrifice for the whole world, for for the salvation of souls." Seeing they had no canon, but for a long time, one after the other, individual popes each added something to the words of the Supper, until they produced something wholly different than what the Lord instituted.[32]

Pope Gregory himself, Flacius pointed out, had advised St. Augustine the Less to incorporate into the mass any customs he might find in England that were edifying.[33] He buttressed his argument by publishing other variant canon texts – notably in his 1557 *Refutation of the Mass*, and appending others to his first edition of Sulpicius Severus' *Chronicles*: the Second Apology of Justin Martyr, the *Stromata* of Clement of Alexandria, and (Pseudo) Dionysius.[34] He pointed out that the Greek canon differed greatly from the Roman, and never claimed to be a sacrifice for the living or dead, much less for souls, nor did it ever claim that God is placated by it, or, as in the Latin canon, that it is carried to heaven by angels' hands.

The epistle and the gospel, he wrote, were not in the liturgy to be prayed, but were for instructing the people. It was a stupid thing, he wrote in the "observations" that he appended to his mass edition, for the deacon to be told, "I give you power to read the epistle and the gospel for the living and the dead..." He ridiculed the priest celebrating private mass (*missa in angulo, Winkelmesse*) "in a deserted corner," who reads the epistle and the gospel to the wall, greets the wall with "dominus vobiscum" and asks the stones to pray with him. The plural forms, *oremus, Dominus vobiscum, pax vobis, habemus ad dominum, gratias agamus*, imply a community. The phrase, *repleti potu*, implies that more than one person had drunk the wine. According to St. Ambrose, in fact, even the words, *introibo ad altare dei*, applied to *all* Christians.

The words, "this do," he wrote, are not an authorization for a ritual; instead, they mandated eating and drinking.

The most telling proof of historical variations in the text of the liturgy[35] was a manuscript, Cod. Guelf. 1151 Helmstedt, known since by Flacius' name (e. g. in the the *Patrologia Latina* 138, 1305 – 1336), as the Missa Illyrica[36]. Before publishing it he sought the expert advice of François Badouin, who, in turn, consulted Georg Cassander.[37] Although Hans Butzmann[38] and Joanne Pierce (see below) have made attempts to re-name it "prayerbook," the traditional name seems destined to survive: in an article that appeared after Butzmann and Pierce made their arguments, Andreas Odenthal still called it "Missa Illyrica."[39]

Flacius himself called it *A Latin Mass Which was Once in Use Before the Roman [mass], About 700 A. D., described in Good Faith from an Old and Authentic Codex*.[40] One third of the text consists of "apologies," confessions of gluttony, drunkenness, fornication, lust, depression, dryness of soul, drowsiness, negligence, anger, covetousness, malice, hate, slander, perjury, lying, vanity, levity and pride. One of the prayers regrets no less than forty-three sins, none of which, it should be noted, have anything to do with Flacius' later teaching on original sin.

In the accompanying essay, "Some Observations on the Antiquity of the Mass," Flacius took issue with Helding's explanation of the word, "mass" as the Hebrew word for "sacrifice." He cited the *Etymologies* of Isidore of Seville (Book VI, chapter 13), Polydore Vergile, *De Inventoribus Rerum*. The correct explanation, he argued, is that the word came from the expression,

33 MGH, *Gregorii Papae Registrum Epistolarum*. Bd. II. Berlin: Weidmann, 1899. 334. Robert McCulloch. "Gregorian Adaptation to the Augustine Mission in England." *Missiology* VI (1978). 328.

34 *Sulpitii Severi sacrae historiae a mundi Exordio ad sua usque tempora deductae, libri II. nunc primum in lucem editi. Item aliae quaedam Historicae appendices, lectu dignissimae*. Basel: Johannes Oporinus, 1556.

35 "... through his [Helding's] confidently delivered and often repeated statements about the apostolic origin of the Roman cult actions, he stimulated the Protestants to historical studies, whose most mature fruit was the publication of Matthias Flacius, Missa Latina ... in the year 1557." Paul Tschakert. "Sidonius." ADB, XXXIV, 166.

36 Cf. Fernand Cabrol. "La Messe Latine de Flacius Illyricus." *Revue Bénédictine* XXII (1905). 151–164; Idem, "La Messe latine de Flacius Illricus." *Dictionnaire d'Archéologie chrétienne et de Liturgie* 5 (1923). 1625–1635.

37 "Notes and Documents." *Bibliothèque d'Humanisme et Renaissance* XL (1978). 538.

38 On the basis of Josef Braun's investigation (see below), Hans Butzmann suggested it be renamed "ordo Missae Sigberti." "Einige Fragen zu Mindener Kreuz und die Adoratio Crucis des Bischofs Sigebert." Hans Nordseid (ed.). *Zwischen Dom und Rathaus*. Minden, 1977. 66.

39 "Ein Formular des 'Rheinischen Messordos' aus St. Aposteln in Köln." *Archiv für Liturgiewissenschaft* XXIV (1992). 333–344.

40 *Missa Latina, quae Olim ante Romanam circa 700. Domini annum in usu fuit, bona fide ex uetusto authenticoque Codice descripta. Item quedam de vetustatibus Missae scitu valdè digna. Adiuncta Est Beati Rhenani Praefatio in Mißam Chrysostomi à Leone Tusco, Anno Domini 1070*.

uersam. Strassburg: Christian Mylius, 1557. PL, 138, 1305–1336. A critical edition has been prepared by Joanne Pierce. See bibliography. Flacius appended an excerpt from Walafrid Strabo's *Rationale Divinorum*, G r – G iij v, and a letter of Beatus Rhenanus to Johann Hoffmeister, G vj r – H iij r, about the Latin translation of the Greek liturgy, *Missa D. Ioannis Chrysostomi Secundum veterem usum Ecclesiae Constantinopolitanae, a forma illa quam Magnus Dionysius depingit, non ita multum evarians, insigne prorsus publici sacrificij specimen, digna planè quam docti piique cognitam ac perspectam habeant, à Leone Tusco Emanuelis Imperatoris Constantinopolitani Joannis F. Latinarum epistolarum magistro, iam olim conversa, regnante videlicet Friedericho Aug. huius nominis primo.* Colmar: Bartholomeus Gryeningerus. 1540. A ij r – B iij v. In reorganizing the cloister library, Hoffmeister had discovered the disputations of Hugo Aetherianus and the translation of the mass of St. John Chrysostom by Leo of Toskana, which he submitted to Rhenanus for an opinion before he had it printed. August von Druffel. "Nachträgliche Bemerkungen über den Augustiner Johann Hoffmeister." ZKG, III (1879). 485–497. Rhenanus observed that those who had heard Hoffmeister's explanation of scripture on the feast days in Colmar, left the church before the offertory, as if they did not care for the mass sacrifice. Whether or not they were adherents of the Reformation, the people longed for the sermon. He ascribed the decline of respect for the mass to the attitude of the priests, who were like mine workers. "At one time there were fewer priests and fewer masses, but the people were not less religious." 487f.

In his publication, Flacius printed his letter to Rhenanus. Recent literature on the letter: The letter is

Flacius argues here that the first form of the mass consisted of the words of Institution and the Lords' Prayer

"ite missa est." Common people, who could not understand the mass, waited for the words, "ite, missa est," to know when to go home.

The Missa Illyrica was denounced by Wilhelm van der Lindt, Inquisitor of the Netherlands, who called Flacius "Delirius Illyricus,"[41] and at the request of the Duke of Alba, Philipp II of Spain put it on the Index of Prohibited Books. Later, Pope Sixtus V did the same.[42] Strenuous efforts were made by Roman Catholic apologists to demonstrate that the strange

Page from Cod. Guelf 1151 Helmst.: the strange "Missa Illyrica"

order was not strange: it was merely the conventional mass, only supplied with more prayers. A century after its publication a legend arose, constructed out of whole cloth, about the destruction of the first edition. Guillaume du Peyrat charged that when the Lutherans read the order more carefully they discovered that it contained Roman Catholic practices. They were embarrassed and attempted to destroy all the copies: "Flavius [sic] Illyricus and his followers ... recognizing that the prejudice made by

discussed by Peter Fraenkel "Une Lettre Oubliée de Beatus Rhenanus: Sa Préface à la Liturgie des S. Jean Chrysostome Dédiée à Johannes Hoffmeister 24 Janvier 1540." *Bibliothèque d'Humanisme et Renaissance* XLVIII (1986). 387–404. Beatus Rhenanus. *Beati Rhenani Praefatio in Missam Chrysostomi, à Leone Tusco, anno Domini, 1070 versam, ad Joannem Hoffmeister, Priorem Augustinensem.* Graz: Akademischer Druck- und Verlagsanstalt, 1957. Flacius refers to the Rhenanus' preface again in the *Catalogus Testium Veritatis* (1562). 573, and in his *Refutatio invectivae Bruni contra Centurias Historiae Ecclesiasticae.* Basel: Johannes Oporinus, 1566. 155–163.

Flacius' own essay, "Quaedam Observationes de Vetustatibus Missae," appended to the mass order, E iiiij r – G r, has been done into English as "Some Observations on the Antiquity of the Mass" by Oliver K. Olson. *The "Missa Illyrica" and the Liturgical Thought of Flacius Illyricus.* Diss., Hamburg, 1966. 147–167.

41 Wilhelm van der Lindt. *Missa Apostolica.* Antwerp: Christopher Plantin, 1589. 102.

42 Colomiés. 13; Friedrich Eberhard Rambach. *Johan Peter Nicerons Nachrichten.* 21. Theil. Halle: Christoph Peter Francke, 1761. 157. Cf. *Index Librorum Prohibitorum Innoc. XI. P. M. Iussu Editus Usque ad Annum 1681.* Prague, 1726. 272. Heinrich Reusch. *Der Index der verbotenen Bücher* I. Bonn: Max Cohen & Sohn, 1883. 410. Quandoquidem non tam missa sit quam ordo missae ... et incerti auctoris nec constet, unde desumta sit, non videtur posthac imprimenda, praesertim quod et orationibus quaedam adjuncta sint, quae lectorem possent offendere, et careat ea canonis parte, quae consecrationem continet. Praefatio etiam M. Flacii Ill. plane haeretica est.

43 *L'Histoire ecclésiastique de la cour ou les antiquités et recherches de la chapelle et oratoire du Roy de France.* Paris, 1645. 217.

44 *Annales Ecclesiastici Francorum.* Paris: Typographia Regia, 1666. 534.

45 *De Liturgia Gallicana.* Paris, 1685.

46 *Bibliographie Instructive ou Traité de la Conaissance des Livres Rares et Singuliers.* Paris: Chez Guillaume Franÿhois de Bure le Jeune, 1763. 171.

47 *Rerum Liturgicarum Libri Duo.* Rome: Angelus Tinarius, 1671. 471–505.

48 *De Antiquis Ecclesiae Ritibus Libri Tres.* Rouen, 1700–1702. I, 482 ff.

49 *La Perpetuité de la Foy Touchant l'Eucharistie defendue contra le Livre du Sieur Claude Ministre de Charenton.* Paris, 1669. 746–753. Arnauld, an associate of Blaise Pascal, cited it as proof of the continuity of Roman Catholicism against Jean Claude, Calvinist minister of Charenton.

50 "Suprimérent tous les exemplaires qu'ils purent trouver..." Op. cit. 13.

51 Op. cit. I, 104n.

52 "Einige Fragen." 75, and "Die Missa Illyrica und die Adoratio Crucis von Minden." *Wolfenbütteler Beiträge* III (1978). 35 f.

53 Op. cit. 335n.

54 "Matthias Flacius Illyricus." *The Dictionary Historical and Critical of M. Peter Bayle* III. London: J. J. and P. Knapton, 1736. 558. Cf. Olson "Missa Illyrica." Idem. "Flacius Illyricus als Liturgiker." *Jahrbuch für Liturgik und Hymnologie* XII (1967). 45–69.

55 *Bibliothèque curieuse Historique et Critique ou Catalogue Raisoné des Livres Difficultes à Trouver* VIII. Leipzig, 1759. 351.

56 *Sammlung.* 1739. 534.

57 "Alter und Herkunft der sog. 'Missa Illyrica.'" *Stimmen aus Maria Laach* LXIX (1905). 143–155. Cf. Klemens Honselmann. *Das Rationale der Bischöfe.* Paderborn: Selbstverlag Des Vereins für Geschichte und

this ancient mass against their new opinions ... the followers of Flacius destroyed all the copies they could."[43] Du Peyrat was under the impression that Flacius had at first considered it an order acceptable to Lutherans, and only later changed his mind – which was not the case. Flacius argued simply that the order was *different* from the Roman Catholic mass order of the 16th century.

The charge that he destroyed all possible copies has crept through the literature, repeated by Charles LeCointe,[44] Jean Mabillon,[45] Guillaume-François De Bure,[46] Giovanni Bona,[47] Edmund Martène,[48] Antoine Arnauld,[49] Paul Colomiés,[50] Josef Jungmann,[51] Hans Butzmann,[52] and most recently by Andreas Odenthal.[53] In his celebrated *Dictionary*, Pierre Bayle dismissed the charge: "... du Peyrat gives no other reason for what he imputes to the Lutherans but the scarcity of the copies of the missal."[54] David Clement observed that "... one would not know how to be astonished enough, how such an assertion, lacking proof and authority, could be followed with such popular credulity, as if it came from the seat of Apollo."[55]

Charles LeCointe was one of the writers who perpetuated the false story about the destruction of copies of Flacius' *Missa Latina*.

534   ANNALES ECCLESIASTICI
Alia.

601. Actiones nostras, quæsumus Domine, & aspirando præueni, & adiuuando prosequere, vt omnis oratio & cuncta nostra operatio à te semper incipiat, & per te cœpta finiatur. Per, &c.

Explicit Ordo de Officio Missæ.

XXI. Matthias Flauius, corruptè Flaccus & Fisius, natione Illyricus ex oppido Albona, vnde & cognomento Illyricus, inter Lutheranos maximum nomen sibi comparauit, præcipuus Author fuit Centuriarum Magdeburgensium, princépsque *Rigidorum Lutheranorum* ita nuncupatorum quòd à doctrina & scriptis Lutheri, quæ vt diuina venerabantur, ne in vocula quidem aut syllaba dissentiendum esse prædicarent. Existimauit autem suarum partium hominibus rem acceptissimam atque vtilissimam se facturum, si Missam euulgaret aliam à Gregoriana seu Romana, quam Ecclesiæ Gallicanæ Germanicæque à temporibus vt ille opinatur Caroli Magni, aut potius vt suprà obseruauimus à temporibus Pipini, aliæque Occidentales postea susceperunt. At tantùmabest ab illo opere Catholicis nocuerit, quin eorum causam validissimè defendit, vt anno post septimo, Christi millesimo quingentesimo sexagesimo-quarto Georgius Wicelius in defensione Liturgiæ Ecclesiasticæ testatus est his verbis. *Matthias Flauius Illyricus edidit repertam Missam Latinam, non triumphans tamen de thesauro tanto aduersus Catholicos, quàm vel cauticenti homini apparet totum illud quod edidit, contra Lutheri Caluinique sectas edidisse, sed & Catholicæ nobis rem longè gratissimam fecisse. Quid enim ibi nisi Missam Latinam, quæ hodie in vsu generali est, insciens imprudensque defendit ? Tantùm abest, vt suo, sectæque more oppugnet, locupletior est illa quidem, plúsque precum continet, sed omnino tamen eadem cum vsitata, cuius etiam dicta factæque omnia passim sequitur, vt diuersam esse confirmare nemo audeat.* Georgius Wicelius Germanus fuit ditionis * Hessen, cùmque decennium fere Luthero adhæsisset, vir impensè doctus, vbi ex lectione Sanctorum Patrum animaduertit Lutheri dogmata tum Euangelio Christi tum vetustis illis Patribus penitus aduersari, rediit ad Catholicos anno Christi millesimo quingentesimo tricesimo-primo. Mox carceri mancipatus est ceu maleficus, Luthero id fieri curante, sed innocentia comperta liber dimissus est, & cùm omnia Lutheranismi mysteria, conditionem, mores, genium intimè nosset, primus totam eius turpitudinem detexit, ac Lutheranis plausibilem illam detraxit Ecclesiæ primitiuæ laruam, quà tecti sese fraudulenter insinuabant. Eam ob causam odium illorum acerbissimum incurrit, calumniisque frequenter est appetitus, nihil tamen animi remisit, ac triginta sex amplius annis, quibus superuixit, hostes Catholicæ fidei non cessauit publicis scriptis oppugnare. Quàm æquum tulerit iudicium de Missa Illyriciana, vt Hugo Menardus in notis ad librum Sacramentorum seu Sacramentale sancti Gregorij vocat, id est, de Missa in lucem à Flauio Illyrico edita, subsequentes obseruationes indicabunt.

XXII. Primò, Illyricus in sua præfatione dicit olim apud Latinos vnicam fuisse celebrandæ Missæ rationem, quemadmodum apud Græcos, & suam ita esse compositam, vt sibi pro omni necessitate, nec olim fuisse Missas de sanctis & Festis. Sed huius sententiæ falsitatem ex ipsa Missa Illyriciana conuincere licet, in qua Introitus, Epistola, Graduale, Euangelium, Secreta, Præfatio, Communio, & Postcommunio non speciatim & particulatim, sed tantùm generatim nominantur sine vlla specificatione aut assignatione alicuius particularis Introitus aut Epistolæ & similium. Quod confirmant

The presence of the barbaric, late Latin word, "diaconibus" was not enough to demonstrate a later date.[56] But Josef Braun noticed that the test mentioned a "rationale," a liturgical neck-piece not in use during Pope Gregory's time. It was evidence enough to prove that the order was written in the eleventh century, and therefore, that it was not a proof of "gregorianism."[57] Valentin Thalhofer argued that the Missa Illyrica is neither a sacramentary nor a mass, but an *ordo*.[58] A Premonstratensian, Boniface Luykx, demonstrated that it is an example of the "Rhenish Mass order."[59] But according to Cyrille Vogel, "This is neither a Gallican Mass before the Romanization process of the VIII century nor a Romano-Frankish type characteristic of the Carolingian era,[60] but a pontifical mass for the church of Minden (Westphalia), composed ca. 1030, and crammed with subjective devotional prayers of the *apologiae* kind."[61]

Joanne Pierce's explanation that the extraordinary prayers represent a simple "sacerdotal spirituality at mass"[62] is inadequate to explain the strangeness of the order. So unusual is the text that Edmund Bishop pronounced it "a liturgical monstrosity."[63] Jungmann recognized that there is a problem. "It is not easy," he wrote, "to understand the world of thought from which this curious seed has come, which speaks to us in an almost terrifying way about consciousness of sin and the misery of sin."[64] The most persuasive explanation for the odd series of prayers is that of Eugene Rosenstock-Heuss, who sets them in the context of the eleventh century power struggle. He suggests that the *apologiae* were a kind of political punishment – an idea that would have interested Flacius! – forced on bishops by that Archbishop of Mainz who attributed the term, "vicar of Christ" to Emperor Conrad II (1042–1039) rather than the pope, and burned a papal bull. The prayers, accordingly, served to lower the bishops' prestige while raising the emperor's.[65]

For three centuries, knowledge of the order was limited to Flacius' *editio princeps*. Despite its appearance in the Roman Index, Roman Catholic scholars Antoine Boucat,[66] Migne in the *Patrologia Latina*,[67] and others, reprinted the text from Flacius' edition. Only in the late 19th century was the manuscript source, Cod. Guelf. 1151 Helmstedt, rediscovered in Wolfenbüttel by Adalbert Ebner.[68]

Because Flacius assigned it to too early a date, the Missa Illyrica failed to illustrate his theory of "gregorianism." But the publication did demonstrate that Helding's argument was quite wrong: the text of the Latin liturgy was *not* complete in the apostolic period, certainly not in Latin. Reacting to official, imperial liturgical fundamentalism, Flacius thoroughly refuted the claim that the Latin liturgy had been uniform throughout history.

Atertum, 1975. 51. That a similar order, Manuscript MR 166 in the University of Zagreb library dates from the eleventh century helps to confirm the dating. Carolus Kniewald. "Ordo et Canon Missae e Missali S. Sabinae MR 166 Saec. XI." *Ephemerides Liturgicae* LXX (1956). 331 f. 35.

58 *Handbuch der katholischen Liturgik*. Freiburg im Breisgau: Herder, 1890–1893. 143.

59 "Essai sur les Sources de l'ordo Missa Prémontré." *Analecta Praemonstratensia* XXII–XXIII (1945–46).

60 As Fernand Cabrol had argued in his cited works.

61 *Medieval Liturgy. An Introduction to the Sources*. Rev. and tr. by William G. Storey and Niels Krogh Rasmussen. Washington: Pastoral Press, 1986. 163.

62 "Sacerdotal Spirituality at Mass: Text and Study of the Prayerbook of Sigbert of Minden (1022–1036)." Diss., University of Notre Dame, 1988; Butzmann. "Einige Fragen." 66.

63 "The Litany of Saints in the Stowe Missal." *Journal of Theological Studies* VII (1906). 123n.

64 Op. cit. 105.

65 *Die europäische Revolutionen und der Charakter der Nationen*. Stuttgart and Cologne: W. Kohlhammer, 1951. 565 f. More on the apologies in Wilhelm Levison. *England and the Continent in the Eighth Century*. Oxford: Clarendon Press, 1950.

66 *Theologia Patrum Scholastico-Dogmatica, sed maxime positiva. Tractatus De Sacramentis, tum in Genere, tum in particulari ... Tomus Quintus*. Rouen: Claudius Jore, 1725. 87–93; Theodor Ittig. *De Bibliothecis et Catenis Patrum*. Leipzig, 1707. 248–249.

67 PL, CXXXVIII, 1305–1336.

68 *Quellen und Forschungen zur Geschichte und Kunstgeschichte des Missale Romanum im Mittelalter. Iter Italicum*. Freiburg im Breisgau: Herder, 1896. 394 f. 397.

1   *Sacrae Caesareae Maiestatis Declaratio, Quomodo in Negocio Religionis Per Imperium usque ad definitionem Concilii generalis vivendum sit, in Comitiis Augustanis. XV. Maii, Anno 1548, proposita & publicata, & ab omnibus imperii ordinibus recepta.* Augsburg: Philipp Ulhard, 1548. Text in Joachim Melhausen (ed.). *Das Augsburger Interim von 1548.* Neukirchen-Vluyn: Neukirchener Verlag, 1970.

2   *A Waying and Considering of the Interim by the honourworthy and highly learned Philip Melanchthon. Translated into Engylshe by John Rogers, 1548.* [London] A iij v.

3   Elmar Neuss and J. V. Pollet. *Pflugiana. Studien über Julius Pflug (1499–1564).* Münster: Aschendorf, 1990. vii.

4   Georg Beutel. *Über den Ursprung des Augsburger Interims.* Dresden: J. Passer, 1888. 88, 97, 112. Otfried Müller. "Schriften von und gegen Julius Pflug bis zu seiner Reise nach Trient 1554." Erwin Iserloh and Konrad Repgen (eds.). *Reformata Reformanda* II. Münster in Westphalia: Aschendorf, 1965. 57.

5   Ibid. 88.

Although the prince might reach a decision of which I cannot approve, I shall nevertheless commit no seditious act, but will either remain silent, go into exile, or else bear the consequences. – Melanchthon

... nothing came to mind more appropriate and useful than if we were to publish some protest against the Interim and all perversions of our teaching. – Flacius

The church would be united eventually, Emperor Charles V believed, by the Council of Trent. But he did not want to wait; at the the "Armored" Diet at Augsburg, September 2, 1547 – June 30, 1548, during which he had the bad grace to parade the captive Lutheran princes, he produced a unity formula, called the "Augsburg Interim": *Declaration of the Holy Roman Imperial Majesty on How Matters are to be Managed in the Holy Empire until the Settlement of a Common Council.*[1] It takes its place historically besides other imperial attempts to rule the church, the *Henotikon* of Emperor Zeno (A.D. 482), the *Ecthesis* of Emperor Heraclius (A. D. 638), and the *Typos* of Emperor Constans II (A.D. 647 or 648).

Charles' law was a clear threat to the Reformation. One London publication explained.

Interim is a booke whiche was at ye Emperoures Maiesties commaundment prynted and put forth about the begynning of June, in this yere of our Saviours birthe 1548, wherein is commaunded that al the cities in Dutchlande that have receaved the worde of god, and made a chaunge of ceremonyes accordyng to the word shal reforme their churches agayne, and turne to the olde popische ordinaunces as a dog dothe to that he hathe spued out, or a washen swyne to the myre.[2]

The new law was formulated primarily by Michael Helding of Merseburg and Julius Pflug of Naumburg, the post-war successors to Lutheran bishops. A third member was Johann Agricola, chaplain of Elector Joachim II of Brandenburg. To call Pflug "a forerunner of the ecumenical movement,"[3] is not satisfactory, since his Interim law was clearly thomistic,[4] and, according to Wolfgang Offele, "proves the scrupulousness with which he [Pflug] wants to hold to the decisions of the Council [of Trent] and thereby submit to the judgment of the [Roman] church." "In the doctrine of justification, already as it was formulated by Pflug," comments Georg Beutel, "the Catholic party had a firm foundation. And here it did not yield."[5] Article XIII specified, moreover, that the church was legitimated by apostolic succession of bishops, who had the power to interpret the scripture and who were furnished with binding traditions and the authority to impose binding laws.

The official theological position of the Holy Roman Empire of the German Nation now was that justification is based partly on inherent righteousness: "Christ's merits and inherent righteousness, by which we are renewed through the gift of love, come together."[6] It happens when "... faith obtains the gift of the Holy Spirit, by which love is poured out in our hearts, which, to the extent it adds faith and hope, we are truly justified by inherent righteousness.[7] "... man," the Interim text reads, "renewed through the Holy Spirit ... is able to produce righteousness with work, and that for the sake of his Son, God wills to be pleased with this weak, inchoate obedience in this wretched, weak nature."[8]

Convinced of his duty to insist on free will, and with a fresh copy of the *Determinatio de justificatione* from the Council of Trent in hand, to reinforce his argument, Pflug tossed the "dead log" into the discussion. The term, *truncus, klotz, plock*, would lumber for decades through subsequent controversies. "The merciful God does not work with man, as if he were a dead log," the Interim laid down, "but draws him willingly, if he is an adult."[9] "The merciful God does not work with man as with a dead log," the Leipzig Interim echoed, "but draws him, so that his will also co-operates if he be of understanding years."[10] Of course God was not dealing with a dead log, Flacius commented; "a dead log can neither love or hate God. But by nature, a man hates and despises God."[11]

To make the law palatable, Pflug coopted two wildly popular practices – the wine cup in communion for lay people, and marriage for priests. Easily understood, the two practices of the "chalice movement" had functioned up to now as a "battering ram" for the Reformation. Only later did Pflug explain that the concessions were not valid without a papal indult.[12] For Wolfgang Offele, the imprecise language of the Interim was ecumenical: "the form and accent of his discourse are also here determined by his [Pflug's] will to peaceableness, 'concern and patience'."[13] For Flacius, the ambiguity was suspicious. "The trick of the papists now is to use some of the statements and speech of our teachers; they want to adorn themselves thereby, just as if they had always had such teachings."[14] The law was written cleverly, so that "the Lutheran would hear his doctrine, the Catholic, his."[15] Flacius identified the ambiguities: the passage about forgiveness could be quoted to defend indulgences; the word, "consecration," could mean Lutheran practice, but Roman Catholics could interpret it to mean the mass canon.

The new law bore down heavily on precisely the place where the Reformation was not yet prepared – the liturgy. Since the seventeen years since the presentation of the Augsburg Confession had been too short to settle ritual questions, the liturgical provisions of the law were especially threatening. Now, the Lutheran churches were commanded to reintroduce invocation of saints, prayers for souls in purgatory, processions, festivals, consecrations, vestments, votive masses, and seven sacraments. Private masses were declared acceptable. That actual communicants were present was not necessary, only "useful."

Nevertheless Melanchthon yielded. The military defeat of the Lutheran princes, he said, was God's will. "I have not fought more fiercely than our princes on the Danube, and trace their defeat not to blind fate, but I know

6 Melhausen. 47.

7 Ibid. 51.

8 Beutel. 112.

9 Melhausen. 49.

10 Henry E. Jacobs (ed.). *The Book of Concord, or the Symbolical Books of the Evangelical Lutheran Church with Historical Introduction, Notes, Appendixes, and Indexes* II. Philadelphia: G. W. Frederick, 1883. 262.

11 *Der Theologen Bedencken odder (wie es durch die ihren inn offentlichem Druck genennet wirdt) Beschluss des Landtages zu Leiptzig ...* [Magdeburg: Michael Lotter] 1550. E v.

12 Julius Pflug. *Correspondance Jacques v. Pollet* (Ed.). Leiden: E. S. Brill, 1977. III. 166.

13 Wolfgang Offele. *Ein Katechismus im Dienste der Glaubenseinheit. Julius Pflugs "Institutio christiani hominis" als katechetischer Beitrag zur interkonfessionellen Begegnung.* Essen: Ludgerus Verlag Wingen, 1965. 33.

14 *Widder die unchristliche Vermanungschrifft des Bisthumbs zu Naumburg.* Magdeburg: Christian Rödinger, 1550. A ij v.

15 O. Müller. 57.

16 Georg Ellinger. *Philipp Melanchthon. Ein Lebensbild.* Berlin: Gaernter, 1902. 534.

17 *Bericht.* 1559. G ij r. Cf. Johannes Herrmann. "Augsburg-Leipzig-Passau: Das Leipziger Interim nach Akten des Landeshauptarchivs Dresden 1547–1553." Diss., Karl-Marx University, Leipzig, 1962. 41.

18 Flacius published the letter in *Gründliche Verlegung des langen Comments.* C ij v – D ij r.; CR, VI, 879–885; MBW, 5139; English translation by Lowell C. Green. *Melanchthon in English.* St. Louis: Center for Reformation Research, 1982. 18–23.

19 *Entschuldigung ... an die Universitet.* H v.

20 "Flacius." 290.

21 *Von der Einigkeit.* C vj v.

22 *Auf das Ausschreiben der zweien Universiteten und die Invectivam Scholasticorum, Antwort M. Fla. Illyrici, darin die Adiaphoristen aus iren eigen Schrifften und zeugnissen irer grewlichen Bulerey mit der Bablyonischen Bestien überwiesen werden ...* Jena: Thomas Rewart, 1568. C iij r.

23 *Melanchthon.* 535.

24 Hartmut Voit. *Nikolaus Gallus: Ein Beitrag zur Reformationsgeschichte der nachlutherischen Zeit.* Neustadt a. d. Aisch: In Kommission beim Verlag Degener & Co., 1977. 126.

25 CR, VII, 462. Otto Clemen. "Briefe sächsischer Staats- und Schulmänner an Melanchthon." KS, VI, 542–556.

that this punishment came to us through our sins."[16] He agreed in advance to negotiations, to accept the Roman Catholic liturgy and even papal authority. He was not the author of the controversy, he wrote, and had never forgotten the old church, whose constitution and discipline he respected. Answering a letter now lost, that Flacius suspected was incited by the emperor himself,[17] in a letter dated April 28, 1548 to Court Official Christoph von Carlowitz,[18] he capitulated and pledged his cooperation.

> ... although the prince might reach a decision which I cannot accept, I shall nevertheless commit no seditious act, but will either remain silent, go into exile, or else bear the consequences. For I also previously bore an almost deformed servitude at times when Luther heeded his own temperament, in which there was much polemical zeal [*philoneikia*], more than his own reputation or the common good. And I am aware that in every age, just as there are misfortunes of storms, so there are some faults in the government which must be stringently endured and concealed by the moderate.

At the same time he reviled Luther. "After the letter to Carlowitz and other writings from him came to light," Flacius went on, "it caused me bitter sorrow that the admirable man, Doctor Luther, his best friend before his death, to whom he had entrusted so much, was portrayed to the enemies of God as a cause for mocking, and at the same time through that witness and blind judgment the Gospel of Christ was hindered."[19] It did not pass unremarked that the same Luther, whose memory was so irritating, he had once praised as divinely-inspired. "None of the very mordant judgments of Flacius over the dead Melanchthon," writes Peter Barton, "was nearly so loveless as that of Philipp over the dead Luther."[20]

Flacius angrily complained that the letter pulled the rug from under steadfast confessors and discouraged the pious. Melanchthon had portrayed the Reformation as a nuisance rather than a movement whose source was in God.[21] It was circulated, Flacius complained, more than any other printed writing of the time, and did more damage than could be expressed.[22] Flacius' reproach, according to Ellinger, is "not totally wrong."[23] Gallus reported that the letter was being used by cities and princely courts as an excuse for accepting the Interim.[24]

In his own defense, Melanchthon wrote:

> I will not excuse myself with many words ... I pray only this, that to one word of that letter, many others of mine about Luther, will be opposed: honorific speeches witten in many places after his death, in the funeral laudation, in the preface to the volume just edited. Then, why is only one word taken out of the letter ...?

> What more do those critics that judge that letter so harshly require of me? Perhaps they do not consider the meaning of *philoneikos*. It is not a fault, but a passion common to heroic natures, which the texts attribute to Pericles, Lysander, Menelaus.[25]

Even less repentant is the statement by the Wittenberg "scholastics," the anonymous group that served as his mouthpiece: "What could be said better?"

Can it be argued in Melanchthon's defense that the letter was at least meant to be kept confidential?[26] Not so, according to Flacius. He knew in advance that it would be read at the imperial court.[27] At Augsburg, where the diet was still in session, the letter, which gave Carlowitz what he wanted – assurance that there would be no opposition in Saxony – caused a sensation. When the emperor read it, he is supposed to have said, "Now you've got him, hold him!"[28] It was "carried around like a monstrance,"[29] and by order of the three ecclesiastical electors, sent to the pope.

In Saxony there was a storm of indignation. Defenders of the Interim were dubbed "Carlevitios."[30] Friedrich von Bezold called the letter "a mixture of truth and lies."[31] Wilhelm Dilthey wrote that "A judgment on this step cannot easily be too hard."[32] Leopold von Ranke wished the letter had never been written.[33] Flacius was very critical; Melanchthon's promise not to be seditious, he observed, was the same as promising to support the emperor:

> ... I would like to see the ecclesiastical polity retained as in the book of Augsburg [the Augsburg Interim], so that authority is allowed to the bishops and the highest bishop. Perhaps by nature I am of a servile spirit, but I really feel that modesty is fitting for good minds, and that the estate of rulers not be undermined. Willingly I also accept the ceremonies which the book prescribes.

> ...It is not only for the sake of public peace but also that the invocation of the common people may not be disturbed that I am ready to yield and to conceal many things.

Hermann Hering calls for understanding; Melanchthon was intimidated by the empire, and anxious to save at least the Saxon church for the Reformation.[34] Georg Ellinger pleads that he was under pressure, and a negative answer might cause an invitation to war; what he wrote openly now was what he had been suppressing for a decade. According to Clyde Manschrek, "Melanchthon was simply admitting that Luther's rashness sometimes made matters very difficult."[35] Franz Lau, however, observes that the ideas in his letter were the same as in his reaction to the Cologne Reformation of 1537, and that at the time of the writing of the Smalcald Articles he had shown himself willing to recognize the authority of the pope.[36] Robert Stupperich argues that the letter cannot be taken as typical.[37] But in the letter, Melanchthon himself had written, "I am laying my whole self bare before you." After reviewing the evidence, Melanchthon specialist Heinz Scheible concluded that the letter was "a well-thought-out expression of Melanchthon's position".[38]

Strict censorship deprived Lutherans of the means by which the Reformation had spread – critical sermons and publications. Any resistance, then, had to be illegal. In spite of the censorship, a flood of anti-Interim publications appeared. "Interim," it was noted, was an adverb – something "joined to the word." And what kind of adverb? "A word of Satan, joined to the Word of God."[39] One verse-smith combined the two names, Pflug (German: plow), and Agricola (Latin: plowman).

26 As James William Richard does. *Philip Melanchthon, the Protestant Preceptor of Germany, 1497–1560*. New York: Putnam, 1898. 332.

27 1559. Liij v.

28 *Entschuldigung ... an die Universitet.* [G iiij r].

29 *Omnia latina scripta.* M iiiij v.

30 Gustav Kawerau. "Gutachten Joh. Agricolas für Christoph von Carlowitz über die Annahme des Augsburger Interims." *Neues Archiv für Sächsische Geschichte und Altertumskunde* I (1880). 268.

31 *Geschichte der deutschen Reformation.* Berlin: G. Grote'sche Verlagsbuchhandlung, 1890. 809.

32 *Weltanschauung und Analyse des Menschen.* 9. Aufl. Göttingen: Vandenhoeck & Ruprecht, 1970. 160.

33 *Deutsche Geschichte im Zeitalter der Reformation* VI. 7. Aufl. Wiesbaden & Berlin: Emil Vollmer, 1857. 1047.

34 *Doktor Pomeranus, Johannes Bugenhagen, Ein Lebensbild aus der Zeit der Reformation.* Halle: Verein für Reformationsgeschichte, 1888. 150.

35 "The Role of Melanchthon in the Adiaphora Controversy." ARG, XLVIII (1957). 169.

36 Franz Lau. "Melanchthon und die Ordnung der Kirche." Walter Elliger (ed.). *Philipp Melanchthon: Forschungsbeiträge zur vierhundertsten Wiederkehr seines Todestages dargeboten in Wittenberg 1960.* Göttingen: Vandenhoeck & Ruprecht, 1961. 98–115, esp. 100 ff.

37 *Der Unbekannte Melanchthon.* Stuttgart: W. Kohlhammer, 1961. 11. Cf. Green. 17.

38 "Melanchthon's Brief an Carlowitz." ARG, LVII (1966). 127 ff.

39 Salig. I, 611.

40 [Ludwig] Götze. "Die Magdeburger Presse zur Zeit der Reichsacht und der Belagerung durch den Kurfürsten Moritz von Sachsen." *Blätter für Handel, Gewerbe und Sociales Leben.* 102 [Beiblatt zur Magdeburgischen Zeitung No. 21] (22. Mai 1976). 162.

41 CR, VII, 167.

42 Hermann Gebhardt. *Thüringische Kirchengeschichte. Zweite Hälfte: Vom Beginn der Reformation bis zur neueren Zeit.* Gotha: Friedrich Andreas Pustet, 1881. 164.

43 "caput enim sceleris, origo omnis improbatis iste Saxoniae dux fuit." *Epistola Pauli III ad Carolum V, Gratulatoria de victoria adversus Protestantis"* 30 May 1547. Josse Le Plat. *Monumentorum ad Historian Concilii Tridentini Potissimum Illustrandam. Spectantium Amplissima Collectio* III: *Monumenta ab anno MDXLI, ad Februarii MDXLVIII.* Louvain: Ex typographia academia, 1783. 644.

Recht listig greift's der Teufel an,
meint uns zu überreden,
Ein Pflug und auch ein Ackermann,
ja neben diesen beiden
ein Weihbischof, der heißt nicht Heinz,
mich dünkt, der Esel sei von Mainz,
haben ein Buch gespeiet,
das sei vermaledeiet
sammt denen, die es geweihet.[40]

The devil is attacking right deceitfully,
and wants to persuade us,
A plow [Pflug] and also a plowman [Agricola],
and beside both of these,
a suffragan bishop, who is not named Heinz,
It seems to me the ass comes from Mainz,
have spewed out a book;
may it be cursed,
together with those who have blessed it.

Pressed by the emperor to accept the Interim law, Johann Friedrich refused.

> I stand before your majesty as a poor imprisoned man. I do not lie. I have confessed the truth and therefore abandon possessions, estate, land and people ... and have nothing but this imprisoned body ... and should I also lose eternal [life] through my recantation? God preserve me from that ... It would be wrong if many thousand people would be led into great scandal through my foolish recantation.[41]

Flacius remarked that Johann Friedrich bore the cross of Christ after him. When that prince's advisors informed him how angry the emperor was when he learned about his refusal, out of a clear sky he heard a peal of thunder. "Ach, ja, you old, strong God," he shouted, "you let it be heard that you still live; you will do it!"[42]

When Cardinal Granvella pressed his prisoner he refused again. His books were therefore taken from him, he was allowed no meat, and his Lutheran chaplain, previously tolerated, had to escape in disguise. "You may take away my books," the prince said, "but you cannot snatch from my heart what I have learned from them, Jesus Christ!" In a letter congratulating Charles V for his victory over the Lutherans, Pope Paul III wrote that "that Duke of Saxony was the chieftain of crime, the origin of all wickedness."[43]

Like Melanchthon, Flacius, too, produced a significant letter on the subject of the Interim. Whereas Melanchthon promised acquiesence, Flacius called for resistance. The undated appeal, addressed to the church in Hamburg, has the appearance of a circular letter to the North German cities.

> Since we are being pressured to despise the truth, all angels and men, especially the faithful, ought to be thinking constantly about what should be done to preserve doctrine and the church of Christ, it seems to me, having considered the matter carefully and having thought about current conditions, that, after prayer, nothing would be more appropriate and useful, than if we, in a dignified and prudent fashion, would publish a protest against the Interim and all perversions of our doctrine, written in the name of all those who would want to sign it.

In it we would assert that no law permits men willing to give a reason for their actions to be killed without a hearing. That Luther, princes and cities confessing our doctrine have appealed so often from the iniquitous condemnation of the pope to a free council; that Caesar himself and the princes promised it so many times. That we demand from Caesar, therefore, the free inquiry promised so many times, and protest before God and men, that he is acting extremely unjustly with us and with the cause of the gospel, violating every right and promise, that we are being murdered unheard, and that we are being cut off by deceptions and violence from that doctrine that we believe is the only truth of Christ.

With Christ's help, there would be many good results. First, perhaps even Caesar himself would be moved by our just claim. I certainly hope that he will be a bit moved, if not out of kindness, at least on account of the the opinion of all those people who are somewhat reasonable, who on the basis of our protest, must necessarily decide that our opponents are dealing with us very unjustly. Thus, his rage against us will be a bit restrained. In secular legal cases no one abandons his rights as carelessly as we are doing in this cause of the Gospel. I have no doubt, then, just as our adversaries are encouraged by our softness and surrenders, that, especially in this case, about which it is possible to speak positively, even in the presence of not too favorable judges, they would be restrained by a steadfast defense of our cause.

Secondly, even if we could not accomplish anything among the tyrants themselves, nevertheless we would strengthen our own people when they saw how unjustly and wickedly the adversaries have put everything in motion against us. In the same way we would attract many among the adversaries to our teaching, lest it come about that even the less sympathetic think about us, "See, that party wants everything done in an orderly and proper fashion; that after indictment their cause be examined lawfully before impartial judges. But the papal party is doing everything excrably, by deception and violence. The party that does not flee the light, surely, is the more just. Likewise, since those are doing everything properly, observing Christian modesty, and gently, but ours are proceeding with the help of fraud, violence, lies and murders, it seems likely that those, not these, are the ones ruled by the Spirit of Christ." Surely it is absolutely true that there is no way that we can speak more plausibly about the present controversy, among ourselves, or among the impious, than by such a protest. If there is anything to be written for our religion, certainly, then it is especially this.

Finally, if the world does not want to recognize our complaints and tears or laughs at them, surely the father in heaven understands, gathers them into his bottle, as the Psalm [56.9] says, and in his own time will wipe them away. God wills that we do it; if not to convert them, then for their judgment.

Enormous good should be expected from the protest itself, since undoubtedly many preachers would sign it, and their agreement would become known. No more useful thing, then, could be done for the church at this time, than this. So faithful men, especially the ministry of the church ought to promote it with the most possible zeal. What we have sensed we can do piously and usefully for the church, we certainly must do. And we must expect and implore help from the Lord, who in his own time will grant his blessing and copious increase on our planting and watering.[44]

44 Carl Hieronymus Wilhelm Sillem (ed.). *Briefsammlung des Hamburgischen Superintendenten Joachim Westphal aus den Jahren 1530 bis 1575.* Hamburg: Lucas Gräfe & Sillem, 1903. I, 90 f.

1 CR, VII, 7.
2 Cf. Horst Rabe. *Reichsbund und Interim.* Cologne and Vienna: Böhlau, 1971. 431 f.; Robert Stupperich. "Melanchthons Gedanken zur Kirchenpolitik des Herzogs Moritz von Sachsen." *Reformatio und Confessio.* Friedrich Wilhelm Kantzenbach and Gerhard Müller (eds.). Berlin and Hamburg: Lutherisches Verlagshaus, 1965. 89.
3 CR, VII, 186.
4 *Bericht vom Interim der Theologen auf dem Landtag zu Meissen versamlet Anno.* M.D.xlviij. [Magdeburg: Christian Rödinger, 1548]. CR, VII, 14.

It is not our responsibility to burden the Lords or subjects with the danger of confession. – Melanchthon

Melanchthon cannot separate from the gospel the sword and fire with which Christ sent it into the world ... Whoever does not want to be the occasion of causing others to suffer the cross, he should not teach Christ, but rather arrange that Christ, together with his cross, be driven out of the city and region, as the Gerasenes did. – Flacius

With the prophets, they must say, "Thus saith the Lord." – Flacius

Elector Maurice arrived in Meissen on July 2, 1548, on a mount named "Düsterer Blick," "Gloomy Look." Riding past the nervous crowds, he made his way directly to the bishop's palace for a conference, with one question in mind: how to answer the emperor "so that the Imperial Majesty can see that we and you, in everything which serves Christian reconciliation, quiet, peace, and unity, and which can take place with God and good conscience, are inclined to conduct ourselves most submissively and obediently."[1]

In the introduction to the Interim text, the participants read that "genuine catholics" were exempted from its provisions; the law applied only to the Evangelicals. Whatever the emperor's original intention may have been,[2] the Interim law now was plainly an instrument for forcing Protestants under the papal obedience. When the city of Wesel, for instance, wanted later to adopt the law, permission was denied, because Wesel had never accepted Lutheran teaching.[3] Opposition to the new law was forbidden, and sermons and publications would be severely censored. They would be required to accept whatever decisions would be made by the Council of Trent.

Nevertheless, the statement formulated at the Meissen meeting was critical. It was clear that if the Interim offered concessions to Protestants – the chalice for the laity and marriage for priests – by the same authority they could be withdrawn. But it was not the prerogative of the imperial government to decide. Those matters could not be regarded as if they were against God's ordinance and those of the Catholic church; they had already been settled by the Scriptures.

... namely, communion under two forms, and the marriage of priests as if they contradicted the Christian religion and the doctrines of the churches, because, praise God ... it is clear that both the articles are grounded in divine scripture, were in use by universal Christendom ...[4]

The conference rejected the Interim's doctrine of justification. Although the text contained "much that is good," it objected to "the many provisos", and "pharisaical leaven" that obscured doctrine, such as the statement that "the merit of Christ joins with inherent righteousness, to which we are renewed through the gift of love."

The most disturbing statement was the section on the power of the bishops, who could reintroduce the old superstitions and abuses. While the men at Meissen showed a willingness to accept liturgical festivals and some minor ceremonies, they rejected votive masses, invocation of saints and pilgrimages. They could accept the seven sacraments, but since oil was not a means by which God forgives sins, there could be no consecration of oil. In fact, there should be no consecrations of salt, or spices either. Ritual action, they wrote, had no divine significance. Christ's sacrifice had happened only once, and could not be repeated in the mass, and its anamnesis (remembrance) in the liturgy was not an "action," but a passive reception of the gifts of communion. The eucharistic prayer, furthermore, was a historical conglomerate and not binding on the church. The estates, therefore, wanted no changes, at least until a free, ecumenical council.[5]

The appalling reality touched Melanchthon at the level of his basic convictions: *the Interim was an imperial law.* There was an inviolable, a holy obligation to obey the authorities. The church, accordingly, had to yield and accept servitude. Although Elector Maurice had promised fidelity to the Augsburg Confession, according to all he had ever taught and believed, serious resistance was impossible. It would be sedition.[6]

Melanchthon's solution was *to separate public from private responsibility.* It was the responsibility of the government, not his, to protect the church. Only the state was able to survey the whole situation and make the proper decisions.[7] "If at my own peril," he wrote, "I should give my own opinion someplace privately, and if I see that the emperor is extremely angry at me, in Socrates' fashion I will simply say that I will not say yes to these sophisms. But even if I do not agree, I will not hinder the powerful from making the decision for the state according to their own decision." "I do not want to burden the lords with dangers because of my confession," he wrote. "I do not want to give our gracious lord a criterion for what His Electoral Grace should do or confess, and thus put His Electoral Grace in great danger." By privatizing the conscience thus, Melanchthon was neatly able to escape both sedition and danger. Flacius called it a triumph for Saxon diplomacy.

Melanchthon was abandoning the authority by which Luther held the princes responsible for what they believed and said. The Albertine Saxon estates were ready to do as their elders had done at Augsburg, but according to Melanchthon's policy, secular rulers, many of whom really did not understand the doctrine, were encouraged to answer the emperor as they wished. The Meissen meeting thus ended lamely with a mere request that the emperor not introduce the Interim in Saxony.

Melanchthon liberated clergymen as well. Personal engagement was no longer required, only personal opinion. *Dixi*, they could say, without endangering themselves or their princes, *et animam salvavi*: "I have spoken and thereby saved my soul." "... others may approve, accept, further on, what they think," Melanchthon explained, "according to their understanding and desire. We decide for nobody, but reveal our simple opinion and let many important and controversial matters pass."[8]

5 CR, VII, 65.
6 Inge Mager. "'Gott erhalte uns Philippum ...' Antonius Corvinus' Mahnbrief an Philipp Melanchthon wegen des Leipziger Interims." *Jahrbuch der Gesellschaft für Niedersächsische Kirchengeschichte* LXXXIV (1991). 90.
7 R. Stupperich. "Gedanken." 93.
8 *Gründlicher und warhafftiger Bericht aller Rathschleg und antwort, so die Theologen zu Wittemberg ... zur Widerlegung des [Interims] ... gestelt, auch was sie nachmals in Mitteldingen geraten ... Von den Professoren in der Universitet zu Wittenberg in Druck verordnet.* Wittenberg: Georg Rhau Erben, 1559. 198b.

9 "Quod me attinet ab ea in mea confessione non discedam. Aliis timidioribus non possum tam fortia consilia praescribere." CR, VII, 222.

10 CR, VII, 85; MBW, 5231, 5233, 5246, 5251, 5253, 5286.

11 CR, VII, 45.

12 CR, VII, 322–326. Ernst Otto Reichert. "'In Tanta Ecclesiarum Mestitia ...' Eine Antwort Niklaus von Amsdorffs an Philip Melanchthon." ZKG, LXXVIII (1967). 263.

13 *Responsio ad Epistolam Philippi Melanthonis.* Magdeburg: [Michael Lotter], 1549. B r.

14 *Ein Buch von waren und falschen Mitteldingen, darin fast der gantze handel von Mitteldingen erkleret wird, widder die schedliche Rotte der Adiaphoristen.* Magdeburg: Michael Lotter, 1549. O iiij r & v.

15 *Quod hoc tempore nulla mutatio in religione sit in gratiam impiorum facienda.* [Magdeburg: Michael Lotter, 1549]. Appendix. Cf. H. von Hase. 77n.

16 *Omnia latina scripta.* D vj v.

17 Ibid. Bb iiiij r.

18 H. von Hase. 75 f.

Melanchthon and Bugenhagen recommended the new policy in all directions, to Paul Eber,[9] to Prince George, to Johann Pfeffinger. In a letter to Margrave John of Brandenburg Melanchthon argued that preachers and teachers should distinguish their answer from the answer of the secular authority.[10]

> ...it is not our responsibility to burden the Lords or subjects with the danger of confession. Each individual, rather, should decide for himself. If we sided with the *Landschaft* it would appear that we wished thereby to put them under obligation to give protection ... we pray that the *Landschaft* itself will decide ... and think about the danger they are in ..."[11]

The effect of that decision, Amsdorf wrote, was that because of the emperor's command, the adiaphora were no longer adiaphora.[12] It freed people, Flacius argued, from God's command. "One hears such murmurs and complaints from Franconia, Hesse, Meissen, the Mark, and Saxony, about D. Philipp," Flacius wrote, "that by his letters he strengthens the godless and discourages the faithful."[13]

> Not only do they not admonish the people to steadfastness, confession, and maintaining truth, something that such people especially, who as the most prominent, stand at the pinnacle, should do most emphatically and earnestly, but through their sweet words, they liberate the people from religion, free from God's command, which earnestly commands steadfastness in truth and confession.[14]

"Do you not know," Flacius went on ...

> ... or do you not want to know, that by your lack of steadfastness and by your faint-heartedness (not to use a harsher term), writing everywhere in Swabia, in Franconia, and elsewhere in the German nation, the hearts of the steadfast and rightly God-fearing Christians are broken and destroyed and the church is overturned.

The crisis called not for opinions or for spectators, but for confessors. What was needed was theologians who, like the prophets, would say "thus saith the Lord!"[15] "You are not supposed to give only your simple opinion," he thundered, "but the immovable truth of almighty God."[16]

Authority in the church was passing to the government. But Flacius demanded that the church authorities take responsibility. "On the basis of their office," he said about the Wittenberger professors, "the theologians should have cried, 'stand fast' ... but they cried 'yield, yield, submit yourself to the Antichrist and the Pharaohs, and you will be saved'." In the mouth of theologians, who are called to be expositors of the divine word, a statement like Melanchthon's was impossible. What can frighten and enfeeble soldiers more, he asked, than seeing their leaders themselves acting confused and trembling?[17]

Preaching in the name of Christ, he wrote, can never be non-binding, mere instruction. For Flacius the preaching office is part of the Office of the Keys, and places the believer under the command of Christ.[18] Churchly authority consists in confessing the confession, in commanding the divine command. Whoever does not exercize the office commited to him to bind the consciences to God's command looses the congregation from obedience, since his action shows that the doctrine preached is not binding in serious situations. Churchly authority is not given once and for all, but consists only in its use. And whoever is unwilling to exericize his office publicly necessarily surrenders his own leadership."[19]

Melanchthon, no doubt, was personally prepared to suffer, but was he willing to require martyrdom from others? On that matter, Flacius confronted him with his own words: "Whoever does not want to be the occasion of causing others to suffer, should not teach Christ, but rather arrange that Christ, together with his cross, be driven out of the city and region, as the Gerasenes did."[20]

"I truly attribute to Philipp many virtues, as all rational people do," Flacius observed, "yet this I cannot yet attribute to him, that he is so wise that he is able to remove from the gospel the sword and fire that Christ sent with the gospel ... into the earth."[21] After the failure of Melanchthon's leadership in 1548, as Otto Ritschl observed, he was no longer the unquestioned leader of the Reformation. He had been reduced to being the leader of the party of the Philippists.

COMPELLING MELANCHTHON TO RESIST

> They should not take counsel secretly with the high priests and afterwards appear suddenly and say, we will have it so. For the church is not their own, like cows that they can deal with and manage as they please. – Flacius

Charles V put the Duchess Sybille and the Young Lords Regent in Weimar, her three sons, on notice. They had only twenty-one days to introduce the Interim in Ernestine Saxony. His prisoner, the duke, however, urged his sons to be confessors. They should be ready to abandon their territories before committing the sin against the Holy Spirit by denying what they knew was true.[1] On July 16 the Young Lords called a consultation of the Ernestine estates in Weimar.

It was a Time of Confession. All of those assembled were conscious of the example of the princes who had signed the Augsburg Confession two decades earlier. The young Ernestine princes were especially mindful of their father's courageous example. By his own steadfast confession under pressure at the imperial court,[2] he had earned a popular title more brilliant than the one the emperor had taken away.

> Johann Friedrich, by the Grace of God Elect Martyr of Jesus Christ, Duke of the Afflicted, Prince of the Confessors of the Faith, Heir to Eternal Life. And after this life, Victor over [Emperor] Charles and Judge of his betrayer.[3]

Flacius' influence was felt from a distance,[4] but old Amsdorf was on the scene to advise and to stir the blood. "We Lutherans remain with our

19 Ibid. 71–78.
20 *Omnia latina scripta.* D r, Appendix; Cf. H. von Hase. 77n.
21 *Responsio ad epistolam ... Melanthonis.* [O vij v].

1 Mentz. *Johann Friedrich.* 286.
2 *Confession H. Johann Friderich des Eltern vor Kayserlichen Majestat gethan zu Augsburg Anno M.XLIX do im auffgelegt von Kay: M. ins Interim zu willigen.* n. p. [1549?]. UN 1702. 393–398.
3 *Des Gefangnen Christlichen Churfürsten, rechter Titel so ihn itziger Zeit, von allen Gottseligen Waren Christen, billich gegeben wird zu Latein und Deutsch in ein Lied verfasset.* [Mag-deburg: Michael Lotter], n. t.
4 Jörg Rainer Fligge. "Herzog Albrecht von Preussen und der Osiandrismus 1522–1568." Diss., Bonn, 1972. 276.

5 *Antwort, Glaub und Bekenntnis auf das schöne und liebliche Interim.* [Magdeburg]: Michael Lotter, 1548. E iiij r.

6 Nicolas von Amsdorf. *Wie sichs mit des Durchleuchtigsten Hochgebornen Fürsten und Herrn, Herrn Johans Friedrich des Eldern weiland Hertzogen zu Sachssen und gebornem Churfürsten, Landgraven in Düringen und Marggraven zu Meissen meines gnedigsten Herrn Christlichen Abschied zugetragen hat.* Jena: Christian Rödinger, 1554. D ij r – D ij v.

teaching and faith forever," he announced. "That I know for certain ... because the Word of the Lord remains forever" – *Verbum Domini Manet in Aeternum.* "Rome, Trier, Cologne, here there is defiance; strike up the pipes and we will dance": "Trotz hie, Rom, Trier, Cölln, pfeifft auff, so wollen wir tantzen."[5]

> As I pray in all submission and humilty, through the mercy which he has shown to the whole human race though the incarnation and death of his own beloved son, our Redeemer and Savior, Jesus Christ, that it will not move the Imperial Majesty to disfavor, that I do not consent to the Interim, but finally persevere in the Ausburg Confession and putting everything else behind, look forward alone, after this wretched, sorry, and troubled life to being able to participate in eternal joy.[6]

The Ernestine estates rose to the occasion with a statement of August 4 rejecting the Interim. To accept the Augsburg Interim, they agreed, was to accept the papacy. It was necessary to put one's trust in God and not in human reason. They rejected twenty-six points, among them whether both bread and wine should be distributed in Communion. That was a question that should not be asked; Christ had already decided the matter. Since it does not impart forgiveness, ordination should not be considered a sacrament. Requiring everyone to fast every Friday and Saturday was the devil's doctrine. "This oiling," they commented on unction in confirmation, "has no scriptural basis, neither command nor promise of the Lord Christ. The unction of the apostles is quite another thing than what is discussed here."[7]

Was it a Time of Confession in Wittenberg as well? A disturbing rumor was going around that Melanchthon had defected. His betrayal of the Reformation would be catastrophic; the possibility was feared as far away as England. "A great sorte openlye saye that he had denyed the trueth," John Rogers reported in London, "or (that I maye use their owne wordes) recanted." "... his denying would do more harme to the trueth in these last

Elector Johann Friedrich at Prayer. Herzog August Bibliothek, signature 925.17 Th. (34).

7 *Der Prediger der Jungen Herrn Johans Friderichen Hertzogen zu Sachssen etc. Sönen Christlich Bedencken auff das Interim.* n. p. 1548. Bieck. 102–122.

8 CR, VI, 926.

The Young Lords of Ernestine Saxony. Lucas Cranach the Younger, printed by Pankratz Kempf. Germanisches Nationalmuseum, Nuremberg H 1700. Max Geisberg. *Der deutsche Einblatt-Holzschnitt in der ersten Hälfte des XVI. Jahrhunderts.* Munich; H. Schmidt [1923–1929]. 666; Max Geisberg. *The German Single-Leaf Woodcut: 1500–1550.* Revised and edited by Walter L. Strauß. 4 vols. New York: Hacker Art Books, Inc., 1974. II, 630; F. W. Hollstein. *German Engravings, etchings and Woodcuts, Ca 1400–1700,* VI. Edited by K. G. Boon and R. W. Scheller. Amsterdam: Menno Hertzberger, 1959. 138. No. 32.

and most perelouse tymes," he wrote, "than any tongue or penn can expresse." But Rogers, later burned alive by Queen Mary, "Bloody Mary" Tudor, for printing an English translation of the Bible, was relieved when he read a printed protest against the law, signed by Melanchthon. He was encouraged by the brave words: "What urges us to confession of the right doctrine, which is preached in our churches, is the earnest command, that the recognized doctrine of the truth of the gospel must not be denied, or persecuted, and we will also commit our danger to God."[8]

In the document, together with Cruciger, Major and Sebastian Fröschel, Melanchthon rejected the eucharistic prayer, private and votive masses, Corpus Christi processions, prayers to saints, and ...

> ... that we are justified or made righteous through love, and the same meaning is also repeated and declared later, so that it may be surely known, that that book is not agreeable to the true doctrine which is ... that a man is made righteous before God ... for Our Lord's sake through faith ... Therefore this is one fault of this book, that it says that love is true righteousness, and pretends that faith is simply a form of knowledge, such as the sort of belief that devils have ... In short, there are so many horrible misuses in the

9 Quoted from Ralph Keen (ed.). *A Melanchthon Reader.* New York: Peter Lang, 1988. 155–167.

10 According to W. Gordon Zeeveld, by introducing the notion of "adiaphora," it was the source of the idea that the Church of England is a *via media. Foundations of Tudor Policy.* Cambridge, Mass.: Harvard University Press, 1948. 140. Cf. Thomas F. Mayer. "Starkey and Melanchthon on Adiaphora: A Critique of W. Gordon Zeeveld." *Sixteenth Century Journal* XI (1980). 39–49.

11 *A Waying and Considering.* A ij r – A iij r. Cf. Francis Augustus Cox. *The Life of Philip Melanchthon.* London: Gale & Fenner; Edinburgh: Oliphant Waugh & Innes, 1817. 475n.

12 Wolf-Dieter Hauschild. "Zum Kampf gegen den Augsburger Interim in norddeutschen Hansa-städten." ZKG, LXXXIV (1973). 60–81.

13 *Bedencken auffs Interim Des Ehrwirdigen und Hochgelarten Herrn Philippi Melanthonis.* [Magdeburg: Michael Lotter], 1548.

14 CR, VII, 127.

15 Emanuel Hirsch. "Melanchthon und das Interim." ARG, XVII (1920). 62–66; cf. MBW, 5280.

16 Bindseil. 282 f.

17 Derk Visser. *Zacharius Ursinus the Reluctant Reformer.* New York: United Church Press, 1983. 234; O. Ritschl. III, 336.

18 *Entschuldigung ... an die Universitet.* B iij v.

19 Ibid. C v.

20 *Liber de veris et falsis, quo integre pro-pemodum Adiaphorica controversia explicatur.* Magdeburg, 1549. 66.

21 *Eine schrifft widder ein recht heidnisch ja epicurisch Buch der Adiaphoristen, darin das Leiptzische Interim verteidiget wird, sich zu hüten für den itzigen Verfelschern der waren Religion, sehr nützlich zu lesen.* Magdeburg: Christian Rödinger, 1549. C ij v.

popish customs and fashion that we shrink and quake for fear when we speak of them, and thus pray that no man may be burdened with setting up such things ... praying to the saints is not right or lawful. Since then this Interim is against the true doctrine in many articles ... we must show a true declaration and answer to it, which we will also do with Christian measure..."[9]

Rogers gratefully translated the text into English and published it as *A Waying and Considering of the Interim by the honourworthy and Highly Learned Philipp Melanchthon.*[10] "...although this his writing be shorte and answere not to al the poyntes of the Interim," he wrote in the introduction, "yet it playnely answereth to the greetest misuses and to the very senowes of the Rome-Bushops moste tyrannouse kyngdome contayned in that boke."[11] The publication stiffened the will to resist in Germany as well. Hans-Dieter Hauschild reports its effectiveness in the North, especially in Lübeck.[12]

At the imperial court the publication of the same text[13] had quite another effect. When the emperor read it, he angrily demanded that Melanchthon be exiled,[14] and dispatched an envoy, Hans von Oppersdorf, to Dresden to see that he was. Elector Maurice was acutely embarrassed and summoned Melanchthon on September 3 to explain the breach of security. Melanchthon was unable to supply either the name of the printer or the place of publication. It had not been printed in Wittenberg, he said, or within the boundaries of the electorate and emphatically denied his own responsibility. He pleaded his thirty years of peaceful activity and emphasized that he always avoided controversies. To strengthen the point he demonstratively tore up a copy.[15]

The Elector was convinced. How, indeed, could he stave off rebellion without the assistance of Luther's own colleague? The explanation letter to the emperor the Preceptor wrote for him cited the amnesty granted Melanchthon in the Wittenberg Capitulation.[16]

Flacius' deliberate breach of state security sprang from his convictions about ecclesiastical authority. Who ultimately has the right to determine doctrine? Melanchthon favored private negotiations;[17] Flacius demanded that they be public. To negotiate in private, he wrote, was to treat members of the church like serfs.[18] "Three or four crawl into a corner, Spanish-fashion, put their heads together and concoct something secret." "They should not take counsel secretly with the high priests and immediately afterwards come forward and say, we will have it so, for the church is not their own, as if it were made up of cattle which they can deal with and manage as they please."[19] The court's presumption in making foundational decisions for the church was illegitimate. "Who let them give the treasure of the church, entrusted to them, to its enemy, when they would even refuse to give a roast on their table to an intruder? Wouldn't they rather throw a beer tankard at his head?"[20] "I would very much like to hear from the Adiaphorists who gave them this power to subjugate the Church of God, which Christ has made free with his blood, to a man, even if he were the holiest."[21]

> Abolish these secret and obviously Spanish deliberations from the church! Let there be upright meetings in the cities. Do not institute an oligarchy in the church, the kind you are always criticizing in government! This is not a matter for two or three people, but for all the faithful![22]
>
> In religious matters and affairs of the church they should deal openly. If they think that with good conscience something should be changed, they should prepare articles and present them to the whole land and all God-fearing churches, and give them time to consider them for several months. A conference should be held thereafter and god-fearing opinions should be heard. Instead of two or three creeping into a corner and putting their heads together in good Spanish fashion ...[23]

Secular government, he argued further, citing Luther, has no right to determine the church's doctrine. "... that is a good and wholesome counsel, that the church should know above all, first, that the power of the keys, that is, the whole government of the church, has been given to her and not to the tyrants of this world or to the antichristian wolves, as was demonstrated by the venerable Doctor Martin of blessed memory in his book to the Bohemians on the ordination of pastors, and elsewhere."[24]

Melanchthon had a negative opinion about the new law as well, which he called "the Augsburg Sphinx."[25] He found its explanation of justification "weak and sophistic," and often expressed his displeasure in letters to his friends.[26] "I do not want to burden my conscience with the book." "It is not possible to approve the Augsburg Book." "By no means do I want to assent to the Augsburg book."[27] It contained "the gravest blasphemies," "the denial of recognized truth," "manifest corruptions,"[28] "great deception."[29] "...this sophistical book," he wrote, "will be the cause of new wars and of greater alienation in the church."[30] "From this negotiation one sees that a terrible fire and great anger has been ignited by the enemies of the gospel in these great deeds."[31] It would be "the trumpet call for new wars and for greater alienation in the churches." "Acceptance of this book is a confession that our churches have hitherto taught wrongly, and have deliberately aroused divisions."[32]

It is not possible to reconcile Melanchthon's early protest that "death would be easier for me than agreeing with the Augsburg Sphinx,"[33] with his meek acceptance of the law in his notorious letter to Carlowitz. Upon close examination, in fact, Melanchthon's statements about the Interim are downright contradictory. To learn what he really thought, Robert Stupperich recommends believing the letters and ignoring the official statements to the Elector.[34]

From private conversations Flacius was aware of Melanchthon's distaste, and it occurred to him that he could enlist Melanchthon for the resistance by making his judgments public. He had to reckon with Melanchthon's anger, of course, but their friendship, he commented once, reached "only as far as the altar; in an emergency one may for the sake of love pull his teacher out of the water, even if that requires pulling his beard."[35] Although his private letters would have served Flacius' purpose even more dramatically, his official opinions were enough to make the point.

22 *Omnia Latina Scripta.* E. Cf. H. von Hase. 84–96.

23 *Entschüldigung ... an die Universitet.* B iij v.

24 *Ein Supplication und demütige bitt einer Christlichen Gemein in Schwaben, an ihren Rath. Darinne sie biettet, das man ihn wolle die Tauffe lassen nach Christi Einsetzung, wie sie es zuvor gehabt haben.* Magdeburg: Michael Lotter, 1550. A iij v.

25 CR, VII, 69.

26 Beutel. 66.

27 Ibid. 80.

28 Ibid. 99.

29 Ibid. 85.

30 CR, VI, 922.

31 CR, VII, 84.

32 CR, VI, 925.

33 Bezold. 809.

34 R. Stupperich. "Gedanken." 91.

35 *Responsio ad epistolam ... Melanthonis.* A iiiij v.

36 *Eine Schrifft der Theologen zu Witten-berg an die Prediger von Nürnberg anno 1540. von der vereinigung der Evangelischen mit den Papisten da-raus man sehr wol mercken kan, was von der jtzigen vereinigung Christi und Belials der wolffe und der schaffe zu-halten sey. Liß diesen brief Christlicher Leser, du wirst schweren er sey widder die Adiaphoristen geschrieben. Item, Eine Schrifft Lutheri und Pomerani an Johann Friedrich Churfürsten geschrieben anno 1541.* [Magdeburg: Christian Rödinger, 1549]. (= CR, III, 958–968).

37 *Eine Vorrede Philippi Melanthoni auf des fürgelegte Buch zu Regensburg. Deudsch ausgangen zu Wittenberg. Darin er unterrichtete, was man von aller Reformation und Vergleichungen so in der Religion mit den papisten fürgenomen wird, halten sol. Not und nützlich zu lesen.* Magdeburg: Christian Rödinger, 1549.

38 "Somnium Philippi de hyaena in comitis Ratisbonensis, 1541." CR, X, 576; CR, XX, 686 f. Otto Clemen. *Studien zu Melanchthons Reden und Gedichten.* Leipzig: M. Heinsius Nachfolger, 1913. 51 f. Clemen. KS, IV, 267 f. Reprint in Nikolaus Müller. *Beiträge zur Kirchengeschichte der Mark Brandenburg im sechzehnten Jahrhundert* I (1907). 121 f.

39 CR, IX, 203; CR, XX, 685–92; Preger. II, 542; Clemen. KS, VI, 338 f.

40 *D. Ratzebergers geheime Geschichte* 103. On the publication of the *Bericht,* H. von Hase. 36.

41 CR, VI, xviij, 924.

42 *Gründliche Verlegung des langen Comments.* B iij r.

43 *Verzeichnis der im deutschen Sprachgebiet erschienen Drucke des XVI. Jahrhunderts.* (VD 16) Stuttgart: Hiersemann, 1983.

44 Martin Boghardt. "Partial Duplicate Setting: Means of Rationalization or Complicating Factor in Textual Transmission?" *The Library,* Sixth Series XV (1993). 306–331.

45 Salig. I, 617.

"Read this letter, Christian reader," he asked, introducing Melanchthon's 1540 letter to Nuremberg, "...you will swear that it is written against the adiaphora."[36] Very useful was also Melanchthon's critique of the Regensburg colloquy of 1541,[37] and his account of a dream he had on the way to the colloquy about a monster with an animal's body, a girl's face and flaming eyes,[38] like a combination of Christ and Belial. Recognizing a vivid image when he heard one, Flacius appropriated it to denigrate the Augsburg Interim.[39] The document prepared at the colloquy was promptly dubbed the "Regensburg hyena"; like the beast, it had been constructed carelessly.

Once the political winds had changed, Flacius noted sourly, the Wittenberg professors wanted credit for the first published protest against the Interim law. Georg Strobel, Melanchthon's eighteenth-century apologist, denounced Mattaeus Ratzeberger, physician to Elector Johann Friedrich, because he "does not give Melanchthon the honor of having been the first to write against the Interim." Ratzeburger he explained, hated Melanchthon.[40] There was never any doubt, of course, that with his colleagues, Melanchthon was the author of such a protest. The question now, however, was who had *published* it? Karl Bretschneider, editor of the *Corpus Reformatorum*,[41] and Melanchthon biographer Karl Matthes believed the Wittenbergers had done it. Another possibility was Andreas Kegel.[42] But certainly, after his demonstrative destruction of a copy of the document at the Dresden court and his explicit denial of responsibility for the printing, no one can seriously give Melanchthon the distinction of having made it public.

Now, four hundred years after the fact, new evidence has come to light. In the course of the preparation of the new Munich-Wolfenbüttel bibliography of sixteenth-century books,[43] librarian Ulrich Kopp noted the complex publishing history of Melanchthon's opinion. Suspecting irregularity, he enlisted his colleague, Martin Boghardt, who determined that one of the editions was a hybrid printing ("*Zwitterdruck*"). Boghardt established that the greater part of it had been manufactured in Magdeburg, but that the first gathering had been printed in Wittenberg.[44] His technical sleuthing uncovered a deception by the Wittenberg printer, Hans Lufft. It was a dishonest attempt to spread the impression that the pamplet had been first printed in Wittenberg during the time of the Interim. and thus that the Wittenbergers could take credit for resisting the imperial government. This is precisely what in his audience with Elector Maurice, Melanchthon had denied.

Credit for the first printed protest against the Interim law, it is clear, is due not to Melanchthon or the other Wittenbergers, but to Flacius. It was the first of his daring exposés of crucial documents and state papers – an unexpected variant of his vocation of manuscript collecting. The details of how he usually did it, if we had them, surely would involve deft espionage. In this case, however, we do know what happened. Andreas Kegel, who opposed the law, lent him the copy of his father-in-law, Caspar Cruciger.[45]

It was Flacius who brought it to Magdeburg printer Michael Lotter[46] quite illegally and at great risk.

Flacius' second exposé was another state secret, the equally negative *Report of the Theologians Gathered in Meissen*[47] of July 2, 1548, discussed above, which he also published illegally. "If the two publications had not been wrung from them," he commented, "and had not been sent to the printer without their knowledge, there would not be one small page which the great persons had written against the Interim. Lo, so manfully have they contended these three years against the Antichrist."[48]

For Melanchthon, the imperial law was inviolate, but for Flacius the times demanded civil disobedience. He therefore defied censorship – and deliberately broke the law. By making state papers public, he was able to compel Philipp Melanchthon – against his will – to speak for the resistance.

46 *Apologia ... Menii.* A iij r.
47 *Bericht vom Interim.* MBW, 5208.
48 *Antwort auff ettliche Beschüldigung D. Gei. Maiors und D. Pommers.* [Magdeburg: Christian Rödinger, 1552]. A iij r.

MELANCHTHON SURRENDERS JUSTIFICATION BY FAITH ALONE

... this holy, delightful work [the Leipzig Interim] had a good beginning at Pegau, for there Christ and Antichrist were somewhat reconciled, namely, in the most important article of all, on justification ... – Flacius

"What treacle!" Flacius said. He was put off by what was flowing from his own pen. Melanchthon had required him to make a copy of the statement on justification from a consultation, August 23 – 25, at the abandoned Benedictine house at Pegau.[1] It was an agreement between the bishops Pflug of Naumburg and Maltitz of Meissen on one side, and Melanchthon, Bishop George of Anhalt, and *Stiftssuperintendent* Förster of Merseburg on the other.[2] No longer was there talk about a new confession; the risk of war was too great. Maurice's new tactic was to forge a common statement with the Roman Catholic bishops in his lands. A letter signed by the bishops might convince the emperor that he was introducing the Interim. In his introductory address, the Elector insisted that he adhered to biblical authority. He asked only that matters that did not conflict with scripture should be yielded – to please the emperor. With Amsdorf and Flacius in mind, he asked the participants to adopt a broad view, so "...that they will not let themselves be moved by stiff-necked people who do not have much to lose."[3]

The initiative at the conference came not from the theologians, but from court officials Georg von Carlowitz, Christoph von Carlowitz, Melchior von Osse, Heinrich von Bünau zu Droyssig and Law Professor Ludwig

1 CR, VII, 120–122. The Benedictine monastery was the probable venue. Offele. 323.
2 Pflug. *Correspondance* III. 672–675, esp. 673, lines 17–22.
3 CR, VII, 112.

4 Ibid. 60n.

5 Ibid. 121 Italics added; MBW, 5268.

6 *Zwei Schrifften zweier gelehrter und frommer menner widder die adiaphoristische Vefelschung. Geselt zu Leipzig, gantz nützlich zu lesen.* Magdeburg: Michael Lotter, 1550. [A iiij r].

7 Ritschl. II, 373.

8 CR, VI, 910.

9 *Gründliche Verlegung aller Sophisterey, so D. Pfeffinger mit den andern Adiaphoristen, das Leiptzigsche Interim zubeschönen, gebraucht.* [Magdeburg: Christian Rödinger, 1551]. E ij v.

10 Ibid. E iij r.

Fachs. George of Anhalt did his best: still unacceptable were the "gross pagan supersititions," blessing sacramental oil, sacramental processions, masses without communicants, the mass canon and the office for the dead.

At Meissen, Melanchthon had begun a statement on justification. At Pegau the bishops of Naumburg and Meissen offered an amendment:

> But that man, renewed and justified though the Holy Spirit, with his works is able to produce righteousness.[4]

The crucial exclusive particle had disappeared: the *sola fide* had vanished. The clear implication was that salvation was not by faith alone, but by faith only *primarily*. Accepted by the Lutherans, it was official. Flacius transcribed the text only reluctantly:

> These new virtues and good works, in those who are reconciled in this way, are also called righteousness, as was said above about infused righteousness, which should not be understood in the sense that on this account a person has remission of sins, or that a person is without sin in God's judgment, *but that man, renewed and justified though the Holy Spirit is able with his works to produce righteousness* and that God will be pleased with this weak, inchoate obedience in the believers in this wretched, fragile nature for the sake of his Son in faith.[5]

To jettison justification by faith was a serious matter. "Dr. Martin Luther of blessed memory," Flacius objected, "insisted on this little word [alone] so sternly and stoutly, that this article gives birth to the church, raises it, maintains and protects it. And that without this article it could not exist an hour."[6] His impression that Melanchthon had abandoned the word, *sola* for the first time at Pegau, however, is incorrect; he had already done so in an *Opinion* of the preceding May.[7] "We do not contend about the little word, 'sola,'" the Wittenbergers had explained, "but say and confess that other virtues must be in us and a good resolution be begun and remain. Nevertheless, beyond these virtues there must be faith in the Son of God, as was said, and must overshadow the other virtues."[8]

The scriptures, of course, St. Paul and even Luther, usually spoke of justification without using the word, *sola*. Then why not speak, Leipzig Superintendent Johann Pfeffinger suggested, as the Bible usually speaks?[9] But sometimes there are good reasons to use other language. An example of a necessary departure from the way the Bible usually speaks, Flacius volunteered, was the philosophical word, "homoousios," in the Nicene Creed, which had played an essential part in defending scriptural doctrine. Now, in a new situation when the Augsburg Interim credited justification to "inherent righteousness" (mentioned four times), and to "love," the word *sola* was necessary. In such high and now important controversial issues as the article on justification, he insisted, "we should not speak as the scriptures usually speak, but with such words by which the truth is presented to the people as clearly as possible according as the circumstances ... demand."[10]

Melanchthon insisted that he was concerned only about rendering the meaning of "sola" more precise. Defending himself from criticism, he wrote to Prince George of Anhalt that he could more easily "bear exile and death than this union of vipers."

> I know that as a wise man you carefully look into the hearts and dispositions of men. Hence I hope you have considered also my motive, and that you are not influenced by the sycophantic writings of Illyricus, who invents *manifesta mendacia*. Never have I said, never have I written, never have I thought, what he says I have said, that is, that the proposition, "we are justified by faith alone," is an absurd trifling about words. On the contrary, I have spoken and written much more in regard to the meaning of the exclusive particles than many others. Not without effort have I corrected the opinion of others who did not properly explain the particle *sola*.[11]

Melanchthon also argues in a somewhat different fashion.

> I reject the insipid, absurd sophistry of consequent obedience, by which sophistry says that the exclusive *sola* excludes not only merit, but also the presentness of obedience. Then the shameless drips (*Tropffen*) say that the new obedience is not present in Elijah, John the Bapist and Paul. But I consciously omit here longer disputation, and admonish all pious, god-fearing hearers that they avoid and flee such foolish buffonery and harmful sophistry.[12]

After the conference, Bishop Pflug observed that if everything depended on Melanchthon, there could be an agreement on the whole papacy.[13] How could the author of the Augsburg Confession have agreed at Pegau that the sinner is justified partly through Christ, and partly by his behavior? "I asked him why he had written that," Flacius remembered, "but he gave me no clear answer."[14]

11 CR, VII, 658 f. Translation from Richard, 350.
12 *Corpus Doctrinae Christianae.* Wittenberg: Hans Krafft, 1576. 726.
13 MBW, 5655.
14 *Grundliche Verlegung ... Pfeffinger.* Eij v.

THE EUCHARISTIC PRAYER AND THE PROTEST OF LAUTERWAR

> From the origin of the world, under the law of nature, by divine inspiration God called forth in the souls of men the rite of sacrificing. – Augsburg Interim

> ...every common prayer and thanksgiving in the church can correctly be called "eucharist," if no offering of the sacrament occurs together with it ... a work that God shows to men, that he has created, renews, upholds and promises us eternal life, cannot be called a sacrifice or a thanksgiving. – Flacius

With the surrender on the doctrine of justification at Pegau, Elector Maurice's politics were making progress. The only matter still unresolved was the form of the liturgy, especially the canon of the mass or the eucharistic prayer. For Luther, the dominical command, "this do in remembrance of me," mandated eating and drinking. According to the Augsburg Interim, the command required a sacrifice. For support, Bishop Pflug cited the "law of nature." Sacrifice was a universal religious practice, from which the church was not exempt.

In the same way as the law of nature has established religion, without which no people

1 Melhausen. 102, 107.

2 MBW, 5434.

3 *Sacri Canonis Missae Paraphrastica Explicatio, cum Declaratione Ceremoniarum.* Augsburg: Philipp Ulhard, [1548].

4 Pflug. *Correspondance* III. 12–133, 138–140; MBW, 5305.

5 Feifel. 182.

lives, so also [the law of nature has established] ceremonies, without which religion neither is nor can be practiced. And among the ceremonies pagans in all times have considered sacrifice the foremost ... from the origin of the world, under the law of nature, God by divine inspiration called forth the rite of sacrificing in the souls of men."[1]

His argument struck Flacius as "approving heathen sacrifice." Crucial to that interpretation was the use of the canon/eucharistic prayer. Its use by the Lutherans was demanded by the Emperor himself,[2] and under his auspices, promoted by Bishop Michael Helding's *Paraphrastic Explanation of the Sacred Canon of the Mass With an Explanation of the Ceremonies.*[3]

Bishop Julius Pflug set out to convince the Lutherans to adopt the prayer. The discussion in the Interim law about an "effective memorial" came from Pflug, who talked about a "eucharistic" sacrifice. The Reformers emphasized that Christ's sacrifice happens only once, quoting Hebrews 9.15:

Nor was it to offer himself repeatedly, as the high priest enters the Holy Place yearly with blood not his own, for then he would have had to suffer repeatedly since the foundation of the world. But as it is, he has appeared once for all at the end of the age to put away sin by the sacrifice of himself.

But there were subtle ways to deal with the statement of Hebrews 9. Instead of saying Christ's sacrifice was "repeated" in the mass, Pflug said, mysteriously, that it was "continued." His statement is not unlike the one adopted at the Council of Trent:

This *oblatio rememorativa*, however, is more than a mere memorial. It is at the same time in truth the sacrifice of the body and blood of Christ, the same that was offered on the cross, none other. Only now it happens in an unbloody fashion. The two sacrifices are the same according to their substance, but different according to the manner and ceremony of sacrificing [*ratio et ritus offerendi*].

In his double memoire of September 18 and October 2, 1548 to Melanchthon and Prince George, Bishop Pflug argued that "the eucharist is not only food for the health of souls, but also an external sacrifice." He attempted to prove it from the Old Testament,[4] and attached an explanation of the canon. The eucharistic prayer, the canon – Pflug wrote, had been instituted by Christ himself. The "perpetual sacrifice" was called up through the *anamnesis* (remembrance) of the church and thus "made effective."

Rather than using Pflug's (platonic) expression, "repraesentatio," however, Trent used the phrase, "Christ establishing the perpetual sacrifice of the new law," *Christus perpetuum condens novae legis sacrificium* Erich Feifel, aware of the recent discussion on the theme since Odo Casel revealed his (pre-platonic) "mystery theology" at the beginning of this century, explains Helding's ideas in the contemporary Roman Catholic fashion: "The mass is no new sacrifice, but a contemporization (*Vergegenwärtigung*) of the one-time sacrifice of Christ on the cross in the form of an image – a commemorative sacrifice (*ebenbildlich Gedenk-opfer*)."[5]

Since post-Caselian theory to a suprising extent is a repetition of

Helding's theory, Flacius' criticism of Helding and of the Interim law is also applicable against the current explanations of the mass as "eucharistic sacrifice" and a contemporization of Calvary: "Formerly in the papacy they taught that the mass is in itself such a holy work, which is valid before God and must be an acceptable propitiatory sacrifice. Now in the Interim they reject the old error and put a new error in its place, that is, that the mass is a thank-offering (eucharist)."[6] Rather than a memorial of Christ, he wrote, the canon/eucharistic prayer is an *oblivional*, and the centerpiece of the whole papal system.[7]

Private conferences between Pflug and Prince George followed in September and October, 1548, and there was another, secret exchange of letters in October and November.[8] Pflug knew that the Evangelicals would never accept that "this do" meant *repeating* Christ's sacrifice. So he said that Christ did not destroy sacrifice, but *fulfilled* it. It was "a clever presentation of Catholic doctrine, in which he maintained both one-timeness of the sacrifice on the cross as well as the sacrifical character of the mass."[9]

In December, Pflug was dismayed to learn that there was an interloper in the discussion, a mysterious "Christian Lauterwar," whose pamphlet *Against the Interim, Papist Mass, Canon and Master Eisleben (Wider das Interim, Papistische Meß, Canonem, und Meister Eißleben durch Christianum Lauterwar, zu dieser Zeit nützlich zu lesen.* [Magdeburg: Michael Lotter] 1549) was selling briskly at the Leipzig Christmas Market[10] and making him a laughing-stock. Following the outline of Johann Agricola's recommendation of the Interim to Christoph von Carlowitz,[11] Lauterwar – "pure," "true" – was the first of five pseudonymous publications written against the Interim.

Lauterwar reported that at Pegau Pflug had complained that Dominicus de Soto, the emperor's Spanish confessor, had introduced false and superstitious material into the Interim text. "Julius Pflug ... in the presence of many reliable men, confessed and said that it was unfortunately true that much in the Interim was still false and superstitious ... a Spanish monk, Dominicus de Soto, had falsified it."[12] "There was something true about it," comments Albert Jansen about Lauterwar's charge.[13]

> As Soto was called to Augsburg in February, 1548, he was at once brought into the Interim negotiations. It is not possible, at least not yet today, to isolate his participation in the formulation. But Soto was aware that the final form of the Interim lacked clarity. Otherwise he would not have pushed through the addition, that the Interim must (with the exception of the last article) agree with the doctrine and practice of the church "if it is understood in the correct sense."[14]

As the Hanseatic theologians demonstrated in their confession against the Interim,[15] De Soto's intervention made the Interim text contradictory. At the electoral court, Rudolf von Beunau suggested that mistakes had crept into the text because there were people present who did not understand Latin very well.[16] But the responsibility was clearly De Soto's.[17] With Malvenda, he had practiced a kind of supervision over the text.[18] And "... the editing of his draft by the Spanish," Jansen continues, "cast suspi-

6 *Etliche greiffliche ... warzeichen* (1549). F iiiij v.

7 *Widder den Auszug des Leipsischen Interims, oder das kleine Interim.* Magdeburg: Christian Rödinger, 1549. B ij r.

8 Pflug. *Correspondance* III. 131–133, 138–140, 148–151. MBW 5270, 5304f., 5321, 5324.

9 Smolinsky. 129.

10 Pflug. *Correspondance* III. 58, 187, 196–197n, 219.

11 G. Kawerau. "Gutachten." 268 f.

12 Ibid. D ij v.

13 "Julius Pflug. Ein Beitrag zur Geschichte der Kirchen und Politik Deutschlands im sechzehnten Jahrhundert." *Neue Mitteilungen aus dem Gebiet historischer-antiquarischer Forschung des thüringischen-sächsischen Vereins zur Erforschung des vaterländischen Altertums* X (1963–64). II, 95.

14 Le Plat, III, 33. Cf. Karl Josef Becker. *Die Rechtfertigungslehre nach Domingo de Soto.* Rome: Verlagsbuchhandlung der Päpstlichen Universität Gregoriana, 1967. 400.

15 *Bekentnuß unnd Erklerung auffs Interim durch der Erbarn Stedte Lübeck, Hamburg, Lüneberg, etc. Superintendenten, pastorn unnd Predigern zu Christlicher und notwendiger unterrichtung gestellet.* Magdeburg: Michael Lotter, 1549. XLV, 37. Jansen (64 f., 78, 122 f.) agrees: there was no agreement between Malvenda, de Soto and Pflug. W. Radtke. "Das Lüneberger Bekenntnis (1549) gegen das Augsburger Interim." *Zeitschrift der Gesellschaft für niedersächsische Kirchengeschichte* XLIV (1939).

16 Jansen. 94.

17 "During the Pegau negotiations, Melanchthon learned that Pedro de Malvenda had changed the words, against the will of the others." "Either Malvenda or Dominicus de Soto, or both at the same time, had inserted a great deal, about which Elector Maurice complained to the Emperor." Salig. I, 568; J. V. Pollet. "La Diète d'Augsbourg 1547/48 et L'Intérim

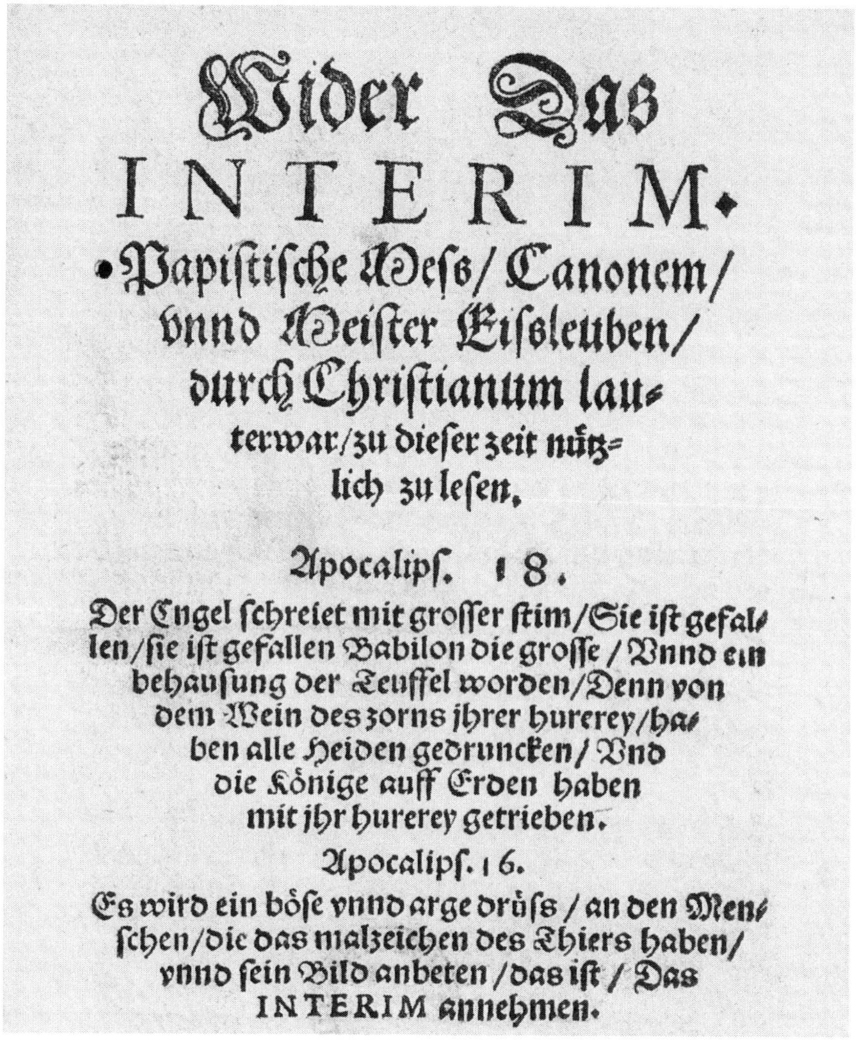

Wider Das INTERIM·

**•Papiſtiſche Meſß/ Canonem/
vnnd Meiſter Eiſßleuben/
durch Chriſtianum lau-
terwar/zu dieſer zeit nützlich zu leſen.**

Apocalipſ. 18.

Der Engel ſchreiet mit groſſer ſtim/Sie iſt gefal-
len/ſie iſt gefallen Babilon die groſſe / Vnnd ein
behauſung der Teuffel worden/Denn von
dem Wein des zorns jhrer hurerey/ha-
ben alle Heiden gedruncken/ Vnd
die Könige auff Erden haben
mit jhr hurerey getrieben.

Apocalipſ. 16.

Es wird ein böſe vnnd arge drüs / an den Men-
ſchen/die das malzeichen des Thiers haben/
vnnd ſein Bild anbeten /das iſt / Das
INTERIM annehmen.

d'Après les Publications Récents"
*Bibliothèque d' Humanisme et Ren-
naissance* XXXVI (1974). 639.
18 Beutel. 73.
19 Ibid. [A iv v].
20 *Wider das Interim.* B ij v.

cion on it."

Lauterwar dismissed Pflug's defense of the mass sacrifice from the Old Testament: The shew-bread of Leviticus 24.5 – 7 has nothing to do with the mass; the narrative of Melchisedek in Genesis 13 describes no sacrifice; Daniel 12.9 – 12 and Malachi 1.11, "in every place incense is offered to my name, and a pure offering" have to do with with Old Testament practice, not Christian worship. The sacrifices of the Old Testament are part of the law, whose task, like that of the schoolmaster in Galatians 3, ends with the arrival of Christ.

Like Luther, Lauterwar insisted that anamnesis, memorial, was not sacrifice, but eating and drinking. "Christ speaks, we should eat his body and drink and thus remember him. But they say, "we should sacrifice him."[19] The mass is not a sacrifice "... for the work which God shows to men, that he has created, renews, upholds us and promises eternal life, cannot be called sacrifice or thank-offering."[20]

> We do not sacrifice, but receive it. The words of institution imply that one does not sacrifice, but receives. Just as it is God who baptizes, absolves, and comforts with the Holy gospel, in the Sacrament of the Altar, it is he who offers us his body and blood. As the work of God, it cannot be called men's sacrifice any more than can absolution and baptism.

It is more accurate to call the sacrament communion, "a work whereby our Lord God shows himself gracious toward us, for just as in Christ's stead the minister baptizes, absolves and comforts in the name of Jesus, he also offers us his body and blood, in order that in the Communion we receive it from him and not (as occurs in the Mass) that we sacrifice, and that is what the words of the meal clearly imply..."[21] Lauterwar ridiculed the "minor canon", the prayer over money and gifts (a term since abandoned by Roman Catholic theologians); it was blasphemous to offer God gifts not yet consecrated.[22] Nor was Pflug's substitution of the word, eucharist, thanksgiving, for the propitiatory sacrifice permissible.

> But that the communion was called "eucharist," by the ancient fathers happened because the reception of the venerable Sacrament of the Altar was followed by a common thanksgiving of the church. For this ceremony was celebrated in the same way by the ancients as now is commonly done in our churches.

> But who cannot understand that this name, Eucharist, or Thanksgiving does not properly pertain to the Sacrament of the Altar? For in this fashion the meal of every Christian could be called "eucharist", since before and after eating he gives thanks to God the Lord for his benefits. And every common prayer and thanksgiving of the churches can rightly be called "eucharist", even when no distribution or giving of the sacrament occurs.[23]

Hans-Christoph von Hase suggests that Flacius hid behind pseudonymns not to protect himself, but to induce people to consider arguments independently of their attitude about him.[24] Lauterwar's identity, as it happened, did remain unknown while the public was learning about the charges against Bishop Pflug. Individual statements, demanded by an angry Pflug from those who had been present at the meeting, all of which denied responsibility for the affair,[25] remain as evidence of the mysterious Lauterwar's success.

21 Ibid. B v – Bii r.
22 Ibid. B iij r.
23 Ibid. B ij r – B ij v.
24 H. von Hase. 37.
25 The statements have been preserved by Ernest Cyprianus. *Tabularium Ecclesiae Romanae Seculi Decimi in qua Monumenta Restituti Calicis Ecclesiastici ... Continentur.* Frankfurt & Leipzig: Wolfgang Ludwig Spring, 1742. 544–547; cf. *Pflug Correspondance* III. 657–677.

FORCED ROMANIZING AND THE PROTEST
OF WAREMUND

1 E. Hopp. "Zur Geschichte des Liedes 'Erhalt uns Herr bei deinem Wort.'" *Beiträge zur bayerischen Kirchengeschichte* VIII (1901). 79–87.
2 Theodor Keim. *Reformationsgeschichte der Reichstadt Ulm*. Stuttgart: C. Belser, 1851. 502.
3 CR, VII, 78.
4 Ludwig Fürstenwerth. *Die Verfassungsänderungen in den oberdeutschen Reichsstädten zur Zeit Karls V*. Göttingen: Dietrische Univ.-Buchdruckerei (W. F. Kästner), 1893. 38; Eberhard Naujoks. *Kaiser Karl und die Zunftverfassung*. Stuttgart: Kohlhammer, 1985.
5 William Robertson. *The History of the Reign of the Emperor Charles V*. III. London, 1763 & Philadelphia: Lippincott, 1857. 181.

Learn the old again, or people will be sent who will teach it to you. You are going to learn Spanish. – Cardinal Granvella

Where the Interim is obstructed, the land must become powder and kindling. – Johann Agricola

The Christian church is obligated at all times to state its doctrine and innocence … especially now, because, against God and justice, the enemies are persecuting our doctrine with sword and fire. – Flacius

Emperor Charles V left Augsburg August 13, 1548 at the head of an army, marched like Nebuchadnezzar on the South, accompanied by bishops to reconsecrate evangelical churches. "Learn the old again," Cardinal Granvella threatened, "or people will be sent who will teach it to you. You are going to learn Spanish." In Ansbach, Nuremberg and Strassburg, there was a ban on singing the hymn, "Lord, Keep Us Steadfast in Thy Word."[1] On August 14, Charles appeared in Ulm; the next day the Bishop of Arras consecrated the altars in the Minister Church and held the first Interim mass. To put Roman Catholics in power, Charles suspended the city's constitution. When, with two exceptions, the Lutheran pastors refused to accept the Interim, Pastors Martin Frecht, Bonaventura Stelzer, Jakob Speiss and Jörg Frecht were arrested and shackled by a single chain.[2] The news from Ulm spread through Germany and beyond, and Frecht and his co-prisoners became famous as confessors and martyrs.

Charles proceeded to rid Speyer of its Evangelical clergy. Nuremberg had already surrendered on June 19. Then Rothenburg, Memmingen, Dinkelsbühl, Windsheim, Kempten, Nördlingen fell. When Kostnitz resisted, a whole suburb was put to the torch as punishment. Had not Agricola warned that "where the Interim is obstructed, the land must become powder and kindling?"[3] The city of Lindau determined that "in secular matters we want to be obedient," but that the emperor could not command their souls. However, after a struggle, the city surrendered on July 13.

To prevent popular uprisings, Lutheran pastors were driven out. To ensure Roman Catholic hegemony, membership in the city councils was taken from the guilds and limited to Roman Catholics, and the guilds were dissolved. The constitutions of Memmingen, Isny, Ravensburg – no less than twenty-five cities altogether – were altered.[4] The new councils were called *Hasenräte* after Charles' agent, Vice Chancellor, Heinrich Hass. It was "an act of power unprecedented as well as arbitrary, which excluded the body of inhabitants from any share in the government of their own community and subjected them to men who had no other merit than their servile devotion to the emperor's will, and gave general disgust; but as they durst not venture upon resistance, they were obliged to submit in silence."[5]

Hass delivered an ultimatim to Regensburg on December 30, 1548: only preachers were allowed who had sworn an oath to God and the saints not only that they would not preach against the Interim, but teach it to the letter.[6] The answer, *A Humble Answer of a Christian City to the Interim Delivered by the Imperial Majesty and a Suggestion of the Preachers of the Same City*, was written by Superintendent Nicolaus Gallus, and published in Magdeburg by Flacius.[7] For five months after Nikolaus Gallus fled, eventually to Magdeburg where he joined Flacius, no church services were held in the city.

Disguised as an official, Johann Brenz narrowly escaped an imperial commission sent by the emperor to arrest him in Schwäbisch Hall, and for eighteen months hid in the Black Forest.[8] A price of 5,000 Gulden was put on the head of Caspar Aquila of Saalfeld for publishing a pamphlet critical of the law, and he had to hide in the castle of Countess Katharina in Rudolfstadt, disguised as a sick woman.[9] The Lutheran prior of the Franciscan monastery in Speyer, who up until now had worn a habit, donned secular clothing and disappeared. Matthäus Alber fled from Reutlingen, Erasmus Sarcerius from Nassau, Martin Bucer from Strassburg, Andreas Osiander and Veit Dietrich from Nuremberg.

The worst fate befell Constance. After vain negotiations, the city was put under the imperial ban. On August 6, imperial troops attacked the city, which fell after a brave defense and a desperate appeal for military assistance. The Reformer Ambrosius Blaurer was banished. The defeated city was forced to accept rule by the House of Habsburg on August 13, and the Interim on August 18. An imperial city was reduced to a provincial city in Habsburg territory. Liliencron has preserved a sad song that begins, "Wann ich denk, mit was großem flyß dem herren got zu ehren 's gotswort ward glert uf rechte wys..." When I think of what great diligence the Word of God was taught in the right way..."[10]

2,000 Spanish troops were employed to occupy Württemberg. Spanish "visitors" harassed the pastors. In Swabia an imperial mandate of October 24th, dismissed all evangelical pastors. At the emperor's insistence, Erhard Schnepf, who had preached hard against the Interim in Tübingen, and later would be Flacius' colleague in Jena, was dismissed. For supporting the Reformation, Duke Ulrich was charged with a felony. He accepted the Interim under pressure, but found a way in May, 1549 to rescue the Lutheran church by appointing some pastors as "catechists" and "pedagogues." Others faced a worse fate.

> The Protestant ministers flee from the cities of upper Germany or move out. Men who have instructed their congregations in Luther's doctrine for a lifetime, reach now for the staff of a pilgrim and move into the unknown, accompanied hour after hour by weeping wives, morose men, their heads down, and tired children, grasping their parents.

> Former monks, who for ten years or longer have preached the Augsburg Confession in their old habit, disappear suddenly from the revenge of the church, disguised in civilian clothing. No one knows where they are. Only the moon eavesdrops on the

6   Robert Döllinger. *Das Evangelium in Regensburg.* Regensburg: Evangelische Lutherische Gesamtkirchengemeinde Regensburg, 1959. 134.

7   *Einer Christlichen Stad untertenick Antwort auff das von Key. Ma. uberschickt Interim unnd ein Radtschlag der Prediger der selbigen Stadt.* n. p. 1548.

8   Johann Erdmann Bieck. *Das Dreyfache Interim.* Leipzig: John Christoph Cörner, 1721. 81 ff.

9   Georg Biundo. "Aquila und das Interim." *Theologische Literaturzeitung* LXXIV (1949). 589; Gebhardt. 187.

10 Rochus von Liliencron. *Die historischen Volkslieder der Deutschen vom 13. bis 16. Jahrhundert* IV. Leipzig: F. C. W. Vogel, 1869. 474.

11 Hans Baumgarten. *Moritz von Sachsen, der Gegenspieler Karls V.* Berlin: Paul Neff Verlag, 1941. 226, 229.

12 *Newe Zeytung, vnd Warhafftige Geschichte, die sich des vergangnen M.D.L. Jahrs den ij. Februa. in der Löblichen Freyen Stadt Strassburg, in unswer Frauwen Thumbstifft dz Münster genant an widerauffrichtung der Grausamen und abschühelichen Gotslesterung Bäbstlicher Messen, so man der Pfaffn Interim nennet, hat beygeben vnd zugetragen, Hievor niemals, yetzund aber durch Blasium Argen von Magdeburg in den Truck gegeben Anno dominj M.D. Lj.* Magdeburg: Michael Lotter, 1551. Identification of the pseudonymn by Emil Weller. "Die Lieder gegen das Interim." *Serapaeum* XXIII (1862). 293. Rochuson Liliencron. "Dichtung über das Interim." *Mitteilungen aus dem Gebiete der öffentlichen Meinung in Deutschland während der zweiten Hälfte des 16. Jahrhunderts* IV. Munich: Verlag der königlichen Akademie, 1874. 155.

13 *Von der Papisten Tauff, und andern Caeremonien oder Kirchendiensten, ob die nach Erkenter und angenomener Wahrheit, durch jemand Christlich zu besuchen und zu gebrauchen sein, durch ein Prediger in Oberdeutschland gestellt.* Magdeburg: Christian Rödinger, 1549.

14 *Ein Supplication*, op. cit.; Paul Warmbrunn. *Zwei Konfessionen in einer Stadt. Das Zusammenleben von Katholiken und Protestanten in der Päritatischen Reichsstädten Augsburg, Biberach, Ravensburg und Dinkelsbühl von 1548 bis 1648.* Wiesbaden: Franz Steiner Verlag, 1983. 96–98.

15 *Form und weiss einer Bisschofflichen ja Erzbischofflichen Visitation am Rein in welcher zu besehen ist wie es künfftig umb die Kirche wird gelegen sein wenn die Bisschoff ihre alte Jurisdiction wider bekommen werden.* [Magdeburg: Christian Rödinger] 1549. A iij v.

16 *Bedencken Etlicher Predicanten, Als*

secret meetings in inaccessible woods on warm September evenings, in which lonely men, who do not look like loiterers, campers or highwaymen, receive baskets with meager nourishment and quickly disappear again into the still shadows.

Thus, the teachers of faith flee from their pulpits into the forests, and in upper Germany alone four hundred Protestant preachers, who cannot submit their consciences to the Interim, wander as homeless beggars.[11]

The Reformation churches had been deprived of political protection, and the emperor's romanizing march encountered almost no serious opposition. At a time before newspapers, Magdeburg pamphlets reported the progress of the devastation, and Flacius was the chief reporter. As "Blasius Arg," he described the riot attending the reintroduction of the Latin mass in the Strassburg cathedral.[12] Another pamphlet reported the anonymous protest of a desperate pastor,[13] and an appeal of Dinkelsbühl's Protestant majority that baptisms be allowed, "according to Christ's institution."[14] All churches in the Rhineland, he reported, "poisoned" by the Reformation were required to surrender of all Lutheran books and to reinstate the Latin cultus. "…if the church was formerly Lutheran, one should first ask whether the mass has been restored, together with ceremonies, sacraments and other services according to the old usage of the church and the order and command of the emperor … if they (the clergy) are married and have offered the sacrament in both kinds, one must lead them back to the usages of the ancient church and command them to observe them."[15]

Flacius also printed evidence of the Counter-Reformation pressure imposed on the Evangelical clergy, the protest of pastors in Swäbish Hall,[16] the formula by which clergymen in the diocese of Mainz were compelled to conform to papal practice,[17] and the oath they were required to make.

I, N. N., unworthy priest and pastor of N. confess here openly (beloved in Christ) that at the instigation of Satan, the enemy of divine truth, and also out of human stupidity, that in time past I fell from the holy congregation, of the Apostolic, Catholic, Roman church, into all kinds of error, especially the new sect of the Lutherans, now hovering, and at the beginning, I have not held to the doctrine of the holy fathers, the councils, the tradition of the same, and have not rendered to the holy Christian vicar, the most holy pope at Rome, due obedience, but, according to the practice of the new sect, have dishonored, reviled, and slandered him, and also defiled myself in my priestly office and estate in a false, supposed marriage, and have not used the holy reverend sacrament of baptism, confirmation, the sacrament of the altar, chrism, unction and consecration, also not matrimony, (as established according to the order of the Holy Common Apostolic, Catholic, Christian, Roman Church), further taught and preached against the office of the holy mass and invocation of the highly laudable Virgin Mary and the dear saints, and against purgatory, and beyond that, have fallen into many other errors, false doctrine, and unchristian heresy and my sheep with a right model of life and doctrine, which I should have improved, I have vexed and hindered in their salvation.

Now, by the inspiration and grace of the Holy Spirit I have turned again to the truth and rule of the said Holy Apostolic Catholic Roman church. So that everyone may know that such happens not insincerely, but from me from totally good will. So I confess openly with mouth and my whole heart, will and whole soul, the right, true Christian Common, Catholic, Roman faith, and condemn and curse all and every heresy, false doctrine and error, especially that of Luther and all those, who now in our times are against the unity of the whole holy common Christian Catholic Roman Church in the German nation and oppose it, in which I have no pleasure and which I formerly praised, taught, and preached. I swear and promise at the peril of my holy and eternal salvation never more to believe, to teach, or to preach such error, as for that reason I have sworn the same living oath on the holy gospel before my legitimate authority.

And I will henceforth never detatch myself or fall away from the same authority, but remain and persist uprightly and steadfastly in the same unity, and pray for God's sake that all those who have been offended by my life, speech and preaching will forgive me and with me willingly return with me to the said unity of the holy common Christian Catholic Roman church and absolve themselves. So I swear and promise that, where the present heresy and error would occur, that I will act, teach and preach against it, so I surrender to the power of the spiritual government. As witness I have signed this paper and confession with my own hand.[18]

In places where no concessions had been made there was devastation. Pastors were murdered even near Wittenberg, their churches reduced to confusion. Flacius reported on the atrocities.

For our enemies have not only wantonly burdened the poor people in Bavaria and Swabia with theft, burning, immorality, and other things, but have also hacked small children apart in pieces, and were incited by their clergy to a degree of atrocity unheard of by any people.[19]

A nervous Bugenhagen ordered his assistant clergy not to mention the Interim or the Lutheran Confessions from the pulpit. The report that three hundred pastors were driven from their churches in Swabia and their wives and daughters raped alarmed Melanchthon.[20] "The Emperor's power is so great now that I do not think the princes can resist him," he wrote.[21] "If the emperor comes he will certainly not be content with a small change. Everyone will be in the same danger, whether they have made some small change or whether they have made none. He wants to abolish all the learned. So, when the teachers have been removed, he wants to restore all the abuses."[22]

Melanchthon found solace in star-gazing. Having studied the eclipse of the moon, and having consulted Ptolemy, he announced that the emperor would die in August of 1548.[23] One had to be patient, then, until he died. When the emperor remained inconveniently alive, Melanchthon consulted Ptolemy again and redid his calculations: the emperor would die in August, 1549.[24]

"It is not necessary," Flacius commented coldly, "that a theologian be so erudite that he derives the future from the stars."[25] To count on the emperor's death from an eclipse was "... completely futile."[26] "When he is dead," he mocked, "we can be steadfast confessors of Christ without fear and danger of suffering." Should one serve two masters, he wanted to know, "so that the Romans would not come and the heavens fall in? According to the prophet Isaiah, tyrants are nothing more than a rod in God's hand. One should be reconciled not with the rod, then, but with the hand ... And even if it were possible to reconcile the rod so that it spares us against the will of the hand, one would have to fear that the hand of Al-

der zu Schwebischen Hall, Der in Hessen und der Stadt N. N. auffs Interim Uberreicht. n. p. 1548.

17 *Fragestücke unde Artikel Auff welche die Priesterschafft im Stifft Meintz zuforderung des Teufflichen Pabsthumbs itzt Examiniert werden.* [Magdeburg: 1548].

18 *Eine Schrifft wie die Pfarrherrn an den Örtern da man die Papisterey widerumb auffricht, die Evangelisch lehr, welche sie Lutherisch nennen, verloben und verschweren müssen.* [Magdeburg: Christian Rödinger] 1548. Reprinted, G. Hertel. "Zur Geschichte der Gegenreformation." *Geschichts-Blätter für Stadt und Land Magdeburg* XXXIII (1898). 407–409.

19 *Etliche greiffliche ... warzeichen.* 1550. N r.

20 Ibid. 312 f.

21 Ibid. 87.

22 Ibid. 192.

23 O. Ritschl. II, 340n.

24 *Gründliche Verlegung des ... Comments.* Gg iij r.

25 *Omnia latina Scripta.* [Dd vj r].

26 *Entschuldigung ... an die Universitet.* I ij v.

27 *Ein Buch von ... Mitteldingen.* [R iiij v]–f.

28 Ibid. S iij r – f.

29 Introduction to Joachim Westphal. *Gründliche Verlegung des Gründlichen Berichts der Adiaphoristen zu diesen bösen Zeiten, sehr nützlich zu lesen.* Magdeburg: Christian Rödinger, 1551.

30 Cod. Guelf. 64.1 Helmst. fol. 66 r. – 67 v.

31 Heldelin. V iij v.

mighty God would throw the rod away, and take a hammer to shatter us completely."[27] "I do not doubt that if our theologians had been more steadfast, and had admonished the people to steadfastness, the Interim would be behind us."[28] The Interim, he wrote, was born out of the fear of the Wittenberg theologians.

He often thought, Flacius recalled, about the exiled pastors of Swabia, who were forced to sleep in the fields.[29] "When I saw that the outrageous devastation, with the compromises and changes of religion was growing, and that our admonitions and pleas to Philipp and all the learned were in vain, I was very depressed," he recalled. How could he not keep faith with his own persecuted students? One of them, Sixtus Caesar (Kayser?), wrote him, describing his experiences in the summer of 1548.

> ... after many consultations in the council because of the adiaphora (as it is called today), therefore, having shaken the dust from our feet, we set out on the Sabbath after St. Lawrence's Day [August 11] 1548, not without great danger to life, directly through the duchy of Württemberg, which was filled with the most cruel Spanish soldiers. On St. Bartholmew's Day [August 24] we arrived at Heidelberg. There, by the wonderful providence of God, all our brothers gathered in the church, and each one told the history of the comedy he had undergone. And we praise and glorify God for all he had done for us, that to all us who were dispersed, he gave one mouth and the same wisdom of convincing apostates.
>
> We wandered together through many dangerous places, five brothers and a sister, having left the security of home, wives and children, and seeking a place to stay, but for 30 weeks not finding one.
>
> How many hardships we were in, how many sorrows of soul we bore, no one can believe unless he has experienced it. For how great an evil it is that well-established churches are so cruelly laid waste, and so many souls scandalized, the genuine and steadfast driven out, you, Domine preceptor, have observed well through to the wisdom given you by experience.
>
> With how many prayers and sighs, have we waited for a candid and free confession from the Wittenbergers. But then, alas, all the doctors of the church were mute.
>
> ... And if you had done nothing more than strengthening us Caesars by your pious publications, I would believe that you had been divinely raised up. Therefore all of us revere your noble gift, and, by the request and mandate of all my brothers, to your reverend worthiness, for such great support shown us in your publications, I give as much thanks as my soul is able to feel, and from my whole heart I pray that God will deign to be with you henceforth, so that you may be able to serve us who are afflicted and his dispersed church a long time.
>
> And I congratulate myself at the good fortune of once having experienced you as a teacher, and having experienced your kindness, present as a spectator during a good part of your great catastrophes. When I read your publications, I seem to see and hear Illyricus in person...[30]

"There was something like a fire in my heart, as Jeremiah writes about himself," Flacius reported, "so that I had to do something."[31] "I did what I could", he wrote, explaining his fiery *Common Protest Against the Horrors of South Germany*, "and published the protest of Waremund."[32] In an intimidated Germany, Waremund broke the silence:

The pope and his bishops promise that they will grant us a free council. But when will they hold it? Why do they tyrannize and rage with sword and fire against us before we are condemned? Why are they destroying our churches? Why with such fuming and raging, are they everywhere persecuting our doctrine? We, who are ready and heartily glad if they permit, to demonstrate at a free council that it is the word of the Lord Christ?

The Christian church is obliged to declare and defend its doctrine and its innocence at all times, especially now, since against God and against the law, the opponents are persecuting our doctrine with sword and with fire ... The pagans formerly thought there was nothing more praiseworthy than for someone to dare to risk his life in knightly struggle to save his honor and that of his fatherland. We are struggling now not for earthly, but for that heavenly fatherland; we are fighting not for our passing honor, but primarily for God's, and then for our eternal honor.

...Therefore, with the apostles, let us rejoice that we can be worthy to suffer something for the sake of the Lord's name. And if it is God's will that we be martyrs, let us run through this temporal death with a joyful confession to the eternal blessedness of the kingdom of heaven ... Most important, at this time all leaders, pastors and curates of souls [*Seelsorger*] should be alert and not be dumb dogs, as the prophet says. But because they see that the wolf, that is the devil and our enemies, is dispersing and scattering the Lord's flock, they should attack, properly and undaunted with the sword of the Spirit ... and not be dumb, frightened dogs who bark at the wolf first when they see him fleeing ... Stand your ground, then, you preachers. Suffer a little, and expect help and salvation from God![33]

Luther's friend, Michael Stifel, wrote appreciatively.

When out of fear everyone only murmured and no one dared open his mouth honestly, God awakened an un-German man, who alerted us ... this man, Illyricus, wrote pamphlets which served the anti-Interim cause. One was called "Waremund," one "Lauterwar," another "Henetus," and another "Azarias." He published them all when no one else dared murmur against the Interim, and many pious men were awakened and turned about, who after that contributed their best.[34]

Having consulted the book of *Revelation* in his cabbalistic fashion, he once had concluded that Luther was the First Angel of the Apocalypse (Revelation 14.6). Now, he announced that the Second Angel was none other than Matthias Flacius Illyricus. "Never having seen you," Stifel wrote to him, "I vehemently love you."[35]

32 *Von der Einigkeit.* [A vij r]; Flacius uses the pseudonym again in the *Gründliche Entscheidung deß langwirigen vnd ergerlichen streits von der Erbsünde.* n. p. 1578. Luther as "wahrer Mund." Preger. I, 113.

33 *Ein gemeine protestation und Klagschrifft aller frommen Christen wieder das Interim unnd andere geschwinde anschlege und grausame Verfolgung der Wiedersacher des Evangelii, allen Gotfürchtigen gewissen, zu dieser betrübtern zeit uberaus sehr nützlich zu lesen. Durch Johannem Waremundum.* [Magdeburg: Michael Lotter] 1548. Bij r, v; Gij r – [Giiij r].

34 Quoted by Johannes Christophorus Wendler. *De Praecipiorum Quorundam Sec. XVI et XVII Theologicorum Lutheranorum ... meritis et scriptis.* Altdorf: Cyril Osterlandus Typis Kohlesii Acad. Typogr, 1710. Cap. 14, v. 9. 123 f.

35 Walter Friedensburg. "Zwei Briefe Michael Stifels an Flacius (1551 und 1552)." ARG, LXIII/LXIV (1919). 247–251.

The Saxon Solution

THE SITUATION OF CONFESSION

1 *Bulla des Antichrists, dadurch er das volck Gottes widderumb inn den eisern Ofen der egiptischen gefengnknis zuziehen, gleichstimmig mit des Meintzischen Rabsakes briefe. Daraus wol zuvernemen, was der Teufel durch seine beide Tugent, das ist, durch den mörderischen Krieg widder die Kirche Gottes, und durch seine Lügen, als da sind, Concilium, Interim, Mittelding, Chorrock, denckt auszurichten.* Magdeburg: Christian Rödinger, 1553. A iij v.
2 *Ein Buch von ... Mitteldingen.* [R iiij r].

> The teachers of the divine word stand as if before Mount Sinai. Behind them is God, who lightens and thunders with his Word and threat. Even if man demanded it, therefore, they cannot yield. – Flacius

> In the situation of confession and incitement to sin, nothing is an adiaphoron. – Flacius

> If the devil and the Antichrist were to ask me to pray the Our Father, I would not do it. – Jost Schalreuter

In discussions with Elector Joachim II of Brandenburg during the activities surrounding the marriage of Maurice's brother, Duke August, to Princess Anne of Denmark, in early October, 1548, Maurice came up with a new idea to stave off an invasion, a Saxon solution. He would have the religious law *modified* for Saxony and Brandenburg. Perhaps a compromise would placate the emperor. He ordered a conference to begin the process at Torgau on October 18th. Thus, once more, the initiative was taken not by the theologians, but by officials of the Dresden court. It was another fateful step toward a state church.

The officials proposed reintroducing as many Roman Catholic ceremonies as possible to please the emperor – the litany procession, chants, vigils, private masses, the reserved sacrament for the sick, solitary masses and the sacraments of Penance, Confirmation, and Extreme Unction. If truth be known, Melanchthon said, they actually preferred the papal rule; it was more convenient.[1] "They think that one should serve two masters so that the Romans do not come and the heaven falls down," Flacius wrote about those court officials who presumed to legislate doctrine. "They want to crucify Christ, that is, they fear men more than God."[2]

The theologians, effectively excluded from influence, could only react. Melanchthon's *Opinion* overlooked some of the controversial matters – private masses, prayers to saints and processions, but he opposed the liturgical formula of Extreme Unction, "through this unction your sins are remitted." God, he said, does not use oil to forgive sins. A report of what an apostle did in this case, with oil, was no basis for calling it a sacrament, and he wondered about the conscience of bishops who said such words. At the end of October the diplomats, Melchior von Osse and Hans von Schönburg, returned from Vienna with the report that the emperor would be satisfied with nothing less than total submission. Not even the permission written into the Interim law for laity to drink from the chalice had any meaning: the only attention the imperial government had given it was Ferdinand's promise to ask the emperor to ask the pope for permission.

After the conference, Melanchthon fell into anxiety and irresolution, regretting the death of the hero who alone would have been able to deal with the situation. Still, he made a brief appearance as a resistance leader on November 10, during the ceremonies for the doctoral promotion of Königsberg Professor Melchior Isinder. On that occasion he repeated Ovid's advice to check evil at the outset – *principiis obsta*. He admonished the students to "remember that you are custodians of heavenly doctrine; consider diligently that God has commended to you a deposit through the prophets, apostles, and lastly also by Luther."

> Since Luther made known this same doctrine of Paul and committed it to us as a deposit to be guarded; let us not permit it to be perverted, and our minds seduced from it by superstitous counterfeits, or it be rejected by invocation of variety or by ambiguity of opinions ... hold on with both hands to the sacrosanct deposit of pure religion entrusted to us by Doctor Luther, and most faithfully preserve it.[3]

Flacius often quoted Melanchthon's judgment on that occasion that the Interim was an "an apple of contention." It troubled him that on that occasion Melanchthon departed from Luther by saying that the gospel produces repentance.[4] For Luther the gospel had no conditions; repentance was produced by the law. But he waited a decade before provoking a public controversy about the proper and the improper use of the term, gospel.[5]

The pamphlet Flacius prepared now to stir up resistance, *That in These Strong Winds, to Please the Devil and Antichrist, Nothing in the Churches of God Should be Changed*, was signed "Hermann," a name probably chosen to stir memories of the German hero, Hermann, and his victory against the Roman legion in the Teutoburg forest.[6]

> After the devil together with the false brothers and public persecutors of divine truth have noticed that the sign of the beast, that is, the blasphemous Interim, cannot penetrate openly in all Christian churches they consider how to attack the truth with cunning. They first suggest fasts or differentiation of food, to be observed on this day or on that. Again, a new manner for confirmation, feast days, bell-ringing and other useless follies, so that by our sanctioning them, the people gradually become accustomed to changes also in important matters. And with the deed, we bear witness that we are ready to accept the Interim and the papacy.[7]

The honor of Christ was at stake, Flacius insisted. Since a formal appeal had been made to an ecumenical council and such a council had been promised, a common statement should be prepared, by which university professors, clergymen and prominent laymen refused to negotiate. He warned against salami tactics – "they begin with changes from the smallest and afterward climb to the highest and every step they sing this song, 'what does this matter?' 'what does that matter?'" "Since the common people do not distinguish important from unimportant matters, any change at all would be perceived as yielding. One must drive out one wedge with another, small fears with the fear of Almighty God."[8] In the battle, the field is full of the fallen pious. The remnant of the troops must know that their

4 *Disputatio Theologica de poenitentia, respondente M. Melchior Isindero Suidnicensi.* Wittenberg: Johan Luft, 1548. Propositio 2.

5 *Bericht.* 1559 [C iv v – D iv r].

6 *Das man in diesen geschwinden leufften, dem Teuffel und Antichrist zugefallen, nichts in den Kirchen Gottes vorendern soll. Durch Joh. Hermannum.* [Magdeburg: Michael Lotter] 1548.

7 Ibid. A ij v.

8 *Ein Buch von ... Mitteldingen.* A ij v – f.

9 *Ein Buch von ... Mitteldingen.* G ij r.

10 *Gründliche Verlegung ... Issleb.* K r.

11 Its history is traced by Martin Schloemann. "The Special Case for Confession: Reflections on the Casus Confessionis (Dar Es Salaam 1977) in the Light of History and Systematic Theology." Eckehart Lorenz, ed. *The Debate on Status Confessionis. Studies in Christian Political Theology.* Geneva: Department of Studies. The Lutheran World Federation, 1983. 47–94.

12 H. von Hase. 61n.

13 Hans-Henning Pflanz. Review of Hans Christoph von Hase. *Die Gestalt der Kirche Luthers. Theologische Literaturzeitung* LXVI (1941). 33.

14 *Luther als Wegbereiter Hitlers? Zur Geschichte eines Vorurteils.* Gütersloh: Gütersloher Verlagshaus, 1993. 77 f.; English translation: *The Fabricated Luther: the Rise and Fall of the Shirer Myth.* St. Louis: Concordia, 1995. 95.

leaders are reliable and that they must be followed. "The teachers of the divine word stand as if before Mount Sinai. Behind them is God, who lightens and thunders with his Word and threat. Even if man demanded it, therefore, they cannot yield."[9] Jost Schalreuter of Zwickau understood precisely what Flacius meant: "if the devil and Antichrist command me to pray the Our Father," he said, "I would not do it."[10] Flacius called for across-the-board resistance whenever there was a *casus confessionis*, a "situation of confession."[11]

During the period of National Socialism, there were churchmen ready to resist the government the moment Nazi persecution of the church reached the stage of a *status confessionis*, that is to say, if they directly imperiled the church's defined doctrine. But that, argued Hans-Christoph von Hase, was not enough. It did not apply to matters not addressed by the Reformation confessions. For one thing, there was nothing in the confessions that applied to the Nazis' racial laws. As a graduate student in New York, he searched in the library at Union Seminary for a useful doctrine to use in the German *Kirchenkampf.* From the Quakers or Puritans, perhaps, he thought. Instead, he found a doctrine of resistance in his own Lutheran tradition, Flacius' teaching about the *casus confessionis.* He announced the Flacian doctrine to his fellow Germans at the last possible moment, in the last theological work the Nazis permitted the Göttingen firm of Vandenhoeck and Ruprecht to print, in 1940.

> The expression, *casus confessionis*, should not be confused with the later expression, *status confessionis.* The *casus confessionis* is an event, the struggle for the gospel, which comprehends everything – teaching and confession, the articles of faith and "adiaphora," and the involvement of life itself.[12]

Von Hase's appeal was lost on one contemporary reviewer, who preferred Melanchthon's teaching that the power of the state was superior to that of the church.

> In the discussion of the adiaphora for faith and the church, especially in Melanchthon flash thoughts of great breadth, which are today becoming significant, because they take into account the needs of the *Volk* and *Reich*, which are included in the formation of the external church.

> The church theoretician [Flacius], in matters that affect the church not only peripherally, could and would not recognize any other authority besides the church.[13]

Nevertheless, in those dark hours, Flacius' definition of the "situation of confession" may not have gone totally unheeded. Uwe Siemon-Netto argues that the last minute plea for an across-the-board resistance influenced Von Hase's cousin, Dietrich Bonhoeffer.[14]

Just before the conference at Altzelle, Professor George Major showed Flacius the copies of *In These Strong Winds* he planned to distribute there. Flacius gave him a manuscript copy of the expanded Latin edition, the text in which he required theologians to insist "Thus said the Lord!" In the Latin version, printed the following Spring, the famous slogan appeared by which the adiaphora controversy is remembered: "In the situation in which a confession is required or which causes scandal, nothing is an indifferent matter" – *Nihil est adiaphoron in casu confessionis et scandali.*

Flacius importuned his colleagues. "I fell at the feet of almost all the scholars," Flacius wrote, "and entreated them not to yield to the enemy." The University dean, Caspar Cruciger, saw the crisis as a clear choice between peace and truth. "I have spoken against it," he protested on his deathbed. But, Flacius noted, his opposition to the Interim was not mentioned at his funeral.[15] He persisted in pressing his case, he reports, with Eber and Major a hundred times and with Melanchthon a hundred times. "Herr Praeceptor," he remembered saying to Melanchthon, "the milder you are, the more stubborn the enemies become ... experience should have taught us how little philosophical mildness serves the church." "Whatever you give up is given up. But whatever you want from them, they have not said, 'yes'; and even if they say it, it will be the same as a 'no.'" "If you run they chase."

> Neither other pious persons, nor you yourself (as I have often understood from your words) doubt that those Achitophels represent traps for your mildness, kindness and simplicity of heart. Now I firmly believe that in your great wisdom and piety you will protect yourself against the plots of the crafty men. Alone that everything is happening secretly, that the rumors of the enemies about what is being yielded and the complaints of the pious are noised about, it seems to me best to satisfy the monstrous pains with which I am afflicted, and ask and lay on [your conscience] that you grant nothing to those godless ministers of Antichrist.

> For at this time in which a faithful witness of truth is required from us, nothing can be yielded and changed in the church from this school from which the truth has come, without provoking a monstrous scandal.[16]

He had ample occasion to plead with Melanchthon, since the Preceptor insisted on approving the lectures of the young members of the faculty in advance, including Flacius' lectures on the psalms.[17] The required "willingness" to obey Melanchthon was later used against Flacius. "... in Wittenberg he was not able by himself to give an explanation for one single psalm or one lecture," wrote Justus Menius. "Herr Philipp wrote it for him ..."[18] The editor of the second edition explained that "These short but most useful commentaries, rich with teaching of many kinds, were dictated some years ago to a certain most ungrateful disciple, his opponent."

As early as his 1534 *Consilium ad Gallos,* however, Melanchthon had been ready to make optional the invocation of the saints, to tolerate withholding the chalice from laymen and the obligation of clerical celibacy, and to approve the jurisdiction of the bishops, even the authority of the pope.[19]

Major had complained about the Interim, and had induced his colleague, Paul Eber, to write against it. He also encouraged Flacius' idea of writing to Prince George of Anhalt, the Bishop of Merseburg, who would be a leader at the conference, noting that many people, even his wife, were worried.[20] Now, however, back from the conference, the former

15 *Ein christliche vermanung zur Bestendigkeit, inn der Waren reinen Religion Jhesu Christi, unnd in der Augpurgischen Bekentnis. Geschrieben an die Meissnische Kirche, unnd andere, so das lauttere Evangelium Jhesu Christi erkant haben.* [Magdeburg: Michael Lotter], 1550. A iij v.

16 Ellinger. *Melanchthon.* 544.

17 *Argumenta Psalmorum Sexaginta, Distributis ordine versuum sentiis, dictata a Matthia Flacio Illyrico in Academia Wittebergensi.* Frankfurt: Petrus Brubach, 1550. In the introduction to the second edition is an observation, "These short but most useful commentaries, rich with teaching of many kinds, were dictated some years ago to a certain most ungrateful disciple, his opponent." *Psalterium Davidis integrum, in quo Psalmi 83 illustrati sunt argumentis et ennaratione P. Melanchthonis.* Wittenberg: Crato, 1561.

18 *Verantwortung Justi Menii Auff Matth. Flacij Illyrici gifftige und unwarhafftige Verleumbdung und Lesterung.* Wittenberg: [Georg Rhau's Erben], 1557. K iiij.

19 Stephan Skalweit. "Die 'Affaire des Placards' und ihr reformationsgeschichtlicher Hintergrund." Stephan Skalweit (ed.). *Gestalten und Probleme der frühen Neuzeit. Ausgewählte Aufsätze.* Berlin: Duncker & Humblot, 1987. 50 f.

20 *Antwort auff ... Beschuldigung ... Majors.* A ij.

21 Neudecker. *Geschichte Ratzebergers.* 220.

22 *Ex Actis Synodicis et Aliis diligenter et fideliter Collecta Expositio eorum, quae Theologi Academiae Wittebergensis et harum Regionum alij, qui his adiunctis fuerunt, in deliberationibus Provincialibus et alioquin extra has, de rebus ad Religionem pertinentibus.* Wittenberg: Georg Rhaus Erben, 1559. Mmm 3 r.

critic of the negotiations had become their defender. Major told his classes that the decisions at Altzelle had been necessary: no house could be ruled without order.

But Flacius lacked the necessary status. "For a long while in Wittenberg," Ratzeberger observed, "he had to suffer in poverty and was dependent on assistance. Among the other professors, therefore, he had no special prestige." More than that, he was not a native German.[21] "Like a drunkard," they explained, "Flacius, who has fallen asleep and dreams of fire, jumps into the street, cries fire, rings the storm bells, wakens the peaceful citizens from their sleep, but what he had seen was only the smoke from the chimney of a bakery."[22]

A CONFERENCE ON THE LITURGY

1 Eduard Beyer. *Das Cistercienser-Stift und Kloster Alt-Zelle in dem Bisthum Meissen.* Dresden: In Commission von F. G. Janssen, 1855. 495, 498.

2 *Wider den Evangelisten des heiligen Chorrocks, D. Geitz Maior.* Basel [Magdeburg: Michael Lotter], 1552. B ij r.

> We have always urged yielding and assisting toward unity, and the true church is always in servitude. – Melanchthon
>
> Christ determines the doctrine, the government the church order. – Melanchthon
>
> No conciliation can be made with the papists in ceremonies unless they agree in doctrine. – Flacius

The 12th-century Cistercian monastery at Altzelle, where eight monks were still in residence,[1] was the venue for the conference from November 16 to 22, 1548 to plan a new Saxon Church Order to fit the Augsburg Interim. Prince George of Anhalt was there. Bugenhagen and Major were there. Melanchthon was there, together with Johannes Forster, Leipzig Professor Joachim Camerarius, Superintendent Johannes Pfeffinger of Leipzig, Daniel Greser of Dresden, Hieronymus Weller of Freiburg and Anton Lauterbach of Pirna. When the Interim crisis was over, George Major and Johann Bugenhagen insisted they were not guilty. But Flacius reminded the world that at Altzelle they had abbetted the liturgical attack on the Reformation. They had been there. *They had been at Altzelle.*[2]

It was the Achilles' heel: a consensus had been reached on doctrinal, but not liturgical reforms. Furthermore, as Otto Ritschl observed, Elector Maurice's promise to his Estates to protect Lutheran doctrine did not extend to ceremonies. Decisions to make broad changes in the liturgy, therefore, were especially threatening. Emperor Charles V's priority for change was not doctrinal, but liturgical.

The emperor's grim recatholicizing campaign was not far from anyone's mind. Just back from Vienna, Melchior von Ossa reported that King Ferdinand was adamant that the Interim law be accepted completely. Meanwhile, the theologians were bluntly told that if there were no concessions Saxony would be laid waste by invasion. They were threatened that lack of cooperation would lead to the church's being denied the income from the monasteries.[3]

Court officials were determined now "to introduce everything not opposed to God's word and that can be done with a good conscience."[4] Their program meshed perfectly with Melanchthon's view that the liturgy, as an external matter, had no doctrinal significance, and his related view that "Christ determines the doctrine, the government the church order."[5] Beyond that, he was not adverse to enforced liturgical uniformity – a *similis forma rituum*. Smarting under the emperor's displeasure, moreover, he had personal reasons for compromising. It was always the church's fate, he argued, to tolerate a certain servitude.[6] "We have always urged yielding and assisting toward unity," he said, "and the true church is always in servitude."[7] Was not compromise preferable to the bitter fate of South Germany?

Two criteria for liturgical change were adopted: (1) that which ancient teachers had taught and (2) that which remained in use "by the other part."[8] Lutheran precedents for what they were doing they found in the rituals of Brandenburg[9] and Merseburg. And had not Luther himself permitted liturgical freedom? It seemed reassuring that "... the prince said to us in his own voice that he did not seek for change in doctrine or any necessary matters..."[10]

The final document of the conference, the "Celle Interim"[11] was signed by Prince George for Meissen, by Melanchthon, by Bugenhagen for the Electoral Circle, and by Melchior von Ossa and Christoph von Carlowitz. It accepted almost wholesale the *ordo romanus*: confirmation, the canonical hours, the Latin language, lights, vessels, chants, bells, vestments, images, festivals (including Corpus Christi), exorcism, fraction of the bread at communion. Extreme Unction was re-introduced cautiously, as a treatment of the sick "according to apostolic command" (Mark 6.13; James 5.14). Fasts were required, oddly enough, as a requirement of *secular* law. Although authority for excommunication and parish visitation was transferred to government consistories, the general government of the church was surrendered to the bishops and the pope, with the wistful provision that they would not persecute sound doctrine and the true worship of God. Pastors who did not conform would be dismissed from office. The next step, it was agreed, was to compile a richer liturgical order based on the elaborate *Heinrichsagenda* Luther had approved, the Albertine Saxon order of 1539,[12] an example of the "ancient and true catholic church."[13]

Significant were the rituals not accepted even under extreme pressure, even while other elements of the Roman order were accepted. There was to be absolutely no chrism in baptism. The eucharistic prayer was such a weighty matter, the theologians wrote, that it should be settled by an ecumenical council. "...in the canon there are still some very difficult and highly important disputations ... indeed, in a proper council, it will be the most important matter."[14]

3 Friedrich Hortleder. *Der Römischen Kayser- und Königlichen Maiestet Auch des heiligen Römischen Reichs geistlicher unnd weltlicher Stände ... Handlungen und Außschreiben ... von Rechtmässigkeit, Anfang, Fort- und endlichen Außgang deß Teutschen Kriegs, Keyser Carls deß Fünften wider die Schmalkaldische Bundsoberste, Chur- und Fürsten, Sachsen und Hessen ... und an den tag gegeben ...* Andere Aufl. II. Gotha, 1645. 930–933.

4 CR, VII, 208.

5 H. von Hase. 54.

6 Ibid. 314; CR, VII, 314, 315, 324.

7 CR, VII, 258.

8 Ibid. 216.

9 Gustav Kawerau. *Johann Agricola von Eisleben.* Berlin: Wilhelm Hertz, 1881. 280.

10 Ibid. 841.

11 MBW, 5359; CR, VII, 215–221.

12 *Kirchenordnunge zum Anfang für die Pfarrher in Herzog Heinrichs zu Sachsen v. g. H. Fürstentumb.* Wittenberg: Hans Lufft, 1539. *Agenda, Das ist Kyrchenordnung wie sich die Pfarrherrn und Seelsorger ... Hertzog Heinrichen zu Sachsen v. g. h. Fürstenthumb gestellet.* Leipzig, 1880. 483–498. Emil Sehling. *Die Evangelischen Kirchenordnungen des XVI. Jahrhundert I, Sachsen und Thüringen nebst angrenzenden Gebieten.* 1. Halbband. Leipzig; O. R. Reisland, 1902. 264–281.

13 Simon Issleib. *Aufsätze und Beiträge zu Kurfürst Moritz von Sachsen (1877–1907).* Leipzig: Zentralantiquariat, 1988. I. 535.

14 CR, VII, 214.

15 *Von der Einigkeit.* [A vi v – f.].

16 Berhard Coppel. "Philomela in Bologna and Wittenberg. Die Nachtigall als Topus, Epigrammstoff und Vogelmaske in der propagandistischen Reformationsdichtung." Richard Joseph Schoek (ed.). *Acta Conventus Neo-Latini Bononiensis. Proceedings of the Fourth International Congress of Neo-Latin Studies.* [Medieval and Renaissance Texts and Studies 37]. Binghamton and New York, 1985. 427 ff.

17 *Von der Einigkeit.* [A vii r].

When he read the decisions from Altzelle, Flacius wept. Driven by ambition, he wrote, the doctors of the church had failed.

> I know that if such a good, strong, courageous protest and warning had gone out from Wittenberg in a timely fashion, our people would have siezed a little Christian courage, that the Interim would not have seen the light.[15]

One wanted a reputation as grammarian, another as philosopher, a third as a scholastic personage. Even the nightingale, *philomela*[16] – he used the name admirers had concocted for Phi[lipp] Mel[anchthon] – had forgotten the first duty of a Christian, confession. It had been a hard, nasty winter, with no music. "Philomela had put the pipe in the sack," he wrote sadly, "and was afraid of the hawk."[17]

1 *Ein prophetische Buspredigt, für die jenigen, so den erkanten und bekanten Christum mit dem Antichrist und seinem hauffen verfolget haben oder noch verfolgen.* Magdeburg: Michael Lotter, 1547.

2 Beutel. 71.

The Elector of Brandenburg promoted a "third way" between Rome and Wittenberg. Lucas Cranach the Younger.

MELANCHTHON PROTESTS THE EUCHARISTIC PRAYER

> ... they also want to burden the church by the reception of the canon, or of other things, which cannot be received without impiety. – Melanchthon

> The whole papacy is in the canon. – Flacius

When the news arrived that the Smalcald League had been defeated and that Elector Johann Friedrich had been captured, the dean of Berlin, George Buchholzer, Reformer of the Neumark and Kurmark, delivered a sermon pleading for the prince, which Flacius promptly printed.[1] In the same city, Johann Agricola, chaplain to Elector Joachim II conducted a *Te Deum.* The Lutherans, he said, had been disobedient rebels.[2] The defeat of the Smalcaldic League, moreoever, was a judgment of God on for the injustice Agricola had suffered defending antinomianism against Luther in Wittenberg.[3]

His prince, Joachim II, was torn between an oath he had sworn before his father that he would be faithful to the Roman Church and his mother's entreaties to accept the Reformation. Accepting the Reformation, he decided, was not a break with Rome, but an opportunity to purify the catholic doctrine of his own land. He convinced himself that he could follow a third way. He would support not the church of Rome nor the church of Wittenberg, but the church of Brandenburg. For him, the Reformation could be reduced to three points: the doctrine of justification, the chalice for laity, and marriage of priests. An imperial law regulating religion, therefore, seemed to him a reasonable step. "The Interim," Flacius wrote, "comes primarily out of the Mark [Brandenburg]."[4]

Whom the populace blamed is suggested by a popular song directed against the prince and his chaplain.

Der Marggraf und der Grickel
Von Augsburg bringen her
Das Interim den grewel,
des leidigen teufels lehr;
derselb sol ihn auch geben,
was sie verdienet han,
müssen darzu auch werden
verspott von jedermann.
Kyrie eleison.[5]

From Augsburg,
The Margrave and the Grickel [Agricola]
bring the Interim, the abomination,
the teaching of the accursed devil;
Therefore they should be given
what they have earned,
they must also be ridiculed by all.
Kyrie eleison.

Joachim was given the popular name, "fat Interim."[6] When he ventured a journey to Wittenberg in January, 1549, Agricola was threatened by peasants with stones in their hands.[7]

Agricola was an ideal agent for carrying out the Elector's religious policy. Approved by the emperor, accordingly, he was named member of the committee to draw up the new Interim law. "Not only was I present at the writing of the Interim," he boasted, with no little exaggeration, "I was the leader."[8] Now the Interim law had a formidable defender in the Evangelical camp. "The Interim would be the best work for unity in the whole empire," Agricola wrote, "and for settling religion through all of Europe." "I can assure you that this Interim, as they call it, will conserve and cleanse the church and return it to its old purity..."[9] "I have made the emperor and the pope Lutheran."[10]

When he boasted that "I have made the emperor and pope Lutheran." Agricola was talking about the emperor who, after the 1521 Edict of Worms, was responsible for burning, hanging, or burying alive of 50,000 Protestants. Janne Lievensonne, a baker, for example, and his friend, Peter van den Broecke, were burned alive at the marketplace in Ghent. Receipts have survived for the ropes the emperor's agents used for torture, for gallows, nails, sacks, straw for kindling fires for burning obdurate men, and linen breeches for drowning unyielding women.[11]

To put Agricola in his place, Flacius published Charles' V notorious *Bloedplakaat*, the "Placard of Blood" of April 29, 1550,[12] that specified male Protestants would be deprived of both their possessions and their lives; women would be burned alive. He appended the Index of Forbidden Books for implementing the April 8, 1546, decision of the Council of Trent, to forbid reading the Bible. Dangerous business! Even printer Michael Lotter took care to obscure the place of publication with a strategic ink smudge. In the introduction, Flacius remembered the countess beheaded for not permitting begging by mendicant monks,[13] and reinforced

3 Walther von Loewenich. "Das Interim von 1548." *Von Augustin zu Luther*. Witten: Luther Verlag, 1959. 393.

4 *Wider das Interim*. C ij v.

5 Liliencron. *Volkslieder* IV. 465; Biundo. *Kaspar Aquila*. 87n.

6 Bezold. 810.

7 Pflug. *Correspondance* III. 119.

8 "Non solum adfui compositioni interim, sed etiam praefui." Quoted by Flacius in *Wider das Interim*. [Ciii r]. Beutel thinks that by "praefui" Agricola meant only that he was at the leading edge of the discussion. Op. cit. 86n.; Cf. CR, VII, 77.

9 Otto Waltz. "Epistolae Reformatorum." I. ZKG, II (1878). 175.

10 Jansen. "Pflug." 189; CR, VII, 77.

11 Jervis Wegg. *Antwerp 1477–1559*. London: Methuen & Co., 1916, 205 ff.

12 *Ordenung und Mandat Keiser Caroli V, vernewert im April anno 1550; zu aussrotten und zu vertilgen, die Secten und spaltung welche entstanden sind, widder unswern heiligen Christlichen glauben und wieder die ordenung unswer Mutter der heiligen Christlichen Kirche. Item ein Register der veworffenen und verbotten Büchern; auch von guten Büchern welche man inn den Schulen lesen mag. Item eine vermanung des Rectors der Universitet zu Löven. Item ein ander Keisers mandat von dem seligen handel im 40. jar ausgangen. Transferirt aus einem gedruckten Brabantischen Exemplar.* [Magdeburg: Michael Lotter, 1551].

13 *Ein kurtzer Bericht von Interim.* C iiij r.

14 *Forma inquisitionis hispanicae insti-tuta in inferiori Germania. Anno 1550.* Magdeburg: Michael Lotter, 1550.

15 Op. cit. 350 f.

16 Liliencron. *Volkslieder.* 145.

17 *Ein Schrifft des Achtbarn und Ehr-wirdigen Herren seliger gedechtnis. Doctoris Martini Lutheri, wider den Eisleben, kurtz vor seinem end ge-schrieben, vormals aber nie im Druck aussgangen.* Magdeburg: Christian Rödinger, 1549.

18 Nikolaus Müller. "Zur Geschichte des Interims." *Jahrbuch für Bran-denburgische Kirchengeschichte* V (1908). 51, 54.

19 Ibid. 97.

20 Christian Wilhelm Spieker. "Bei-träge zur Geschichte des Augsbur-ger Interims, Meistens aus dem königlichen geheimen Staats- und Kabinetts-Archiv zu Berlin." *Zeit-schrift für Historische Theologie* XXI (1851). 362.

21 Wartenburg. "Nachwirkung." 247.

22 N. Müller. *Geschichte.* 65.

23 Ibid. 75.

the report of persecution in the Netherlands with a report about how it was carried out, *Form of the Spanish Inquisition in nether Germany.*[14]

James William Richard criticizes Flacius for not criticizing Agricola sufficiently: "that Flacius was actuated chiefly by malice toward Melan-chthon is evidenced by the fact that he had but little to say against Agrico-la and the Elector of Brandenburg, who from the beginning abetted and promoted the Interim as its chief patrons."[15] But Richard was ill-informed. Agricola was criticized in many pamphlets that Flacius signed, and for many of which he was obviously responsible, even if his name did not appear. In one, Agricola was portrayed as donkey.[16] Another quoted Luther; "Eisleben is driven by the devil, who has completely captured him. After my death you will experience what kind of noise he raises."[17]

The emperor now asked Joachim to win Maurice of Saxony for the im-perial law.[18] Joachim explained to Maurice that he had to choose between the theologians and the emperor.[19] Maurice readiness to do it, understand-ably, was not entirely unrelated to his concern to have his son, Prince Frie-drich, named bishop of Havelberg.[20] The theologians were often not al-ways led by the Holy Spirit, Joachim wrote to Maurice; they could lead to sedition. "... through our scholars the poor people are being seduced in a deplorable and evil way and are being brought to insurrection."[21] The real cause of the Peasants' War, the first rebellion against divinely-instituted authority, was Luther. After the reading of the epistle at mass in Thomas Müntzer's revolutionary Altstadt, he recalled, a song had been sung incit-ing the peasants to kill the princes and burn their houses. The second re-bellion was the struggle against the emperor by princes and imperial cities in the Smalcaldic war. Now, in the murmuring of the theologians were seeds of a third rebellion. Knowing that his own theologians would follow the lead of the Saxon theologians, he advised Maurice to ignore them. He should recall how they had denounced him from the pulpit. If they could do what they wanted, the Elbe would not have enough water to drown the elector. He should remember the Peasants' Revolt.

> After Doctor Martin Luther in 1521 was, as they say, imprisoned, the game began, and they wanted to be too much like Luther. That was the beginning of iconoclasm. Soon, the Anabaptists and the Sacramentarians followed ... After that they wrote that one should kill the *Pfaffen* and monks and wade in their blood, and at Alstadt at the end of the epistle, they sang publicly that the princes should be killed and their houses burned ... they recommended that the nobility and all authorities should be exterminated and murdered ... the poor are now deplorably and evilly seduced by the learned and incited to sedition...[22]

The Interim law, in contrast, was a conservative force, a means to pre-serve political stability. Its ceremonies were provided for the sake of order and discipline. For Brandenburg he provided an elaborate liturgy since man was "not only spirit, but also flesh and blood." Criticism of the Interim was the same as mixing into business of the princes. "About the ceremonies and external usages, everyone is obligated to be obedient to his author-ity."[23] He proposed an eucharistic prayer without any invocation of saints.

It should be accepted, he argued, on the basis of tradition. "...many pious ancient Christians and martyrs, some of whom shed their blood for the sake of the Christian faith, made use of this hundreds of years ago and never charged that it was an outrage, as do these hair-splitting fellows."[24] If the old *Pfaffen* were allowed again among them, they would lose the whole religion. Therefore it would be better, and much more advisable ... to accept the Interim.[25] "Whoever does not accept the Interim," his chaplain, Agricola, echoed, "is not a Christian, because in two years all of Europe will come to the gospel; it will be effective in France, Poland, and the whole world." To influence Saxony, he sent ahead a formal Opinion on the law.[26]

Maurice agreed to a conference to plan for introducing the Interim into Saxony and Brandenburg. Their meeting would be a sham, Melanchthon warned; it was planned to restore the papistic mass and the papacy. In Flacius' presence he worried that Agricola would press for the eucharistic prayer/mass canon, something that could not be received without impiety.[27] On December 11th, he wrote that he suspected the Margrave had sent Maurice a copy of an edited eucharistic prayer.[28] "If Luther were alive now," Agricola wrote, "and only heard that the mass ... was only a commemorative and eucharistic sacrifice he would live ten years longer for joy..."[29] The night before the conference, Melanchthon dreamed that a neighbor came and asked him for a glazier, a request he interpreted as a demand to sing a papal mass.[30]

The difficulty was not simply the text of the prayer, as the Brandenburgers assumed, and as is still widely assumed. But, as Flacius understood, it involved something that can be called the hermeneutics of ritual: meaning is born not only by words, but also, independent of words, by rituals. Primary at the moment was the matter of ritual direction. Enclosing the Words of Institution in a prayer makes them part of the prayer. Luther recognized, however, that the initiative in the mass – Christ's testament – necessarily made the divine Word central. In his mass orders he freed Christ's words at the Last Supper, from their ritual framework, and thereby yielded the sacramental initiative to God.

Rather than (as with baptism) something that God does, the mass canon/eucharistic prayer *necessarily* transforms the liturgy into something the church does. Imbedding the Words of Institution in a framework of prayer, necessarily gives the initiative to the church. Since "power" to read the canon would be once again the prerogative of the clergy, the theory for medieval clericalism was lurking in the wings. The church, moreover, would be susceptible again to dubious doctrinal notions inseparable from ritual – according to the old rule, *lex orandi lex credendi* – and not only sacrifical ideas. In Flacius' view, therefore, the threat that the eucharistic prayer would be thrust on the church was a matter of staggering importance, and the kernel of the Interim crisis. "The whole papacy," he warned, "is in the canon."[31]

Just before the conference Flacius pleaded with Melanchthon not to accept the prayer. "To achieve conciliation with the papists in ceremonies

24 Ibid. 76.
25 Ibid. 69.
26 G. Kawerau. "Gutachten." 267–280.
27 CR, VII, 297.
28 Ibid. 234.
29 G. Kawerau. "Gutachten." 278.
30 *Eine Entschuldigung an einen Pfarher.* [Magdeburg: Christian Rödinger]. Biij v.
31 *Widder den Auszug.* B ij r.

32 Bindseil. 582.

33 "Prefatio in sylvam de Missa M. Fl. Illyr. Anno 1548 paulo ante Juterbacensia comitia Philippo oblatam." *Omnia Latina Scripta.* [J vj v – J vij v].

is not possible," he wrote, "unless they first agree with us in doctrine."[32] Thinking he might not have have been eloquent enough, he sent Melanchthon a memorandum and appended a collection (*silva*) of sources on the history of the liturgy.[33]

The meeting of the two Electors took place December 16 and 17 at the castle of Jüterbog, situated between Saxony and Brandenburg, Joachim had invited Elector Maurice, Prince George, the Bishop of Merseburg,

The 1548 Jüterbog conference.

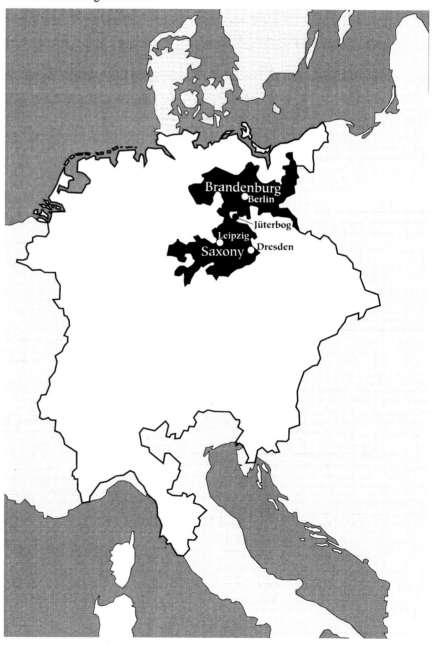

Bishop Pflug of Naumburg, Melanchthon, Johann Pfeffinger, Joachim Camerarius, and Daniel Greser. They began by agreeing that in the liturgy, tradition was the authority. "In the adiaphora everything should be maintained that the holy fathers have maintained." It was an idea, Flacius commented, which was enough in itself to bring back the papacy.[34] The text they began with was the statement from Altzelle.

Prince George, however, opposed the restoration of the eucharistic prayer/mass canon so ardently recommended by Agricola.

> If the papists are now on the proper path, it follows that they themselves either have to abolish or reform their canon. But if they want to allow it to remain unchanged, they prove that they have not changed its meaning, and you have not acted uprightly by vexing the congregation of God and assisting in the decline of right doctrine. If the canon was godless twenty years ago, as you wrote against it, it is no better new; it is and remains the canon and what tasted better than, now tastes like sugar and honey.[35]

The sermon that Prince George was talking then about was the one Agricola had preached at the Diet of Speyer in 1526. Flacius promptly published it.[36]

The two Electors conferred first with Bishop Pflug, and afterwards with Agricola, George of Anhalt, Melanchthon, Pfeffinger, Camerarius and Greser. They were asked whether the canon could be modified. Agricola maintained that the prayer could be used if were edited to removed offensive doctrinal statements.[37] There was a sharp exchange between the Elector and Prince George. Melanchthon read a paper on the subject, "Refutation and Explication of Recent Sophisms, by which the Blasphemies of Private Masses and the Canon are Depicted Idolatrously."[38] In the evangelical liturgical orders, he insisted, all essential parts of the mass were retained: consecration, distribution, reception, prayer for forgiveness, and thanksgiving.

The emperor was coming closer to his goal. An agreement, the Jüterbog decree, was signed on December 17, and Albertine Saxony and Brandenburg thus adopted the Interim law. Somehow, Flacius found a copy and published it.[39] After the conference, the Jüterbog agreement was made a concomitant text to the Augsburg Interim in Brandenburg.[40]

After the conference, Agricola spread a rumor that Saxony and Brandenburg had accepted both the Interim and the eucharistic prayer. In reality, it was the resistance by Melanchthon and George of Anhalt that had prevented its adoption.[41] "Although we could make no decision about the canon," reads the official report approved by the two electors, "we will continue to confer."

Melanchthon was convinced that by preventing the use of the eucharistic prayer he had saved the Reformation. "The controversies about the canon," Melanchthon wrote, "were of the highest importance to me, and I thank God, if I succeed in preventing that these impieties are forced on the pastors."[42] "The action at Leipzig makes no change in the church," he reported, "because the contention concerning the mass and the eucharistic prayer is postponed for further consideration."[43]

34 *Ein Brief der Prediger zu Hamburg an die Theologen zu Wittenbergk in welchem gehandelt wird von Mitteldingen zu dieser Zeit sehr nützlich zu lesen.* Magdeburg: Christian Rödinger, 1549. A iiij, C iij r.

35 Otto Vogt. *Dr. Johan Bugenhagens Briefwechsel.* Stettin: In Komission bei Leon Saunrers, 1888–1889. 548.

36 *Von der Messe und ihrem Canone Magistri Johannis Agricolae Eysleben Lehre und schrifft welche er auff dem Reichstag zu Speyer in der Epistel zu den Colossern gepredigt und folgend Anno. M.D. XXVII. zu Wittenbergk im Druck offentlich hat ausgehen lassen. Dem Interim so er ytzt hat helffen stellen gantz entgegen Daraus sein geyst zuvermercken.* Magdeburg: Christian Rödinger, [1549]. Cf. UN, 1707, 823–825.

37 CR, VII, 249 f.

38 Ibid. 234–247.

39 *Hertzogs Moritzen zu Sachsen und des Margrafen zu Brandenburg, beyder Churfürsten, Vereinigung des Interims halben.* n. p. [1549]. B iij v. 82; Cod. Guelf. 82 Helmst. f. 200–207; Reprinted in Hortleder. III, 3, cap. 86. CR, VII, 248 ff.

40 N. Müller. *Beiträge.* 120.

41 J. Hermann. 102.

42 CR, VII, 342.

43 Ibid. 292. Ranke comments: "although they had yielded to pressure, they still had not violated the evangelical doctrine in essence." Op. cit. V, 84.

1 *Ein Christliche Vermanung.* C ij v.
2 *Gründliche Verlegung ... Issleb.* D iij r.
3 J. Hermann. 137.
4 *Entschuldigung ... an die Universitet.* E iiij.
5 Op. cit. 67.
6 *Ein Buch von ... Mitteldingen.* P ij v – f.
7 H. Jacobs. II, 260.
8 CR, VII, 258.
9 J. Hermann. 64.

The holy people came forth like Moses from God's cloud and presented the Christian people with their lawbook and Gospel. – Flacius

Hardly was there one Interim, or hellish devil, disguised as an angel of light ... when lo, there is already another devil, disguised as an angel of light much more beautiful than the first ... that is a new Interim. – Flacius

Early in the morning of December 21, 1548, the Elector Maurice and his brother, Duke August, mounted their horses and proceeded from their lodgings on the marketplace to the Church of St. Thomas in Leipzig, followed on their mounts by the bishops Maltitz of Meissen and Pflug of Naumburg. So many meetings! Flacius reported the wonderment of some Jews at the Leipzig marketplace. Didn't they already know what their religion was?[1] One eminent Spaniard in Wittenberg asked him, "What do you think about these wanton people? Yesterday they threw out their old religion and accepted a new one. Today they accept another. And tomorrow, when they are forced to, they will accept still another."[2] The miners in Freiburg prayed that the Elector would not surrender the Reformation.[3]

The possibility raised in the public mind by the Leipzig negotiations, Flacius warned, that religious doctrine was negotiable, brought with it the threat of yawning atheism. People could be counted on to draw their own conclusion: "See, our great teachers are doing that and more. Without doubt, if the doctrine were true, they would have acted more steadfastly. I no longer know which teaching is right and which is wrong. Who knows? Maybe religion is only a human dream, the one as well as the other."[4] It was a sixteenth-century foretaste – so Hans-Christoph von Hase – of the subversive Ludwig Feuerbach of the nineteenth.[5] When the people see "that the great scholars do and act in a totally different way than they spoke and acted previously," Flacius cautioned, "they are upset, and begin to doubt all the teaching, they become disgusted and abandon the teaching entirely."[6]

The proceedings began at the Rathaus with an urgent appeal by the Elector, on the basis of the Jüterbog agreement, to give up as much of Lutheran doctrine and practice "as can happen with God and a good conscience." In his mind, the new statement on justification, together with the provisions for both kinds in the sacrament and priestly marriage, met all the Reformation requirements. "It is our judgment that obedience should be rendered to Roman Imperial Majesty, and such disposition should be shown that His Imperial Majesty and everyone may note that we are all inclined to quiet, peace and unity."[7] At the request of court officials the theologians, George of Anhalt, Melanchthon, Daniel Greser, Joachim Camerarius and Johannes Pfeffinger listed what they were willing to yield in order to avoid war. The church, it was explained, is in servitude all times, albeit only "an external fleshly servitude."[8] Someone thought up a slogan for the proceedings: "in necessary matters, fidelity; in the rest, yielding."[9]

That meant that operative authority at the Leipzig conference was not scripture, Flacius objected, but tradition. The emperor had instructed Elector Maurice to conduct his negotiations with the lay Estates and not with the theologians.[10] The laymen aquitted themselves well. Wiser than the scholars, Flacius wrote, they were more inclined to defend the Reformation; they were not overwhelmed by the reputation of the theologians or fooled by parliamentary tricks. Representatives of the cities protested against the reinstitution of the Corpus Christi festival and Extreme Unction, as well as against provisions about baptism, which gave no guarantee against the restoration of chrism. The power of the bishops, they said, was built on the power to bless the oil for confirmation. The knights were skeptical. "How does one come to the place that one has such bishops, under whose jurisdiction the pastors and preachers preach the pure, upright Christian doctrine without impairment, conduct spiritual ceremonies, and are protected therein?" The counts opposed the use of chrism in baptism, confirmation, and required ordinations by bishops. They demanded German hymns and collects.

Flacius complained that the conference was manipulated in a high-handed Spanish fashion. The maneuver of the parliamentary tricksters was to overcome the opposition of the superintendents meeting at the home of the superintendent of Leipzig.

> Then, when the deception and the noose had been made, they called the other Superintendents together without warning, so that through their tricks the rope could be brought over the horns, and they did not give them enough space to consider it.[11]

Since there was no protest, the next step was to convince the lay Estates. Their doubts were overcome by Melanchthon's prestige.

> One cannot say or think enough how greatly the theologians have sinned. First, in the work of many days and secret puffing together with the godless bishops [Pflug and Maltitz], they patched together some nets and deceptions. Then, without warning they suddenly suggested to the committee of the whole land ... and immediately pulled the rope around the neck, and beyond that, when they (the Estates) did not accept their godless suggestion, they pressed them intensely. In sum, there the shepherds became not dumb dogs ... but wolves.[12]

On December 24, 1548, an agreement was completed, and was signed for the evangelicals by Johann Forster, Caspar Cruciger, George Major, and Philipp Melanchthon. The final document[13] combined the doctrinal agreement from Pegau and the liturgical decisions of Altzelle. They had "mixed their slush," Flacius wrote, "with the two dishes cooked up by the theologians at Pegau and Celle."[14] "The holy people came forth like Moses from God's cloud and presented the Christian people with their lawbook and gospel."[15]

But what right did the *government* have to decide on church doctrine? What right did it have to interfere with internal church matters? "It is godless," Flacius objected, "that laws are made through which Christian freedom is destroyed and the church is brought again into a Babylonian prison."

10 *Der Theologen Bedencken.* [B iv v].
11 *Gründliche Verlegung ... Issleb.* [H iiij f.].
12 *Entschuldigung ... an die Universitet.* F iij r.
13 PKMS, IV, No. 212. MBW, 5387. TRE, 16. 235.
14 *Der Theologen Bedencken.* [B iiij r].
15 Ibid. C r.

16 *Widder die newe Reformation.* [B iv v].

17 *Der Theologen Bedencken.* [K iiij v].

18 *Gründliche Verlegung des ... Comments.* M iij v.

19 Baumgarten. 238.

20 CR, VIII, 840. On Melanchthon's responsibility for the text, see MBW, 5387.

21 Carl Schmidt. *Philipp Melanchthon. Leben und ausgewählte Schriften.* Elberfeld: R. L. Friderichs, 1861. 526; MBW, 5387.

22 Twesten. 70.

23 Sehling. I, 102.

24 Text in Albert Kirchhoff. "Die 'Famoss' Schrifften." *Archiv für Geschichte des deutschen Buchhandels.* N. F. V (1880). 116–159.

25 PKMS, IV, 289.

26 *Eine Schrifft ... widder ein Heidnisch Buch.* D r.

The agreement was not made in the presence of the superintendents, he pointed out, but written rather by the bishops, sometimes with two, three, or at most five of the Saxon theologians involved. The bishops, moreoever, announced that the decisions made in Leipzig would be interpreted according to the Augsburg Interim. To go into effect, they decreed, the two concessions to the Protestants – marriage of priests and both species in the sacrament – would require a papal indult. The fact that there was no pained outcry but only silence from the Wittenberg theologians meant that the bishops' interpretation had been accepted.[16] Together with the obligatory surplice, it was a requirement, Flacius commented, powerful enough to introduce the whole Augsburg Interim.[17]

It was holiday time and someone derided it in what appears to be a parody of a Christmas hymn.

> An Interim so shameful
> Is born to us today
> From shameful Adiaphorists
> To lead the poor astray
> Were the Interim not born to us
> Many poor souls would remain unlost.[18]

By having Melanchthon lead the proceedings, Maurice wanted to appear to defer to the higher insights of the theologians."[19] Melanchthon claimed that he had not signed the Leipzig articles, and announced that he was not satisfied with the document.[20] He could not, however, evade responsibility. For one thing, it reflected his own teaching.[21] And, "As the minutes show," Flacius wrote, "Philipp was presiding."[22]

The emperor's plans for enforcing the Interim were developing rather well in January, 1549, even in the lands that had been central to the Reformation, Hesse and Saxony. In an edict of March 5, Maurice enforced the Leipzig Interim's provision that no meat could be slaughtered or sold during Lent. It was necessary because of inflation, a shortage of meat – and the decision of the recent Landtag. It was not to be mistaken for Roman Catholic practice, he explained, but was purely a secular matter.[23] To eliminate opposition, Maurice, still wary of insurrection, issued a censorship edict on January 10, renewed on June 26, 1550.[24] When he left Saxony temporarily, he left instructions that if preachers taught suspiciously they should be dismissed, and asked especially that court preacher Johann Weiss, Leonhard Beyer of Zwickau and Wolfgang Pfendtner of Annaberg be monitored. If they criticized the Leipzig decisions the government should step in.[25]

Ethics, too, were under attack in the wake of the Leipzig decisions. On the basis of Luther's Postil for the Seventeenth Sunday after Trinity, it was being said that "love conquers all."[26] It followed, Flacius said, that outside the articles on which salvation depended, one should not resist the government. To avoid danger, one should be obedient. Nor is one obligated for the sake of God's other commandments to endanger wife and child. But such ideas, Flacius objected, would destroy the moral order. The thief would say that he, with his wife and child, was in danger of starving or dying in the cold, and therefore God would excuse him for stealing. The rapist could argue that he was overcome by love. Since God excused him, so should man, because love conquers all.[27] The agument, *proximus sum egemet mihi* – that I may do what serves me and is useful – is epicurean; it implies that one should obey man rather than God. But even in a situation of great emergency, one should hold God's commandment higher than the life of his wife, child and neighbor, and higher than his own.

Since the finaly document[28] from the Leipzig meeting never became law, Günther Wartenburg chooses careful terms for it: Recommendation for an evangelical Interim Order for Electoral Saxony or, simply, Leipzig Articles.[29] Contemporaries called it *Bedencken* (Opinion), then *Beschluß* (Decision).[30] Even those terms were not accurate, according to Flacius, because everything had been decided in advance;[31] evil was at work.

This time, censorship, which effectively silenced the Wittenbergers, worked in his favor. Making up their minds about the new religion law, Saxons had only one pamphlet to read, the work of a mysterious Carolus Azarias Gotsburgensis, *Against the Worthless Devil Who Has Disguised Himself Again as an Angel of Light, That is, Against the New Interim*. Friedrich Loofs agreed with Flacius; the theological content of the Leipzig document makes "Interim" an appropriate name.[32] It was a fulfillment, the mysterious Azarius continued, of II Corinthians 11.14: "Satan disguises himself as an angel of light." "Hardly was there one Interim, or hellish devil, disguised as an angel of light, when lo, there is already another devil, disguised as an angel of light much more beautiful than the first ... that is a new Interim."[33]

Another Interim! By linking the Leipzig decisions in the popular mind with the imperial law, Flacius (Azarius was his latest pseudonymn) had brought off his most spectacular propaganda coup. Heinz Scheible's sober demurer that "the insufficient differentiation between Augsburg and Leipzig Interim made for confusion to the present day"[34] is quite true. But the modifications approved by Melanchthon at Leipzig, as Otto Ritschl observed, could not have saved the Reformation.[35] Confusion was just the point.

The most successful propaganda is what is not recognized as such, and every historian who mentions a "Leipzig Interim" without a hint that the term was ever controversial gives evidence of Flacius' stunning victory. By identifying the provincial decisions from Leipzig with the imperial law from Augsburg, Azarius/Flacius unleashed popular resentment, deftly depriving Elector Maurice of his Middle Way – his Saxon Solution. "Another Interim! Try to explain the fine distinction to the people! Augsburg Interim – Leipzig Interim? Even Wittenberg tongues, would falter – the people hear only 'Interim.'"[36]

27 Ibid. A iij r.

28 PKMS, IV, No. 212.

29 "Philipp Melanchthon und die sächsische-albertinische Interimspolitik." *Lutherjahrbuch* LV (1988). 74. Cf. Hermann. 119–129, 132.

30 *Der Auszug des Beschlusses oder der vorleuffer des Leipsischen Interims. Aus einem gedruckten Exemplar gedruckt. Mit einer Vorrede M. Flacij Illyrici.* Magdeburg: Christian Rödinger, 1550. A ij r.

31 *Der Theologen Bedencken.* C ij v.

32 *Leitfaden zum Studium der Dogmengeschichte.* 4. Aufl. Halle: Max Niemeyer, 1906. 867.

33 *Wider den Schöden Teuffel, der sich jtzt abermals in einen Engel des liechtes verkleidet hat, das ist wider das newe Interim, Durch Carolum Azaiam Gotsburgensem.* [Magdeburg: Christian Rödinger], 1549. A iij v.

34 "Philipp Melanchthon (1497–1560)." TRE, 22, 382.

35 O. Ritschl. II, 328.

36 Baumgarten. 24.

1 *Von der Einigkeit.* [A iij v].
2 Ibid. B r.
3 *Etliche greiffliche ... warzeichen.* A iiij v.
4 Ibid. [V viij v]; *Omnia Scripta Latina.* M vj v.
5 *Von der Einigkeit.* B v.
6 On March 29th, Melanchthon wrote that Förster would be the Hebraist if Flacius did not return. CR, VII, 356.

Although people were saying that one should keep quiet to stay out of trouble, someone had to speak up against the church's weak leadership. – Flacius

[The] bright light of the non-authoritarian elements of the Reformation [could be found] in the cloudy and misty districts of the North, the Hanseatic City Reformation. – Heinz Schilling

When it occured to Flacius that he might lead the resistance, he hesitated. "The church leaders were" highly learned people with a great reputation and favor," he reflected, "but I was unlearned, unknown, despised and especially inept at writing German. More that, I was a foreigner, they were native, and I was alone, since I knew of no one who would take sides with me."[1]

> How could I, a poor, unskilled foreigner, lonesome man, have hoped that I could deal with the great people and not rather have been worried that I would rather be thrown out of Germany with rotten eggs? For I had the whole world against me, papist and evangelical, great and small, learned and unlearned.[2]

> I would have had to be less intelligent than a block or a stone to have begun such a great controversy with the adiaphorists from an evil desire for bickering and disunity, for great possessions or honor, rather than from hope of divine assistance in a just cause. For I had to take into account that they were highly educated, highly thought of and approved. I, on the other hand, was unlearned, unknown, despised and especially inept at writing German.[3]

He would also have to resign his professorship at the largest and most prominent German university, his ample salary of 100 Florins annually, the promise of promotion and his leisurely schedule of four lectures a week. Those who dared to write against the Interim law lived under the threat of the gallows. Speculation about the identity of Theodor Henetus and Christian Lauterwar was growing; remaining in Wittenberg was more dangerous.

Yet resistance was imperative. It was certainly not possible at Wittenberg, where everything was settled by two words: *autos epha* – "he himself [Philipp Melanchthon] has said it."[4] But Melanchthon, far different from the bold leader that Luther had been, was uncertain. "Everyone," Flacius remembered about the Spring of 1549, "was trembling, vacillating and seeking out where he could find grace and favor among the persecutors." "Although people were saying that one should keep quiet to stay out of trouble, someone had to speak up against the church's weak leadership."[5]

Difficult as it was, Flacius made the decision to leave Wittenberg. Entrusting his lectures to Johannes Aurifaber,[6] leaving his pregnant wife behind, and in time to avoid witnessing the liturgical changes announced for Easter, 1549, he headed north, to where the Reformation was still intact. Lübeck, Bremen, Lüneburg, Braunschweig, Hannover, Hildesheim, Göttingen and Einbeck were resisting the Interim law.

He stopped first at Magdeburg, a city stricken by the imperial ban, which meant, for example, that tradesmen's wagons could be attacked by anyone without fear of punishment. It was clear that sooner or later the city itself would be attacked. The suggestion that he resettle there reminded him of his frail constitution. If there were a siege, he would have to eat dried fish, meat and bacon, which he had difficulty tolerating.[7] His hosts laughed and said it would never happen.

In Braunschweig he visited the friends he had made when he taught there. From Lüneburg, we have the report that "the Superintendent and the other theologians ... consulted with him and were pleased with his attitude toward the Interim."[8] Perhaps his visit had some influence on their public protest.[9] In Hamburg he conferred with Westphal, Jacob Bordingus, and Conrad Gerlacus, and the Superintendent Johann Aepinus.[10]

Poking about the Hamburg harbor, he found a ship bound for London that would deliver a copy of his *De Vocabulo Fidei* to the Archbishop of Canterbury. The friendly attitude Melanchthon had shown toward him in the introduction of the book, meanwhile, had changed suddenly and irrevocably. Flacius' departure had been an intolerable show of independence, and for the rest of his life Melanchthon remained implacably hostile to the student he had once cherished. On the day Flacius left Wittenberg, Melanchthon, as a guest at a party hosted by printer Hans Lufft, complained to Johannes Aurifaber about the *Azarias* pamphlet *Wider den Schnöden Teufel*. The next day he asked him to write to Flacius, "so that he doesn't hasten to condemn me." The letter was duly sent, with a request "to spare the name and honor of our Praeceptor."[11]

Melanchthon pronounced him an *echidna illyrica* (Illyrian viper),[12] one incapable of dealing theological issues,[13] and a "runaway slave." That was a racial slur, since Latin does not distinguish "Slav" from "slave." Flacius had been "provided with many kindnesses by our academy and me. Truly we have nourished a serpent in our bosom. His forehead ought to be inscribed with the brand," he went on, "as the king of Macedonia once branded on a soldier, a 'thankless guest'!"[14] Melanchthon even imagined that Flacius was plotting to murder him.[15] From Meissen came Johann Pfeffinger's echo, with a pedantic twist. "Those who are not thankful to their preceptors are like the vipers that Pliny describes, who, because they do not want to remain in their mothers' body until they are fully born, so that they can come to the light, they begin to tear open their mothers' sides."[16]

Why did Flacius leave Wittenberg? Melanchthon never considered that it might be a matter of conscience. At first, he accepted his explanation that he did not want to witness the changes in the liturgy, but soon he wrote to Prince George of Anhalt that Flacus had left because he believed he could launch his attack against him better from another place.[17] "What was there that was not called on to explain it" one commentator asks, "envy, personal hate, inborn love of controversy? But the real root of his zeal is

7 *Von der Einigkeit.* B v.
8 Ritter. 31.
9 Radtke. 60n.
10 Ibid. E r.
11 Walter Friedenburg. "Ein Brief Aurifabers an Flacius (1549)." ARG, XX (1923). 65.
12 CR, VII, 532.
13 Ibid. 286.
14 Ibid. 450.
15 CR, VII, 481.
16 Johann Pfeffinger. *Grüntlicher und warhafftiger Bericht der vorigen und jetzigen für und nach dem Kriege ergangen Handlungen, von den Adiaphoris oder Mitteldinge.* Leipzig: Bapst, 1550.
17 Ibid. 356.

18 Anonymous. Review of Preger. *Zeitschrift für die gesamte Lutherische Theologie* II (1965). 327.

19 CR, VII, 449.

20 *Widder die newe Reformation.* A iij r – f.

21 Franz Dominicus Häberlin. *Neueste Teutsche Reichs-Geschichte* III. Halle: Gebauers Wittwe and Jacob Gebauer, 1776. 483. D. G. J. Planck. *Geschichte der Entstehung, der Veränderungen und der Bildung unseres protestantischen Lehrbegriffs* IV. Leipzig: Siegfried Lebrecht Crucius, 1796. 184; O. Ritschl. II, 325–327; Karl Mathes. *Philipp Melanchthon. Sein Leben und Wirken.* Altenburg: Julius Helbig, 1846. 307.

22 *Carmen de Natalibus, Parentibus, Vita, Moribus, Rebus gestis eiusdem Flacii Autore N. Bucholcero.* 1558. Clemen. KS, VI, 11.

23 Ellinger. *Melanchthon.* 455.

24 *Widder die newe Reformation.* A iij v.

25 *Refutatio vanissimi Adiaphoristarum Commenti de Logo Verbo.* Jena [Christian Rödinger der Ältere], 1558. A iiij v.

26 *Apologia ... Menii.* [B iij v].

27 *... an die Universitet.* A iij v – f.

passed over in silence, because in this way it was easier to deny the justification of the controversy that Flacius was carrying on."[18]

Melanchthon's ultimate explanation was that Flacius was disappointed at not being promoted. "I do not know the source of his hate," he said, "except that we did not give him Cruciger's place."[19] Melanchthon's friend and biographer, Joachim Camerarius, agreed: Flacius was motivated by ambition. From his pulpit, Pfeffinger announced that Flacius left Wittenberg because he did not get Cruciger's deanship.[20] The explanation has been passed down from one writer to another.[21] Noah Bucholzer made the charge in Latin verse.[22]

> Functus erat fato Cruciger, munusque vacabat
> Quod petere audebat nemo, licet omnibus esset
> Ingenii donis instructus et artibus amplis,
> Illyrico soli tantae fiducia laudis
> Atque animus talem fuit accepturus honorem ...
> At minus ista sibi postquam succedere sensit,
> Ingentes odii flammas concepit, et unum
> Tollere constituit vel deformare Philippum

> Cruciger suffered his fate, and his position was vacant.
> No one dared seek it, however well-equipped
> with all the gifts of talent and great skills.
> Only Illyricus had the confidence [to seek] such glory,
> and the pride to grasp such an honor ...
> But when he realized that those things were not going well for him,
> he began to feel vast flames of hate,
> and decided to destroy or disgrace one Philipp.

Flacius protested that he had never even applied for the position of dean, either at the university or with the prince. If he really had been maneuvering for the deanship he would not have been undiplomatic enough to compare the Wittenberg professors with St. Peter sinking under the waves. He had written against the adiaphora before Cruciger's death, and, according to the rule Melanchthon always emphasized,[23] the effect cannot precede the cause – *effectus non potest esse ante causam.*[24] Committing a capital crime and getting banned and condemned, he observed wryly, was not a smart thing for an ambitious man to do,[25] and hardly the best way to become famous: *Qui tollit aliqua media is non cogitat per ea crescere:* anyone who employs such methods surely is not planning to become great.[26]

Flacius explained that his motivation was concern for the cause of the gospel, a cause for which he had already forsaken family, friends and homeland.

> I truly do not know why, having left my fatherland, my patrimony and everyone most dear, with the opposition of the impious world, I set out for Germany for the sake of the Holy Scriptures, to completely unknown people, and why I spent eight years of study in Wittenberg where I heard many excellent disputations of Luther and others on the constancy necessary for standing up for the truth if I am not obliged to retain faithfully and confess and teach those things I learned there. As God is my witness, I am concerned with nothing more than that the pure religion of Christ remains unfalsified.[27]

On September, 1548, Aepinus had sent a formal statement to the imperial government that Hamburg opposed the cup. The city "could not commit a deadly sin by abandoning God's Word. The Emperor should let them remain with the Christian religion, according to Christ's institution."[28] In Aepinus Flacius had found a bold ally and advisor. Aepinus gave him the crucial advice: Flacius should settle in Magdeburg, a city still unconquered, where the presses were still free.

28 "Answers of Cities." August von Druffel. *Briefe und Acten zur Geschichte des sechszehnten Jahrhunderts mit besonderer Rücksicht auf Bayerns Fürstenhaus* III, 1546– 1552. Munich: M. Rieger, 1882. 109– 130.

THE SURPLICE, SYMBOL OF STATE DOMINATION OF THE CHURCH

The poor folk look mostly at the ceremonies because they fill the eyes. Flacius

Freedom of order is definitively limited by the confession. It is characteristic that the "folk-missionary" standpoint is asserted here by the Lutheran, Flacius: "The poor folk look mostly at the ceremonies, because they fill the eyes, whereas doctrine cannot be seen." – Dietrich Bonhoeffer

The adiaphorists say that it has to do only with a surplice ... but look ... at how wide the surplice is; it covers the whole Antichrist. – Flacius

1 Druffel, 1882. 131.
2 Pflug. *Correspondance* III. 63n.
3 H. von Hase. 33.
4 *Gründliche Verlegung ... Pfeffinger.* C ij r.
5 *Gründliche Verlegung ... Issleb.* C ij.
6 MBW, 5655. No. 19.
7 CR, VII, 342.

Charles V was very interested in what was going on in Evangelical churches. One result was that in the Fall of 1548 fewer German hymns were being sung in Saxony. The Emperor "was very pleased," Andreas Hügel reported, "with the churches of these lands, because they were provided with ceremonies, and was displeased with some churches in the empire, where few ceremonies were carried out."[1] On April 15, he issued an order requiring that the mass be used "in all its points, without explanation, gloss, or change." A compliance report was required in a month's time.[2] Pastors who refused to sing the mass were exiled.[3] Special intensity was devoted to the eucharistic prayer. "Philipp often said to me with clear words," Flacius recorded, "that they pressed hard about the canon."[4]

The Emperor found a weak spot. Since there had been little time to arrive at a consensus on ritual matters, the liturgy was an Achilles' heel. From Pirna, from Meissen, from Dresden, one heard reports that imperial pressure was working; the liturgy was changing. In Meissen, Flacius learned, some preachers were persecuted because they denounced the Interim in their sermons.[5]

Fearful and always accustomed to cooperating with governmental authority, Bugenhagen instructed his deacon not to criticize the emperor and not even to mention the Interim law in sermons. Melanchthon counseled a conscience-stricken candidate to submit to authority and accept ordination according to the Roman order;[6] he advised one pastor not to protest, but to assign objectionable ceremonies to his deacon.[7] When Major was

8   *Wider den Evangelisten.* [A iv v] – B r.

9   Neudecker. *Geschichte Ratzebergers.* 208 f.

10 *Gründliche Verlegung ... Pfeffinger.* G v.

11 *Widder die newe Reformation.* E iij r.

12 Alfred Chalybaeus *Die Durchführung des Leipziger Interims.* Chemnitz: Oehme, 1905. 35. CR, VII, 384 f.

13 *Auf die künstliche, Spöttische und Bitterhöhnische Oration, So D. Ziegler zu Leiptzig am Ostermontag widder die bestendigen Lutherischen recitiert hat 1549, beurische und einfältige antwort.* Magdeburg: Michael Lotter, 1549.

14 *Oratio de coniunctione et unitate Christianorum contra non necessarias separationes, et aemultationes perversas, recitata in templo collegii Paulini a Bernhardo Ziglero S. Theologiae doctrine, feriis secundis paschalibus.* Leipzig: Valentin Papa, 1549.

15 *Widder die newe Reformation.* D ij r.

16 Ibid. D v.

criticized for administering Extreme Unction, Melanchthon consoled him by saying that no one could satisfy the opinions of the Stoic critics.[8] Suspicion spread about the correctness of Melanchthon's view: that everything internal (doctrine) is the responsibility of the church, whereas everything external (liturgy) is the responsibility of the state.

There were reports of bribes. Daniel Gresser had been offered a thousand Gulden if he would practice Roman Catholic ceremonies in Dresden. Johann Pfeffinger, who was using salt and candles at baptisms,[9] practicing chrism and "every part that tastes like the papacy that had survived and was tolerated anywhere,"[10] and was rumored to have sung the mass in Latin,[11] was appointed dean of the cathedral at Meissen simply for being cooperative. The ceremonial at St. Nicholas' in Leipzig,[12] which drew the wrath of Amsdorf[13] was defended by Professor Bernhard Ziegler: Lutheran churches, he argued, should not differ unnecessarily in liturgical matters from Roman Catholic churches.[14]

Yet if one accepted the evangelical Nihil Rule, *extra usum nihil est sacramentum* – that outside the use, there is no sacrament – how could one march in a Corpus Christi procession, in which the altar bread ("host") had been separated from its normal use and carried about as an object of adoration? The foremost liturgical expert in the evangelical camp, Prince George of Anhalt, still Lutheran coadjutor bishop of Merseberg, dealt with the scandal by finding a way to celebrate the Feast of Corpus Christi with an edited ritual. How could one deal, however, with the *confiteor* prayer, addressed to Mary and the saints, and meant to be read aloud by the priest?

> I confess to Almighty God, to blessed Mary, ever virgin, to John the Baptist, to the holy apostle Paul, to all the saints ... I beseech the blessed Mary, ever virgin, blessed Michael the archangel, blessed John the Baptist, the holy apostles Peter and Paul, all the saints, and you, brethren, to pray to the Lord God for me.

Flacius demanded honest resistance. Priests, he wrote, should read a common confession, to which the congregation should answer amen.[15] Major, who cautiously recommended substituting a psalm, drew his scorn.[16] The faint-hearted, he charged, were being dishonest. They also were able to dissemble with the help of the mysterious Latin language. "One will murmur a psalm with his sacristan, the other perhaps a fable out of Aesop, the third something from *Til Eulenspiegel*, etc. Only the people and the emperor think that they have spoken the proper *Confiteor* and that therefore they keep peace with the godless."

Meanwhile, through the winter George of Anhalt had been toiling on that great experimental task assigned him at Altzelle, compiling a liturgical order, carefully evangelical but in the Roman tradition. As model, he recognized the ceremonies described by (Pseudo-) Dionysius. The similarity between the Lutheran mass orders and Dionysius' was a proof that those orders adhered to the tradition. "And this very form that we observe in the mass," Melanchthon reported in approval, "was done a thousand years ago, as Dionysius clearly witnesses."[17] According to his instructions,

Prince George had begun with the elaborate 1539 *Heinrichsagenda*,[18] approved by Luther himself, consulting, among others, the order of Cologne produced when that diocese was Lutheran. Although he had assistance from Camerarius, Pfeffinger, and Bugenhagen,[19] his work was promptly dubbed *Georgsagenda*.[20]

The order began with the formula, "accept the salt of God's wisdom; may it lead you to eternal life," and included the elevation, Latin hymns, confirmation, public penance, a liturgical calendar and the obligatory use of the surplice (*superpellicium*, "over the fur"), a variation of the alb (*vestis alba*, "white garment"),[21] cut very wide to allow shivering clerics in northern churches to draw it over warm clothes. Significantly for those interested in liturgical reform, he omitted the ceremony of "churching of women" after childbirth, candles at baptism, consecrated oil for confirmation (the sources of dissension at Jüterbog), and the eucharistic prayer.

Melanchthon provided an introduction,[22] and the clergy of Dresden, Leipzig and Wittenberg prounounced it tolerable.[23] On March 18, the manuscript was delivered to the court.[24] To approve the new work, which he hoped would placate the Emperor, Elector Maurice announced a conference for April 10 through 13 at Torgau. Summoned were the bishops, Estates and knights, and theologians – among others, Melanchthon, Pfeffinger, Gresser, and Camerarius.

At the conference, Bishop Pflug spoke out against the *Georgsagenda*, because it was not in agreement with the Augsburg Interim, and warned against publishing it without the approval of the emperor. At the same time, Maurice was listening to warnings by Christoph von Carlowitz that King Ferdinand was seriously pressing for the acceptance of the Interim and intolerant of alterations.

To stiffen the backs of the conferees, Flacius had given them copies of his pamphlet, *In These Strong Winds*. It was from this expanded, Latin edition that the statement comes remembered as the theme of the Adiaphora Controvery: *Nihil esse adiaphoron in casu confessionis et scandali*: In the situation of confession and incitement to sin, nothing is an adiaphoron.[25] In church on April 10, to open the conference with prayer, the conferees were forced to listen to Flacius' argument, delivered in the opening sermon by Gabriel Zwilling, once a monk in Luther's Black Cloister. Now in the presence of the very prince who had stolen land and title from Elector Johann Friedrich, the daring Zwilling prayed for the deprived and imprisoned prince, and, as if he were reading directly from the text of *In These Strong Winds*, he denounced the liturgical order, saying it would lead back to the papacy.

The Estates refused their approval. The order contained material not discussed at Leipzig, and three hundred pages, it was agreed, were too much to read at the conference, They requested a theological Opinion whether the new liturgy agreed with the Word of God.[26] Even before the war, the liturgical predelictions of Georg of Anhalt had aroused opposition,[27] and Zwilling's sermon had stirred up latent resentment.

17 Ibid. 366.

18 Aemilius Ludwig Richter (ed.). *Die Evangelischen Kirchenordnungen des Sechzehnten Jahrhunderts* I. Weimar, 1846. 207 ff.

19 Eike Wolgast. "Bugenhagen in den politischen Krisen seiner Zeit." Hans-Günter Leder (ed.). *Johannes Bugenhagen. Gestalt und Wirkung.* Berlin: Evangelische Verlagsanstalt, 1984. 111n.

20 *Agenda, wie es in des Churfürsten zu Sachsen Landen in den Kirchen gehalten wirdt.* Hrsg. v. Emil Friedberg. Halle: Verlag der Buchhandlung des Waisenhauses, 1869; Sehling. I, 91 ff.

21 Albert Chalybaeus investigated whether the Interim's pressure for wearing the garment resulted in its permanent use. "Sind 'Alba' und Krause durch das Leipziger Interim in Sachsen eingeführt worden?" *Beiträge zur Sächsischen Kirchengeschichte* XX (1906). 214–241.

22 MBW, 5473.

23 CR, VII, 362.

24 Emil Sehling. *Die Kirchengesetzgebung unter Moritz von Sachsen (1544–1545) und Georg III von Anhalt.* Leipzig: Deichert, 1899. 108

25 *Quod hoc tempore.* A vij v; H. von Hase. 77n. 16.

26 *Auff die Unterredung so (nach Ubergebung der Schrifften) die neue Kirchenordenung belangend zu Torgaw geschehen, Freitags nach Judica M.D. XLIX Durch Joannem N. Pfarrherr zu N.* Magdeburg: Christian Rödinger, 1549; CR, VII, 363–66.

27 J. Hermann. 3, 11.

28 PKMS, IV, No. 331.

29 Text in Kirchhoff, "Schriften." 157 f.

30 Salig. I, 631.

31 Otto Clemen. *Beiträge zur Reformationsgeschichte aus Büchern und Handschriften der Zwickauer Ratsschulbibliothek.* 2. Heft. Berlin: C. A. Schwetschke und Sohn, 1902. 42.

32 *Widder die newe Reformation.* E iij v.

33 Preger. I, 80.

34 *Ein Buch von ... Mitteldingen.* M ij r. *Entschuldigung ... an die Universitet.* [B iv v].

35 *Omnia Scripta Latina.* Z iij r.

36 PKMS, IV, No. 387.

37 CR, VII, 416.

38 MBW, 5565. Zwilling & Schultheis persisted in their resistance. MBW, 5570, 5574.

Zwilling's sermon was of the audacious kind that can be preached only once. The following day, April 11, he compounded his offense by submitting a formal complaint that prohibiting meat sales during Holy Week was blasphemous.[28] Already on January 10, 1549, Elector Maurice had issued a decree (renewed on June 24) forbidding satirical books, rhymes and pictures.[29] On April 24, the angry Elector dismissed him from office.

Michael Schultheis, his deacon and father of the celebrated composer, Michael Praetorius, was arrested as well. When Georg Mohr, Zwilling's successor at Torgau, demanded that he wear a surplice, he refused,[30] and on March 6 submitted a confession, that repeated Flacius' arguments from *In These Strong Winds*:

> Since because a confession of faith is required of us, no change should be made at this time. By approving or accepting the most inconsequential thing I would have to abandon Almighty God, to deny the Lord Christ, to pray to the devil and serve him, and also to deceive and mislead Your Electoral Grace and burden Your Grace with unnumbered sins and God's eternal and temporal wrath. That I should, will, and cannot do.[31]

Under cover of darkness, Zwilling and Schultheis were spirited to the Wittenberg Castle and imprisoned. The news provoked a protest by Flacius.

> The kind, faithful old man, Herr Gabriel, pastor at Torgau, was not only driven out of office, but also betrayed and, in sum, robbed of all his pay, so that ... he is now tormented with prison and hunger. Such inequality between the fortunate and unfortunate Lutheran preachers is astonishing to me, and I do not know how to deal with it. I ask, therefore, Herr Pfeffinger to explain the reason for such inequality.[32]

Flacius laid the blame on Pastor Mohr, at whose services the Burgomaster was now requiring attendance.[33] In Flacius' judgment, he was a wolf who had usurped the place of a shepherd.[34] "Mohr, with the help, or rather by the instigation of Balaams and Achitophels [court officials], drove out two truly pious and faithful preachers who refused to accept the newest changes."[35]

After being mistreated by the guards, Zwilling and Schultheiss were summoned to a hearing conducted by Melanchthon, Bugenhagen and George Forster on June 12.[36] The Wittenberg theologians denounced them as "fanatics" and "mentally unbalanced." Melanchthon, who seems never to have understood motivations for resistance, expressed his frustration to Georg of Anhalt:

> Gabriel and a deacon were sent here because they contend that it is idolatry and desertion of truth to put on a linen vestment ... I would rather go into exile than contend continually with such obstinate men.[37]

The Wittenbergers demanded written refutations, but Schultheis pointed out that as yet there was no formal order to introduce the Interim. Bugenhagen, Forster and Major reported to the Elector that their efforts had been useless.[38] The Wittenbergers described their treatment of the prisoners as "friendly, Christian, and earnest,"[39] a judgment shared by Heinz Scheible, who says they acted with consideration (*schonend*).[40] Flacius, on the other hand, considered the coercion atrocious. "We," he thundered, "have contended with the spiritual sword of the Word of God alone, but they with stones and the fist!"[41]

Schultheis was banned from the country and accepted a parish in ducal Saxony. Zwilling was allowed to stay in his Torgau house, but not allowed to function, except as chaplain to the Elector's wife and mother. The bitterness among the populace was so great that Zwilling's parishioners boycotted the church and thereby provoked a threat from the Burgomaster. In spite of an invitation for an audience with the Elector, talks with court officials, and a visit to the count of Barby, he did not yield.

For Maurice, preaching against the Interim was sedition. He turned high-ranking clergymen out of office and cited the dismissals to the emperor as evidence that he was accepting the Interim. The dismissals included Superintendent Jakob Klappe of Grossenhain, Wolfgang Pfendtner of Annaberg,[42] Leonhard Bayer of Zwickau, Wolfgang Fues of Chemnitz, and Cyriakus Spangenberg.[43] Flacius added the names of Christopher in Torgau and Christoph Zobel in Freiberg. On January, 10, Maurice demanded that Johannes Weiss, pastor in Zwickau, be dismissed.

For Flacius, accepting the Interim was to accept papal supremacy. To prove it, he published a letter by Archbishop Sebastian von Hausenstamm of Mainz to the city of Kassel which revealed the plan, in Flacius' terms, "to bring people back into Egyptian bondage." He dubbed it "a Rabsake letter," since it reminded him of the letter of the Assyrian general Rabsake (Rabshakeh) to King Hezekiah from II Kings 19, 10–13. The archbishop was carrying out the intent of an August 31, 1548, bull of Pope Paul III, *Benedictus Deus*, to the the bishops of Fano, Verona and Ferentino, *legati a latere* to Germany, about how to deal with the Interim. Again, Flacius was able to find a copy and to print it,[44] again suggesting details we will never learn – how he was constantly able to obtain such documents.

In a gloss, he observed that the Pope was ignoring the concessions made to the Protestants in the Interim law – marriage of priests, and both kinds in the sacrament. Von Heusenstamm ignored them as well, and demanded that married clergy be forced to abandon their wives and everyone who had received communion under both kinds be required to confess it to a priest. For the love of the Fatherland. "Ah," commented Flacius, "what love that is!"

In their answer, which he also published, the Hessian clergy insisted that they had not left the universal, old, true catholic and Christian church.[45] "You should answer the princes and publicly announce in the sermon," Flacius demanded, "...that you have been put in office by the Holy Spirit, and not through the bishops' hands, by the secular lords."[46] "It is not true," Flacius insisted, speaking for both of them, "that we condemn the surplice itself."[47] "I know very well that putting on a fool's cap is an indifferent matter."[48]

By permitting it in the Interim law, Bishop Pflug had deftly co-opted one symbol that the simplest peasant could understand, the chalice for laymen.

39 PKMS, IV, No. 387.
40 "Philipp Melanchthon." TRE, 22, 382.
41 *Von der Einigkeit.* B iiiij v.
42 PKMS, IV, No. 98.
43 Cyriakus Spangenberg. *Hennebergische Chronika, d. uralten Grafen zu Henneberg.* Meinigen: Griesbach, 1768. 1755. Quoted by J. Döllinger. II, 281; Ritschl. II, 346.
44 *Bulla Antichristi, de retrahendo populo Dei in ferream Aegiptiacae servitutis fornacem, Maguntini Rabsakes blasphemis literis consona. Ex qua facile animadverti potest, quid satan per utraque suam virtutem, scilicet, per patricidiale bellum contra Ecclesiam Dei susceptu, & per mendacia concilium, Interim, Adiaphora & Chorrock efficere conetur.* n. p. 1548. The German edition: *Bulla des Antichrists,* op. cit.
45 *Antwort der Predicanten in Hessen auff die Schrifft des Bischoffs von Meintz oder Rabsakesbrieff. De Abrogatione matrimonii der Prediger und von der Dispensation mit dem Bapst zu halten vom brauch des Sacraments sub utraque specie, welche ihnen von Fürstlichen Rethen zu Cassel für gelesen, den fünften tag Augusti diss XLIX. Jahrs.* Magdeburg: Michael Lotter [1549].
46 *Antwort auf den Brief etlicher Prediger in Meissen, von der frage, Ob sie lieber weichen den den Chorrock anziehen solen.* Magdeburg: Christian Rödinger, [1553]. [A iv v].
47 *Gründliche Verlegung ... Issleb.* H v.
48 *Widder den Auszug.* B r.

Der unschüldigen Adiaphoristen Chorrock/darüber sich die unrugige und Störrische Stoici mit ihnen zancken.

M. FL. ILL.

Flacius. *Der unschuldigen Adiaphoristen Chorrock, darüber sich die unrugige Störrische Stoici mit ihnen zancken.* Illustration by Pankratz Kempf.

---

49 *Ein Buch von ... Mitteldingen.* [Q iv r]. Dietrich Bonhoeffer. *Gesammelte Schriften* II. Ed. by Eberhard Bethge. Munich: Christian Kaiser, 1965. 271.

50 J. Hermann. 12. Wearing the surplice was not rigidly enforced in Meissen. Johannes Voigt. *Briefwechsel der berühmtsten Gelehrten des Zeitalters der Reformation mit Herzog Albrecht von Preussen.*

Now, Flacius and Gallus recognized that by demanding the use of the white surplice, the Elector had delivered to them an even more potent symbol. "The poor folk see mainly the ceremonies," said the people's missionary" (Dietrich Bonhoeffer's description of Flacius) "because they fill the eyes."[49]

A group of pastors in Meissen, facing the choice between wearing it and dismissal from office, wrote, asking whether they could conform. Vestments were not really an important matter, and the surplice had never been abandoned in Meissen.[50] The answer was a resounding "no." "Those who put on the *alba vestis*," Flacius insisted, "condemn and persecute

Luther's doctrine."[51] "...whoever puts on a surplice denies Christ's teaching."

He reinforced the defiance with a torrent of pamphlets. "Every week in Magdeburg new tracts flew..." one complaint read, about the broadsheet in which "The surplice was so depicted that when one lifted it a gang of monks and Pfaffen and the whole papal rabble could be seen. With the picture ... they wanted to give the impression that where the surplice was done again, there one had fallen from the pure doctrine of the gospel and had again accepted the whole papacy."[52] Another[53] was fitted out with a flap that (until lifted) hid the errors hidden under its skirt. "You can see

Kìnigsberg: Im Vertrage der Gebrüder Bornträger, 1841. 444. That the surplice had been retained after the introduction of the Reformation in Reutlingen is reported by Gustav Bossert. "Brenz und der Streit um den Chorrock." *Blätter für Württembergische Kirchengeschichte* XXX (1926). 114.
51 FS, 1723, 894.

52 *Endlicher Bericht und Erklerung der Theologen beider Universiteten, Leipzig und Wittemberg ... belangend die Lere.* Wittenberg: Hans Lufft, 1570. H iij v.

53 The drawing is attributed by Geisberg to Master BP, and the text to Flacius. It is the only known publication prepared in that way. Harry Oelke. *Die Konfessionsbildung des 16. Jahrhundert im Spiegel illustrierter Flugblätter.* Berlin, New York: de Gruyter, 1992. 309 f., 463.

54 *Ein rechter ... Rabsakesbrieff.* C iij r.

yourself, poor Christian," the broadsheet explains, "how wide the surplice is, namely that it covers the whole Antichrist."[54]

The white surplice had become a red flag – a flowing, flapping, persuasive, *unavoidable* symbol of the subjection of the church. It had to be resisted *because the government commanded it.*

DEFEAT OF THE INTERIM LITURGY

1 Salig. III, 612.
2 Wartenberg. "Nachwirkung." 245.
3 Ibid. 248 f.
4 Ernst-Otto Reichert. *Amsdorf und das Interim: Erstausgabe seiner Schriften zum Interim mit Kommentar und historischer Einleitung.* Diss., Halle/Saale, 1955. 129.
5 CR, VII, 389 f.; Emil Sehling. *Kirchengesetzgebung unter Moritz von Sachsen (1544–1549) und Georg III von Anhalt.* Leipzig: Deichert, 1899. 91–120.
6 H. von Hase. 33.
7 MBW, 5512.
8 Conrad von Orelli. "Johann Pfeffinger." RE3, 15, 253.
9 CR, VII, 457.
10 Ibid. 416.

[Liturgical change] will be the window through which the wolf will enter the evangelical fold. – Flacius

Slim and handsome at 29, the elector appeared at Grimma in boots and spurs to makes an appeal to a conference held from April 20 to May 1, 1549, to approve the Interim liturgy. At his conference now, Maurice faced clergymen who were bitter opponents of the Interim – Pfendtner of Annaberg, Klappe of Grossenhein, Fues of Chemnitz, and Wolf of Colditz. He had read Flacius' attacks, he said, and those of his associates. Such attacks would no longer be tolerated; his mandate of April 25 was directed against the "Münster spirits." The ghost of Thomas Müntzer was no imaginary threat. When the emperor pressed the eucharistic prayer on the counts of Mansfeld, they replied that accepting it would set off a revolt by the miners.[1] The clergy had stirred up resistance in Döberln, Mühlberg and Oschatz.[2] Behind them was an angry populace. Peasants were preparing another uprising.[3]

Christoph von Carlowitz cautioned the elector that King Ferdinand was pressing the Interim and warning about any deviations.[4] The Grimma meeting did end with the Interim liturgical order,[5] a decision clearly understood as bowing to the prince's pressure.[6] For "important reasons," Maurice announced, it would not be published[7]; it was introduced largely *pro forma.* Seven years afterward in 1555, when Pfeffinger recommended to Elector August that it be re-introduced in the interest of liturgical uniformity, Melanchthon cautioned that doing so would lead only to disunity.[8]

Melanchthon's advice now was to publish a brief exerpt from the Leipzig papers (the "Leipzig Interim"). If the liturgy were changed, the popular cry would go up that "the gospel has been changed."[9] Public opinion had to be taken into account. "... so great is the stubbornness in some that if the mandate were published there will be more disorder. I hope that the court does not hurry in publishing these mandates."[10] "...if it is decided that something must be changed now, it is my humble opinion and humble plea, that our most gracious Lord will not permit extensive publications about it, because there would certainly be opposition writing, and even if the same abusive writings are groundless, the great masses have an appetite for it, and with it comes contempt for religion, authority, and of any moral people; but His Electoral Grace should issue short edicts, like the law on selling meat. Such brief commands give less excuse for new disputes."[11]

A limited run of the *Excerpt from the Decision of the Recent Leipzig Landtag of Christmas, 1549* was printed at Dresden in early August.[12] Reassuringly, the elector explained that he was not restoring old abuses. Besides an obligatory fast on Friday, passed off as a secular law – Melanchthon's suggestion – it required only a few things: psalm singing, elevation of the host, the feast of Corpus Christi, and the surplice.

Maurice had appealed to church leaders "that through your writings you should warn all pastors and preachers in our lands, and admonish them henceforth to cease such speaking and preaching, and to excuse us in the sight of the common man..."[13] But taking no chances, he backed his *Excerpt* with an order of July 4 (renewed August 2), putting the the clergy under police supervision.[14] Once again, Flacius charged, the secular authorities had violated the church by making religious decisions in secret. "This game is not new in the world, but it has often happened that some lords and learned men have put their heads together (as has happened now at Augsburg, Celle, Pegau, Jüterbog, Leipzig, Grimma, Torgau, Dresden etc.) and fashioned the divine doctrine according to their convenience."

Police supervision of the church made for a poisonous atmosphere. Complaining was a punishable offence. "Adiaphorists" tended to take sides with the court. Flacius accused George Mohr of Torgau of recruiting informers.

> Again and again they incite secret betrayers, as Mohr has done in Torgau, who observe gestures, sighs and complaints of everyone who cannot praise the new falsifications. That sighing and weeping is forbidden to Christians, is like what happened long ago through such informers under the tyrants, Nero, Domitian and other godless emperors...
>
> If afterwards, such desperate traitors, pretend ... that they did it only because they were paid for their treason, or are otherwise dissatisfied, my adiaphorists are soon there and arrange to have them thrown into the tower by their Spanish and Hussar lords, Burgomasters, judges, mayors and other slaves of the devil where they are judged and martyred.[15]

To muffle controversy, the *Excerpt* was distributed very slowly. It arrived at Wittenberg and Leipzig only in late September. It arrived on October 3 in Meissen, where the Elector exerted great pressure for its adoption.[16] In many places it did not appear at all.[17]

Flacius struck again. Once more he published a secret state document, illegally: *The Excerpt from the Decisions or the Forerunner of the Leipzig Interim. Published from a Printed Copy.*[18] He followed it up with his own harsh evaluation: *Against the Excerpt from the Leipzig Interim or the Little*

11 Emil Friedberg. *Agenda, wie es in des Churfürsten zu Sachsen Landen in den Kirchen gehalten wirdt.* Halle: Verlag der Buchhandlung des Waisenhauses, 1869. 6.

12 *Auszug aus dem Beschlüss jüngst gehaltenen Landtags zu Leipzigk in Weynachten des neunundviertzigsten Jahrs.* Dresden, July 4th, 1549. Cod. Guelf. 82 Helmstedt fol. 196r–197v and Cod. Guelf. Aug. 12.9 2° fol. 439r–440v; Chalybaeus. *Durchführung.* 73–76; CR, VII, 426–428.

13 Ibid. 67.

14 Einführungsmandat. 82 Helmst. Bl. 395. Printed in *Der Theologen Bedencken.* M ij v – M iiij r; Chalybaeus. "Durchführung." 77–78.

15 *Widder die newe Reformation.* E iiij v f.

16 Chalybaeus. *Durchführung.* 20.

17 Ibid. 10.

18 *Der Auszug des beschlusses oder der vorleufer des Leipsischen Interims. aus einem gedruckten Exemplar gedruckt.* Magdeburg: Christian Rödinger, 1550.

19 *Widder den Auszug.* Op. cit.

20 *Des Ehrwirdigen und tewren Mans Doct. Marti. Luthers seliger gedechtnis meinung, von den Mitteldingen, durch M. Joachimum Westphalum Pfarrhern zu Hamburg zusammen gelesen. Eine gemeine Regel von allen Caeremonien M. F. Ill.* Magdeburg: Michael Lotter, 1550.

21 *Auf die Künstliche ... Oration.* C j v.

22 Bieck. 151.

23 Karl Binke. "Zu Johann Walters Stellung als Hofkappelmeister in Dresden." *Jahrbuch für Liturgie und Hymnologie* V (1960). 235–43.

24 Ellinger. *Melanchthon.* 542.

25 Sehlung. *Kirchengesetzgebung.* 114.

26 *Bulla Antichristi.* A iij r.

27 Pflug. *Correspondance* III. 60 n. Friedberg. *Agenda.* 6.

28 J. Hermann. 154.

29 Sehling. I, 102.

30 F. Westphal. *Zur Erinnerung an Fürst Georg den Gottseligen zu Anhalt.* Leipzig: Im Kommissions Verlag von Rudolph Haupt, 1907. 69.

31 *Durchführung.* 8; Emil Friedberg. *Agenda, wie es in des Churfürsten zu Sachsen Landen gehalten wirdt.* 1869. *Zeitschrift für Historische Theologie* XL (1871). 36 f.; Voigt, *Bugenhagens Briefwechsel.* 450; Martin Stupperich. *Osiander in Preussen, 1549 Ë 1552.* Berlin and New York: Walter de Gruyter, 1973. 97.

32 Friedberg. *Agenda.* Druffel. I, 141 ff. raised the question whether the order published by Friedberg was exactly the same as the order read at Grimma.

Interim.[19] Luther's hymns should not be considered suspect. There was no mention of faith in the discussion of the sacrament. The unction described in Acts 19 was not the basis for a sacrament called "extreme unction," but like the narrative of apostolic healing with handkerchiefs, it was one of the apostolic miracles. For good measure, he published Joachim Westphal's collection of Luther's statements on the adiaphora.[20]

It was proper, Amsdorf commented, to sing, whistle, and play the organ as long as you like, but not if the ritual brought with it doctrinal aberrations. "Is anyone made better, pious, sober and moderate," he asked, "by eating fish on Friday?"[21] He called the new liturgy the "the Koran of Antiochus." Antiochus was the Hellenistic king who sacrificed a pig in the Jerusalem temple and set off the Maccabean revolt, and Antiochus was Maurice. When the *Georgsagenda* was read aloud to a group of church officials in Leipzig, Superintendent Pfentner denounced it as "fool's work" – how else should one judge introduction of the epiclesis of baptismal water, consecration of salt, processions? Superintendent Daniel Gresser of Dresden wept. Superintendent Ziegler of Cottbus declared he would rather be decapitated than confuse people with such material.[22] In Dresden, Johann Walther, court composer and *Kapellmeister*, wrote to Flacius and Amsdorf that he had advised his wife, his child, and the boys' choir not to take communion at services held according to the new liturgy.[23]

Understanding and influencing public opinion was not Melanchthon's strong point.[24] Flacius, on other other hand, had long since mastered the art of propaganda. Once again, he organized an elaborate campaign, this time against the the liturgical order he called "the Great Pontificale."[25] "The devil is especially interested in the liturgy," Flacius announced. "When he has it, he has everything." "Liturgical changes will be the window through which the wolf will enter the evangelical fold."[26] We know from Melanchthon that Flacius' campaign was carried on in Magdeburg, Erfurt, Halle, Saxony, Prussia and Denmark.[27] Once again, as he had during the siege of Magdeburg, he forced the Elector to react. In June, 1549, Maurice felt constrained to make a journey to persuade King Ferdinand to lessen the diplomatic pressure.[28]

According to a contemporary report, Flacius' campaign against the liturgical order was "unbelievable."[29] One souvenir is a coin showing the head of Georg von Anhalt, with the inscription: "I hate those concilators more than the open enemies of religion."[30] Although Chalybaeus considered Melanchthon responsible for the successful opposition,[31] Bugenhagen and Major gave the credit to Flacius. After his assault, the four hundred-page ritual of Prince George was banished to the Saxon archives.[32]

Let them be consoled by this assurance, that fundamental principles are faithfully retained in our churches, namely, the uncorrupted ministry of the gospel, all the articles of faith, and the use of Christian sacraments without alteration. – Melanchthon

What they are boasting about, that "we have changed nothing yet," they do not have because of their steadfastness or free confession, but rather because of the pains, danger and distress of those who have opposed the present deceptions. So they need not boast so much, "we have changed nothing yet, we have changed nothing yet." Yes, dear fellows, you would have changed all too much, if you had not been hindered by others. – Flacius

While Flacius sounded the alarm against the Interim law, Melanchthon offered soothing words: nothing had been changed.

> The same doctrine that appears in our books is taught in all respects. There is the same use of the sacraments that there was before the war ... But Flacius Illyricus exclaims that the doctrine is changed, and that certain ceremonies formerly abolished have been restored ... The voice of all the teachers in our churches and schools openly refutes this calumny ... I refer to the whole body of doctrine written in the *Loci Communes*.
>
> ...I have written this brief reply to the clamors of Flacius not so much on my own account as for the sake of our churches in general, among whom many pious minds are deeply wounded by his writings. Let them be consoled by this assurance, that fundamental principles are faithfully retained in our churches, namely, the uncorrupted ministry of the Gospel, all the articles of faith, and the use of Christian sacraments without alteration.[1]

There were soothing words from Bugenhagen as well.[2] Indeed, it was he who had attempted to introduce the *Excerpt* in Wittenberg, but his plan was hindered by the insubordination of his assistant, Albert Christian. "...it was prevented and scattered, thank God," Flacius commented, "and not thanks to them."[3] For a Merseburg synod, George of Anhalt also had soothing words[4]: nothing had been changed.

But the public was deliberately being kept in the dark. The *Excerpt* revealed only part of the planned religious changes: the secret Leipzig decisions were much more extensive. The Wittenbergers were crying, peace, peace, Flacius wrote, when there was no peace.[5]

How could he make clear what was in store for Saxony if the Interim was put into use? Defying the censor once more, Flacius published the records of the Leipzig conference, his most daring exposé. When Melanchthon raised the cry that he had falsified the text,[6] Flacius replied that he had carefully compared several copies – one borrowed from a nobleman (unnamed), one from the Burgomaster of Zwickau, another from a Leipzig delegate, Winsheim, and one with Melanchthon's own penned-in corrections.[7]

Was his outcry frivolous? Now that the deliberations were for all the world to read,[8] the Saxons could decide for themselves. About to happen

1 *Epistola Phi. Me. ad lectorem in qua respondetur Flacio Illyrico*. Wittenberg: Josef Klug, 1549. A ij v.
2 To the king of Denmark. Andreas Schumacher. *Gelehrter Männer Briefe an die Könige in Dännemark von Jahr 1522 bis 1633* I. Copenhagen & Leipzig: L. H. Lille, 1758. 125.
3 *Auff den Ausschreiben der Zwei Universitäten*. Op. cit.
4 Albert Fraustadt. *Die Einführung der Reform im Hochstift Merseburg*. Leipzig: Friedlein & Hirsch, 1843. 208.
5 *Widder die newe Reformation*. B ij v.
6 CR, VIII, 840.
7 Bindseil. 580.
8 *Der Theologen Bedencken*. English translation in Henry E. Jacobs (ed.). *The Book of Concord*. Vol. II: *Historical Introduction to the Book of Concord*. Philadelphia: G. W. Frederick, 1883. 260–272. CR, VII, 259–264.

9 Jacobs. II, 262.

10 *Der Theologen Bedencken.* E ij r.

11 Jacobs. II, 267.

12 Ibid. II, 269.

13 *Eine Schrifft widder ein Heidnisch ... Buch.* C ij r.

14 *Widder die newe Reformation.* [C iiiij v].

15 *Gründliche Verlegung ... Pfeffinger.* F ij v; Bjarne Hareide. *Die Konfirmation in der Reformationszeit. Eine Untersuchung der lutherischen Konfirmation in Deutschland 1520–1584.* Göttingen: Vandenhoeck und Ruprecht, 1971. 264–273.

was a religious reversion, beginning with the Thomistic doctrine of justification signaled by Bishop Pflug's terms, "dead log" or "block."

> Although God does not justify men by the merit of the works which they perform, but out of grace, freely and without our merit, and the praise is not ours, but Christ's through whose merit alone we are justified from our sins; nevertheless, God does not deal with men as with a block, but draws them in such a way that, if they have arrived at the age of discretion, their will cooperates with his.[9]

"Here lies buried the papist *meritum de congruo*," Flacius commented, "and a small piece of free will."[10]

To Melanchthon he wrote, "...you maintain that the teaching has been preserved pure and integral in the whole adiaphoristic action. I ask you through Christ, that you reflect on those things a little higher, and repeat the whole action in your mind, and not persist in this assertion against your conscience and manifest evidence. For we can clearly prove the opposite. For nowhere in the Leipzig formula can *sola fides* be found, but, rather, the contrary: good works are necessary to salvation." The document had more to say about virtue. "Therefore it is certainly true that these virtues, faith, love, and hope and others must be in us and are necessary for salvation."[11] From Hamburg came the comment that men would be led to believe "that acceptance of faith in Christ, the proffered grace and salvation, stands in the free will of man, which he can accept or not when he comes to good reason or understanding."

Flacius pointed out treacherous ambiguities in the official text. "Ancient ceremonies" at baptism could mean consecrated salt and chrism. Ceremonies "dependent" on confession, could mean satisfaction. "Singing" at funerals could mean votive masses. "Consecration" in the mass could mean the canon. In the discussion of the mass, moreover, the medieval term, "fruits of the mass" was used instead of any mention of the faith of the believer.

The article on confirmation specified that children "be confirmed and established by the laying-on-of-hands and Christian prayer and ceremonies."[12] "How is that different," Flacius asked, "from the notion that the sacrament brings God's grace with it?"[13] Why does their Leipzig Interim bring God's grace to confirmation, and why must it be performed by a bishop?[14] Confirmation was not mandated by Christ and was therefore not a means of grace. It was "episcopal monkey-play," a piece of "anti-Christianity."

Since confirmation was not a means of grace, the emphasis, Flacius decided, should rather be on instruction. Why could it not be conducted as an examination by a pastor or chaplain, as, indeed, was practiced in many places? Flacius suggested a rite consisting of examination, confession of faith, and prayer. It could even be repeated annually.[15] His ideas were reflected in a sixteenth-century verse.

> Firmung ist ein guter alter brauch,
> wens nicht thut ein beschorner hauff
> mit crutz drücken und schmiren,

> Sonder die jugent wird verhort
> fur den gmein an pillichen ort,
> das sie im glauben nicht irren.[16]

> Confirmation is a good ancient practice,
> if it is not done by a shorn chief
> with imprinted cross and daubed oil,
> But rather the youth are examined
> before the congregation in a suitable place,
> that they do not err in faith.

Where confirmation did not disappear entirely in evangelical territories, as in Hesse, Flacius' model was followed.[17] If the church were to conduct the Leipzig ceremonies, simple folk would not be able to distinguish between Catholic and Evangelical confirmation. Why should it be made as similar as possible to the Catholic rite? Conformity would demonstrate weakness and the lack of the will to follow a clear principle.

> Flacius' critique convinced a group within the Lutheran Reformation to reject confirmation without considering whether it should be replaced by another rite. Flacius' critique of confirmation was based on his conviction that it belongs essentially to the adiaphora ... In many places, confirmation disappeared completely under Flacius' influence, since it was thought that no justification could be found for such an act. It happened so in several provincial churches in Germany and also in the evangelical churches of the Nordic countries.[18]

At Leipzig, the sacrament of Extreme Unction, with modifications, had been approved:

> Although in this country the unction has not been in use for many years ... such unction ... according to the apostle, may be hereafter practiced, and Christian prayer and words of consolation from the Holy Scriptures be spoken over the sick...[19]

But what did it really mean to practice unction as the apostles did? They used the oil to work miracles, a charism the contemporary church did not routinely have. "For it is impossible to do it now according to apostolic usage; the dear apostles healed the sick with their shadows (Acts 5), with oil (Mark 6, James 5), with their handkerchiefs and aprons (Acts 19) and by other means."[20]

> I admit that he [Luther] said he would permit unction if it were done according to the Gospel, Mark 6 and James 5. That is true ... but because the Adiaphorists do not have such gifts, the quotation from Luther is not relevant unless they prove beforehand that they have such gifts."[21]

The basis of a sacrament, Flacius insisted, was not imitating something the apostles did. "According to apostolic usage" was the same as "according to papal usage."

The Leipzig articles would transfer the churches back to papal authority."...all ministers should be subject and obedient to the chief and other bishops..."[22] The chief bishop? Who was that? Not someone in Wittenberg, Calcutta or Never-Never-land (*Schlaraffenland*), Flacius explained, in case anyone wondered. The chief bishop was the one sitting in Rome.[23] It helped just as little to avoid the word, "pope," as to hope that the bishops

16 Liliencron. "Dichtung." 158.
17 Paul Graff. *Geschichte der Auflösung der alten gottesdienstlichen Formen in der evanglischen Kirche Deutschlands* I. Göttingen: Vandenhoeck & Ruprecht, 1937. 317.
18 Carl-Gustaf Andrén. "Die Konfirmationsfrage in der Reformationszeit." *Zur Geschichte und Ordnung der Konfirmation in den Lutherischen Kirchen. Aus den Verhandlungen des Internationalen Seminars des lutherischen Weltbundes in Loccum 1961 über Fragen der Konfirmation.* Ed. Kurt Frör. Munich: Claudius, 1962. 53.
19 Jacobs. II, 269.
20 *Wider den Auszug.* [A iiij r].
21 *Gründliche Verlegung ... Pfeffinger.* G v.
22 CR, VII, 260; *Der Theologen Bedencken.* Gij v; Jacobs. II, 268.
23 *Gründliche Verlegung ... Issleb.* M r.
24 *Eine Schrift widder ein Heidnisch ... Buch.* C ij v.

25 *Gründliche Verlegung ... Issleb.* F ij r.
26 Op. cit. 80.
27 "Affaire." 50.
28 CR, VII, 266.
29 *Responsio ad epistolam ...*
   Melanthonis. A iiij.
30 *Der Theologen Bedenken.* G ij r.
31 *Bericht.* 1559. [H iiij r].
32 *Von der Einigkeit.* C ij v–f.

would carry out their office according to God's command.[24]

"It is to be hoped," Melanchthon wrote, "that through God's grace there will be such bishops."[25] "Melanchthon thought he could dare this dangerous game," writes Hans-Christoph von Hase about the situation in 1549, "because on the basis of his estimation of the political situation, one could reckon only with a short period of the Interim, and he hoped that "the matter would be delayed."[26] "Who would have expected," asks Stephan Skalweit, referring to Melanchthons approval of episcopal and papal jurisdiction in the 1534 "Concilium ad Gallos."[27] "that the most famous Lutheran would under certain cicumstances recognize even the authority of the pope, that he...approved the jurisdictional power of the bishops...?"

The knights asked how one could find such bishops.[28] The negotiators showed which bishops they had in mind, Flacius wrote, "when they recognize Pflug and the bishop of Meissen, obvious persecutors of the gospel, as their lord bishops and promise humbly to come to agreement with them on the remaining articles."[29] "The adiaphorists have a strong faith, since they have counted the sheep with the wolf, and earnestly admonished him to tend, and on no account to eat them." "Lieben Herren," he pleaded, "what you have yielded is yielded, what you want from them, to which they have not yet said 'yes,' and even if they said it, will be just the same as 'no.'"[30] Hoping that they would act correctly was like hoping that wolves would be pious.[31] How long would agreements with the Lutherans last after the bishops had regained power? "Alone, the jurisdiction of the pope and the bishops can totally destroy our churches."[32]

PART THREE: MAGDEBURG

God's Chancery

AT THE SIGN OF THE DRAGON

> Here, in these ungrateful German lands, no one dares to print anything against the Interim except the highly praiseworthy, ancient, Christian, imperial city, Magdeburg. There is God's chancery. – Caspar Aquila

> The authoritative voice of the Evangelical Church now sounded from Magdeburg, and no longer from Wittenberg. – Hans Christoph von Hase

For the military chieftains of the Smalcald League after the disastrous battle at Mühlberg in April, 1547, Magdeburg was the last redoubt. Unbowed, they applied their skills to prepare for the inevitable siege: Kaspar Pflug, commander of the Bohemian army, and Baron von Heydeck, commander of the Württemberg army, Count Albrecht of Mansfeld and Count Christian of Oldenburg. Led by the political party of Levin of Emden, which included Andreas Birkicht, the city's secretary, and Heinrich Merkel, the city was defiant. Through Ebeling Alemann, the city announced that it was ready to fight for political and religious freedom – for the ancient liberties granted by Emperor Otto I, and for the Augsburg Confession.[1] In "The Complaint and Prayer of a Saxon Maiden," the *Magd* on the city's coat-of-arms refused to dance with the emperor. "Let there be no jewel on my body," she sang, "until Germany is free again." Besides Germany's heroes, Hermann and Emperor Otto I, she predicted, a third would come: Jehu, anointed by the disciple of Elisha, avenger of Israel, who would destroy the house of Ahab and the priests of Baal.[2]

The tension mounted. On May 13, just days after Flacius' arrival, the imperial bann was spoken again. Since Frau Tucher was Elisabeth Flacius' sister, the family found shelter in the household of Archdeacon Stephan Tucher, pastor of the church of SS. Ulrich and Levin. His brother-in-law was a kindred spirit, who published *The Last Sermon of Doctor Martin Luther*[3] for the faithful at a time when "everyone was attempting to falsify Luther's teaching."

Flacius was also welcomed warmly by a group of refugees, clergymen who called themselves "Christ's exiles." The most prominent was Bishop Nicolaus von Amsdorf, forced out of the diocese of Naumburg-Zeitz. When the generals decided to raze monastery buildings to protect the areas not guarded by the Elbe river, a taunt came from Wittenberg about stealing and plundering. Was that godly work? Amsdorf answered that the demolition was indeed a good thing – a work of the Holy Spirit.[4]

There was no possibility of employment for Flacius by the church, since he was not ordained. At first, funds arrived for him from friends – from

1 *Der von Magdeburgk Entschüldigung, Bit unnd gemeine Christliche Erinnerunge*. Magdeburg: Michael Lotter, 1549. A iij v – f.
2 Bezold. *Geschichte*. 814.
3 *Die letzte Predigt Doctoris Martini Lutheri*. Magdeburg: Michael Lotter, 1550.
4 *Antwort auff der Wittenberg Lästerung – Quasi Magdeburgenses praedando velint defendere Evangelium*. Magdeburg, 1549. Text in Hortleder. II, 1046 f.

The House at Breiter Weg 141, "Zum Lindwurm." Courtesy of Stadtchronist Alfred Heidelmayer, Kulturhistorisches Museum, Magdeburg.

5 "Quod mihi praeter preces etiam pecuniarum adiumentum polliceris, habeo ingentes gratias." Flacius' Letter of August lst to Poach. Otto Clemen. *Handschriftenproben aus der Reformationszeit.* Zwickau: F. Ull- mann, 1911. No. 20.

6 Radtke. 60n.

7 If "causa Dei" in the records of Prior Heinrich von Hademstorpe meant Flacius' cause. "Ein Beitrag zur Lebens Geschichte des Vlacich oder Flacius Illyricus," by "Wd." *Allgemeiner Litterarischer Anzeiger,* July 10th, 1798. 1102.

8 Voigt. *Briefwechsel.* 30.

9 *Widder die newen Detzel, oder ausrüffer der Ablas Bullen und Antichristischen Jubil yars.* Magdeburg: Michael Lotter, 1550. B r

10 Cod. Guelf. 139b Helmst.; Rapularius. 669 Helmst.; *Catalogus* 1562. 210; Paul Lehmann. *Mitteilungen aus Handschriften* I. Munich, 1922; Verlag der Bayerischen Akademie der Wissen-schaften, 1951. 29–31. Hansgeorg Löbel. "Die Reformtraktate des Magdeburger Domherrn Heinrich Toke." Diss. Göttingen 1949. 9 f., 150 ff.; K. Zeumer. *Quellensammlung zur Geschichte der deutschen Reichsverfassung im Mittelalter und Neuzeit.* 2. Aufl. Tübingen 1913. Nr. 167.

11 *Catalogus.* 1562. 555 f.

12 "Heinrich Toke und die Kirchenreform in der Kirchenprovinz Magdeburg." Hildegund Hölzel. "Heinrich Toke und der Wolfenbüttler Rapularius." Dissertation, Göttingen, 1994. 20–89. Flacius' Use of the Rapularius 130–131. Cf. Ernst Breest. "Heinrich Toke. Domherr zu Magdeburg." *Geschichtsblätter für Stadt und Land Magdeburg.* XVII (1883) 43–72, 97–146.

13 *Duae veteres prophetae ac pia Eccle-*

Andreas Poach,[5] from Lüneberg[6] and from Hildesheim.[7] Eventually he earned his daily bread as supervisor for the intrepid printer, Michael Lotter, Breiter Weg 141, in a house called "Zum Lindwurm" – the Sign of the Dragon. From that house and from the other printshops poured a torrent of protest. "Here in these ungrateful German lands," Caspar Aquila wrote to the Duke of Prussia, "no one dares to print anything against the Interim except the highly praiseworthy, ancient, Christian, imperial city, Magdeburg. There is God's chancery."[8]

Magdeburg was another place for finding manuscripts. In the introduction to a tract he published against Julius III and his officer of plenary indulgence for visiting Roman altars, Flacius quotes the prior of the Magdeburg Benedictine house: Luther had admitted he was a heretic. The proof was that Luther had written to the pope, "pestis eram vivens, moriens tua mors ero papa" – "living, I have been a pest; dying, I will be your death." What should one make of someone so unschooled as to think that the Latin word, *pestis*, meant "heretic"?[9]

Another manuscript he found was an example of a "Rapularius," literally, "a serving of turnips" (from *rapum*, Latin for turnip). It was a kind of scrapbook of texts assembled by Heinrich Toke, containing first-hand information about the 1432 Council of Basel.[10] Toke, also author of the 1433 conciliar tract, "Queritur an ecclesia,"[11] had been Professor at Erfurt and lector and canon at Magdeburg. Because of his campaign for church reform, he qualified as one of those Flacius selected for his famous *Catalog of Witnesses to the Truth,*[12] especially for his part in combatting the cult of the bleeding altar bread in Wilsnack, Brandenburg. From the

Rapularius, Flacius printed in the *Catalogus* and separately, a prophecy of the renewal of the church by Hildegard of Bingen, the Benedictine abbess (1098–1179), which, he said, anticipated the sixteenth-century Reformation.[13]

At the Franciscan monastery, *Unsere Liebe Frau*, in nearby Bergen, he found two copies of a satirical letter, first attested at Avignon in 1351, in which the devil thanks the pope for help in the fight against Christ, signed, "your special friend, Beelzebub." In his publication, Flacius attributed it – mistakenly – to Bishop Nicolas Oresme of Lisieux († 1382).[14] Elsewhere he found and published a twelfth-century letter with a similar, harsh criticism of the corruption of the clergy by Archbishop of Canterbury Pierre de Blois.[15]

The "Rapularius". Cod. Guelf. 139 b Helmst,

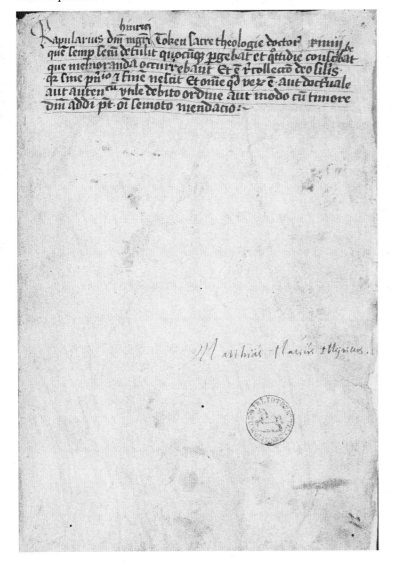

siae Dei instauratione ad nostra tempora pertinantes S. Prophetia de politicom et ecclesiasticorum certaminum eventu. n. t. n. p.

14 *Epistola Luciferi ad Spirituales circiter ante Annos centum ut ex codicis vestutis apparet, descripta Autore Nic. Oresme.* Magdeburg: Michael Lotter, 1549. The first printing in Paris is no longer known. There was another one in Strassburg in 1507. There were a great many copies of the letter about, and Flacius eventually disovered two others. Cf. Clemen. KS, II, 350–352, where other possible authors are named. Otto-kar Lorenz. *Deutschlands Geschichts- quelle im Mittelalter seit der Mitte des 13. Jahrhunderts.* 3, III, 1887. 397 ff. Wilhelm Wattenbach. "Über erfundene Briefe in Handschriften des Mittelalters, besonders Teufelsbriefe." *Sitzungsberichte der Königlichen Preussischen Akademie der Wissenschaften zu Berlin.* 1892. I, 91 ff.; Flacius' attribution to Oresme was mistaken. F. M. Meunier. *Essai sur la vie et les ouvrages de Nicole Oresme.* Paris, 1557, quoted by M. Curtze. "Bemerkung zu dem Aufsatze: 'Geistliche Scherze des Mittelalters II." *Anzeiger für die Kunde der deutschen Vorzeit* XVI (1896). 10.

15 *Wie iemmerlich und schendtlich der Bapst sampt seinen Bischoven und Geistlichen, die arme Scheflein Christi durch die Officialen schindet. Durch den Hochgelehrten und grossen praelaten Petrum Blesensem, welcher für cccc jaren gelebt hat.* Magdeburg: Christian Rödinger, n. t.; Preger. II, 553, PL, CCVI, col. 1005–1052. Polman. "L'Elément." 190n.

16 Cod. Guelf. 656 Helmst. Oscar

Doering. "Reste der ehemaligen Il-senburger Klosterbibliothek." *Zeit-schrift für Bücherfreunde* I (1897–98). 629 f.

17 *Catalogus.* 1562. 581 f. Quoted by Hans Volz. *Die Lutherpredigten des Johannes Mathesius.* Leipzig: M. Heinsius Nachfolger Eger & Sievers, 1930. p. 77. Hans-Jürgen Schönstädt. *Antichrist, Weltgesche-hen und Gottes Werkzeug.* Wies-baden: Franz Steiner, 1978. 300 f. Eduard Jacobs. "Bruder Henning von Himmelpforten, sein Zeugnis von Andreas Proles und der von demselben als nahe bevorstehend bestimmt geahnten Kirchenerneu-erung." *Zeitschrift des Vereins für Kirchengeschichte der Provinz Sach-sen* XIV (1917). 110.

18 CR, VII, 660.

19 Hartmut Voit. "Gallus und das Interim. Eine anonyme Druck-schrift aus dem Jahr 1548." ARG, LXV (1974). 277–285.

20 *Eine Disputation von Mittelding und von den itzigen verenderung in Kir-chen die Christlich und wol geordnet sind aus dem Latein verdeudscht.* Magdeburg: Christian Rödinger, 1550. [B iij v] – C v. CR, VII, 547, 600.

21 Gallus' authorship is attested by a note in a Wolfenbüttel copy, sig. 183.28 Th (2). Cf. Leonhard Theobald. *Die Reformationsge-schichte der Reichstadt Regensburg* II. Nuremberg: "Die Egge," 1951. 202; Gottlob von Polenz. *Geschich-te des französischen Calvinismus.* Go-tha: Friedrich Andreas Perthes. II, 1860. 80.

22 Kettner. *Clerus Magdeburgensis, Cle-rus Ulrico-Levinianus.* 236 ff.

23 *Confessio et Apologia Pastorum & reliquorum ministrorum Ecclesiae Magdeburgensis.* Magdeburg: Mi-chael Lotter, 1550.

24 *Geschichte des deutschen Protestan-tismus in den Jahren 1551–1581* II. Marburg: R. G. Elwert, 1852–1859. 42 ff.

25 *Die Entstehung und Fortbildung des*

At the Ilsenburg monastery at Wernigerode in the Harz Mountains, Flacius found manuscripts of Bishop Halitgarius of Cameracensis and Rhabanus Maurus.[16] At the same place he found 95-year-old Henning Smeth, retired inspector of fortifications and former lay brother at the monastery of Porta Coeli (*Himmelspforte*, Gate of Heaven). It was the monastery Luther had visited, August 6, 1517, to discuss the ninety-five theses with Vicar General von Staupitz. Smeth related the 1497 prophecy made by Andreas Proles, Prior of Porta Coeli, after meeting Luther as a boy in Magdeburg. "Dear brothers, Christendom needs a great renewal, and I see the same already near in spirit ... God the Lord will awaken a great hero ... who will take over this work of Reformation and oppose error. God will give him the courage to dare to resist the high magnates. Through God's goodness, you will see the salutary service of this man."[17]

On November 11, St. Ulrich's church welcomed a new pastor, Nicolaus Gallus. Melanchthon commented tartly that in Magdeburg there were now two "sons of Cyclops."[18] Lest anyone think Flacius had influenced him to join the resistance, however, Gallus noted that he had opposed the Interim before even hearing about Flacius. As Superintendent in Regens-burg, he had taken an early stand against the Interim, and was the author of Regensburg's protest.[19] During his stay in Wittenberg, he had sounded the alarm against the Interim, preaching on the stirring call in Isaiah 8.20: "To the teaching and the testimony! Surely for this word which they speak there is no dawn!" During the war, he complained, the Wittenberg theolo-gians had spoken bravely, but now their word was weak. He announced that he was taking up the anti-Interim cause at Flacius' side.

> Illyricus has done the same as St. Paul, who rebuked Peter when he did not conduct himself rightly according to the truth of the Gospel ... I must freely and publicly support the witness which...the Word of God...gives to the Illyrian, that is, that he is especially called from God thus to undertake this matter ... But God be praised and thanked, that he soon gave someone who could judge this adiaphoristic spirit and dared to oppose it.[20]

On August 13, 1550, Flacius' brother-in-law, Stephan Tucher, died. He lived long enough, however, to read a new Confession Gallus had written[21] in the name of the Magdeburg clergy. On his deathbed, he asked that his name appear as signatory.[22] It was the *Confession, Instruction, and Warning,* of April 13, 1550.[23] Until the Formula of Concord," wrote Heinrich Heppe, "no confession had such a broad ecclesiastical significance."[24] For the first time, Heppe explained, it argued that as the prophet sent from God, only Luther was a valid authority in the church.[25] He argued, on the contrary, that the authentic Reformation "idea" began with Luther, but was worked out in the Melanchthonian Augsburg Confession, and further developed in the formation of the United Church. An apologist for the Union between the Evangelical-Lutheran and Reformed Churches in Germany, Heppe called Gallus' text the "first specifically *Lutheran* con-fession."[26]

It is not without interest that this "first Lutheran confession" was the source of a doctrine of military resistance. The Magdeburg Confession is, in fact, a significant document in the history of political science. Expanding the right of the hereditary German dukes to resist the emperor, Gallus claimed the right for the city government. "There can be little doubt," wrote W. D. Cargill Thompson, "that Calvin, Beza, and the English Marian exiles were drawing on a well-established Lutheran tradition when they propounded the theory of the right of inferior magistrates to resist their superiors."[27]

Flacius, who as a lay person did not sign the document, recognized its theological influence. "After they had rejected it in the Leipzig Interim," Flacius wrote about the Wittenbergers, "until, finally, the Confession of the Magdeburg Pastors appeared, they began to remember it again, they had forgotten the Augsburg Confession."[28]

Gallus' confession derives the right of armed political resistance from Luther.[29] Since his other concerns very often took precedence, it is misguided, of course, to think Luther's political axioms can be discerned from his day-to-day decisions.[30] But Gallus understood Luther's axiomatic position, as one understands, say, Euclid. His observation about the square of the hypotenuse has a life of its own, independent of whatever he might have·thought or done in various life-situations. Luther's basic insight about the relationship between the two realms, too, has a life of its own, independent of his judgments in changing situations.

During the time of the Smalcaldic League, the Saxon jurists, to whose thought Gallus had access through Levin of Emden, combined Luther's axiom about the two realms with an ancient German intepretation of the imperial constitutional tradition, which assigned primary authority not to the emperor, but to the dukes. If the emperor misused his delegated power, the dukes (lesser magistrates), as the authorities that had delegated their powers to him originally, were duty-bound to oppose him militarily. Gallus boldly expanded the duty to include the governments of cities, especially God's government, His chancery at Magdeburg.

Luthertums und die kirchlichen Bekenntnisschriften desselben von 1548– 1576. Kassel: J. G. Krieger, 1863. 213.

26 *Philipp Melanchthon, der Lehrer Deutschlands.* Nuremberg: Joh. Aug. Koch, 1860. 147.

27 "Luther and the Right of Resistance to the Emperor." *Church, Society and Politics.* Oxford: Blackwell, 1979. 200, 202.

28 *Gründliche Verlegung ... Pfeffinger.* C iij v.

29 Quentin Skinner. "The Origins of the Calvinist Theory of Revolution." Barbara C. Malument (ed.). *After the Reformation. Essays in Honor of J. H. Hexter.* Manchester: Manchester University Press, 1980. 317.

30 Gordon Rupp. "Those have, I think, over-simplified who have found in Luther the beginnings of the right of resistance by inferior magistrates, though the City of Magdeburg was to make an outright declaration of the duty of armed resistance later ... correspondence with his Prince in the early 1540's about the situation in Saxony in relation to Duke Henry and Maurice of Saxony, shows how reluctant he always was to encourage any kind of military action, still less preemptive war. "Luther and the Castle Coburg, 1530." *Bulletin of the John Rylands University Library of Manchester* LXI (1978). 204.

1 Preger. II, 484 f. n.
2 *De locorum Theologicorum D. Philippi Melanthoni Orthodoxa puritate et utilitate, Adsertio & subscriptio praecipuorum aliquot doctorum.* Frankfurt am Main: [Paul Reffeler], 1579. A iiij v.
3 Heldelin. [X iv r].
4 *Entschuldigung ... an die Universitet.* D ij v.
5 Ibid. [J iiij v].
6 Ibid. A iij r.
7 *Responsio ad epistolam ... Melanchthonis.* P ij v.
8 *Widder die newe Reformation.* E v.
9 *Von der Einigkeit.* B ij v.
10 CR, VII, 658.

No authority, whatever it is, has a right to forbid a pastor pure teaching. – Flacius

Lex orandi lex confitendi. – Olson

Although there was no university in Magdeburg, Flacius continued teaching, with lectures on Greek and Hebrew, the Gospel of St. John, and Melanchthon's 1548 *Erotemata Dialectices.*[1] One of his classes at SS. Ulrich and Levin is remembered because of his fervent recommendation of Melanchthon. He held up a copy of the *Loci Communes* before the young people present and with tears in his eyes, kissed it. Rather than lose that book, he told them, he would choose to perish.[2]

When his hope for a change of heart in Wittenberg was disappointed, he decided to carry out the first step of the *ordo progrediendi in reprehensione* Jesus had laid down in Matthew 18.15: "If your brother sins against you, go and tell him his fault, between you and him alone." It was a painful step; it would convince Melanchthon he was an enemy.[3] "As God is my witness," he remembered, "I really wanted to live in the most friendly and brotherly way ... I have no pleasure in war..."[4] It was necessary, nevertheless, to confront Melanchthon with his fault. In a letter of June 8th, he implored Melanchthon to change "so that the Antichrist be resisted, and windows not be opened to him." "For God's sake," he wrote, "consider the bodies of Christians who have been slaughtered, either by the papacy or by epicurianism. For God's sake, stop following the jurists...!"[5]

He was not so dull, Flacius wrote in his own defense, that he did not recognize his debt to a great teacher. Something more important than friendship was involved. "In such a short time I have not completely become a stone and a lump so that I do not know or recognize that I have much for which to thank my teachers. But I also know that Christ strictly demands that we prefer him and his religion, not only to teachers, but also to parents and children and to life itself."[6] "I consider that friendship goes as far as the altar, not beyond," he wrote, "for Christ gravely commands us to prefer the purity of the gospel to all men."[7] "The most important and highest thankfulness a disciple can show to his preceptor in my judgment is this, that, especially in religion, he defend the teaching the preceptor has given him ... according to his highest ability and fight for it."[8]

If Melanchthon were concerned about unity, Flacius commented, he would have answered his letter at once.[9] But he did not. His reaction was hostile. How dare anyone suggest that the Preceptor had done wrong? He berated the student who brought the letter, and submitted it to general ridicule. He could more easily bear exile and death, he said, than this venom of vipers.[10] From Pythagorus he had learned that the way to deal with opposition was to ignore it.

Nor did the rector of the University answer a similar letter. So Flacius took the third step in the *ordo progrediendi*: "If he refuses to listen to them, tell it to the church," and the counsel "to admonish them publicly before the church" [Matthew 18.16]. "I was forced by the command of Christ, he explained, "to say these things to the church." He published an open *Apology to the Wittenberg School in the Matter of Adiaphora*,[11] the first of what have been called his "classics of resistance." *The Apology* is memorable for the first appearance of the accusatory term, "adiaphorist."

To Andreas Hoppe, pastor of St. Sebastian's in Magdeburg, Flacius' criticism demonstrated lovelessness. "Love has gone cold," he said, "as we can also see in our theologians. For Illyricus now has published a slanderous book, in which, against the truth, he reviles Philipp, and wants to force him to public repentance."[12] Face to face, Flacius answered him that he was opposing not Wittenberg doctrine, but the Leipzig Interim. Love implied preventing godlessness and corruption, not fostering them. Melanchthon's own admonition that evangelical doctrine should be passed on unchanged to posterity was in contradiction with what he was actually practicing.

"God is a great and stern God," he thundered in his second resistance classic, an *Admonition to Steadfastness*. "God wants to be feared no less than the Lord of this world." Its status as classic was reinforced in 1906, when it was reprinted during a part of the campaign by the Old Lutherans of Breslau in resisting coerced union with Calvinists.[13] It was dedicated to the imprisoned Elector Johann Friedrich, who, he thought, was bearing Christ's cross after him. Fear was spreading like a thick fog, so that "we can hardly tell true from false, and the truth seems to be less true than it was before and the false less false." The deceptions of the Interim worked like a wedge. First the narrow edge of the minimal *Excerpt*, and afterward, papal rule. It was thus no trivial matter to wear a surplice or to tolerate the expulsion of God-fearing pastors, and to stand by idly while frivolous ones took their place.

> No authority, whatever it is, has a right to forbid a pastor pure teaching, for when the authority calls someone to preach the gospel, it has done what its office demands. But when it forbids the gospel to be preached and demands that the pastor move away, it is acting against its office.[14]

But the evangelical churches were in extreme peril. After the military defeat, no ruler had survived to protect the church. Pastors and congregations were on their own. In the new situation, Flacius did not hesitate to demand martyrdom. Once more, he invoked the *clausula Petri*, Acts 5.19: "We ought to obey God rather than men," and not shrink from demanding martyrdom. A government that no longer rewards good and punishes evil, he wrote, is no longer God's authority, but the devil's and should not be obeyed. How should one resist? "To one who is willing," he promised, "nothing is too difficult. If we had true zeal for God's word, we would find a thousand ways by which we could be useful in maintaining the truth."

11 *Entschuldigung ... an die Universitet.*

12 Ignaz von Döllinger. *Die Reformation, ihre innere Entwicklung und ihre Wirkungen im Umfange des Lutherischen Bekenntnisses.* II. Arnheim, Josua Witz, 1853–4. 238.

13 *Dr. Matthius Flacius Illyricus: Eine christliche Vermanung zur Beständigkeit in der wahren Religion Jesu Christi. Mit einem Vorwort wider den Byzantinismus, Opportunismus und Unionismus unswerer Tage von Dietrich Schwertfeger.* Eberfeld: Verlag des Lutherischen Büchervereins, 1906.

14 *Ein Vermanung zur bestendigkeit in bekentnis der warheit, Creutz, und Gebett, in dieser betrübten Zeit sehr nützlich und tröstlich.* Magdeburg: Michael Lotter [1549]. [D iiij r].

15 CR, XXI, 511; *Der Theologen Be-dencken.* D iiij v, J vj r; Franz Lau. "Adiaphora." RGG3, I, 93–96; Wolfgang Trillhaas. "Adiaphoron. Erneute Erwägung eines alten Begriffs." *Theologische Literatur-zeitung* LXXXIX (1954). 457–62; Bernhard J. Verkamp. "The Zwing-lians and Adiaphorism." *Church History* XL (1973). 486 f.

16 CR, VIII, 841.

17 H. von Hase. 52.

18 *Ein Vermanung zur Bestendigkeit.* [A iiij v].

19 Marcus Tulius Cicero. *De Finibus Bonorum et Malorum.* Cambridge: Harvard University Press; London: William Heinemann Ltd., 1951. 272 f.; Margaret Ressor. "The 'Indifferents' in the Old and Middle Stoa." *Transactions and Proceedings of the American Philosophical Asso-ciation* (1951). 102–111; Eward F. Meylan. "The Stoic Doctrine of In-different Things and the Concep-tion of Christian Liberty in Calvin's Institutio Religionis Christianae." *Romanic Review* XXVIII (1937). 135–145.

20 CR, VII, 292–296.

21 Ibid. 295.

22 CR, VII, 383.

23 Mager. Op. cit.; Ritschl. II, 348.

It was not such a deplorable thing as they fancied to die for Christ's sake. Those who had no other option should "take the cross on their shoulder, go willingly to death and confess the truth steadfastly, with one mind." In persecution, a pastor may flee – as Jesus and the apostles did – but he should return as soon as possible. It was better, however, to stay and risk the danger ... to renounce the world, in which no one becomes a citizen, but is only a guest. Steadfastness could help to induce the rulers to abandon their plans: "they cannot or would not kill us all at one time."

To understand the adiaphora controversy it is necessary to distinguish two levels. The first level is political, a struggle for the freedom of the church to determine its own life, a refusal to be ruled even in secondary matters by the state. The second level concerns the precise nature of the church's inner life, especially the form of the liturgy. The introduction of the Greek word, *adiaphoron*[15] (Latin *res media*; German *Mitteldinge*, Eng-lish indifferent matters), into the controversy was the source of no little vexation. Although Melanchthon blamed court officials for introduc-ing it,[16] the fact is that he had been employing it for some time.[17]

"What kind of word is 'adiaphora'"? Flacius heard someone ask in Torgau. "I think the accursed devil himself invented it. Now everything is adiaphora, whether one prays to God or the devil."[18] The word is part of the vocabulary of the Stoic philosophers. *Diapherein* means "to separate," "to make a difference." With the addition of an alpha privative, the word becomes *adiapherein* – "*not* to make a difference." For the philosopher Zeno, *adiaphora* were matters that made no difference – the ones that led neither to eudaemony nor harm.[19]

Which were the liturgical practices that made a difference, and which did not make a difference? The question was put to Melanchthon by the pastors of Berlin in a letter of January 7, 1549.[20] They did not know yet what had been decided at the Jüterbog conference, and asked for more information. They also called for clear liturgical guidelines: exactly which rituals were to be reckoned as adiaphora.[21]

A well-thought-out reply would have laid a new foundation for liturgics. But Melanchthon disappointed them. He was already on record, of course, against consecration of oil and salt, which he considered magical, adora-tion of images and Corpus Christi processions with a consecrated host.[22] Now, however, he limited himself to quoting the Augsburg Confession, "Our churches are falsely accused of abolishing the mass. Actually, the mass is retained among us and is celebrated with the greatest reverence." His generalities did not satisfy Antonius Corvinus. Just before being imprisoned for resistance to the Interim, he urged Melanchthon to demonstrate his old steadfastness.[23] How could some ceremonies be classed as adiaphora if pastors were being sent to prison for not practicing them? Christ, he wrote, did not come to bring peace, but a sword.

The pastors of Hamburg, too, wanted clear liturgical guidelines and made the same request as their colleagues in Berlin had done in a letter of April 16, written by Johann Aepinus.[24] They objected to the ground rule adopted at Jüterbog, "In the adiaphora everything should be maintained that the holy fathers maintained."[25] All faithful pastors were obligated to resist such a rule, and to surrender their office rather than being besmirched by it. Rituals had their limits; if they were the occasion for restoring abuses and impiety they could be nurseries for superstition and snares for consciences. The church of Hamburg, they explained, had maintained the Reformation tradition, but now they needed assistance from Wittenberg. It was important to determine *exactly* which ceremonies were to be avoided, and which were consonant with sound doctrine. If there were no clear word, the result would be chaos.

In his answer to the Hamburg pastors,[26] Melanchthon disappointed again; he wanted to remain flexible, he said, and referred once more in general to the authority of tradition, especially of the early church. He may have feared that pursuing the matter might lead to the sedition he feared.

At this point, Flacius entered the discussion with a third resistance classic, the *Book About True and False Adiaphora*.[27] It began with Aepinus' themes from the Hamburg letter. Flacius' viewpoint was conservative. Adiaphora, in fact, were willed by God – *in genere*. "That I teach that no ancient ceremonies should be preserved in the churches," he wrote, "is not true."

True adiaphora, he wrote, are hymns, lections, readings, the time of services, the liturgical year, ringing of bells, the choice between leavened or unleavened bread in the sacrament, distinctions between teachers and hearers, and clerical rank "so they do not sit on the wheel before they have mastered the rudder." As examples of the church's freedom to determine the adiaphora he cited the early church's arbitrary transfer of the Sabbath to the first day of the week, and the separation of the date of Easter from the date of the Passover.[28]

False adiaphora are what God has clearly forbidden. But there are also – and here is a root of the adiaphora controversy – temporary adiaphora. "All ceremonies and rites, however indifferent they are by nature, cease to be adiaphora: when coersion, the false idea that they are worship and have to be performed, and when denial, scandal, manifest occasion of impiety are added, and when they do not edify the church of God, but destroy it and become an affront to God."[29]

In contrast to Melanchthon, for whom all ceremonies were matters of indifference, he understood the ancient tradition, *lex orandi, lex credendi* – the law of prayer is the law of believing. Cult and doctrine, he said, "cohere together, and are connected."[30] That is another way of saying that there is an intrinsic meaning in ceremonies (apart from the words associated with them), and that the ritual meaning must not contradict what the church teaches otherwise. "It is ... an event of highest importance in church history," comments Hans Christoph von Hase, "that as the first in Lutheranism, Flacius clarified the relationship between cult and church order."[31]

But he went one step farther. He was also the first to demonstrate the

24 CR, VII, 367–382.
25 *Ein Brief der Prediger zu Hamburg.* A iiij, C iij r; CR, VII, 248, 370.
26 CR, VII, 382–386.
27 *Ein Buch von ... Mitteldingen.* Op. cit.
28 In addition to those *public* adiaphora, he lists *private* adiaphora – the individual's choice of times for prayer, the decision to give up delicious food, fasting the better to pray, abstaining from sexual intercourse, and secular adiaphora – upon which "the whole religion of the monks" was built – such as clothing, food, housing.
29 *Omnia Latina Scripta.* [A r].
30 Bibl. 1899. 103.
31 Op. cit. 33. Stephan Skalweit observes the same thing: "Probably for the first time in the history of Lutheranism, Flacius saw clearly their inner connection." *Reich und Reformation.* Berlin: Propyläen, 1967. 361.

32 Biundo. *Kaspar Aquila*. 75n.
33 Ritschl. II, 330.
34 *Ein Buch von ... Mitteldingen*. Q iij v.

inner relationship between cult and *confession*.[32] Melanchthon had maintained that the adiaphora had nothing to do with it, that "confession is not in the adiaphora" – a position Ritschl called an "artificial fiction."[33] Instead, Flacius insisted that "It is true, more than true, that confession is in the adiaphora."[34] Ritual, accordingly, is a kind of language that must function responsibly. "...we confess and declare the faith of our heart not only with words, but also with deeds and external gestures. In confessing, actions cannot conflict with words." Thus at Flacius' hands, to the ancient insight, *lex orandi, lex credendi*, was added another rule. Call it the rule of *lex orandi, lex confitendi*.

CAN THE GOVERNMENT DETERMINE THE LITURGY?

1 *Gründliche verlegung ... Issleb*. A iij v.
2 *Eine freidige vermanung, zu klarem und öffentlichem bekentnis Jhesu Christi, wider die Adiaphoristisch Davidianistische und Epicurische Klugheit des heuchelns und meuchelns sehr nützlich zu lesen. Gestelt durch Civlium einen Italiener*. Magdeburg: Michael Lotter, 1550. B r.
3 Cf. Wilhelm Preger. "Flacius von den kirchlichen Mitteldingen." *Zeitschrift für Protestantismus und Kirche* XXXV (1858). 165–186.

The magistrate should be the protector not only of the second table [of the Law], but also of the first... – Melanchthon

The state is the protector of both tables. But in secular office. – Flacius

Flacius also had a traditional view about the prerogatives of the church. "When someone says that the church has the keys, and that the bishop is their servant, again, that the secular power can and should serve the church in that which is Christian and right... That is not papist, but Christian and evangelical."[1] The "Adiaphora controversy" was a controversy about the church's independence: it became a bitter wrangle about the separation of church and state. A decision that the government could rule on the adiaphora would lead in the direction of absolutism. "O what a terrible day, one to weep for," Flacius wrote, "on which Constantine became a Christian!"[2] On the other hand, a decision that only the church could rule on the adiaphora would lead in a direction toward freedom (how could a state be absolutist if the church was free?).

It went without saying that every secular government that accepted the Reformation recognized the authority of the Bible to settle the chief religious questions. But it did not take long before it was discovered that effective power over the church could be exercized by whomever had the right to adjudicate secondary questions – the adiaphora. It was a new chapter in an old struggle of church and state.[3] *The adiaphora controversy can be understood only if it is seen primarily as a quarrel about the relationship between church and state.*

Charles V's law presumed his right to rule the church. By claiming the right to determine the *adiaphora*, Protestant princes claimed the same right. It was the crucial premise not only of the state churches in Germany but of the Elizabethan Settlement in England.

The most prominent protagonist of the right of the the prince to rule over the church was Philipp Melanchthon. "Just as the father of a family is a minister and executor of the church in his family," he wrote, "...so is the magistrate minister and executor of the church in the republic."[4] "The civil power is part of the church, as Constantine piously says."[5] "The magistrate is the *custos utriusque tabellae legis*", Melanchthon continues, guardian, that is, of both tables of the law – commandments one through three, and four through ten.[6] "Our intention," he explained, "is to give God those things which are God's and to Caesar what is Caesar's, as the authority designated by God, and to yield everything which can be done without offending God."[7] For Melanchthon, God's claim was over what was internal. External matters were the realm of the state. "Ecclesiastical traditions are civil laws," he argued, "and their enforcement in no way pertains to spiritual government."[8] "Christ determines the doctrine, the government the church order."[9] There should be, therefore, no controversy about the liturgy. "Here a spiritualizing of the 'ceremonies' [churchly usages] in Melanchthon comes to light," comments Peter Meinhold, "which makes it clear how near humanism and spiritualism stand with regard to churchliness."[10]

The quarrel was in the first instance about *who decided* about the liturgy – the church itself, or the state. "...he [Melanchthon] says that the governmental authority has power for the sake of peace to change the ceremonies of the church," Flacius complained, "and that the churches should therefore show obedience to it. *That is the most important basis of the adiaphoristic error.*"[11]

The analyses of the Adiaphora Controversy by Clyde Manschrek and by Bernard Verkamp ultimately fail because they did not identify the Adiaphora controversy as a church-state issue. Manschrek saw it as a solely doctrinal dispute. "...if they [the adiaphora] were really non-essentials, a controversy could hardly arise. Since a dispute did arise, another element must have been involved, and that other element in the Reformation period was the theological concept of justification."[12]

Verkamp advances what Gordon Rupp called an imaginary adiaphoristic theory.[13] He agrees essentially with Melanchthon, who wrote that he who forbids circumcision errs just as much as those who demand it. He disagrees with Flacius' argument that "one cannot really be true to ones Christian liberty except that one actually rejects those ceremonies which the 'tyrant' is trying to impose." "For a Karlstadt or a Flacius Illyricus to insist to the contrary that certain external actions must of necessity be rejected as proof of one's liberty is but a new type of 'tyranny' which must be opposed no less than the 'tyranny of Antichrist.'"[14]

"Everywhere," Flacius observed with growing dismay, "one sees the secular rulers reaching for the keys of the church, wanting to prescribe what the preachers teach, what they pray, sing, how they rule the church, whom they should bind and loose. That can by no means be tolerated, for Christ distinguishes the offices..."[15] According to the logic of Johann Pfef-

4 CR, XVI, 124.

5 CR, XII, 497.

6 CR, XVI, 87.

7 *Gründlicher und warhafftiger Bericht.* 196.

8 Themes for Discussion on the Sixth Day (1522). Thesis 22. Charles L. Hill. "Some Theses of Philip Melanchthon." *Lutheran Quarterly* VI (1954). 247.

9 H. von Hase. 54.

10 *Philipp Melanchthon, der Lehrer der Kirche.* Berlin: Lutherisches Verlagshaus, 1960. 44.

11 *Widder die newe Reformation.* B ij v. italics added.

12 "Role." 165.

13 G. Rupp. Review of Verkamp, *American Historical Review* LXXXIV (1970). 1361.

14 Bernard J. Verkamp. *The Indifferent Mean: Adiaphorism in the English Reformation to 1554.* Athens and Ohio: Ohio University Press and Wayne State University Press, 1977. 107.

15 *Von der Einigkeit.* D vij r.

16 *Widder die newe Reformation.* [B iiij r].

17 *Ein Supplication und demütige Bitt.* A iij v.

18 CR, III, 225.

19 *Gründliche Verlegung ... Issleb.* A iij. Italics added.

20 *Eine Schrifft ... widder ein Heidnisch Buch.* C r.

21 *Gründliche Verlegung ... Isleb.* A iij r.

22 WAB, V, 616.

finger, a Turkish conquest of Europe would be followed by the adoption of Turkish adiaphora.[16]

Quoting Luther's Letter to the Bohemians, he insisted that the church had the right to determine its own order. "In religion," he wrote, "the church is completely free. It cannot, therefore, be a servant of any man." "But that is a good and wholesome counsel, which the church should know above all, that the power of the keys, that is, the whole government of the church, has been given to her and not to the tyrants of this world..."[17]

Did the state have jurisdiction over both tables of the Law? Melanchthon said yes: "The magistrate should be the protector not only of the second table, but of the first."[18] Flacius said no: It was the duty of the state to protect the church, but not to assume ecclesiastical authority. "The state is the protector of both tables. *But in secular office.*"[19] Melanchthon, he argued, was mistaken. "...he often repeats that in external things one must be obedient to the government." There are two kinds of external things, secular and spiritual. In secular matters one should be obedient to them, in spiritual matters not. Baptism is an external matter, but the government has no authority over it.[20] Pfeffinger was mistaken as well. "...that he [Pfeffinger] alleges that the state authority is a guardian of both tables of God, is correct. But in secular office. That according to scripture they should open the door to Christ and nourish the church according to the scripture is also true. But it should not be its Lord. The right to, and the use of the keys belongs to the church."[21]

Pfeffinger, like others, invoked a statement of Luther's that Hans-Christoph von Hase called "adiaphoristic peace-music."

> Question: whether certain external usages should be restored in the church, so that unity can be established everywhere, so that we will not be denounced as schismatics because of unnecessary matters, or whether one should hold fast to Christian freedom?

> Answer: Where there is no unity in important matters, what does it matter if many of these unimportant matters are given or taken? But if there is unity in the important matters, we will yield and suffer in these unimportant matters, and do what we should and what they want. For where Christ maintains his own, we will gladly, for his sake, give up our own.

> But so that they do not think that we want to be right, although the important matters remain controversial, for my part, I am willing and ready to accept all such external usages for the sake of peace, insofar as they do not burden my conscience. That I have always offered in almost all my books. Would to God that they, too, mean to accept them. But to burden consciences thereby, that my Christ cannot tolerate.[22]

"When a Christian government for its own reasons ... desires uniformity of ceremonies or adiaphora in its lands," Pfeffinger echoed, "...I as a poor, simple Christian am not minded to oppose it, and thereby to lose my vocation and churches." Indeed, why *not* yield under pressure? There was no reason to object to anything which could be introduced "without offense to God's word and good conscience." "I believe and maintain that in all things that are not against God, one should be obedient to the secular regular authority." He appropriated Luther's language.

Where Christ Jesus maintains his own, that is, the right doctrine of God's word, right use of the most venerable sacraments and the ceremonies or adiaphora are not considered service to God necessary in salvation, but for discipline and order for the sake of peace and unity ... so I will heartily abandon my own, that is, be reconciled as far as possible with other churches in external matters that are not against God, and which can happen according to the circumstances of each place, and not condemn the others for some disunity about some indifferent matters, nor call them renegade Christians and Mamalukes, for I believe and maintain that one should obey also secular authority in all things that are not against God, and thus in these things as well.[23]

But the present crisis was quite different from Luther's situation. What authority did Pfeffinger have, Flacius wanted to know, for delivering the church to the government? "This big Junker Cathedral dean," he fumed, "thinks that the church, together with its ceremonies, is his, and that therefore he can deal with them the way he likes. Not so, dear Adiaphorist, it all belongs to the church and to Christ, her head..."[24]

There are two kinds of false adiaphora, Flacius objected. First, ceremonies that by their nature are forbidden, and second, temporary adiaphora – those imposed on the church. Interim ceremonies had been thrust on the Church entirely against her will and thereby constituted a serious violation of her freedom. Secondly, they contradicted the will of God, who does not desire the re-establishment of ceremonies that have long served idolatry and which on that account had already been abolished previously. Thirdly, they have not been ordered by "pious and enlightened" men. Thus, whatever they may once have been, "they are no longer [true] adiaphora, but are rather the impious commands of the Antichrist" and as such "may in no way find a place in the church."

Chief among Flacius' pseudo-adiaphora were the ceremonies Charles V was imposing in an attempt to re-establish the papacy. To submit under such conditions would inevitably mean a loss of faith. Far from being edifying, then, the ceremonies would be a scandal for the Christian community and for that reason must be rejected. "In a time of confession and scandal there are no adiaphora."

Friedrich Loofs called the controversies of the second Reformation generation "pathological."[25] Otto Ritschl, on the contrary, thought the controversies were of major importance, "an event of the first rank."[26] But during a time that absolutist notions were becoming more important, Flacius' struggle for a church free from state domination was significant indeed.

Flacius' arguments in the Adiaphora controversy were ultimately unsuccessful in Germany, but had a significant influence in England. The standard Puritan work, *The Fortresse of Fathers* which quotes parts of the letter from the Hamburg ministerium by Johann Aepinus, and from Flacius' *Book about True and False Adiaphora*, was where many Englishmen first learned about an "adiaphoron," that "...hit signifieth a thing whereof is made no matter, whether a man kepe hit or do not kepe hit." Whereas the Anglican presupposition was the same as Melanchthon's (the Elizabethan Settlement was built on the notion that the queen had the right to determine

23 *Von den Traditionibus, Ceremoniis, oder Mitteldingen, Christlicher warer Bericht allen lieben Christen in disen letzten und gefehrlichen zeiten nützlich zu wissen.* Leipzig: Nicolaus Wolrab, 1550. [C vij v–C viij r].

24 *Widder die newe Reformation.* C ij v. Here is an exception to Gordon Rupps' statement that the Reformers "did not accost each other by saying. 'Ah! I see you are an adiaphorist!'" Review of Verkamp. 1361.

25 Op. cit. 897.

26 Op. cit. II, 328.

27 *The Fortresse of Fathers, ernestlie defending the puritie of Religion and Ceremonies, by the trewe exposition of certaine places of Scripture: against such as wold bring in an abuse of Idol Stouff, and of thinges indifferent and do appoinct th'authority of Princes and prelates larger than trueth is. Translated out of the Latine for there sakes that understand no Latin by I. B.* 1566. B t r–c v.

28 Leonard J. Trinterud. *Elizabethan Puritanism.* New York: Oxford University Press, 1971. 82.

29 *Verantwortung vom Logo von dem Wort oder son Gottes und etlichen andern aufflagen.* [Jena: Thomas Rebart] 1561. D ij v.

30 John Henry Primus. *The Vestments Controversy.* Kempen: J. H. Kok, 1960.

the adiaphora), the Puritans' question was Flacius' question: "whether it be a "mortall sinne to transgresse civil lawes which be the commaundements of civill Magistrates." Their answer was Flacius' answer: "it lieth not in the power of any man to ordaine any worshippings of God, withowte the commandment of God."[27]

> The Divel could not have found, or devised anything more crafty or subtill, to destroy the trew worshipping of God, and to overthrowe the truew chirch of Christ: then the chaunging, and bringing in of thinges called indifferent.

"The quotations from Epinus [Aepinus] and Flacius came to be regarded as standard by the English bishops – in short, they were anything but *ex parte* pronouncements elicted for a purpose..."[28] The "four general rules" for worship by Puritan Thomas Cartwright, for instance, come straight from Flacius' *Book about True and False Adiaphora.*

> 1. That they offend not any, especially the Church of God.
> 2. That all be done in order and comliness.
> 3. That all be done to edifying.
> 4. That all be done to the glory of God.

Flacius, it should be noticed here, did not share the Puritans' – biblicistic – presupposition that the adiaphora were also limited to those mentioned in the New Testament itself. "That I teach that no ancient ceremonies should be preserved in the churches," he wrote, "is not true."[29] But that notion apart, both on the continent and in England, resisting the surplice meant refusing to betray the church into the power of the state. The English Vestarian Controversy,[30] an extension of the Adiaphora Controversy, was fought over the same flowing, white symbol as in Lutheran Germany – about "the chorrok which we commonlie call in English a surplesse." Flacius had helped raise the delicate problem of the Queen's authority.

[Flacius] fayneth properly, but lyeth not. – William Baldwin

Flacius influenced not only English politics, but also English letters. His one work of fiction, which appeared in London in 1549, was directed against the tyrant responsible for the murder of Baldo Lupetino: *Wonderfull Newes of the Death of Paule, the III last byshop of Rome, Where in is Truly Set Out the Abominable Actes of His Most Mischevous Life, and of Diverse Thynges that After his Death Have Happened, Written in Latin by P. Esquillus and Englished by W.B. Londoner.* The "W. B." in the title is most likely William Baldwin,[1] the most representative religious and moralistic writer of the reign of Edward VI. It is "...a highly visual and, at times, grotesque satire," writes Stephen Gresham, "woven through a tapestry narrative. The narrative itself moves steadily from Pope Paul's reception in hell to a recounting of the pope's 'mischevous deeds,' including the abuse of his own daughter, to the final casting of the pope into a lake of fire."[2] William Ringler has summarized the story.

> When Pope Paul III dies, my Genius brings me to the pope's palace, where I see Dracolicus carry him to hell. We see him change into a foul hag, clothed in a dress on which are figured his most notable crimes, and sit on a spotted beast with seven heads and ten horns. His son, Peter Aloysius, meets him and berates him for having said that there was no hell, so that he had thought he could commit crimes without punishment.
>
> We follow Paul III to the city of Pluto, where his crimes are engraved on pillars of adamant: he forces his sister to become the mistress of Alexander Borgia and poisoned his mother; after he was made a cardinal he begot a son; when he became pope, he committed incest with his daughter, Constance; he overcame the Perusines and drove Ascanius Colona from his kingdom; he gave Parma and Placentia to his son; he cast horoscopes and gave bribes; he led the forces of the church against Christians and desired to "swim in the blood of the Lutherans."
>
> Genius then shows me the feast prepared by Pluto at which the kings of the earth engendered with the whore with the golden cup, after which they were thrown into a pond of brimstone to be punished forever. "This is the end of the great Bishop Paul." Then Genius leads me back to earth, as before us was led the seven-headed beast with the cup on its back – gifts which Pluto was sending to Paul's successor. So we return to Rome, and I write this to you, my Forius. Halcyon days will come again. Adieu.[3]

In the same book, Englishmen read about the pope's son, awaiting his father in hell,

> ...wrapped in a Goates skinne, ryd vpon a Goate, that was so byg, that he seemed to be greater then a bul. At his brest in stede of a golden Bull, hong a great Priapus ... About Peter Aloysius [Pier Luigi] were Catamites [boys kept for unnatural purposes] innumerable ... And in theyr banners ... they had images of Priapus.

An account followed of the rumored homosexual violation of the twenty-four year-old bishop of Fano by the Pope's son, Pier Luigi Farnese.[4] A triumphal arch recorded the sordid deeds.

1 King. 371. George B. Parks, however, in "William Barker, Tudor Translator." *Papers of the Bibliographical Society of America* LI (1957). 134, attributes it to William Barker.

2 "William Baldwin: Literary Voice of the Reign of Edward VI." *The Huntington Library Quarterly* XLVI, 1981. 112.

3 *Beware the Cat by William Baldwin, the First English Novel.* William A. Ringler, Jr. and Michael Flachmann (eds.). San Marino, California: Huntington Library, 1988. 124 f.

4 Cf. George B. Parks. "The Pier Luigi Farnese Scandal: An English Report." *Renaissance News* XV (1962). 194 ff.

5 *Wonderfull Newes of the death of Paule the III. last byshop of Rome, where is truly set out the abominable actes of his most mischevous life and of diverse thynges that after his death have happened. Written in latin by P. Esquillus and Englyshed by W. B.* London: T. Gaultier, n. t. B iij v.

6 George Gordon Coulton. *Medieval Panorama. The English Scene from the Conquest to the Reformation.* Cambridge: Cambridge University Press, 1944. 697.

7 Op. cit. 375 f.

8 Peter Partner. *Renaissance Rome 1500–1559.* Berkeley: University of California Press, 1976. 203.

9 Oskar Schade. *Satiren und Pasquille aus der Reformationszeit.* Hannover: Carl Rümper, 1863. 44–47.

10 *Epistola de Morte Pauli Tertii Pontificis Maximis [et] de qua iis, quae post mortem acciderunt.* Piacenza [Basel: Oporinus] ca. 1549. Flacius admits authorship in the German version: *Ein Sendbrieff, P. Aesquilli von dem tode Pauli des dritten Babsts dieses namens, Item was ihm nach seinem tode begegnet ist.* Magdeburg: Christian Rödinger, 1549. King traces the subsequent use of the pseudonymn, "Aesquillus." Op. cit. 373n.

In the vpper parte of this Arche, Peter Aloysius, wrought by force vnnaturallye with the Bysshope Fanensis, whereof that good yong man dyed. And there his father Paule smylying, dyd absolue him.[5]

The morals of the papal family were, of course, a legitimate Reformation theme. Paul III lost all claim to be called merciful, since he had decreed that all Englishmen captured in battle be enslaved[6]; nor could he claim to be disciplined, since he fathered two bastard children. His ascent to the papal throne in 1534 had been possible because his sister, Giulia Farnese, was the mistress of the notorious Pope Alexander VI, hence his informal title, *il cardinale della gonnella*, the petticoat cardinal. The following is King's summary of his life.

Alessandro Farnese (* 1468) rose to favor under the patronage of Rodrigo Borgia after his sister Giulia had a scandalous affair with the cardinal. Appointed to the cardinalate in 1493 soon after his patron was crowned as Pope Alexander VI (1492–1503), Farnese became Legate of Ancona in 1502. Julius II legitimatized his natural offspring, Pier Luigi, Paolo and Costanza. As the senior cardinal and Dean of the College of Cardinals, Farnese was elected pope in 1534 as a transitional figure who was not expected to reign long. In actual fact, fifteen years remained to his life. He detached territory from the papal states to create the hereditary Duchy of Parma and Modena for Pier Luigi and made his grandsons, Guido Sforza and Alessandro Farnese, cardinals.[7]

Pope Paul III was a frequent subject of pasquinades. The term, "pasquinade," derives from the satirical notes that Roman citizens stuck to the statue of Pasquino (Pasquinus, Pasquille), erected in Rome in 1501 in the Piazza Navona. One pasquinade had Paul III dying in childbirth, having aborted two stillborn cardinals,[8] a reference to his two grandsons.

At the pope's death, two other pasquinades appeared in Magdeburg, "A Te Deum of Pope Paul III" by Erasmus Alber[9] and *A Letter on the Death of Paul III, Pontifex Maximus.* The latter was dated November 11, 1549, the day after the death of the eighty-one-year-old pope, and signed "Publius Aesquillus," a reconstruction of the name, "Pasquillus."[10] Publius Aesquillus turns out to be none other than Flacius. The story that the Londoners were reading, was a translation of Flacius' only exercise in fiction. After William Thomas' *Historie of Italy* of 1549, Flacius' tale was only the second written description of contemporary Italy to be found in London. It was as good, Baldwin thought, as the story of "Robin Hode," and he recommended it enthusiastically.

It is wonderfull (good Reader), to see the sundry diversities of wittes what meanes they invente to declare [and] publishe suche thynges as they thinke necessary to be known, some under the colour of fayned histories, some under the persons of specheles beastes, and some under ye shadow of dreames and visions, of which thou haste here a notable and wurthy example.

Flacius' story was the main source of John Bale's account of Paul III in the *Acta Romanorum*. It was popular in England, since it satisfied an "insatiable curiosity about Italy." According to John King, the story was "extremely important as the earliest shift toward the imported standards of Italianate and neoclassical satire that would take hold in England by the end of the century."[11]

Not only did Flacius influence the English satirical tradition; he has a place in the history of the novel. When in 1979, William A. Ringler listed *Wonderfull Newes* among forty-eight works of early English fiction, he recognized Flacius' minor place in the history of English literature because of his influence (especially his first-person narrative),[12] on William Baldwin's novel, *Beware the Cat*,[13] a "robust and sly, direct and wildly ... witty" work, and "arguably the most enjoyable work to come out of the brief Reformist days of Edward VI."[14]

Was Flacius' story mere fiction? Only in its form, according to Baldwin. It was written as a service to "al christen men, especially princes..."

> ... to the intent that all Englishe men myghte thanke God the more for his aboundant mercy, in delivering them through knowledge of his truth from the tiranny of so corrupt and stinking an heade, and the better love and obeye our soveraygne lord and kyng, theyr head by God appoynted...

The facts, Baldwin assures us in his introduction, were accurate: "he fayneth properly, but lyeth not."[15]

11 King. 371. cf. 360, 374.
12 William A. Ringler. "'Beware the Cat' and The Beginnings of English Fiction." *Novel* XII (1979). 126.
13 Ibid. 113, 117; Baldwin. *First English Novel* xvi; King. 387.
14 Arthur F. Kinney. Review in *Modern Philology* LXXXVII (1990). 396; Another edition: William Baldwin. *Beware the Cat.* New London: Connecticut College, 1963.
15 *Wonderful newes.* Introduction.

LUTHER'S VOICE FROM HEAVEN

> I have hoped that even if they despised my entreaties and those of other dutiful men, those men would esteem the voice of Luther, as if admonishing them from heaven.
> – Flacius

A significant part of the history of the printing of Luther's works is the uneasy period between 1548 and 1552, when under imperial pressure Magdeburg had drastic need of the Reformer's authority.[1] Especially effective was Flacius' collection[2] of Luther's letters from the Coburg castle to Melanchthon during the Diet of 1530. In those letters, the contrast became evident between Luther's firm stand at Augsburg in 1530 and at Smalkalden in 1540 and Melanchthon's vacillation.[3] Written at castle Coburg in the days after the presentation of the Augsburg Confession to the 1530 imperial Diet, the letters warned Melanchthon against compromise with the Roman Belial and chided him for pussy-footing (*Leisetreterei*).

Flacius published the letters not only in the original Latin, but also in German translation.[4] He published them again in 1567 for the victims of the Belgian Council of Blood.[5] The collection achieved a kind of canonical status; the Jena edition, which normally published only the original texts, made an exception for Flacius' German version. Save for the Weimar edition, the Jena precedent was followed in subsequent editions of Luther's

1 *Der ander Psalm Davids durch D. Martinum Luther heiliger gedechtnis ausgelegt, Darin auff die leuffte und hendel der weltgelerten itziger Zeit so meisterlich geantwortet und den armen betrübten Christen so reicher trost Lehr und Unterweizung vorgelegt wird gleich als hette er den heilige Geist sonderlich mitfingern auf diese Zeit und tage weisen wollen.* Magdeburg: Christian Rödinger, 1550

Ennaratio 53. Capitis Esaiae prophetae ev. praelectionibus Reverendi patris D. Martini Lutheri, summa fide & diligenter collecta, Anno 1546, nunc (hoc 1550. anno) primum in lucem aedita. Magdeburg: Michael Lotter, 1550.

Die Letzte Predig Doctoris Martini Lutheri Heiliger gedechtnis, So ehr gethan hat zu Wittenberg am andern Sontag nach Epiphanias Domini den xvij. Januarij. Im M.D. Xivj. Jahr. [Magdeburg: Michael Lotter], 1549.

D. Martini Luthers auslegung uber den
129. Psalm Verdeutscht. Zu diesen
betrübten Zeiten fast nützlich zu lesen.
Auch desselbigen etliche Trostbrieff
an betrübte Personen. Magdeburg:
Michael Lotter, 1559.
Parvus Catechismus Pueris in Schola
nuper auctus per Mart. Luth. [Magde-
burg: Michael Lotter, 1550].
Der Spruch Esaie am XXXV. Ausgelegt aus den Schrifften d. Martini Luth.
seliger gedechtnis. Per N. E. E. N.
1548.
Von der Entheubtung Joannis des
Teufers durch der Fuchs-König Herodem. [Magdeburg: Michael Lotter,
ca. 1550].

2   WA, 30/II, 698.
3   Bedenken Doctoris Martini Lutheris
auff den Reichstag zu Augsburgk im
XXX. Yare gesellet. Item ein ander Bedencken auff der Tag zu Schmalkalden
den Ersten martij, des 40. Yars. Der
Theologen so zu solcher zeit daselbst
gewesen welcher namen zu Trücke verzeichnet. Zu diesen ferlichen Zeiten
nützlich und von nöten zu lesen. Damit jederman bericht werden was in
Religionssachen nachzugeben oder
nicht könne nachgegeben werden.
[Magdeburg: Michael Lotter],
1548.
4   Etliche Brieffe des Ehrwirdigen Herrn
D. Martini Luthers seliger gedechtnis an die Theologos auff den Reichstag zu Augsburg geschrieben, anno.
M.D. XXX. Von der der vereinigung
Christi und Belials, Auss welchen man
viel nützlicher Lehr in gegenwertiger
gefahr der Kirchen nemen kan, Verdeudscht. Item, etliche andere Schrief-
ten, nützlich und tröstlich zu lesen.
[Magdeburg: Christian Rödinger,
1549]. WAB, 14, 400–408.
5   Sommige trooslijke vermaningen in
saken die dat haylighe Gootlijcke
woort aengaen, in diese bezoefden tijds
seer nytteliycken ende Troostelychen te
lesen door M. Lutherus. Wesel, 1567.
6   Etliche tröstliche Vermanungen in
Sachen das heilige Göttliche Wort
betreffend, zu dieser betrübten Zeit
sehr nützlich zu lesen. Dr. Martinus
Luther Anno 1530 ... Mit diesen
Sprüchen hat sich der heilig Mann und
teure Held D. Martinus Luther
getröstet Anno 1530, da ihn die Ai-
daphoristen mit ihrer philosophischen
Klugheit und gottlosen Vereinigung

works. His second Luther collection, *Some Comforting Thoughts*,[6] quotations from various Luther letters, offered "ever-fresh, brimming-over
springs of religious power."[7]

The possibility that there might have been differences between Luther
and Melanchthon was new to the public. For Melanchthon, who apparently had lent them to him, the printed collection was a betrayal of trust.
Since the secrets of friends, of whatever kind, should not be revealed –
even letters – he had not acted as an honest man.[8] But the letters, Flacius

Etliche tröstliche ver-
manungen in sachē das heilige Got-
liche Wort betreffend/ zu dieser betrübten zeit
sehr nützlich vnd tröstlich zu lesen.

D. Martinus Luther
Anno M. D. XXX.

Zum Christlichen leser.

Mit diesen sprüchen hat sich der heilige Man vnd
taure held D Martinus Luther getröstet/Anno 30.da jhn
die Adiaphoristen mit jhrer Philosophischer klugheit vn
Gottlosen vereinigung Christi vnd Belias sehr geplagt
vnd geengstiget haben.Solche grosse schmerzen verstehet
vnd fület nicht ein jeder.Weil wir nun sehen/das jhn solche Göttliche trostsprüche nicht betrogen/sondern getrö-
stet/vnd jhn aus seiner freunde/des alten Adams klugheit
vnd aus der feinde list vnd gewalt / scheinbarlich heraus
gerissen/vnd in ewige freud gebracht haben. Ey so last
nur vns/ Jhr armen betrübten/ vnd verlassene Christen/
solche Prophetische rede als ein liecht/welchs im finsternis
leuchtet/nachfolgen.Dann Gottes Wort soll ja ein liecht
sein vnserer füsse/ vnd so wenig als der Himlische Ewige Vater zum lügener werden kan/also wenig kan vns
auch das Heilige Gottes Wort/das da viel fester
denn Himel vnd erden stehet / feilen vnd be-
triegen. Gott gebe vns seine gnade/
AMEN.Matt. Fla. Illy.

Christi und Belials sehr geplagt und geängstiget haben... Magdeburg: Christian Rödinger, 1550; See, WAB,14.400–407. Nr. VIIa–VIIIc, 587– 592; WAB, 5, 1609, 1611; WA, 30, II, 697–699; Johannes Haussleiter. "Matthias Flacius als Herausgeber von Luthers Koburger Briefen und Trostspruchen." *Neue Kirchliche Zeitschrift*, 1917. 149–187. Gustav Kawerau. "Die 'Trostschriften' als eine der ältesten Quellen für Briefe Luthers." ARG, XIV (1917). 187 ff. 191 ff.

7 WA, 30/II, 698. The first to suspect that the arrangement of the collection was not Luther's, but Flacius's, was Ernst Ludwig Enders. "This writing, that was taken over into the collected works of Luther … did not come from Luther, but was put together by Flacius." *Dr. Martin Luther's Briefwechsel.* Calw & Stuttgart: Verlag der Vereinsbuchhandlung 1898, Bd. VIII, 53n. He was followed by Steinlein, "Kritische Bemerkungen zur neuesten katholischen Lutherbiographie [Schluß]." *Neue Kirchliche Zeitschrift* XII (1911). 519 f. Julius Köstlin. *Martin Luther, sein Leben und seine Schrifften.* 5. Auflage nach des Verfassers Tode fortgesetzt von Gustav Kawerau. Berlin: A. Dunker, 1903. II, 655, suggested that it had been assembled partly by Flacius, but also partly by Luther. Here there is a mention, but no citation, of an edition of the *Thoughts* in 1530. Haussleiter, "Herausgeber," thinks this theory is somewhat too clever. Cf. WA, 30/II, 696 ff.

8 "Hamburgi accepi literas Vitemberga, in quibus erat scriptum grauiter accusari me a Dominis, quod nec liberalis nec honesti hominis officio functus sim, qui Epistolas Lutheri ediderim, non enim esse patefacienda amicorum secreta, cuius modi sunt etiam literae." *Entschuldigung … an die Universitet.* [Magdeburg: Christian Rödinger] 1549. F iiij r – v.

9 WAB, XIV, 401n.

10 *Entschuldigung … an die Universitet.* [F iiij r].

said, were addressed not only to Melanchthon; the Holy Spirit had written them to the whole church.[9] "…because I have hoped that even if they despised my entreaties and those of other dutiful men, those men would esteem the voice of Luther, as if admonishing them now from heaven."[10]

Jena aspired to be the New Wittenberg as the true guardian of Luther's literary remains. The Jena edition of Luther's works, eight German volumes from 1555 to 1558 and four Latin volumes from 1556 to 1558, became the standard Luther text until the 19th century. Controversy was

11 Nicolaus von Amsdorf. *Das die zu Wittenberg im anderen Teil der Bücher Doctoris Martini, im Buch "Das diese Worte Christi (Das ist mein Leib, etc.) Noch feststehen," mehr denn ein Blatt, vier gantze Paragraphos versetzlich aussgelassen haben wie folget.* Magdeburg: Michael Lotter, 1549. A 4 a f. The paragraphs omitted: WA, Vol. 23, lines 277.33 through 281.27 and 283.1 through 4. LW, 37, lines 147 to 149.26.

12 Reinhold Jauernig. "Die Konkurrenz der Jenaer mit der Wittenberger Ausgabe von Martin Luthers Werken." *Luther Jahrbuch* XXVI (1959). 80; Eike Wolgast. "Der Streit um die Werke Luthers im 16. Jahrhundert." ARG, LIX, (1968). 177–202; WA, 60, Introduction.

13 Eike Wolgast. *Die Wittenberger Luther-Ausgabe.* Frankfurt am Main: Buchhandlung der Vereinigung, 1982. 200 f.

14 *Bericht von der Wittenbergischen Tomis der Bücher des Ehrnwirdigen Herrn Doctoris Martini Luther. Wider Matthes Flacium Illyricum.* Wittenberg: Hans Lufft, 1558. A iij r.

15 Gustav Georg Zeltner. *Kurtz-gefaßte Historie Der gedruckten Bibel-Version und anderer Schriften D. Mart. Lutheri...* Nuremberg and Altdorff: Joh. Dan. Tanberg Erben, 1727. 87 f.

16 "Extract aus der Historia ecclesiastica manuscripta des Gothaischen Consistorial-Raths D. Cypriani, darinnen die Historia Tomorum Lutheri, aus denen Original-Acten des Waymarischen und Gothaischen Archiv abgehandelt wird." FS, 1726. 738.

17 *Apologia ... Menii.* [F iiij r].

18 *Bericht von der Wittenbergischen Tomis.* Op. cit.

19 Christoph Walther. *Ein Register aller Bücher und Schrifften des Ehrnwirdigen Herrn Doctoris Martini Lutheri seliger gedechtnis welche in die Eilff Deudsche Theil und in die sieben Latinische Tomos, zu Wittenberg gedruckt sind. Item Etliche Bücher und Schrifften welche in den zwelfften Teil, wils Gott in kurtz gedruckt sollen werden nach diesem Register verzeichnet.* Wittenberg: Hans Lufft, 1558.

20 Wolgast. "Streit". 199.

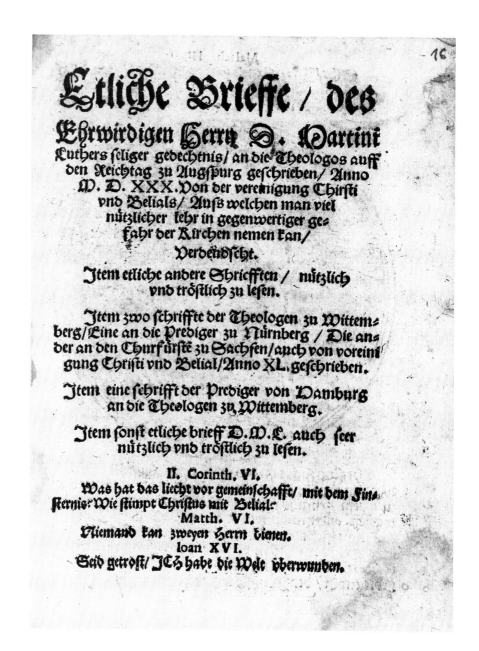

transformed into scholarly precision beginning with a charge by von Amsdorf in 1549 that the Wittenberg edition had omitted parts of a text critical of Martin Bucer's teaching on the sacrament, and Luther's warning to beware of "sacramentarianism." The charge was part of the larger controversy whether Melanchthon was attempting to falsify Luther's doctrine of the sacrament. It was obvious, Amsdorf wrote, that the Wittenbergers wanted to shield a heretic.[11]

Having heard of the plan of Duke Johann Friedrich the Middler to publish a new edition, Flacius and Gallus proposed in a letter of December 21, 1552, that he call George Rörer from his exile in Denmark to be the editor. Rörer had left Wittenberg during the recent crisis "solely because he wanted thereby to be faithful to his master."[12] Since it was well-known that Rörer had been Luther's secretary, his cooperation gave the new project an aura of legitimacy. In the first volume, which appeared in 1555, Amsdorf summarized the cause against the earlier edition: it had omitted parts of texts, altered others, included the works of other authors, used translations rather than original languages, and had adopted a thematic arrangment rather than a chronological one. Mixing what Luther had written while he was still a monk with those which reflected his mature position gave a false impression.[13]

Christoph Walther, editor of the Wittenberg edition answered that the omissions had been ordered by Luther himself, who had changed his mind about Bucer's doctrine.[14] Perhaps Walther was lying; he had also been accused earlier of deliberately omitting or altering passages from Luther's texts in favor of the Calvinists.[15] Rörer would scarcely have restored the omitted words in the Jena edition had Luther actually given such an order. Flacius and others charged that the court had ordered a cover-up of the Interim, which involved too much mildness toward the Zwinglians. And the words were restored later even to the text of the Wittenberg edition. Doubt is cast on Walther's statement because he made the claim only after Rörer's death. Suspicion for having given the order to change Luther's sacramental doctrine falls on Melanchthon and his son-in-law, Caspar Peucer.[16] But the question whether Luther authorized the changes has never been resolved.

In a tract against Menius, Flacius repeated Amsdorf's reproach.[17] It provoked a lengthy reply by Walther, meant, perhaps, to advertise his edition,[18] and a register was added to the Wittenberg edition, in which he (correctly) argued that Luther's order was preserved, along with accurate transcriptions.[19] In the end, Walther's efforts were without success. Amsdorf's original reproach led to the charge of crypto-Calvinism.

The insistence that only Luther's own works be included in the edition was due to the determination to emphasize Luther's influence over that of Melanchthon. The greater success of the Jena volumes, according to Eike Wolgast, was largely due to the determination of the Magdeburg theologians to make it so.[20] Everything would appear in the language originally used, a chronological arrangement, and exact rendering of Luther's own text.[21] Later editions have followed the Jena, not the Wittenberg edition.[22] The Jena rules[23] thus happily transformed theological passion into a standard of scholarly accuracy.

21 *Sammlung.* 1726. 751 f.
22 Wolgast. "Streit." 197.
23 1. Nihil addatur et adimatur scriptis viri Dei. 2. Maneant in ea lingua, qua scripsit autor. 3. Nihil inseratur, quod authoris non est. 4. Ordo et series annorum diligens servetur. 5. Adantur in marginis asterici in quo quid erroris occurit. 6. Seorsim contextatur historia Lutheri, quae simul index sit. Reinhold Jauernig. "Zur Jenaer Luther Ausgabe." *Theologische Literaturzeitung* LXXVII (1952). 754; D. Cyprian. "Extract aus der Historia ecclesiastica manuscripta des Gothaischen Consistorial-Raths D. Cyprian, darinnen die Historica Tomorum Lutheri: aus denen original Acten des Waymarischen und Gothaischen Archiv abgehandelt wird." FS, 1726. 735–766.

Siege

TRUE MAURICIANS

1 On the siege: Sebastian Bessel-meyer. *Gründtlicher Bericht des Magdeburgischen Kriegs, Schlacht, Belagerung und fürnemsten Scharmüzteln. Und alles was sich von beyden teylen, Innen und ausserhalb der Stadt, Von Anfang bis zum ende zugetragen hat. Auffs kürtste warhafftiger verfasset, denn zuvor mit unfleiß Im Druck zu Basell ausgangen ist.* Magdeburg: Christian Rödinger, ca. 1552; Heinrich Merkel. *Warhafftiger, aussfürlicher und grundlicher Bericht von der Altenstadt Magdeburgk Belagerung, so die Röm. Key: May: Carolus Quintus sampt Churfürsten, Fürsten und Stenden des Heiligen Römischen Reichs etc. Anno 50 am 16. Septembris angefangen und bis auff den 9. novembris Anno 51. continuirt: Und wie endlich die Stadt vortragen und zur Aussönung wider kommen.* Magdeburg: Paul Donat, 1587; Elias Pomerius. *Warhafftige, Grundtliche unnd Eygentliche Beschreibung der uber-jährigen Belagerung der kayserlichen freyen Reichstadt Magdeburgk.* Magdeburg: Johann Francken, 1622; Friedrich Wilhelm Hoffman. *Geschichte der Stadt Magdeburg.* Neu bearbeitet von Gustav Hertel und Friedrich Hülsse. Magdeburg: Albert Rathke, 1855. II, 1–32; Salig. II; Liliencron. IV, 499–520.
2 Friedrich Heer. *The Holy Roman Empire.* London: Weidenfeld & Nicolson, 1968. 29. Cf. MGH. *Scriptores* III, 1896. 20–41.
3 Adalbert Joseph Herzberg. *Der heilige Mauritius: Ein Beitrag zur Geschichte der deutschen Mauritiusverehrung.* Düsseldorf: Schwann, 1936. 83.

... we can consider it an honor that we are worthy to suffer shame and persecution for the sake of Jesus' name ... and to become true mauricians ... his history is almost the same as our deeds. – Magdeburg Pastors

It was the last time the voice of the people was heard in Germany until the eighteenth century. – Karl Brandi

Hellersleben, just outside Magdeburg, was reduced to ashes. Eight hundred men had been captured and hundreds were wounded, victims of the marauding troops of twenty-one-year-old Duke George of Mecklenburg, who took sides with the Catholic Magdeburg *Stift*. The long-dreaded military attack on the city had begun.[1] It was September 22, 1550, the Day of St. Maurice, the ancient commander of the Theban legion, who had chosen death rather than fight against Christians.

Six hundred years earlier, in 922 A. D., preparing for battle against the Hungarians, Emperor Otto I had...

... invoked all the saving powers and forces he knew: St. Lawrence, to whom on the morning of the battle he vowed a bishopric at Merseburg in the event of victory; the Archangel Michael, standard bearer of the empire, and of the hosts of heaven, whose battle ensigns pulsed with divine energy ... and the lance of St. Maurice ... linking him directly with the saving energy which flowed from Christ the conqueror.[2]

In 1843, Archduke Matthias of Austria visited the Magdeburg Cathedral and took the relics of St. Maurice away. In that Protestant city no longer, it was said, were they estimated.[3] The cult of St. Maurice – indeed, all "estimation" of dead bones – ended with the Reformation.

No longer a credible source of military energy, according to Lutheran teaching about saints, St. Maurice remained an example. To honor him, then, was to resist the emperor's army – even though the attackers had a battle ensign emblazoned with St. Maurice's image, and St. Maurice's sword. It is not without interest that when the survival of the Reformation was at stake,[4] its defenders identified themselves with a black African. "As it is written," read the proclamation of the city council, "the praiseworthy knight, the dear St. Maurice, together with all his legions, shed their blood when they refused to serve the Roman emperor against Christians."[5]

The true Mauricians were not those who had contact with his relics, the Magdeburgers insisted, but those who had laid down their lives at Hellersleben.

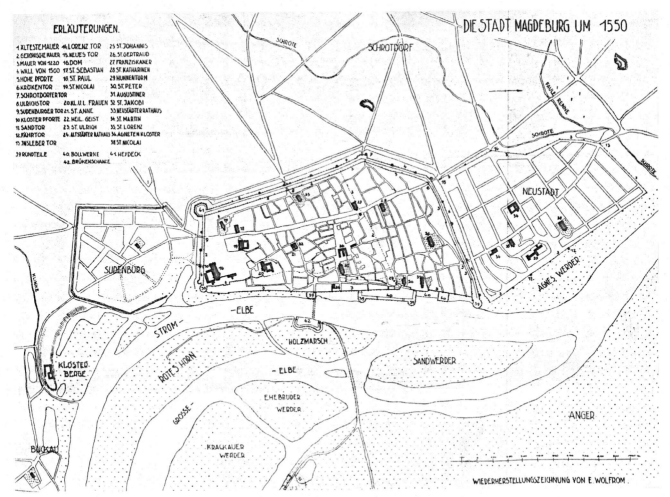

Magdeburg about 1500. Erich Wolfrom. *Die Baugeschichte der Stadt und Festung Magdeburg*. Magdeburg: City of Magdeburg, 1936.

St. Moritz. Statue in the Magdeburg Cathedral.

Our suffering is holy because it is based on God's Word. Those who died on St. Maurice's day did not die in vain. St. John's prophecy was being fulfilled – the devil wanted again to enthrone the Antichrist. We are disobedient children. The Lord is just, but we are unjust. He wants to test whether we will remain with him under the cross.

...we can consider it an honor that we are worthy to suffer shame and persecution for the sake of Jesus' name ... and to become true mauricians. We remember the example of dear Maurice rather than others, because in the papacy he was patron here in Magdeburg and his history is almost the same as our deeds. For like him and his men we did not want to sacrifice to idols according to the command of the emperor, nor offer any help against Christians.[6]

The siege army numbered sixteen or twenty thousand; the Magdeburg garrison, in contrast, counted 3,000. In Flacius' prayer, those three thousand were the biblical seven thousand, the faithful remnant.

169

4 Ritschl. II, 328.

5 *Der von Magdeburg Ausschreiben an alle Christen.* Magdeburg: Michael Lotter, 1550. B iij v; Gude Suckale-Redlefsen. *The Black St. Maurice.* Houston: Menil Foundation, Munich & Zürich: Schnell & Steiner, 1987.

6 *Christlich kurtze erinnerung an ihre Christliche gemeine und all Christen ausserhalb, gegenwertrige Verfolgung betreffend, so wir in und uber der bekentnis des Evangelii Christi allhie zu Magdeburg itzt leiden.* Magdeburg: Michael Lotter, 1550. C ij r.

7 *Eine freidige vermanung.* A ij r.

8 Friedrich W. E. Roth. *Augsburg Reformationsgeschichte IV: 1547–1555.* Munich: Theodor Ackermann, 1911. 296; *Gründliche Verlegung des ... Comments.* B iij v – f.

9 Liliencron. *Volkslieder* IV. 497.

O Lord Jesus Christ, thou Son of the Living God, whom the Eternal and Almighty God hast annointed over his holy mountain Zion, that is, over the church, against the raging and fury of the kings and princes, and to whom he has given an inheritance and possessions unto the ends of the earth, protect the seven thousand elect and graciously guard them and break the godless Ahabs and Baalites like an earthen vessel with the iron scepter.[7]

The mood at the 1547 "Armored Diet" at Augsburg had been triumphal. At the 1550 Diet, in contrast, spirits had been dampened by reports that Matthias Flacius was preventing the execution of imperial law in Magdeburg. There were demands for military action,[8] and Elector Maurice, the Judas of Meissen, was charged with subduing the city. Determined to lead events rather than to be led by them, he appeared on the scene on September 29 and took over the siege army. Some versifier, ending each line with the sound, "-ich," put in his mouth an appropriate apology.

> Für Magdeburg zu ziehen verpflicht' ich mich,
> Dieselben zu verderben undschuldiglich,
> Welchs mein Bundgenossen und ich
> jetz under vorhaben ganz haimblich.
> Unswer kainer kommt davon, das weis ich.
> Der Teufel kom und hole mich
> Und alle meine gesellen, das wünsche ich,
> Die hell wartet unser ganz herrlich,
> Ade, Evangelium, Gott gesegne dich![9]

> I bind myself to appear before Magdeburg,
> to destroy it innocently,
> Which plan my allies and I
> have decided secretly.
> None of us will escape, that I know.
> Let the devil come and take me
> and all my men, that I wish.
> Hell waits for us.
> Farewell, gospel. God bless you.

Not adverse to using strong measures, Maurice imprisoned the entire city council of Torgau on September 30 when they refused to pay taxes to finance the siege.[10] On November 29 the besiegers burned the Magdeburg *Neustadt*.

Reporting to the emperor on the progress of the siege was General Lazarus Schwendi. The English diplomat, Roger Ascham, wrote about his persecution of Protestants.

> ... this Lazarus Swendi is a tall and a comely personage, and being brought up in learning under Oecolampadius at Basel, making more account of his tall stature than any beauty of the mind, began to be weary of learning, and became desirous to hear some brag in the world, and so made a soldier, marred a scholar; and because he would make a lusty change from the fear of God and knowledge of Christ's doctrine, he fell to be a perverse and bloody papist, ever at hand in any cruel execution against the poor Protestants ...[11]

From his pulpit, Wolfgang Ruppert, chaplain to Duke Albrecht Alcibiades of Brandenburg-Kulmbach, denounced the siege as sin.[12] There was talk

Elector Moritz in blackface as Saint Moritz in the Leipzig *Rathaus*.
Courtesy of Günther Wartenberg.

10 F. Joel. "Herzog August von Sachsen bis zur Erlangung der Kurwürde. Schluß." *Neues Archiv für Sächsische Geschichte und Altertumskunde* XIX (1898). 271.

11 Acham. 37.

12 Matthias Simon. *Evangelische Kirchengeschichte Bayerns*. Nuremberg: Selbstverlag des Verfassers, 1952. 256.

13 F. Roth. 318.

14 Emil Körner. *Erasmus Alberus. Das Kämpferleben eines Gottesgelehrten aus Luthers Schule*. Leipzig: M. Heinsius Nachfolger, 1910. 127.

about the Roman Cerberus and the Spanish Geryon. If the Spanish were free to enter Germany, all Europe would be lost.[13]

The talent of the veteran officers in the city began to make itself felt when military fortunes began to improve. On December 19, Magdeburg troops attacked a cavalry camp at Ottersleben and captured 263 horses and "like swine and cattle" in Alber's song, 225 prisoners.[14] Another

15 F. Roth. 319.

16 Götze. 172.

17 Heinrich Wilhelm Benson. *Das Verhängnis Magdeburgs*. Schaffhausen: Hurter, 1858. 64. Besselmeyer. B iij.

18 H. von Hase. 91.

19 *Deutsche Geschichte*. 248.

20 *Die kirchliche Reunionsbestrebungen während der Regierung Karls V.* Freiburg: Herder, 1879. 424.

21 Eduard Jacobs. "Ein bisher unbekanntes, während der Belagerung von Magdeburg im Jahre 1550–1551 gedrucktes niederdeutsches Gesangbuch nebst einer Übersicht über die geistig-literarischen Schutz- und Trutzwaffen des Belagerten." *Geschichtsblätter für Stadt und Land Magdeburg* VI (1871). 184.

22 Bezold. *Geschichte*. 811.

23 Karl August von Hase. *Kirchengeschichte auf der Grundlage akademischer Vorlesungen* III. Leipzig: Breitkopf & Härtel, 1891. 187.

24 *Ehrendenckmal*. 44.

trophy was the battle ensign of St. Maurice. Next day's report was even better; Magdeburg troops captured Duke George of Mecklenburg himself. At the news, jubilation broke out in Augsburg.[15] In Magdeburg, the widows of the men who died in battle on St. Maurice's day demanded immediate execution. But cooler heads prevailed. For the duration of the siege, January to November, the duke was imprisoned in the house where Flacius was employed, at the Sign of the Dragon.

The news of Magdeburg's resistance raced through Europe. At Augsburg, songs were sung about its knights of Christ, about bold sermons and appeals. In Hamburg appeared *Two Writings of M. Joachim Westphal, pastor of Hamburg, in the first, it is demonstrated that those who resist the present changes of doctrine, are not quarreling about Petty Matters*.[16] According to Magdeburg historian Heinrich Merkel the city resisted "so that also foreign nations could sense ... old, steadfast German hearts and spirits, for whom God's word, their Fatherland and freedom were dear."

On the Tuesday after St. Andrew's Day, December 2, there was an assembly before the Magdeburg *Rathaus*. Soldiers formed ranks in the middle and citizens lined up on both sides. Together with the council and two Counts of Mansfeld, Albrecht and Karl, they swore to be true in life and in death, to stay together on the walls and the embankments, on water and land, and to fight against the foe to the last drop of blood.[17] They had a right to freedom, they insisted, based on membership in the Hanseatic League.[18] It was a political movement important to know for those who would like to find anti-absolutist strands in German history. According to Karl Brandi, the Magdeburg resistance was "the last time the voice of the people was heard in Germany until the eighteenth century."[19]

According to the ultramontaine historian, Ludwig Pastor, the Magdeburg resistance was purely political, based on aversion to anything positively churchly.[20] The songs that have survived, however, speak of the religious motivation of the Magdeburgers, who identified their faith with that of the ancient Maccabees.

> Thut wie die Machabeer
> und streittet für gottes wort,
> Griefft an die landtsverherer
> rechnet den grossen mord
> Im Teudtschen landt begangen.[21]

> Do as the Maccabees did
> And strive for God's word.
> Attack the land's betrayer;
> Avenge the gross murder
> done in the German land.

A stanza was added to the hymn, "Lord, Keep Us Steadfast in Your Word," a prayer for the imprisoned elector.[22] Someone had seen him at the head of an army of angels in the sky, protecting the city.[23] At 12 o'clock daily the bells of all parish churches were rung for prayer in the homes, and on the open squares the workers would pause for prayer.[24]

Müssen wir darüber sterben
lob, er und preis sei gott,
Der uns dann heisst ererben
das ewig leben dort.[25]

If we must die because of it,
Praise, glory and honor be to God
Who has promised us
that we will inherit eternal life there.

A religiously indifferent population, Waldemar Kawerau observed, "would scarcely have risked their life and freedom for the faith."[26]

25 Franz M. Böhme. *Altdeutsches Liederbuch*. Hildesheim: Georg Olms & Wiesbaden: Breitkopf and Härtel, 1966. 505.
26 Erasmus Alber in Magdeburg." *Geschichtsblätter für Stadt und Land Magdeburg* XXVIII (1893). 5.

WHO CAN FIGHT JERUSALEM?

All those who let themselves be used against us and their fellow Christians, persecute not only Christians, but our Savior Jesus Christ himself. – Magdeburg City Council

Absolutely no one will allow himself to be used against Jerusalem and Our Lord God's Chancery. – Valerius Kraukau

Just as the Smalcald League had done, the Magdeburgers insisted that they were loyal to the emperor in secular matters.[1] Following Luther's distinction between the two realms, however, they would not tolerate the emperor's authority in religious matters. The distinction was lost on Elector Maurice. For him, the city was simply seditious.

The bold verses of Erasmus Alberus reinforced the impression.

Macht unterm Adel Meuterei,
daß kein treu Mann bei Fürsten sei...[2]

Cause a mutiny among the nobles
so that no faithful man be with the prince...

To his chagrin he had to bear being called "the Judas of Meissen."

Moritz, du rechter Judas,
was hastu gethan!
Du bringst uns die Spanier,
die schenden frau und man;
Du bringst her die Maraner
in unser vaterland
darzu Italiener,
ist dir ein ewig schand!
Kyrie eleison.[3]

What have you done, Maurice, you Judas?
You bring us the Spaniards
who disgrace woman and man:

1 For example, in *Christlicher Bericht aus heiliger schrift, wie ferne man dem Oberherrn Gehorsam schuldig sei, auch wie unnd in welcherlei fellen man den verderblichen Tyrannen möge widerstand thun. Allen Christen, sonderlich den Kriegsleuten, nützlich zu lesen.* [Magdeburg: Michael Lotter, n. t.].
2 Götze. 171.
3 Liliencron. IV, 464.

4 Acham. 52.
5 Karl Erich Born. *Moritz von Sachsen und die Fürstenverschwörung gegen Karl V.* Darmstadt: Wissenschaftliche Buchgesellschaft, 1972. 77.
6 Wartenberg. "Nachwirkungen." 246, 250.
7 *Ausschreiben an alle Christen.* A iij r.
8 Baumgarten. 255.
9 J. Hermann. 130 f.
10 PKMS, IV, No. 701.

you bring us the Marons and Italians
to our Fatherland
You are eternally disgraced!
Kyrie eleison.

The day that Charles V invested him with the stolen title of Elector someone fixed a defiant note to the gate of the house he occupied – *Seu dux, seu princeps, seu tu dicaris elector, Maurici, es patriae proditor ipse tuae!*[4] "Whether you are called duke, prince or elector, you are a traitor to your fatherland."

There were rumors that the sons of Johann Friedrich were plotting to regain their lost territory.[5] What if they were to ally themselves with France? Lazarus Schwendi talked darkly about a new *Schweizerei.* Wars were being planned, he said, as in Switzerland, to drive out princes, lords, and nobles. If the resistance were not subdued, a conflagration would surely break out.[6] The goal of the late war, according to popular consensus, was to destroy the Augsburg Confession, and peasants dug bulwarks only under duress. If the religion were changed, Maurice was warned, there would be a rebellion, the fighting would be worse than in the Peasants' War, and not even one out of a hundred of Maurice's subjects would remain loyal.

"All those who let themselves be used against us and their fellow Christians," the Magdeburg City council made it known, "persecute not only Christians, but our Savior Jesus Christ himself."[7] It is no longer an echo that sounds from the Lord God's Chancery, but a fanfare for attack. "Did not that echo in this year 1550," asked Hans Baumgarten, "grow with the fruits in the field?"[8] "The common man," Maurice realized, "is very attached to the city."

But asks Baumgarten,[9] what was there to win in a war against Magdeburg? Military failure and great costs, or – at best – the sad, harmful reputation of having betrayed "our Lord God's Chancery" to the papists and the enemies of freedom? Moritz frantically sent spies, reporters, eavesdroppers to Berlin, Munich, Hesse, Denmark, Paris, the imperial court.

It was an agitated Maurice who appeared before the Landtag at Torgau on October 12th, only days after the siege had begun. The siege, he pleaded, was both right and necessary. Magdeburg was guilty of acts of violence, of breach of the peace, and of criticizing his theologians in Wittenberg and Leipzig. If the nobles were to refuse to follow their liege lord and support the Magdeburg siege, Maurice wanted to know, what would prevent the peasants from doing the same? He attempted to frighten the estates by reading from one of Magdeburg's leaflets.

> Deutzsch landt hette keine not,
> wurden die vom Adel
> von jedem schock
> fier Mandel geschlagen todt.[10]

> Germany would have no problem
> if the nobles were killed –
> four mandels for every shock.

Fifteen sheaves of grain, as everybody knew, made a mandel. And four mandels made a shock. Eliminating four mandels per shock, then, was a clear call for killing. The court at Dresden had identified the revolutionary firebrand. The new Thomas Müntzer was Matthias Flacius Illyricus.[11]

But was there really danger of revolution? Gallus dismissed comparisons with the chaotic revolutionary Anabaptist kingdom in Münster in Westphalia. No one could expect perfection, he wrote, but the mercenary troops were no different than they were elsewhere. At least some of their women were proper wives and not prostitutes. Discipline was being maintained in the city; the authorities had been admonished to enforce proper behavior, and no fornicator was admitted to communion.[12]

Nor were the Estates concerned. There was no need to ruin the city, they decided. Rather, the imperial bann should be suspended, and negotiations with Magdeburg conducted with kindness. They pressed the Elector to get guarantees from the emperor that the Lutheran confession would not be displaced. They even dared suggest that Maurice resign in favor of his brother, Duke August.

At a meeting at Jüterbog the elector appealed for assistance to the Estates of the Imperial Circle, the lands adjacent to Saxony, including vassals on church lands of the Magdeburg and Halberstadt dioceses, but they also refused. At Zörbig he appealed to the Saxon knights. Led by *Krieghauptmann* Asmus von Könneritz, even under threat of losing their fiefs, they refused to fight against Magdeburg.[13] Valerius Kraukau explained: "Absolutely no one will allow himself to be used against Jerusalem and Our Lord God's Chancery."[14]

11 "Für den Dresdner Hof ... 'Müntzerisch' wäre damit gleich flacianisch." Wartenberg. "Nachwirkungen." 249.

12 *Ein sendbrieff Nicolai Galli Pfarherrn zu S. Ulrich der alten Stadt Magdeburgk an einen andern Pfarrhern ausserhalb zum bericht gegen etlicher leichtfertiger Leut schmehung, als ob keine zucht noch Erbarkeit inn dieser belagerung mehr bei uns fürhanden.* Magdeburg: Michael Lotter [1551].

13 Julius von Könneritz. "Weigerung der Leipziger Ritterschaft, gegen Magdeburg zu ziehn, und das hierauf von Kurfürst Moritz gegen dieselbe, so wie gegen deren Führer, den Oberhauptmann von Könneritz eingeleitete Verfahren, 1550 ff." *Archiv für die Sächsische Geschichte* IV (1886). 134. PKMS, IV, No. 802.

14 PKMS, No. 729.

GOD'S SCRIPTORIUM

> Illyricus and his adherents have so permeated and tormented the churches of these lands and the schools of Wittenberg and Leipzig with the adiaphora that it would be no wonder if the child in the cradle in these lands would sigh and cry against them.
> – Nikolaus Selnecker

Surrounded by a hostile army, one might reasonably have concluded that Magdeburg had been been reduced to silence. "During the siege," Flacius wrote, "when we were surrounded by our enemies so that no one could go in or out, they began to defend their most beautiful *Adiaphoristerei*, to lay one cross after the other on the troubled Christians and, together with the enemies, to persecute the church of God."[1]

But it was Wittenberg that was silenced; the Wittenbergers were obedient to the censorship laws. Thus, the only printed comments on the Interim were the denunciations from Magdeburg, "Gottes Schreibstube"–

1 *Wider den Evangelisten.* A ij r.

2 Friedrich Hülsse. "Beiträge zur Geschichte der Buchdruckerkunst in Magdeburg." *Bibliographiae Reconditae* I. Amsterdam: Schupper, 1966. 636–738; Johannes Voigt. "Über Pasquille, Spottlieder und Schmähschriften aus der ersten Hälfte des 16. Jahrhunderts." *Raumers Taschenbuch* IX (1838). 429–473.

3 "Des Flacius Erbsünde-Streit." *Zeitschrift für Historische Theologie* XIX (1849). 139.

4 CS, XVI, 594.

5 Mirković, 1960. 498.

6 H. von Hase. 14.

7 "Reformationszeitliche Bildpolemik auf rheinischem Steinzeug." *Bonner Jahrbücher* CLXXIX. Cologne: Rheinland-Verlag, 1979. 275.

8 *Bericht*. 1559. H ij r.

Precationes Miserae & afflictae Ecclesiae quae est in Belgico, quae in hisque praesentibus periculis à solo Christo tota pendet. Zwey Gebethe der Elenden Hochbetrübten Christlichen Kirchen im Niderlande/welche in der jetzo ihr vorstehnden eussersten Jahr vnd verfolgung/allein an dem Herzen Christo henget. [Hamburg: Joachim Löw, ca. 1566]. Herzog August Bibliothek, signature 527.29 Quod. (20).

God's Scriptorium. Writing feverishly, Erasmus Alber, Nicolaus von Amsdorf, Nicholas Gallus and Flacius poured out a torrent of propaganda.[2] "Here, in these ungrateful German lands," wrote Kaspar Aquila, who may have originated the term, "no one dares to print anything against the Interim except the highly praiseworthy, ancient, Christian, imperial city, Magdeburg – there is God's chancery." Eduard Schmid commented that Flacius was convinced that if he did not keep on writing the truth would be suppressed.[3] For Caspar Schwenckfeld he was "like the nine-headed Hydra, which eventually was beheaded by Hercules, but in the place of every one that was cut off, developed two heads."[4]

The flood of pamphlets was produced by courageous printers, Christian Rödinger in the Lödischenhof and Michael Lotter at the Sign of the Dragon, Breiteweg 141. Something new was happening: the newly-invented printing press had been harnessed to change the course of history.

Members of nine craft guilds read the pamphlets and turned them into incendiary speeches.[5] Students, businessmen, nobles and peasants defied the law, slipping out of the city to hawk the fiery words. A Frankfurt bookseller reported selling a Zentner (750 kilograms) of Magdeburg books; another, a ton.[6] One colporteur was arrested for selling a pamphlet against Duke August at the gate of the University of Leipzig.

Bishop Pflug had subtly cast the law in Lutheran language to make it acceptable to the evangelicals. But in selling skills he was no match for the Magdeburgers, who invented a proto-logo that even the illiterate could understand. "Apparently," wrote Ingeborg Krüger, "it was in Magdeburg that the form of a personification of the Interim originated, the 'Interim Dragon,' which established itself as almost canonical."[7]

The Interim dragon had three heads. Its angel's head suggested its seeming innocence. Its pope's head, however, with the triple crown, showed its true goal, subjecting the Evangelical churches to papal authority. Its Turk's head suggested that, in the end, the law would lead to unbelief. Since symbols need not be unambiguous, however, the three heads could also suggest the three Interims, Regensburg, Augsburg, Leipzig, or the three authors, Pflug, Helding, Agricola. The dragon's tail among stars betrayed the family resemblance to the monster of Revelation 12.3: "And another portent appeared in heaven; behold a great red dragon, with seven heads and ten horns, and seven diadems upon his heads. His tail swept down a third of the stars of heaven, and cast them down to earth." One of its feet is a toad's (godlessness?), the other an eagle's talon (imperial power?).

On Magdeburg's coins, Jesus exorcizes the dragon with the words, "Packe di[ch] Satan du Interim!" ("Begone, Satan" Matthew 4.10). Four hundred years after the Interim crisis, Europe is almost dragon-free, but, as our illustrations show, he still prowls in scattered museums, spewing flame on printed pages, on coins, and even on beer mugs.

The logo was not Flacius' invention: "I have never had a dragon or a dragon-head painted."[8] The idea may have been Amsdorf's, who had once

The Interim Dragon. *Das Interims und interimisten warhafftige abgemalte figur und gestalt daraus yderman sonderlich bey dem Bretspiel und der großen Kanen mit Bier yr andacht und messig leben erkennen kan.* Illustration by Pancratz Kempf. Germanisches Museum, Nuremberg. Strauß I, 502. No. 1; the music arranged for performance in J. Wolf, op. cit.; cf. *Lutheran Quarterly* VII (1953). 293–314.

9 Francis Pierrepont Barnard. *Satirical and Controversial Medals of the Reformation. The Biceps or Double-Headed Series.* Oxford: Clarendon Press, 1927.

10 Cod. Guelf. 12.9 Aug. fol. 158. Reproduced, with commentary, in Wolfgang Harms (ed.). *Deutsche Illustrierte Flugblätter des 16. und 17. Jahrhunderts* II. Munich: Kraus International Publications, 1980. 10.

11 *Christliche vermanung etlicher Theologen zu Wittenbergk an alle Christen, sonderlich an die Deudtschen Kriegsleut, nechst verschiener jare und itzt schwebende Kriegshandlung wider die Christen betreffend auffs newe wieder in Druck ausgangen.* Magdeburg: Michael Lotther, 1551.

12 *Gründlicher Bericht aus heiliger schrift, wie ferne man dem Oberherrn Gehorsam schüldig sei, auch wie unnd in wellicherlei fellen man den ver-*

The Interim Dragon. Illustration from *Schöner Lieder Zwei.* Herzog August Bibliothek, signature 925.17 Th. (27).

come up with the image of a cardinal who, upside-down, revealed the face of a fool.[9] Or, since there is an original sketch of the dragon[10] in the collection at Wolfenbüttel called *Interimistica Wigandi,* it may have been Wigand or an artist he had engaged.

The siege of Magdeburg is a significant chapter in the history of psychological warfare. Pamphlets were tossed over the enemy lines for the siege soldiers to read. One of them was the Wittenberg pamphlet from the Smalcald war that Gallus recycled: *Christian Warning of Certain Theologians in Wittenberg to All Christians, especially to German Soldiers about the military matters of the Last Year and Now Pending Against the Christians, Again Published in Print.*[11] Another was an anonymous *Thorough Report from the Holy Scriptures, to what extent one is obligated to the Authorities, how and in which cases one can resist the destructive tyrants. For all Christians, especially military personnel, useful and comforting to read.*

> ... if they serve as military leaders who knowingly serve an evil purpose, such as is now being done, to protect the Antichrist and all his abominations and to reintroduce them, and on the contrary to despoil the gospel with human additions, or even to destroy it, they are truly the devil's own, with body and soul.[12]

The Interim Dragon. Cod. Guelf. 12.9 Aug. 2°. fol. 158.

derblichen Tyrannen möge widerstand thun. Allen Christen, sonderlich den Kriegsleuten, nützlich und tröstlich zu lesen. [Magdeburg: Michael Lotter, 1552]. A iij v.

13 . "Ein Lied und Vermahnung an die Landsknechte, daß sie der armen Christenheit und ihrem Vaterlande beistehen und die Verräter und Verheerer desselben straffen wollten." *Lob der Wetterau, Enthaltend die "Kurze Beschreibung der Wetterau" (1552), zwölf auserlesene Fabeln aus Wetterau und Hessenland, sowie als Anhang fünf geistliche Lieder.* Ed. Helmut Bode. Frankfurt am Main: Waldemar Kramer, 1978. 62.

14 *Klerliche Beweisung, das alle die jenige, welche die schrifften widder das Interim und Mittelding feil zuhaben und zu lesen verbieten, item, die zu dieser zeit, die von Magdeburg (aus waserley weise solches geschehen mag) verfolgen oder verfolgen helffen, Christum den Son Gottes warhafftiglich selbs verfolgen. Geschrieben zur warnung an alle Christen, auff das sie sich für dieser grawsamen, Teufflischen wüterey fleissig huten.* Magdeburg: Michael Lotter, 1550.

Alber encouraged the Magdeburg garrison with *A Song and Admonition to the Troops, that They Assist Poor Christendom and their Fatherland, and that they Punish the Betrayers and Ravagers.*[13] Flacius' contributions to the psychological assault were *Clear Demonstration that everyone who forbids selling or reading publications against the Interim and Adiaphora, and, in whatever way it happens, persecutes those from Magdeburg or assists in persecution, is really persecuting Christ the Son of God himself. Written as warning to all Christians, so that they energetically avoid this horrible, devilish madness,*[14] and *That all Persecutors of the Church of Christ in Magdeburg are Persecutors of Christ. Written as a Warning to all Christians and especially to the Military Personnel of the Enemy.*

> Some will say, I am a subject, a layman, a foot soldier, a peasant. I really cannot judge which side is persecuting the true religion or defending it. God, therefore, will not be angry with me for persecuting the Gospel unknowingly.

The excuse was unacceptable. "If you are a Christian," Flacius wrote, "you really have to recognize Christ's cause and not allow yourself to be used so foolishly, so that you slaughter Christians as if you were asked to slaughter swine or sheep."[15]

Although much of Flacius' hasty writing – "delightful stream-of-consciousness prose," Ronald Diener called it – would have benefitted from an editor, "His age and all history would have been much the poorer without his lively, spirited polemics, written in an adopted language that he made ring with memorable alliterations, metaphors and neologisms."[16] About his propaganda, Otto Ritschl comments

> For this task he was enabled no less by his many-sided, thorough education, as by his tireless energy and his great publicistic skill ... Although in his rapidly written and hastily printed polemical writings linguistic mistakes or less than apt expressions appear, still in all, the style of the Illyrian is notable for skill of expression, richness of graphic images, appropriate comparisons, and smooth flow of thought. His language is easily understandable, clear and popular, and what he said he knew how to present with an extremely impressive eloquence. His discourses are consistently carried by his religious enthusiasm and passion, now by an unrelenting earnestness of his admonitions and demand, now in a vehement action against his opponents, but also sometimes in moving tones of a longing, never extinguished, for peace and theological unity.[17]

His propaganda was astonishingly effective. "Illyricus and his adherents," Nicolaus Selnecker complained, "have so permeated and tormented the churches of these lands and the schools of Wittenberg and Leipzig with the adiaphora that it would be no wonder if the child in the cradle in these lands would sigh and cry against them."[18]

Christina Hasslinger, a doctoral candidate in advertising at the University of Vienna, reported on Flacius' propaganda campaigns: "It is of great importance," Flacius wrote about the public, "what kind of illusion is made for people at first." "The first fancy that comes into their heads, is very important." Flacius repeated ideas again and again – the same arguments, the same quotations, the same biblical passages, illustrations and appeals. "One must explain it to them again and again."[19] Sometimes the arguments were woven into fresh contexts, and sometimes treated from new points of view. He isolated specific target areas – Hamburg, Magdeburg, Königsberg, Naumburg, Austria, Bavaria, and had a sense of the rhythm of a controversy. He recognized "the great simplicity and laziness of the common man, who almost always thinks that the latest book and the latest answer confute the earlier one." If an opponent did not answer immediately he would publish another attack, pointing out that his opponents' silence betrayed shaky foundations.

Flacius was also aware of the power of illustrations. "One must explain the matter to them with all diligence," he wrote, "magnify it, and inform them with powerful and moving words and picture the matter before their eyes."[20] "What one sees moves one more than what one hears."[21] In one pamphlet by "Janus Zymaius," one of Flacius' pseudonyms, appears "Frau Interim," dressed in armor, crowned, and holding a scepter.[22] Another, which makes a distinctly modern impression, is a colored comic strip in the style of the medieval *biblia pauperum*. In the first squares Elector Maurice is keeping company with Joseph's treacherous brothers and, later, as Judas, betrays Jesus. In the seventh square, he betrays Johann Friedrich.[23]

The Interim Dragon. Johannes Wolf. "Ein Spottdruck auf das Augsburger Interim." *Zeitschrift für Bibliothekswesen* XL (1921).

The Interim Dragon. on Magdeburg coins. Rudolf Schildmacher. *Magdeburger Münzen.* Magdeburg, 1936.

15 *Das alle Verfolger der Kirchen Christi zu Magdeburg Christi den Herrn selbst verfolger sindt. Geschreiben zur Warnung an alle Christen und sonderlich an das Kriegsvolch der Feinde.* Magdeburg: Michael Lotter, 1551. A iij v.

16 Diener. 46, 358.

17 Op. cit. II, 358 f.

18 *Christliche und Notwendige Verantwortung.* F iij v.

19 *Verlegung des kurtzen Antwort des Schwenckfelds.* [Magdeburg: Michael Lotter, 1554]. A v.

20 Christina Hasslinger. "Die religiöse Propaganda des Matthias Flacius Illyricus und seiner Epigonen. Ein Beitrag zur Flugschriftliteratur der Reformationszeit." Diss., Vienna, 1970. 112 f., 23 f.

21 *Erklerung der schendlichen Sünde der jenigen, die durch das Concilium, Jnterim und Adiaphora, von Christo zum Antichrist fallen: aus diesem Prophetischen gemelde, des 3. Eliae seliger gedechtnis, D. M. Luth. genomen.* [Magdeburg: Christian Rödinger, 1550]. B iij v.

22 *Ein Arglichs new Lied, von der zart schönen Frawen Interim, auch von zucht, ehr und lob irer Schöpffern.* [Bern: Math. Aparius], 1552. Attribution to Flacius by E. Weller, "Lieder." 293; Karl Schottenloher. *Flugblatt und Zeitung.* Berlin: R. C. Schmidt, 1922. 207. "Die heilig Frau Sant Interim," Bern: Math. Aparius, 1552, reprinted in Lilliencron, "Dichtung." 142 f.

23 Reiner Gross, Manfred Kobuch and Ernst Müller (eds.). *Martin Luther 1483–1546: Dokumente seines Lebens und Wirkens.* Weimar: Hermann Böhlaus Nachfolger, 1983. 286–288.

Flacius. *Vergleichung Francisci mit Christo et Libro Conformitarum, das ist aus der Barfusser Bibel abgedruckt.* Illustration by Monogramist BP. Handschriftenabteilung, Staatsbibliothek zu Berlin Preussischer Kulturbesitz. YA307gr; Geisberg 654 f.;Geisberg/Strauß II, 619; Hallstein VI, No. 18.

Flacius. *Unterschied zwischen der wahren Religion und falschen Abgöttischen lehre der Antichrists in den fürnehmsten stücken.* Illustration by Cranach the Younger. Kupferstichkabinett, Staatliche Museen zu Berlin Preußischer Kulturbesitz. H. 18. Geisberg III, 854; Geisberg/ Strauß 654 f. St. Francis (upper right) portrayed as equal to God.

A good research theme, according to Hildegard Zimmermann, would be Flacius' collaboration with artists.[24] According to F. J. Stopp, "... the Cranachs, both the elder and younger, produced a number of sheets from Wittenberg, which made up in forthrightness what they lacked in artistic skill and which were copied later in the century, by a whole series of further polemicists, such as Matthias Flacius Illyricus."[25] With "Master BP" (Bastian Palm?),[26] of the Cranach workshop, Flacius published a pamphlet attacking the Erfurt Franciscan Konrad Kling, and the *Book of Conformities* between Christ and St. Francis by Bartholomaeus of Pisa. It was Bartholmaeus' view that there was "no difference between them, except that Christ did not wear the holy garment,"[27] probably referring to St. Francis' hood. "Oh holy father Francis," so went his prayer, "deliver us from all temptation and give us eternal life, Amen."[28] Equating St. Francis with God was blasphemous, Flacius judged; he attacked the notion in a broadsheet illustrated by another Cranach woodcut, in which the false religion was indicated by Francis' occupying a place at the right hand of God, "The True Religion of Christ and the False."[29]

24 "Vom deutschen Holzschnitt der Reformationszeit." ARG, XXIII (1926). 106.

25 "The Early German Broadsheet and Related Ephemera: A Bibliographical Survey." *The Transactions of the Cambridge Bibliographical Society* II (1970). 85.

26 Walter Leopold Strauss. *The German Single-Leaf Woodcut, 1500–1600* II. New York: Abaris Books Inc., 1975. 502.

27 Oelke. 309.

28 Kurt Victor Selge. "Ein Magdeburger Flugblatt: Flacius Illyricus und die franziskaniche Sonderfrömmigkeit im Streit um das Interim." *Communio Viatorum* XXV (1982). 219–226. Max Geisberg. *Der deut-*

sche Einblatt-Holzschnitt in der ersten Hälfte des 16. Jahrhunderts VI. Munich: H. Schmidt, 1923–1929. No. 921; Idem. *The German Single-Leaf Woodcut: 1500–1550.* Revised and edited by Walter L. Strauss. New York: Hacker Art Books, Ind. 1974. No. 921. Cf. Clemens. KS, VIII, 174; Hildegard Zimmermann. "Vom deutschen Holzschnitt der Reformationszeit." ARG, XXIII (1926). 106; Nikolaus Paulus. "Konrad Kling, ein Erfurter Domprediger des 16. Jahrhunderts." *Der Katholik* IX (1894). 146 ff.; Gustav Kawerau. *Jahresberichte über neuere deutsche Literaturgeschichte* XXV (1894). 5, II, 6; WA, 23, 13 ff. 321 ff.

29 "Unterschied zwischen der waren Religion Christi und falschen Abgöttischen lehr des Antichrists in den fürnemsten stücken." Angelika Marsch. *Bilder zur Augsburger Konfession und ihrem Jubiläen.* [Weißenborn]: Anton H. Konrad, [1980]. 37; Strauss. II, 508.

30 "Examination." 43.

31 *Von der Einigkeit.* B v r.

32 *Entschuldigung ... an die Universitet.* J iiij r.

33 Op. cit. K ij v – f. He specifies the *Bericht der Wittenberger* and Flacius' answer; Justus Menius' *Bittere Warheit* and *Verantwortung, Bescheid* and Flacius' *Widerlegung*; Heshusius' *Antidotum* and Flacius' *Responsio*; Andreae's *Epistel* and Flacius; *Refutatio*.

34 Mentz. *Johann Friedrich.* 296.

35 *We Condemn. How Luther and 16th-century Lutheranism Condemned False Doctrine.* St. Louis: Concordia, 1967. 138.

36 Kling. "Flacius." RE, 2, II, 410, 413.

37 Op. cit. 13.

38 Op. cit. II, 366.

39 Op. cit. 301.

40 CS, XIII, 221.

41 Johann Gottfried Weller. *Altes aus allen Teilen der Geschichte* I. Chemnitz: Johann Christoph Stössel, 1762. 22. A photographic reproduction of the letter Weller quotes appears in Clemen. *Handschriften-*

It has been assumed that the two parties were equally guilty of *ad hominem* charges. "There was much name-calling on both sides," wrote Clyde Manschrek.[30] But Flacius argued otherwise. "...all my writings," he insisted, "deal primarily with the matter itself for the sake of truth and the Church of Christ. Theirs, however, are abuse, slander and calumny of my person and my brothers, needlessly to crush and condemn me."[31] "I have truly not said anything about anyone's private life; from that you can conclude that I have no appetite for saying evil of anyone." "As God is my witness, I am concerned with nothing more than that the pure religion of Christ remains unfalsified."[32]

Flacius' pupil, Caspar Heldelin, suggests that if one examined his exchanges with the Wittenberg faculty and with Menius, Heshusius and Andreae, one would find that Flacius avoided personal polemics." "... if one reads his books and compares them with their writings and publications, a Christian must simply marvel about the great patience and mildness that he employs to refute ... the infamous pamphlets."[33] Duke Johann Friedrich, for one, even considered his polemics too gentle.[34] Hans-Werner Gensichen, who notes that in the Flacius-Melanchthon correspondence a great deal of space was devoted to a tally of the insults and offenses on both sides, reports that "the letters of Flacius in particular, place constant emphasis on the primacy of the matter itself."[35] An encyclopedia article reports that "as much as possible [he] spared the persons and reproached them without mentioning their names."[36] According to August Twesten, he "could justifiably assert that, when one compared his polemical writings with the scornful and abusive writings that came from Wittenberg against him, one had to find his replies milder, at least in as far as he held fast to the matter itself, not to the externals of personalities."[37] Otto Ritschl came to the same conclusion.[38]

Paul Piur admired Flacius' German translation of Petrarch, which, he thought, was "marked by Luther's power and vitality."[39] Flacius' German edition of Luther's *Letters of Comfort* was so good that, despite a rule in the Jena edition about preserving the original language, it was made an exception. His German made such a good impression on Caspar von Schwenckfeld that he could not believe he was an Italian.[40] But his own statements give another impression. "In me, I think" he wrote, "is fulfilled the prophecy of Christ that if they remained silent, the stones would cry out. Writing German, I am clearly a stone, crying out."[41] Perhaps Otto Ritschl is correct, that he did, in fact, master German.[42] At any rate, we know that Albert Rolevink was his amanuensis in Wittenberg and that as an eighteen-year-old he followed him to Magdeburg, to transform his Latin handwriting[43] into German.[44]

During the siege, "these most turbulent times of Mars,"[45] Flacius had began to investigate the Hussite movement, and worked on *Certain Rules and Tracts* for interpreting the Bible,[46] a preliminary study to his *Clavis Scripturae Sacrae.* In it he quotes a letter of Luther from June 30, 1540, to George Rörer, reproduced by Hans Volz,[47] about the discrepancy between

The Interim Dragon. Siegburger Interims-Schnelle. Rheinisches Landesmuseum, Bonn.

proben. No. 20.

42 *Op. cit.* II, 358.

43 Specimens in Ficker and Winkel-
mann. II, No. 90; Georg Mentz.
Handschriften der Reformationszeit.
Bonn: A. Marcus and E. Weber,
1912. plate 17b; Clemen. *Handschriftenproben.* 20; Konrad Ziegler
(ed.). *Juli Firmici Materni V. C. de
errore profanarum religionum.* Leipzig: B. G. Tuebner, 1908. Tafel ii.

44 *Biographische Woordenboek van Protestantische Godgeleerden in Nederland.* Alfering 29. The Hague:

The Interim Dragon. Tankard.
From M. L. Solon. *The Ancient Art
Stoneware of the Low Countries and
Germany.* London: Chiswick Press,
1892.

183

Martinus Nijhoff, 1959. 24.
Hülsse. "Beiträge" XV (1880). 359;
Friedrich Gottlieb Kettner. *Clerus
Petrinus.* Magdeburg: Johann Sie-
gelers Witwe 1731. 588.

45 Sillem. I, 119.
46 Regulae et Tractatus. Cf. Keller.
108–11; Moldaenke. 138.

Tankard from Raeren-Neudorf. National Museum, Copenhagen.

two Old Testament passages.

He also managed to complete his *Paralipomena Dialectices*,[48] a contribution to the long Western discussion on "method,"[49] and a further development of his 1547 Wittenberg lectures. According to Josip Talanga, who concluded that it does not reflect the influence of Melanchthon, it was one of the better efforts in a flood of contemporary works on dialectic.[50] How influential it was is not clear. Talanga thought it remained without influence and "isolated,"[51] whereas Hans Emil Weber called it "a prophecy of the future development," and thought that it influenced the Heidelberg Catechism.[52]

Grammar, Flacius argued, is a part of philosophy.[53] Paul, in fact,[54] wanted a doctor of the church to be a good dialectician. As demonstration, Flacius quoted I Timothy 1.2, II Titus 2, and I Timothy 3. The only correct division of logical methods was Galen's: analytic, synthetic and definitive, which he illustrated with a chart, also published separately.[55] Whereas logic is limited to the synthetic method, theology can make use of all three.[56] But he considered the synthetic method the most suitable one for theology. "it should begin with the simplest elements, principles or causes, and then go on by combining them, until the whole body has been constructed and the wished-for endpoint is reached."

We will probably never learn how he informed himself, how he was able to find the secret material he published. Melanchthon suggested that some of his charges were of his own invention. "Now mark this crafty man: in order to excite suspicion and inflame hatred, he misinterprets and also attributes to others sayings of his own invention, that he might appear not only to have witnesses, but agents at his command." Although Flacius discounted such reports,[57] Ronald Diener names one probable informant: William Eccius.[58]

During those difficult months, Matthias and Elizabeth lost a new-born son. His father longed to join him, so dark was the situation. Once, a six-pound bomb crashed through the roof and destroyed his bed. Another time, a twenty-five pounder landed in the kitchen, filling it with stones. Altogether, his house was hit five times by cannon fire.[59] But all through the siege, he persisted at reading and writing.[60] "Nothing irritated him more," Caspar Heldelin remembered, "than being kept from his studies and his tasks."[61]

47 *Martin Luthers Deutsche Bibel.* Hamburg: Friedrich Wittig, 1978. 92. Cf. WAB, 9, 165–167.

48 *Paralipomena Dialectices, Libellus lectu dignissimus, et ad Dialecticam Demonstrationem certius cognoscendam, cuius etiam in Praefatione prima quaedam principa proponuntur, apprime utilis.* Basel: Jacobus Parcus, 1558.

49 Neil W. Gilbert. *Renaissance Concepts of Method.* New York: Columbia University Press, 1960. 111.

50 Op. cit. 119.

51 Ibid. 128.

52 *Der Einfluss der protestantischen Schulphilosophie auf die orthodoxe lutherische Dogmatik.* Leipzig: Deichert, 1908. 22.

53 Cf. *Clavis.* II, 59, 652.

54 Ibid. II, 55.

55 *Declaratio Tabulae Trium methodorum.* [Jena: Donat Richtzenhahn, ca. 1560]. On p. 88 of the *Paralipomena* he quotes Galen: Dividit igitur ordinem Galenus principio Artis medicae seu parvae in tres species. Primam appellat analysin seu resolutionem, secundam synthesin seu corruptionem, tertiam definitionis explicationem. Talanga. 129n.

56 *Paralimpomena.* 99. The three methods are described by Wilhelm Gass. *Georg Calixt und der Syncretismus.* Breslau: Gosohorksky, 1846. 46 f. and C. H. Ratschow. *Lutherische Dogmatik zwischen Reformation und Aufklärung* I. Gütersloh: Gütersloher Verlagshaus Gerd Mohn, 1964. 38 f.

57 *Bericht.* 1559. H r.

58 Op. cit. 169.

59 Bindseil. 587.

60 Wedel. 27.

61 Op. cit. [K iv r].

1 Paul Drews. *Petrus Canisius, der erste deutsche Jesuit.* Halle: Verein für Reformationsgeschichte, 1892. 35.

2 Jansen. 108.

3 Peter Brunner. *Nikolaus von Amsdorf als Bischof von Naumburg: eine Untersuchung zur Gestalt des evang. Bischofsamtes in der Reformationszeit.* Gütersloh: G. Mohn, 1961. 145.

4 Op. cit. 19.

5 Christian G. Müller (ed.). *Epistolae Petri Mosellani ... aliquorum virorum doctorum seculi XVI pleramque partem ad Julium Pflugium ipsiusque Iulii Pflugi nondum editam.* Leipzig, 1802. 63.

Perhaps with Bishop Julius the doors will be open for the [Jesuit] order to penetrate Saxony, the source and headquarters of heresy and establish itself where the devil has established his kingdom, and the heretics have their sanctuary and home.
– [Saint] Peter Canisius

The bishops of Merseburg and Naumburg seemed to be the spiritual arsenals where North Germany would be brought under the obedience of the Roman See.
– Albert Fraustadt

Thus did these two consuls sport together. And thus perish the truth and the church of God. May God have mercy on us. – Duke Johann Friedrich II

Nikolaus von Amsdorf had been installed as Bishop of Naumburg-Zeitz by Martin Luther himself. But in May 1547, soon after military victory, Charles V evicted him and replaced him with Julius Pflug, the main author of the Augsburg Interim and a learned man, able to hold his own with scholars like Melanchthon. From the Habsburg perspective he was ideal: he thought of the schism as source of the evils of the time, and was committed to restoring religious and political unity. Once installed in Naumburg, he reclaimed secular authority for the bishopric, which under Lutheran leadership had been separated from spiritual leadership. His goal was church reform, but within the papal obedience, and he pursued it according to the imperial *Formula Emendorum* of July 9th, 1548, which was incorporated into the Recess of the Diet, and meant for territories unaffected by the Reformation.

The Jesuit, Peter Canisius, had been hopeful. "Perhaps with Bishop Julius the doors will be open for the [Jesuit] order to penetrate Saxony, the source and headquarters of heresy, and establish itself where the devil has established his kingdom, and the heretics have their sanctuary and home."[1]

When Pflug arrived he found only one unmarried priest. He attempted to recruit others by offering them high salaries, but attracted only four. Beyond the *Hauptkirche* in Zeitz and the cathedral church in Naumburg all other churches conducted Lutheran services.[2] The seminary he founded lasted only until his death. In spite of all of his efforts, the diocese remained evangelical, so well had Bishop Amsdorf done his work. "Amsdorf's episcopal activity, despite its brevity and in spite of the many impediments, consolidated the Lutheran Reformation in the region of the *Stift*, so that all of Pflug's counter-reformatory efforts during his seventeen-year reign remained fruitless."[3]

Modern assessments of Pflug vary. For Albert Jansen, he was motivated not so much by a love of righteousness, as a search for honor.[4] Christian Müller saw his goals as primarily political; for him the Holy Roman Empire had "a grandeur almost absolute, to which he referred everything, and according to which he measured other values."[5] Wolfgang Offele

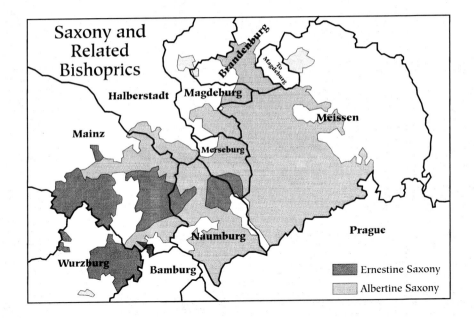

Saxony and Related Bishoprics

Halberstadt · Magdeburg · Brandenburg · To Magdeburg · Meissen · Mainz · Merseburg · Naumburg · Prague · Wurzburg · Bamburg

■ Ernestine Saxony
▢ Albertine Saxony

6 Op. cit. 28.

7 *Die Reformation in Deutschland.* 3. Aufl. Freiburg im Breisgau: Herder, 1949. II, 217.

8 Offele. 153.

9 O. Müller. 58.

10 *Christlich Ermanungen, welche die Seelsorgere des Stiffts Naumburg bey dem Sacrament der Tauffe: bey dem Sacrament des Altars: bey der Verehlichung: bey den Krancken: gebrauchen sollen und mögen.* Erfurt: Melchior Sachsse in der Archen Noe, 1550.

11 *Widder die unchristliche Vermanungs-chrifft* [A iiij r].

12 *Auf die Vermanung Julii des Bepstlichen Bischoffs, darin er die Evangelischen vermanet, das sie sich wider zur Bepstischen Synagoge bekeren wolten. Antwort M. Flacii Illyrici aus des papsts Recht, dist. 40. Si papa.* Jena: Christian Rödinger, 1554.

13 *Widderlegung des Catechismi.* B r.

argues that his goal was not political, but ecclesiastical unity.[6] "His purpose," according to Joseph Lortz, however, "was to make the church stronger against the enemy, Luther.[7]

As was to be expected, Pflug's romanizing campaign drew Flacius' ire. He rejected Pflug's catechism, *Institutio Christiani Hominis,* patterned in part after Luther's Small Catechism,[8] as aristotelian.[9] He took issue with the presuppositions of his handbook for priests, *Christian Exhortation,* which gave directions for administering baptism, preparation for communion, premarital instruction, and sick visitation.[10] Marriage does not mediate the divine forgiveness, he argued, that, by definition, a sacrament does. Since Turks and Jews also marry, the institution is to be considered part of the secular order.[11] Marriage as sacrament is not a part of the catholic tradition; neither Rhabanus Maurus nor Dionysius had called it a sacrament.

To Pflug's appeal to the Saxons to return to the pope, Flacius published an *Answer.*[12] Pflug's *Christian Admonition and Reminder of Julius, Bishop of Naumburg to his People,* called the "blind book" because it lacked place or date, appealed for a "return to the church." Instead of merely saying "church, church, church," Flacius commented, "he should explain what the church is. Is it the pope of Rome together with his cardinals, chaste and holy courtesans, prelates and clergy, who believe neither in God, angels, devil or hell? Is it built on Francis, Dominicus, holy water, mass, good works, chastity of monks and nuns, letters of indulgence, pictures, bones and clothes of dead saints and such fools' work?" "...with what right," he wanted to know, "does he become bishop against the knowledge and will of the congregations? Which devil had given three or four godless, epicurian cathedral canons might and power, so that they can ordain, that they can set over the flock of the Lord a wolf of their own choice?"[13] The

14 Pflug. *Correspondance*. III, 321.

15 Liliencron. "Dichtung." 141.

16 Erwin Iserloh (ed.). *Katholische Theologen der Reformationszeit* II. Münster: Aschendorff, 1985. 214.

17 Fraustadt. 213.

18 Feifel. 30.

19 Heppe. *Geschichte* I. 211n.

20 *Sacri Canonis ... Explicatio*. Op. cit.

21 *Vermanung an die umbstehenden bey dem heiligen Ambt der Messe*. Frankfurt an der Oder: Cited by O. Mueller. 64.

22 *Institutio ad pietatem Christianem secundum doctrinam Catholicam, complectens Explicationem Symboli Apostolici, Orationis Dominicae, Angelicae Salutationis, Decalogi, et septem sacracamentorum*. It was printed together with the minutes of the provincial synod of Mainz, May 6th – 24th, 1549, *Constitutiones Concilii Provincialis Moguntini Sub ... Sebastiano Archepiscopo Moguntino ... sexta Mai an. MDLXIX celebrati*. Mainz: Behem, 1549.

23 *Widderlegung des Catechismi*. B v.

bishop did not answer. "Illyricus is not worthy," he explained, "to dispute with under my name."[14]

After the military defeat, on December 6, 1550, Michael Helding, whose sermons at the Augsburg Diet had so pleased the Hapsburg brothers, was enthroned, and reclaimed secular authority. A song directed against Helding expresses the hostility against him.

> Seht zu, der unvershempt Bachant
> das Euangelium ganz verdampt,
> den glauben schendt und lobt die lieb;
> also thun alle bebstische dieb.[15]

> Behold, the shameless bachant
> totally damns the gospel,
> reviles faith and praises love.
> All papist thieves do the same.

Although the senior of the cathedral chapter insisted that Helding promise not to make religious changes,[16] Heldings' plan was to restore the Roman obedience. The two bishops worked together, and were considered a team for recatholicizing North Germany. "The bishoprics of Merseburg and Naumburg seemed to be the spiritual arsenals whence North Germany would be brought under the obedience of the Roman See."[17] "Already in Merseburg," writes Erich Feifel, "it was no more so very much about the Interim, but the uncompromising introduction of Catholic doctrine."[18] "Thus did these two consuls sport together," commented Duke Johann Friedrich II, "and thus perish the truth and the church of God. May God have mercy on us."[19]

Although the *Formula Emendorum* was meant for non-reformed territories, Helding used it as a guide for his re-catholicizing program in Merseburg. It was also the basis for his *Explanation of the Holy Canon of the Mass*,[20] published under imperial auspices and at imperial expense. Pflug, in turn, made use of Helding's *Explanation* for his *Admonition to those Attending the Holy Office of the Mass*.[21] While he was still in Mainz, Helding had published a catechism, *Institutio ad Pietatem Christianum*, for the scions of the nobility,[22] with which the pope was so pleased that he created Helding Bishop of Sidon, Lebanon, *in partibus infidelium*.

Flacius accused Helding with being careless about the biblical context, and for treating his texts simply as tags around which, in medieval fashion, he could teach anything. He challenged Helding's statement that (Pseudo-) Dionysius was the pupil of St. Paul mentioned in Acts, and assigned him instead a fourth century date. He took issue with the idea that penance was a sacrament separate from baptism. "That he teaches falsely and incorrectly is apparent in that he makes a big separation between baptism and penance and makes of it a separate sacrament."[23] Baptism was not just the first in a series of initiations, but was valid for one's whole life.

To reinforce his argument that biblical unction was a medical practice, he quoted from another old manuscript.

> Lord, look mercifully on this, your servant, and help him in this bed of pain and sorrow. Lay your hand on our hand so the illness may not despise our hand, but take fright before the invocation of your name and flee, so that he comes again to his health, arises from bed...[24]

Extreme Unction, lacking a christological mandate, was not a sacrament, but a mere imitation of something the apostles did. "It is not necessary that one make a sacrament out of all the deeds of the apostles and the Lord Christ."[25]

Biblical authority for the use of holy water, Helding said was the prophet, Elisha, who had cured a fountain by using water and salt. "Therefore we should consecrate water, so that it can blot out sin, and give life and salvation to those who are sprinkled." Criticizing "holy water," Flacius denounced the formula, "may this blessed water blot out your sins, and be salvation and life to you," *aqua benedicta deleat tua dilecta sit tibi salus et vita.*[26] Sins could not be forgiven by enchanted water. He objected to the teaching that "sanctified salt and water make the body healthy, and that they drive out sickness and the devil." Helding defended the importance of relics: just as important as baptism was the hood of St. Francis. He erred, Flacius said, just as he did about baptism, justification, penance, confirmation, extreme unction, the Ave Maria and the consecration of physical things.

The demand that the Lutheran clergy abandon their wives made the bishops' own sexual behavior an appropriate theme;[27] and Flacius charged Helding with having sired eight illegitimate children.[28] Demonstrable is that he had at least one son, Theodosius. Simon Widman thinks he sired the son while serving as *Domschulmeister*[29] – an office reserved for clerics.[30]

Recent admirers of Helding have dismissed the morals charge with the excuse that they were made by Flacius. That is the answer of Albert Fraustadt.[31] Erich Feifel, undisturbed by Helding's "foregoing philological details," asks that criticism of the bishop be put off until there is an authority more reliable than Flacius, because Flacius' "tendency to irrelevance and defamation is so obvious here, that it does not seem appropriate to linger any longer."[32]

They follow a sixteenth-century precedent. Georg Witzel, formerly a student at Wittenberg and a Roman Catholic convert, was offended that Flacius even dared to raise his voice against the bishop.

> It should not surprise the pious, learned Bishop Michael, still less distress him, that he is denounced by this great slanderer as unchristian and unkind. Do not believe that there is a slander word heard in the wide world, with which he does not molest and put down this honorable man with such untruth. Can we expect that the one who does not spare God's children, all saints, all sacraments, and the whole ancient service of God, but rather disrupts, tramples, and destroys everything, would spare our persons and names?[33]

Helding himself attacked his accuser in a seventy-page "Defense against Matthias Illyricus," in a preface to another catechism published under imperial auspices, the *Brevis Institutio.*[34] He echoed Melanchthon's charge

24 Ibid. [D iii r].

25 Ibid. D v.

26 *Verlegung der Apologia Sydoni.* B v.

27 Melanchthon reports, e. g., "Ad Rhenum horribilis confusio est, sicut meus frater mihi scribit. Multi pastores pelluntur in exilium cum familiis; alii coniuges dimittunt et coniugium negant metu, contra conscientiam." CR, VII, 297.

28 Ibid. [E iiij r].

29 *Eine Mainzer Presse der Reformationszeit im Dienste der katholischen Litteratur.* Paderborn: Ferdinand Schönigh, 1889. 18, 37, 61; Smolinsky. 125; Paulus. "Helding." 411.

30 Fritz Hermann. *Die evangelische Bewegung in Mainz im Reformationszeitalter.* Mainz: In Kommision bei Hermann Quasthof, 1907. 16 f.

31 Op. cit. 233.

32 Ibid. 15, 17f.

33 *Publicum Ecclesiae Sacrum.* A ij v.

34 *Brevis institutio ad christianam pietatem secundum doctrinam Catholicam.* Mainz, Ivo Schoeffer, 1549.

35 Druffel, 1546–1551. 775; Smolinsky. 130.

The Last Supper, Memorial of Joachim of Anhalt. Lucas Cranach the Younger, 1565.
St. John's Lutheran Church, Dessau.

that "Delyricus" had denied the divinity of Christ and the Holy Spirit.
Flacius, moreover, was a revolutionary – and a non-German.

In 1564 the Naumburg-Zeitz diocese reverted to Saxony; the Merseburg diocese in 1561. Both had already been reformed so thoroughly that
reconquest was impossible. In a report to the emperor, October 7, 1551,
another evidence of Flacius' effectiveness, Helding blamed his failure on
propaganda: "The Interim was represented to the people as a falsification
of the Gospel..."[35]

In the chancel of St. John's Lutheran Church in Dessau hangs a painting
in which Lucas Cranach the Younger depicted prominent reformers with
Christ at the Last Supper. Whereas Luther is separated from Christ by

Abendmahl. Circle of Georg Lemberger. Martin Luther. *Ein Betbüchlein mit einem Kalender und Passional.* Wittenberg: Hans Lufft, 1529; WA, X, II, 359.

Bugenhagen, Melanchthon, understandable in a painting commissioned by a princely house so close to the Preceptor, is seated next to the Lord. In the popular mind, the yellow-coated Judas figure is Flacius.

Although the assumption is not new, art scholars have been cautious since, unlike the frontal depictions of the others that reproduce known portraits, the Judas is painted in profile and thus not identifiable in the same way. Proof of his identity, however, is apparent from the knife he

Umkreis des Georg Lemberger: Abendmahl, Holzschnitt. In: Martin Luther: Ein Betbüchlein mit einem Kalender und Passional, ... Wittenberg: Hans Lufft, 1529.

wears at his waist. As our illustrations suggest, in contemporary woodcuts (often used as models for paintings) of the Last Supper, knives are often seen lying on the table. The knife in the Cranach painting, in contrast, is worn at the waist of the Judas figure in the manner of a dagger. That is the proof that the figure of the Jew is meant to be Flacius. The dagger is the famous *culter flacianus*, the imaginary knife, well-known at the time the painting was made, by which Flacius was supposed to have defaced books.[36]

37 *Von der Einigkeit.* C iij r.

38 Oswald Gottlob Schmidt. *Georg von Anhalt des Gottseligen Leben.* Leipzig & Dresden: Justus Raumann, 1864. 155; Fraustadt. 255.

Hans Wechtlin (1480/85–after 1516). The print appeared in various books published by J. Knobloch and J. Grüninger in Straßburg; Johann David Passavant. *Le Peintre-Graveur.* 6 vols. Leipzig, 1860–1854. III, 331.

Hostility against Flacius in Dessau is not difficult to understand. In 1550, Flacius had lodged a protest against Prince George."The jurisdiction of the popes and the bishops alone can completely destroy our church, as the Leipzig Interim clearly presents and establishes. And Prince George himself assisted in Sidonius' ascending the throne!"[37] In response, Prince George's brother, the reigning prince, directed a complaint against Flacius to the Magdeburg government.[38] Melanchthon, moreover, influenced the

39 CR, VII, 356.
40 Salig. III, 240.
41 Roth. IV, 146 f.
42 Warmbrunn. 280.
43 Roth. IV, 345.

Ulrich Holtzmann. *Ein newes Lied.*
Wie die Predicanten der stat Augspurg
geurlaubt unnd abgeschafft sind worden
den XXVI. Augusti Anno Domini M.D.
LI. geschehen [Augsburg]:
[Kriegstein], [1551]. Staats- und
Stadtbibliothek, Augsburg.
Aug. 1035.

princely house In 1549 he wrote to Prince George that Flacius had left Wittenberg to find "a place from which to attack him."[39] In 1551, he succeeded in persuading the dukes to expel Flacius from his refuge in Cothen. In 1559 he told Prince Joachim that Flacius was a *Landläufer*, and again reminded him of Flacius' criticism of his brother.[40]

On June 26, 1547, with his Spanish troops, Charles V occupied Augsburg, and although the population was nine-tenths Lutheran, he appropriated the cathedral. The "half emperor," Bishop Anton Perrenot Granvella of Arras, restricted the Lutherans to St. Anne's, St. Ulrich's, St. George's, Holy Cross and the Franciscan church. Wolfgang Musculus was driven out of the city for having written against the law. Refractory clergy were threatened with stationing of Spanish troops. Cardinal Otto Truchsess von Waldburg erected a victory monument, and gave tribute to Charles V. for restoring religious unity. In July, 1548, Colonel Count Hans of Nassau, entered Augsburg through the Red Gate at the head of 1,500 troops. Known as the "preacher catcher", for his persecution, he was a supporter of the Dominican, Johann Fabri, whose sermons, according to Pontien Polman, made him Flacius' *adversaire classique*.

On August 2, a Roman Catholic bishop of Augsburg was installed; on August 3rd, the republican constitution of the city was changed to give the Roman Catholic patricians the deciding voice, and the semi-democratic voices of the guilds were silenced. On July 28 the clergy were ordered to make a final decision about wearing the surplice.[41] On August 12 some of them complied; others – under Flacius' influence – resisted.[42] When the schoolmasters were made to decide on the Interim, five out of the nine Latin teachers accepted it, and ten of the twelve German teachers. On August 17th and the days following, the emperor called Lutheran clergy and teachers from Regensburg, Memmingen and other cities to Augsburg, to answer for their disobedience. On August 26, 1551, a few days before the Council of Trent was reconvened, and a month before the siege of Magdeburg began, all the Lutheran pastors of Augsburg were summoned to appear before the Imperial Vice Chancellor, Georg Sigmund Seld, and the Bishop of Arras.

The pastors were asked individually whether they accepted the Interim law. Except for four, the clergy refused to wear the surplice. "Now one hears publicly their own confession," Seld said, "that they are renegade, Lutheran scoundrels!"[43] The scene on August 28 has been remembered in verse.

> So hor ich wol, sprach drutzlich
> des bischofs von Arres rat,
> ir haltent sei n(it) nutzlich,
> das kaiserliche Majestat
> gut mittel und articula macht
> in geistlichen dingen wie in weltlicher sach.
>
> ... der bishof zu der stunden
> ergimmet an den ort.

Wutend und tobend er da sprach:
habe dich hinaus, du bestia!
des auch gar bald geschah.[44]

I have heard, the counsellor
of the bishop of Arras, spoke insolently,
that you think it is not useful,
that Imperial Majesty
makes good means and articles
in spiritual matters as in secular.

...the bishop on that hour
was angry at that place
furious and raging he spoke:
get out, you beasts
and it happened soon.

The bishop gave the Lutheran clergy three days to leave the city. The city took on the aspect of a house of mourning. One Pastor, Bartholomäus Bertlin, whose pregnant wife had told him before to take no account of her or her child, asked for permission to see her before his departure. The bishop answered, "what he calls a wife is only a whore."[45] Caspar Huberinus, convinced to accept the Interim by Vice Chancellor Seld, his brother-in-law, was called to Augsburg by the emperor, and therefore considered a traitor by the evangelicals and by Flacius, who prepared a tract against him.[46]

With Michael Helding, Johann Fabri was assigned by Cardinal Otto Truchsess with the task of preaching in the Augsburg cathedral church. Despite the attempts of the city council to convince him to adopt a milder tone, he defended the Roman tradition, thundering against the Lutherans daily from the cathedral pulpit. The Catholic church, he announced,

> ...has not alone the external letters, but also the correct sense and understanding of the letters and that through the rule of the Holy Spirit, who had led the Catholic Church from the beginning and would never abandon her. But the heretics had only the letter, which they understand and explain according to their head, against the consensus and understanding of the Catholic Church. They want to know better than the whole Christendom of the whole world; therefore errors and schisms flow to destruction of souls, for Christ says, whoever does not hear the church should be to you a heathen and publican.[47]

The Reformation, Fabri said, had brought thorns and thistles; Germany's troubles came from the "sweet sugar-words" about justification by faith.

> The sweet sugar-preachers, who strengthen the people in their evil, say: the Lord has atoned for us, good works are impure and sins, a good, pious, honest life, with fasting, prayer, church attendance, confession, service to God, is papistic and hypocritical, the Lord has earned heaven for us, our doing good is all in vain. That and similar are the sweet sugar words with which they call and shout, "peace, peace! Heaven is open, only believe, and you are already just and an heir of heaven."

> ...the Catholic church is pure, clean, just, clean and upright; you are certain of it, for the Holy Spirit tolerates no falsity or error in his great house that he rules, teaches, instructs and maintains. The Catholic religion is the true one, because it is in agreement with the apostolic doctrine as it was handed down from the ancient fathers.[48]

44 Ulrich Holzmann. *Ein newes lied wie die Prädikanten der stat Augsburg geurlaubt unnd abgeschafft sind worden, den XXVI Augusti Anno Domini M.D. LI geschehen.* Augsburg, 1551; "Verhandlung über die Ausweisung der Augsburger Prediger." Druffel, 1546–1551, 226.

45 M. Simon. 258.

46 *Contra quaedam interimistica et Adiaphoristica scripta, quae a multis Gasparo Huberino tribuuntur. Item locus Brentii, praesentibus Christi & Belial Conciliationibus admodum conveniens.* Magdeburg: Christian Rödinger [ca. 1550]; Friedrich Roth "Kaspar Huberinus und das Interim in Augsburg." *Beiträge zur bayerischen Kirchengeschichte* XI (1905). 201–218.

47 Roth. IV, 301.

48 Ibid. 252.

49 *Was die Evangeliche Meß sey, Grund-liche und Christenliche Anzeigung auß der Heiligen Geschrifft, unnd auß den alten heiligen Kirchenlehrern.* Dillingen: Sebastian Meyer, 1556.

50 *Antwort auff das unnütz, unrain, irrig geschwetz Mathie Flaccij Illyrici, so er geschriben wider das büchlein genant Rechter weg. Und auff seine dreyvnd-zwantzig sectische Argument, so er geschriben an Osterreich und Bayern wider die Euangelische Meß.* Dillin-gen: Sebastian Meyer, 1558. [K iiij v – f.].

51 *Refutatio Missae. Widerlegung des sophistischen Buchs des Schwartzen Münchs von der Opfer Mess, anno 1550 ausgangen.* Straßburg: Samuel Emmel, 1557.

52 Ibid. D r.

53 Ibid. D iij v, D v.

On November 16, 1550, the city council acted to bind the Lutheran teachers to Fabri's catechism. In *What the Evangelical Mass Is*,[49] like Held-ing, Fabri argued that the mass had been passed down from the apostles unchanged. He backed it up with a curious geographical definition of catholicity.

> The office of the holy mass has been held by arrangement and rule of the Holy Spirit in Italy, in Spain, in Gaul, in Germany, in Poland, in Hungary, in Bohemia, in the is-lands of the Ocean Sea, in England, in Scotland, in Scotia, in Hibernia, in Sweden, in Norway, in the Mediterranean, in Sicily, in Crete, Cyprus, Rhodes, Sardinia, Corsica, by the Greeks, by the Russians, by the Muscovites, by all who confess Christ in Syria, in Armenia, in India, in Ethiopia, in Palestine, at Jerusalem, at Bethelehem on Mount Sinai, in the newly-discovered land in America, in Peru, which new land, found by God's providence, is more than 3000 miles long and more than 5000 wide."[50]

Flacius answered him with a *Refutation of the Mass*.[51] To call the whole mass a prayer, to talk about "praying the mass," Flacius argued, was absurd; only some of the elements were prayers. Some were praise and thanksgiv-ing to God, some instruction, and some the communion of the people. The Epistle and Gospel were appointed to be read in the church and to be teaching, but not to be used as a prayer. "I cannot marvel enough how such stupid blindness has come upon the popes and bishops that when they ordain a deacon, they say, 'I give you the power to read the Epistle and Gospel for the living and the dead.'" "As if a woman in Spain has a hundred Epistles and Gospels mumbled for her son or husband who is sent to India somewhere, or is imprisoned by the Turks or lies under the sea. It is supposed to give him a great deal of help! ... as if it helped those who hear it in an unkown tongue, and do not know what the priest is grunting...

> ... when the *Pfaff* turns around, and so often speaks Dominus Vobiscum, the Lord be with you, as if he wanted to greet the people, but either no one is there, or because he says it in Latin, no one understands.[52] He speaks the Pax Domini to the stones, prayers for those who are present – but no one is there. He thinks he is doing a great deed for those for whom he murmurs the mass, whether they are present or in Calcutta, dead or living.[53]

There was not a word in the biblical narrative, he argued, about sacrifice. If the mass sacrifice had been such a precious thing the apostles would have written about it. The Letter to the Hebrews, chapter 5, talks about a sacrifice that has no sequel. There is no purgatory, for it can never be proved either by Holy Scripture or from the most ancient writers. There-fore it is a horrible abuse that the body and blood of the Lord is sacrificed and consumed for the sake of nothing. The basic form of the mass, the recitation of Christ's Words of Institution, is backed up by the Popes, Innocent and Gregory, by Platina, Polydore, Biel, Valafrid, and Sabellicus. Both the "major canon" and the "minor canon" were added several hundred years later.

In *On the Advent and Origin of the Roman Bishop from Peter to Julius III*, Fabri pleaded "do not be so disturbed by the abuses of some Roman bishops that you despise, dishonor or slander the chair left behind

Against Flacius, Johann Fabri defended papal succession

54 *Von Ankunfft und herkommen der Römischen Bischöff von Petro biß auf Julium den Dritten, Und die Namen aller Cardinäl so yetzund Anno Domini M.D.L. bey Leben seind. Auch von des Römischen Reichs Monarchey, und ordenlichen Succession, oder volgung der Römischen Kaiser, von Julio Cesare, biß auf den großmächigsten Kaiser Carolum den fünfften.* Augsburg: Ph. Ulhart [1550]. [A iv r].

55 *Ein Nützlich Beychtbüchlin, wie der Mensch sich seiner Sünd erinnern unnd die bekennenen sol.* Augsburg; Philip Ulhart, n. t.

56 *Verlegung zweier schrifften eines Augsburgischen Münchs, mit Namen Joannes Fabri, von des Bapsts Primat und von der Beicht.* Magdeburg: Christian Rödinger [1550]; Nikolaus Paulus. *Die deutschen Dominikaner im Kampf gegen Luther (1518–1563).* Freiburg im Breisgau: Herder, 1903. 244, argues that since Fabri's book was dated October 7, 1550, the date of Flacius' preface, August 20, 1550, cannot be correct, and must therefore have been published in 1551.

by Christ ... Although the evil life of the bad Roman bishops should be hated, Peter's chair, which they occupy, and the key and power given and committed to them by Christ, should be honored."[54] The neglect of both the highest Christian authorities could only bring harm. Against this book and his *Useful Book for Confession*[55] Flacius reacted immediately with a *Confutation of Two Writings of an Augsburg Monk, John Fabri by Name, on the Pope's Primacy and on Confession.*[56] In an appendix he argued that private confession was introduced not by Christ, but by Pope Innocent III in the decretum, *Omnis Utriusque Sexus*, in 1215. Another appendix was a treatise first published at Augsburg in 1520, an argument that St. Peter had never even been at Rome, refueled the controversy about papal authority. It had appeared originally at Augsburg in 1520, one year after Luther's challenge

57 Antoine Jan Lamping. *Ulrichus Velenus (Oldřich Velenský) And His Treatise Against the Papacy.* Leiden: E. J. Brill, 1976. 3n.

58 *Trattato nel quale con certissimi ragioni nella sacra Scrittura, si manifesta, come Pietro Apostolo non mai fu a Roma, ne anco pati in quella il Martirio; La onde si vede quanto debolmente il Romano pontefice si vanta di esser successore dei Pietro.* Regensburg: Johann Burger, 1567.

59 *Olympiae Fulviae Moratae Opera Omnia, quae hactenus inveniri potuerunt.* Basel, 1579. 118 f.

60 "Von des Ulrich Velenus Schrifft, das Petrus nie nach Rom gekommen sey, und den Schrifften dagegen." *Sammlung von Aufsätzen zur Erläuterung der Kirchen-, Literatur-, und Sittengeschichte.* Ulm, 1827. 149.

61 "Zur Literatur des Petrus-Sage," Appendix to *Paulus der Apostel Jesu Christi.* Stuttgart: Becher & Müller, 1845. 671–677.

62 *Peter: Disciple-Apostle-Martyr.* Philadelphia: Westminster Press, 1953. 72. Cf. K. Werner. *Geschichte der Apologetischen und Polemischen Literatur der Christlichen Theologie* IV. Schaffhausen, 1865. 52.

63 *Zapadle dilko bratrske vedy.* [A Forgotten Work from the Science of the (Bohemian) Brethren]. Prague: Vestnick kralovske ceske spolecnosti nauk [The Royal Bohemian Society for Science], 1926. 1–28.

64 Lamping. 182.

65 Ibid. 186.

66 Ibid. 182 f.; Cullmann. 77; F. Baur. 317; see below, "Who Wrote the Centuries?"

67 *Quod Petrus Romae fuerit, et ibidem Primus Episcopatum gesserit, atque sub Nerone martyrium passus fuit; Et an fundamentum Ecclesiae dici possit.* Dillingen: Sebastian Mayer [1552].

68 Henry de Vocht. *History of the Foundation and the Rise of the Collegium Trilingue Lovaniense 1517–1550* III. Louvain: Librarie Universitaire, 1954. 476. The tract, however, was reprinted several times: *Testimo-*

Flacius edition of *Petrum Romam non Venisse* was the first appendix of his Confutation of Johann Frabri

to papal authority at Leipzig, and just before Luther burned the papal bull, *Exurge Domini.* It is now referred to as *Petrum Romam non Venisse* to avoid the confusion of its various titles.[57] Two of the titles were Flacius' – one in German, "Eighteen Proofs that St. Peter Did Not Come to Rome;" and one in Italian.[58] Flacius did, in fact, publish little in Italian. Nothing, for instance, seems to have come of the 1553 request of the noted humanist, Olympia Fulvia Morata, that he make an Italian translation of Luther's works.[59] Unaware of Flacius' mastery of Italian, Georg Veesenmeyer

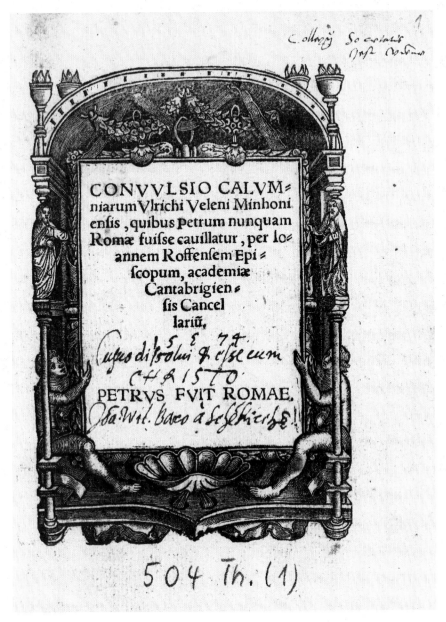

CONVVLSIO CALVM=
niarum Vlrichi Veleni Minhoni.
enſis, quibus petrum nunquam
Romæ fuiſſe cauillatur, per Io=
annem Roffenſem Epi=
ſcopum, academiæ
Cantabrigien=
ſis Cancel
lariū.

PETRVS FVIT ROMAE.

504 Th. (1)

An Answer to Velensky from England

explained, "If we had something else Italian by Flacius, I would be inclined to attribute the translation to him."[60]

Ferdinand Christian Baur concluded that the *Petrum Romam non Venisse* was written by Flacius,[61] and Oscar Cullmann considered the name, "Ulrich Velensky," attached to the tract a pseudonym.[62] But there really was an Ulrich Velensky. He came from Mnichov, and was the author of the book. Writing in Czeck in 1925, F. M. Bartos settled the question of authorship, and also that Flacius was the translator.[63] Building on Walden-

nium Scripturae et Patrum Petrum Apostolum Romae Fuisse; primumque ibidem Episcopum, et sub Nerone martyrium passum; ac fundamentum Ecclesiae dici. Cum Epistola Mamerani praefixa eiusdem argumenti. Dillingen, 1553. Further editions in Paulus, *Dominikaner*, 245. Cf. Polman. "Historien." 31.

69 Nicholas Sanders. *De Visibili Monarchiae Ecclesiae Libri Octo.* Louvain: J. Foulerus, 1571. Robert Bellarmine. *Disputationes de controversia Christianae fidei adversus huius temporibus haereticos.* 1586; Wilhelm van der Lindt. *Panoplia evangelica, sive de verbo dei evangelico libri quinque* IV. Cologne: M. Cholius, 1560. Cf. Lamping. 184 ff.

70 Lamping. 151 f.

71 *Der recht Weg: Welcher weg oder straß der glaubig wandeln oder gehn soll, daß er komme zu der ewigen ruh und friden.* Dillingen: Sebald Mayer, 1556.

72 It had been printed as *Epistola Divi Hulderici Augustensis Episcopi, Adversus Constitutionem de Cleri Coelibatu, plane referens apostolicum scriptum.* Wittenberg, 1521.

73 *Epistola S. Huldrici episcopi Augustani, adversus constitutionem de cleri coelibatu, circiter ante sexcentos et 50 annos, ad Pontificem Nicolaum Primum, ad Defensionem coniugij Sacerdotum, scripta, ex qua apparet, quam impudenter Papistae S. patres jactent. cum et vita et doctrina cum S. Patribus plane ex Diametro Pugnent.* Magdeburg: Michael Lotter, n. t.; *Des h. Hulrichs etwa vor sechshundert jaren Bischoffs zu Augsburg schrifft wider das ehelos Leben der Priester, itzt sehr nützlich zulesen. Mit einer vorrede M. Fl. Illyrici wider den Münch zu Augsburg.* Magdeburg: Michael Lotter, 1553; Reprinted in Flacius' *Antilogia Papae: Hoc est, De corrupto ecclesiae statu, et totius cleri papistici perverssitate...* Basel: Johannes Oporinus, 1555. 161– 166 ff. and in *Catalogus Testium Veritatis*, 1556. 101–109; 1562. 99–108; Johann Herold. *Monu-*

menta s. patrum Orthodoxographa. Basel: Heinrich Petri, 1555. 1254–1257; MGH. *Libelli.* I, 1891. 254–264; Preger. II, 553; Further printings, and changing judgments on the letter: Samuel Schelwig. "Concentrirte Untersuchung wegen Hulderici, Episc. August. Brieff an den Papst Nicolaum I. von verbothener Priester-Ehe." UN, 1710, 137–41; Clement. KS, IV, 502 ff.; Polman. "Historien." 60; Paulus. *Dominikaner.* 253n.

74 *Antwort auff das ... geschwetz.* [B iv r].

75 Engelbert M. Buxbaum. "'Von der Priestereh' Die sogenannte Ulrichsepistel – ihre Verbreitung, Bekämpfung und zeitliche Einordnung." Walter Brandmüller, et al.: *Ecclesia Militans. Studien zur Konzilien- und Reformationsgeschichte Remigius Bäumer zum 70. Geburtstag gewidmet* II. Paderborn, et al.: Ferdinand Schöningh, 1988. 407–415; Paulus. *Dominikaner.* 253.

76 *Ein newer Antichristischer radtschlag oder bedenken des Saltzbürgischen Bischoffs und anderer verfolger Christi, wie sie die Warheit des heiligen Evangelii auzurotten gedencken.* Magdeburg: Michael Lotter, 1554.

77 *Vermanungk an die verfolgte Christen in Bistumb Saltzburgk und Beierland.* Magdeburg: Michael Lotter, 1554. Salig. III, 187.

78 *Des h. Merterers Christi, Georgen Scherers letzte bekentnis, welcher umb der warheit Christi willen, von dem Antichristischen Wolffe zu Saltzburgk, grawsamlich ist ermordet worden. Mit einer Vorrede M. Fl. Ill. An die verfolgete Christen im Bistumb Saltzburg, und Beiern.* [Magdeburg: Michael Lotter], 1554.

79 Josef Schmid. "Des Cardinals und Erzbischofs von Salzburg Mattheus Lang Verhalten zur Reformation." JGGPO, XIX (1900). 153.

80 Franz Ortner. *Reformation, Katholische Reform und Gegenreformation im Erzstift Salzburg.* Salzburg: Pustet, 1981. 64 f.

81 Ludwig Rabe. *Historien der Mar-*

sian arguments, Velensky argued that the papacy was a product of the legal position of the church dating from the time of Constantine and of the myth of the Donation of Constantine, exposed in the mid-fifteenth century by Lorenzo Valla.

Luther had been impressed, but not wholly convinced, by Velensky's chronology. For him the main question about the papacy was not historical, but theological: whether obedience to him was necessary for salvation. The papal party insisted that Peter had been in Rome for 25 years. But since he stayed in Jerusalem eighteen years, according to the biblical account, four years in Pontus and seven in Antioch, if that had been followed by 25 years in Rome, he would have been dead long after Nero's reign. Flacius observed merely that it "is not settled" whether Peter ever was at Rome, a statement that Lamping takes as evidence that for Flacius, too, the question was secondary. His words are "to be taken as a cautious indication that no absolute certainty can be obtained regarding this matter, although the available data argue in favor of a denial of Peter's having been in Rome."[64] Since Flacius demonstrably is not responsible for the text of the Magdeburg Centuries, all statements that assume he was the author, including those of Robert Bellarmine on Peter's reaching Rome,[65] are worthless.[66]

The first printing of Fabri's answer, *That Peter was at Rome, and in the Same Place as Primate Administered a Bishopric and Suffered Martyrdom under Nero: And whether he can be Called the Foundation of the Church.*[67] in which he repeated the arguments of John Cochlaeus and John Fisher. The edition was destroyed by Christopher Fugger, to whom it was dedicated; he feared the harm it could do to his business.[68] Flacius was answered also by Nicholas Sanders, Robert Bellarmine and the Inquisitor of Friesland, Wilhelm van der Lindt.[69] Because of Flacius' reprint, the *Petrum Romam non Venisse* was placed on the Index in 1559 and 1564.[70]

Answering Fabri's *The Right Way*,[71] Flacius re-published[72] *On the Continence of the Clerics*,[73] a tract critical of the new obligation of clerical celibacy written shortly after the Roman synod of 1074 which required it. He attributed it to Bishop Ulrich of Augsburg. In his answer,[74] Fabri, followed by Bellarmine, Baronius, Possevino and others,[75] correctly challenge Flacius' attribution.

Against the persecutions of the Lutherans from 1554 to 1556 by Salzburg Archbishop Michael of Keuenberg, Flacius published a document from von Keuenberg's chancery, *A New Anti-Christian Opinion by the Salzburg Bishop and Other Persecutors of the Church, How they Plan to Eradicate the Truth of the Holy Gospel.*[76] And for those unfortunates, Flacius addressed an *Admonition to the Persecuted Christians in the Bishopric of Salzburg and in Bavaria.*[77]

Only Flacius has preserved the memory of Reformation martyr George Scherer. He was a victim of the bishop of Salzburg, Cardinal Matthias Lang, former chancellor to Emperor Maximilian I, and a supporter of the Habsburg religious policy. In 1554, Flacius published the confession

Scherer had written in prison, just before the execution, *The Last Confession of Georg Scherer, the Holy Martyr, Who for the Sake of Christ's Truth was Horribly Murdered by the Antichristian Wolf at Salzburg.*[78] He reports that he was beheaded and burned in Ratstadt, near Salzburg, for Lutheran preaching, April 13, 1528. Lang had been able to coerce the population of his diocese to pay him homage only by introducing an army from the Tyrol. As Scherer was led to the place of execution, so (non-Flacian) legend has it, he addressed the spectators, and then prayed fervently and, announced with a loud voice that he would give a sign of his innocence. After he was beheaded, he fell on his stomach and lay there as long as it took leisurely to eat an egg (or, according to another version, as long as it took to recite the Our Father, the Creed and the Ten Commandments). Then his body turned slowly on its back, the right foot over the left and the right hand over the left, making the sign of the cross.[79]

Franz Ortner, who offers no basis for his doubts, called Flacius' report "very doubtful." He suggests that Scherer may have been the monk Georgius from the Franciscan monastery in Judenburg mentioned in visitation records, whose preaching had created "much disorder" in some mountain communities. Scherer had possibly been treated as one of the Anabaptists, who, according to the Archbishop's instructions of November, 1527, were considered "disturbers of the peace," and were to be burned alive, or, if they showed repentance, decapitated.[80]

When the confession was reprinted in Ludwig Rabus' *History of Martyrs,*[81] Flacius' report about Scherer became a part of Reformation tradition. The story was reprinted two hundred years later. The sad occasion was history repeating itself: on Reformation Day, October 31, 1731, another Salzburg bishop, Leopold Anthony von Firmian, expelled 20,000 Lutherans. Thus, Scherer's last confession has become part of the tradition of the Salzburger refugees:

> If we had to earn heaven with our own works, Christ would have become man in vain; he would have suffered in vain, he would have died and risen in vain.

tyrer. Straßburg, 1572. II, 467 ff. Idem, *Geschichte der Märterer* II. Frankfurt, 1584. 467–470; Johann Gottlieb Hillinger. *Memoria Schaereriana, das gute Andencken des Evangelischen Märtyrers Georg Schärers.* Saalfeld, 1732, Frankfurt and Leipzig, 1732; Idem. *Beytrag zur Kirchen-Historie des Ertz-Bischofthums Saltzburg.* Saalfeld: Christoph Michael Köhlern, 1732; Johann Georg Schelhorn. *Historische Nachricht vom Ursprung, Fortgang und Schicksale der Evangelischen Religion in den Salzburgischen Landen.* Leipzig: Bernhard Christoph Breitkopf, 1732. 124–140; D. Koch. "Georg Schaerer, ein evangelischer Märterer." *Die Wartburg* XIX (1930). 93–95. Gerhard Florey. *Bischöfe, Ketzer, Emigranten: Der Protestantismus im Lande Salzburg von seinen Anfängen bis zur Gegenwart.* Graz, Vienna and Cologne: Hermann Böhlau, 1967. 18–21.

How often both during our seige and before, but you have condemned not only the preachers, but also the whole city, with various statements and jeers, publicly and privately, in lectures, sermons and publications, like a second monomonastery ...
– Flacius

Johannes Bugenhagen announced in the pulpit that because they were obedient to the authorities, those who died while digging fortifications for the siege troops encamped before Magdeburg died as Christians.[1] He ordered that the emperor and the new Elector be included in the prayer of the church. He encouraged foreign students to write home that Flacius was an errant spirit, a traitor, and a false brother.[2] Churches had nothing to do with politics, George Major said; the citizenship of Christians was in heaven. Taking part in the war against Magdeburg, was a service to God, Magdeburg should be destroyed with fire and sword.[3] "If I had Illyricus," Major was heard to say, "I would tear him apart alive."[4]

Against the accusation that Magdeburg was interested primarily in secular gain, a pamphlet appeared under the pseudonym (Flacius'?), W. Rhodius, *That the Persecution of the Magdeburgers does not Concern Secular Matters or Church lands, but is basically a matter of God's Word and Confession.*[5] The Wittenbergers, not they, were the source of disunity. Amsdorf agreed: *That Doctor Pomer [Bugenhagen] and Doctor Major with their Adiaphorists have ... Caused Vexation and Division.*[6] Flacius complained about Wittenberg's attacks on Magdeburg.[7] Why was it that the income of St. Ulrich's church in Magdeburg had been cut off?[8] Why was it that all right-believing churches and their teachers were persecuted, while the adiaphorists had high salaries and the favor and gifts from the great lords? Because they recommended that the emperor's orders be followed.

In the *Truly Grounded Answer of the Preachers of Magdeburg to the Accusation of their Enemies that they, too, have God's Word in the pure content of the Augsburg confession as well as those in Magdeburg, and what they have dared on that basis to enter against and accuse against the city,*[9] he denied that Wittenberg could claim fidelity to the Augsburg Confession. For those who had taken the wrong side, Flacius and Gallus printed *A Penitential Sermon for the Public Sinners.*[10] The root cause was their subservient attitude toward government. Flacius accused them of "jack-booted theology."[11] Not so long ago, during the war, he remembered, George Major had written the **highly** political *Heavenly Bann*, in which he declared Charles V and Paul III outlaws, and incited military resistance against him.[12] Gallus recalled that during the late war they had acted differently; we have seen above that to prove his point he reprinted their wartime pamphlets. In the preface to his letter to Bohemia five years earlier, Bugenhagen had done the same.[13] But that was then.

1 *Antwort auf ... Beschüldigung ... Majors.* C iij r.

2 *Eine Entschuldigung an einen Pfarher.* A v.

3 J. Döllinger. II, 150.

4 Quoted by Flacius, *Antwort auff ... Beschuldigung ... Majors.* A iij r – v.

5 *Daß die Magdeburg nicht umb Weltlichen Sachen oder Pfaffengüter sonder im grunde umb Gottes Worts, und des Bekentnis willen verfolget werden.* Magdeburg: Christian Rödinger, 1551.

6 *Das Doctor Pomer und Doctor Major mit jren Adiaphoristen ergernis und zurtrennung angericht, Unnd den Kirchen Christi unüberwuntlichen Schaden gethan haben. Derhalben sie und nicht wir zu Magdeburg von Teuffel erwegt seint wie sie uns schmehen und lestern.* Magdeburg [Michael Lotter], 1551.

7 Bindseil. 588.

8 *Widder die newe Reformation.* C v.

9 *Der Prediger zu Magdeburgk ware gegründte Antwort auff das rhumen irer Feinde das sie auch Gottes Wort reine inhalts der Augsburgischen Confession so wol als die zu Magdeburg haben. Und was sie daraus mehr wider die Stadt einführen unnd fürgeben dürfften.* Magdeburg: Michael Lotter, 1551. Kettner. *Clericus Ulrico-Levinianus.* 201, makes Gallus the author. Voit. *Nicolaus Gallus.* 162, reports a second printing.

10 *Bußpredigt für die öffentlichen Sünder jtziger zeit, die falschen Brüder, Nemlich für die Verlasser verleugker, Abtrünnige und Verfolger ihrer eignen Religion an ihren Brüdern.* n. t. n. p.

11 *Entschuldigung ... an die Universitet.* H iij.

12 *Ewiger: Göttlicher Almechtiger Maiestet Declaration wider Kaiser Carl: König zu Hispanien, etc. Und Bapst Paulum den Dritten.* Wittenberg: Hans Lufft, 1546.

13 *Erklerung der schendlichen Sünde.* A ij r.

But then they still had a prince who said the same war was persecution. And since they were in the same danger with him, they, too, said it was persecution. But now, after they, with their beautiful adiaphorism have reconciled the whore and the beast, and have a lord who says it is not persecution, they, too, say it is not persecution. Now they are writing a secret confession, because the lord wants it so. They are theologians very obedient to the government.[14]

On November 14, 1550 a papal Bull was published by Julius III, summoning the second period of the Council of Trent, to begin on May 1, 1551. The Germans had appealed for a fair general council; they were granted, instead, a *papal* council. How long, Flacius asked, has all of Germany sought a free Christian council? How often had both the emperor and pope promised it? But until the present day, they had not been bold enough to allow it.[15] "It is known publicly that the pope orders the whole process according to his own will ... put his four *Amptsverweser* whom he calls *legati a latere* over the whole pile, like kings and monarchs do. Finally, the council, therefore, was not free, and has begun a war against our churches."[16]

The return to Trent from Bologna was a triumph for the victorious emperor. He wanted the Protestant Estates to send representatives, and promised them a safe conduct. From besieged Magdeburg came a plea that Melanchthon and Brenz stay away from the council, as Christ had stood silent before his accusers, and as the ancient Church Fathers had absented themselves from councils of which they were suspicious. Evangelicals would, by their presence, give Trent a legitimacy it should not have, and which would end hopes for a free council in Germany. Maurice asked Melanchthon, Bugenhagen and Camerarius to discuss the affair with him on February 12, 1551, in Dresden. They recommended that Prince George of Anhalt with other theologians be sent to Trent. Melanchthon insisted that the previous decisions of the council could not be taken into account, and that the proceedings must begin anew. And the pope could not be president or judge.

On December 13 Melanchthon received the order to be in Nuremberg on January 11, where he would receive further orders. There was no instruction or travel funds. Melanchthon came back to Wittenberg on March 20. In 1548, at the Armored Diet of Augsburg, the Protestants had been promised that the council would not come under the pope's leadership, and the decrees already passed would be negotiated again. When the Emperor promised the Protestants a safe-conduct to Trent and a hearing in the council, the Elector summoned Melanchthon, Bugenhagen, and Camerarius to Dresden in January, 1551, to hear their views in the matter.

It was decided that Melanchthon should not go to Trent, but he was commissioned to prepare a new confession of faith. He retired to Dessau, where from May 6 – 10 1551 he wrote *The Confession of the Doctrine of the Saxon Churches*,[17] It was signed, on June 10, 1551 only by clergymen – all Superintendents of Electoral Saxony, with the professors of Wittenberg

14 *Antwort auff ... Beschuldigung ... Majors.* A iiij r.

15 *Ein kurtzer Bericht vom Interim.* B iij v.

16 *Erklerung der schendlichen Sünde.* [A iiij v].

17 *Confessio Doctrinae Saxonicarum ecclesiarum synodo Tridentinae oblata, anno Domini MDLI.* Basel, 1552. CR, XXVIII, 370–467.

18 Heinrich Heppe. *Die Confessionelle Entwicklung der altprotestantischen Kirche Deutschlands.* Marburg: Elwert, 1854. 143.

19 *Confession. Das ist, ain Bekandnuß der Sächsischen Kirchen lerr, welliche dem Concilio zu Triendt in dem MDLI. Jar ist überantwort worden. Darinnen ain yeder Christenlicher Leser sehen kan, wer von der allgemeinen Christenlichen Kirchen abgetretten sey, Und an wem es ligt, das kain Gotsälige ainheligkait in der Kirchen auffgericht wirt. Durch M. Johan Maisperger von Augspurg verteütscht.* Augsburg: Philipp Ulhart, 1552.

20 *Ein Register der hundert Beshwerungen damit Deudschland von dem Bapst und den seinen jemmerlich beschwert, und uberladen, ja gentzlich verterbt wird, auffm Reichstage zn Nürneberg Anno 1532, angefangen und Anno 1523 geendet, von dem Reich dem Bapst ubersendet.* Magdeburg: Christian Rödinger, 1550.

21 *Recusationschrift der Christlichen Augspurgischen Confessionsverwandten Stende wider das vermeint von Bapst Paulo dem dritten, weilandt zu Trient indicirt und angefangen Concilium, sampt einer gebürlichen prouocation und erbietung, auff ein allgemein oder National, frey, Christlich und unparteisch Concilium inn Deudtschen Landen.* [Magdeburg: Michael Lotter], 1551.

22 *Protestatio contra Concilium Tridentinum cum norma synodi & Scripta quaedam Papae et Monarcharum de eo Concilio ad cognoscendem veritatem admodum lectu utilis, nunc primum in publicum edita.* Magdeburg, 1551.

23 *Was und wie man sich zu dem künfftigen Concilium zu Trydent versähen möge. Auch was gutts davon zu verhoffen.* Magdeburg: Michael Lotter [1551].

24 *Eine prophetische abconterfeihung des Tridentischen Conciliabuli. Durch Martinum Luther.* Magdeburg: Christian Rödinger, 1551.

25 *Ein grausam meer Wunder, den Bapst bedeutende, zu Rom gefunden, und zu*

and Leipzig, all the clergy of Pomerania, the theologians of the Margrave Johann of Brandenburg, the theologians of the Margrave George Friedrich zu Ansbach-Bayreuth, theologians of Mansfeld, Stolberg and Königstein, and the theologians of Württemberg, Strassburg and the University of Greifswald. Together with Brenz's *Confessio Würtembergica* it was meant to be read at the second session of the Council of Trent. Bringing together themes from the latter editions of his *Loci Communes* and the altered Augsburg Confession, it was a "finished development" of Melanchthonian doctrine,[18] having "wholly other character" than Luther's.

The Magdeburg critique of the Repetitio, as it was called, was published in Augsburg.[19] Flacius also reprinted the text of the German *Gravanima* against Rome, from the Nuremberg diet.[20] In March, 1551, Flacius and Gallus reprinted the 1546 protest from Nuremberg of the Estates of the Augsburg Confession, who had appealed for a non-partisan council, against the newly-assembled council in Trent, *Protest of the Christian Estates Related to the Augsburg Confession Against the Presumed Council*,[21] in which they called for a "universal, free, Christian council, outside the control of a single party" to judge their cause, and in which they listed seven reasons for rejecting Trent. In their glosses, Flacius and Gallus observed that by first calling a council, postponing its opening and changing its venue until he could mount an open attack on the Evangelicals, the pope was attempting to destroy the gospel with deceit and brute force. Since they were convinced that Charles V and Paul II had coordinated a conspiracy, they blamed the pope for sending Evangelical leaders, both in church and state, to the grave or to prison by means of murder and arson. Flacius published his own rules for conducting a proper council,[22] and reasons for avoiding the council the pope had called.

The official Magdeburg reaction to the approaching council was *What and how one should expect from the future Council in Trent. And what Good can be expected from it.*[23] How could a council be "universal" when there were no representatives from Africa, Greece, Hungary, Poland, France, and England? How could it be free if it was dominated by the pope? How could it be an ecumenical council, since those whom the pope convicts and persecutes with an army as enemies will have little freedom and peace, let alone what he has in mind in his *scrinium pectoris*?

Flacius recyled the tract in which Luther denounced the original announcement of the council, "The Pope Grants a Free, Christian, Universal Council in Germany,"[24] illustrated with a caricature of the Pope Paul III riding a swine. It referred to the peasant notion that a swine could be ridden if distracted with ordure. Flacius commented that when Luther published it the tract had been considered a fool's fantasy, but had proved to be divine wisdom. He also reprinted Melanchthon's *Papstesel* tract, in which the papacy is portrayed as a "sea-wonder," a feminine form with the head of an ass, scales on the breast, an elephant's foot instead of a right arm, the right foot of an ox, the left of a claw. The tail is a dragon's head and on one side of her hip there is a man's head.[25]

FLACIUS' AND GALLUS' REASONS FOR REJECTING THE COUNCIL OF TRENT

1. The pope has no right to call a council. In the Old Testament and in the early church, councils were called by political leaders.

2. Papal legates had promised the Diet that a free council would be held in Germany. Trent was not a German city, nor was it safe, since the pope had placed Protestants under the ban.

3. Because sympathizers with Rome controlled it, and because, in violation of New Testament and patristic practice, the laity was excluded, the council was not universal.

4. Since the Evangelicals had already been condemned, it was not a free council.

5. Since it would not listen to the Word of Christ, it was not a Christian council.

6. Although Christians were in attendance, as could be seen from the pope's doctrinal errors and the moral turpitude, they represented Satan, not God.

7. The pope could not be the final judge in a matter to which he was a party; yet his legates completely controlled the council.

From the Protestation contra Concilium Tridentinum

Wittenberg erstlich A. 23. und darnach abermal A. 46. mit der auslegung Philippi gedruckt. Magdeburg: Christian Rödinger [1550].

26 non caste, sed caute famula amare. Cf. Clemen. KS, V, 11 f.

27 Etliche greiffliche ... warzeichen, 1549 [A iiij v].

In the *Varia Doctorum ... poemata* Flacius printed "A citation of Paul III ... to the clergy," inviting them to the council. It had come to his attention, the pope said, that the laity wanted to reform the clergy and fire their kitchen personnel (concubines). Therefore, in consultation with the college of cardinals, he had called a council to Trent to make decisions about the matter. The council would not be conducted according to the Holy Scripture, since there was an easier way to destroy heretics. One need only mobilize the secular powers against them. One member of the chapter after another explains why he cannot obey the papal command. The senior finally summarizes the explanations, that they want to love their servants cautiously, not chastely.[26] In Trent, they had made patchwork out of the Holy Scripture. By the same token one could mix togther all of Eulenspiegel from the Bible, and afterwards say that Eulenspiegel was based on scripture.[27]

28 *Was von dem jetzt ausgeschriebenen Tridentischen Concilio zu halten sey. Drey Gesprech.* [Magdeburg: Michael Lotter], 1542. C iij v.

29 *Scripta quaedam papae et Monarchum, de concilio Tridentino, ad cognoscendam veritatem admodum lectu utilis nunc primum in lucem edita.* Basel [Magdeburg?], n. t. On the dating, cf. Robert Kolb. "The German Lutheran Reaction to the Third Period of the Council of Trent, 1563." *Lutherjahrbuch* LI (1984). 63–95. Kolb makes the terminus ad quem 1554.

30 *Von der grewlichen Uneinigkeit, Zwitracht, Secten und Rotten der Bepstlichen Religion und Kirchen, Jtziger zeit sehr nützlich zu lesen.* Jena: Thomas Rebart, 1559.

31 Walther Gose (ed.). *Reformationdrucke. Von den Anfängen Luthers bis zum Ende des 16. Jahrhunderts.* Nuremberg: Antiquariat M. Edelmann, 1972. 47.

32 *Warer Grundt und Beweisung das die unrecht handlen die jren Predigern verbiten das Antichristisch Bapstum mit seinem grewlen zustraffen...* [Magdeburg: Christian Rödinger, 1550].

33 *Dass itzund die rechte zeit sey, Christum und sein Wort zu bekennen und auff keine andere zu warten sey. Etliche Sprüche, das man den Adiaphoristen nicht trawen noch gleuben sol.* [Magdeburg: Christian Rödinger], 1551.

34 *Disputatio de Adiaphoris, & mutatione praesentis status pie constituarum ecclesiarum.* Magdeburg: Michael Lotter, 1551.

35 *Der von Magdeburg verantwortung alles vnglimpffs so ihnen in ihrer Belagerung von der magdeburgischen Baals Pfaffen und andern ihrem unnd den Christen Feinden begegenet.* [Magdeburg: Christian Rödinger, 1550].

36 *Wider den Evangelisten.* A j f.

At Trent, the Protestants were heard, not in the plenary session, but in a congregation, January 24, 1552. At the end of the first session, a pamphlet appeared in Magdeburg, *What one should think of the Tridentine Council, now called. Three Conversations.*[28] Between 1554 and 1560, Flacius also published *Certain Writings of the Pope and the Monks*, which included correspondence between Pope Paul III and his legates with representatives of Charles V, and a Protestation of King Henry of France, dated August 12, 1551, read by J. Amyot before a preparatory meeting of the Council. In the preface, Flacius made the claim that the documents demonstrated how the pope had deceived monarchs and mocked the delegation from Württemberg and Strassburg that had gone to Trent. The document would show the council was neither universal, free, Christian, or legitimate. It ended with a reference to the coincidence of the calling of the council and the German (Smalcald) war.[29]

A later pamphlet against the council was *On the Horrible Disunity, Dissension, Sects, and Rabble of the Papal Religion.*[30] As Sigismund Cephalus (the pseudonym may be an anagram for Flacius' name),[31] Flacius criticized the Wittenberg ban on speaking against the papacy.[32] All those who had participated in the siege, Amsdorf wrote, contended against God, Christ and his Word, have sinned against the Holy Spirit.[33] Because of complaints that the Magdeburg theologians had attacked the Wittenbergers without warning, Gallus published a letter from 1549 to Melanchthon and Bugenhagen, illustrated with a list, summarizing the main points of the controversy on the adiaphora.[34] Against harsh criticism the city issued an apology.[35]

"They had concocted plans to fool the military victors and thus avoid martyrdom," Flacius thundered. "Avoiding the cross, they have abandoned their brothers in the cross, have come to terms with the Antichrist, and through their Interim have made way for his abomination and ... have persecuted the Christians. To them that is pure unity." "During the siege," Flacius wrote against the Wittenbergers, "when we were surrounded by our enemies so that no one could go in or out, they began to defend their most beautiful *Adiaphoristerei*, to lay one cross after the other on the troubled Christians and, together with the enemies, to persecute the church of God."[36]

The present time ... will not stand for much disputation ... but demands that ... all Christians, every Christian, confess with whole, steadfast hearts. – Flacius

To be as effective as possible, cannon barrages against Magdeburg were timed most often for Sunday mornings during church services. One cannonball landed on the residence of the Cathedral dean and wounded Countess Anne of Mansfeld. A sunny presence in a difficult time was Erasmus Alber, who said he relied on the words of Luther, in chapters 14 through 17 of his commentary on St. John. He produced up-beat songs, such as "Hear from Me a New Song about How the Pope Has Cooked for Us."[1] When a friend gave him a fish to fry, the story goes, he asked him to remain for supper. There was no firewood, of course, but the Lord would provide. Hardly had he finished speaking when a cannonball loosed a beam of his house. Firewood! He had forseen it.[2]

The defenders hoisted their own cannons to the church towers " the cathedral, St. Sebastian's, and St. James'. They were used with telling effect by *Büchsenmeister* Andreas Kritzmann, who is remembered as a hero of the resistance.[3]

The really difficult times began on November 28 when Elector Maurice took the Neustadt. But the military imagination of the exiled generals made itself felt. On the stormy night of December 20, 1,400 men pulled white shirts over their armor as camouflage in the new snow. Like Moses during the battle with the Amelekites, Burgomaster Hans Ebeling promised them as they slipped quietly out of the Sudenberg gate, until they returned he would remain on his knees.[4] In summer they played another trick.

> It is reported among us for certain, that the Magdeburgers deceived the enemy by an extraordinary stratagem on the 15th of June. They sent out young men in women's clothes to gather forage, and added a guard of soldiers to accompany them. The enemy, supposing them to be really young women, made an attack upon them, as though certain of their prey. The pretended females made a show of fight, the guard hastened to their defence. At last the young men threw off the mask, and appeared in arms. After this victory having become somewhat more elated, they again attacked the enemy, when they brought into the city three or four wagons laden with the slain bodies of the Magdeburgers. It is reported, however, that not less than five hundred of the enemy were slain. This statement is given by the messenger who has come hither from Magdeburg.[5]

Since the siege guns had been positioned at some distance, Magdeburg's cattle were able to graze just outside the walls, and only once did the 400,000 Magdeburgers have to eat horse meat. As a contribution to morale, Flacius brewed up some beer. It was *anise* beer, since he substituted anise for hops. It is not clear whether he had learned the art in his homeland, or whether he aquired the skill somewhere in Germany. From the history of beer, at least, we know that at the time it was not unknown, and

1 Alberus. *Wetterau.* 62.
2 Franz Schnorr von Carolsfeld. *Erasmus Alber.* Dresden: L. Ehlermann, 1893. 98.
3 Götze. 173.
4 Eberhard von Alemann. *Geschichte des Geschlechts von Alemann.* Magdeburg, 1911. 99.
5 Letter of John Burcher to Henry Bullinger, August 3rd, 1551. Hastings Robinson (ed.). *Original Letters Relative to the English Reformation.* Cambridge: Cambridge University Press, 1947. 579.

Johannes Pomarius. Beschreibung des Newen S. Jacob Thorms. Magdeburg, 1583.

6 Heinrich Knaustius. *Fünf Bücher von der Göttlichen und Edlenn Gabe der Philosophischen hochthweeren und wunderbaren Kunst, Bier zu brawen.* Erfurt: Nicolaus Schmach, 1614. 91. For the reference I am thankful to Dr. Hans G. Schlutze-Berndt of the Gesellschaft für die Geschichte und Bibliographie des Brauwesens, Berlin.

7 "sich wol hat trinken lassen." Wilhelm Raabe. *Unseres Herrgotts Kanzlei: Eine Erzählung von Jacob Corbinus.* Göttingen: Vandenhoeck & Ruprecht, 1969. 362, quoting Merkel, op. cit.

8 *Geistliche Ringeltänze. Aus der heiligen Schrift. Vor die Jugend.* Magdeburg: Hans Walther, 1551. Cited, Götze. 177.

9 *Ein christlich Gebet der Kirchen und Kriegsleute zu Magdeburgk, sonderlich in treffender Not, wieder ihre Feinde, durch die Prediger daselbs gestellt.* Magdeburg: Michael Lotter, 1551. According to Kettner, *Clericus Ulrico-Levinianus.* 201, Gallus was the author.

10 *Ein Form zu Beten und Gott anzurufen in dieser gegenwertigen not und trübsal.* [Magdeburg: Michael Lotter, 1550].

11 *Das II. Capit. Syrach, der XII und XCIV. Psalm mit kurtzen ausslegungen.* Magdeburg, 1551.

12 *Warer Bericht und Trost aus dem sechsten Capitel des Propheten Baruchs, allen betrübten gewissen, so in diesen kümmerlichen zeiten des Interims und Adiaphora halben nicht wissen, wie sie sich halten sollen.* Magdeburg: Christian Rödinger, 1550.

13 *Ein geistlicher Trost dieser betrübten Magdeburgischen Kirchen Christi, das sie diese Verfolgung umb Gottes worts, und kein andern ursachen halben, leidet.* [Magdeburg: Michael Lotter, 1551].

14 *Kleriche beweisung.*

15 *Christlich kurtze erinnerung.* 3n.

16 *Ein kurtzer Bericht vom Interim.* B iiij v.

17 *Responsio ad epistolam Philippi Melanthoni.* A vj.

was put to use as a *digestif* as well as a cure for colic.[6] Given a glass to sample, city secretary Heinrich Merkel pronounced Flacius' brew potable.[7]

The Magdeburgers suffered no shortage of encouraging words. The Time of Confession had arrived and the contrast was clear; it was a struggle between Christ and Belial. In church they sang "Lord Keep us Steadfast in Your Word." Songs were provided for young people,[8] for the the garrison[9] and for the citizens.[10] Flacius recommended reading the twelfth and the ninety-fourth Psalms: "Help, Lord; for there is no longer any that is godly." "Rise up, O judge of the earth; render to the proud their deserts! ... Can wicked rulers be allied with Thee, who frame mischief by statutes?" and the second chapter of *Syrach*.[11] Gallus recommended the fiery words from *Baruch* 4.21.[12]

> Take heart, my children! Cry out to God, and he will rescue you from tyranny and from the power of your enemies. For I have set my hope of your deliverance on the Everlasting; the Holy One, your everlasting savior, has filled me with joy over the mercy soon to be granted you.

It was a struggle between Christ and Belial; Flacius assured the Magdeburgers that they were suffering for the Word of God, and for no other reason.[13] He warned those outside the city that those who opposed Magdeburg were persecutors of Christ, since the Interim's changes were perversions of the recognized Christian religion, and since whoever persecuted innocent Christians because of their faith, persecuted Christ.[14] The same message was announced in a pamphlet prepared by the Magdeburg clergy on October 16th: *A Short Christian Reminder of the Pastors and Preachers of Magdeburg to their Christian Congregation and Concerning all Christians Outside the Current Persecution. That Now in Magdeburg We Are Suffering in and About the Confession of the Gospel of Christ.*[15]

"The present time," Flacius cautioned, "will not stand for much disputation, but demands that ... all Christians, every Christian, confess with whole, steadfast hearts."[16] "I see that even Christ knew no other way ... than steadfast confession, fervent appeal for help to God, and patience on the cross."[17]

The fear of suffering, he wrote, was worse than suffering itself.[18] He held up the memories of Christian martyrs: the woman of Odessa, who was asked by a military officer if she knew that the Emperor Valen would have everyone who entered the church killed. "That I have heard," the woman answered, "and therefore I am hurrying there with this child, so that we my die with the other Christians and be martyrs." Others were Basil, from chapters 32 and 36 of Cassiodorus' sixth century *Tripartite History*,[19] and Simeon from Book VII, Chapter XXVI, of Sozomenus' *Ecclesiastical History*.[20] One should be prepared for a martyr's death.

> It is not such a deplorable thing to die for Christ's sake, as the Interimists and Adiaphorists imagine. It is also possible that through such steadfastness of Christians the rulers may be persuaded to give up their plans, because they cannot or will not want to kill all of us at one time.[21]

On March 7, when the Elbe was finally free from ice, mercenary soldiers were dispatched upstream in two ships and twenty-two small boats, Lieutenant Colonel Hans Winkelbricht in command. They sank the whole enemy fleet. And on April 14, with a dismayed Maurice watching from the river bank, Magdeburg won a second naval battle.

On March 20, the Magdeburgers obediently brought half the silver they owned to the Rathaus to finance the resistance. Their resolve was remembered in a reaction Flacius heard from one the prisoners of war: "And if Magdeburg were bound on a chain, and Our Lord God in heaven held the chain with the hand, still it would want to wage war." The statement became well enough known to be quoted by angry Imperial General Wallenstein in 1628 during his unsuccessful siege of Stralsund.[22] For David Chytraeus in Rostock, Magdeburg was Bethulia. Like the other Bethulians somewhere in ancient Samaria, the Magdeburgers were in peril of losing their religion. "Now therefore" he was putting words from the book of *Judith* into their mouths "let us set an example to our brethren." "...their lives depend on us, and the sanctuary, the temple and the altar rest on us ... For if we are captured, all Judea will be captured and our sanctuary will be plundered; and he will exact of us the penalty for its desecration."[23]

Toward the end, Amsdorf published a pamphlet, warning everyone who had assisted in the war or the siege to repent. They had resisted God, Christ, and his holy Word and had sinned against the Holy Spirit. Unless they repented, they would all perish.[24] And only a few days before capitulation, October 28, the day of St. Simon and St. Jude, conscious that freedom of the press was in danger, Flacius and Amsdorf published a final statement, starting, as they had done before, with the *clausula Petri*, *Acts of the Apostles* 5:29: "one must obey God rather than man."[25]

The search for a diplomatic solution had advanced far enough in the fall of 1551, that agreement was within reach. The final negotiations, authorized by the emperor, took place on November 4 and 5. The city renounced allegiance to the Smalcald League, agreed to pay reparations of 50,000 Gulden to the cathedral chapter, surrendered twelve cannons to the elector of Brandenburg, and recognized the Magdeburg *Erzstift*, Electoral Saxony and Brandenburg. Furthermore, the city promised not to make any treaty against the emperor and the Austrian house. After thirteen months, the siege ended on November 7, 1551. 2,000 footsoldiers and 130 mounted troops marched throught the open gates, and a rumor went around that Flacius would be hung on the city wall.[26] The next day, November 8, Flacius wrote to Conrad Gerlach for advice. Should he stay or leave?[27] The next day, Maurice himself made his entrance, accepted the key to the city, acknowledged the homage of its citizens, pronounced an amnesty, and confirmed the city's rights and freedoms.

On November 13 the pastors were summoned to the house of George Sturm to meet with Saxon officials, Fachs, Mordeissen, von Carlowitz, and von Gersdorff, to discuss the articles of capitulation "the most extraordinary," Ranke observed, "of anything that has ever come under the desig-

18 *Ein Vermanung zur gedult und glauben zu Gott, im Creutz dieser verfolgung. Geschrieben an die Kirche Christi zu Magdeburg.* Magdeburg: Christian Rödinger, 1551. A ij r. He thus anticipated Michel de Montaigne, "The thing of which I have most fear is fear," Francis Bacon in 1623, "Nothing is terrible except fear itself," the Duke of Wellington, "the only thing I am afraid of is fear," Henry David Thoreau, "Nothing is so much to be feared as fear," and Franklin Roosevelt, "the only thing we have to fear is fear itself." Clifford D. May. "Biden and the Annals..." New York Times, September 21, 1987.

19 *Eine schöne historia von der standhaftigkeit des heiligen mans Basilij beschrieben in der tripartita historia und ander schone exemple mehr itzt zu dieser zeit sehr tröstlich und nützlich zu lesen.* Magdeburg: Christian Rödinger, 1549.

20 *Ein sehr schöne Historia von der standhafftigkeit im Bekentnis und leiden des heiligen mans Simeonis welcher ein oberster Superintendent gewesen ist in Persia und von seinen gesellen aus den andern buch Sozomenis.* Magdeburg: Christian Rödinger, n. t.

21 *Eine freidige Vermanung; Ein Christlich Vermanung.* G ij r.

22 Götze. 177.

23 *Judith.* 8.21,42.

24 *Eine erinnerung an die Deudschen, das die einfeltigen ihre Sünde, so sie diese Fünff jar her gethan haben, erkennen und bekennen sollen, sich bekehren und bessern, Auff das sie selig und mit dem hauffen nicht verdampt werden.* [Magdeburg: Christian Rödinger], 1551. B iij v.

25 *Deren zu Magdeburgk so widder die Adiaphora geschrieben haben, ihres vorigen schreibens beschlus auff der adiaphoristen beschuldigen und lesterung die zeit ihrer belagerung und jtzt zum teil neulich unter diesen friedenshandlungen wider sie abgangen.* Magdeburg: Michael Lotter, 1551.

26 Schnorr von Carolsfeld. 855.

27 Sillem. I, 118.

28 Op. cit. 513.

29 Göttingen. ms. theol. 162.
    Bl. 213 r–217 v.

30 Friedrich Wilhelm Hoffmann.
    Geschichte der Stadt Magdeburg.
    2 Bde. Magdeburg: Albert Rathke,
    1855. 306.

31 "tamquam Leo generosus latran-
    tem catulum neglexit." *Lipsia, seu
    Originum Lipsiensium Libri IV.*
    Leipzig & Martisburg: 1689. III,
    399. Quoted by Ritter. 47.

nation of 'explanation.'"[28] The emperor's instructions were to require the Interim, but Fachs explained that Maurice would be faithful to the grave to the Word of God as explained in the Augsburg Confession. Only the secular provisions of the late Imperial diet would be put into effect. Reversing his policy of the year previous, he announced that would also tolerate the Magdeburg liturgy, a concession for which Pastor Lukas Rosenthal expressed thanks.

Pastors were to admonish their parishioners to obey authority and to pray for the Council of Trent and for Christian unity. Then it was Gallus' turn to speak. The clergy were not responsible for the attacks on the Elector, he said. They would not deny they had written those books by which they had portrayed the superstition of the Antichrist to simple people, and had clarified the gospel. They could not condemn that. In the Leipzig Interim, some theologians had departed from the right doctrine of justification, repentance and the sacraments and had betrayed the evangelical church to the pope. The term, "highest bishop," could be understood in no other way than of the pope. Although there may have been political reasons among the members of the council, the attack on the city was religious. What evil would have come had the Magdeburg church not been steadfast!

The Magdeburgers chose not to promise to obey the imperial edict of January 1551 ordering that Protestants submit to the decisions of the Council of Trent. They had retained the earlier teaching and were ready to give an account of it, whereas at the diets of 1548 and 1551 there were many who accepted the Council of Trent and persuaded others to do so. Since the Council had continually damned the holy religion and since one could expect from it only persecution of true Christians, one could pray only that God direct it.[29] Better to pray that the council be confounded. As for the request for loyalty to the legitimate government, they had consistently practiced it and would continue to do so.

Dr. Fachs did not conceal his anger against what the Magdeburg printers had been producing. No longer would satirical rhymes and songs be tolerated. Nor could Maurice be any longer accused of having departed the true faith. Intolerable as well were reports that Magdeburg had resisted for the sake of God's word, and that the gospel would have been lost except for Magdeburg's faithfulness. Only poor Alber, who had asked the world whether a such a thief (Maurice) should be given legal custody of his plunder, was punished. "Too vulgar even for a peasant,"[30] he was driven into exile. But instead of having the Sons of Cyclops killed on the city walls, Maurice let it be known he had nothing against them: a clause in the capitulation paper specifically guaranteed freedom to Gallus and to Flacius. Elector Maurice, according to the imperious Saxon Chancellor, David Pfeiffer, dealt with Flacius "as a noble lion ignores a barking puppy."[31]

A Second Beginning

THE REVOLT OF THE PRINCES

Flacius and Maurice of Saxony saved the Reformation. – Georg Ellinger.

... if Luther's work were saved then, it is special measure thanks to Flacius.
– Gustav Kawerau

... it is certainly not too much said, if one therefore regards him as the rescuer of an independent Protestant movement. – Lutz Geldsetzer

1 Born. 25.
2 Op. cit. 1645. 1270–1271.
3 n. p. [1631].
4 Spieker. 358.

Luther's reform survived because the faithful resistance of Magdeburg succeeded. But even in Magdeburg, the great deeds of God's Chancery have never been marked by a memorial holiday. After the Thirty Years' War the memory of religious conflict was unpopular. And during the period of German absolutism, resistance against political authority was no less unpopular. Another reason is that the outcome was less than heroic: the struggle between Christ and Belial ended with negotiations.

After Maurice's army entered the city, the Saxony chancellor began a speech, "after the city surrenders ..." He was emphatically corrected by Levin of Emden. Magdeburg was coming to terms, not surrendering, *vertragen*, not *ergeben*. "Ja," said the Elector, and so it was.[1] Magdeburg was showered with praise. Some of it has been preserved in Friedrich Hortleder's collection of political documents[2]; the most famous tribute is the elegy by Petrus Loticius, *De Obsidione Urbis Magdeburgensis*,[3] revived after the later siege of 1631. In the last century, the defiance of the Magdeburgers was celebrated in the novel by Wilhelm Raabe, *Unseres Herrgotts Kanzlei. Eine Erzählung.*

Resistance had been growing since the Mühlberg defeat. Margrave Hans of Brandenburg (Küstrin-Neumark) came to realize that he had been betrayed. He had been assured that the war in which he fought on the side of Maurice was solely secular. The truth, he now saw, was that it had been a religious war – a war to elminate the Evangelical faith. At the the 1547 Diet he invoked St. Peter's clause: we ought to obey God rather than men. He would never accept the *Gemengel*, he said, the hotch-potch of the Interim. Rather than to surrender to the Council of Trent, he announced that he had chosen to fight: "better a sword than a pen, better blood than ink!"[4]

In February 1550, with Duke Albrecht of Prussia, Duke Johann Albrecht of Mecklenburg and Count Volrad of Mansfeld, he organized a new military alliance, the Königsberg Defense League, to protect the

5 J. Hermann. 134.
6 "Examination." 104.
7 PKMS, IV, 36.

Augsburg Confession and to rescue Magdeburg. Maurice learned about the Lutheran alliance, and felt a noose tightening around his neck. But always a strategist, he determined not to be led by events. He would lead them. Indeed, he had his own reasons for resenting the emperor – the arrogant behavior of the Spanish troops in Augsburg, the imprisonment of Landgrave Philipp of Hesse, his father-in-law, and the plan, called the "Spanish Succession," to make Charles' son Philipp the next emperor. That, in Maurice's words, would mean "good night, Germany." He had been rewarded, moreover, after the war with only the Electoral Circle around Wittenberg, not the whole of Saxony. That meant that his cousins were still in power in the *other* Saxony. His spies told him they were plotting revenge. Less than three weeks into the siege, he offered Magdeburg an armistice. Still influenced by Flacius' propaganda, the officials refused the offer.[5] Although Manschrek's assertion that Flacius had taken on "the role of a dictator"[6] is an overstatement, officials were influenced by his calls for firmness, and it took them a long time to take Maurice's diplomatic initiatives seriously.

In spite of Flacius' determination to portray the situation in black and white, General von Heideck came to realize the potential of Maurice's advances.[7] Count Volrad and Count Johann von Mansfeld slipped out of the city, and with the assistance of Jan Laski of Poland, collected money from the Hanseatic cities and from Queen Jane Grey of England, and troops from those just dismissed by the Duke of Mecklenburg. On December 13th, 1550, Maurice left the siege and travelled to Verden to negotiate with Baron von Heideck and Count Albrecht, who had assembled an army of 4,300 foot soldiers and 300 mounted troups from the area of Bremen and Verden, ready to defend the Lutheran cause.

On January 11, just as he had once put himself at the service of the emperor, Maurice had himself formally named commander-in-chief of the new alliance. He met with Margrave Hans in Dresden on February 20, 1550. A formal basis for a revolt was laid at Verden, January 7, 1551. The treaty united the Königsberg League, the cities of the south, Electoral Saxony, and Hesse. Maurice promised to do nothing that would limit German liberty, and it was agreed that the allies would cooperate with King Henry II of France "for the preservation of the religion freedom of the Germans." It was carefully aimed not at the House of Habsburg, but at the emperor alone. To demonstrate that he was "no Mameluke," Maurice promised to preserve the Evangelical faith; he would give up the siege against Magdeburg, protest against the Council of Trent, and protect the Augsburg Confession.

The princes who assembled at Königsberg on February 26 were uneasy about a Habsburg family treaty of March, 1551, making King Philipp of Spain successor to the imperial throne. That meant certain Spanish servitude. They organized a new military alliance, the Torgau League of May 1551, to protect the Reformation. And Prince Maurice – at the same time his troops were killing its citizens – promised to support

8 CR, VII, 902–905.

Erasmus Alber. Christ as Victor over the Interim Dragon. Kupferstichkabinett,
Staatliche Museen Preußischer Kulturbesitz, Berlin.

Magdeburg. In October, 1551, at a meeting in Lochau and in a treaty with
King Henry II of France at the Chateau Chambord on the Loire, Maurice
conspired to attack the emperor. The king's price was possession of the
Imperial vicariates of Metz, Toul, and Verdun. Melanchthon warned
against the revolt, calling it sedition; the emperor was the proper authority.[8] Nevertheless, on January 15, 1552, a treaty was made with the king.
Meanwhile, the real blood his siege troops required of the Magdeburgers
deceived the emperor. But in May 1551, serious negotiations with Magdeburg began.

Under the mottos, "Liberation from the breastly Spanish servitude,"
and "Freedom for the Gospel," Maurice and his allies attacked the Emper-
or. Taken off guard, the Emperor escaped to Villach in Austria, and the
balance of power changed. The 1552 "Revolt of the Princes" accomplished
what the Smalcald League could not. Charles had almost succeeded in

9 Benno von Bundschuh. *Das Wormser Religionsgespräch von 1557 unter besonderer Berücksichtigung der kaiserlichen Religionspolitik.* Münster: Aschendorff, 1988. 9.

10 Götze. 179.

11 Op. cit. 44.

12 "O felicem Saxoniae Bethuliam, Per cuius constantiam, Deus, propemodum amissam Germaniae libertatem, tum Christianum, tum civilem, restituit!" *Saxonia* IV. Leipzig: Hennius Grosius, 1599. 442.

Christ Overcoming the Interim Dragon. 1552. Cranach pupil Peter Rodelstatt of Gottlandt. Kupferstichkabinett, Staatliche Museen Preußischer Kulturbesitz, Berlin; Hollstein X, 194. No. 6; Passavant 194. No. 6.

realizing his "great plan" – to disempower the Protestant princes politically, and to force recognition of the Council of Trent.[9] But when he took flight through the Brenner Pass in the dark of night of May 19, his dreams of a universal monarchy, a Roman Catholic Habsburg superstate, vanished. The Magdeburg resistance had confounded the plans of the emperor.

> In point of fact, nothing was more harmful to the emperor's reputation than the siege, as the example that, after all the other imperial estates had been crushed, that one single city, completely alone, dared tell the mighty emperor whose empire was spread over the old and new world, that his power came to an end in the matter of the Christian faith, that in the spiritual realm there was no master and subject, an idea that had its most brilliant validation for all those who did not recognize the drive that worked in secret – that is, for almost the whole world, precisely in the course of the siege.[10]

"It was no small thing to take up the game of war with Charles and Granvelle," Eduard Böhl observed, "and Maurice won."[11] David Chytraeus praised the modern Bethulia.

> fortunate Bethulia of Saxony,
> through whose constancy
> God has restored Germany's freedom, almost lost
> both Christian and civil.[12]

A stately victory cup in the silver collection at the Lübeck *Rathaus* still expresses the elation in the North at the news of Maurice's victory: Christ trampling on the Interim dragon.

13 *Von Anrichtung des newen Evangelii und der alten Libertet oder Freyheit Teutcher Nation. An die Römisch Kayser. Majestat geschrieben.* Cologne: Heinrich Mameranus, 1552. Quoted, Paulus. *Dominikaner.* 250.

14 *Beweisung das nicht die unsere Christi.*

15 A. Cornelius. "Kurfürst Moritz gegenüber der Fürstenverschwörung in den Jahren 1550–1551." *Abhandlung der Historischen Klasse der Königlicher Akademie der Wissenschaften.* Bd X, Abt. III. 637.

16 H. von Hase. 24.

17 *Das römisch-deutche Reich im politischen System Karls V.* Munich and Vienna: R. Oldenbourg, 1982. 187.

18 "Luther and the State: The Reformer's Teaching in its Social Setting." James D. Tracy (ed.). *Luther and the Modern State in Germany.* Kirksville, Missouri: Sixteenth Century Journal Publishers, 1986. 40.

19 Aloys Meister. *Gebhardts Handbuch der Deutschen Geschichte.* 6. Aufl., 2. Bd. Stuttgart, Berlin & Leipzig: Union Deutsche Verlagsgesellschaft, 1923. 90.

20 Friedrich Hülsse. *Die Stadt Magdeburg im Kampfe für den Protestantismus während 1547–1550.* Halle/Saale: Verein für Reformationsgeschichte, 1872. 58 f.

21 *Ehrendenkmal.* 52.

Roman Catholic writer Nicolas Mameranus, who under the patronage of imperial chancellor John von Naves, served as a war correspondent, was critical of the revolt. "Is that evangelical? Is that Christian? Is that the liberty of the Germans? I think that you learned your gospel from the Alcoran of the Turks: shed blood, spread anxiety and need, despoil land and people, murder, rob, burn, steal, yes, all wantonness."[13] Lutheran doctrine, Mameranus charged, was "new and seditious." In his answer, Flacius wrote that it was the papacy that was new and seditious.[14]

But could the Judas of Meissen be transformed suddenly into the Savior of the Reformation? Considering Moritz' motives, A. Cornelius concluded that he had acted for himself. "By no means did the half-sovereign aristocracy of the empire draw the sword for their subjects, let alone for the sake of the German people."[15] The attack on the emperor did, incidentally, result in the liberation of Johann Friedrich, "the Magnanimous," and thereby it lived up to the claim of being the *vindex libertatis Germaniae et captivorum principum*, avenger of German freedom and of the captive princes. It is worth noting that Maurice asked the emperor's brother Ferdinand *not* to free the cousin he had robbed of the electoral title.

Magdeburg encouraged opposition in the surrounding regions, and created a resistance front.[16] The political fallout of the city's fierce act of confession was profound, and, according to Heinrich Lutz, "difficult to over-estimate."[17] It is difficult therefore to credit the statement of Thomas J. Brady, that "the right to resistance was endorsed with enthusiasm nowhere in Lutheran Germany."[18] "The impression that went out from Magdeburg, was so strong that the clergy also in those surrounding lands, whose governments were not exactly opposed to the Interim, for example, in Electoral Saxony, Hesse, Brandenburg, submitted and practiced resistance, partly because of the strengthening of their personal attachment to the Evangelical cause, and partly out of fear of the aroused public opinion."[19]

"Metz and Magdeburg," wrote Friedrich Hülsse, "are the cities on which Charles' V politics for a Spanish-Hapsburg world monarchy break up"; And Magdeburg was "the rock on which the politics of Emperor Charles V foundered."[20]

The Magdeburg theologians knew something significant had been achieved.

> If this city with its example and steadfastness, and with the printing of Christian writings, had not resisted the papistic deceit and falsification, the papacy through its multifarious Interim and Adiaphora would have long ago expelled the gospel of Jesus Christ and again taken the churches ... Therefore, all churches, which still have maintained something of the true religion, have such a mercy from the Grace of God through our toil and cross.[21]

Otto Ritschl agreed.

> ... if the lower Saxon churches, especially the church of Magdeburg, enriched by the spiritual strength which accrued to it in the many refugees from the South, and the unerringly certain leadership of the aged Amsdorf and the great Illyricus, which

released all religious passion, had not opposed the imperial as well as the electoral church politics with their powerful witness for a Christianity in Luther's sense, Maurice of Saxony would hardly have learned to respect Protestantism as a power for which it really paid to exchange the favor of Charles V for his irreconcilable enmity. The *modestia* and *moderatio* of the Wittenberg theologians would never have undertaken his strike against the Ehrenberger Clause.[22]

"It is to him almost exclusively," Wilhelm Maurenbrecher wrote about Elector Maurice, "that thanks should be given for the public recognition of Protestantism in the empire."[23] But there is little reason to think that Maurice would have taken action had he not been forced to do it. In turning on the Emperor, he was reacting to the force originating in Magdeburg. Twesten asks, "For who would argue that Maurice would have decided to attack the emperor if he had not been forced to do it because of the impossibility in the previous way of winning the agreement of the Protestant party and of his own subjects, essential for maintaining his position and for carrying out his plans?"[24] "It cannot be denied," Karl Heussi wrote, "that Protestantism was rescued through a determined resistance against the Interim by the Gnesio-Lutherans."[25] It was Flacius, according to Mirković, who convinced Maurice to turn on the emperor.[26] "The denunciations of Flacius delivered a terrible blow to the Augsburg Interim," writes J. V. Pollet, "from which it hardly recovered."[27]

Taking Flacius into account, then, Georg Ellinger divided the credit. "Flacius and Maurice of Saxony", he wrote, "saved the Reformation."[28] Others give most of the credit to Flacius. In his introduction to his edition of Flacius' rules for interpretation, Lutz Geldsetzer pronounces him the "rescuer of an independent Protestant movement."[29] "His critique was devastating," according to Gustav Kawerau. "If general opposition arose in Saxony and North Germany in which the people's soul proved more powerful than the complaisance of the politicians and the mediating formulae of the weak-willed theologians, if Luther's work was saved then, it is in special measure thanks to Flacius."[30]

Was Flacius, then, the "new Müntzer" Maurice had feared? The Saxon chancellor, David Pfeiffer, thought so.[31] And so did Melanchthon, who charged him with "terrorizing the princes."

> For though Illyricus cries out vehemently that the churches should be deserted, and the princes alarmed by the fear of sedition, I should not choose to be the author of such wretched advice. It is plain that we must endure much greater burdens in the cause of literature and religion than mere duress – as the hatred of the great, the insolent contempt of the populace, the malevolence of hypocritical friends, the dissensions of the teachers, poverty, persecution, and other evils which accompany even a quiet government: but these turbulent time produce many greater miseries.[32]

Johann Pfeffinger echoed Melanchthon.

> Freedom is nothing for unruly people, even when they [Flacius and associates] are angry at us because we do not seek the extension of freedom, which would have happened, as they say, if with our outcry, we had threatened the princes with the disapproval of the people and with revolt. But our purpose is not to produce mutiny and to stir up the common man against his proper government.[33]

22 O. Ritschl. II, 328 f.
23 Op. cit. 140.
24 Twesten. 10.
25 Karl Heussi. *Geschichte der theologischen Fakultät zu Jena.* Weimar: Herman Böhlaus Nachfolger, 1954. 25.
26 Mirković, 1960. 150.
27 Pflug. *Correspondance.* III, 63.
28 *Melanchthon.* 544.
29 *Matthias Flacius Illyricus: De Ratione cognoscendi Sacras Literas.* Düsseldorf: Stern-Verlag Janssen & Co., 1968. Introduction.
30 G. Kawerau. RE3, VI, 83; Idem. "Matthias Flacius." *New Schaff-Herzog Encyclopedia* IV. 322.
31 *Lipsia.* 397. Quoted by Ritter. 30n.
32 CR, VII, 479.
33 *Gründlicher und warhafftiger Bericht.* 22b.

34 Niceron. XXIV, 8.
35 Op. cit. III, 558.
36 Ritter. 153.
37 *Ein Buch von … Mitteldingen.* G ij r.
38 Ibid. D ij r.
39 *Ein Christliche Vermahnung…* [A iiij v].
40 Ibid. G ij r.
41 Böhl. 49.
42 *Gründliche Verlegung … Issleb.* [C iiij r].
43 *Eine Entschuldigung an einen Pfarher.* A ij v.
44 *Antwort auf den Brief etlicher Prediger.* Cij v r.

Melanchthon's reproach was also echoed in Jan Pierre Niceron's biographical sketch of Flacius: "What good could one expect from a man who dared to say that one should keep the respect of princes by means of fear of sedition?[34] "He made no scruples," wrote Pierre Bayle, in the same tradition, "to declare that princes were to be kept in awe by the fear of insurrections."[35] Flacius' eighteenth century biographer, Johan Balthasar Ritter, agreed that he was a rebel. "Flacius did not say so in so many words … that the people should be stirred up to revolt, but that is obviously what he had in mind – to convince the princes that there would be a rebellion if the old order were reimposed."[36]

Once more citing the *clausula Petri*, however, Flacius made a distinction between sedition and religious resistance.

> Therefore, when worldly people cry that in such a matter one must be obedient to the government, the leaders should answer, one must obey God rather than man. And if they say, the Romans are coming, the preachers should say, one must fear those who can destroy body and soul more than those who destroy the body alone … They should also warn all people most vigorously to steadfastness in the acknowledged truth, but they should never advise sedition.[37]

"I do not know of anything in my writings which could be called seditious," he wrote. He had taken no part in the political calculations or diplomacy. He agreed with his friend, Aepinus: "We should do what pertains to us, and commend the outcome to the Lord through our prayer."[38] "I contend with no one about great palaces, about land or people, but I take pains to heal Christian hearts who are confused and deeply bounded by the Interim and Adiaphora and admonish them to steadfastness."[39] "Through such Christian steadfastness the church has often confounded the godless plan of the tyrant."[40]

The Interim controversy had a lasting effect on the theological tradition in the expectation of precision of thought. "The necessity to define the pure doctrine more precisely against the ambiguity of the Interim was a heritage that remained from that time."[41]

"By our outcry and by nothing else," Flacius wrote, looking back on events, "they were forced to resist the papist error a little more …"[42] The scholar turned agitator and had frustrated the cherished plan of the Emperor himself. "With our writing, through the grace of God, it [the Leipzig Interim] was arrested."[43] And he had saved the Reformation. "Through our outcry (be it ever so childish) the new falsification and establishment of the papacy was prevented."[44]

A few eyes saw the possibilities in the change in the imperial house. In those months Flacius developed a plan for the Centuries. – Andreas Burkhardt

1 A. Burkhardt. 19.
2 Consultatio de conscribenda accurata historia ecclesiae. Text in Schottenloher, *Ottheinrich*. 147 f.
3 Preger. I, 416 f.
4 Böhl. 42.
5 Preger. II, 280.

There was a new pastor at SS. Ulrich and Levin, Johann Wigand. He succeeded Nicolaus Gallus, who rolled away to Regensburg with family, servants and furniture piled on two wagons. In Halle there was a new Magdeburg archbishop, fourteen years old. Power was flowing from Charles V to his brother, Ferdinand, who had the stomach to deal with a distasteful situation. And when the beloved prince Johann Friedrich came home to Weimar, someone saw a white cross in the sky.

The treaty of Passau of July 23, 1552, that gave them legal rights, marked the end of Charles' campaign of romanizing the Evangelical churches. Recognizing the possibilities,[1] Flacius determined to embark on two foundational projects, on which he would labor for most of his career. The first was a church history, "a scholarly and accurate history of the church from the time of Christ up to our own times."[2] The second was a Bible study guide, "scholarly glosses or a very brief explanation of the text of sacred scriptures."

He described his vision for the church history in a letter of March 7, 1552, to Hartmann Beyer in Frankfurt.

> I am going about with a great plan, which, of course, outreaches my own powers, but which, if it is carried out, could be extraordinarily useful for the church. First, I want to write a catalog of all the men that before Martin Luther of blessed memory fought the pope and his errors. Then I would wish that a church history would be written, in which in a certain order and in sequence it would be demonstrated how the true church and its religion gradually fell off the track from that original purity and simplicity in the apostolic time because of the negligence and ignorance of teachers, and also partly through the evil of the godless. Then it must be shown that at times the church was restored by a few really faithful men, and why the light of truth sometimes shone more clearly, and sometimes under the growing darkness of godless entity was again more or less darkened – until, finally at our time, when the truth was almost totally destroyed, through God's unbounded benefice, the true religion in its purity was again restored.[3]

Sometime about March 10, having been expelled from Cöthen by the prince of Anhalt at Melanchthon's urging, Flacius returned to Magdeburg and to bookselling. Evidence of the business remains in his correspondence. "A certain pastor in Augsburg," he wrote to Joachim Westphal, for instance, "asked me especially to send him your book on baptism ... if you have any extra copies of the publication, I ask that you send them to me. I pray that you let me know whether you still have any copies of Major's book on the sacrament. I would like to buy twenty or thirty from you."[4]

Flacius visited the book fairs in Leipzig and Frankfurt, the latter in 1555, 1561, 1565 and 1566.[5] He built up a network of sales agents and distributorships which became big business. In Leipzig he distributed

6 Diener. 300 ff.

7 *Bibliothek Palatina. Katalog zur Ausstellung von 8. Juli bis 1. November 1986. Heiliggeistkirche Heidelberg. Textband.* Ed. Elmar Mittler. Heidelberg: Edition Braus [1986]. 456.

8 Christ. "Zur Geschichte." 51.

9 Georg Müller. "Quellenstudien zur Geschichte der sächsischen Hofprediger. II: Daniel Grieser. Superintendent zu Dresden und Hofprediger des Kurfürsten August." *Zeitschrift für kirchliche Wissenschaft und Kirchliches Leben* IV (1887). 19.

10 Rudolf Schäfer. *Philipp Melanchthons Leben aus den Quellen dargestellt.* Gütersloh: Bertelsmann, 1894. 248. Flacius' judgment on Maurice can be found in Cod. Guelf. 722. Helmst. fol. 227, "Iudicium Illyrici de Morte mauritii."

11 Druffel. IV, 270 f.

12 *Bedencken von dem Kriege der Anno sechs, sieben- und viertzig im Landt zu Meissen unnd Sachsen gefurth ist, gestellt durch Christian Aleman, mit einer kurtzen Vorrede Christof Cunrads.* Basel: Barth. Stehle, 1557.

13 Albrecht Kirchhoff. "Beiträge zur Geschichte der Pressmassregelungen und des Verkehrs auf den Büchermessen im 16. und 17. Jahrhundert." *Archiv für Geschichte des Deutschen Buchhandels* II (1879). 45.

14 Suckale-Redlefsen. 265.

books published in the Rhineland; in Nuremberg he engaged the printer, Johann vom Berg as agent. By 1566 he had capitalized a distributorship which sold books on consignment.[6] The authors of the recent catalog for the exhibition of books from the Vatican library formerly in the library at Heidelberg, found evidence of his high-placed clients: "Striking is the great number of prints of Matthias Flacius Illyricus. That suggests a close relationship with Ulrich Fugger, and on the other hand, a special relationship to [Elector] Ott-heinrich."[7] It is not unlikely that Flacius was the unnamed buyer of 1553[8] who negotiated Fugger's purchase of the library of his teacher, Egnazio.

In 1553 there was also a new prince in Dresden. Elector Maurice died on July 11 from a wound in a battle at Sievershausen against Margrave Albrecht of Brandenburg. "God so loved the world," his chaplain read to him, "that he gave his only-begotten son." "What a wonderful statement," said the wounded Maurice. "Who would not gladly die with it?" Maurice died at the age of 32 – like Julian the Apostate, it was said. Over his dying body the chaplain read the words, "Lord, into Thy hands I commend my spirit." In Dresden there was a funeral sermon on the text, "Blessed are the dead who died in the Lord."[9] Melanchthon agreed that he had died "in true invocation of God and Christian confession."[10]

But had he confessed his sin? Had the dying Maurice repented of the Sin of the House of Wettin, the sin of stealing the electorship? Duke Johann Friedrich asked Amsdorf to find out. But Amsdorf could comment only that "if he had recognized and confessed such sin, had called on God for grace, had asked the Elector for forgiveness and had returned what he had taken, then he would have had a true faith and would have done honest fruits of repentance."[11]

But he had not. If the Dresden court were to admit that the Smalcald War indeed had been a war of religion, simple logic would make the Albertine princes persecutors of religion. Elector August, Moritz's successor, suspected that a new book that labelled the late war a religious war[12] had been written by Flacius, and intervened with the Frankfurt Book Fair to have the book censored. Christian Aleman, and Christof Cunrad, were not pseudonyms of Flacius, but of Jena law professor, Basilius Monner.[13] By organizing the Princes' Revolt, Maurice had done a good deal to change the image as "Judas of Meissen." More than simply signifying "something of the magical power of a black knight," as was suggested in a recent publication,[14] the blackface portrait in the Leipzig *Rathaus* of Maurice as St. Maurice should be understood as part of the continuing effort to project a positive image of the Albertine dynasty, and, possibly, a reply to the Magdeburg claim to be the true Mauricians.

Protecting himself against the machinations of the Ernestine princes meant establishing the legitimacy of his throne. "August's keen perception that he had to protect himself on the one hand from Bohemia and on the other side from revenge from his cousins in Thuringia had a great effect on the Reformation churches. The ruse of the Albertine house was based on

15 Druffel. IV, 252 ff.

Bedencken vonn dem

Kriege/ der Anno/ic.ſechs/ſiben/vnd viertzig im land zů Meiſſen vnd Sachſen gefůrt
iſt/wo für er zůhalten ſey/geſtalt.
Durch Chriſtian Aleman/mit einer
kurtzen vorrede Chriſtoff
Cůnrads. *(vij.1584.47.)*

Pſalm xxxvij.

Erzürne dich nicht vber die böſen/ſey nicht neidiſch vber die vbel
thåter. Dann wie das gras/werden ſy bald abgehauwen/ vnnd
wie das grüne kreut/werdē ſy verwelcken. Hoffe auff den HER-
REN/vnd thů gůts/bleib im lande/ vnd nere dich redlich. Hab
deine luſt am HERRN/der wirdt dir geben/was dein hertz wün-
ſchet. Befehl dem HERRN deine wege/ vnd hoffe auff jhn/Er
wirds wol machen. Vnd wird deine gerechtigkeit herfür bringen/
wie das liecht/vnd dein Recht wie den mittag. Harre deß HER-
REN/vnd warte auff jn/erzürne dich nicht vber den/dem ſein můt
wille glücklich fort ghet. Stehe ab vom zorn/ vnd laß den grim̃/
erzürne dich nicht/das du auch vbel thůſt. Denn die böſen
werden außgereüttet/die aber deß HERRN
harren/werden das land
erben.

Gedruckt zů Baſel M. D. LVII.

Elector August blamed Flacius for Basilius Monners' critique of the war.

the betrayal of the evangelical cause; now its security lay in alliance with the Catholic house of Hapsburg."[15]

His policy also meant keeping the Saxon clergy in line. Two pastors, Christoph and Solomon, announced in the pulpit in Torgau that Duke Maurice had stolen the land, and prayed publicly that God would ask August to return it, so that the House of Saxony could live in quietness, peace and unity. They were immediately summoned to appear before the burgomaster, who informed them that the government was not to be criticized.

The next month, September 19, 1552, Melanchthon held court on them and warned them not to criticize Elector August. On October 22, the twenty-first Sunday after Trinity, Martin Wolf preached before August in

16 Salig. III, 219.
17 McNair. 153.
18 *Historia Certaminum*, preface.
19 Rule. 489.

the chapel at Colditz castle and touched the same nerve. The Smalcald war and the siege of Magdeburg, he said, had been fought against the gospel, and that whoever had assisted the emperor was guilty of innocent blood. The court should repent for having caused the war, and the Elector should return his ill-gotten possessions to avoid God's judgment. He praised the Magdeburg theologians as witnesses for truth and as martyrs, and prayed against the Elector.[16] The next day he was ordered to report to the Elector's dining room and made to account for his sermon. At 3.00 p.m. he delivered to chancellor Kysewetter a written statement, stating that Elector Johann Friedrich and Magdeburg had been persecuted for the sake of the gospel.

Again, Melanchthon was available to enforce the Elector's will. With Superintendent Daniel Gresser of Dresden, in a hearing, he attempted to induce him to change his mind. Wolf, however, insisted he had made no mistake; the Elector had no right to tell him what to preach.

Wolf was therefore imprisoned in the tower of Hohnstein castle. No one, not even the jailer, was allowed to speak to him. He was badly fed and forced to suffer sixteen days of cold weather. Despite the pleas of eighteen of the nobility and of the Superintendent, the clergy of the Leisnig diocese, and the pastors of the superintendency of Colditz, who said that he had done "what he had to do," the Elector was adamant. Preaching, he said, was only for "edification and improvement." Wolf's sermon had been seditious. On January 13, he was released from prison, and expelled from Saxony.

August's wrath was felt also by David Schaefer, whose story was similar to that of Wolf. When court chaplain Nikolaus Selnecker dared denounce the three devils at the court, licence, dissimulation, and patronage, and to preach against hunting, he was dismissed, despite pleas by Gresser and others.

Meanwhile, the inquisition in Flacius' homeland had begun in earnest.

> The mills of the Roman inquisition were comparatively slow in beginning to grind, but once they got going, they ground exeeding small, so that the policy of total suppression was far more successful in Italy than it was in any other country of Christendom except Spain. Indeed, as I have hinted, we could claim with perfect justice that not only were the glowing embers of crypto-Lutheranism in Italy efficiently, effectively and ruthlessly stamped out before the end of the sixteenth century, but the very ashes themselves were all swept out of sight under the ornate carpet of the Tridentine church.[17]

"Open the portals of your empire," Flacius wrote to Doge Francesco Venier, "to the Son of God."[18] But he wrote in vain. "Throughout the Venetian territory the inquisitorial plague prevailed; but the secrecy of that tribunal, and the contempt of Italian historians toward heretics, hide their names, and we have only the general statement of foreign writers that their brethren of the Venetian republic everywhere suffered bonds, poverty, and death.[19] An anguished Altieri wrote from Venice:

> The persecution here increases every day. Many are seized, of whom some have been sent to the galleys, other condemned to perpetual imprisonment, and some, alas! have

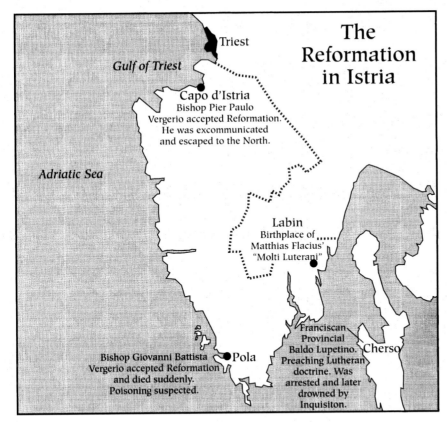

20 McCrie. 221.
21 C. de Franceschi. "*L'Istria. Note Storicha Parenzo*, 1879. Quoted by E. Schatzmayer. Beiträge zur Geschichte des Protestantismus in Istrien und Triest. II." JGGPO, XV (1894). 60.

The Reformation in Istria

Triest

Gulf of Triest

Capo d'Istria
Bishop Pier Paulo Vergerio accepted Reformation. He was excommunicated and escaped to the North.

Adriatic Sea

Labin
Birthplace of Matthias Flacius' "Molti Luterani"

Franciscan Provincial Baldo Lupetino. Preaching Lutheran doctrine. Was arrested and later drowned by Inquisiton.

Cherso

Bishop Giovanni Battista Vergerio accepted Reformation and died suddenly. Poisoning suspected.

Pola

The Inquisition succeeded in elimination: The Reformation from Istria

been induced, by fear of punishment, to recant. Many also have been banished along with their wives and children, while still greater numbers have fled for their lives. Matters are come to that pass, that I begin to fear for myself; for though I have frequently been able to protect others in this storm, there is reason to apprehend that the same hard terms will be proposed to me; but it is the will of God that his people be tried by such afflictions.[20]

The inquisitor, Giovanni Della Casa, moved against Vergerio in 1544, after he had been denounced by a friar. Two weeks later, having got permission from the pope's son, Cardinal Pier Luigi Farnese, he took action against the bishop.

In that same year, Della Casa sent a commission of the inquisition to Flacius' homeland, and Annibale Grisonio, probably a member of the new Theatine order, was named inquisitor. The Reformation had had a great success in Istria. Preachers had "flooded in,"[21] on one side from Venice and on the other by the county of Mitterburg (now Pisono) on the border of Carinthia, and the Bishop of Capo d'Istria, Pier Paulo Vergerio, and his brother, Bishop Giovanni Vergerio of Pola had become Lutheran converts. "Is it not a marvel," Flacius wrote about Pier Paulo, "that there is a learned bishop abroad who was in the good graces of the pope, and was a

22 *Widder den Auszug.* B ij v.
23 Schutte. 183.
24 Ibid. 238.
25 McCrie. 224–226.
26 Mirković. 1960. 130.

great lord, who left his riches for the sake of confessing the Lord Christ, and willed to move into misery and now, two days' journey from Milan, writes and publishes against the pope?"[22]

From the pulpits of Capo d'Istria, Grisonio now read the menacing papal bull, requiring all, under pain of excommunication, to inform against those suspected of heresy, and to deliver up whatever prohibited books might be in their possession. Those who confessed that they had read the New Testament, he charged under threat to abstain from that dangerous practice. Those who confessed and sought forgiveness would be treated with lenity, but those guilty of concealment would be condemned. The city council of Capo d'Istria called him fanatic.[23]

Not satisfied with public denunciations, in search of heretical books, Grisonio forced his way into houses. He subjected the rich to private penance, and the poor to public recantation. At first, only a few individuals were induced to inform, but gradually, fear of denunciation changed the public climate. Ties of consanguinity and gratitude were disregarded; sons, it is reported, did not spare fathers, wives their husbands, nor clients their patrons. It was their Catholic duty, Grisonio insisted, to stone the Lutherans.[24] Ascending the cathedral pulpit, he urged his hearers to kill their bishop.

> You see the calamities which have befallen you for some years past. At one time your fields, at another your olive trees, at another your vines have failed. You have been afflicted in your cattle, and in the whole of your substance. To what are all these evils to be ascribed? To your bishop and the other heretics among you. Nor can you expect any alleviation of your distress until they are punished. Why do you not rise up and stone them?[25]

Grisonio moved on to Pola. Bishop Giovanni Battista Vergerio of Pola, Flacius' native diocese, had accepted Luther's teaching in 1532, under the influence of his brother, Bishop Pier Paulo. On June 24, 1549, Ambrosius von Vernicci of Milan testified before an Inquisition court that young girls and shepherds were discussing questions of the faith, and that soon all the inhabitants of Pola and Wodnjan would be Lutheran.[26] In the account of Pier Paulo Vergerio's conversion, there is a hint of what might have been.

> Now you shall tell me (O Fatherland), that what I say about the Reformation perhaps could have taken place if my brother the bishop of Pola had not died, if I had not departed, if those two authoritative doctors, M. Ottonello Vida and M. Francesco Grisoni, had not died – one my cousin, the other my nephew, and if some citizens had not been driven out, others forced to recant, and others struck quiet by fear ... Let me answer this question, Fatherland, and I will say no more.

Anne Jacobson Schutte comments that Giovanni "probably shared his brother's religious views, but was not officially suspected of heresy until after his death in 1548." His Lutheran views, however, were well-known.

> He [Pier Paulo Vergerio] went immediately to the city of Pola, where his brother, Giovanni Baptist Vergerio was bishop, and through the help and support of God explained to him the true basis of the gospel, and later announced to the nobility in Istria in pious

Welschland [foreign parts] the conversion of these two brothers to the Lutheran faith. A great commotion followed. And the pope did not cease asking the illustrious Venetian doge daily to extirpate the Lutherans from his territories, completely and totally to destroy the new doctrine brought about by those Venetians to the highest detriment of the papal throne and the Roman church.[27]

As reflected in the rising arrest statistics, Grisonio did his efficient best. One of the Inquisition's crimes, it was reported, was the murder by poisoning of the bishop,[28] mourned by his brother.

> It is most certainly true that the Bishop of Pola, of blessed memory, my brother, through me came into the knowledge of the truth a short time after I did. He learned it with all his soul and powerfully supported its being preached in Pola and throughout his diocese. I surmise that it was also the cause of his death, and that with his usual craft the Antichrist, the murderer, has eliminated him. I know for certain that my dear brother was affected by spiritual regeneration and that he was among the number of the true soldiers of the Living Christ.[29]

On June 8, 1549, Pope Paul III expressed to the doge and the Senate satisfaction for "granting your arm and favor to our representative for extirpating heresies in your province, Istria." He asked them to pursue the matter "without respect of any person."[30]

As he wrote to Pier Paulo, Flacius believed the murder report.

> For I hope that it will happen to the glory of God and the salvation of many, not only in our Istria, where through you and through your brother, the Reverend Doctor Giovanni Baptista Vergerio, Bishop of Pola, a man of distinguished piety and a martyr of Jesus Christ (whom the Roman wretches put under with poison), the Gospel of Christ has been planted, that those men will be greatly strengthened when they remember you, your constant confession, exile, and numerous difficulties in sealing the truth of Christ ...

> When I recently read your book in which you describe the most cruel persecution after your leaving, in Iustinopolis [Capo d'Istria] and in the whole of Istria, through certain Grisonios and Busdragos, incited by a most foul nuncio, Della Casa, slaves of Antichrist, where the noblest men were harshly tormented ... I lamented."[31]

He was surprised that the doge and senate would tolerate such goings-on, since they had always been very friendly to their subjects, and since Istria had been very faithful in the war against Emperor Maximilian. Flacius doubtlessly hoped that the recent military developments might convince the Venetian senate to stop persecuting Protestants, but the persecution continued.[32] The Venetian rulers were aware that Maurice's soldiers had stopped marching far away.

In the summer of 1552, Flacius had embarked on his historical enterprise. One of his priorities in Italy and Istria was finding a manuscript copy of Dante's *De Monarchia*, which was little known at the time. He reports finding two or three pious men who promised to help.[33] While he was still in Italy, he visited Pier Paulo Vergerio. "Matthias Illyricus was with me," he wrote to Heinrich Bullinger, "with whom I discussed a great deal about the eucharist."[34] He promised to help him collect books, and it is "more

27 Giovanni Vergerio. *Von der wunderbahren Bekehrung Petri Pauli Vergerii Justonopolitani Bischoff, erwehlten Päpstl. Cardinals und Gestantes in Teutschland wider D. Luther*. n. p. 1699. Unpaginated.

28 McNair. loc. cit.

29 Jo. Georg Schelhorn. *Apologia pro Petro Paulo Vergerio Episcopo Iustinapolitano adversus Joannem Casam Archiepiscopum Beneventanum*. Ulm & Memmingen: Gaumiano, 1754. 15.

30 Quoted by Ludwig von Pastor. *Geschichte Papst Pauls III (1534–1549)*. Freiburg im Breisgau: Herder, 1928. 714.

31 *De Voce et Re Fidei*. A ij v – f.; A vj r – v.

32 Mirković, 1960. 133.

33 Ibid. 135n.

34 Traugott Schiess (ed.). *Heinrich Bullingers Korrespondenz mit den Graubündern* I. Nieuwkoop: B. de Graff, 1968. 253.

35 Ernst Schaumkell. *Beitrag zur Entstehungsgeschichte der Magdeburger
Centurien*. Ludwigslust: Hins-
dorff'sche Hofbuchhandlung (Carl
Kober), 1898. 20.

36 Schutte. 18.

37 Natko Devčić. *Labinska Vieŝtica*.
Zagreb: Union of Yugoslavian
Composers, 1960. A transcription
for piano, the gift of the composer
to the author, with text in Croatian
and German, can be found in the
Herzog August Library, Wolfenbüttel. Cf. Josip Andreis. *Music
in Croatia* V. Ed. Stanley Sadie.
London: MacMillan, 1980. 5079.

than probable"[35] that he kept his promise. Before he left, he warned Flacius to avoid "tragedies."

But tragedies were happening. In 1552, a good many in Southern Europe called themselves Lutheran. But not for long. In Vergerio's Capo d'Istria, the episcopal records for 1536 to 1549, the time of his episcopacy there, have disappeared.[36] In Flacius' Labin, the many *Luterani* soon disappeared, and records of their disappearance no longer exist.

The sad history became the theme of an opera, "The Witch of Labin," by Croat composer Natko Devčić, produced a dozen years ago in Zagreb. It stars the baritone, Matthias Flacius, "a Protestant thinker, daring, determined, and intelligent." The screams of his soprano sweetheart, the imaginary Marylin, were meant to summon up thoughts of those long out of mind: forgotten Croats who suffered for their evangelical faith.

> Hear, hear, how she cries out;
> She is being martyred on the torture rack
> Her poor body is being stretched;
> hear her cry out, Marylin...[37]

THE MARTYRDOM OF BALDO LUPETINO

> He deserves a place in the Protestant martyrology, since after he had been imprisoned twenty years because he was suspected of heresy, he was thrown into the sea.
> – Pierre Bayle

> A worthy man, whose name should not be left out of the martyrology.
> – Johannes Hoornbeck

Baldo Lupetino, *Il piu gran Luterano del mundo*. Courtesy of Tullio Vorano

The demise of Pope Julius III brought no relief; in 1555 a fiercer pontiff occupied the throne – Paul IV (1555–1559), Giampietro Carafa, who became notorious as the first Counter-Reformation pope. One souvenir of his pontificate is the oath he required in 1556 of some unfortunate Italians.

> I swear and loath and curse it that I have often praised and recommended the Lutherans and that I have possessed and read their books...

> I promise therefore and swear as above, that I now believe firmly with my whole heart and confess with my mouth everything that the Holy Mother Church believes, holds, preaches and observes on the Most Holy Sacrament of Communion, the freedom of the will, attendance at mass, the power of all the saints, the writings accepted and approved by the Holy Church, on predestination and the merit of good works.[1]

Meanwhile, often in solitary confinement, Flacius' mentor was still alive. But the pope, particularly vexed by "that cursed nest of conventual friars minor" in Venice[2] demanded that the provincial, Baldo Lupetino, be burned alive.[3] The Venetian government, more merciful than the Inquisition – perhaps through the intervention of Vergerio – [4] commuted his death sentence to life imprisonment. In the North he was not forgotten. Caspar Schwenckfeld had sent 20 gulden to him and to Pietro Citadella.[5] But in vain did Duke Christopher of Württemberg intercede for him, September 9, 1555, with Doge Marcantonio Trevesan. The doge explained that Venice could not interfere with the Inquisition.[6]

Lupetino had been an unsatisfactory prisoner. On one occasion in 1552, he wrote for assistance to the daughter of King Louis XII of France, the Duchess Renée of Ferrara, for which trespass he was kept on bread and water for five months.[7] When in 1556, bearded now, emaciated and suffering from from gout, scurvy and eye injury inflicted by a fellow-prisoner, he appeared before the Tribunal of the Inquisition, he was charged with writing Latin poems in praise of the Gospel, of having sent letters to the Patriarch of Venice and of having written satires against those who oppressed freedom of conscience. Taking his own advice – *non recantare anzi cantare* – Baldo refused to recant, and, instead, wrote a confession.[8]

On August 20, 1556, the sentence was pronounced. Baldo would be drowned in the middle of the night; his demise would be "hidden, secret, without sound, without noise,"[9] a method calculated to induce terror locally, and to preserve a reputation for openness and tolerance abroad. As Della Casa duly reported to the pope, Baldo was formally degraded. The degradation ritual was conducted in the chapel of San Theodoro, as prescribed in *Licet ab omnia*, the night of September 17, 1556. The Patriarch and his vicar were required to be there, together with the Inquisitor and his commissar, the fiscal, the papal nuncio, and the three *savi*. The ceremony finished, the prisoner was turned over to the police.

Although much of the persecution escaped reporting, the Venetian archives preserve records of 1,560 Inquisition trials from 1541 to 1592;[10] the Venetian lagoon was the scene of twenty-five official drownings.[11] How they were carried out has been described by Rosius de Porta.

> At the dead hour of midnight the prisoner was taken from his cell and put into a gondola or Venetian boat, attended only, besides the sailors, by a single priest, to act as confessor. He was rowed out into the sea beyond the Two Castles, where another boat was waiting. A plank was then laid across the two gondolas, upon which the prisoner, having his body chained, and a heavy stone affixed to his feet, was placed; and, on a signal given, the gondolas retiring from one another, he was precipitated into the deep.[12]

On one such dark midnight, November 20, 1556, Baldo Lupetino earned his place in the martyrology[13]. His last words were a plea for a free, ecumenical council.[14]

Flacius' words about his death were restrained.

> The Reverend Baldus Lupetinus, sprung from a noble and ancient family, a learned monk and provincial of the order to which he belonged, after having long preached the word of God in both the vulgar languages in many cities, and defending it by public disputation in several places of celebrity and with great applause, was at last thrown into close prison at Venice by the Inquisitor and the papal legate. In this condition he

1 E. Schatzmayr. "Beiträge zur Geschichte des Protestantismus in Istrien und Triest II." JGGPO, XV (1894). 75 f.

2 Martin. 39.

3 Pio Paschini. *Venezia e l'inquisitione romana da Giulio III a Pio IV*. Padua: Editrice Antenore, 1959. 104; Bonet. 456.

4 Schutte. 229.

5 CS, XII, 623.

6 Theodor Schott (ed.). *Briefwechsel zwischen Christoph, Herzog von Württemberg und Petrus Paulus Vergerius*. Stuttgart: Literarischer Verein, 1875. 85.

7 Elze. *Geschichte*. 20.

8 A copy of the confession was sent by the German consul, Philip Walther, to Augsburg. CS, XI, 487–498.

9 "occulte, secrete, sine sonitu et sine strepitu … se faza morir summerso molto, et pero, che ipse summergatur in profundum maris … facta prius degradatione." Comba. 70.

10 Paul F. Grendler. *The Roman Inquisition and the Venetian Press, 1540–1605*. Princeton: Princeton University Press, 1977. 57.

11 Martin. 69.

12 Quoted by M'Crie. 233 f.

13 Pierre Bayle. "Matthias Flacius Illyricus." *Dictionary Historical and Critical of Mr. Peter Bayle*. Seond edition, Vol. III. London: J. J. and P. Knapton, 1930. 557n.; Johannes Hoornbeck. *Summa Controversiarum Religionis Editio secunda*. Trajecti ad Rhenum: Joannis a Waesberge, 1568. 652.

14 Karl Benrath. "Italien, reformatorische Bewegungen im XVI. Jahrhundert." RE3, 9, 530.

15 *De sectis.* 43 f. Translation from M'Crie. 235.
16 Bonet. 466.

continued, during twenty years, to bear an undaunted testimony to the gospel of Christ; so that his bonds and doctrine were made known, not only to that city, but almost the whole of Italy, and by it to Europe at large, by which means evangelical truth was more widely spread.

Two things, among others, may be mentioned as marks of the singular providence of God toward this person during his imprisonment. In the first place, the princes of Germany often interceded for his liberation, but without success. And, secondly, on the other hand, the papal legate, the inquisitor and even the pope himself laboured with all their might, and by repeated applications, to have him from the very first committed to the flames as a noted heresiarch. This was refused by the doge and the senate, who, by an express decree, when he was at last condemned, freed him from the punishment of the fire.

It was the will of God that he should bear his testimony to the truth for so long a time; and that, like a person affixed to a cross, he should, as from an eminence, proclaim to all the world the restoration of Christianity, and the revelation of Antichrist. At last, this pious and excellent man, whom neither threatenings nor promises could move, sealed his doctrine by an undaunted martyrdom, and exchanged the filth and protracted tortures of a prison for a watery grave.[15]

Were the years of his suffering of no consequence? Worth considering is the relationship between Lupetino's forced impotence in the South and, during the same period, his protegé's intense activity in the North. Was his martyrdom in vain? Not according to Jules Bonet, who commended him to the thoughtful pilgrim.

… the traveller, moved by melancholy evocations of the past, who goes from San Marco to the Rialto, where he lets himself be rocked gently the length of the Grand Canal between rows of tomb-like palaces. Leaving Venice on the Lido route he can easily recall the funerary tragedies whose secret is guarded by the sea.

Or if of an evening in some side street he suddenly hears the hymn of an evangelical congregation, reborn, so to speak, from their ruins, he easily associates the pious melodies with the unknown martyrs of the sixteenth century … Spirits of Algieri, of Spinola, of Baldo Lupetino, of so many other confessors, obscure or illustrious, your witness is not lost! By no means was your sacrifice in vain![16]

1 Reusch. *Indices.* 206.

ANTI-PAPAL STATEMENTS

The pope's violence is always great, but in the matter of the inquisition, it is really indescribable. – Venetian ambassador

Collation is the mother of truth. – Flacius

Pope Paul IV (Giovanni Pietro Carafa, 1555–1559) banned printing, possessing, or even reading, the bible. He forbade that "all bibles in the vulgar languages, German, Gallian, Spanish, Italian, or Flemish, whether in manuscript or printed, be read or owned without the permission of the Sacred Office of the Holy Roman Inquisition."[1] For combatting the Reformation he gave the Dominican order almost unlimited power, and the "Holy Office" of the Inquisition functioned like a police force. According to a contemporary chronicler, the pope's head was like "the Vesuvius of his native city ... ardent in all his actions, wrathful, hard, and inflexible, undoubtedly moved by an incredible zeal for religion, but a zeal often lacking in prudence, and breaking out in eruptions of excessive severity." So cruel were his methods that General Seripando of the Augustinians called them "inhuman"; a Venetian ambassador called them "indescribable."[2] At the news of the pope's death in 1559, the people of Rome destroyed his statues, stormed the Inquisition's Roman prison, burned records and released seventy captives.

A protest from a prison cell in Venice obviously could make no impression on the all-powerful Inquisition. But what Baldo could not do, Flacius could attempt in Germany; he had his collection of manuscripts, not a powerful weapon, but *something*. Anthologies, he believed, were important in establishing truth: "collatio is the mother of truth," *collatio sit mater veritatis*.[3] With one *sylva* ("forest"), as "John Free Life" he demonstrated that salvation by faith alone had been a frequent theme in the Middle Ages.[4] His *Little Forest of Songs* was a collection of medieval religious songs.[5] In the first year of the savage new pontificate, he published an anthology that attacked the roots of papal power: *Anti-papal Statements, that is, on the Corrupt State of the Church and the Perversity of the Whole Papistic Clergy, Written by Some Ancient Authors*.[6] It is listed in the British Library

2 Edward Burman. *The Inquisition, the Hammer of Heresy*. Wellingborough: The Aquarian Press, 1984. 159.

3 *Verlegung des unwarhaftigen unbegründten Berichts Hansen Funckens, von der Osiandrischen Schwermerey*. [Magdeburg: Christian Rödinger, 1554]. A iij r.

4 *Sylva Quaedam Tetimoniorum ex propriis Papistarum, atque s. Patrum atque Ecclesiasticorum Scriptorum libris collecta, qua meridiana luce clarium indicatur, probatur, & convincitur: quod coram divino judicio, sola Fiducia gratiae & misericordiae Dei propter Christum sine ullis nostris meritis iustificemur & salvemur. Autore Ioanne Freyesleben*. Nuremberg: Gabriel Heyne, Jr. 1556.

5 *Sylvula carminum aliquot adversis, piis, et eruditis vitis conscriptorum; quibus variae de religione sententiae & controversiae brevissime explicantur*. n. p. [1553].

6 *Antilogia Papae: hoc est, de corrupto ecclesiae statu, et totius cleri Papistici peruersitate, Scripta aliquot veterum authorum, ante annos plus minus CCC, et interea: nunc primum in lucem eruta, et ab interitu vindicata*. Basel: Johannes Oporinus, 1555.

7 Bibl. 1899 102, 113.

8 Evidence that Flacius was the editor is to be found in the preface to his *Various ... Poems*, in the *Catalogus* (834, 947), and in a letter of Oporinus to Nidbruck of February 12th, 1555. Cf. A. Burchardt, op. cit. 25 and Diener. 137 f.; Karl Gauss. "Der Basel Reformationspfarrer Wolfgang Weissenburg." *Christlicher Volksfreund* LXI. Basel (1925), 487, relying on the 1608 edition of the *Catalogus*, claims that Flacius' name was surpressed by Weissenburg. But according to Flacius, "Antilogiae sine meo nomine prodierunt et tamen ado non possunt distrahi, ut me Oporinus aliquoties oraverit, ut meam illis praefationem addicerem, se initium esse recursum." Bibl. 1899. 105, 113.

9 *Antilogia* 543–583. Printed separately: *Confutatio Primatus Papae*. Magdeburg: Christian Rödinger, 1550. Reprinted in F. Brown. *Appendix ad Fasciculum rerum expetendarum et fugiendarum.* London, 1690. 17–164; German edition: *Widder die vermeinte gewalt und Primat des Bapstes, zu dieser Zeit, da die gantze welt sich befleisset, den ausgetriebenen Antichrist, widderumb in den tempel Christi zu setzen, nutzliche zu lesen.* Magdeburg: Christian Rödinger, n. t.

10 Analysis of the argument in Bruno Gebhart. "Die Confutatio Primatum Papae." *Neues Archiv der Gesellschaft für ältere deutsche Geschichtskunde* XII (1887). 517–129.

11 Peter Paul Albert. "Die Confutatio Primatus Papae, ihre Quelle und ihr Verfasser." *Historisches Jahrbuch der Görresgesellschaft* XI (1890). 439–490; Bruno Gebhart. "Matthias Döring der Minorit." *Historische Zeitschrift* LIX (1888). 259; Cf. Ludger Meier. "Zur Frage nach des Verfassers der Confutatio Primatus Papae." *Scholastik. Vierteljahrschrift für Theologie und Philosophie* XI (1936). 539–562.

12 Following Flacius, Melchior Gold-

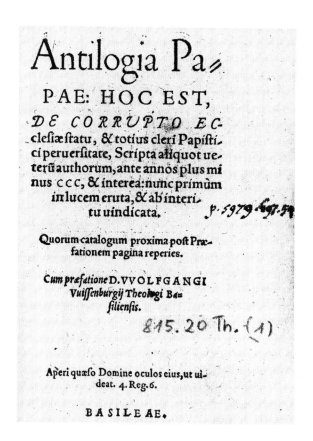

catalog under the name of the Basel professor, Wolfgang Wissenburg, who wrote the preface. Flacius had been asked by Oporinus to write the preface, because without his touch, it would sell too slowly,[7] but he did not, because of the potential danger to Nidbruck.[8]

One of the anti-papal statements, which the editor of the 1667 edition of the *Catalogus* called "golden," was a protest from the time of the fifteenth-century Council of Basel against papal police power, the *Confutation of Papal Primacy*.[9] A continuation of the anti-papal tradition of the Franciscans at the court of Emperor Louis the Bavarian,[10] the *Confutation* was sent on behalf of Duke Sigmund of Austria by Matthias Döring, one of two rival Franciscan Vicars General, to the Council of Basel.[11] Flacius attributed it mistakenly to Gregory Heimburg, rival of Pope Pius II.[12] According to Georges de Lagard, however, he had made only a *demi-erreur*;[13] the text is a rehearsal of the second *dictio* of the *Defensor Pacis* of Marsilius of Padua,[14] introduced by Heimburg to the court of the Utraquist King Jirik of Podebrady.

By finding the tract, Flacius unwittingly fulfilled his own wish. About an anti-papal tract given to Cardinal Nicolas of Cusa by some Franciscan Provincial when he was travelling through Germany in 1451 and 1452,[15] he wrote, "Would that we had that writing!"[16] He already owned it – and had published it twice,[17] in 1550 and 1551.[18] The title's claim – for advertising purposes, perhaps, therefore, that it was first printed here ("nunc prima edita") is incorrect. The *Confutation* contained a section on Jesus' command, "render unto Caesar the things that are Caesar's" (Matthew 22.21), and a historical summary beginning with praise of the politically-unabitious early church, and ending with the period of the investiture controversy and the Hohenstaufen dynasty.

Another "golden tract" from the collection was *The History of the Controversy Between the Roman Bishops and the Sixth Synod of Carthage and the African Church*,[19] an exposé of a fraudulent claim of Pope Zosimus (417–418). In a letter to a synod of Carthage, May 25–30, A. D. 419, the pope falsely certified that a decision making the pope a court of appeal for accused bishops, originated at the 325 Council of Nicaea. In reality, it was a decision of a 342 synod at Serdica (modern Sophia). Authentic texts from Alexandria and Constantinople revealed that Nicaea had, in fact, *forbidden* such appeals.[20] Flacius repeated the charge against pope Zosimus in the *Excerpt from Some Old Reformations of the Church*.[21]

The tract had no influence on the Doge and Signorie of Venice, to whom it was dedicated. It did, however, have an influence in England. In a Reformation controversy in England, it was quoted by M. Harding.

> That Pope Zosimus corrupted the Nicene Council, never did any honest man say it from the beginning of the world. No man ever said it but Illyricus or bawdy Bale.[22]

But Harding was mistaken; Flacius and Bale were not the first to report it. The scandal had been aired at the Council of Florence, said Bishop Jewel, by Cardinal Bessarion, among others, long before Flacius and Bale were born.

> It were very hard for you, M. Harding, to say that all these were unhonest men, or of ill disposition, or the maintainers of the succession of lies. They lived in the light and commendation of the world above an hundred and forty years ago, long before either Flacius Illyricus or John Bale was heard of. They said openly in the council of Florence, that pope Zosimus had falsified the council of Nice; and further they were able to prove it, and that otherwise they would not have said it. Mark, therefore, M. Harding, the truth and courtesy of your words. Thus you say; "Never did any honest man thus say from the beginning of the world."[23]

An authentic *editio princeps* among the *Statements* is the "Transfer of Empire" by Marsilius of Padua, which challenged the curial theory that the coronation of Charlemagne gave the popes power to transfer civil power from one state to another.[24] Challenging papal power in the secular realm, Marsilius denies papal *plenituto potestatis*, the notion that authority for granting all political power was vested in the pope (the power that Paul IV was working to restore). The *translatio imperii* doctrine had been developed in the period after 800 A.D. papal coronation of Charlemagne. Marsilius insisted that the pope's coronation ceremony was only a formality. He defended the right of a council to depose popes, and argued for the separation of church and state.

Included as well was the sensation of Paris in the summer of 1256, a report of the attempt of the University of Paris to prevent infiltration of

ast also attributes the pamphlet to Heimburg. *Monarchia S. Romani Imperii.* Hannover: Typis Thomae Willierij, impensis Conradi Biermanni & consorti, 1562. 557– 563. The attribution was first challenged by Io. Arnold Ballenstedt in his *Vitae Gregorii de Heimburg. Brevis Narratio.* Helmstedt: Drimborn, 1727. 7.

13 Georges De Lagarde. *La Naissance de l'Esprit Laique au Declin de Moyen Age. III: Le Defensor Pacis.* Louvain and Paris: Editions Nauwelaerts, 1970. 370 f.

14 Albert. "Confutatio." 462 ff., compares the two texts.

15 *Catalogus*, 1562. 806. Peter Paul Albert. *Matthias Döring, ein deutscher Minorit des 15. Jahrhunderts.* Stuttgart: Süddeutsche Verlagsbuchhandlung [D. Ochs], 1982. 488.

16 *Catalogus*, 1562. 551.

17 Albert. "Confutatio." 488. Cf. 444n.

18 *Scriptum contra primatvm Papae, ante annos 100 compositum. Item, M. Fl. Ill. de eadem materia.* Magdeburg: Christian Rhodius, 1550.

19 Also printed separately:. Op.cit.

20 Charles Munier. *Concilia Africae a. 345–a. 520.* Turnhout: Brepols, 1974. 89–161; Cuthbert Hamilton Turner (ed.). *Ecclesiae occidentalis monumentis antiquissimae, canonum et consciliorum Graecorum interpretationes Latinae* I. Oxford: Clarendon, 1899. I, 460–462, 496–598, 571. Cf. Myron Wjtowytsch. *Papsttum und Konzile von den Anfangen bis zu Leo (440–461).* Stuttgart: Anton Hiersemann, 1981. 226–264, esp. 255 ff.; Polman. *L'Element.* 167 f.

21 *Auszug etlicher alten Reformation der Kirchen, in den Handlungen mit den Geistlichen sehr nützlich zu wissen. Item, eine überaus feine Historie von Bepstlicher gewalt, die sich zur Zeit Cypriani, ungefehr 250 Jar nach Christo zugetragen*, 1556. n. p.

22 Jewel. 340 f.

23 Ibid. IV, 340 f., cf. 613.

Dominicans and Franciscans, Guillaume de Saint-Amour's "On the Perils of the Last Times," a text which was burned by Pope Alexander IV.[25] The monks, Saint-Amour wrote, were the "ungodly men" of Revelation, and the intruders of II Timothy 3.6, who creep into houses and "after their own lusts heap to themselves teachers." In retribution, the author was deprived by the pope of all dignities.[26]

Another was a quotation from the 1404 *Speculum Aureum* of Johannes Engelschalk attacking the simony of the curia,[27] an appeal by Gregory Heimburg on behalf of Duke Sigmund of Austria to an ecumenical council rather than to the pope and an amusing sermon in which the Cistercian abbot of Sedichenbech (Sichem, Westphalia), in the interest of peace and quiet, imposed a miraculous silence on Westphalian frogs.

On the themes of the *Antilogia* Flacius also published several other separate pamphlets. *The Source and Origin of Purgatory*[28] was a section from the Dialogs of Pope Gregory I. A letter of Nilus Cabasilas, uncle of the celebrated fifteenth-century Bishop of Thessalonica, Nicolas Cabasilas, denounced the notion of papal infallibility and backed the conciliar idea – power of ecumenical councils over the pope.[29] He had started a publication trend.

> After the first writings of Flacius Illyricus published in Basel and the related source publications offered the greatest possible space to the historical argumentation, a great and growing public campaign began ... on the model of the Flacian opuscula and related to the old conciliarist-patriotic positions of the publications from the time of Hutten, meant to undergird the claims to power of the emperor, and to undermine those of the pope.[30]

24 *Antilogia*. 210–252. It was included at Nidbruck's suggestion. Bibl. 1896. 7; 1897. 205. Reprinted, Simon Schard. *De jurisdictione, auctoritate et eminentia imperiali ac potestate ecclesiastica*. Basel: Oporinus, 1566; Felice Battaglia. *Marsilio da Padova e la filosofia politica del medioevo*. Florence, 1928. 196–207; Judy Collete & Jeannine Quillet. *Marsile de Padoue. Ouvres Mineures, Defensor Minor, De Translatione Imperii*. Paris: Centre National de la Recherche Scientifique, 1979.

25 *Antilogia*. 210–252.

26 James Dawson. "William of Saint-Amour and the Apostolic Tradition." *Medieval Studies* XL (1978). 49; Hastings Rashdall. *The Universities of Europe in the Middle Ages*. New edition, F. H. Powicke and A. B. Emden (eds.). Vol. I. Oxford: Clarendon Press, 1936. 344 ff.; Y. H.-J. Congar. "Aspects ecclésiologiques de la querelle entre Mediants et séculiers dans le seconde moitié du XIIIe siècle et le debut du XIVe." *Archives d'Histoire Doctrinale et Littéraire du Moyen Age* XXXVI (1961). 151; Christine Thouzellier. "La Place du de Periculis de Guillaume de Saint-Amour dans les Polémiques Universitaires du XIIIe Siècle." *Revue Historique* CLVI (1927). 69–83; Michel-Marie Dufeil. *Guillaume de Saint-Amour et la Polémique Universitaire Parisienne 1250–1259*. Paris: A. et J. Picard, 1972.

27 *Antilogia*. 252–561; *Catalogus*, 1556. 935 f. Further printings listed in Theodor Brieger. "Zu Jakob von Jüterbog." ZKG, XXIV (1903). 138.

28 *Fons atque Origo Purgatorii*, 1555. n. p.

29 *Nili Thessaloncensis libellus de primatu romani pontificis a M. Fl. Ill. in latinum sermonem conversus*. Frankfurt: David Zephelius, 1555.

30 A. Burckhardt. 10.

A Catalog of Witnesses

THE CATHOLIC TRADITION

The German Reformation is imperfectly described when it is considered an appeal to scripture versus tradition. It was rather an appeal to history. – Mark Pattison

It was as if that unseen congregation of the most profound, noblest spirits, which from the beginning were the light of the world, the salt of the earth, had found a voice with which to greet the confessor of the evangelical doctrine as their brother in faith.
– August Twesten

Whereas similar works of the Englishmen, Robert Barnes and John Bale, were "enterprises of destruction," according to Jean-François Gilmont, Flacius' *Catalog of Witnesses*[1] was a positive enterprise.[2] Mirković sees in it "a thousand-year struggle for man and peoples striving for freedom and who wanted to live out their religious feelings according to their fashion."[3] A more careful examination, however, shows his theme was not religious feelings, but the authoritative tradition of the church. "Basically we have the impression," writes Harald Wagner, "that Flacius was not so concerned about the individual witnesses as the continuity – the catholicity – of the church itself."[4] "It was," August Twesten wrote, "as if that unseen congregation of the most profound, noblest spirits, which from the beginning were the light of the world, the salt of the earth, had found a voice with which to greet the confessor of the evangelical doctrine as their brother in faith."[5]

According to Eberhard Gothein, "The Renaissance and Reformation agree in that they consciously effect an abrupt break with historical continuity ... The biblical piety is nothing else than the Renaissance principle [*ad fontes*], transferred to the religious area."[6] Ignoring the Middle Ages is, indeed, characteristic of the tradition stemming from the Swiss Reformation, where Reformation has often been understood as New Testament "primitivism," or "restorationism." According to Theodore Dwight Bozeman, that notion is a "reversion undercutting both Catholic and Anglican appeals to a continuity of tradition, to the first, or primitive, order of things..."[7]

The *Catalogus*, on the other hand, reflects what Hans Lietzmann called "the good Lutheran notion of the continual presence of the pure Gospel in the catholic church."[8] "Flacius," Haikola comments, "knew only the *una sancta ecclesia Catholica*, which exists from the beginning of time to the present and remains to the end of days, to which true believers in all the world belong."[9] From the *Libri Carolini* of Charlemagne, newly published by Jean du Tillet in Paris, 1549,[10] Flacius cited the decision of the Synod

1 *Catalogus Testium Veritatis, qui ante nostram aetatem reclamarunt Papae.* Basel: Oporinus, 1556; Second edition: *Catalogus Testium Veritatis, qui ante nostram aetatem Pontifici Romano, eiusque erroribus clamarunt; iam denuo longe quam antea, & emendatior & auctorior editus.* Straßburg: Paul Messerschmidt, 1562.
2 "Martyrologes." 89.
3 Op. cit. 1560. 527.
4 *An den Ursprüngen des frühkatholischen Problems: die Ortsbestimmung des Katholizismus im älteren Luthertum.* Frankfurt am Main: Josef Knect, 1973. 28.
5 Op. cit. 15.
6 *Grundlagen.* 586.
7 *To Live Ancient Lives: The Primitive Dimension in New England Puritanism.* Chapel Hill: University of North Carolina Press, 1988. 11.
8 Hans Lietzmann. *Die Reformation und ihre Wirkungen in der Theologischen Fakultät der Universität Jena.* Leipzig: A. Deichert'sche Verlagsbuchhandlung Werner School, 1917. 154.
9 Moldaenke. 87.
10 PL, XCVIII, col. 989–1247. Polman. "Historien" 59.

11 *Catalogus*, 1556. 870; 1562. 508. Ferdinand Piper. *Einleitung in die Monumentale Theologie.* Gotha: Rud. Besser, 1876. Nidbruck visited Tauler's grave. Bibl. 1897. 214.

12 *Catalogus*, 1562. 390. First published in the *Carmina Vetusta.*

13 Jewel. 888.

14 Op cit. 322.

15 C. Frank. 235.

16 Haye, 1992. 32.

17 C. Frank. 238.

18 Haye, 1992. 35.

of Frankfurt 794, which like Luther, took a position against adoration of images, and against the Second Nicene Council. He recognized the marks of that true church in the carving of the grave-plate of the fourteenth-century Dominican, John Tauler, who, like Luther, pointed to the Lamb of God.[11] He found the same faith in a Premonstratensian breviary.

> Adiuvent nos eorum merita.
> Quos propria impediunt scelere?
> Excuset eorum intercessio,
> quos propria accusat actio?
> At tu qui eis tribuisti
> Coelestis palmam triumphi,
> Nobis veniam non denegas peccati.[12]

> Do their merits help us,
> whose own sins shackle?
> Does intercession of those excuse,
> who are accused by their own action?
> But you, who gave them
> the palm of heavenly triumph
> do not deny us forgiveness of sin.

When Flacius introduces the Apostle Peter as witness, when his documents reveal that purgatory, private masses and papal primacy were never recognized by the church in Greece, Asia, Macedonia, Mysis, Valachia, Russia, Muscovy and Africa,[13] he, of course, makes common cause with the Swiss Reformation.

But he had a significantly different notion of Christian history. Unlike the Swiss, Mark Pattison writes, "The German Reformation is imperfectly described when it is considered an appeal to scripture versus tradition. It was rather an appeal to history."[14] "The whole work [Flacius' *Catalogus*] in its structure and execution is so contrasted, so that it shows us that the Middle Ages are a connecting bridge between the times of the Church fathers and the sixteenth century."[15] Whereas "... the humanists – at least according to their understanding – consciously turn away from the linguistic, literary and spiritual culture of the Middle Ages to concentrate on the 'purer' sources of antiquity, the author of the *Catalogus* concentrates essentially on the 'discovery' of the Latin literature of the Middle Ages, evaluation of their contents, and its critical classification."[16] As many commentators have observed, he stood "in obvious contradiction to many of his contemporaries and fellow religionists, who deplore the Middle Ages as an intermediate epoch, and greet the Reformation as the rebirth of the original Christian idea."[17]

The *Catalogus* took a significant step forward by opening up medieval studies. "... for the first time," Thomas Haye writes, Flacius "acquainted his public with the wide spectrum of medieval literature."[18] "It is the entire Middle Ages that Flacius made an object of critical examination," Fumaroli wrote, "an open digging site for the 'archeologists' of the repub-

IOHANNIS TAVLERI *Bildnüs, wie selbiges zu Strasburg auff seinem Grabmahl zu finden*

HAB: Portraitsammlung. Flacius' witness, John Tauler, points to the lamb of God.

19 *Fumaroli 8, discussing the Centuries.*

20 *Catalogus Testium Veritatis. Historia der Zeugen, Bekenner und Märterer, so Christum und die evangelische warheit hierher, auch etwa im Reich der Finsternis warhafftig erkenent ... erstlich widersprochen.* Tr. Conrad Lauterbach. Frankfurt: Johann Schmidt, 1573. CCXXVIII, r. Professor H. J. Real of the University of Bochum supplied the connection to Swift.

21 *A Tale of a Tub with Other Early Works 1696–1707.* Herbert Davis (ed.). Oxford: Basil Blackwell, 1939. 74.

lic of letters.'" He was able thus to elevate historical erudition to the rank of an auxiliary science in theology.[19]

    There was also a good deal of foolishness to be rejected. According to H. J. Real of the University of Bochum, the idea for the "multiplying of the Virgin's milk" in Jonathan Swift's *Tale of a Tub* came from the *Catalogus*. Flacius' reported that "the Franciscans show Christ's blood, the Cistercians Mary's milk."[20] Lord Peter, in Swift's work, "swore he had a cow at home, which gave as much milk at a meal, as would fill three thousand churches, and what was yet more extraordinary, would never turn sower."[21]

22 *Catalogus*, 1562. 424.

23 Ibid. 65–67.

24 A. Burckhardt. 33.

25 Hermann Dörries. "Von Boniface zu Luther." *Materialdienst des Konfessionskundlichen Instituts Bensheim.* 22 Jg. No. 4. July–August 1960. 45.

26 Burman. 159.

27 Thomas Erastus. *De Astrologia Divinatrice Epistolae ... in lucem aedita, opera et studio Ioannis Iacobi Grynaei.* Basel: Peter Perna, 1580. 208. Romeo de Maio thinks his reference to the Antichrist was influenced by Flacius. "Anche Thomas Erastus, evidemente influenzato dal Flaccius [sic] affermo che Savonarola ritenne Alesandro VII Antichristo." "Savonarola, Alesandro VI ed il mito dell' Antichristo." *Riforme ed miti nella Chiese del cinquecento.* Naples: Guilda, 1975. 33.

28 C. Frank. "Die Manifestation des Antichrists." Op. cit. 77–84. Gottfried Seebass. "Antichrist." TRE, IV, 32 f.; Michael Wolter. "Der Gegner als endzeitlicher Widersacher. Die Darstellung des Feindes in der jüdischen und christlichen Apokalyptik." Franz Bosbach (ed.). *Feindbilder. Die Darstellung des Gegners in der politischen Publizistik des Mittelalters und der Neuzeit.* Cologne, Weimar and Vienna: Böhlau, 1992. 23–40.

29 *Catalogus*, 1562. 508.

30 *Das der Bapst mit seinem hoffe die recht Babilon und Babilonische Hure sey. Durch den hochgelarten Franciscum Petrarcham einen Welcher, der für 250 jarn gelebt hat.* [Magdeburg: Christian Rödinger, ca. 1550].

31 Francesco Petrarch. *Petrarch's Book Without a Name. A Translation of the Liber sine Nomine.* Tr. Norman P. Zacour. Toronto: The Pontifical Institute of Medieval Studies, 1973. 115 f.

Nor should some well-known historical figure be counted as catholic teachers: Gratian, Peter Lombard, Francis of Assisi, and Dominic, he argued, were guilty of perverting the tradition.[22] Since he was critical of Roman influence, he was critical of Boniface[23] and his mission to Germany[24] but praised him for freeing the country from Arianism.[25]

"At first this institution was a temperate and lenient tribunal ... but above all when the superhuman reign of Carafa [Paul IV] held sway, the Inquisition aquired such a reputation that from no other judgment seat on earth were more horrible and fearful sentences to be expected."[26]

Talk about a papal Antichrist was an old tradition, as Luther had observed the term was used by the Florentine reformer, Girolamo Savonarola about Paul IV's mentor, the unsavory Alexander VI (Alexander Borgia).[27] In his *Catalogus*, Flacius was the first to bring the tradition together,[28] with statements by Joachim Calaber, Bishop Florentinus, Heinrich of Herford, the early Franciscans, Hayabalins, John Wycliffe, John Huss and Luther. The high-point of the talk about a papal Antichrist was the pontificate of Paul IV, when "antichrist" was the most-used epithet for the pope.

As witness, Flacius quotes Francesco Petrarch on the Avignon papacy (1309–1377). Petrarch identified the papal court with Babylon, that "sits upon many waters (Revelation 17.1-2; 18.3)."[29] In letter 18 of his *Liber Sine Nomine*, which Flacius published separately,[30] Petrarch asked whether Avignon recognized itself as the whore of Babylon. "If he [St. John] was right in saying that there was written on her forehead 'Babylon the Great' (Revelation 17.5), then you are Babylon the Small. Small indeed in the circumference of your walls, but in vice and the corruption of souls, in infinite greed and the heaping up of every wickedness, you are not just great, but rather huge, immense, and certainly the words that follow apply to you alone and to no other: 'Babylon, the mother of harlots and abominations of the earth" (Revelation 17.5). In the same letter, Petrarch repeats a story about one Avignon figure, the old lecher.

> Well now, there was a certain little old fellow of that crowd who deserves a place in all the annals. The man was as lusty as a goat. If there is anything lustier and smellier than a goat, he was it. He dared not sleep alone, fearing either mice or ghosts. He found nothing more depressing or more wretched than celibacy. Daily he celebrated new nuptials, and was betrothed again and again in casual encounters, though he was as empty of mouth as he was full of years – he was well over seventy, with scarcely seven teeth left. He employed a hunter of young maidens who was one in a million, in every way equal to the demands of his master's lust. His raps and snares were to be found in all the streets and all the houses, especially of the poor: here some money, there a necklace, here a few rings, there a little flattery, here the left-overs of some banquet, there all sorts of food – whatever deviousness captures the female fancy. Then he kept his fingers crossed, and meanwhile sang: for he was in fact a cantor, though he had transferred his voice from the altar to the theatres and the bawdy houses. I knew the man, pointed out to me by the finger of the crowd. He was said to have been accustomed with his skills to entice a lot of game into the jaws of that old wolf.[31]

Against Pope Calixtus II (1119–1124), who at the Lateran Council of

1123 forbade the marriage of priests, Flacius printed a contemporary protest against the new "sodomitic celibacy."

> O bone Calixte, mundus totus perodit te.
> quondam presbyteri poterant uxoribus uti:
> Hoc destruxisi, postqam tu Papa fuisti.[32]

> O good Calixtus, the whole world detests you.
> Formerly, priests could have wives
> You destroyed that, after you became pope.

Meanwhile, according to Fumaroli, the *Catalogus* entry on the Council of Constance (1414–1418) "destroyed the myth of a medieval Christianity assembled around the Roman pontiff."[33]

The Roman Catholic counter-attack on the *Catalogus* as an "inverted Index Prohibitorum" or Catalogus Testium Falsorum was somewhat illogical, since among the witnesses are not a few popes – Gregory (for refusing the title of "general bishop"), Gelasius (for insisting on both bread and wine for the laity in communion), Innocent III (for permitting worship in the people's language and insisting that priests not abandon their wives), as well as Simplicius, John VII, Leo VII, Leo XII and John XXII.[34]

In view of the clearly unsuitable persons counted in the papal succession – the Avignon popes, for example, and not least Paul III and Paul IV, who persecuted the Gospel itself – basing the catholicity of the church on the *successio personarum*, the succession of *persons*, was unthinkable.

Flacius, instead, based the Lutheran concept of catholicity: not on a *successio personarum*, but the *successio doctrinae*: the catholic succession through the centuries was passed on by those who taught faithfully. "Good God," he wrote, "how many pious men, for the past seven hundred years, wanted to see the cleansing of God's temple that has happened in our time."[35] What Martin Luther had taught, he argued, had *always* been taught, beginning with the apostles. "We do not concede to the papists that they are the ancient church," Luther had said, "but we Evangelicals stand in conformity with the ancient church."[36] Flacius said the same: "Whoever reads the writers or fathers of that age diligently, easily observes that in most articles their judgment agrees with our doctrine."[37]

The donnish opinion of A. G. Dickens that Flacius awarded his witnesses with "a sort of posthumous membership in the Lutheran Church,"[38] is not shared by other commentators. Paul Piur wondered how he could include Petrarch, who "is really no spiritual relative of Luther or Calvin."[39] Carlos Gilly thinks he made a mistake by citing Rodrigo Sanches de Arevalo, an ardent papalist.[40] "On closer examination," Thomas Haye reports, "many 'testes veritatis' turn out to be authors with no specifically Protestant alignment…"[41] The denial of papal infallibility by the fifteenth century Bishop Nil Cabasilas, for one, is characteristic of the Eastern Church.[42] Mirković explains that Flacius' goal was not a specifically Lutheran or even German truth." It was, rather, "…the truth of Methodius the Illyrican, the Croatian Glagolitic, the old Slavic church, the south

32 *Catalogus*, 1556. 243.
33 Op. cit. 8.
34 Cf. "Päpste als Wahrheitszeugen." C. Frank. Op. cit. 61–76.
35 *Cleri Fletus. Est deploratio perditae maliciae Clericorum seu Spiritualium Antichrist, olim ante annos 100, vel amplius ab aliquo pio, templi Domini repurgationem videre cupiente, conscripta.* Magdeburg: Christian Rödinger, 1549. I ij r.
36 "Wider Hans Worst." WA, 51, 480; LW, 41, 195.
37 *Catalogus*, 1562. [A 5 v].
38 *Contemporary Historians of the German Reformation.* London: Institute of German Studies, 1978. 17.
39 Piur. xiii.
40 *Spanien und der Basler Buchdruck bis 1600.* Basel and Frankfurt am Main: Lichtenhan, 1985. 112.
41 Haye, 1992. 38.
42 *Catalogus*, 1562. 520; PL, CXLIX, 699–730.

43 Mirković, 1960. 270.
44 *Catalogus*, 1556. 935.
45 Haye, 1992. 25.
46 Polman. *L'Element.* 173.
47 *Catalogus*, 1562. [A vj v], [A ij v].
48 Ibid. [A vj v].
49 H. Wagner. 28.
50 A. Burkhardt. 28 f.
51 Jutta Krimm-Beumann. "Der Traktat 'De investura episcoporum' von 1109." *Deutsches Archiv für Erforschung des Mittelalters* XXXIII (1977). 37–83.

Title page from Gotthold Ephraim Lessing. *Berengarius Turonensis,* 1770.

French Waldensians, the English church and the Czech Hussites."[43]

Altogether (depending on how one counts), the witnesses cited numbered about six hundred and fifty. Among them were Hegesippus, Dionysius, Irenaeus, Basil, and Augustine to Otto of Freising, William of Ockham, Hugh of St. Victor, St. Bernard, Thomas Aquinas, Tauler, Savonarola, St. Hildegard of Bingen, St. Brigitta, St. Louis, Valdez, Huss, Wycliff, Philipp the Fair, Louis of Bavaria. Carlos Gilly noticed how many Spaniards were listed – Alphonse de Spina, Sanchez de Arevalo, Jeronimo Paul, Arnaldus de Villanova, Claudius of Turin, Jaime II of Aragon, Gironi Paul. As a Venetian, Flacius did not overlook Italians – Joachim of Fiore, Jean de Roquetaillade, Arnold of Villanova, Pierre Jean d'Olivi, Seganelli and Colcini, Dante, Marsilius of Padua, Occam, Dietrich of Niem.[44] He made a distinction between witnesses to the truth and testimonies to the same. Eusebius, is presented, for example, only as a medium for passing on information."[45]

How *could* one trace catholicity, then, taking into consideration the existence of evil in the church – the "mystery of iniquity" [I Thessalonians 1.7].[46] Flacius' solution was his remnant doctrine, expressed first in his song text collections, "Yet I will leave seven thousand in Israel, all the knees that have not bowed down to Baal, and every mouth that has not kissed him [I Kings 19,18 and Romans 11.4]." The Evangelical-Lutheran church thus did not turn its back on the catholic tradition: recognizing that in every generation there was a faithful remnant was quite another thing from the "conscious break" made in Switzerland.

Nor did Flacius think of that remnant as a "little flock." "The literature on the Catalog, in our opinion," Harald Wagner writes, "emphasizes too little that the 'witnesses' are merely representatives of a much larger group. In every age there were many witnesses. "There always were not few, but many doctors and hearers," Flacius wrote, "who agreed with us and not our opponents"[47] "...where there was one teacher, who thought more correctly, there were also a great many listeners..."[48] "That is the point," Wagner says. "Wherever pure doctrine was represented and taught (even if only in the form of a confession against Rome), there had to be 'listeners,' whose totality represented the true church of God."[49]

Without giving evidence of the German nationalism of South-German humanists,[50] Flacius is often favorable to the emperors. During the periods of Constantine, Charlemagne, and Louis the Pious, he discerned an independent church. He approved the supervision Otto I excerized over the Roman see. One section, "The Unfortunate Emperors," was a vehement introduction to the investiture controversy. From 1109, the time of the Concordat at Worms, he printed an anonymous tract, "That the investiture of bishops should be done by emperors,"[51] in which emperor Henry V was described as a sacrifice to papal terror. The papal campaign against the Hohenstaufens he saw as as an encroachment on imperial authority. In his entry about the chief propagandist for Hohenstaufen emperor Frederik II, he cites Piero della Vigna's argument against the pope's right to depose the

Emperor.

> Piero della Vigna, chancellor of Emperor Frederic II, flourished three hundred years ago, that is, about 1230. He wrote many letters to many in the name of the emperor, especially about the excommunication and deposing of Caesar, an enormity and abomination done then by the pope ... He contended that the pope did not have the civil sword, nor any right to dismiss an emperor ... The same Piero wrote a book on the power of the emperor against the pope, in which without doubt, he asserted that the pope has no power in political matters over the emperor. For which the pope also excommunicated him.[52]

Maximilian I is cited as a sponsor of the German *gravanima* against the papacy.[53] Frances Yates was intrigued by the possibility that Flacius' quoting a letter of Pico della Mirandola, urging the Emperor Maximilian to reform the church might mean he was attempting to claim the Italian neoplatonists for the imperial cause.[54]

One of the more important discoveries of the philosopher Gotthold Ephraim Lessing (1728–1781), first announced to his father on July 27, 1770, was that the sacramental doctrine of Berengar of Tours (ca. 1010–1088) was the same as Luther's. To demonstrate it, he called attention to the Berengar manuscript (Codex Guelf. 101 Weissenburg) he had found in the Wolfenbüttel library.[55]

Lessing's contemporaries among Lutheran theologians had rejected Berengar. Rostock professor Johann Fecht, for instance, considered his popularity at the University of Helmstedt was proof of cryptocalvinism.[56] But Lessing found one exception, Matthias Flacius, "a man who at least wants to see with his own eyes." "Among the older theologians of our church, I know only one who judged Berengar more leniently and favorably, and that is Flacius, who, however, had no more data for his better opinion than the others did for their worse one."

> Therein he [Lessing] is the most brilliant representative of his age, going far beyond the usual representation of the Enlightenment: a passionate theologian, for whom it was important, over against a questionable doctrine of communion, freighted with massive realism, which, moreover, falsely pretended to be legitimate, to defend it, by seeing in him [Berengar] a forerunner of Lutheran doctrine.[57]

"One is aware," Lessing wrote, "of the undismayed diligence of this man, the immense labor ... with which he sought everywhere for that which, in his view, was useful. Still, he knew no more about Berengar than what everyone knew."[58] R. B. C. Huygens concluded that Flacius, on the contrary, was the only one since the Middle Ages who had been aware of Berengar.[59]

But Wolfenbüttel librarian Lessing was not completely informed about his own library, and erred about Flacius. He did not know that Flacius had used the same manuscript; in fact, that he once had discovered and had *owned* it.[60] When he did not publish the Berengar text himself, Flacius probably made a mistake as well. Since Lessing was able to claim the discovery, he astonished the learned world, and earned credibility for himself

52 *Catalogus*, 1562. 470. Cf. Peter Segl. "Die Feindbilder in der Politischen Propaganda Friedrichs II. und seiner Gegner." Bosbach. Op. cit. 41–71.

53 *Catalogus*, 1556. 1007; 1562. 572.

54 Ibid. 995 f.; 1562. 586; Frances Yates. *Astraea: The Imperial "Theme" in the Sixteenth Century.* London and Boston: Routledge and Kegan Paul, 1975. 45n.

55 *Berengarious Turonensis: oder Ankündigung eines wichtigen Werkes desselben in der Herzoglichen Bibliothek in Wolfenbüttel befindlich, welcher bisher völlig unerkannt geblieben.* Braunschweig: Waisenhaus, 1770.

56 *De Origine et Superstitione Missarum.* Rostock and Leipzig: 1725. 1024.

57 Horst Althaus. "Marginalien zu Lessings Wolfenbüttler Berengarforschung." ZKG, LXXII (1961). 344.

58 *Sämtliche Schriften.* 3rd ed. Karl Lachmann and Franz Muncker (eds.). Stuttgart: G. J. Göschen, 1895. XI, 64 f.

59 "A propos de Bérengar et son Traité de l'Eucharistie." *Revue Bénédictine* LXXVI (1966). 134. "A mon avis, il est significatif, qu'on ne trouve aucune trace, qu'aucune allusion n'y soit faite chez les contemporains, ne meme au cours des siècles suivants jusqu'à Flacius Illyricus."

60 Which has recently appeared in photographic reproduction. *Berengarius Turonensis Rescriptum Contra Lanfrannum, Faksimile der Handschrift Wolfenbüttel Cod. Guelf. 101 Weissenburg.* Mit einer Einleitung von Wolfgang Milde. Turnot: Typographi Brepols Editores Pontifici, 1988; The parallel text edition: *Berengarius Turonensis. Rescriptum contra Lanfrannum [De Sacra Coena adversus Lanfrancum].* Ed. Robert Burchard Constantyn Huygens. Tournhout: Brepols, 1988.

61 Op. cit. 237.

62 Op. cit. 1992. 38.

63 Preger. "Flacius." ADB, VII, 95; Franz von Wegele. *Geschichte der deutschen Historiographie seit dem Auftreten des Humanismus.* Munich and Leipzig: L. Oldenbourg, 1885. 330.

64 Polman. "Historien." 36.

65 Haye, 1992. 30 ff. 33.

66 *L'Element.* 228 f.; Cf. Klaus Herbers. "Die Päpstin Joanna. Ein kritischer Forschungsbericht. *Historisches Jahrbuch* CVII (1988). 178.

67 C. Frank. 66 f.

68 A. Burckhardt. 92.

69 Ibid. 29.

70 My thanks to Charles Béné of the University of Grenoble for allowing me to make use of his manuscript article on the Goulart editions.

71 Marcella Roddewig. "Flacius, Vergerio, Foxe, Wolfius, Mornay und der erste Übersetzungsversuch aus dem Paradiso vom Jahre 1573." *Deutsches Dante Jahrbuch* XLIV/XLV (1957). 105.

In the *Catalogus* Flacius defined the catholicity of the church.

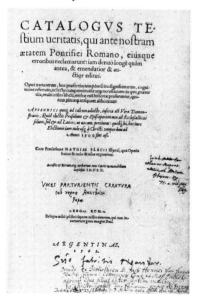

in the eyes of his duke. He was thus able to avoid the censorship that might have prevented publication of his famous "Wolfenbüttel Fragments," and thus advance the cause of the German Enlightenment. The Fragments, which he passed off – dishonestly – as another manuscript discovery, spread doubts about the divinity of Christ.

Flacius' idea of historical data strikes one as advanced: he used excerpts from texts, summaries, paraphrases, synod minutes, letters, decretals, gravanima, tracts, reports of visions, laws, capitularies, historical chronicles, and satires. In her investigation, Christiana Frank noticed the "indisputable precision of his working method." "The reproach of having worked all too grandiosely," she writes, "of having adopted statements of his witnesses blindly and uncritically, the suspicion of false citation and impure method can be rejected."[61]

Reacting to the reproach of Pontien Polman that most of the witnesses were from the thirteenth to the nineteenth centuries and very few from the sixth, seventh, eighth and ninth, Thomas Haye found, on the contrary, that "the material cited in the Catalog gives a proportionally thorough and appropriate picture of the tradition of Medieval literature."[62] Haye also resolved the disagreement between Wilhelm Preger and Franz von Wegele on the one side, who emphasized his use of original manuscripts,[63] and Polman on the other, who reported that he used primarily printed texts.[64] Of 430 entries in the 1562 edition, Haye reports 90 citations from texts already in print and 60 from manuscript sources.[65]

Flacius had a sharp eye for the question of authenticity. Haye calls attention to his "rich arsenal of philological methods with respect to authenticity, authorship and dating," and, disagreeing with Pontien Polman, notes that he did not put his critical skills to work for any theological purpose. Although Polman accuses him of making use of the legend of Pope Joan,[66] which appeared in the Centuries, Flacius did not credit the legend.[67]

The *Catalogus* came to be used, as Trithemius' volume had been used before it, as a research guide. Flacius' old friend, Heinrich Pantlin, in his 1563 *Martyrum Historia* made use of the *Catalogus*,[68] as did Jean Crespin in his 1570 *Histoire des Vrays Tesmoines.* Calvinists discovered that the *Catalogus* was a good source of ammunition for polemics[69]; Simon Goulart's 1597 and 1608 editions doubled the size of the volume, with new material, e. g., Guillaume Budé's record of the murder of Frenchmen by Pope Julius II.[70] Among Lutherans, it influenced the *Confessio Catholica* of Johann Gerhard. The German translation by Lutheran pastor Conrad Lauterbach in 1573 (above) is of interest in the history of literature for the first German translation of Dante,[71] and as a possible source of the Faust legend.[72] An interesting use to which it was put recently, was the identification of a painting of Johannes Schering by Lucas Cranach the Elder in the Musée des Beaux-Arts in Brussels.[73]

Although possibly undervalued in the universities,[74] dominated as they were by followers of Melanchthon,[75] it was nevertheless a best-seller, a

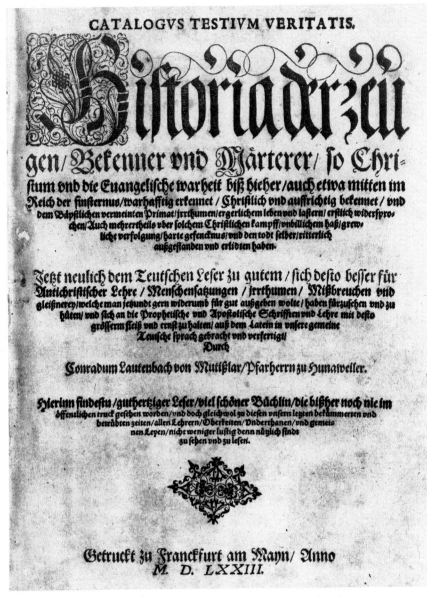

CATALOGVS TESTIVM VERITATIS.

Historia derzü

gen/ Bekenner vnd Märterer/ so Christum vnd die Euangelische warheit biß hieher/ auch etwa mitten im Reich der finsternus/ warhafftig erkennet/ Christlich vnd auffrichtig bekennet/ vnd dem Bäpstlichen vermeinten Primat/ jrrthumen/ergerlichem leben vnd lastern/ erstlich widersprochen/ Auch mehrertheils vber solchem Christlichen kampff/ vnbillichem haß/ grewliche verfolgung/ harte gefencknus/ vnd den todt selber/ritterlich außgestanden vnd erlidten haben.

Jetzt neulich dem Teutschen Leser zu gutem/ sich desto besser für Antichristischer Lehre/ Menschensatzungen/ jrrthumen/ Mißbreuchen vnd gleißnerey/ welche man jetzundt gern widerumb für gut außgeben wolte/ haben fürzusehen vnd zu hüten/ vnd sich an die Prophetische vnd Apostolische Schrifften vnd Lehre mit desto grösserm fleiß vnd ernst zu halten/ auß dem Latein in vnsere gemeine Teutsche sprach gebracht vnd verfertigt Durch

Conradum Lautenbach von Mutißlar/ Pfarherrn zu Hunaweiler.

Hierinn findestu/ guthertziger Leser/ viel schöner Büchlin/ die bißher noch nie im öffentlichen truck gesehen worden/ vnd doch gleichwol zu diesen vnsern letzen bekümmerten vnd betrübten zeiten/ allen Lehrern/ Oberkeiten/ Vnderthanen/ vnd gemeinen Leyen/ nicht weniger lustig denn nützlich sind zu sehen vnd zu lesen.

Getruckt zu Franckfurt am Mayn/ Anno
M. D. LXXIII.

The German translation of the *Catalogus* may be a source of the legend of Faust.

"much-read folk-book." "Where do these whirlwinds not rage, these lions roar, these scorpions creep?" Wilhelm Eisengrein asked, alarmed that even the uneducated masses were reading it. "Oh, the gluttonous and unruly teeth of the heretics, who abandon themselves to lust and to Venus, to greed and simony and to the loathsome and monstrous crimes and who lie, face to face with the cross of Christ!"[76]

In opposition to the *Catalogus*, Robert Bellarmine,[77] Nicholas Sanders,[78] and Eisengrein[79] produced their own collections of source-documents. There was no avoiding Flacius' influence. The counter-catalogs were obliged to adopt his method, the use of primary sources.

72 Helmut Häuser. *Gibt es eine Gemeinsame Quelle zum Faustbuch von 1587 und zu Goethe's Faust?* Wiesbaden: Guido Preston Verlag, 1973. Idem. "Zur Verfasserfrage des Faustbuchs von 1587: Konrad Lautenbach." *Euphorion* LXVI (1972). 151–173.

For this sumary of Häuser's comparison I am grateful to Thomas Haye.

	Lautenbach, 1573	Flacius, 1562
Famulus motif	fol. 141.	p. 227
Books of magic	fol. 138v.	p. 223
Appearances of spirits	fol. 138v.	p. 223
24-hours of compact	fol. 141r,	p. 226
Sorcerer's apprentice	fol. 138v.	p. 223
Pact with the devil	fol. 143r,	p. 230

73 Hjalmar Sander. "Zur Identifizierung Zweier Bildnisse von Lucas Cranach d. Ä." *Zeitschrift für Kunstwissenschaft* IV (1950). 35–48.

74 Polman. *L'Elément.* 109n.

75 Schönstädt. 100.

76 Luzian Pfleger. "Wilhelm Eisengrein, ein Gegner des Flacius Illyricus." *Historisches Jahrbuch* XXV (1904). 774.

77 *De Scriptoribus ecclesiasticis.* Rome, 1613. Cf. C. Frank. 9.

78 Op. cit.

79 *Catalogus Testium Veritatis Locupletissimus, Omnium Orthodoxae matris Ecclesiae Doctorum, exstantium & non exstantium & in Bibliothecis latentium.* Dillingen: Sebald Mayer, 1565.

1 A. Burckhardt. 88.
2 August Wilhelm Dieckhoff. *Die Waldenser in Mittelalter.* Göttingen: Vandenhoeck & Ruprecht, 1851. 5.
3 "Die wissenschaftliche Waldenserforschung beginnt mit Flacius' *Catalogus Testium Veritatis.*" Johann Martini. *Die Waldenser und die hussitische Reformation.* Vienna & Leipzig: Heinrich Kirche, 1910. 17; Gustav Wolf. *Quellenkunde der deutschen Reformationsgeschichte.* Gotha, 1915–1922. I, 179.
4 Evan Cameron. *The Reformation of the Heretics. The Waldensians of the Alps 1480–1580.* Oxford: Clarendon Press, 1984. 244. Cf. 230 ff.; 233, 240, 246 f. *Catalogus*, 1562. 424–447.
5 Ritter. 65.
6 *Confessio Waldensium de plerisque nunc controversis dogmatibus ante 134. annos contra claudicantes Hussitas scripta, nostris[que] temporibus statui, ac rebus pulchre correspondens.* Basel: Oporinus, 1568.
7 Cameron. 245.

Scholarly Waldensian research began with Flacius' Catalogus Testium Veritatis.
– Gustav Wolf

Flacius gets credit for calling attention to the dispersion throughout Europe of the movement of Waldensians.[1] Although the collection of Waldensian writings he planned was never completed,[2] he also gets credit for initiating scholarly research about the movement.[3] Since for him they were a clear example of the faithful remnant, he gave them a large place in the *Catalogus*. Evan Cameron has summarized the entry.

> A short account was given of how Waldo was suddenly converted into a pious ascetic at Lyon around 1160; then Flacius described how Waldo fell out with the Church, and was expelled from the city with his followers. Then, without any explanation or reference, a list of supposedly "Waldensian" articles of faith was appended. These asserted the sole sufficiency of scripture; the sole mediation of Christ; the non-existence of purgatory; two sacraments; the rejection of the mass, human traditions, and the primacy of the pope; they also urged that communion be taken in both kinds, claimed the church of Rome was Babylon, rejected indulgences and clerical celibacy, and said the church of God resides in the hearers of His word. These articles were immensely influential; but their origin is unknown, and their correspondence to the belief of the Waldenses studied above is fairly remote.[4]

On the basis of the report that they had been active in Lyon, Flacius began his investigation of the Waldensians by requesting Hartmann Beyer, "...that you might deal diligently with the Lyon merchants, if some of them sell there at the fairs and are pious men, that they might endeavor to inquire carefully in their libraries, if any history of the Waldensians or other writings of theirs can be found there. Indeed, they first rose up four hundred years ago."[5] Here, he was quoting the 1431 Confession of the Hussite Taborites, which he published in 1568, but which he considered a Waldensian document.[6]

> Thereafter Flacius quoted Sleidan on the persecutions in Provence. More original, however, was the first introduction of a device which was to shape the rest of the debate: argument around medieval texts. Flacius quoted a long excerpt from the so-called "Pseudo-Reinerius treatise," an influential medieval summary of the beliefs and morals of the Eastern German Waldenses.
>
> Some parts of this text were welcome, as when pseudo-Reinerius prized the humility, simplicity, and chastity of the heretics; other parts where he criticized their doctrine required an antidote. For instance, when the medieval text claimed the Waldenses had a vow of poverty, Flacius commented in the margin that only persecutions taught them to be poor. To the allegations that the Waldenses condemned excommunication, oath-taking, or marriage, the marginalia asserted that the heretics condemned the abuse of the thing, not the thing itself. At other times, Flacius tried to discredit his text by claiming that another author, for example, Pius II, had not made such allegations.[7]

The manuscript, a first-hand report of his activities in the diocese of Passau by a thirteenth-century inquisitor, has been analyzed by Alexander Patchovsky. A *unicum*[8] that Cameron says shaped the debate on the Waldensians, it was attributed by Flacius to the Italian Dominican, Rainer Sacconi. When it later became clear that the author was German, Wilhelm Preger suggested the name, "Pseudo-Rainer."[9] It is now called the "Passauer Anonymous."

In a letter of March 13, 1555 to Pastor Antonius Bodenstein of Thorn, Flacius complained about the negotiations supported by the Prussian duke between the Lutherans and the Bohemian brethren. They could not only weaken the evangelical cause against Rome, but confuse Lutheran doctrine itself. Since they teach that certain ceremonies are essential, they show their lack of understanding of Christian freedom. Their understanding of baptism was ethical, and they made reception into a congregation into a ritual almost equivalent to baptism. Luther himself had complained about the Brethren's contempt for scholarship.[10] Here for the first time, Joseph Mueller remarks, Flacius sees the nature of the Brethren as a free church as opposed to a folk church[11]: "their account of religion and form of churches and ceremonies will not be sufficiently suitable for encompassing large cities and whole peoples."[12]

When Pastor Bodenstein complained that the liturgical uses of the Brethren were going to be forced on the Lutheran congregations in Prussia,[13] Flacius addressed himself to the Seniors of the Unitas Fratrum in Prague. "Your churches," he wrote to the Bohemian Brethren, "were especially seven thousand men, who these four hundred years since they began, never bowed their knees to the Antichrist."[14] Even Aeneas Sylvius (Pope Pius II) found no fault with the Waldensians; he urged them to be true to the faith of their forefathers.[15]

Flacius had touched a sensitive nerve. The Seniors, who received the letter on January 7, 1556, were proudly convinced of their independent origin. In the name of the Seniors, Jan Czerny wrote back that they would have been happy to comply with Flacius' request for documentary evidence had the archives in Leitomischel not been burned and the archivist, Johann Augusta, not been imprisoned. On the origin of the church, Czerny wrote that the founders of the Brethren were Bohemians, pupils of Jan Rokycana (1397–1471), the Archbishop of Prague and spiritual leader of the Hussite Utraquists (a name derived from the slogan about the sacrament, "sub utraque specie"). They had already had conversations with the Waldensians in Italy. They rejected the names, "Waldensians" and "Picards" and said that there were no Waldensians in Bohemia.[16] A recent author comments:

> The statements of Flacius about the relationships between Bohemian Waldensians in Lombardy already in the first half of the fourteenth century have proved at least partly false. The source for his statements about the gathering of collections for the Lombard Waldensians was not the Acts of an Inquisition in Bohemia and Poland about 1330, but an Inquisition Handbook from Prague from the first half of the fourteenth century. Taken into this Handbook was the composite work of the Passauer Anonymous, a question-scheme, that mentioned the collection gathering.[17]

8 Cod. Guelf. 311 Helmst. lv–42 v; Alexander Patchovsky. *Der Passauer Anonymus. Ein Sammelwerk über Ketzer, Juden, Antichrist aus der Mitte des 13. Jahrhundert.* Stuttgart: Hiersemann, 1968. 3 f., 7 ff.

9 Cf. Margaret Nickson. "The 'Pseudo-Reinerus' Treatise. The Final Stage of a Thirteenth Century Work on Heresy from the Diocese of Passau." *Archives d'histoire doctrinale et littéraire du Moyen Age* XLII (1967). 255–314.

10 Schaumkell. 42; Gottlieb. 447 f.

11 Joseph T. Mueller. *Geschichte der Böhmischen Brüder* III. Herrnhut: Verlag der Missionsbuchhandlung, 1931. 49.

12 "Eorum ratio religionis formaque Ecclesiarum ac ceremoniarum non satis erit apta ad complectandas magnas civitates et integras gentes." Anton Gindely. *Quellen zur Geschichte der Böhmischen Brüder.* Vienna: Kaiserlich-königliche Hof und Staatsdruckerei, 1859. 275 f.

13 Ibid. 281.

14 Dietrich Kurze. *Quellen zur Ketzergeschichte Brandenburgs und Pommerns.* Berlin and New York: de Gruyter, 1975. 324.

15 Ibid. 275 f.

16 Peter Brock. *The Political and Social Doctrines of the Unity of Czech Brethren in the Fifteenth and Early Sixteenth Centuries.* The Hague: Mouton, 1957. 279.

17 Martin Schneider. *Europäisches Waldensertum im 13. und 14. Jahrhundert.* Berlin and New York: de Gruyter, 1981. 74, citing Alexander Patschovsky. *Die Anfänge einer ständigen Inquisition in Böhmen. Ein Prager Inquisitoren-Handbuch aus der ersten Hälfte des 14. Jahrhunderts.* Berlin and New York: de Gruyter, 1975.

18 Otakar Odložilík. "Two Reformation Leaders of the Unitas Fratrum." *Church History* IX (1940). 253–263.

19 Cf. Hermann Plitt. "Über die Lehrweise der böhmischen Brüder in Betreff der Rechtfertigung durch den Glauben und der Werke des Glaubens." *Theologische Studien und Kritiken* XLI (1868). 581 ff.

At the same time, the pressure of the Inquisition made them amenable to closer relations with Protestant Germany, and they promised to send the same Jan Blahoslav with whom Nidbruck had spoken, one of the four Seniors and official archivist, to Magdeburg, who would give a complete report. Blahoslav was the right man for the mission, since unlike the Hussite writer, Peter Chelčický (1390–1460), he had pressed for participation in higher education and wider affairs.[18] With one or two companions, Blahoslav arrived on the Thursday after Pentecost, May 28, 1556. He presented Flacius with some doctrinal publications and a letter from Czerny, which again made the point that the Bohemian Brethren had not developed out of the Waldensians; one could just as well argue that the origin of Luther's movement was with the Brethren! He also gave Flacius some official publications of the Unity's teachings. Flacius gave his guest some old books on the Waldensians which also had to do with the historical development of the liturgy.

Flacius presented him with a copy of the Catalogus, and showed him the "Missa Illyrica" manuscript, a demonstration, he said, that the mass once lasted so long it could not have been celebrated every day, as the papists were claiming, and that in the Middle Ages both species had been given to the people. He reported that his edition of Huss' works was ready for the press in Nuremberg and promised to send a copy. On the sensitive matter of doctrine, he said that the Bohemian Brethren had a much purer doctrine than either Huss or Rokycana,[19] and that the doctrine of justification was different in the Latin and German texts of Brothers' confession. Flacius pointed out discrepancies in their doctrinal statements. Sometimes they said that sacraments administered by unworthy ministers were invalid; at other times they were valid. Whereas the Latin version of their *Apology* identified justification with regeneration, as the Lutherans did, in the document they had submitted to Duke Albrecht of Prussia, their teaching was double justification, like that in the Interim. He suggested to Blahoslav that the Bohemian seniors make corrections.

Blahoslav said he did not have to stand for this, and pointed out the discrepancy between the doctrine of St. Paul and St. James. The earlier Luther differed from the later Luther. And Lutherans also had doctrinal disagreements. Before they criticized others for disunity, why didn't they unify themselves? Why wasn't there even a spark of love between the Lutheran parties? The answer, according to Flacius, was that the Wittenbergers had departed from the right doctrine. When Flacius pointed out that the Confession criticized the Prussian church and those who agreed with it. Blahoslav said he had not taken part in the preparation of the text. Flacius was not satisfied with their liturgical order and was disturbed by the report of a Lutheran pastor who was required to be re-ordained when he transferred to the Unity.

When Blahoslav expressed interest in the Magdeburg liturgy, it was explained to him that the communicants kneel when they come to communion, and that they themselves took the bread from the paten – a detail of interest for the Bohemians, for whom ritual nuances asserted the rights of the people in the face of priestly prerogatives.

On Friday, when Wigand and Judex joined them, they discussed the Unitas Fratrum, especially in Prussia. Flacius had exact knowledge of the situation of the Brethren in Prussia, probably from Bodenstein.[20] He complained that in Prussia the Brethren had made it difficult for Lutherans to take communion. When they discussed the Brethren's attitude to Osiander, Flacius attempted several times in vain to get Blahoslav to express his own opinion. He did venture that some talk about "imputation", the others about "infusion of God's gifts," but insisted that it was an unneccessary quarrel – merely about terms.[21]

On the following day Blahoslav left the city. They parted politely, Blahoslav reported, "and although not very pleased with each other, we did not show it. The sum of what I have seen is this: the people are relaxed, used to drinking, dancing and singing, but distinguished from others that they do not shoot birds before the Wednesday after Pentecost ... But I also noticed that the Magdeburg clergy thunder against the pope, the Interimists and the Adiaphorists in their sermons more than is usually the case among the Lutherans." Blahoslav, Flacius concluded, was indifferent to theological problems, and more concerned with maintaining the distinctiveness of the Unitas Fratrum. About Flacius, Blahoslav wrote, "He is a zealous and learned man; he means to be upright; but his highmindedness, obstinacy, and determination never to yield, stand in his way. He might compete with Osiander in pride, quarrelsomeness and inaccessibility to argument. While disputing with me he became so angry that his hands trembled."

On the way to Wittenberg, his next stop, Blahoslav noticed that even the people who did not understand the theological controversies, in the taverns in Magdeburg territory passionately took sides with Flacius and around Leipzig and Wittenberg with Melanchthon. He found the same bitter spirit in Wittenberg. If the situation went on, he wrote, it would lead to the defeat of both parties. After leaving Wittenberg after only a day for Leipzig, the party encountered Melanchthon, his son-in-law, Caspar Peucer, and Peter Antonius in Schmidberg. Peucer called Flacius "an unlearned ass," "arrogant" and "deceitful."[22]

Back in Bohemia Blahoslav dug into his archives and published a small volume,[23] the first history of the Moravian church, to disprove Flacius' assumption of a Waldensian background. According to one Moravian historian, since the point was important to Blahoslav, it can be supposed that it was compiled with great care.[24] But according to Peter Brock, Blahoslav deliberately omitted Chelčický's early influence on the movement, overemphasized the part played by Rokycana and the Utraquists at the beginning of the Brethren's history, and "in his efforts to prove Flacius Illyricus wrong ... goes too far when he writes ... 'there were no relationships with the Waldensians.'"[25]

20 Jan Kvačala. "Die Beziehungen der Unität zu Flacius und Laski." JGGPO, XXX (1909). 149.

21 "Ihr fugt ad imputationem motus quosdam spiritus sancti hinzu, quo corda apta redduntur ad credendum, et regenerationem ponitis iustificationis effectum. Die unswere sagen, der eine Teil est imputatio, der andere donorum infusio, id est effici mentem talem ut credere possit, et inde sequuntur bona opera etc. Der Unterschied besteht also fast nur in vocibus, worüber man sich nicht zu streiten braucht." J. Müller. Geschichte. 50.

22 Anton Gindely. Geschichte der Böhmischen Brüder I. Herrnhut: Verlag des Missionsbuchhandlung, 1931. 422 f.

23 Summa quaedam brevissima collecta ex variis scriptis Fratrum, qui falso Waldenses vel Piccardi vocantur, de eorundum Fratrum origine et actis. 1556; Jaroslav Goll. Quellen und Untersuchungen zur Geschichte der Böhmischen Brüder. Prague: J. Otto, 1878–1882. 118.

24 Edmund de Schweinitz. The History of the Church Known as the Unitas Fratrum or the Unity of the Brethren. 2nd. ed. Bethlehem, PA: The Moravian Publishing Concern, 1901. 144.

25 Op. cit. 278 f.

1 *Catalogus.* 1562. 93 f. Scholars call the "Praefatio in librum antiquum in lingua saxonia conscriptum," "preface A," and "Versus de Poeta et Interpret huius codicis" "preface B." *Catalogus.* 1562. 93–94. Cf. Willy Drogman, "Die Praefatio in librum antiquum Lingua Saxonia conscriptum." *Jahrbuch des Vereins für niederdeutsche Sprachforschung* XLVIII–LXX (1943–47). 242–263.

2 Gerhard Meissburger. *Grundlagen zu Verständnis der deutschen Mönchsdichtung im 11. und 12. Jahrundert.* Munich: Wilhelm Fink Verlag, 1970. 52–65, 81–86.

3 J. A. Schmeller. *Heliand oder die altsächsische Evangelien-Harmonie. Erste Lieferung: Text.* Munich, Stuttgart and Tübingen, 1839. The English translation by Mariana Scott. *The Heliand Translated from the Old Saxon.* Chapel Hill: The University of North Carolina Press, 1966, does not include the preface.

4 *Catalogus.* 1562. 93 f.

5 "Zur Heliandfrage." *Zeitschrift für deutsche Philologie* IV (1873). 67.

6 Kurt Hannemann. "Der Humanist Georg Fabricius in Meissen, das Luthermonotessaron in Wittenberg und Leipzig und der Heliandpraefatiokodex aus Naumburg a. d. Saale." *Filologia Germanica* XVII (1974). 8.

7 A. Wagner. "Die Heliand Vorreden." *Zeitschrift für deutsches Altertum* XXV (1881). 173–181.

8 "Omnia omne opus per vitteas distinxit." Cf. Hermann Paul. *Grundriß der Germanischen Philologie* II/1. Straßburg: Karl J. Tuebner, 1893. 203.

9 Ibid. 327.

10 "Die Lösung des Rätsels der Heliandpraefatio." *Forschungen und Fortschritte* XV (1939). 327–329.

11 "Über den Heliand." *Zeitschrift für deutsche Philologie* I (1869). 277.

The inclusion of the Heliand preface makes the Catalogus Testium Veritatis immortal.
– Konrad Burdach

To support the *Catalogus* claim of the catholicity of the Reformation, the reprinting of "A Preface to an Old Book Written in the Saxon Language"[1] was right on target. At the time, Emperor Charles V, author of the *Bloedplakaat*, was responsible for persecution and death by live burial or burning of those who dared read the Bible in the vernacular. In striking contrast, the son of Charlemagne, King Louis the Pious (814–840), as the text explains, not only permitted Bible translation, he *sponsored* it.[2] Scholars now agree that the text is none other than the preface to the first book of German poetry, the *Heliand*, a ninth-century narrative of Jesus' life done into 5,932 lines of alliterative verse. The name applied to it in 1830 by J. A. Schmeller, "Heliand"[3] (in modern German, "Heiland"), means "savior."

Clearly, Charles' savage persecutions of Bible-readers were a novelty. "Seven hundred years ago," Flacius wrote, appealing to tradition, "it was not considered a sin, but rather the highest piety, to translate the Holy Scripture ... into the vernacular."[4] According to J. W. Schulte in 1873, the preface was much too satisfactory. It fit too perfectly into Flacius' program, and therefore it must be a forgery.[5] A forgery? The dark suspicion was one of the elements that made it "the most controversial preface in world literature."[6]

The more intense the research, however, the more medieval it appeared.[7] Schulte's thesis was finally refuted when it was noticed that the text explains that it was divided *per vitteas* (episodes).[8] Given the state of philology at the time, Flacius could not possibly have known the word, *vittea* (German: *fitten* or Old English, *fitt*). It could not, therefore, have been a forgery. Once again, Flacius had offered persuasive evidence for the Lutheran claim to catholic tradition. Although "the Preface does serve the Lutheran *Tendenz*," wrote Kurt Hannemann, "the Heliand preface was "no Protestant invention."[9]

Hannemann offered further proof that Flacius did not write the preface himself in his doctoral dissertation. The dissertation was lost during the second World War, but he reconstructed it in a 1939 essay, "The Solution of the Riddle of the Heliand Preface."[10] Unfortunately, Flacius had neglected to specify from which manuscript he had copied the text. "It would be very difficult," M. Heyne had observed, "to detect Flacius' sources."[11] Hannemann overcame the difficulty, however, when he determined to "look over the wall" at a different discipline. His proof was in a letter from George Fabricius, rector of St. Afra's school in Meissen, to his brother, already in print for a half century:

I am sending you a preface from an old German book from which you can tell that the best and the truly German emperors of Germany did not prohibit the Holy Scripture to the common man, as ours does by means of the Belgian Mandates, and as the whole papacy practices. You may share it with those in Jena who are preparing their history. D. Illyricus owns the geneaology of the emperor Lothar the Saxon. If you could get hold of it for me you would be doing me a great favor."[12]

Convinced, with Konrad Burdach, that the *Heliandpraefatio* makes the *Catalogus Testium Veritatis* "immortal,"[13] Hannemann praises Flacius' the "preface action" – finding and publishing the text – as a miracle. He had rescued an irreplaceable text from oblivion at the last possible moment. The *Catalog* also has the distinction of publishing the first German version of the preface, in the 1573 translation by Conrad Lautenbach.[14] "If Flacius had done nothing more than save the *Heliand* preface," Hannemann wrote, "he would, as an immigrant, have done enough for German studies."[15]

Having demonstrated that there really had been a manuscript behind the text printed in the *Catalogus*, Hannemann attempted to solve other related questions, and concluded that the manuscript from Luther's library that Melanchthon called "monotessaron," was a manuscript Flacius borrowed from Melanchthon and did not return.[16] Discussing the loan, Clemen, who offers no proof he did not return it, simply accepts the (false) legend of the "culter Flacianus."[17] But Hannemann's identification of that particular manuscript as the source of the *Heliand* preface, according to Kurt Beckey, was "all too daring."[18] Hardly any of the major problems surrounding the *Heliand*, as a matter of fact, have been solved;[19] *Heliand* research is in a "desperate situation."[20]

The thousand-plus books and articles on the work,[21] however, do yield up one piece of useful information for Flacius biography. From all those books and articles emerges evidence to refute another charge: Flacius was not a forger.

12 Herman Peter (ed.). *Jahresbericht der Fürsten- und Landesschule St. Afra in Meissen.* 1892.

13 "Einführende Worte nebst einer Abhandlung über die Nationale Aneignung der Bibel und die Anfänge der Germanischen Philologie." *Festschrift Eugen Mogk.* Halle: Max Niemeyer, 1924. 267.

14 Friedrich Wilhelm. "Eine deutsche Übersetzung der Praefatio." *Münchner Museum für Philologie des Mittelalters und der Renaissance* I (1911/12). 362–365.

15 "Humanist." 8.

16 According to Otto Clemen. "Eine Heilandhandschrift in Luthers Besitz." *Zentralblatt für Bibliothekswesen* XXXVI (1919). 257.

17 Olson. "Bucherdieb."

18 Hans Vollmer. *Bibel und deutsche Kultur* X. Potsdam: Athenaion, 1940. 471 f.

19 Ludwig Erich Schmidt. *Kurzer Grundriß der germanischen Philologie bis 1500.* Vol. 2: *Literaturgeschichte.* Berlin: De Gruyter, 1971. 248.

20 Heinz Rupp. "Forschungen zur althochdeutschen Literatur 1945–1962." *Deutsche Vierteljahrsschrift für Geistesgeschichte* XXXVII (1964). 39.

21 Johanna Belkin and Jürgen Meyer. *Bibliographie zu Otfried von Weissenburg und zur altsächsischen Bibeldichtung (Heliand und Genesis).* Berlin: Erich Schmidt, 1975.

1 Frano Cale. *Dante i Slavenski Svijet/ Dante e il Mondo Slavo*. Zagreb: Jugoslavenska Akademija Znanosti, Umjetnosti, 1984. 40. Marcella Roddewig. "Mattia Flacio Illyrico: Fortuna d'un Interprete Dantesco Nei Poesi del Nord." Ibid. 553. Cf. 492.

2 *Catalogus*, 1556. 868, 1562. 505.

3 Dante. *Monarchy and Three Political Letters. With an Introduction by Donald Nicholl*. New York: The Noonday Press, 1954. 91.

4 *Catalogus*, 1556. 838, 1562. 490; *Inferno* XIX. 115–117; *De Monarchia* III. X, 10–12.

5 Questus est ante annos amplius 150. Dantes Florentinus in suo quodam Italico poemata, Evangelium Christi in templis taceri, & tantum fabulas, ac meras nugas, Syculis gerris vaniores, Ecclesiae Dei proponi, regemque Christi vento pasci. Negat tam multas esse Florentiae fabulas, lacerosque panniculos, quam multae vanissimae fabulae in suggestus annuatim a Monachis effuntiatur. *Regulae et Tractatus*. A ij r – A ij v.

6 Es hat zwar billich der Dantes sich in seinen italienischen reimen vor 200. jaren beklagt, das nicht so viel kleiner zurissenen leplein und nestel zu Florentz verhanden weren. Als viel fabeln des jars auff der Cantzel an stat Göttlichs worts von München dem volck fürgesagt worden, und das sie also ihre arme und ihres unglücks unverstendige aber doch darumb unentschuldigten scheflein widder heim bringen, mit wird geweidet. *Eine köstliche Osterpredigt, zu Andtorff vor kurtzer zeit von einem Münch gehalten, das mann den Ketzern nicht leichtlich gleuben soll*. [Magdeburg: Christian Rödinger, 1550]. A ij r.

7 Op. cit. 91

8 Roddewig. "Flacius, Vergerius ..." 114.

[Dante] showed that the pope was not superior to the Emperor, nor had he any rights in the Empire... – Flacius

Credit for first mention of Dante Alighieri in Germany has been given to Flacius for the Dante Entry in the 1556 *Catalogus*.[1]

Dante of Florence flourished 250 years ago. He was a pious and learned man, as many writers and above all his own writings testify. He wrote a book, which he called the Monarchy. In it he showed that the Pope was not superior to the Emperor, nor had he any rights in the Empire, wherefore he is condemned by some as a heretic. He also wrote not a little in the Italian tongue, in which he censured many things in the Pope and his religion.[2]

Dante qualified as witness because he wanted to reduce the popes' political power, arguing that papal interference in the political realm was the root of evil. Flacius had this passage in mind:

Thus we have quite adequately shown by the congruity that their arguments involve that the authority of the Empire in no way depends upon the church.[3]

He goes on to name Dante as the first to recognize the Donation of Constantine as an eighth-century forgery. It was based on a fifth-century legend that after Pope Sylvester cured him of leprosy and influenced his conversion to Christianity, the Emperor Constantine handed over all imperial rights and power to the Roman Church.[4]

The record should be corrected: Flacius had already quoted Dante in 1551,[5] and probably earlier, depending on the date of the sermon he published as an example of the foolishness of an Antwerp monk[6] who cites Dante. Flacius' quoting him in the *De Monarchia* is remarkable, since at the time it was unknown in Germany, England, and even in Italy. "... it is very curious," writes Schmitthenner, "that in Magdeburg Flacius could quote a passage from the *Monarchia*. At that time this tract had not yet been printed, and in its own fatherland it was completely forgotten. It was Flacius who from its obscurity first brought it to light."[7] He passed over material in the Inferno more damaging to the papacy,[8] and chose themes which fitted into the scheme of the *Catalogus*, for example, the complaint of Fulco of Marseilles about subordinating scriptures to the decretals.[9]

Adolf Schmitthenner thinks Flacius learned about the manuscript of the *Monarchia* by reading Vergerio's publication of the Index of Prohibited Books. But from his printed correspondence with Nidbruck, we know he had been trying to find the manuscript since 1552, that three or four men in Italy promised to send him the manuscript, and that he was waiting for it impatiently.[10] Oporinus had the manuscript by 1554, and the first edition appeared in 1559 as part of a collection, together with texts by Andreas Alciati, Aneas Sylvius and Jordanus of Osnabrück.[11] Flacius, who, as we have seen, often had reasons to omit his name from publications, may even

The facsimile reads:

§63

femina sanioris doctrinæ à Vualdensibus. Habue-
runt amplius quàm per 40 annos, multos sectatores,
præcipuè in Cisalpina Gallia, & proximis alpibus.
Tandem uerò à Papa non tantùm isti duo doctores,
sed & ingens auditorum numerus, crudeliter inter-
fecti sunt. Tribuuntur eis præterea quædam incom-
modæ sententiæ, quin & promiscuæ libidines: quæ,
ut suspicor, magna ex parte mendaciter à papisticis
eis adscribuntur, sicut & Vualdensibus promiscuæ
libidines falsissimè Papistæ tribuunt.

Dantes.

DAntes Florentinus floruit ante annos 250. fuit
uir pius & doctus, ut multi scriptores, &
præsertim ipsius scripta testantur. Scripsit librum,
quem appellauit Monarchiam. In eo probauit, Pa-
pam nõ esse supra Imperatorem, nec habere aliquod
ius in Imperium, ob eamq́; rem à quibusdam hære-
seos est damnatus. Scripsit & uulgari Italico sermo-
ne non pauca, in quibus multa reprehendit in Papa,
eiusq́; religione. Quæritur alicubi prolixè, intermis-
sam esse uerbi Dei prædicationem, & pro ea prædi-
cari à monachis uanissimas fabulas, eorumq́; nu agis si-
dem haberi: atque ita oues Christi non uero pabulo
Euangelij, sed uento pasci. Dicit alibi, Papam ex pa-
store factum lupum, uastare Ecclesiam, non curare
una cum suis spiritualibus uerbum Dei, sed tantùm
sua decreta. Alicubi in Conuiuio ama-
torio, æquat coniugium cœ-
libatui.

Tau-

The Dante entry in the 1556 *Catalogues.*

have served as editor; Michael Caesar thinks it possible.[12] G. A. Scartazzini is convinced that, in any case, Flacius was behind its publication:
"there is no doubt that the spirit of Flacius gave the impulse" to the publication.[13] Schmitthenner agrees.

One can suspect that the actual editor, whether it was Matthias Flacius or Paulus
Vergerius or a third, or the printer Johannes Oporinus attributed it falsely to the fa-

9 It is Fulco of Marseille, not Petrus (as Flacius has it) on the decretals which place the scriptures behind the selfish interests of the clergy. Emil Feuerlein. "Dante unter den 'Wahrheitszeugen.'" *Literarische Beilage des Staatsanzeigers für Württemberg*, 1881. 13.

10 Bibl. 1896 9, 15; Roddewig. "Flacius, Vergerius..." 101; note 3, takes credit for being the first to bring the Flacius-Nidbruck correspondence into the context of Dante scholarship. Cf. her "Matija Vlačić Ilirik i Petar Pavao Vergerije i Recepzije Dantea u Sjevernoj Europi." *Dometi*, 1984. 57–61.

11 *Andree Alciati Jureconsulti clariss. De formula Romani Imperii Libellus. Accesserunt non dissimilis argumenti: Dantis Florentini de Monarchia, libri tres. Rudolphi Carnotensis De Translatione Imperii libellus. Chronica M. Jordanis, Qualiter romanum Imperium translatum sit ad Germanos. Omnia nunc primum in lucem edit.* Basel: Oporinus, 1559. A German translation by Johann Herold appeared in Basel in 1556.

12 Dante. *The Critical Heritage (1314?– 1870).* London: Routledge, 1989. 273.

13 "Non c'e dubbio che lo spirito de Flacius diede l'impulso anche a queste due pubblicazioni." *Dante in Germania* I. Milan and Pisa: G. Heipli, 1883. 11. Early editions of Dante in Germany are listed by Theodor Osterman. *Dante in Deutschland: Bibliographie der Deutschen Dante-Literatur 1416–1027.* Heidelberg: Carl Winter, 1919. 93–96. Cf. A. Burckhardt. 198.

14 Op. cit. 93.

15 *Regulae et tractatus,* A ij v.

16 Scartazzini. I, 29 f.; "Die Behauptung, daß Dante die Ehe dem Coelibat gleichsetzt ist unrichtig. Eine derartige Stelle findet sich nicht im Convivio." Emil Sulger-Gebing, "Dante in der deutschen Literatur bis zum Erscheinen der ersten vollständigen Übersetzung der Divina Commedia (1767/69)." *Zeitschrift für die vergleichende Literaturgeschichte.* N. F. VIII (1895). 234; Hermann Grauert. "Dante in Deutschland." *Historisch-polemische Blätter für das katholische Deutschland* II (1897). 90; Friedrich Wagner. "Dante In Deutschland: Sein staatlich-kirchliches Bild von 1417–1699. *Deutsches Dante-Jahrbuch* XVI (1934). 31.

17 *Catalogus,* 1556. 868; 1562. 509. *Il Convivio,* with commentary by G. Busnelli and G. Vandelli. Florence: Felice Le Monnier, 1964. 355 f.; Dante. *The Banquet.* Tr. Christopher Ryan. Saratoga, PA: Anma Libri, 1989. 196.

18 "Flacius, Vergerius..." 102n.

19 Ibid. 101n; Piero Chiminelli. *La Fortuna di Dante nella Christianita Riformata.* Rome: "Bilychnis," 1921. 65n.

20 "Flacius und Dante." *Zeitschrift für die gesamte Lutherische Theologie und Kirche* XXVIII (1867). 695; Another survey of the theme, Flacius and Dante: Mirko Deanović. "Dante interpretato da Mattia Flacio Illirico [Vlačić]." *Studia Romanica et Anglica Zagrabiensis* XIX–XX (1965). 161–170.

mous law expert on his own, so that there would be an opening for the book in Catholic circles, and to be able to recommend it to jurists. However that may be, there is no doubt about the connection between the edition of the *Monarchia* and the *Catalog of Witnesses to the Truth.*[14]

Since it had already been printed several times in Italy, his use of the *Divine Comedy* is easier to understand:

> In one place [*Paradiso* XXIX, 94–97, 103–107] he complains at length that the preaching of the word of God is discontinued and that instead, monks preach vain fables, which are believed. And so Christ's lambs are fed not with the true substance of the Gospel, but with wind.

> He says in another place [*Paradiso* IX, 132–135] that the pope, once a pastor, has become a wolf, and, together with his clergy, ravages the church, attending not to the word, but only to his decretals.

"Why is it necessary," he mused on the Dante quotations, "to report that Christ's flock is fed with wind? ... Why is it necessary to prove by Dante's testimony or by other signs, that Holy Scripture has been abandoned under the Antichrist, and for it, a thousand other vain ... fables and human traditions are turning in the hands and hearts of men, since there are many men still living (among whom I am one) whom sad experience teaches ... it?"[15]

The *Catalogus* entry on Dante concludes with a reference to the *Convivio*: "In another place, the *Convivio amatorio,* he equates marriage with celibacy." Giovanni Scartazzini, Emil Sulger-Gebing, Hermann Grauert, and Friedrich Wagner were not able to identify the passage.[16] Marcella Roddewig, however, found it in *Convivio* IV, 28, sentence 9: *ma eziando a buona e vera religione si puo tornare in matrimonio stando* ["Even those who are still in the married state can devote themselves to a life that is in the full and true sense, religious ..."].[17] Flacius, she objected, misinterpreted the passage. Dante emphasizes only that marriage is not an excuse for not "turning to religion."

> The fact that Dante speaks here in a restricted way about marriage in old age, probably little bothered the theologians who were concerned about justification. Decisive for him here was the confrontation between a monastic life and one not bound to the rule of any order. That Dante did not think of the "tornare a religione" and "curo religioso" in principle as the opposite to life under a monastic order, must have escaped a man, who, more uncompromising than his Reformation contemporaries, insisted that "in the hour of confession there are no adiaphora."[18]

She claims credit for being the first to identify the passage, but Piero Chiminelli had already done it in *The Fortune of Dante in Reformed Christianity.*[19] Even earlier, in 1867, H. O. Köhler had identified it in his article, "Flacius and Dante."[20]

In the expanded edition of 1562 Flacius – *cosa singolare*! – included the quotations noted above: Dante's complaint that the popes preferred their decretals to scripture, [Canto IX, 133–142], about the papal use of the ban and interdict against enemies and the substitution of money for repentance [Canto XVIII, 127–136] and the complaint of Beatrice that sermons were being transformed into fables [Canto XXIX, 97–126]. These passages are interesting for Dante research, since the first German (partial) translation of the *Paradiso* appeared in the German edition of of the *Catalogus* in 1573 by Conrad Lautenbach. The next one, by August Wilhelm Schlegel, known for translating Shakespeare, was in 1794. The first Dante translation into Dutch was that of M. Boerove in 1633.[21] The *Catalogus* translation of sections from the *Paradiso*, wholly independent of the better-known version by John de Serravale, is to be attributed to Flacius himself. In view of what we know about his untiring work habits, Roddewig's argument that he had no time in Jena to translate 66 lines from his native Italian into Latin is not convincing.

The *Catalogus* Dante entry was copied by John Foxe,[22] by Johannes Wolf,[23] and by Philippe du Plessis Mornay.[24] Themes from Paradiso XXIX, 97–104, and the critique of the sermons of the monks, both of which were emphasized by Flacius, suggest his influence on the first mention of Dante in America by John Clapp in New York in 1679.[25] Recently Donna Mancusi-Ungaro observed that "Dante the poet, spiritual pilgrim and passionate exponent of the potential of faith has *always* upstaged Dante the philosopher and political theorist. His originality in reinterpreting the Roman ideal of government has not been overlooked, but his political role has been relegated to a lesser office just as the so-called 'minor works' have been demoted before the divine poem."[26] Dante the poet, she says – whom Flacius obscured for two centuries – dare not obscure the other Dante.

"Always" is an overstatement. According to Ernst Robert Curtius, Dante's reputation as a classical poet began in the century after the death of Goethe [1832].[27] Prior to that, convinced by the *Catalogus*, continental scholars thought of him as a political writer. Flacius' judgment was echoed by Pierre Bayle, who wrote that the *Divine Comedy* "contains some things, which those that favour the Popes are not pleased with, and which seem to signify that Rome is the Seat of Antichrist."[28] Bayle's opinion was accepted during the Enlightenment. Gotthold Ephraim Lessing, for example, influenced by Bayle, did not include the *Divine Comedy* in his discussions of esthetics.

> Thus, knowledge of Dante's poetry, was not only postponed, but also impeded by the polemic to which Flacius had given the impulse, since now a conscious resistance by the educated had to be overcome. The gifts of the great poet began to be appreciated dispassionately for the first time when the period of polemics was far behind.[29]

21 Roddewig. "Fortuna." 557; Idem. "Flacius, Vergerius..." 100–149.

22 Caesar, 278 f., assumes he took it from the editio princeps of the *Monarchia*.

23 Johannes Wolf. "Lectiones Memorabilies et Reconditae," *Omnia Opera*. Frankfurt am Main: Hered. Henningi Grossi, 1671. 498 ff.

24 Philippe de Mornay. *Mysterium Iniquitatis, seu Historia Papatus*. Salmurii: Porthaeus, 1612. 971–973. Cf. Roddewig. "Fortuna." 558; Idem. "Flacius, Vergerius ..." 132 ff., 138 ff.

25 Roddewig. "Fortuna," p. 557.

26 *Dante and the Empire*. New York et al.: Peter Lang, 1987. 1; Italics added.

27 "Dante as Classic." *European Literature and the Latin Middle Ages*. Princeton: Princeton University Press, 1953. 348.

28 Bayle. II, 594.

29 Schmitthenner. 97; Cf. Grauert. 642.

1 *Documents of the English Reformation.* Gerald Bray (ed.). Minneapolis: Fortress, 1994. 78. Cf. Walter Ullmann. "This Realm of England is an Empire." *Journal of Ecclesiastical History* XXX (1979). 175–203.

2 *The Acts and Monuments of John Foxe.* ed. Josiah Pratt. 4th edition. London, The Religious Prace Society, 1877. vii–viij.

3 *The Ecclesiasticall History of John Foxe*, London: John Daye, 1570. I, 485.

4 *Acts and Monuments*, London: R. B. Seeley and W. Burnside, 1837. VI, 466.

5 "Queen Elizabeth as Astraea." *Journal of the Warburg and Courtauld Institutes* X (1947). 38. Jewel. II, 913.

If most of these witnesses came from Flacius, that made no difference in the effect on English readers. – William Haller

For England, the influence ... of Flacius cannot be too highly estimated. – Marcella Roddewig

It was as if Flacius' *Catalogus* was meant for England. The 1533 Act in Restraint of Appeals (to papal courts) made claim for England to the imperial title.

> Where by divers sundry old authentic histories and chronicles it is manifestly declared and expressed that this realm of England is an empire, and so hath been accepted in the world, governed by one Supreme Head and King having the dignity and royal estate of the imperial crown ...[1]

"Briefly, let Constantinus be never so great," John Foxe wrote to Queen Elizabeth, now become empress, "yet wherein is your noble grace to him inferior?"[2] With the glory of empire came the power to guarantee the good – to be the bulwark against Antichrist. St. Paul had warned long ago that the "mystery of iniquity" was already at work (II Thessalonian-sonians 2.8 f.). Antichrist could be restrained, it had long been said, by the Holy Roman Empire. Tertullian, Augustine, Ambrose, and Chrysostom had said so. In a passage crucial for importing the ancient tradition to the new empire in England, Foxe agreed:

> ... forasmuch as Antichrist cometh not before the destruction of the empire, therefore, such as go about to have the empire exinct are forerunners and messengers in doing so of Antichrist... It is the great honor of the Roman Empire that the Antichrist, the adversary of Christ and his members, will not come unless first the Roman empire is entirely destroyed.[3]

He applied the tradition to the English queen.

> ... at the change whereof Queen Elizabeth was appointed and anointed, for whome the grey-headed father so earnestly prayed in his imprisonment: Through whose true, natural and imperial crowne, the brightness of God's word was set up to confound the dark and false-vizored kingdom of antichrist.[4]

After Foxe, the imperial theme was the central idea of Elizabethan ideology. It was taken up by the likes of William Tyndale, Edward Grindal, James Pilkington, and John Bale. "...it is in its religious use of the imperial theme," according to Frances Yates, "that Elizabethan imperialism is, perhaps, most strongly characterized, for the Royal supremacy over both church and state – the key-stone of the whole Tudor position – owed its sanction to the tradition of the sacred empire."[5]

Translating the religious prerogative from the Roman to the English empire, Foxe was quoting Jordanus of Osnabrück:

It is the great honor of the Roman Empire that the Antichrist, the adversary of Christ and his members, will not come unless first the Roman empire is entirely destroyed. When the Roman Empire has been destroyed, therefore, there will be such tribulation ... as is read in Matthew [24.11] and Mark [13.19].[6]

How, then, did Jordanus jump from thirteenth century Germany to sixteenth century England? Paget Toynbee thought that Foxe found the quotation at the Oporinus press in Basel, where he worked during his Marian exile.[7] The passage does occur in the collection from Oporinus' press famous as the first edition of Dante's *De Monarchia*. But Frances Yates spotted the quotation, *Item nota quod cum Antichristus venturos non sit, nisi prius Imperium destruatur*, in the *Catalogus* (where the name was spelled wrong).[8] "Foxe's reference to 'Jornandus' [sic]," she observed, "does not in itself prove that he had studied the volume in which Dante's work first appeared, for he is simply quoting the quotation from Flacius Illyricus."[9]

Since the outrageous inquisitorial activity of Paul IV among other things, had made Englishmen ready to believe the worst about the papal office, they listened to Bishop John Jewel when he brought up the ancient tradition of the papal Antichrist, quoting the Franciscan Joachim of Fiore ("Antichriste is longe sithence borne in Rome, and yet shal be higher avaunced in the Apostolique See"), Theodore of Niem, Boccacio, Baptista Mantuanus "the Mantuan," Valla, Petrarch ("Rome is the whore of Babylon ... the mother of idolatry") and Dante ("Rome, the whore of Babylon"). Dante had even harsher things to say about the papacy, reports Marcella Roddewig; his quotations show Jewel was quoting from the *Catalogus*.[10] He was "probably using as his guide the Catalog," wrote Yates, "compiled by Flacius Illyricus."[11]

Marjorie Reeves demonstrated that John Foxe copied Flacius' entry on Joachim of Fiore.[12] The comparative study needed probably would reveal even more dependence.[13] For a moment, S. R. Cattley, editor of the *Acts and Monuments*, could argue that Flacius had copied Foxe: "Illyricus was indebted to Foxe, rather than Foxe to Illyricus."[14] But Samuel Maitland, librarian at Lambeth Palace, demonstrated that Foxe had copied Flacius' entry on the Waldensians, giving extensive proof in parallel columns,[15] and in a long series of nineteenth-century pamphlets, he demonstrated Foxe's borrowing from Flacius of entries on Petrarch, Savonarola, Orthuinus Gratius, Arnulphus, Eneas Sylvius, the Letter of Lucifer, and the Letter of St. Ulrich. "Will he deny that he was copying Illyricus?" he asked. "It seems quite impossible."[16]

Just as it had in the formation of the Protestant ideology of England, the *Catalogus* thus played a role in its decline. To attack Foxe's view of Christian history, the high churchmen understood, was a way to attack the Protestant Reformation itself.[17] The most severe attack on Foxe among Maitland's successors was made by Sydney Lee.

It has been conclusively shown that his chapter on the Waldenses is directly translated from the "Catalogus" of Illyricus, although Illyricus is not mentioned by Foxe among the authorities whom he acknowledges to have consulted. Foxe claims to have

6 Alexander von Roes. *De Translatione Imperii und Jordanus von Osnabrück de Prerogativa Romani Imperii*. Herbert Grundmann (ed.). Leipzig: B. G. Tübner, 1930. 15; Georg Waitz (ed.). *Des Jordanus von Osnabrück Buch über den Römischen Reich*. Göttingen: Dieterische Buchhandlung, 1868.

7 *Britain's Tribute to Dante in Literature and Art*. London: Published for the British Academy by H. Milford, Oxford University Press, 1921. Idem. "John Foxe and the 'Editio Princeps' of Dante's Monarchia." *Dante Studies*. Oxford: Clarendon Press, 1921. 109–110.

8 *Catalogus*, 1562. 507.

9 *Theme*. 46; On Foxe's use of Flacius: William Haller. *Foxe's Book of Martyrs and the elect Nation. The Meaning and Relevance of Foxe's Book of Martyrs*. London: Jonathan Cape [1663]. 167, cf. 162.; and James Frederic Mozley. *John Foxe and His Book*. London: SPCK, and New York: Macmillan, 1948. 201 f. Since, as is clear from the last chapter, Flacius would have been involved even if Toynbee were correct, because he was the mover behind the first edition of the *Monarchia*.

10 "Flacius, Vergerius ..." 128.

11 *Theme*. 41; "Elizabeth." 40.

12 Marjorie Reeves. *The Influence of Prophecy in the Later Middle Ages: A Study of Joachimism*. Oxford: Clarendon Press, 1969. 478.

13 John F. McNeill "John Foxe. Historiographer, Disciplinarian, Tolerationist." *Church History* XLIV (1974). 228n.

14 *Acts and Monuments*, 1837.I, 233 ff.

15 *A Review of Fox the Martyrologist's History of the Waldenses*. London: Printed for J. G. and J. Rivington, 1848. 13–21.

16 Ibid. 18.

17 Rosemary O'Day. *The Debate on the English Reformation*. London and New York: Methuen, 1986. 29.

18 Sydney Lee. "John Foxe (1516–
    1587)." *Dictionary of National
    Biography* XX. London: Smith,
    Elder, & Co., 1889. 149.
19 Mozley. 139, 201.
20 Quoted by George Townsend. *The
    Acts and Monuments of John Foxe* I.
    London: Burnside & Seeley, 1853.
    98; note 3. On p. 58. Townsend
    notes that Foxe carried on a Latin
    correspondence with Flacius.
21 *English Literature in the Sixteenth
    Century excluding Drama.* New
    York: Oxford University Press,
    1954. 299.
22 John F. H. New. "The
    Whitgift-Cartwright Controversy."
    ARG, LIX (1964). 203.
23 John Whitgift. *The Works of John
    Whitgift, Bishop of Salisbury.* John
    Ayer (ed.). Cambridge: Parker
    Society, 1851. I, 448.
24 Whitgift. I, 448 f.
25 Op. cit. 162.

consulted "parchment documents" on the subject, whereas he only knew them in the text of Illyricus' book. This indicates a loose notion of literary morality which justifies some of the harshest judgments that have been passed on Foxe.[18]

Why did Foxe not give Flacius his due? In 1940, James Mozley noticed that rather than being embarrassed by Flacius, his attitude toward him was friendly,[19] and he demonstrated it by quoting a letter about attacks on the *Centuries* by Nicholas Harpsfield (*alias* Alan Copus),[20] Omitting Flacius' name was due simply to his casual work habits. He answered Maitland, "as it seems to me," comments C. S. Lewis, "with complete success."[21]

Quotation of Flacius in England is nowhere so clear as in the controversy between John Whitgift and Thomas Cartwright, "the epitome of the Anglican-Puritan struggle within the Church of England."[22] "...you cast a mist before your readers' eyes," Whitgift said to his opponent. Cartwright had been "heaping up out of Illyricus needless proofes." Cartwright explained he had been too busy to do research himself. He had relied on Flacius' book because it was easy to use: his expression was that it had *commodity*. "For, lacking opportunities divers ways, I was contented somewhat to use the collection to my commodity, for the more speedy furtherance in other matters..."[23]

At question was the matter of who selected bishops.

> And that this election continued in the church until within a ccc. years, at what time there was more than Egyptiacal and palpabel darkness over the face of the whole earth, It may appear in a treatise of Flaccus [sic] Illyricus which he calleth an addition unto his book that he intituleth the Catalogue of the Witnesses of the Truth; of whom I confess myself to have been much holpen in this matter of the choice of the church touching the ministers; especially in the Emperors' Edicts which are before cited. For, lacking opportunities divers ways, I was contented somewhat to use the collection to my commodity...

When Cartwright admitted he had quoted Flacius, Whitgift replied, "You do well to confess the help that you had by Illyricus..."

> ... for it could not have been unespied, seeing you have, almost *verbatim*, drawn all the authorities and reasons that you use in this cause out of him.

Then Cartwright turned the tables. Whitgift himself, it developed, had also been quoting Flacius.

> And truly I marvel with what face you can so opprobriously object unto me, "other men's collections" and "lack of reading the ancient writers," when as is evident that your whole book consisteth of other men's notes and collections; and that you yourself have scarce read any one of the authors that you have alleged; eighteen authorities at least you have borrowed of Illyricus in this cause ...[24]

"If most of these witnesses came from Flacius," comments William Haller, "that made no difference in the effect on English readers."[25] With or without attribution, the *Catalogus* was functioning precisely as Flacius had planned; the point was user-friendliness, or, to use Cartwright's old-fashioned word, *commodity*. Explaining his method, Flacius, in fact, used the same word – *commode*.[26] The nineteenth-century charges of plagiarism by S. R. Maitland and others, therefore, are irrelevant: Jewel, Cartwright, Foxe – whoever – were welcome to quote his catalog. "...many very important and useful histories and even complete texts are included here," Flacius wrote, "that cannot be found in printed books, and that cannot otherwise be found except in this book." "I will relate [these things] to gratify those who perhaps do not have the book at hand."[27] Because so many men were gratified, it is clear, in Roddewig's words, that "For England the influence ... of Flacius cannot be too highly estimated."[28]

26 *Catalogus*, 1562. 212c. (182).
27 Ibid. A ij v.
28 "Flacius, Vergerius ..." 132.

The First Comprehensive History of the Church

VERY NATURAL FOOTPRINTS

1 *The Golden Legend of Jacobus de Voragine.* Tr. Granger Ryan and Helmut Ripperger. New York: Arno Press, 1969. vii.

2 *Refutatio invectivae Bruni.* 17.

3 *Les Légendes Hagiographiques.* Brussels: Societé des Bollandistes, 1905. 8, 12.

4 *Les Passions de Martyrs et les genres littéraires.* Brussels: Societé des Bollandistes, 1921. 321.

Christianity means the activation of memory. – Hans Küng

He rendered an especially great service to historians in putting at their door an enormous documentation, arranged systematically, for the polemicists of his party. – Pontien Polman

The deeds of Alexander the Great, of Hannibal, Caesar, Plato and Socrates had long since been registered, the Spanish humanist, Jan Luis Vives, was saying. But no one had written a history of the apostles, martyers, and the heroes of the church. More than a thousand years had passed since the *Historia Ecclesiastica* of Eusebius of Caesarea had appeared in 323 A. D. But the work Vives missed soon appeared. Published from 1559 to 1574, the *Ecclesiastica Historia* of Matthias Flacius, called the "Magdeburg Centuries," became the first comprehensive history of the church in more than a millenium.

One might speculate whether the Reformation would have happened as it did if accurate knowledge of the actual history of the church had been available. What was thought to be church history came largely from legends of the lives of saints, especially from The Golden Legend collection by the Dominican Archbishop of Genoa, Jacobus de Voragine, a popular folk book of the Middle Ages, written between 1263 and 1273. About Voragine, quoting Vives, or possibly Erasmus,[1] Flacius wrote, "O how unworthy this history of saints ... which is called 'Golden Legend.' Why it is called .golden' I do not know, since it was written by a man with a mouth of iron and a heart of lead."[2]

A similar complaint appears in the first *Century* volume. "Many are occupied with describing and praising persons. They commemorate some man, his nature, how holy he was, how wonderful a life he lived, how much he fasted and prayed, which miracles he performed, living and dead; yet none of them expresses doubt whether they accord with truth ..." Modern scholar Hippolyte Deleheye of the Bollandists, whose business it has been by means of modern research methods to examine and correct the lives-of-saints tradition, agrees with Flacius. He admits that the wonderful works attributed to the saints by Voragine are "not consistent with history," but are "imaginary deeds, presented with "artificial passions."[3] "Everything produced in the *genre* is necessarily that of fantasy."[4]

Flacius was dissatisfied not just with the inaccuracy of the biographical legends, but with the centrality of biography itself. His great discovery, writes Heinz Scheible, was that the actions of Christ's church consist primarily in doctrine.[5] The subject of church history should be the church itself, and specifically, the church's teaching. Better than relying on pious imagination was activating memory, to use Hans Küng's phrase.[6] The better way was to quote primary sources, "the very natural footprints," as he called them, "of events."[7] "[Flacius] rendered an especially great service to historians," Polman commented, "in putting at their door an enormous documentation, arranged systematically, for the polemicists of his party."[8] Adapting the Venetian tradition of Aldus Manutius, he assembled a massive collection of primary sources, an *accumulation gigantesque*,"[9] meant "to overwhelm the adversary under the weight of undeniable documentation…"[10] "Thus, with overwhelming force," writes von Wegele, "the critical principle inherent in Protestantism in contrast to Catholicism found expression in its application to history."[11] After the appearance of the *Centuries*, church history could no longer be written in either ecclesiastical camp without documentation.

Leopold von Ranke credited Flacius for laying bare "the cloudy figures, through which the hierarchical power had hidden its origin," "the great ecclesiastical fiction that had been built up in the course of time."[12] By insisting on primary sources, Flacius contributed to overcoming the lives-of-saints tradition. "One may see the influence of a Flacius Illyricus and his source criticism," wrote Zacharias Rivander, "in criticism of impertinent, lazy and idle monks, who patched together fables, by which they falsified good and honest histories…"[13]

This influence also helped change "history-obscuring pamphleteering" (*geschicht-klitterende Pamphletismus*), as Arno Duch observed,[14] and through Flacius' follower, Cyriacus Spangenburg, the fanciful tradition known as the history of dynasties.

> Modern critical *Landesgeschichte* in Thuringia … begins with Spangenburg … The historiography of dynasties in the tenth century began with proficient monks, who legitimated the power of their lord by means of an authentic or imaginary family tree from the royal dynasty. The critical provincial history of a Cyriacus Spangenburg put aside the legitimacy of the Middle Ages, the holiness of blood and their late medieval derivatives, and replaced them with the scholarly legitimacy of source…[15]

Flacius also took on the ciceronian tradition of the humanists as well,[16] specifically the tradition of *artes historicae*, a *genre* which dates back to Suetonius and Jerome. Its practioners, including Flacius' mentors, Egnazio, in *De Exemplis Illustrium Virorum*, and Melanchthon, in the *Carion Chronicle*.[17] produced stories about illustrious men, *viri illustres*, that, just like the lives of the saints, were more inspiring than accurate. (That the eighteenth-century *Bibliotheca Ragusina* treated Flacius himself as a *vir illustris* may strike one as irony.)[18] Flacius, Fumaroli notes, "left the limits of the humanist *artes historiae* to be able to enter the theological, but also the juridical framework of the syllogistic structure … The humanist philosophy intervenes here to establish the text and the discussion of its authenticity … The critical erudition, of which Flacius was one of the fathers, detaches history from rhetoric…"[19]

5 Scheible. "Plan". 137. Harald Zimmermann. *Ecclesia als Objekt der Historiographie*. Vienna: Hermann Böhlaus Nachf. 1960. 62–80.

6 *On Being a Christian*. Garden City, N. Y.: Doubleday, 1976. 121.

7 Schaumkell. 5.

8 "Historien." 62.

9 Ibid. 55

10 Fumaroli. 8.

11 *Geschichte*. 334.

12 Ranke. V, 355.

13 Quoted in Hans Patze and Walter Schlesinger (eds.). *Geschichte Thüringens II: Das Zeitalter des Humanismus und der Reformation*. Cologne: Böhlau Verlag, 1967. 139.

14 Op. cit. 417.

15 Hans Patze. "Landesgeschichtsschreibung in Thüringen." *Jahrbuch für die Geschichte Mittel- und Ostdeutschland* XVI/XVII (1968). 135.

16 Fumaroli. 10.

17 Diener. 83.

18 Seraphimus Cerva. "Matthias Flaccus" [sic]. *Bibliotheca Ragusina* II. Zagreb, 1977. 425–443.

19 Fumaroli. 8.

20 Op. cit. II, 26.
21 Op. cit. 316.
22 Wegele. 333; Wilhelm Wattenbach. *Deutschlands Geschichtsquellen im Mittelalter. Deutsche Kaiserzeit.* Hrsg. Robert Hotzmann. Berlin; E. Ebering, 1938–43. 9.
23 Ibid. 182, 430 f.

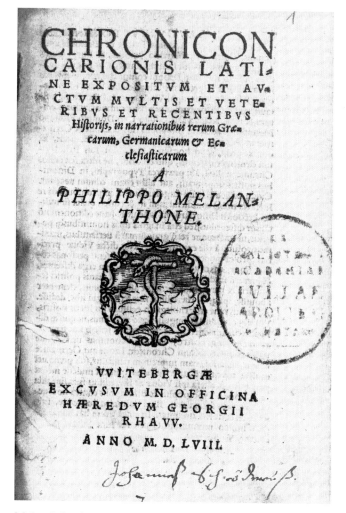

Melanchthon's history still follows the tradition of Cicero.

"Protestant Church history was brought into being by the Interim," wrote Adolph von Harnack, "Flacius being its father."[20] According to Ronald Diener, "... the refutation of the Magdeburg Centuries," was also responsible for modern Roman Catholic church history. To defend their tradition against the attack, Flacius' opponents were forced to use his means – primary sources. Thus, the counter-histories "gave direction, shape, and even content (in the negative sense) to the Catholic histories and history writing of the last third of the seventeenth century."[21] For both Franz Xaver von Wegele and Wilhelm Wattenbach the Centuries were "epoch-making."[22]

Flacius' plan was backed almost immediately by Maximilian, Archduke of Austria, King of Bohemia, the future Emperor Maximilian II (1564–1576). "We are graciously pleased," he wrote to Flacius and his co-workers, "not only by your work and its dedication, but ... would offer assistance and help to organize [it] to its full stride."[23]

But we are ahead of the story. For some time Flacius had been thinking about launching his historical enterprise. In March, 1554, he circulated a *scheda* ("piece of paper"), which can be given credit for outlining *the* Protestant conception of Church History,[24] a "Consultation on Writing an Accurate and Erudite History of the Church."[25]

> Useful it would be that a church history be written, organized to show through a succession of ages how the true church and her religion declined to the worse from a first purity and simplicity that she had in the age of the Apostles, while falsehood and errors were gradually on the increase, in a succession of ages and men. Declined to the worse, that is, partly on account of the malice of impious men; and contrariwise, somehow renewed again and again by some truly pious men.

> The light of the truth used to shine more clearly for a time, and then it would be more or less obscured by the lengthening shadows of impiety for a time, such that finally in these most recent ages, after truth had been so far removed, by the magnificent gift of God true piety is again restored to a healthy condition.

> Indeed, it could be demonstrated in this history that there were in all ages men who held to and followed the truth of the religion which pious men now embrace, that there were always, I say, seven thousand [I Kings 19.18, Romans 11.3] who hated Antichrist and his abominations and purely embraced Christ and his piety.

> In this work, many other consolations would be proffered for the pious: then indeed, they would meet all that but single argument of the papists who always keep crying out that the true church of Christ never defected, but has always remained in all ages, but that our church is new, born recently, in the last thirty years, was always its own thing: therefore they, not we, are the true, catholic and eternal church of God.[26]

On November 10, Flacius sent a copy of his proposal to the twenty-seven-year-old Caspar von Nidbruck,[27] in Vienna, counsellor to King Maximilian. Nidbruck, who was about the same age as Maximilian, also served Emperor Charles V, and (soon) Emperor Ferdinand.[28] As a student Nidbruck had heard Flacius' lectures on Aristotle's *Politics*,[29] and had amassed a personal collection that Pope Pius IV denounced as "a Lutheran library."[30] Mail service was slow in those days, and the letter sent November 10th arrived on February 28. Nidbruck immediately discerned in the proposal a religious obligation, and answered the next day. "I recognize that I owe this to God and to the church that according to my talent I devote my labors to the propagation of truth things, and I pray God ... that he will make me a vessel of mercy and salvation for myself and other faithful."[31] He was able to search for documents in Italy, Gaul, Poland, Spain, even in Turkey.[32]

Flacius could have recruited no more valuable ally than Nidbruck, who had access to the royal library at Vienna, the forerunner of the Austrian National Library. Having studied at Strassbourg, Orleans, Erfurt, Padua, Bologna, besides Wittenberg, he was master of Latin, Greek, French, Italian and Spanish, and the central figure of a humanist circle at the University of Vienna.[33] It was to him that the Swiss humanist, Conrad Gessner dedicated his *Bibliotheca Universalis*, known for opening new possibilities in the history of literature.[34]

24 Polman. *L'Element.* 215.

25 Consultatio de conscribenda accurata historia ecclesiae usque ad nos in qua potissimum doctrinae ac religionis forma, quo tempore ac loco qualis fuerit, diligenter exponetur. Schottenloher, *Ottheinrich.* 147–157.

26 Diener. 6, 527 f.

27 Bibl. 1896. 6–9; On Nidbruck: Josef Stummvoll. *Geschichte der österreichischen Nationalbibliothek I. Die Hofbibliothek (1368–1922).* Vienna: Georg Prachner Verlag, 1968. I, 67–71; Idem. "Die Praefekten der Bibliotheca Palatina Vindobonensis." Die österreichische Nationalbibliothek Festschrift. Vienna: H. Bauer, 1948; ADB, 52, 628 f.; Otto Clemen. "Kaspar von Niedbruck als Büchersammler." *Zentralblatt für Bibliothekswesen* LIX (1942) 168–169; Schulte *Beiträge.* 70–88; Clemen. KS, VI, 524 f.; Schaumkell. 20–58; Against Schaumkell. 41.

28 Bibl. 1896. 2.

29 Heldelin. Aa iij r.

30 Bibl. "Nidbruck und Tanner." 383.

31 Adalbert Horawitz. "Beiträge zu den Sammlungen von Briefen Philipp Melanchthons." *Sitzungsberichte der kaiserlichen Akademie der Wissenschaften. Philosophisch-Historische Klasse* LXXVI (1874). 319–323.

32 Bibl. 1899. 99.

33 Grete Mecenseffy. *Evangelische Lehrer an der Universität Wien.* Graz, Vienna and Cologne: Hermann Böhlaus Nachfolger, 1967. 17.

34 Georg Loesche. "Der Briefwechsel des Mathesius." JGGPO, XI (1890). 32.

35 Review of Bibl. "Nidbruck und Tanner." *Mitteilungen des Instituts für österreichische Geschichtsforschung* XXI (1900). 698–70.

36 A. Burckhardt. 35.

37 R. Döllinger. 228.

38 Lieselotte von Eltz-Hoffman. *Protestantismus im Hause Hapsburg.* Bad Rappenau-Obergimpern: Johannes-Mathesius Verlag, 1978. 25.

39 On the basis of the exchange of letters between Nidbruck with Matthias Collinus, Viktor Bibl. had a "certain impression" that Maximilian had assisted. JGGPO, 1897, 49. Cf. Gottlieb. Theodor Gottlieb. "Zwei Schriften über die Magdeburger Centurien." [leview] *Göttingische Gelehrte Anzeigen* CLXIV (1902) 451, who insisted that Maximilian had been tricked by perfidious courtiers," demanded proof. He "tried in every way to mitigate the major conclusion of Bibl.: that Maximilian had become patron of both the Magdeburg Centuries and of Protestantism on the basis of deep convictions." (Diener. 359 f.), Schaumkell (Op. cit. 9), had said that Maximilian's collections were "förderlich" to the Centuries enterprise. According to Gottlieb (446) Schaumkell should not have quoted Schulte. It was not to be found in the Nidbruck-Tanner correspondence, something which Bibl. (16) admitted. Even if it could be shown that Flacius got books from the royal library, did that prove that Maximilian knew about it? (Gottlieb. 250, 452).

40 Theodor Brieger. "Ein Brief Maximilians II. und Melanchthon." *Theologische Studien und Kritiken* XLVI (1873). 727; Cf. Bibl. "Nidbruck und Tanner." 394; Robert Holtzman. *Kaiser Maximilian II. bis zu seiner Thronbesteigung (1527–1564).* Berlin: C. A. Schwetschke und Sohn, 1903. 206.

41 Maximilian to the Centuriators. Transcription and translation from Diener. 182, 430 f.; Schottenloher. "Handschriftenschätze." 70.

Franz von Krones erred when he wrote that Nidbruck was "anxiously concerned to conceal his own relationship to Flacius from the heir to the throne, since Maximilian II was and remained aloof from the contentious Flacius."[35] During the period in which the Centuries initiative was taken, Maximilian favored Lutheranism, although, as the centuriators were aware, he tended toward Philippism.[36] In 1566 Maximilian warned the Elector Palatine, Friedrich III, against Calvinist doctrine, especially in "the sacrament of the Holy Supper and True Presence of the Body and Blood of Christ ... in which the Calvinist sect departs from the doctrine and holding of both religions, that is, the old religion and that of the Augsburg Confession."[37] At one point, he conceived a plan to flee to Germany, openly to confess his Lutheran faith, enlist the German princes to join a rebellion against his Father, and assist the Reformation to victory in the whole empire.[38]

Maximilian's support for Flacius' project has been questioned from the Roman Catholic side.[39] That he did support the Centuries undertaking, however, is probable from a letter of Melanchthon,[40] and proved conclusively by his own 1553 letter to the centuriators.

> Honorable, learned, especially dear [friends]: We have received your writing of April 14th, 1559 and with it the letter of the first century of the church history, which you dedicated and addressed to our name. We have also profited from it in part – as much as we have had time and will to do up to now. And we have observed it in your Christian, steadfast industriousness, pain, and work, as you showed and proved in the compilation of such a great work. Doubtless the very same [work] will extend the edification of the Holy Gospel and right worship of God, as well as for yourselves, for your honor and esteem.
>
> Thus, we are graciously pleased not only by your work and its dedication, but inasmuch as we, at the leave of divine help, would offer assistance and help to organize [it] to its full stride, to the same and also yourselves together or individually, publicly to offer gracious thanks, we were well inclined and disposed earlier.
>
> Therefore, in connection with your writing, we did not want to withhold our gracious and approving opinion. And accordingly, you know that formerly our honorable, learned, trusted, beloved Caspar von Nidbruck, Doctor of Laws, our Counselor, allowed to go to you from Regensburg on loan to you in 1556 for the above-mentioned work, a number of books out of our library together with an inventory with our gracious permission. So that you would have [them] delivered again with its [their] box and returned – as we have no doubt that you would do so without [our asking]. Issued in Vienna on October 29th, 1559, the eleventh year of our Bohemian reign.[41]

> Considered formally, the Centuries are essentially nothing else but excerpts, systematically arranged source material. – Arno Duch

> For the practical purpose the centuriators pursued, no more suitable form could have been found. – Eduard Feuter

Flacius' organization of his history into units of one hundred years each has been criticized as faulty periodization. François Bauduin called the work a "shapeless mass,"[1] Antonio Possevino, wrote that it was "patched together, without base, without order,"[2] A. G. Dickens thought it "rigid and often meaningless,"[3] Joseph Priestly, "artificial and unnatural,"[4] Franz Xaver von Wegele, "unhistorical,"[5] Jean-François Gilmont, "not authentic history."[6] Walter Nigg[7] and Pontien Polman have expressed similar reservations.[8] An arbitrary period of a hundred years, they would agree, is no periodization at all;[9] proper periodization begins by discerning significant events within the flow of time.

But the human, natural explanation of history presupposed in the histories of their contemporaries in Italy, remarks Eduard Fueter, made no impression on the centuriators. "Mysterious divine interventions are again the *ultima ratio*."[10] Assuming that Flacius was indeed attempting periodization, what scheme might have expressed "Christonomy," his conviction that the impulse that creates history comes from *outside* history "like a gentle rain"?[11] What periodization scheme can express the Christian conviction that the initative in history comes from God?

The reproach misses the mark in any case, since the division into centuries was not intended as periodization, but simply as a means by which to render a massive collection of source material easily usable, for refuting the charge that the Reformation was new, and for demonstrating its catholicity. "Considered formally," Arno Duch discerned, "the Centuries are essentially nothing else but excerpts, systematically arranged source material."[12]

One could have adopted a chronological order. But that would have resulted in a jumble – "imperial diets and wars next to failed harvests and cases of misfortune."[13] It was Nidbruck who suggested, instead, a topical order (by commonplaces, *loci communes*), the arrangement Melanchthon had adopted for his systematic theology, but which he considered wrong for historical writing.[14] "The whole historical work," Nidbruck wrote, "should be arranged according to certain commonplaces, so that one thing is not confused with another."[15] The key, to use a modern term, was user-friendliness. "The individual materials will stand out better," Nidbruck continued, "if they are distributed according to their own logical position than if they were to be all mixed up in chronological order. Certainly it is a much happier and more useful arrangement for the reader, if

1 "Magnam video rerum molem atque silvam. Veror ne informis materia sit." Michael Erbe. *François Bauduin (1520–1573). Biographie eines Humanisten.* Gütersloh: Gütersloher Verlagshaus Gerd Mohn, 1978. 115.

2 *Bibliotheca selecta.* Cologne, 1607. Book XVI, Section IV, Chapter 8, p. 351.

3 A. G. Dickens and John Tonkin. *The Reformation in Historical Thought.* Cambridge, Mass.: Harvard University Press, 1985. 29.

4 George Huntston Williams. "Joseph Priestly on Luther." Jaroslav Pelikan (ed.). *Interpreters of Luther. Essays in Honor of Wilhelm Pauck.* Philadelphia: Fortress, 1968. 127.

5 Op. cit. 333.

6 "Flacius Illyricus." 325.

7 *Die Kirchengeschichtschreibung. Grundzüge ihrer historischen Entwicklung.* Munich: Beck, 1934. 56 f.

8 "Historien." 55.

9 Karl Heussi. "Centuriae." *Harnack-Ehrung. Beiträge zur Kirchengeschichte ihrem Lehrer Adolf von Harnack zu seinem 70. Geburtstag (7. Mai 1921), dargebracht von einer Reihe seiner Schüler.* Leipzig: J.C.Hinrichs,1921. 328 ff.; Idem, *Altertum, Mittelalter und Neuzeit in der Kirchengeschichte: Ein Beitrag zum Problem der historischen Periodisierung.* Tübingen: J. C. Hinrichs, 1921. 13.

10 Feuter. 252.

11 Simon Verheus. *Zeugnis und Gericht: Kirchengeschichtliche Betrachtungen bei Sebastian Franck und Matthias Flacius.* Nieuwkoop: B. de Graaf, 1971. 68.

12 Op. cit. 418.

13 Scheible. "Plan." 23.

14 Fraenkel. Review of Scheible. In his review of the same book, Wilhelm Neuser came to the same conclusion. *Theologische Literaturzeitung* XCIII (1968). 126.

15 "Consilium meum extemporate. Inscribenda historia Ecclesiastica." Cod. vind. pal. 9737k, transcribed by Diener. 567.

16 Bibl. 1896. 14 f. Translation, Diener. 46.

17 Op. cit. 417.

18 Schaumkell. 37.

19 *The City of God.* New York: Modern Library, 1950. 610 f.

20 Johann Andreas Schmidt (ed.). *Introductio Sagittarianae [Caspar Sagittarius] in Historiam Ecclesiasticam.* Jena: Io. Felix Bielck, 1718. II. 137–151; Erbe. 262–269. cf. 114 f.; Daniel Gerdes. *Scrinium Antiquarium sive Miscellanea Groenigensis Nova* VI, Pars. I. 1760. 560–573.

21 Scheible. "Plan." 7, 8l; Schaumkell. 40; Heinrich Berger. *Calvin's Geschichtsauffassung.* Zürich: Zwingli-Verlag, 1955. 15; Nigg. 544; Bibl. "Melanchthon und Nidbruck." 45–47.

22 Rudolf Schwarz. *Johannes Calvins Lebenswerk in seinen Briefen* II. Tübingen: J. C. B. Mohr (Paul Siebeck) 1909. 164f.

23 Diener. 415 f. Guilielmus Julius Mangold (ed.). *Andreas Hyperii. De Methodo in Conscribenda Historia Ecclesiastica Consilium.* Marburg: Elwert, 1866. Also printed in Gerdes. Tom V, Part I. 560–573.

24 Discussed in Scheible. *Enstehung.* 19–28, 43 ff.

25 "Cupio enim eam inde a Christi resurrectione inchoari." Bibl. 1896. 7; Böhl. 17; Cf. Harald Zimmermann. "Über das Anfangsdatum der Kirchengeschichte." *Archiv für Kulturgeschichte* XLI (1959). 12 f.

he could in individual places put his hands on the materials of a certain type brought together in some spot, as it were, in a heap."[16] The arrangement according to commonplaces was a good solution. "For the practical purpose," in the judgment of the historiographer Eduard Feuter, "the centuriators pursued, no more suitable form could have been found."

In a planning meeting, Gottschalk Praetorius read a paper based on Melanchthon's *Elementa Rhetorica*, and argued against organization around commonplaces. It would interrupt the historical sequence, he thought; the history should, instead, be organized according to the rules of Cicero and Quintillian. At first, Flacius did consider producing a conventional history. The first part, he thought, should be written like Livy, with a uniform presentation of the church. The second part, then, could be be organized around themes, in the style of Suetonius. But in the end, the theological motives triumphed over historical ones; Nidbruck's "rhetorical-loci-method" led to an organization around sixteen *loci*: characteristics of the period, propagation of the church, persecution, doctrine, heresy, liturgy, polity, schisms, councils, outstanding churchmen, heretics, martyrs, miracles, the Jews, non-Christian religions and changes in the political order. Thus, its organization made it not primarily a history, but "a kind of cornucopia," as it calls itself in the introduction, meant for easy use in polemics. "How paltry is the charge of tendentiousness," Arno Duch observes, "in comparison with the grandiosity of the thought and its execution. In that agitated age there is hardly an important work without a polemical intention."[17]

The deliberations that led to that decision constitute an interesting chapter in the discussion carried on since antiquity *de methodo*, how to organize knowledge. The question could not be avoided; the text had to be divided somehow. Just how long should the historical divisions be? Five hundred years, perhaps? Like Melanchthon, Flacius at first thought of units of about five hundred years. Discretely omitting mention that Flacius was involved, Nidbruck polled the experts: Melanchthon, John Calvin, Conrad Gesner, Simon Schard, and Arnold Arlen.

The replies have been collected by Heinz Scheible in his "Plan of the Magdeburg Centuries." George Tanner (who included a comment deploring Flacius' thanklessness to Melanchthon) recommended the traditional four-monarchy order[18] used by St. Jerome and St. Augustine[19] on the basis of the second chapter of Daniel. There was found King Nebuchadnessar's dream of the statue with a golden head, a silver breast, a bronze midriff, and iron legs, the four-monarchy order (usually taken as the Assyrian, Persian, Grecian, and Roman empires). François Bauduin approved the *loci* arrangement,[20] Calvin and Gesner did not. Calvin pointed out that such an organization was unprecedented; it would necessarily involve repetition.[21] He suggested periods of ten years.[22] Andreas Hyperius thought fifty years would be appropriate.[23]

The decision was to divide the work into periods of 100 years.[24] Since Flacius also chose to begin the Centuries with birth of Christ,[25] each hundred years following is logically a *centuria domini*. The numbering of the years fits so well with the *anni domini* that the combination seems inevitable. A new term was born, making possible the useful (if unscientific) expression, *fin de siècle*, and generally pervading the culture. As Johannes Burkhardt has demonstrated, our notion of, "century," became current about 1800.[26] Before Flacius, "century" meant a hundred of anything. After him it means – exclusively – one hundred years.

26 *Die Entstehung der modernen Jahrhundertrechnung.* Göppingen: A. Kümmerle, 1971.

IMITATING THE BEES

No other church-historical work was to have been initiated and carried through as far as it went, with a clear awareness of the task that church history in general must perform, and in accord with so definite and methodical a plan. – Ferdinand Christian Baur

... so that they imitate, as it were, the organization and honey-making of bees. – Flacius

"Now I have joined these four to myself," Flacius wrote to Nidbruck, discussing the progress of his church history, "all known and completely trustworthy, not so much that they work but that they oversee and mutually discuss everything and know all – what has been given, what has been received – lest with only one person someone be suspected of something."[1] Nowhere in Europe, writes Paul Lehmann, never since the time of the Alexandrians, had there been such teamwork.[2] His team (*collegium, collegiolum, quinquevirate*), was a novum, a fictitious person: he had created a corporation.

One Sunday morning in February 1556, the five young men, all of them associated with the resistance, met to decide on working methods. Diener imagines a jolly dinner at the St. Ulrich parsonage after the church service. At Wittenberg, they were ridiculed as schoolboys. At 34, Flacius was the eldest. Johann Wigand,[3] pastor of SS. Levin and Ulrich, was 34; Deacon Matthias Judex, was 25. The remaining members were the school con-rector, Gottschalk Praetorius and the physician, Martin Cope. The group assembled again at 3.00 p.m., and compiled rules for the newly-hired writer, Basilius Faber, who would supervise volumes I–III. Faber apparently took the place of Hermann Hamelmann, who was unable to appear.[4] It was a good choice; Faber later distinguished himself as the originator of modern lexicography in Latin for Germany. His *Thesaurus Eruditioni Scholastici* is an ancestor of the Latin-English lexicon of Andrews, Lewis and Short.[5]

They met again in a few weeks and agreed on precise, hand-written working rules, which can still be examined at Wolfenbüttel.[6] "No other church-historical work," Ferdinand Christian Baur wrote, "was to have

1 Bibl. 1898. 102.
2 "Geisteswissenschaftliche Gemeinschafts- und Kollektivunternehmungen in der geschichtlichen Entwicklung." *Sitzungsbericht der bayerischen Akade mie der Wissen-schaften, Philologisch-historische Klasse,* 1956. Heft 5, 39 f. Reprinted in *Erforschung des Mittelalters* IV. Stuttgart: Anton Hirschmann, 1961. 380 ff.
3 Diener. 15–17; FS, 1738. 601–620
4 Sillem. I, 17 f.
5 Diener. 229.
6 Cod. Guelf. 11.20 Aug. 2° The rules are explained by Scheible, "Plan."

7 *Ferdinand Christian Baur on the Writing of Church History.* Peter C. Hodgson (ed.). New York: Oxford University Press, 1968. 83.

8 Ritter. 65.

9 Scheible. "Plan." 110.

10 Texts in Diener. 531–567.

11 Ibid. 417.

12 Cod. Guelf. 64.1 Helmst. f. 73.

13 Johann Nepomuk Kelle. *Otfried von Weissenburg Evangelienbuch: Text, Einleitung, Grammatik.* Regensburg: G. J. Manz, 1856–81. XXI. It is identified as the Vienna codex by Paul Piper. *Otfrids Evangelienbuch.* Paderborn: Ferdinand Schoenigh, 1878. I, 44.

14 Sigfrid von der Gönna. "Beatus Rhenanus und Otfrid von Weissenburg." *Zeitschrift für Deutches Altertum und Deutsche Literatur* CVII (1978). 254 ff.

15 Op. cit. 127.

been initiated and carried through as far as it went, with such a clear awareness of the task that church history in general must perform, and in accord with so definite and methodical a plan."[7] Flacius specified that he needed "… rather not one, but three or four people: two to seek out and gather materials from wherever, a third to compose the collected materials in writing, as it were, imitating the organization and honeymaking of bees."[8] The team developed into a happy enterprise; everyone involved felt free to criticize the leadership and each other.[9]

Their most important agreement, described in the *Method*,[10] was to divide their project into three activities – collecting, arranging, and writing. To the Architects was given the task of deciding which authors were to be read, by whom, and in which order. They were expected to have read Eusebius, and to have a text of Nicephoros handy, together with texts of church fathers, councils, and chronicles. Each collector and writer would keep three notebooks, one to record what was not clear or what needed more work; a second for a record of what went into a volume and what belonged to a book already worked on, and a third for suggestions for improvement. They were expected to read the books and manuscripts rapidly to determine whether they contained anything of value, to carry the plan of the whole series in their heads, especially the chapter divisions, and to copy their sources exactly.

The beginnings were difficult, "like rolling a great stone," Flacius thought.[11] If nothing were produced, financial backers would suspect Flacius of dishonesty. He urged Nidbruck to send what he had promised, or, in case he had found a better partner, to let him know so that he would not be working in vain. Nidbruck answered that he had not known how difficult it would be to find sources from the first century. Flacius was relieved in 1553, when his friends in Lindau, Matthias Roth, George Necker and Tobias Rupp, sent a letter of credit.[12] Recruiting personnel was not easy; he hired two writers at his own expense. Finally, on October 31, two fully-packed barrels arrived by ship on the Danube, one marked "A" for Flacius, another marked "B." Manuscripts meant for Flacius were inked either with an "F" or the Greek letter Phi, for Philos, "friend." Opening the first barrels was an event of considerable importance, since (although it has been assumed that it appeared first in 1563),[13] it is likely that the priceless manuscript of the Gospel Harmony of Otfrid of Weissenburg was waiting in the "A" barrel.[14] The governor, Cope, kept books and prepared a quarterly audit. Every Saturday morning the collectors and writers gave a report, and their difficulties were turned over to the inspectors for solution.

Gradually, they were deluged with great masses of material. Were they able to distinguish what was genuine from what was not? "Before making damning judgments about the centuriators' gullibility," Diener cautions, "the modern observer might take into consideration that the centuriators were the first people in modern times to deal with works that were subsequently proved to be spurious, precisely because they were brought into the purview of modern historiography by their presence …"[15] The letter

Jesus wrote to King Abgarus of Edessa that they mentioned in column II of volume I caught the attention of Arno Duch. They noted that the letter was controversial; Duch concluded that they had no criteria for distinguishing authentic documents from forgeries.

> In general, the effort of the Centuries to use good and authentic sources is unmistakable, but they did not have a method for source criticism and could also not discriminate between primary and secondary sources.[16]

As it happens, however, they did have a guide, possibly influenced by François Baduin,[17] and most probably written by Flacius,[18] "On the manner of collecting, rules for judging and exploring whether books, which are often attributed to authors are, in fact, of errors." It cautioned them to be critical of style, subject matter, contents, and to make use of any light thrown on it by other reliable authors or catalogues. So armed, they were suspicious of *Shepherd of Hermas* and the correspondence between St. Paul and Seneca.[19] Their exposé of the notorious forgery, the Pseudo-Isidorian Decretals, an important prop of the papacy,[20] which along with the exposure of the Donation of Constantine by Laurentius Valla, ranks as a masterpiece of detection. The proofs they offered were conclusive. All that remained to be determined was the exact time the forgery was perpetrated.[21]

Word that the centuriators copied their sources as carefully as the *Method* required comes from Ranke.[22] Wegele went further and said that they "prepared a new path for accuracy."[23] Working on the *Monumenta Germaniae Historica*, Ernst Dümmler compared medieval manuscripts of letters of St. Boniface with the centuriators' summaries of them – and found them accurate.[24] Using manuscripts of Hrabanus Maurus and Berno of Reichenau, Arno Duch did the same, and announced that the "excerpts remained reasonably true to the wording of the text itself."[25] Ernst Perels discovered the same in Flacius' own work.[26] Their passing modern tests of reliablility means that investigators who venture to blow the dust off the vast Latin tomes of the Centuries have a chance of recovering the contents of manuscripts otherwise lost forever.[27]

16 Op. cit. 420n.
17 "Baduin's Rules." Cod. Guelf. 11.20, 39a–41a. Scheible. "Plan." 69–90, 79a.
18 Diener. 562–566.
19 Feuter. 251.
20 "De epistolis decretalibus ut vocant. Seu Pontificum." *Ecclesiastica historia ... congesta per aliquot studiosus et pios viros in urbe magdeburgica.* Cent. II. Basel, 1560. Chapter. 7, col. 147, 59 ff. Horst Fuhrmann. *Einfluss und Verbreitung der pseudo-isidorischen Fälschungen* I. Stuttgart: Anton Hiersemann, 1972. 5. Fuhrmann discusses Flacius' theme, the "mysterii iniquitatis fundamenta" from II Thessalonians 2.
21 Ranke. V, 335.
22 Ibid.
23 Op. cit. 332.
24 "Über eine verschollene Fuldische Briefsammlung des neuenten Jahrhunderts." *Forschungen zur Deutschen Geschichte* V (1865). 373.
25 Op. cit. 419.
26 "Ein erhaltener Brief aus der verschollenen Fuldaer Briefsammlung." *Neues Archiv der Gesellschaft für ältere deutsche Geschichtskunde* XXX. 1905. 145–147.
27 Wattenbach. *Geschichtsquellen.* 9.

1 "Nidbruck und Tanner." 383.

2 Bibl. 1899. 86.

3 Stummvoll. 70.

4 Ferdinand Mencik. "Caspar Nydbruck's Verhältnis zu den Calixtern in Böhmen." JGGPO, XVIII (1897). 51. George Loesche. *Luther, Melanchthon und Calvin in Oesterreich.* Tübingen: J. C. B. Mohr (Paul Siebeck), 1909, p. 143: "Illos [the Magdeburgers] iuro quod ad historicum opus attinet, nam studium et diligentiam ipsorum *in hoc instituto* [in the enterprise undertaken] non possum non commendare." Cf. Gottlieb. 447; Schaumkell. 41 f.

5 Gindely. *Geschichte.* 430.

6 Mecenseffy. 17.

7 Christoph Schöttgen. "Das Leben Marcus Wagners eines bekannten Thüringischen Historici und Pfarrer zu Bussleben." Johann Georg Brückner. *Sammlung verschiedener Nachrichten zu einer Beschreibung des Kirchen- und Schulenstaats in Herzogthum Gotha* I. 12. Stück. Gotha: Christian Mevius, 1757. 59 f.; Heinrich Schneider. "Die Bibliotheksreisen des Marcus Wagner." *Zen-tralblatt für Bibliothekswesen* L (1933). 678–682; Schulte. *Beiträge.* 94–148 (an account Gottlieb 48, calls "vortrefflich"); James A. Baxter (ed.). *Copiale Prioratus Santiandree.* London: Oxford University Press, 1930. xx–xxxi; C. P. C. Schönemann. "Umrisse zur Geschichte und Beschreibung der Wolfenbüttler Bibliothek [I]." *Serapeum* IV (1843). 86 f.; Preger. II, 127, 418–21; ABD, 40, 531; RE3, 6, 90.

8 Patze. "Landesgeschichtsschreibung." 132.

9 Loesche. "Briefwechsel." 32.

10 Schottenloher. "Handschriftenschätze." 65.

The historical enterprise was taken up in lordly fashion and with great élan by Caspar von Nidbruck, to whom all doors were open. Viktor Bibl suggests that Nidbruck made the Centuries enterprise his priority over his responsibility to the royal library.[1] When Flacius asked him to pursue Hungarian sources he called on the Bishop of Grosswardein, Matyas Zabardi. He called on Duke Christopher of Württemberg and Elector Otheinrich of the Palatinate to facilitate obtaining manuscripts from Hungary, Italy, Corsica, Transylvania, Poland, Russia, Greece and Turkey. He asked the Venetian ambassador to Vienna for help in Corsica,[2] and the royal ambassador to the Porte, Ghislein von Busbeck, for help in Istanbul.

Nor was it difficult to find allies in Bohemia. Czech professors were required to send manuscripts from the Collegium Caroli III in Prague and from Nymburg.[3] He enlisted Thaddaeus Hajek (Nemikus), Cuthenus the poet, Thomas Mitis, and Melanchthon's former student, Matous Kolin (Matthaeus Collinus). Kolin alerted Nidbruck about libraries, the Hasenburg library in Dubuyne library in Budnye, and libraries in Königgrätz, Klattauer and Ney-Bydzover. He recruited two or three young men weekly to read Latin and Bohemian books and either copy or summarize them. That Nidbruck established an historical institute in Prague, however, is not true. It was based on a misreading of the Latin word, "instititum," "that which has been undertaken."[4]

In 1555, responding to Flacius' urging, Nidbruck asked Kolin to concentrate on finding agendas, breviaries, ritual books, psalters and legends of saints from Huss', time to the present, and especially the writings of John Huss. When Flacius heard that Peter Codicillus was giving up translating Huss, he sent word by Kolin that he should persevere and complained to Jan Blahoslav about the laziness of the Bohemians, who had produced no Huss edition.[5]

Flacius suggested that in Vienna itself Nidbruck could consult Wolfgang Lazius, expert on the *Völkerwanderung* and a member Nidbruck's own humanist circle.[6] For six months, Nidbruck was host to Flacius' student, Marcus Wagner,[7] who discovered there a letter of Gregory of Nazianzus and one of Alcuin. Maximilian was pleased to grant him a title, *antiquitatum inquisitor.*[8] Nidbruck rewarded him with a letter of recommendation and financial support for further travel.[9]

In 1556, while Nidbruck was in Regensburg for the Diet, Marcus Wagner worked at Gallus' house on books that Nidbruck had sent. One does not, of course, borrow costly manuscripts from the King of Bohemia lightly. Nidbruck had to consider the possibility of Flacius' death. Most practical, it was determined, was to ship them to Regensburg, the highest point of navigation on the Danube, where Gallus was Superintendent, and thence overland to Magdeburg.[10] Would the governments of the two cities accept the responsibility?[11] Since the Regensburg council had confidence in Gallus, there was no difficulty there. The Magdeburg council was more reluctant. And so Flacius came up with the novel idea of a corporation – a five-man collegium. Together with him, Johann Wigand, Martin Copus, Mathäus Judex and Gottschalk Praetorius would assume responsibility for the borrowed texts. The first substantial shipment was sent on March 13, 1554. In all, from Vienna, Nidbruck sent 175 manuscripts.[12]

The Centuries enterprise was represented in Italy by several agents. One was the diplomat Humbert Languet, who was dispatched to look for canons, decretals and acts of early Greek synods.[13] He set out July 10 to Milan, armed with a letter of recommendation to Cardinal Jean du Belay. His letter of July 26 is the earliest evidence of the search for a copy of Dante's *De Monarchia*.[14] He returned not with manuscripts, but with books only, purchased in Bologna, Venice, Rome and other cities. Flacius was not pleased.

George Tanner, also one of Flacius' former students,[15] was more productive.[16] He reported a discovery by a papal legate of a sure rule for distinguishing Protestants from Catholics: "Whoever always has Christ in his mouth, are most certainly Lutherans."[17] The saying may have had widespread currency; Flacius once wrote that "Everyone who introduces Christ, Christ, into his sermon is certainly Lutheran, Lutheran, Lutheran."[18]

"Good God," Tanner wrote after seeing the Marciana library in Venice, "what lot of old Greek theologians and historians!" Tanner's researches have been summarized by Karl Schottenloher:

> In Italy especially the legal scholar, book expert Georg Tanner was active for Flacius and Nidbruck. Tanner sought in vain, admittedly, to obtain access to the Marciana library in Venice. Since misappropriation had taken place there, the decision had been made sharply to limit access to the collection. Tanner was permitted only to use the catalog and to borrow manuscripts according to it. His request for a recommendation from King Maximilian for library visits was refused by Nidbruck on discretionary grounds. Thus, Tanner often stood before closed doors.
>
> The librarian of the Dominican monastery Giovanni e Paolo in Venice told him that the books of the cloister were not yet chained, and that it was impossible for him to sit with him for the length of his visit. On the other hand, Tanner was able to enter the library of the S. Antonio de Castello monastery, donated by Cardinal Domenico Grimani, and do thorough research. His further journeys were made to Padua, Florence, and Rome.[19]

Nidbruck recruited the Romanist, François Duaren at Bourges, and the student Simon Schard for investigating French libraries. Schard helped him make contact with Michel de l'Hopital, the first president of the Chambre des Comptes, and later chancellor.[20] He suggested hiring the Netherlands medievalists, Georg Cassander and Cornelius Wouters, but in the end, sent Wilhelm Radensis to Cologne to copy their manuscripts.[21]

He also investigated libraries himself during his diplomatic travels; in hand, Flacius' list of desiderata.

11 The agreement, Ibid. 67–69.
12 Stanislaus Hafner. "Südslawische Rara und Rarissima in der österreichischen Nationalbibliothek." *Festschrift Josef Stummvoll*. Ed. Josef Mayerhöfer and Walter Ritzer. I. Vienna: Brüder Hollinek in Komm. 1970. 165.
13 Bibl. "Nidbruck und Tanner." 43–45.
14 Roddewig. "Flacius, Vergerius..." 125.
15 Scheible's statement, "Plan" 91, that the Magdeburgers did not know Tanner, is innacurate. On Tanner, Schaumkell. 35–39.
16 Bibl. "Nidbruck und Tanner." 379–430.
17 Ibid. 389.
18 *Etliche greiffliche ... Warzeichen.* D iv v.
19 Karl Schottenloher. "Handschriftenforschung und Buchdruck im XV. und XVI. Jahrhundert." *Gutenberg Jahrbuch* (1931). 95 f. "Wir wissen nicht, was alles Tanner geleistet hat." Bibl. "Nidbruck und Tanner." 43. On Tanner's second visit to Venice, Bibl reports that he had "leider nichts erfahren können." Ibid. 47. Gottlieb comments that if Tanner had had good fortune elsewhere, he would have reported it. Op. cit. 450.
20 A. Burckhardt. 53, n.
21 *Illustrium & Clarorum virorum Epistolae Selectiores, Superiore saeclo scriptae vel a Belgia vel ad Belgas in Centurias* II. Ed. Pierre de Bart. Lugduni Batavorum: Ludovicus Elzevirius, 1617. 71–74.

22 A. Burkhardt. 21.

23 Ibid. 31.

24 *Codex epistolaris Carolinus: Oesterreichische Nationalbilbiothek Codex 449.* Einleitung und Beschreibung, Franz Unterkircher. Graz: Akademische Druck- und Verlagsanstalt, 1962. MGH, Epp., III, 469; A. Nürnberger. "Die Bonifatiuslitteratur der Magdeburger Centuriatoren." *Neues Archiv der Gesellschaft fr. ältere deutsche Geschichtskunde* XI (1886). 29–35; Otto Meyer. "Reims und Rom unter Gregory VIII. Ein Vortrag. (Analecta Centuriatoria I)." *Zeitschrift der Savigny-Stiftung für Rechtsgeschichte, Kanonistische Abteilung* XXVIII (1939). 438 f.

25 *Sancti Bonifacii Epistolae, Codex Vindobonensis 751 der österreichischen Nationalbibliothek, Faksimile Ausgabe der Wiener Handschrift der Briefe des heiligen Boniface.* Graz: Akademischer Druck- und Verlagsanstalt, 1971.

26 Bibl. "Nidbruck und Tanner." 394; R. Holtzmann. 206.

27 Diener. 55 ff.

28 *Ein Procession so die Hispanier am Tage Marian Scheidung, welcher ist geweset den 15. Augusti Anno 1554 zu Wien bey den Barfüssern München gehalten haben. Darumb gedruckt das alle Christlich hertzen deste klerer Beestliche Abgötterey in diesen Heidnischen Spektakel merken und dagegen Christliche lere suchen und annemen.* 1554. n. p.

29 Bibl. 1897. 220.

30 Ibid. 51.

31 Ibid. 21 f.

32 Bibl. 1896. 5.

Furthermore, for his task, beside other printed books, those others must be sought out, as much as possible, namely, first, the oldest liturgies ("agendas") that were in use before Gregory [I]; second, inquisitions and trials conducted against pious men before recent ages; third, writings composed by pious men against Antichrist and his abominations of which many may be found here and there in old libraries; fourth, books written by papists against right-thinking men, for also from these something could be gained that pertains to history; fifth, chronicles and annals of individual places must be examined, in which mention of religious conflicts might be made often; finally, old people must be interviewed, whether they remember from somewhere or other that formerly there was a right-thinking or -teaching man either in all religion or in some part of it. Indeed, these authors I want to have, namely: the Inquisitiones of Nicolaus Eymeric, printed; the Monarchia of Dante, Caesarius [von Heisterbach] on heresies; the theological works of Johann von Wesel, Jean de Jandun, Arnoldo de Villanova; finally, all the others that can somehow demonstrate other vestiges of those seven thousand pious men, but especially as many as we can have of other materials about the Waldensians.

In 1552 Nidbruck appeared in Basel, and met with the printers Oporinus and Petri, and asked them to look for texts that Flacius wanted. Manuscripts from Vienna, Augsburg and Magdeburg began to appear from the presses in Basel. The result of his visit was a series of historical publications which can be considered by-products of the Centuries.[22] Eventually, the Centuries enterprise stimulated so much printing activity in Basel that other printers had to be enlisted.[23]

In the spring of 1554, he wrote that he hoped to visit thirty libraries. Later, he reported he had visited one hundred. His most important discoveries were two manuscripts important enough to be have been published in facsimile editions just recently, a collection of letters prepared by the order of Charlemagne himself[24] and another of the letters of St. Boniface.[25]

From the Flacius-Nidbruck correspondence, 1552 to 1557, one may even gather that Nidbruck, also a financial contributor to the enterprise,[26] was the real leader. At one point, indeed, Flacius offered to turn the leadership over to him.[27]

Meanwhile in Vienna, the Counter-Reformation was gaining ground. Flacius registered his dismay about the discouraging circumstances by printing an account of a Franciscan Assumption Day procession in Vienna.[28] At Rome questions were being asked whether Maximilian would be a suitable emperor, and a warning to him against priestly influence appeared in the first volume of the Centuries.

More dangerous for Nidbruck, the main Protestant influence on the imperial heir apparent was his relationship to Flacius. Flacius' publications of manuscript texts, which could be traced to Ulrich Fugger, to the Elector Otto Heinrich, or to even to him, made him nervous. To avoid detection, he would write from nowhere – "Utopia,"[29] and he insisted that letters to him be addressed to "philos" or "amicus." Once, to keep the relationship secret, he asked Kolin to correspond with Flacius directly.[30] Another time, he asked Basel professor Wolfgang Wissenburg to serve as a go-between.[31] Flacius, for his part, cautiously signed his letters to Nidbruck with the names, Theodor Henetus, Andreas Petri, Johannes Hoppius, Petrus Henius, Petrus Hoppius, P. Oppius, Johan Tullius, and – Peter Pan.[32]

But on January 27, 1556, an alarmed Nidbruck wrote without using a pseudonym.

> In sum, dear Herr Illyricus, we are in great danger. God knows that I often wish that with my wife and children I were with you. I am unhappy to be in this wretched suffering. I have no greater enemy than my own flesh. It hinders me a great deal, for it is like a dog that is used to good cooking, and if he is thrown out one door, he goes again in another.
>
> May our dear Lord God do that with me, and grant salvation to these lands, over which God's wrath has finally come. It is as if our Lord God wants to give these lands totally to the devil, because the clergy is turning so violent here, that it seems that they want to introduce the Spanish inquisition with coercion and trickery ... All pious Christians will have to yield, or to confess, or one will have to lie. Here there is a great trouble and distress. May the dear Father in heaven strengthen and comfort us with his rich spirit, for the sake of Jesus Christ, His Son. Amen.[33]

Jesuit Peter Canisius, who seemed to be everywhere – now in Bohemia and Bavaria, now in Austria – arrived that same year. On April 2, 1556, Maximilian reported that he was "under persecution at Vienna," and refused to take part in the Corpus Christi procession.[34] He was soon forced to dismiss Sebastian Pfauser, his Protestant court-preacher. "Deus flectat eum", Tanner reported ominously about the prince, "God is turning him."[35] Then, on September 26, 1557, only a little over thirty years old, Nidbruck died suddenly on a diplomatic mission in the Netherlands. His instructions had been to deal with King Philip II of Spain about the relationship of Metz, Toul and Verdun to the Empire. The death of the vigorous young diplomat raised the dark suspicion of poisoning.[36] With Nidbruck's death, Maximilian's support for the Centuries ended.

The tragic circumstances should have been taken into account in *Buchgeschichte*, for example, by Herman Heimpel, who accuses Flacius of theft of manuscripts, including the fifteenth-century Wolfenbüttel manuscript 32.10 Aug. 2°.

> Who had thrown them out of the nest [Vienna]? Matthias Flacius Illyricus. This one had borrowed them from Regensburg to Magdeburg – and not returned them. Only so did 32.10 with many other books of the library-sinner Flacius finally come to Wolfenbüttel. In Wolfenbüttel one knew that in the religious controversy the persecuted persecuter treated books rudely. The founder of the library, Duke Julius, in the Library Ordinance of 1572 commanded that damage to books should not be allowed "as in several places Illyricus is supposed to have done." 32.10 Aug. fol. lies in Wolfenbütel because a scholar did not return a book, did not observe library rules – and because world history so willed.[37]

As it has been demonstrated elsewhere, the famous accusation that Flacius treated books rudely, was part of a deliberate plan hatched at the court at Dresden to defame him, and has no basis in fact.[38] Heimpel's report that fourteen similar manuscripts had already been dutifully returned to Vienna is a demonstration of Flacius' *bona fides*. In light of Nidbruck's catastrophic death, however – almost certainly a murder – and the inevitable chaos that ensued, one can hardly consider the non-return of a random manuscript a serious "library sin."

33 Cod. Guelf. 20 Noviss. 2° 32r.
34 Heer. *Empire*. 182.
35 A. Burckhardt. 33.
36 Georg Loesche. "Zur Melanchthon's vierter Säkularfeier. Melanthon's [sic] Beziehungen zu Österreich." JGGPO, XVII (1897). 9.
37 "Habent sua fata libelli. Wolfenbüttel Cod. 32.10 Aug. fol." *Wolfenbüttler Beiträge* III (1978). 62 f.
38 Olson. "Bücherdieb."

39 Polman. "Historien." 59.

40 Bibl. 1896. 15.

41 *Ottheinrich.* 47.

42 Paul Lehmann. *Eine Geschichte der Alten Fuggerbibliothek* I. Tübingen: J. C. B. Mohr (Paul Siebeck) 1959. 147. Schottenloher. *Ottheinrich.* 47.

43 *Sulpitii Severi ... historiae.*

44 || Halm. "über die handschriftliche überlieferung der Chronik des Sulpitius Severus." *Sitzungsbericht der königlichen Bayerischen Akademie der Wissenschaft. Philosophisch-historische Classe* II. 1865. 38.

45 Paul Lehmann. *Franciscus Modius als Handschriftenforscher.* Munich: C. H. Beck, 1908. 130. Michael Andrieu. *Les Ordines Romani du Haut Moyen Age I: Les Manuscrits.* Louvain: Spicilegium Sacrum Lovaniense, 1931. 429 f.

46 Konrat Ziegler. "Zur Überlieferungsgeschichte des Firmicus Maternus de Errore." *Rheinisches Museum für Philologie.* N. F. LX (1905), 424. Ziegler's statement that Preger did not know about the Firmicus edition is mistaken. Cf. Preger. II, 560. A list of modern studies on *De Errore* is given by Konrat Ziegler. *Julii Firmici Materni v. c. De Errore Profanarum Religionum.* Munich: Max Hueber, 1953. 37.

After Nidbruck's demise, the main responsibility for the historical work reverted to Flacius. The mid-sixteenth century was favorable for historical research because of the new availability of printed materials. Flacius was able to consult the bibliographies of Trithemius, the printed Annals of Bavaria by John Turmair (Aventine), Sebastian Franck's *Weltchronik*, Mutius' *De Germanorum Prima Origine*, the works of Wolfgang Lazius, Johannes Carion's *Chronik* with its sequels, and the history of Johann Sleidan. Available also were new editions of the Greek Church Fathers by Willibald Pirkheimer, of Tertullian by Beatus Rhenanus, of other patristic works by Erasmus, a history of the bishops of Strassburg by Jakob Wimpfeling, Albert Krantz' history of the Saxon and Slavic bishops, Kaspar Bruschius' history of bishops and monasteries, Petrus Crabbe's acts of church councils (which Luther had used in preparing *On the Councils and the Churches*), and a new edition by Eli Phili (Jean du Tilet) of Charlemagne's *Libri Carolini*, which included the condemnation by the synod of Frankfurt of the adoration of images.[39]

More significant is Flacius' use of original manuscripts. The invention of printing had led to a general devaluation of manuscripts, and Flacius succeeded in preserving many of the most valuable ones. "He rescued much from libraries, comments Bernhard Bischoff, "which would in the meanwhile have been ruined."[40] Karl Schottenloher lists some of the places in Germany in which he found them: Berge near Magdeburg, Heilsbronn, St. Michael's in Hildesheim, Hirtzenhagen, Magdeburg, Melk, St. Egidien, Nuremberg, the Hospital of Holy Spirit, Nuremberg, Pöhlde, Augustinian Cloister, Regensburg, Sittich in Carinthia, Schottenkloster, Vienna.

On April 28, 1555, Flacius visited the Palatine library at Heidelberg where Elector Otto Heinrich had built up an impressive collection from the collections of German monasteries and by purchasing manuscripts in the Orient. Here, too, Flacius is arbitrarily accused of wrongdoing. Schottenloher accuses him of writing his name on the manuscripts he inspected.[41] Since it is known that as a dealer he sold manuscripts to Ulrich Fugger (who, in turn, donated manuscripts to the Heidelberg library) and also to the Elector himself,[42] it is just as probable that he inscribed his name while they still belonged to him.

Among the treasures Flacius found in Hildesheim, October 6, 1554, were the poems of Venantius Fortunatus, a collection of letters by Archbishop Hinkmar of Rheims; and the sole surviving manuscript of the Chronicle of Sulpicius Severus, which he published in 1556.[43] Identified as Flacius' manuscript by Hieronymus de Prato,[44] it is one of several Flacian manuscripts now in the Vatican library, part of the booty from the Thirty Years' War.

In Ansbach, at St. Gomber, he found a copy of the Ordo Romanus. At Frankfurt he visited the Frauenbrüder monastery. At the monastery of St. Michael in Lüneberg, he found a copy of Arnobius' *Adversus Gentes*.[45] It was most probably at Minden, possibly travelling with funds provided by Ulrich Fugger,[46] that he found the manuscript, now lost, of the preface discussed above to the Heliand,[47] the ninth-century liturgical manuscript that bears his name, Missa Illyrica,[48] and possibly the handsome pergament Chronicle of Heinrich of Herford.[49] At Minden he also found the only surviving copy of Roman Senator Firmicius Maternus' *On the Error of Profane Religions*, which is crucial for knowledge of the religions of Mithra, Cybele, Attis, Demeter, Ceres, Adonis, and other vanished cults. The thirty-six page pergament manuscript was probably written in Sicily in the year 347 A. D. For Flacius, Maternus' horrified descriptions of what went on during cult meetings and his appeal to the sons of Constantine, Constantius II (337–361) and Constans (337–350), to take action against them, was an example of "struggling against error." Until Conrad Bursian found the manuscript again in 1855 in the Vatican library,[50] Flacius' first edition,[51] was the only text available and was reproduced, for example, in the twelfth volume of the Patrologia Latina. Since the ink of its tenth century scribe from Monte Amiata Abbey in Tuscany has faded and because the two at-

47 F. Kluge. "Zur Herkunft der Heliand-Praefatio." *Korrespondenzblatt des Vereins für niederdeutsche Sprachforschung* XXXVII (1919/21). 7; Braun. 150.

48 Cod. Guelf. 1151. Helmstedt.

49 Cod. Guelf. 11a Helmst., according to Loris Sturlese of Pisa, who has investigated the manuscript for possible connections to Boccacio.

50 Conrad Bursian. *Iulii Firmici Materni de Errore Profanarum Religionum Libellus.* Leipzig: Breitkopf und Hartel, 1856. III.

51 *Julij Firmici Materni v. c. De Errore Profanarum Religionum ad Constantium et Constantem Augustor. Liber.* Strassburg: Paulus Machaeroporeus for Johannes Oporinus, 1562. The letters, "v. c." stand for "vir clarissimus," the honorific title given to Roman Senators.

Flacius' edition of Maternus' *De Errore* was based on the only surviving manuscript.

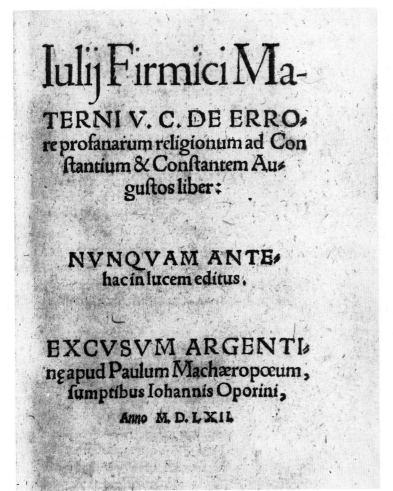

At Reichenau, Flacius made a sensatioal discovery, the Capitulare de Villis, written at the court of Charlemagne in the eighth century. Cod. Guelf. 254 Helmst., fol. 15v, 16r.

tempts since at re-inking make it very difficult to read, the first edition – the text Flacius used – continues to be "of high worth" in establishing the true text.[52]

It was probably at a Franciscan house in Munich that he found a fourteenth-century manuscript with material on the relationship between church and state.[53] At Nienburg, he obtained Helmst. 311.[54] At Regensburg, he visited the Augustinian monastery in June 1554. We have a description by Karl Schottenloher[55] of a monastery visit at Reichenbach.[56] At Reichenau,[57] making use of a catalog from 821 A. D., Flacius was able to obtain the famous *Capitulare de Villis* of Charlemagne, the *Lex Allemannorum* and the Letters of Pope Leo III.[58]

Assistance in finding Polish sources presented itself when Andrezej Frycz Modrzewski (Modrevius) appeared in Magdeburg. He was on a journey to Braunschweig as secretary to Bishop Jan Drohojowski of Kujawy in the entourage of King Sigismund August. The visit can be dated, therefore, in March, 1556, the time of the wedding of Polish Princess Sophie to the Duke of Braunschweig. Modrzewski, who probably knew Flacius from his student years in Wittenberg, reports finding him completely surrounded by books. Flacius invited his guest to speak Polish, and said he would have no difficulty understanding, since his native Croatian was merely a different Slavic dialect.[59] We know that Bishop Drohojowski paid Flacius a visit as well, since it was the subject of intelligence relayed to Aloysio Lippomani, the ruthless nuncio of Pope Paul IV in Poland, and thus part of Drohojowski's downfall.

Lippomani's arrival in Poland had cast the dark shadow of the Counter-Reformation over the land. He imposed a formula written in Louvain which forbade the bishops to introduce reform, and urged the king to use violent means against the Reformation. He thus provoked a denunciation by Modrzewski:

> For I see that you Romans regard this method as being the best way to remove heresy; some of your leaders admit ... they have advised various kings, including our own, to stamp out heresy by the execution of certain persons.[60]

There was much more for Modrzewski to discuss that day. Since Flacius had arranged for its publication, and since it was dedicated to Modrzewski's sovereign, Flacius would certainly have shown him a copy of *Chrzescijanskie Napominanie*[61] by Marcin Krowicki, modelled after Luther's "To the Christian Nobility." Krowicki appealed to the Polish nobility to break with Rome.[62] Since King Sigismund August had given him financial assistance to publish it, they would also have discussed Flacius' edition of the letter of Archbishop Nilus Cabasilas of Thessalonica on papal primacy.[63] They probably also spoke of Biernat of Lublin, whose *Raj Duszny* [Paradise of the Soul], published in Cracow in 1513, is the oldest book printed in Polish still extant. Flacius had included it as a witness in the *Catalogus Testium Veritatis*, now just off the press. That Biernat qualifies as a witness in Flacius' sense was confirmed recently by Czeslaw Milosz in *The History of Polish*

52 Ziegler. "Überlieferungsgeschichte." 424.

53 Hermann Theobald. *Beiträge zur Geschichte Ludwigs der Baiern*. Mannheim: J. Ph. Walter, 1897. 8.

54 Patschovsky. *Anfänge*. 155.

55 "Reichenbacher Handschriften in der Flaciusbibliothek." *Zentralblatt für Bibliothekswesen* XXXIV (1917). 71–82.

56 Maximilian Weigel. "Michael Katzbeck, der letzte Abt des Klosters Reichenbach." *Zeitschrift für bayerische Kirchengeschichte* XVIII (1909). 12.

57 Schottenloher. "Handschriftenschätze." 65–82.

58 *Karls des Großen Capitulare de villis*. (Cod. Guelf. Helmst. 254 der Herzog August Bibliothek.) Hrsg. u. eingl. von Carlrichard Brühl. – Stuttgart: Müller und Schindler 1971.

59 Andreas Fricius Modrevius. *Opera Omnia* III. Panstwowy Instytut Wydawniczy, Academia Scientiarum Polona, 1955. 120.

60 Stanislaw Kot. "Opposition to the Pope by the Polish Bishops, 1557–1560. Thee Unique Polish Reformation Pamphlets." *Oxford Slavonic Papers* IV (1963). 40.

61 [Magdeburg: Michael Lotter, 1554].

62 Stanislaw Kot. "Odnosaji Matije Flacia Ilirika prema reformaciji u Poljskoi." [Relationship of Matthias Flacius Illyricus to the Reformation in Poland]. *Sisicev Zbornik*. Zagreb, 1929. 149 f., 153.

63 *Nili Thessalonicensis libellus*.

64 London: Macmillan, 1969. 49.

65 *Gründliche Verlegung ... Pfeffinger.* D ij v.

66 *Sulpicii Severi Sacrae historiae.* Halm, 37, criticizes the edition; M. Godeau called it "excellent." Niceron, Tom 24, 21; On Flacius as editor. Polman. "Historien." 27–73; Critical edition: Carolus Halm. *Sulpicii Severi Libri Qui Supersunt* I. Vienna: Apud C. Geroldi Filium Bibliopolam Academiae, 1866. 1–105; On the title, "Chronicle," and other editions, Jacob Bernay. *Gesammelte Abhandlungen.* H. Unsere (ed.). Bd. II. Berlin: Verlag von Wilhelm Herzt, 1885. 196–200; August Potthast. *Wegweiser durch die Geschichtswerke des europäischen Mittelalters bis 1500.* 2. Auflage. Bd. II. Berlin: W. Weberg, 1896. 1039.

67 J. Jasnowski. *Nikolaj Czarny Radziwill.* Warsaw, 1939. 372 f.

68 C. K. von Andel. *The Christian Concept of History in the Chronicle of Sulpicius Severus.* Amsterdam: Adolf N. Hakkert, 1976. 137.

69 Kot. "Odnosaji." 153.

70 A. A. van Schelven. "Die Maagdeburgse Centurien als getuigenes van Reformatorische Samenwerking." *Nederlands Archief voor kerkgeschiedenis.* N. S. XXXIX (1952). 5.

71 Agostino Pertusi. "Giovanni Battista Egnacio (Cipelli) e Ludovico Tuberone (Crijeva) tra i primi Storici Occidentali del Populo Turko (vi assunto)." *Venezia e Ungheria nel Rinascimento.* Ed. Vittore Branca. Florence: Leo B. Olschki Editore, 1973. 482.

72 Letter of Drohojowski to Flacius, June 15th, 1556. Theodor Wotschke, "Francesco Stancaro." *Altpreussische Monatschrift* XLVII (1910). 496 ff.

Literature, who observed that "he was following the path taken a little later by Luther."[64]

Nor would Flacius have missed the chance to express his anger about the behavior of Melanchthon and the Wittenberg theologians and the Polish bishops who followed the example of Wittenberg softness at the parliament of Piotrkow (Petricovia) a year earlier, in 1555, and the negative results for the Reformation in Poland. Had they held firm, he was sure, they might have won political equality with Roman Catholics for adherents of the Reformation. Since, invoking the notion of "adiaphora," the Wittenbergers had accepted most of Roman Catholic practice, Flacius reported, the bishops saw no reason to change their religion.[65]

The same year he had published the Chronicle of the presbyter, Sulpicius Severus (360–ca. 420 A. D.),[66] which he had found in Hildesheim and which he published that year and dedicated to Nicolas Radziwill, Woiwoden of Wilna. The introduction to the Chronicle, in which Flacius urges Radziwill to oppose the movement, is the first indication extant of Polish anti-Trinitarianism.

> Since about the middle of the 50's he showed a tendency toward the advancing anti-trinitarian movement in Lithuania and Little Poland. Flacius Illyricus must have known about it already in 1556. In that year he dedicated an edition of the Sacra Historica of Sulpicius Severus to the prince and challenged him to combat the doctrine of the Arians and Servetians."[67]

In a popular style, Severus gives an account of history from the creation to 403 A. D., "with an eye to the imminent coming of the Antichrist and the horrors which would accompany it."[68] Flacius thought that conditions in Poland were deteriorating, like those described by the ancient Aquitainian writer.

The manuscript of the Chronicle, the only one extant, is now also in the Vatican library (Vatican Lat. 825). Appended to the edition, meant to undergird his "Gregorian" thesis about the liturgy, are liturgical texts dating from before Pope Gregory I – the Second Apology of Justin Martyr, sections of the Stromaton of Clement of Alexandria, and from Dionysius the Areopagite, whom, on the authority of Erasmus, he dates from the fourth century. And in a work now lost, also dedicated to Radziwill, Flacius polemicized against Peter of Goniadz.[69]

For Flacius' historical enterprise, the visit was profitable. When the manuscript search came up in the discussion, in the fashion of the dreamers who knew about the secret treasure of Byzantium, Modrzewski waxed eloquent about about fabulous manuscripts in Kiev.[70] Having returned to Poland, Modrzewski enlisted Stanislaus Orzechowski, once a student in Venice,[71] and in Wittenberg. A married priest, he, too, was a victim of Lippomani. Orzechiwski also wrote for assistance in finding manuscripts to Bishop Jakob Uchanski of Chelmza. Bishop Drohojowski undertook a search in Lithuania; his brother, Stanislaus, in Moscow and Bulgaria.[72]

Marcus Wagner, who found it prudent to insist that he was not Flacius' spy,[73] reports that in Flacius' employ he visited all the most important libraries in Denmark, Austria, Bavaria, and the Palatinate. His most successful journey was to Scotland.[74] Since the journey was financed by King Christian III of Denmark, the arrangements for the journey were probably made by the royal chaplain, John McAlpine. Flacius would have known him from Wittenberg and, as a former Dominican prior at Perth and graduate of St. Andrew's, he could have given detailed advice about where to look.

Wagner brought back a distinguished collection – a copy of Pseudo-Turpin, a biography of Charlemagne from Coupar Angus, a collection (Cod. Guelf. 411 Helmstedt) which included a letter of the council of Basel to the Scottish king, a collection of thirteenth-century texts (Cod. Guelf. 1108 Helmstedt) from Cloister Aberbrothik, one of which tells the story of how King Hungus of the Picts brought the relics of St. Andrew the Apostle to Scotland, and another containing letters of Cola di Rienzo.[75] Flacius gave his own titles to the Scottish manuscripts. One from from Aberbrothik (Cod. Guelf. 499 Helmstedt) he called "the Poet Claudian";[76] a fourteenth-century vellum volume (Cod. Guelf. 1029 Helmstedt), he named "A Very Old Sermon on Christ's Resurrection." Since it is to be found among the manuscripts from the Heidelberg in the Vatican library (Pal. lat. 65), he apparently sold another, a twelfth-century psalter written in Irish script, to Ulrich Fugger.[77]

Centuries later, Scotsmen have made their way to Germany to investigate his treasures. Facsimile editions of the manuscripts Wagner rescued from the vermin and the damp have since appeared – The Chronicle of Scotland of John of Fordun,[78] indispensable for Scots history to A. D. 1385; the letters (Copiale) of James Haldenstone, fifteenth century prior of St. Andrews (Helmstedt 411)[79]; and – "a fitting act of Scottish piety" – a facsimile edition of the great musical manuscript (Helmstedt 628) known as "W1."[80]

In 1556 Flacius learned there were copies of Aesop's Fables and satires that would undergird his anti-papal protest in the library at Fulda[81] – with pictures of wolves dressed up like monks, a preaching cuckoo, a fox preaching to geese, a cat with mitre and staff preaching to mice.[82] His first visit to Fulda was probably shortly before 1561,[83] where he copied manuscripts by hand. His copy of the letters of Rhabanus Maurus, enshrined in the *Monumenta Germaniae Historica*,[84] was most likely done there,[85] as was his copy of Nicolaus of Lyra. He brought away with him the capitulary of Charlemagne from 789,[86] a collection of capitularies from before 830 A. D., now lost, but published in 1607 by Johannes Pistorius the Younger in the *Scriptores Rerum Germanicarum*. Flacius had sold it, or given it to, Count Eitel Friedrich I of Hohenzollern-Hechingen.[87]

It may have been on the same visit that he also carried away the important Old High German *Fuldaer Beichte*,[88] from the ninth or tenth century, that he published in 1573, together with the text of Otfrid of Weissenburg.[89]

73 Preger. II, 420–421.

74 Baxter. *Copiale*. xx–xxxi.

75 Konrad Burdach and Paul Piur. *Briefwechsel des Cola di Rienzo*. Bd. II, Zweiter Teil. Berlin: Weidmannsche Buchhandlung, 1928. 292 ff.

76 Ludovicus Jeep. *Quaestiones criticae ad emendationem Claudiani, Panegyricorum Spectantes*. Naumburg: Paetzius, 1869.

77 Baxter. *Copiale*. xxxj f.

78 Cod. Guelf. 538 Helmst. Published as *Johannes de Fordun Chronica Gentis Scotorum*. William Forbes Skene (ed.). 2 vols. Edinburgh: Edmonston and Douglas, 1871–1872.

79 Baxter. *Copiale*. xxii n., Baxter confuses Matthias Flacius Illyricus with Matthias Garbitius Illyricus.

80 Baxter. *Music Book*; Roesner, "Origins," discusses the Scottish background of Helmst. 628.

81 *Catalogus*, 1562. 409; Grimm. *Reinhart Fuchs* CXCII; Karl Christ. *Die Bibliothek des Klosters Fulda im 16. Jahrhundert. Die Handschriften-Verzeichnisse*. Leipzig: Otto Harrassowitz, 1933. 181, 199. cf. 228.

82 Franz Falk. *Beiträge zur Rekonstruktion der alten Bibliotheca fuldensis und Bibliotheca laureshamensis*. Leipzig: Otto Harrassowitz, 1902. 14.

83 Christ. *Fulda*. 181, 199; Paul Lehmann. *Johannes Sichardus und die von ihm benutzten Bibliotheken und Handschriften*. Munich: C. H. Beck, 1911. 99.

84 "Epistolarum Fuldensium Fragmenta, Ex Octava Nona et Decima Centuriis Ecclesiasticae Historiae." MGH. *Epistolarum*. Tomus. V, 517–533.

85 Duch. 419.

86 Cod. Guelf. 496a Helmst.

87 Lehmann. *Mitteilungen*. 6.

88 Theol. 231, University library, Göttingen.

89 Lehmann. *Sichardus*. 100.

90 Dümmler, 372, commenting on Preger, II, 422, cf. p. 442.

91 Schaumkell. 52n.

92 Schönemann. 87n.

93 Ludwig Rockinger. *Die Pflege der Geschichte durch die Wittelsbacher.* Munich: Verlag der Königlischen Akademie, 1880. Beilage XI. 1.

94 *Scriptores Rerum Germanicorum. Veteres iam primum publicati Scriptores* VI. Frankfurt: Clausius Marinus & haeredes Iohannes Aubrii, 1607.

95 *Fuldensium Antiquitatum Libri Quatuor.* Antwerp, 1612. 366.

96 *Historia Fuldensis* I. Frankfurt am Main: Johannes Beniamin & Andreae Henr. Hort, 1729. 66.

97 Nicolaus Serarius (ed.). *Epistolae S. Bonifacii Martyris, Primi Moguntini Archiepiscopi, Germanorum Apostoli: Plurimumque Pontificum, Regum & aliorum, nunc primum e Caesarae Majestatis Viennensi Bibliotheca luce, notisque notae.* Mainz: Michael Demen, 1629. 286. Michael Tangl believed Serarius' charge was false. "Studien zur Neuausgabe der Bonifatius-Briefe. I." Neues Archiv der Gesellschaft für ältere deutsche Geschichtskunde XL. 712 n. 7.

98 *Epistolarum Quas Romani Pontifices ... miserunt ad Principes et Reges Francorum.* Ingolstadt: Andreas Angermanrius, 1613. 6.

99 Franz Unterkircher. *Die datierten Handschriften in Wien ausserhalb der österreichischen Nationalbibliothek bis zum Jahr 1600.* Vienna: Verlag der österreichischen Akademie der Wissenschaften, 1981. xif.

100 Scimus autem, Matthiam Flacium Illyricum eiusque socios in perficienda Octava et Nona centuria ecclesiasticae historiae non solum minore epistolarum collectione usos esse, sed his etiam maioris copiae epistolis, quae in uno codice Vindobonensis (non Carlsruhensi, ut Dümmlero videbatur in Forschungen zur deutchen Geschichte V, 371, n 2.) hodie inveniuntur. Itaque praeter Fuldensem codicem etiam alia subsidia illis praesto

Since he was paid well in those days, there is no need to assume he stole them. Furthermore, as Ernst Dümmler asks about one of them, "who guarantees that the monks considered that manuscript worth owning?"[90] The monks were quite aware of what he took. He reports that he had wrested (*extorsi*) unedited documents from the monks after a great deal of trouble.[91] The word, *extorsi*, of course, all things being equal, would imply an extended argument rather than stealth. Flacius himself comments, "It is said among Philipp's followers that I had made use ... of my knife when I was not able to copy the old manuscripts fast enough. But when and where have they ever seen that? The Roman monasteries have never made that reproach against me."[92]

Flacius' word, however, was interpreted later to undergird the *culter flacianus* legend, "known to all barbers": Flacius wielded a knife, by which he defaced books, when he was not stealing them under his long sleeves. The first time the charge was made that he had damaged books in the Fulda library, as far as has been determined, was in a 1595 letter to Duke Maximilian of Counter-Reformation Bavaria by Marcus Welser, thirty-four years after the first visit: "...I was informed that a goodly treasure of manuscripts are to be found in two age-old cloisters, Fulda and St. Gallen, which at one time had very learned monks. And although Flacius Illyricus to a large extent damaged (*gestimlet*) the library, still that which remains, is worth the effort...[93]

The charge was repeated by Johannes Pistorius[94], by Christopher Brower,[95] and by Johannes Fridericus Shannat.[96] In 1629 Nicolas Serarius did the same: "There was once a third copy [of the letters of St. Boniface] as well in the extraordinary store of books in the library at Fulda. But they were later taken by that most foul flying harpy, Illyricus, and cut and torn."[97] In 1613 the Jesuit, Jakob Gretzer, charged that Flacius had copied the Boniface letters from Onofrio Panvino's *De Votis Pontificum Romanum*.[98] The reverse is true: Panvini copied the letters from the Centuries.[99] Subsequent research[100] has shown that the Boniface letters quoted in the Centuries were copied from the Vienna codex 751,[101] not the one from Fulda,[102] or the collection at Carlsruhe, as Dümmler thought.[103] Nidbruck's letter of November 1, 1554, shows that he obtained the manuscript and sent it to Flacius after September 27, 1555, and that it was returned to Vienna. Serrarius identifies his informant as a Lutheran preacher who had seen a Boniface manuscript at the University of Helmstedt, and who told him about Flacius' putative habit of defacing and stealing books. Who was that Lutheran preacher? According to A. Nürnberger, he was probably Artopäus von Zwoll, a man who had been dismissed from service for the Centuries for carelessness and a disorderly life.[104]

In the decades before the Decrees of Trent, the Fulda Abbots seem to have been relatively indifferent confessionally. In 1573, shortly before Flacius' death, he was received at Fulda in a friendly fashion by the Abbot – an honor not accorded to accused thieves. Flacius' friend, Adolf Hermann Reidesel auf Eysebach, whose estate in Hesse was near the Fulda

Abbey, was able to assist him in borrowing books from the Fulda library, and assumed responsibility for their return.[105]

According to Theodor Gottlieb, the role of established libraries in the preparation of the Centuries has been overestimated.[106] Aldus Manutius' passion for classical texts lived on in the North; Flacius was primarily concerned with manuscripts. Since after Gutenberg's invention of moveable type, manuscripts were generally devalued, the Venetian passion preserved a great many manuscripts which otherwise would have been lost.

WHO WROTE THE CENTURIES?

> Thus, with overwhelming force, the critical spirit in Protestantism in contrast to Catholicism found expression in its application to history. – Franz von Wegele

> The question is not how much of the centuries Flacius wrote, but rather, did he write any of it. – Ronald Diener

Thanks to Flacius' organization, the gigantic history, covering thirteen hundred years, appeared in the relatively short time, from 1559 to 1574, an "application of the Analogy of Faith to history itself."[1] According to Ranke, the Centuries exposed "the great ecclesiastical fiction, which had been built up in the course of time."[2] "Thus, with overwhelming force," writes Franz Xaver von Wegele, "the critical spirit in Protestantism in contrast to Catholicism found expression in its application to history."[3] It was "an encyclopedic handbook of church history and the history of dogma,"[4] "the first work of church history of such quality since Eusebius of Caesarea," "the historical equivalent of Calvin's Institutes," "the foundational work of all modern church history writing,"[5] an "unbelievable and almost impossible" achievement.[6] "Protestant historiography was occasioned by the Interim," wrote Adolf von Harnack, "and Flacius is the Father."[7]

Volume I, comprising the first three centuries, arrived in mid-1559, after Flacius had come to Jena: *The Ecclesiastical History of the perfectly conceived church of Christ, as to situation, propagation, persecutions, periods of peace, and as to doctrine, heresies, ceremonies, government, schisms, councils, important individuals, miracles, martyrdoms, religions other than Christianity, the political position of the Empire, all comprehended in a clear manner according to centuries; compiled with great diligence and honesty from the best historical, patristic and other writers, by a group of studious and devout men at Magdeburg.*[8]

Appropriately to a century in which Europeans were being drawn into closer contact to other cultures, for the first time, the Centuries included notices on other religions. The claim that the series traces the catholic

fuisse liquet. Philippus Jaffé (ed.). *Monumenta Moguntina* [Bibliotheca Rerum Germanicarum III]. Berlin: Weidmann, 1866. 13, n. 5.

101 *Sancti Bonifacii Epistolae*, op. cit.; Michael Tangl. "Die Briefe des heiligen Bonifatius und Lullus." MGH. *Epistolae Selectae* I. xii.

102 Nürnberger. 29–32; Cf. Bibl. 1895. 105.

103 Op. cit. 371.

104 Nürnberger. 36 ff.

105 Cyriacus Spangenburg. *Adelspiegel.* Smalkalden: Michael Schmuck, 1591. 70. This establishes Flacius' connection to Riedesel which Diener, 173, discussing the dedication to him of the tenth Century volume, was not able to determine.

106 Op. cit. 466.

1 Moldaenke. 317.

2 Op. cit. V, 355.

3 Op. cit. 334.

4 Scheible. "Plan." 90

5 Respectively, Schaumkell. 7; Eberhard Gothein. *Reformation und Gegenreformation.* Munich and Leipzig: Duncker and Humblot, 1924. 99. Elert. I, 428.

6 Schönemann. 86.

7 Op. cit. 316.

8 *Ecclesiastica Historia, integram Ecclesiae Christi ideam, quantam ad locum, Propagationem, Persecutionem, Tranquillitatem, Doctrinam, Hereses, Ceremonias, Gubernationem, Schismata, Synodos, Personas, Miracula, Martyria, Religiones extra Ecclesiam, et statum Imperij politicum attinet, secundum singulas Centurias perspicuo ordine complectens; singulari diligenti & fide ex vetustissimis & optimis historicis, patribus, & aliis sciptoribus congesta: Per aliquot sudios & plios viros in urbe Magdeburgica.* Basel: Johannes Operinus, 1562. The letter of transmittal by the printer is in Steinmann. 156 f. The introduction to Volume I in German translation is printed in Peter Meinhold. *Geschichte der Kirchlichen Historiographie* I. Munich: Karl Albert, 1967. 279–295.

9 Diener. p. 359

10 Elert. I, 430.

11 Schaumkell. 48.

12 "Narratio actionem et certami-
    num" in Konrad Schlusselberg,
    Haereti-corum Catalogus. Frankfurt:
    Excusis typis I. Suari, Impensis
    P. Kopfii, 1601. XII, 802–257, 813.
    Diener says Twesten over-
    emphasizes Flacius' part: "Flacius
    was not the author." Op. cit. 19, 22;
    Scheible. *Entstehung.* 13.

13 Scheible. "Plan." 38n., 45.

14 Diener. 399 f.

15 *Syntagma seu Corpus doctrinae
    Christi, ex novo testamento tantum,
    Methodica ratione, singulari fide &
    diligentia congesta.* 2 vols. Basel:
    Johannes Oporinus, 1558. Cf. O.
    Ritschl. I, 1908. 139. Ritschl's com-
    parisons have been reviewed and
    found accurate by Keller, 100; The
    section on the doctrine of the
    church is compared with that of
    Caesare Baronius in Harald Zim-
    mermann. "Ecclesia." 59 ff.

16 Diener. 20.

17 Moldaenke. 316, cf. 319n.

18 Preger. I, 59 f.

19 Heldelin. O iij r, cf. H iv r.

20 *Kirchliche   Überlieferung   und
    Autorität im Flaciuskreis.* Berlin and
    Hamburg: Lutherisches Ver-
    lagshaus, 1964. 87. Cf. Clavis. II,
    37, 676.

21 Op. cit. 32n.

22 "Entstehung." 13.

tradition of the church appears in the introduction, "that this same form of doctrine, which we now have in our churches by the vast favor of God is that same old doctrine..." It was the "perpetual consensus in the doctrine of single articles of faith in all ages." In contrast to Melanchthon's philosophically-influenced *loci*, it was a consciously biblical dogmatics, the beginning of the discipline of the History of Dogma.[9] In it, the scholarly study of the liturgy reached an unprecedented high point. The chapter "On the Place and Propagation of the Church" reminded Werner Elert of Adolf Harnack's *Geschichte der Mission und Ausbreitung des Christentums in den ersten Jahrhunderten.*[10]

When Flacius left Magdeburg for Jena, he was supreme governor, chief captain, *summus gubernator*, the *summus nauclerus*, of the Magdeburg Centuries.[11] But by now the actual work was being carried on by his collaborators – "by the labor of others," he explained, "rather than my own."[12] In the early exchange with Nidbruck he says that he would gather materials and leave the writing to others.[13] His 1552 letter to Hartmann Beyer of Frankfurt makes it clear it was to be a communal project.

> ... this attempt of ours is not a one-man job, but many will have to expend their hard labors to get the job done. And I believe that I am less adapted for this writing task, because I am deficient especially in the requisite historical writing style, and because I cannot carry out so many different tasks, and finally because I am distracted by taking on all kinds of truth-saving causes. Therefore, I believe it is absolutely necessary that the work go on with one master who earns a bit of salary for several years, with just a few colleagues occupied with this job.[14]

Nevertheless, it was widely assumed that Flacius had written the text of the *Centuries* until Otto Ritschl noticed that the two chapters on doctrine from the first volume were almost identical with parts of the *Syntagma* of Matthaeus Judex and Johann Wigand. Flacius, therefore, could not be held responsible for their ideas about the New Testament apocrypha.[15] That raised the question whether Flacius had done any of the writing at all.[16]

In spite of Flacius' name on the title pages of the successive volumes, Günter Moldaenke made no use of the Centuries since he was not sure of their authorship.[17] That Flacius made use of the *Syntagma* is no proof that he was not the author, according to Joachim Massner, who follows Preger's argument based on style.[18] It could be merely a long quotation within a larger text he had written himself. He cited Flacius' practice of extensive quotation. Caspar Heldelin, who knew Flacius personally, probably echoes him when he writes that the first volume expresses "his opinion on all articles and points of our faith."[19] Nor does that mean that he wrote it.

According to Massner, Flacius was at least the co-author of the prefaces,[20] a judgment with which Harald Wagner agrees.[21] Scheible, in contrast, writes that Flacius' name is rightly connected to the Centuries since he planned them, but not because he was the author.[22] He concludes that Flacius was substantially (*massgeblich*) involved with the prefaces. Ronald

Diener, however, citing Wigand's writing that "it will be necessary that you [Flacius] adorn the preface," for a reason "which it is not now necessary to say," argues that Flacius' name on the title pages implied no more than simple courtesy. "Any use of the Magdeburg Centuries," he writes, to construct or reconstruct a Flacian theology or a Flacian politics, is, by definition, mistaken – even down to the introductions and dedications."[23]

Whatever the decision is about the prefaces, it is clear that Flacius cannot be assumed to be the author of the text of the Centuries themselves. Its appearance in *Century* IX,[24] does not prove, for example – as A. G. Dickens and John Tonkin seem to imply,[25] and Valerie R. Hotchkiss[26] states – that Flacius was responsible for the inclusion of the legend of a Pope Joan;[27] Christiana Frank, noting that it is not to be found in the *Catalogus*, has shown that Flacius did not credit the legend of a female pope.[28]

Accusations based on differences between the *Centuries* and his arguments elsewhere, that Flacius was inconsistent, it follows, are without worth – beginning with Robert Bellarmine's list of *Contradictiones Illyrici*.[29] Many writers have made that mistake – about Meister Heinrich the Poet, the "Letter of St. Ulrich," the Old Saxon Heliand, the coronation of Charlemagne, the Council of Nicaea, St. Peter, the institution of the sacrament.[30] It is no longer possible, therefore, for a discussion of the Magdeburger Centuries to begin, as Polman does, with the words, "Aux yeux de Flacius…"

23 Diener. 22n. Among authors whom Diener thereby implicitly criticizes Verheus, Op. cit., and Ernst Walter Zeeden's "Die Flacianische Geschichtstheologie." *Martin Luther und die Reformation im Urteil des deutschen Luthertums.* Freiburg: Herder, 1952. Bd. II: Dokumente. 41 f.

24 500–502. Klaus Herbers. "Die Päpstin Johanne. Ein kritischer For-schungsbericht." *Historisches Jahrbuch* CVIII (1988). 174.

25 Op. cit. 29; cf. Polman. *L'Element.* 228 f.

26 "The Legend of the Female Pope in the Reformation." *Acta Conventus Neo-Latini Hafniensis.* Rhoda Schnur (ed.). Binghamton and New York: Center for Medieval and Renaissance Studies, State University of New York at Binghamton, 1974. 498, 500 f., 505.

27 Op. cit. 25.

28 C. Frank. 66 f.

29 *Opera Omnia* IV, pars 2. Naples: Joseph Giuliano, 1859. 38–41. According to Lamping, 186n, Bellarmine knew he was not the author of the Centuries.

30 Dörries. 45; Grauert. "Magister Heinrich." 36; Buxbaum. 413 f.; Hannemann. 77; Whitgift. 142 f.; Werner Goez. *Translatio Imperii.* Tübingen: J. C. B. Mohr (Paul Siebeck), 1958. 293; Polman. "Historien." 61; Cullmann. 73; Jean Porthaise. *De Verbis Dominis Hoc Facite pro Oecumenico Concilio Tridentino, adversus Sophistias nebulas Matthiae Flacii Illyrici.* Antwerp: Emanuel Philipp Tronaesius, 1567. 111.

Sour Work

MAJOR RUMBLES INTO THE CHURCH

1 Gustav Kawerau. "Eine Episode aus dem Kampfe der Flacianer mit den Melanchthonianern." *Theologische Studien und Kritiken* LV (1882). 324–343.

I say openly and with clear and plain words, that no one will be saved through evil works, and no one will be saved without good works, and I say further, that whoever teaches otherwise, even an angel from heaven, is accursed. – Georg Major

All governments, ancient or modern, try to foster unity. Although the emperor was defeated in 1552, the imperial government persisted in its attempt to restore the unity of Christendom. Nor was disunity tolerated within the evangelical camp. Only a month after the siege of Magdeburg was lifted, on December 10, a formula for reconciling the Melanchthonians at Wittenberg and the Lutherans at Magdeburg was proposed by the pastor of St. Nicolas in Zerbst, Theodore Fabricius, to the Magdeburg clergy. Fabricius, who two years later would be the main influence in turning Anhalt away from Luther and the "Illyrian sect" to Melanchthon's "Philippists," now appeared as the representative of certain "Christian persons," undoubtedly political persons. He proposed amnesty.

1. An end to controversy.

2. (Unpublicized) forgiveness for Wittenberg.

3. Praise for Magdeburg's fidelity in defying the pope.

4. Assurance that Magdeburg would be consulted about doctrinal decisions.

Fabricius explained the scheme to Flacius the same evening in Cöthen. For Flacius, however, it was no solution at all. Fabricius struck him as resembling inexperienced physicians, who "cover the wound in fine fashion so it heals outwardly, but inwardly they allow the pure poison and broken bones to eat around themselves even more."

This hasty pacification between those who confess Christ and those who deny and persecute him, reverend fathers and brothers in Christ, has so disturbed and saddened me, or, rather, as I believe, the Holy Spirit within me – that it can hardly come as a surprise that what I am about to write are the judgments of a sad and disturbed soul. If I had not heard that the Reverend Doctor Amsdorf had resisted the negotiations I would not, without the most profound sorrow of soul, have written even this ... The articles and conditions for peace suppress all confession and disputation, whether it be just or unjust, true or false. It is concerned only for a meeting, but when the right hands have been joined, we will promise that we will thereafter keep silence ...[1]

The way to unity was not a middle way between Melanchthon and Luther, but a change of heart in Wittenbergers. "I wanted to be quiet," he remembered, "and especially to avoid this work, which I am not especially good at." But, inevitably, he was caught up again in "sour work."[2] Together with Gallus, he recommended a public discussion of the disputed matters.[3]

Much of the Interim's theology is indistinguishable from the teaching of Melanchthon. Melanchthon's associate George Major, to point to the most important issue, defended the Augsburg Interim's statement about good works: "... that these virtues, faith, charity, hope and others must be in us and are necessary for our salvation."[4]

> For man must not be a stone or a block, which does neither evil or good. But faith and the Holy Spirit and Christ, who dwells in us through faith, are active and powerful in us and drive us so that we live according to the Spirit, not according to the flesh, and produce all the fruits of the Spirit. For it is impossible that a man has true faith and does not at the same time have all kinds of good works. The sun cannot exist without shining, so where Christ and the Holy Spirit dwell in a man, faith shines forth through good works ... Therefore it is certainly true that these virtues, faith, love, and hope and others must be in us and are necessary to salvation.[5]

Melanchthon had written, "Our obedience, that is, the righteousness of the good conscience or works, which God commands us, must necessarily follow reconciliation. Although God gives us eternal life out of grace for Christ's sake and not because of the worthiness of good works, yet good works are necessary for salvation, because they ought necessarily to follow reconciliation."[6] Aware that he differed from Luther, Major invoked Melanchthon's authority for his assertions.

> I will condemn them until they improve themselves. I intend to remain Maius, Major and Maximus against the will of all, and will rather lose my head or life over it. I have taught thus: Good works are necessary for faith to salvation, and so it is usual, and printed in Philipp's German *Loci* while Luther was still living. Although for his own reasons, Dr. Martin Luther did not completely approve of it, still he did not completely disapprove of it.[7]

Should Flacius defend Luther's position against this challenge? Should he return to doing the unpleasant "sour work"? How could he not? "Very often I have wanted to quit writing," he wrote. But just then, Major "rumbled into the church with his news about good works,"[8] tossing Bishop Pflug's dead log into the discussion once more. In such important matters one must resist. "... the Spirit and the command of God overcame the Old Adam in me, so that I decided that one must obey and fear God more than all men."[9]

Why was Major saying such things? Did the statements merely slip out in the heat of controversy, as Major claimed?[10] Were they mere dogmatic clumsiness?[11] Was it an offense against philosophical language?[12] Bad grammar?[13] Or was he motivated by money? Flacius charged him with taking a bribe.[14] He reported the exact amount was 6000 Thalers.[15] "You avaricious Judas," he raged, "how has greed, the root of all evil, changed you, so that now you dare publicly to accuse and damn our church, as if it had perverted good order and morals, but praise the Antichrist and still want to be thought of as innocent." "I will obliterate you," he promised,

2 *Eine Entschuldigung an ... ein Pfarherr.* A iiij r.

3 *Provocation oder Erbieten der Adiaphoristischen sachen halben, auf Erkenntnis und urteil der Kirche.* Magdeburg: Michael Lotter, 1553. A iij v.

4 Melhausen. 54.

5 *Auff des Ehrenwirdigen Herrn Nicolas von Ambsdorff schrifft, so itzung neulich Mense Novembri Anno 1551, wider Georgen Major öffentlich im Druck ausgegangen. Antwort.* Wittenberg: Rhau, 1552. C v–f.

6 CR, XXI, 429.

7 Salig. III, 324.

8 *Von der Einigkeit* [B vj v].

9 Heldelin [V iv r].

10 J. Döllinger. II, 171.

11 Paul Tschackert. *Die Entstehung der lutherischen und der reformierten Kirchenlehre sampt ihren innerprotestantischen Gegensätzen.* Göttingen: Vandenhoeck und Ruprecht, 1910. 545 f.; Christian Heinrich Zeiblich. *Historische Lebens-Beschreibungen derer Stiffts-Superintendenten in Merseberg von der Reformation an biß zu unsern Zeiten.* Leipzig: Braun, 1752. 44; Salig. I, 638; CR, VII, 1061, VII, 64.

12 Haikola. *Gesetz.* 344.

13 "... daß der Mann gegen die Grammatik oder gegen den philosophischen Sprachgebrauch gesundigt habe." Planck. IV, 489.

14 *Antwort ... auff Beschuldigung ... Majors.* H iij v.

15 *Wider den Evangelisten.* A ij v.

16 *Ein   Christliche   Vermahnung.*
D iij r–f.

17 Op. cit. II, 169n.

18 Salig. III, 62. Strobel. *Ratzeburgers...
Geschichte.* 126.

19 Salig. I, 619.

20 Christianus [A viij r].

21 J. Döllinger. II, 169.

22 *Das Doctor Pomer und Doctor Maior
mit iren Adiaphoristen ergernis unnd
zurtrennung angericht, Unnd den
Kirchen Christi unüberwintlichen
Schaden gethan haben. Derhalben sie
und nicht wir zu Magdeburg vom
Teuffel erwegt seint, wie sie uns schmehen und lestern.* Magdeburg: [Mi-
chael Lotter], 1551.

23 *Auff ... Ambsdorff schrifft.* C v–f.; Cf.
Robert Kolb. "Georg Major as
Controversialist: Polemics in the
Late Reformation." *Church History*
XLV (1976). 455–468.

24 CR, VIII, 411.

25 *Eine kurtze Antwort auf das ... Comment.* A ij v.

26 Planck. IV, 483 f.

"and grind you up!"[16] Josef Döllinger commented that the charge was "not without grounds."[17] In the judgment of August Salig the charge was was true. Major had been summoned to the country estate of Dr. George von Kommerstädt, Counsellor for Ecclesiastical Affairs at the Dresden court. He explained to Major how convenient it would be if a man in his position would support the official religious policy.[18] Kommerstädt thoughtfully arranged matters so that he could continue to draw his Wittenberg salary while at the same time serving as Superintendent at Merseburg.[19] It did not escape notice that in the second edition of his *Psalterium* he withdrew his cricism of the Elector.[20] Justus Jonas testified that with a house full of daughters without dowrys, he needed the money.[21]

Amsdorf counter-attacked in *That Dr. Pomer [Bugenhagen] and Dr. Major Have Caused Vexation and Confusion and have Done Insurmountable Damage to the Churches of Christ.*[22] Major's *Answer* set off the "Majorist Controversy."

> This I confess: I have previously taught and still teach and want to teach my whole life, that good works are necessary for salvation; and I say openly and with clear and plain words, that no one will be saved through evil works, and no one will be saved without good works, and I say further that whoever teaches otherwise, even an angel from heaven, is accursed.
>
> How does that suit you? Because I know that it is the right, prophetic, apostolic doctrine if it is understood correctly.[23]

The source of trouble was understanding the slippery word, "necessary." One could, in fact, talk about the necessity of good works correctly by distinguishing between good works as a necessity (*necessitas*) for salvation, and good works as something every Christian owes to God (*debitum*). "*Necessarium* and *debitum*, however, first of all," Melanchthon explained, "do not mean *extortum coactione*. But the eternal, immutable order of divine wisdom and the Lord Christ and Paul themselves use these words, *necessarium* and *debitum*."[24] The former, which applied to the *forum justificationis*, was unacceptable because it implied merit; in the *forum obedienciae*, on the other hand, it was tolerable. One could, that is to say, reject *necessitas meriti* while defending *necessitas debiti* and *necessitas conjunctionis*. Or one could condemn *necessitas consequentis* and defend *necessitas consequentiae*.

But Flacius called for plain talk. Words should be understandable in their natural meaning, and not require special explanations.[25] The statement, "good works are necessary for salvation," he insisted, implies causation. "It is certain that the expression, when someone says that it is necessary for this or that work, means the same as if one says: this is a cause of the work, or, through this or that one accomplishes that work."[26] "However one understands Major's statement, the words 'necessary for ...' always express something proceeding, impelling, effecting, bringing about." "No one says fruits or leaves are necessary for a tree, wine or grapes are necessary for a vineyard, or that living is necessary for a house, riding is necessary for a horse."

The Mansfeld clergy had decided to tolerate Major as Superintendent only under the condition that he teach rightly – which led to his complaint that everything was denounced if it was not stated in the very words of Luther's postils. His critics were not fit to be judges of the preaching office, but only for sweeping out the asses' stalls of the popes.[27] When, to great jubilation, Duke Johann Friedrich returned from imperial captivity, Major was dismissed from office.

Shortly after, he published a defense, *A Sermon on the Conversion to God of St. Paul and All Godfearing Men*,[28] which Flacius dubbed "the Long Comment."[29] Major sought to relieve the pressure by determining that good works were not necessary for salvation, exactly, but for *retaining* salvation. But Amsdorf insisted that he was still teaching the necessity of merit. Melanchthon, who said he had always advised Major to give up the controversial terminology, nevertheless defended him. "... we cannot abandon this proposition: new obedience is necessary in all the converted. If anyone will not endure this, we regard him as antinomian and an enemy of God."[30]

Stirring up a controversy was clearly called for, however difficult it was in a society terrorized by official threats of retaliation, and however illegal. Flacius' preliminary challenge was *Against the Evangelist of the Holy Surplice, Doctor Avarice Major.*[31] In a *Short Answer to Dr. Avarice's Long Comment on Good Works*,[32] he argued that Major's teaching could not apply to children who die soon after baptism, or to deathbed conversions. Since forgiveness and salvation were the same, and since, by definition, an act is not "good" before conversion (Ephesians 2), how can good works be necessary? What could a pastor do to comfort a penitent who asked whether "I, a poor lost sinner, can be saved?" If Major answered "yes" he would condemn himself; if he says "no," he is responsible for plunging the sinner into despair. He quoted Bernhard's sad admission, "Perdite vixi" (I have lived badly). His attack on Major, against whom he used Luther's word for untested theologians, "tongue-thresher," *Zungendrescher*, were carried on so relentlessly and thoroughly that its effect still remains. No preacher could avoid or dismiss it, none could claim neutrality, and no other Reformation controversy had such a powerful and far-reaching influence on the form and content of religious instruction.

To make conversion, which God alone effects, a good work, as Major did, is to confuse God's work and ours.

> The other sophistry is that he says conversion, faith and renewal are also good works, through which sophistry he means to win easily, and completely to overturn our position ... but in the scripture and church, good works are called fruits, or the Christian life of a new man.[33]

Amsdorf joined the controversy with his *Short Instruction on D. George Major's Answer, That He is Not Guilty, as he Tragically Boasts*,[34] and Gallus with his own *Answer*.[35] When he returned from Italy in the summer of 1552, Flacius discovered that Amsdorf's, Gallus' and his own replies to

27 J. Döllinger, II, 281.

28 *Ein Sermon von S. Pauli und aller Gottfürchtigen menschen bekerung zu Gott.* Leipzig: Wolfgang Günther, 1553.

29 Salig. I, 639; Ritschl. II, 377n.

30 CR, IX, 552.

31 *Wider den Evangelisten.*

32 *Eine kurtze Antwort auff das ... Comment.*

33 *Ibid.* A ij r.

34 *Ein kurtzer Unterricht auff D. Georgen Majors Antwort das er nit unschüldig sey wie er sich tragice rhümet. Das gute werck zur seligkeit nit von nöten sind. Das Gute werck zu einem Christlichen leben hie auff erden nötig sind.* "Basel." [Magdeburg: Michael Lotter], 1552.

35 *Auf des Herrn D. verantwortung und Declaration der Leiptzigischen proposition, wie gute werk zur seligkeit nötige sind, zum zeugnis seiner unschult, das er mit der Leiptzigischen handlung nichts zu thun habe. Antwort.* Basel: [Magdeburg: Michael Lotter], 1552.

36 *Bericht*, 1559. H ij r.

37 *Bedencken das diese Proposition oder Lere nicht nütz noch war sey unnd ohne ergernis in der Kirchen nicht möge geleret werden. Das gute werck zu seligkeit nötig sind, und unmoglich sey one gute werck selig werden. Gestellet durch die Prediger zu Mansfelt unnd unterschreiben von andern Predigern der selben Herrschaft.* Magdeburg: Michael Lotter, 1553.

38 *Sententia docentium in ecclesiae Lubecensi, Hamburgensi, Luneburgensi, de doctrina necessitatis bonorum operum ad salutem.* Schlüsselberg. VII, 592–608.

39 Op. cit. II, 326.

40 Op. cit. 25.

41 Bernard Lohse. "Lehrentscheidung ohne Lehramt." *Kerygma und Dogma* XXVI (1980). 174–187.

42 Gustav Frank. Review of Preger, op. cit. 722.

Major bore the imprint, "Basel," although they had been printed by Michael Lotter in Magdeburg; the small type Lotter used speaks of his embarrassment. Flacius was innocent of the deception, he wanted known: he had been out of the country when his book was printed.[36]

The Mansfeld clergy joined the cause, signing a statement prepared by Wigand.[37] Hamburg, Lübeck and Magdeburg reacted with a formal censure,[38] The pastors of Hamburg sent Flacius a letter with the observation that those who preach repentance and condemn vice were hated everywhere.

Major's defense of necessary good works was no isolated phenomenon. The controversies of the Late Reformation, adiaphorism, majorism, synergism, Otto Ritschl wrote, "belong together."[39] Christina Hasslinger agrees: "Problems which were considered solved," she wrote, "kept arising in a new context ... the numerous doctrinal polemics did not develop chaotically and without relationship to each other. A consistent line, rather, can be drawn from the first to the last controversy."[40] Having once again taken up the onerous burden of "sour work" in defense of Luther's legacy, Flacius never again laid it down. In a period without an institutionalized teaching office,[41] his polemics served the church as "a principle of stability."[42]

RADICAL SCHWÄRMEREI, MAGISTERIAL SCHWÄRMEREI

1 *Vom fürnemlichen stücke punct oder artickel der Schwenckfeldischen schwermerey.* [Magdeburg: Michael Lotter, 1553]. [B iv v].

2 CS, XI, 208.

3 *Von der Hailigen Schrifft, jrem Innhalt, Ampt, Rechten Nutz, Brauch und Missbrauch.* [Ulm: Varnier, 1551]. CS, XII, 425.

I see how God the Lord has attacked the Lutherans bodily. So they will soon be attacked spiritually as well in a few years and in many demonstrations that their doctrine has no permanence or foundation. – Caspar von Schwenckfeld

The lion is dead; now I have to do only with foxes and hares. – Attributed to Andreas Osiander

Surveying the new situation in the church after the Princes' Revolt, Flacius was dismayed by the activity of ambitious and creative spirits; "everyone wants to overcome Dr. Luther's teaching and thereby win his spurs."[1] Even before the siege guns aimed at Magdeburg fell silent, there had been disturbing thunder in the East. In Silesia, Caspar von Schwenckfeld, marshalling his battalions, had served notice that, just as God had attacked the Lutherans militarily, he would "soon attack them spiritually."[2] He made the threat from Malachi (2.1) his own: "And now, O priests, this command is for you. If you will not listen ... I will send the curse upon you." His first salvo, *On the Holy Scripture*, was aimed at the Bible. Luther was wrong, he said, about the clarity of scriptures. The Bible is obscure, not clear, he wrote, but is "a book of seven seals."[3] "There is nothing good in Lutheranism. No one can become pious before God by means of Luther's teachings." His second salvo, *On the Gospel of Christ and the Misuse of the Gospel* aimed at preaching. Luther was wrong again, he said. The sermon was "a Wittenberg idol." One of his lieutenants pressed the attack:

> Lutheranism has a heathen, epicurian, warlike essence ... since in general neither faith, love, discipline, honor, piety, prayer, virtue, fear of God is felt, either among young or old. It is clear from their fruits that there is no faith, no love, no word of God in the land, as the prophet Hosea says in Chapter 4 [1,2], but blasphemy, murder, robbery, envy, usury, affliction, gluttony have taken over. One vile deed can hardly escape another, and one blood-shame comes after the other, so that the situation in the land is wretched.[4]

Schwenckfeld had internalized "certain mystical principles"[5] that governed his understanding of the Bible. The words of Matthew 3.17 "This is My beloved Son," were not spoken by the voice of God; they came out of a cloud.[6] His certainty that "the logos cannot fully enter into concrete facts and actions,"[7] reinforced for him by Cyril of Alexandria's dictum, that "it is impossible that God be introduced into our domicile through a creature,"[8] governed his understanding of Jesus. "The Son of God," he insisted, was only a name, he argued, a hypostasis of the Father.

Since his philosophical presuppositions implied a "certain hostility to nature,"[9] he rejected the *media* of grace, word and sacraments. God, he explained, accomplishes the salvation of the souls of men through the one mediator, Jesus Christ, in the Holy Spirit, not through means, but totally apart from means of creatures or externals. God teaches the internal man not through externals, but through his own spirit. One should not rely on the Bible, but on "a living, internal scripture, written by God's finger."[10] "Over the whole life of Schwenckfeld," in fact, according to Gottfried Maron, "can be written the slogan he himself chose as heading for his arguments against Flacius: *contra media*."[11]

For his part, Flacius had no respect for "spiritual interpretation" that made hash of logical discourse. "If I say that Schwenckfeld's ass eats grapes, I would not mean that Schwenckfeld is an ass, or that he himself eats grapes, but my idea would be that Schwenckfeld and his ass are two different animals. When Paul says that the prophets preached the gospel of Christ, 'gospel' and 'Christ' are two different things."[12] Nor did he have patience with someone whose mind was so disorderly that (as in the *Corpus Schwenckfeldianorum*!) "he repeats everything ten times."[13]

> But Stinkfield is himself a mad and foolish *Schwärmer*, who out of the whole of godliness and Christian teaching produces a horrifying chaos or confusion ... he cooks, brews, mixes, confuses and obscures everything together, so that finally one is completely robbed of all knowledge and distinction between God and divine things.[14]

"What kind of mad saint is he," Flacius asked about Schwenckfeld, "for whom the Word of God is God's very essence, the Gospel is God's essence, the word of hearing is God's essence, faith is God's essence, our renewal is God's essence, our righteousness before God is God's essence, all the gifts of the Holy Spirit are God's essence?" Like the ancient Valentinians, Marcionites, Samosatenes and Servetians, he wrote, Schwenckfeld

4 CS, XV, 61.

5 Heinrich Wilhelm Erbkam. *Geschichte der protestantischen Sekten im Zeitalter der Reformation*. Hamburg and Gotha: Dr. Martin Sändig, 1848. 416n.

6 *Fünffzig Grobe Irthumer der Stenckfeldischen Schwermerey aus seinen eigen Büchern trewlich zusammen gelesen und verzeichnet, damit sich die einfeltigen christen desto fleissiger für seinem Gifft schewen und hüten*. Jena: Thomas Rebart, 1558. A iij r.

7 *Vom Evangelio Christi und vom Misbrauch des Evangelii*. n. p. [1553]. CS, XII, 974; PL, 26, 456.

8 CS, XII, 974.

9 Dorner. *History*. 188; Idem. *Geschichte der protestantischen Theologie* I. 2. Aufl. Munich: J. G. Cotta, 1867. 168; Erbkam. 416n.

10 CS, XII, 461.

11 Gottfried Maron. *Individualismus und Gemeinschaft bei Caspar von Schwenckfeld*. Stuttgart: Evangelisches Verlagswerk, 1961. 83. CS, XIII, 370. Schwenckfeld's pastoral practice, in which he made use of the *verbum externum*, was not consistent with his theory. Johann Anselm Steiger. "Das *verbum externum* in der Seelsorge – Theologie des Spiritualisten Caspar Schwenckfeld von Ossig." *Neue Zeitschrift für Systematische Theologie und Religionsphilosophie* XXXV (1993). 133–149.

12 *Von der heiligen Schrifft und irer Wirckung, widder Caspar Schwenckfeld*. Magdeburg: Michael Lotter, 1553. [A iiij v–f.]. Reprinted in CS, XIII, 384.

13 *Verlegung der kurtzen Antwort*. A ij r.

14 Ibid. C iij r–f.

15 *Fünfzig grobe Irrthumer.* A ij v.

16 George Hunston Williams and Angel M. Mergal (eds.). *Spiritual and Anabaptist Writers. Documents Illustrative of the Radical Reformation.* London: SCM, 1957; Philadelphia: Westminster, 1, 1957. 34.

17 George Hunston Williams. *The Radical Reformation.* 3rd rev. (ed.). Kirksville, MO: Sixteenth Century Journal Publishers, 1992. 1268; Dörner. *Geschichte* I. 168; Erbkam. 416n; Maron. 159, 173.

18 "Enthusiasm," from Greek "en" [in] and "theos" [God], is a technical term, denoting a direct relationship to God. "Schwärmer" carries the negative connotation of "fanatic."

19 Smalcald Articles. BSELK, 455 f.; Tappert. 313.

20 *Von der heiligen Schrift.* A iij v; CS, XIII, 382 f.

21 Götz von Selle. *Geschichte der Albert-Universität zu Königsberg in Preussen.* 2. Aufl. Würzburg: Holzner Verlag, 1956. 37.

22 Joachim Mörlin and Georg von Venediger. *Von der Rechtfertigung des glaubens, gründlicher wahrhafftiger bericht aus gottes Wort etlicher Theologen zu Königsberg in Preussen. Wider die newe verfürerishe und Antichristische Lehr Andreae Osiandri, darinnen er leugnet das Christus in seinem unschüldigen leiden und sterben unswer Gerekchtigkeit sei.* Königsberg: [Hans Lufft], 1552. Dij r, K iiij v.

23 *Von dem Einigen Mittler Jhesu Christo und Rechtfertigung des Glaubens. Bekantnus.* Königsberg: [Hans Daubmann], 1551. 332.

24 Wilhelm Möller. *Andreas Osiander. Leben und ausgewählte Schriften.* Elberfeld: R. L. Friedrich, 1870. 490.

25 Marinus Johan Arnstzen. *Mystieke rechvaardingsleer. Een bejdrage ter berodeling van de theologie van Andreas Osiander.* Diss., Amsterdam. Kampen, 1956. Quoted by Jörg Fligge. "Zur Interpretation der osiandrischen Theologie Herzog Albrechts v. Preussen. ARG LXIV

babbled about the Father's thought and did not know what he was babbling about.[15]

What kind of saint, indeed? A great deal of effort has been dedicated to finding precise words. Schwenckfeld was a "revolutionary spiritualist," a "christocentric spiritualist," a "gnosticising mystic," a theoretical mystic, an "evangelical spiritualist,"[16] or perhaps a "biblicistic, gnosticizing, christosophic mystic"?[17] Whatever the nuance, Flacius saw in him a man that fit Luther's definition of enthusiast – of a *Schwärmer.*[18]

> In short, enthusiasm clings to Adam and his descendants from the beginning to the end of the world. It is a poison implanted and inoculated in man by the old dragon, and it is the source, strength, and power of all heresy, including that of the papacy and Mohammedanism. Accordingly, we should and must constantly maintain that God will not deal with us except through his external Word and sacrament. Whatever is attributed to the Spirit apart from such Word and sacrament is of the devil.[19]

Who could be more *schwärmerisch* than Schwenckfeld? "Each one will boast happily of his faith or spirit or his internal Holy Scriptures, and, as the Anabaptists already do, cry 'spirit, spirit, the spirit.' For the Schwenckfelders the scripture is governed by the spirit, not the spirit by the scripture."[20] "What more *Schwärmerei,*" Flacius asked, "could the *Schwärmer* produce?"

In Prussia, Andreas Osiander, who presided over the the Samland diocese, was planning an assault. "The lion is dead," he is supposed to have said. "Now I have to do only with foxes and hares."[21] The target of his attack was justification by faith. Luther was wrong, he said: justification had nothing to do with the crucifixion. After fifteen hundred years, Christ's blood had dried up. Historical information about it was "colder than ice."[22] Instead, justification comes about by God's indwelling, and is a recognition of God (in man) by God. He was operating on the dictum he quoted in a letter to Flacius: *in Deum non cadit accidens* – "accidence cannot be attributed to God."" Although sin lives in the flesh," he explained, "it is like a drop against a whole, pure sea."[23] A disciple said that it was like a big whale (righteousness) swallowing a little whale (sin).

What kind of theologian was Osiander? A "pantheist," a "gnostic of faith," a "speculative mystic,"[24] a "word mystic"?[25] "Osiander says that the eternal essence of God is our righteousness before God," Flacius wrote. "It follows that I must deal with God through his essence, that is, I must deal with God without any means and mediator."[26] That is to say that for Osiander justification comes about by direct contact with God, which Flacius recognized as Luther's definition of *Schwärmerei.*

Hoping to win approval for his favorite theologian, on October 5, 1551, the duke put the question to all the princes, estates and cities related to the Augsburg Confession. He sent them copies of Osiander's confession[27] and requested a formal reaction. One copy arrived in Magdeburg, and was forwarded for evaluation to Flacius in Cöthen.

Osiander had been creative. Instead of pronouncing a sinner righteous, he taught that God *made* him righteous: one said not *justum pronuntiare*, but *justum facere*.[28] A sinner was made righteous when, as it were, God's being was poured into him – *natura divina homini quasi infunditur*. Enough pouring, and sin was dissolved. That is quite a different notion than "forensic justification," that on the basis of Christ's work, righteousness is *reckoned* to sinners.

Indeed, why should he not take sides with Osiander, "I, who was in such misery, if it had to do only with temporal goods, honor, security of life, and revenge against those who disfavor, as the adiaphorists picture me? Especially, because it seemed as if Osiander had won the game, and because then one did not hear of anyone who wrote against him."[29] Osiander had already claimed Flacius' approval in print. Duke Albrecht counted on Flacius' approval; had they not stood together in opposition to the Interim? If Flacius' judgment was positive, the duke gave to understand, he would be rewarded with money and gifts and be elevated as Bishop Matthias Flacius of Samland.[30]

It was a dazzling prospect. A positive evaluation would bring financial security to the young family, doubly exiles, and social eminence. Elizabeth's reaction is unknown, but when her husband had finished studying the confession, the vision of life in an episcopal palace vanished. Osiander's system, Flacius saw, was not a mere shift of emphasis, but so subversive of Reformation doctrine that negotiations were impossible and amnesty was out of the question. On March 20, 1552, then, there was a brief flash of moral glory in Cothen when Flacius did the right thing and sent off a negative evaluation.[31] "I wanted rather to contend for the truth with my enemies in Wittenberg than against the truth with Osiander, who then was my friend."[32]

From both sides, Schwenckfeldian as well as Osiandrian, has come the charge that Flacius did not understand. Selina Gerhard Schultz, Schwenckfeld's American biographer, complains that none of Schwenckfeld's opponents, beginning with Luther, had read him correctly. "One of the tragedies of Protestant Christianity is the failure of Luther to comprehend the spiritual qualities of the Silesian reformer."[33] Nor did Flacius comprehend "spiritual interpretation." "Like Pharisees," she writes, they "could and would not understand him."[34] Schwenckfeld, an untrained layman who disdained both clergy,[35] and theological discourse dismissed "this crude literalist theologian, Illyricus," as a "creaturist"[36] and *homo aristotelicus* who "cannot grasp such spiritual matters."[37] But in recent studies, both Gottfried Maron[38] and Rudolf Keller[39] report otherwise. Unlike others, they report, Flacius understood Schwenckfeld thoroughly.

Duke Albrecht complained that Flacius misunderstood Osiander.[40] A contemporary, Franziscus Stancarus, disagreed; "many have written against Osiander, but none of them understands him except Amsdorf and Illyricus..."[41] Modern writers have discovered the same: "Flacius knows what he wants," according to Wilhelm Möller, "and a consistent

(1973). 246.

26 *Verlegung des Bekentnis Osiandri von der Rechtfertigung der armen Sünder durch die wesentliche Gerechtigkeit der hohen maiestet Gottes allein.* Magdeburg: Christian Rödinger, 1552. B r.

27 *Von dem Einigen Mittler.* An analysis of the confession and more on the duke's appeal in M. Stupperich, *Osiander in Preussen.* 195–211.

28 O. Ritschl. II, 464.

29 *Von der Einigkeit.* C r.

30 Ibid. C v. Bishop Georg von Polentz of Samland, who had accepted the Reformation, had died April 28th.

31 *Verlegung des Bekentnis Osiandri;* Someone to whom Flacius had sent a copy for comment was responsible for an unauthorized publication: *Confessionis Andreae Osiandri de iustificatione, in qua acerbe de impie insectatur adflictas Ecclesias, earumque ministros, qui hactenus doctrinam in Aug. Conf. comprehensam sonuerunt. Refutatio erudita & pia, scripta Magdeburgi.* Frankfurt: Petrus Brubach, 1552.

32 Preger. I, 218n.

33 CS, IX, 30.

34 *Caspar von Schwenckfeld von Ossig (1489–1561).* Pennsburg and Pennsylvania: The Board of Publication of the Schwenckfelder Church, 1977. 334.

35 CS, XII, 834.

36 Maron. 84.

37 CS, XIII, 542.

38 Op. cit. 10.

39 Op. cit. 79.

40 Jörg Rainer Fligge. "Herzog Albrecht von Preussen und der Osiandrismus 1522–1568." Dissertation, Bonn, 1972.

41 Franz Koch. "Fünf Briefe des Professors der Theologie Franziscus Stancarus aus den Jahren 1551, 1552 und 1553." ARG, III (1905/6). 407. Cf. Hirsch. *Osiander.* 9n.

42 W. Möller. 490 f.

43 *Wort und Geist.* 73

44 Karl Alfred von Hase. *Herzog Albrecht von Preussen und sein Hofprediger.* Leipzig: Breitkopf and Härtel, 1879. 181.

Two Enthusiasts

Above, Andreas Osiander, magisterial Schwärmer

Below, Caspar von Schwenckfeld, "radical" Schwärmer

HAB: Portraitsammlung

Anno M. D C V I.

application of the concepts which he opposed to the speculative mysticism of Osiander, gives him a more solid and clearer position against him than most of the other opponents have shown."[42] Richard Grützmacher agreed: "In spite of all the hardness of his polemics, one must admit that he had thoroughly understood the opposite side."[43]

Since his letter to Albrecht arrived in Königsberg open, it created a stir. Had Flacius left it open deliberately to publicize his dealings with the duke? The question was never solved, and the duke did not pursue the matter. Following the custom of the day, he sent Flacius two hundred Thalers for dedicating the book to him, with the request that the money not be put to use against Osiander and with the suggestion that Flacius work toward unity. How could Flacius be an opponent of Wittenberg, the duke wanted to know, and at the same time an opponent of Osiander?

On July 6, Flacius replied, offering to return the money if accepting it meant he would no longer write as he believed. He had not opened the letter; if someone had wanted to know the contents, he would have sent them a copy. It did not worry him that Osiander had seen the letter; he had written the truth. But since the duke kept nothing secret from Osiander and Aurifaber it was impossible to keep their correspondence confidential, and he would no longer pursue it. He saw that the enemies of Christ had misused the duke's name and seal. The duke had enlisted Aurifaber to write the letter and although he would rather have avoided it, he had to say something to him. It was important that the duke read the letters in a calm mood, apart from those who would turn their sense upside down. Despite Flacius' reaction the duke pursued him, explaining that Osiander had had nothing to do with preparing the letter – only Aurifaber, and that the money he had sent was a simple demonstration of grace, not a bribe. Since he had not yet read Flacius' refutation, he would not discuss it. He required only that his writings be received by Flacius as graciously as Flacius' letters to him were, and that he should not become suspicious so quickly.

As a parody on the Our Father suggests, in Prussia, Osiandrism was less than universally popular.

> Our Father, unworthy, hellish Father Osiander,
> Who art now in Königsberg in Prussia,
> Eradicated be thy name.
> Thy will never be done,
> Neither in Prussia, nor in all of Christendom.
> Give us not from thy mammon and unjust usury, by which thou blindest many.
>
> Forgive us our debts, so we cannot pay our debtors.
> And lead us not into thy heretical Schwärmerei,
> But deliver us from all devilish teaching and your unheard-of soul-murder,
> Which thou thyself teachest, spreadest, and defendest.
> Such do for the sake of thy dear son [Andreas Aurifaber] and his dog-art.[44]

Within Prussia resistance was led by Joachim Mörlin, who as a Lutheran, refused to recognize Osiander's authority as church official. Where he was able, he excommunicated Osiandrians, and would not allow them to be godparents. Now, in Duke Albrecht's view, the obdurant Lutheran resistance was no different than the revolutionary opposition of Thomas Müntzer.[45]

According to a widespread report,[46] Osiander boasted about how resistance would be dealt with. "The three great A's will keep us out of danger – the Almighty, Albrecht and Adam, the executioner, who will in the end chop off my opponents' heads on the marketplace."[47] If it was religion backed by the hangman, which in view of the duke's patronage seems to be the case, official Prussian Osiandrism must be assigned to Williams' George category, "magisterial Reformation."[48] Since political radicalism connotes opposition to established authority, the episode is instructive: Osiandrism was "magisterial," and once again, Lutheranism – Flacius in the vanguard – was "radical." If one wants to be careful about terminology, moreover, the word, "radix" (root), may suggest that Williams' other term, "radical" is more appropriate to politics than to religion.

Schwenckfeld's "Christocentric spiritualism," his "revolutionary spiritualism," "gnosticizing mysticism," and his "biblicistic, gnosticizing, christosophic mysticism," granted, are not precisely the same as Osiander's "gnosticism of faith," and "word mysticism." The gnostic tendency, for one thing, is less obvious in Osiander than in Schwenckfeld.[49] Schwenckfeld ascribed justification to the glorified flesh of Christ, whereas Osiander emphasized essential righteousness in the life of the justified. Whereas Schwenckfeld had no use for the external word, for Osiander the internal word has a certain relationship to the external word,[50] as in his discussion of St. Paul's dictum that "faith comes by hearing" (Romans 10.17).

A contemporary, Franziscus Stancarus, noted however that "Osiander's followers have this in common with those of Schwenckfeld: that love, righteousness, and wisdom, by which a man is made righteous and wise by God, are themselves the essence of God."[51] "That the infused love, which is also God, is our righteousness," Flacius wrote, "that man's renewal is righteousness, teach the pope, Osiander and Schwenckfeld."[52] Osiander's teaching that the *opera ad extra* of the Trinity are undivided and that justification takes place "without any media and mediator,"[53] sounded very like Schwenckfeld. Schwenckfeld admitted it.

> First, I consider Osiander correct for writing that we should not believe imputed righteousness alone, extra nos, because of Christ's obedience, that is, by an alien, imputed justification outside ourselves, but to be saved, we must have the true and essential righteousness, the right substantial justice of God.[54]

Ferdinand Christian Baur noticed the common attempt of Osiander and Schwenckfeld to continue the doctrine of Servetus, "that God and man stand in an ontological, immanent relationship to each other."[55] For Schwenckfeld, man "has become everything that God is."[56] Osiander's identification of man with God, Flacius complained, required people to fall down and worship him.[57] In *Proof that Osiander Holds and Teaches that Divinity Lives in the Orthodox as in the Humanity of Christ Itself*, Flacius

45 Fligge, 1972. 186.
46 Fligge, 1973. 11.
47 Karl August von Hase. *Kirchengeschichte.* 202.
48 *Radical Reformation.* xxiv et passim. Williams, 27, correctly calls the word, "Schwärmer" "a term of derision." A recent critique of William's terminology: Aart de Groot. "The Radical Reformation Revisited." *Nederlands archief voor kerkgeschiedenis* 73 (1993). 199–207.
49 H. Weber. *Reformation.* I/1, 284.
50 Rainer Hauke. "Sola dei iustitia. Die theozentrische Rechtfertigungslehre des Andreas Osiander (1498–1552): Eine mislungene Belehrung der forensischen Rechtfertigungslehre?" *Belehrter Glaube: Festschrift für Johannes Wirsching zum 65. Geburtstag.* (eds.). Elke Axmacher and Klaus Schwarzwäller. Frankfurt am Main et al: Peter Lang, 1994. 115.
51 *Lutheranae trimembris Theologiae Epitome,* 1558. Cited by Hirsch. *Theologie.* 9n.
52 *Fünfzig Grobe Irrthumer.* D iij r.
53 *Verlegung des bekentnis Osiandri.* B r.
54 *Von Osianders Meinung bei der Justification C. S. Bedencken und Judicium.* CS, XIII, 873.
55 *Lehrbuch der christlichen Dogmengeschichte.* 3. Ed. Tübingen: Fues, 1867. 320.
56 H. Weber. *Reformation.* I/1, 284 f.
57 *Wider die Götter in Preussen. Das nur eine einige wesentliche gerechtigkeit Gottes sey, die nemlich, so inn den zehen geboten offenbahret ist. Ein kürtzer, heller und klarer bericht vom verdienst und gerechtigkeit Christi.* [Magdeburg: Christian Rödinger, 1551]. Cf. *Sammlung,* 1774. 636–641.

58 Op. cit. 333.

59 Hirsch. *Osiander*. 27–40; Reuchlin. 116–172, 131 f., 152 f.; Pico della Mirandola. 31, 36. Neoplatonism. Gottfried Seebass. *Das reformatorische Werk des Andreas Osiander*. Nuremberg: Selbstverlag des Vereins für Bayerische Kirchengeschichte, 1967. 80–82.

60 Hirsch. *Osiander*. 165 ff.; Selle. 36; Gerhard Müller. "Zum Verständnis Schwenckfelds." *Festgabe Karl Müller*. Tübingen: J. C. B. Mohr (Paul Siebeck), 1922. 145–170. Here. 150. Horst Weigelt. *Spiritualistische Tradition im Protestantismus: die Geschichte des Schwenckfeldertums in Schliesien* [Arbeiten zur Kirchengeschichte 48]. Berlin: de Gruyter, 1973. 45; accepts Hirsch's assertion; Erbkam. 416n. O. Ritschl. II, 456, 483; Seebass. *Werk*. 71 ff.; Johannes Tauler. "Christian Instruction in and an Understanding of the External and Inner Word of God." CS, XIV, 349–357; E. Emmet McLaughlin. ("Spiritualism and the Bible: The Case of Caspar Schwenckfeld 1498–1561"). *The Mennonite Quarterly Review* LIII (1979). 285; Roth. "Ein Braunschweiger Theologe des 16. Jahrhunderts: Mörlin und seine Rechtfertigungslehre." *Jahrbuch der Gesellschaft für niedersächsische Kirchengeschichte* L (1951). 67; Richard Grützmacher. "Schwenckfeld." RE3, 18, 76, 57–58. Schwenckfeld learned from Augustine, German mysticism – especially Tauler, possibly the Bohemian Brethren.

61 *De Jesu, nomine Christi servatoris nostri proprio, contra Osiandrum. De Jehova nomine veri Dei proprio.* Wittenberg: Hans Krafft der ältere, 1552.

reported Osiander's boast that but for his thick skin, divinity would shine right through, like light from a lantern.

> Osiander wants to be God, and tells us that divinity dwells in him, and in all true Christians in the manner in which it dwells in Christ's humanity. And, as Christ's humanity is one person with divinity, so they are also one person with God. It follows that all men should fall before Osiander or Holy Man and pray, 'behold at this place there is inflation, on the other there is war and at the third there is pestilence. Help the whole world, just as one did when Christ was on earth, and still does. It also follows that Osiander created heaven and earth, as the Son of Mary created.

> Osiander is not only the Son of Mary, but the true, eternal almighty God. Is that not the error of all errors, and the first error of Adam and Eve, and the black dragon itself, who wanted to be Gods?

"The Osiandrian justification doctrine," Ferdinand Christian Baur noted, is built on a basic viewpoint, which recurs in the most varied forms, which builds a constant opposition to Lutheran dogma."[58] That basic viewpoint was that of their sources, Reuchlin, Pico della Mirandola,[59] the Cabbalah of Hassidic Judaism[60] – the source of Osiander's fanciful etymology – corrected by Flacius in *On the Proper Name of Christ Our Savior, Against Osiander. On Jehovah, the Proper Name of the True God.*[61]

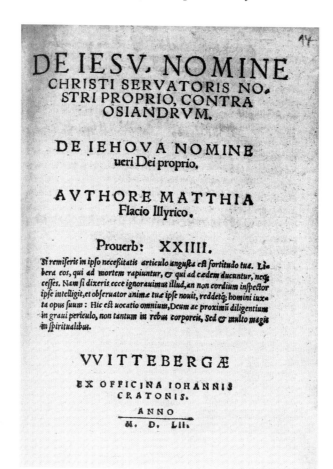

Flacius' critique of Osiander's Cabbalism

If Flacius' report is true, Schwenckfeld's following was not necessarily pacifist. "A few months ago the *Schnaphan* whom Stinkfield shelters sent a letter to the preachers and burghers of Augsburg, theatening that he would persecute and attack, in the most terrifying way he could, whoever preached or spoke against his prophet."[62] Nevertheless, a great political and social gap lay between the puissant Osiandrians and the persecuted Schwenckfeldians.

As we have seen, despite their significantly different political and social status, in a technical sense Osiandrists and Schwenckfeldians were both enthusiasts. If one prefers to look beyond phenomena to presuppositions, the term, "enthusiast" or "Schwärmer" may yet commend itself as more appropriate theologically than Williams' terms. According to Flacius "The Osiandrists and the Schwenckfeldians are the best of comrades."[63]

His motivation in combatting both groups was not political, but solely theological. As his eighteenth-century bibliographer, Johann Balthasar Ritter, observed, Flacius fought his theological battles *sine personarum respectu*.[64] His duty as theologian was to distinguish the Christian faith from what it was not.

> But dear God, all zeal is now burned out. With the exception of a very few Christians, no one concerns himself about the saving truth, whether it remains pure or falsified. The greatest part sees through its fingers, interprets, glosses and convinces everyone that black is white, night is day, wolf is sheep ... they say you should understand the Interim, the canon as well, Osiander's ideas are not so bad, Schwenckfeld's either; one should judge adiaphorism and Majorism in the best light ... etc. That is now modesty, candor, Christian meekness, mildness, thankfulness, and, in sum, the total sum of godliness, etc. May the eternal, almighty God awaken the spirit of his own...[65]

Combatting enthusiasm, he was as little moved by sympathy for the vulnerable Schwenckfeldians as by awe of the powerful Osiandrians. Against Schwenckfeld's twelve attacks, Flacius answered with nine[66]; against Osiander, depending on who is counting, fifteen to twenty-five, a torrent of paper: *Comforting Contradiction of the Reverend Doctor Martin Luther and Matthias Flacius Illyricus Against the Statements of the Raven, Osiander,[67] On Righteousness, Against Osiander,[68] A Brief and Clear Narrative of Osiander's Argument with their Confutation and our Proof Against Him on Justification by Faith,[69] Against the New Heresy of the Dikaeusists on Christ's Saying, John 16,[70] Test of Osiander's Spirit on Justification Through Infused, Essential Righteousness,[71] A Brief Table Against Osiander,[72] Theologians in a Synod held in Custrin,[73] Proof that Osiander holds and teaches that Divinity inheres in the right believers, as in the Humanity of Christ himself. And that consequently that Christians are gods and must be prayed to, as the Man Jesus Himself,[74] Narration of Osiander's arguments, with their Confutation,[75] A Warning to All Estates of the Christian Church in Prussia, on Osiander's Doctrine.*[76]

The theologians at Wittenberg did not share Flacius' willingness to do sour work. In five years, from 1550 to 1555, Flacius calculated, they

62 *Vom fürnemlichen stücke.* [A iv v].

63 *Das das thewre Bludt oder gehorsamlich leiden Christi die ware, recht und einige Gerechtigkeit sey, dadurch wir für God gerecht, im wolgefellig und selig werden. Geschriben an F. D. in Preussen durch Matth. Flacium Illyricum.* [Nuremberg: Johann vom Berg and Ulrich Newber], 1552. vii r.

64 *Ritter.* 36.

65 *Bekandnus von etlichen irthumen Maioris. Item Etliche Spruche Menij.* n. p. 1557. [C vj r].

66 *CS,* XVI, 1052.

67 *Tröstl. Gegenspräch des Ehrw. Herrn D. M. Lutheri und Matthie Illyrici, wider des Rabe Osiandri Primarij spruch.* n. p. 1552.

68 *Von der Gerechtigkeit wider Osiandern, Nützlich zu lesen.* Magdeburg: Christian Rödinger, 1552.

69 *Kurtze und klare erzelung der argument Osiandri mit ihrer verlegung, und unserer beweisung wider ihn, von der gerechtigkeit des glaubens.* Magdeburg: Christian Rödinger, 1552.

70 *Wider die newe ketzerey der dikaeusisten, vom spruch Christi Joan. am XVI. Der Heilig Geist Wird die Welt Straffen umb die Gerechtigkeit, das ich zum Vater Gehe.* Magdeburg: Christian Rödinger [1552].

71 *Probe des Geistes Osiandri von der Rechtfertigung durch die eingegossene wesentliche Gerechtigkeit Gottes.* Magdeburg: Michael Lotter, 1552.

72 *Eine kurtze Tafel wider Osiandrum auf einen gantzen ausgeschlagenen Boten.* n. p. n. t.

73 *Theologen in gehaltenem Synodo zu Custrin ausgangen. In massen solchs An Graf Albrechten dem Eltern, Hertzogen in Preussen auf seiner F. D. Schreiben und zugeschicht worden.* Frankfurt: Johan Einhorn, 1552; Salig. II, 999 f.

74 *Beweisung das Osiander.* op. cit.

75 *Erzelung der Argument Osiandri mit ihrer Verlegung.* Magdeburg, 1552.

76 *Ermanung an alle Stände der Christlichen Kirche in Preussen, Osianders Lehre halben.* Magdeburg: Christian Rödinger [1552]. With Gallus.

77 *Apologia ... Menii.* A iij v.

78 Bernard Willkomm. "Beiträge zur Reformationsgeschichte aus Drücken und Handschriften der Universitätsbibliothek in Jena." ARG, IX (1911/1912). 246.

79 His veerse was not directed at the "Gentle Proposals." Willkomm. 246.

80 "Gigantes clamore assini dissipati." *Scriptorum publice propositorum a gubernatoribus studiorum in Academia Witebergensi.* Tom. II, 1562. X, 7a; CR, X, 631; Clemen. *Studien.* 51 f.; Idem. "Anschlag." KS, VI, 558–575.

An Ass crowned by Four Asses. Cranach workshop. Reproduced from Martin Luther. *Ein neuwer fabel Esopi... Vom Lawen und Esel* [Wittenberg: Georg Rhau, 1528]. WA, 26, 551; Strauß I, 154.

did not write even one publication against Osiander that mattered.[77] The few exceptional pamphlets by the Wittenbergers, he complained, were unsatisfactory. They "had neither head, heart, or form, no clear 'yes' or 'no.'"

Instead of joining Flacius against Osiander, Melanchthon ridiculed his campaign[78] with a mean-spirited verse,[79] "Giants Scattered by the Noise of an Ass."[80] It appeared in print not once, but twice. When Flacius protested,[81] Melanchthon denied publishing, although not having written it. Flacius did not believe him.[82] The poem is based on a story from Ovid's *Metamorphoses*[83]: heaven-storming giants could not be frightened off by Zeus or Pan, but they fled when a raucous signal to attack was given by Silen's ass. "Not otherwise," Melanchthon concludes, "will the sophists ... take flight against the true God, bringing many excuses, when they are held back by the terrible shriek of an ass. This is the end of the war of the foolish chatterers."[84]

It was illustrated by a recycled woodcut, not unusual in the Cranach workshop. This case is especially interesting, since the original application is unknown. The woodcut seems intended to ridicule some academic: two disciples (young asses) armed with halbards, are ready to defend their master (a larger ass), while two other asses hold a crown over his head. Made of manure, the crown suggests that their praise was exaggerated. The picture was already inappropriate when it was used to illustrate Luther's *New Fable of Aesop on the Lion and the Ass* in 1528[85]; it was just as inappropriate for illustrating the poem about the Flacian asses. No matter. It was a signal for Melanchthon's troops to attack.[86] In case anyone wondered, Johannes Gallus, now leader of his own poets' circle in Erfurt, identified the foe.

Qui non pium Melanchthonem
Virum volit dignissimum,
Asellus est, illum Deus
Severterque puniet.[87]

Whoever does not want to honor
the pious Melanchthon as a very worthy man,
is an ass.
God will severely punish him.

81 *Von der Einigkeit.* B iij r.
82 "Nam quod scribis de versibus asellorum iam bis a vobis editis, nunquam audivi te invito esse evulgatos, et sententia eorum manifesta est." Letter of September 18th, 1556. Bindseil. 583; Clemen. "Alte Einblattdrücke." KS, VII, 97 f.
83 *Metamorphoses* with an English translation by Frank Justus Miller. Cambridge, Mass.: Harvard University Press, 1966–1969. 11, 311.
84 W. H. Roscher. *Ausführliches Lexikon der griechischen und römischen Mythologie.* Leipzig: B. G. Tuebner, 1884–1937. I, 2, 1646.
85 WA, 26, 551. Related to a woodcut in the Jena University Library. Willkomm. 245–261.
86 Salig. III, 226 f.
87 Georg Ellinger. *Geschichte der neulateinischen Literatur Deutschlands im sechzehnten Jahrhundert* II. Berlin: Walter de Gruyter, 1929–1933. Cf. CR, X, 301 f.

IN THE BEGINNING, THE LAW?

In an abstract sense ... the statement, "good works are necessary for salvation," can be tolerated in the doctrine of the law. – The 1556 Synod of Eisenach

For Flacius, justification was not a quality, but an action: "...that the justification of the sinner is the fulfilling of the law, that Christ dies for us and he is reconciled to us" (Romans 8). "The fulfillment of the law is Christ" (Romans 10). Christ fulfilled everything the divine law required, and the fulfilling of the law is completely ours. God is seen as the judge who punishes transgression, and Christ in our place has offered to God the obedience required by retributive justice. Our share in eternal life is a

1 *Verlegung des Bekentnis Osiandri.* A iij v.
2 *Geschichte der Ethik.* Leipzig: Felix Meiner, 1932. 251.
3 *Christus Victor. An Historical Study of the Three Main Types of the Idea of the Atonement.* Translated by A. G. Hebert. New York: Macmillan, 1951. 127.
4 Haikola. *Gesetz und Evangelium.* 247.
5 Ibid. 35, 80.
6 Lauri Haikola. "Die reformatorische Anthropologie." *Studien zu Luther und zum Luthertum.* Uppsala: A. B. Lundequista Bokhandeln und Wiesbaden: Otto Harrasowitz, 1958. 11.

reward for the righteousnss of Christ, which is imputed to us. As Flacius explained:

> The controversy between us and Osiander is primarily about what our righteousness is, by which we are justified before God. He says that it is the essential righteousness of God. We say it is the righteousness of Christ's obedience or fulfilling of the law, in which all suffering and action of our mortal life are comprehended.

"I truly cannot see," he commented, "what is false or not correct in this argument."[1] Several recent theologian, curious about what led to Lutheran orthodoxy, have been eager to explain their insights about what was wrong: in teaching *forensic* justification, Flacius neglected *effective* justification. "One could not defend the Anselmian satisfaction theory and the Melanchthonian doctrine of imputation," wrote Ottmar Dittrich about Flacius' confutation of Osiander, "more rationalistically and in a less Lutheran manner."[2]

According to Gustav Aulén, Flacius "describes the imputation to us of Christ's obedience as a transference made by God at the request of both parties, Christ and men. Consequently, he prefers to speak of the forgiveness of sins as granted, not *gratis*, but *precario*; the former term would not only be partly true, but the latter he regards as strictly accurate."[3] Luther's fundamental thought, Aulén goes on, that in one aspect, law is a tyrant and an enemy, from whose power Christ came to set men free, was thus lost. The controversy against Osiander, he determined, was the chief turning-point from Luther to Lutheran orthodoxy.

"When Flacius says that through Christ's satisfaction God has become our debtor," wrote Lauri Haikola, "that lies wholly on the line of Melanchthonian thought."[4] He argued that Flacius' approval of the law as a way to salvation in the abstract meant that faith was an inner fulfilling of the law – and meant that Flacius came close to teaching Thomas Aquinas' *lex aeterna*. He did not follow Luther's distinction in the great Galatians commentary between **righteousness of faith** and the **righteousness of the law**, and had not dealt as seriously as Luther had with the idea that **the law is coercive.**[5]

> For Luther the absolute law is hidden and cannot be known. The command to Adam not to eat from the tree in the middle of the garden, for example, was not an insight into general ethical principles. Instead of living out his life against the background of a timeless, abstract, philosophical law, man lives in a series of "situations of creation" within the flux of time. Dependent, he must learn what is required of him again and again. Melanchthon's idea of an absolute law, on the other hand is inevitably transformed by the human mind into a mastery of the future, and then into a doctrine of free will.[6]

Reviewing a book of Haikola's, Wilhelm Maurer summarizes:

> The consciously rigorous Luther pupil, Flacius, is so dependent on the scholasticism of the later Middle Ages that he is able to maintain the most central concepts of the Reformation doctrine only by giving them another interpretation. That is true especially for the concept of law. It is understood, as by Thomas Aquinas, as an expres-

sion of God's will of eternal and objective validity, as an expression of the divine creative will, which holds the whole cosmos together. The written law, then, is merely a corroboration of the *lex naturae*, already written in men's hearts in the original situation of paradise, the knowledge of which, however, for the most part, had already been lost in the Fall into sin.

Originally this law was meant to be the way of salvation. In this sense, the gospel became its substitute. In terms of its content – fulfilling the divine will – the gospel is subordinated to the law; the latter was prior to the former and reaches its original goal in it. Only with regard to its function is the law, in the form it was given through Moses, useful to the Gospel. And effective in the meanwhile, only as taskmaster leading to Christ, as it awakens terror and remorse over sin and prepares for the comfort of the gospel.

It is clear that the coordination of the gospel with the law results in a moralizing of theology, which constantly pushes toward the opposite principle of antinomianism, without being able to grant its consequences. This tension between moralism and antinomianism, which occurs first in Melanchthon, established itself in the development of post-Lutheran theology after Flacius and to a large extent altered the great paradoxes of repentance and faith, sin and righteousness, judgment and grace, by which the original theology of Luther was governed.[7]

All of Osiander's opponents, in fact, according to Emanuel Hirsch, were Melanchthonians. Osiander himself could see all of them sitting around in a circle of an evening around a song-leader, Philipp Melanchthon. Whatever Melanchthon sang, they repeated after him. "If sixty thousand have written against me," he complained, "it still is nothing but the one song of Philipp."[8] "Their eagerness to condemn, their measureless injustice," Hirsch accuses, "made them unable to see the point where they could learn from Osiander."[9] Their central notion, he continues, that God's righteousness is retributive justice, derived from Anselm of Canterbury.[10] Thus, Flacius transmitted Luther's teaching in a faulty fashion. "The pre-Lutheran idea of the divine righteousness, admitted by preference into the Anselmian-Melanchthonian scheme perverted the original Protestant conception of God."[11]

Hirsch, in turn, has also been criticized. Martin Stupperich detected a hidden agenda: Hirsch began by assuming an identity between Osiander's doctrine and Luther's. When it became clear that Hirsch was not proving the point, he found it necessary to call all Osiander's opponents "Melanchthonians."[12]

Critics have also taken note of the legal presuppositions of the decision of the Synod of Eisenach in 1556. During a formal Visitation of the churches in Ernestine Saxony in 1554, Amsdorf insisted that the members of the Visitation commission sign a document rejecting George Major's statement that good works were necssary for salvation. Justus Menius refused. Such a statement, he said, would exacerbate the tensions between the two Saxonies. Appealing to an agreement reached at Naumburg in February 1554 that the two sides refrain from controversy, he resigned. Suspicion of Menius' own theology led to a synod at Eisenach – more of a legal hearing than a synod, perhaps, to judge from the participants –

7 Review of Haikola, *Gesetz und Evangelium bei Matthias Flacius Illyricus*. ARG, XLV, (1954). 122. Cf. Haikola. "Melanchthon's and Luther's Lehre." 97 f.

8 Hirsch. *Theologie*. 267.

9 Ibid. 242.

10 Ibid. 250.

11 Ibid. 181, 246.

12 *Osiander in Preussen*. 364.

13 Published in an appendix to Flacius' *De Voce et Re Fidei*, 1563; II, 191–204, and in Christian Francis Paullinus. *Historia Isenacensis*. Frankfurt am Main; Bauer, 1698. 155–170.

14 *Erhard Schnepf, der Reformator in Schwaben, Nassau, Hessen und Thüringen.* Tübingen: Osiander, 1870. 93.

15 CR, IX, 232.

16 J. A. Dorner *History.* 394.

17 *Verantwortung vom Logo.* D ij v.

18 *History.* 394.

August 1 to 5, 1556. Duke Johann Friedrich the Middler himself presided.

The subject was whether the law had any relevance in the life of a forgiven sinner. The formal decision at Eisenach gave birth to a new theologumenon, "abstract law." "In an abstract sense ... the statement, 'good works are necessary for salvation,' can be tolerated in the doctrine of the law."[13] Menius signed the agreement with reservations. But neither Flacius nor Wigand had any compunctions about signing the statement when it was sent to them in Magdeburg. According to Julius Hartmann, Flacius' signing was an exercise of tolerance![14]

Amsdorf signed as well, but on second thought he changed his mind. Thus began the "second antinomian controversy." The main question now was whether, in addition of the two uses of the law defined in the Smalcald Articles, the political and the theological (bringing the sinner to repentance), there is a "third use" of the law after conversion. Flacius' first concern was to prevent the confusion of justification and renewal. "The principal basis of Majorism and Meniism," he determined, "... is that newness and rebirth through the Holy Spirit is a part of justification."[15]

Although as a corrective he emphasized forensic justification, Flacius did teach that newness – the effective element – was part of conversion. If that element was lacking in seventeenth-century dogmatics, it may not be Flacius' fault.[16] "There has never been any doubt," he wrote, "that we are reborn from God through the Holy Spirit for Christ's sake." The charge had been made...

> ... that I teach that God justifies us with words alone, which also is not true. I say that God powerfully reckons to us the righteousness of his son, as he powerfully reckons all the sins of the whole world to Christ. And through this reckoning we stand before God. Thereafter he renews us with his Holy Spirit.[17]

True, admits J. A. Dorner. Flacius did teach renewal as part of conversion, but it had only "mediate importance" for him.[18] The difficulty inherent in Lutheran Orthodoxy may have its origin in the choices made by the next generation: what themes from the controversies of the post-Lutheran generation should have been passed on?

Doctor Mörlin ... and Illyricus, the shepherds of Christ's flock. – Prussian song

An amateur theologian, the Duke of Prussia had his own way of explaining Osiandrian justification. Sin is a spark of fire; justification happens when it is extinguished by an ocean. "Although there is still sin in us, which rises up in our flesh, yet in faith we have such infinite righteousness or piety, against which all sin is like a spark of fire in a great ocean."[1] But for him, his friend's passing would have been the end of the movement. His loyalty was evident when after Osiander's death, October 17, 1552, a rumor went around that he had got his just deserts: the devil had broken his neck. The duke ordered the body exhumed and laid out in a church, his neck unbroken, for everyone to inspect.[2]

In a last reply to his critics Osiander strung together examples of his critics' criticisms and his own comments on a poster, which he called *Beer Sample*.[3] It offended some Königsbergers enough that they tore down the poster from the walls. Flacius and Gallus prescribed an *Antidote*.[4]

With the compliance of the duke, the Prussian church was systematically reconstituted – osiandrized – by his appointee, Johannes Funck. Funck also purged anti-osiandrian churchmen and professors at the University of Königsberg, and replaced them with his partisans. Flacius took aim at the new leader: *Against three Blasphemous and Sophistic Argument of Funck, which he recently Spread in Prussia Against the Precious Blood of Christ and the People*.[5] In his reply against the critic he called "Mats Flax" Funck did not hesitate to use his magisterial advantage by calling him seditious.[6]

Convinced that Osiander's axioms were underpinnings for an entirely different religion, Flacius appealed to the duke himself to accept the orthodox view of justification, based on Jesus' crucifixion: *That the Precious Blood or Obedient Suffering of Christ is the True, Right, and Sole Righteousness Through Which We Become Pleasing Before God and are Saved*.[7] Osiandrism was the devil; Funck, Eichorn, Jugendteufl, and Aurifaber were claws of the devil. The worst of them was Funck, who taught that Christ's blood had flowed in vain. To separate redemption from justification, he wrote, was a "fine sophism."[8] Against him, in *Explanation of St. Paul's Romans 3 [.1]*, Flacius insisted that "the righteousness of God has been manifested apart from the law."[9]

Meanwhile, the evaluations of Osiander's Confession the duke had solicited from abroad had arrived, almost all of them negative. The exception was the evaluation from Württemberg. At a synod there, June 1, 1552, fourteen theologians and pastors had determined that the controversy was merely a matter of words. Heartened by the Württemberg support, on January 14, 1553, and ignoring the other judgments, the duke

1 Fligge. "Osiandrismus." 236.

2 [] Roth. 59.

3 *Schmeckbier. Aus D. Joachim Mörlein Buch. Aus M. Michael Rotings Buch. Aus dem Nüremburgischen Ubu Buch. Aus Justi Menii Buch. Aus Mathiae Illyrici und Nicolai Galli Buch. Aus Johannes Policari Buch. Aus Alexandri Halesii Buch. Aus Nicolas Amsdorffs Buch. Aus Johannes Knipstro Buch. Das ein Kurtze Anzaigung etlicher ... Stück und Artickeln die in Iren Buchern wider mich begriffen sein ...* Königsberg: Hans Weinreich, 1551.

4 *Antidotum auff Osiandri gifftiges Schmeckbier.* Magdeburg: Christian Lotter [1552]. Against the same publication Flacius published *Zwo fürnehmliche Gründe Osiandri verlegt, zu einem Schmeckbier.* Magdeburg: Christian Lotter [1552].

5 *Widder drei Gottislesterische unnd Sophistische Argumenta des Funckens, welche er newlich in Preussen widder das tewre blut Christi und die Leute gestrewet hat.* n. t. n. p.

6 *Wider des unverschempten holhipplers unnd Auffrürischen Lugners Mats Flax Eillirrn ... Nottwendige gegenwehr, Schutzrede unnd widerleg u n g bis auff besere gelegenheit*, 1555.

7 *Das das thewre Bludt.* op. cit.

8 Fligge, 1972. 258.

9 *Explicatio loci Sancti Pauli Rom. 3. Nunc autem revelata est Justicia Dei sine lege etc. In quo tum propositio ac scopus Epistolae ad Rom. continetur, tum tota ratio Iusticiae ac Justificationis exponitur. Contra Osiandrum.* Wittenberg: J. Lufft, 1553.

10 *Ausschreiben an unsere alle liebe ge-trewen und landschaften wie sich die ergerliche zweispalt uber den Artikel von unswer armen sünde Rechtferti-gung erhaben.* Königsberg, 1553.

11 *Des Herrn Johan Brentii und anderer Wirtenbergischen Theologen, Declar-ation über Osianders disputation von der Rechtfertigung, sampt ihres Glau-bens Bekentnis, daraus leicht jedem zu vernemen, was Brentius und genante Theologen, im Grunde von Osianders newen lere halten. Mit Vorrede M. Fl. Il. u. Nic. Galli an die Preussi-schen Kirchen.* Magdeburg: Michael Lotter, 1553.

12 *Brentii und Osiandri meinung, vom Ampt Christi und Rechtfertigung des Sünders.* Magdeburg: Michael Lot-ter, 1553.

13 "Ein new christlich liedt von dem verdechtigen und zweyfelhafftigen Abscheidt der Pfarhern im Fursten-tum Preussen den 17. Septembris Anno 1554." Ernst Bizer. "Analec-ta Brentiana." *Blätter für Württembergische Kirchengeschich-te* LVII/LVIII (1957–58). 321 f.

14 Fligge, 1972. 218.

15 *Verlegung des unwarhafftigen ... be-richts.*

16 *Die fürnemste und gröbsten irthumb Irthum Osiandri, sampt einer Vor-manung an die Christen in Preussen.* Eisleben, 1555.

17 Fligge, 1972. 186.

issued an edict.[10] Henceforth, sermons had to conform to the Württemberg interpretion.

Mörlin called the new law a "devil's mandate." Although they should normally be obedient to authority, he told his hearers, in this case, they should not. He was abruptly turned out of office. In solidarity with Mörlin and the internal Prussian opposition, Flacius and Gallus argued that the Württemberg *Declaration* did not support Osiandrism.[11] Nor could the Osiandrians appeal to II Peter 1.4, "that through these [promises] you may become partakers of the divine nature," or I John 3.2, "when he appears we shall be like him." Flacius also produced a collection of earlier state-ments by Brenz and Osiander that contradicted the duke's argument, including quotations from the Brandenburg-Nuremberg Church order they had produced together.[12]

He continued his campaign to foment resistance within Prussia itself, not without popular effect, as one Prussian song shows:

> Wittenberg ist vergessen,
> Der Luther gilt nicht mehr,
> Brentius hoch gesessen
> hat allein recht lehr.
> Wirtenberg ist draus worden
> Das hoch gelobte landt,
> Muss Christi schaf ermorden
> O wehe der Sund und schand.
> ...Doctor Morlein der werde
> Dazu Illyricus
> die hirten Christi herde
> Und Justus Menius.[13]

> Wittenberg is forgotten,
> Luther counts no more.
> High-handed Brenz alone
> has the correct doctrine.
> Württemberg, outside,
> the highly-praised land,
> must murder Christ's sheep.
> Alas, the sin and shame.
> ...the worthy Dr. Mörlin,
> and with him, Illyricus,
> and Justus Menius, [are]
> the shepherd's of Christ's flock.

In May, 1553, the ministerium of Osterode publicly rejected the Württemberg position. A synod in Saalfelt, May 29, 1554, condemned Osiander's doctrine. Prussian nobles Kaspar von Nostiz, Burggraf Pack-mohr, Antonius von Borcke, and Wilhelm von Truchsess, made a collec-tion of money for Flacius for writing a new attack on Funck.[14] The result was a *Refutation of the Untrue, Baseless Report of Hans Funck on the Osian-drian Schwärmerei.*[15] In "The Most Prominent and Worst Error of Osian-der,"[16] he listed Duke Albrecht's errors. To the duke, the opposition was seditious. The Lutherans were infected with "the spirit of Müntzer."[17]

Now Württemberg furnished more support, in the form of a confession of January 30, 1553, signed, among others, by Jakob Andreae,[18] and a *Confession and Declaration of the Württemberg Theologians* of June 30, 1554. The Württemberg theologians had done a deep disservice, Flacius lamented. Their statements guaranteed a destructive, decade-long religious struggle, a struggle, for one thing, that was a contributing cause of Poland's alienation from the Reformation.[19] Osiander's notions, the Württembergers asserted confidenctly, were "true, pious, genuinely Christian."

But the duke gradually noticed that his defenses were not working, and permitted a synod in Königsberg in 1554.[20] Although the synod accepted the Württemberg *Declaration and Confession*, it required that it be interpreted on the basis of the Augsburg Confession.

But some pastors wanted a clearer statement. On the basis of the negative judgments from outside Prussia, they demanded a clear break with the Osiandrists. The duke acceded, but said that first he had to have advice about how to proceed. Both sides turned to authorities outside Prussia. The clergy directed its request to Flacius, for forwarding to the Magdeburg church and churches in Saxony.[21] Flacius' own judgment was *A Christian Warning and Admonition of Matthias Flacius Illyricus to the Church of Christ in Prussia on the Last Recess.*[22] There was no palliative; one doesn't treat a broken bone by treating the skin.

18 UN, 1711. 242.
19 M. Stupperich. *Osiander in Preussen.* 325–328.
20 Preger. I, 287
21 Preger. I, 287.
22 *Christliche Warnunge und Vermahnunge an die Kirche Christi in Preussen den nechsten Abschied belangende.* Magdeburg: Michael Lotter, 1555. A ij r, A v. Preger. I, 287.

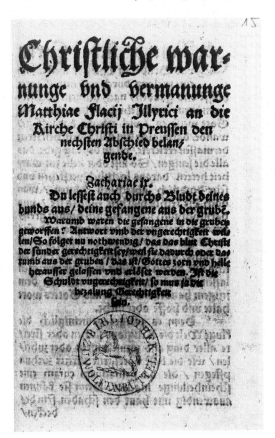

The clear break with Osiander demanded by Flacius

23 *Ein Sendtbrieff des Durchleuchtigsten, Hochgebornen Fürsten und Herrn, Herrn Johann Albrechten von Mechelburg an Illyricum geschrieben, von der osiandrischen Ketzerey.* [Nuremberg: Georg Merkel]. n. t. B iij.

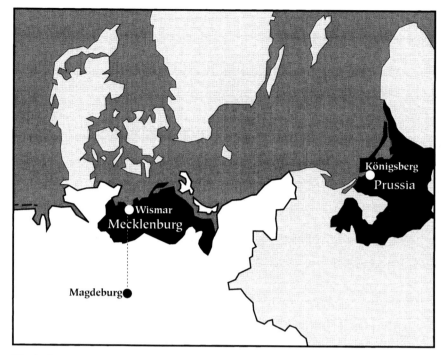

Flacius' winter journey, 1555.

The responses from Magdeburg, Braunschweig, Lübeck and Lüneberg were in essential agreement. All Osiandrist preachers were to be dismissed and excommunicated until they agreed to certain statements. Flacius, too, backed the demand for recantations.

> Since every Christian is obligated to confess publicly, what he thinks about the pending and disputed teaching of his time, as now, about the heresy of the pope and of Osiander, he will be so much the more obligated to confess publicly what is right or not right in the heresy that he himself has poured out. It follows therefore, that recantation is God's command, and all amnesty, that is, all forgetting, should be completely condemned.[23]

The marriage of the Duke Johann Albrecht of Mecklenburg to Anna Sophia, only daughter of Duke Albrecht of Prussia, announced for February 24, 1555, opened up a new possibility: his new son-in-law might influence Duke Albrecht. Flacius accordingly braved the February cold and set off to lay the Osiandrian problem before the bridegroom. In Wismar, however, the duke was not available.

Flacius seems to have expected that the aristocrats could be diverted from their entertainments to discuss a matter that was obviously important. There is nothing we can divine about his personality (self-pitying?) without hearing his tone of voice when he commented that the poor Christ was not welcome at princely festivities. He requested, without success, a meeting with the ducal physician, Andreas Aurifaber, Osiander's son-in-law, and had to settle with talking to the chancellor, Johann von Lucka.

Despite his disappointment, the Wismar trip had not been in vain. Somehow, he had caught the interest of Duke Johann Albrecht[24] who, with his brother, Duke Ulrich, would take a personal interest in the controversy from now on. At the end of December Flacius wrote to Johann Albrecht, arguing that the difficulties in the Prussian church would be healed only when Andreas Aurifaber and Funck were driven out.

On August 11 of the same year, affixed to church towers and Rathäuser in Prussia, appeared a new mandate from the Duke Albrecht,[25] granting anmnesty to all Osiandrians who would teach according to the Augsburg Confession and the provisions of the last Recess. But he also decreed the decisions by Württemberg church ("the most famous church") were binding for the duchy. Under pain of dismissal, all clergy should teach the new doctrine according to the new compromise formula, and to cease the controversy. Any doubt that the Osiandrian church qualified as "magisterial" in the sense of George Williams is dispelled by the mandate's provision that whoever opposed Osiandrism was guilty of a *crimen laesae maiestatis*.

Quoting Jesus, "I have not come to bring peace, but the sword," Flacius called for resistance,[26] and published the text of the mandate with his own scathing commentary. "God deliver his poor church," he wrote, "from all tyrants and false teachers for the sake of his son, Jesus Christ!"

Now Johann Albrecht took it on himself to still the controversy. The more he thought about the problem, the more he was convinced that Flacius was right and Osiander wrong. Eventually, at a 1556 Reisenberg synod, in the presence of both dukes, Funck admitted his error and asked for forgiveness. He promised to teach according to the Augsburg Confession and the *Loci Communes* and to give public notice of his promise. In his own handwriting, Duke Johann Albrecht reported to Flacius that with Funck's recantation, peace had been restored to the Prussian church.[27]

It was the begining of the end. In 1561, the Prussian estates began to accuse the duke of oppressive taxation, interference with their privileges, and arbitrary encroachments on the constitution of the church. They appealed to their feudal lord, the King of Poland, who sent a commission to investigate .They decided against the duke. Martin Chemnitz was called to establish order, and in 1567 in a new doctrinal norm accepted at a synod in Königsberg, Osiander was condemned. On the Königsberg marketplace, with two other Osiandrians, Funck was decapitated.

24 Julius Wiggers. *Kirchengeschichte Mecklenburgs*. Parchim and Ludwigslust: Hinstroff'sche Hofbuchhandlung, 1840. 147.

25 *Des Durchleuchtigsten Hochgeborrnen Fürsten und Hern Albrechten des Eltern Margraffen zu Brandenburg inn Preussen, zu Stettin, Pommern, der Cassuben und Wenden Hertzogen, Burggraffen zu Nürnberg und Fürsten zu Rügern, etc. Mandat*. Königsberg: Johann Daubman, 1555. Friedrich Spitta. *Bekenntnisschriften des Herzogs Albrecht von Preussen*. Leipzig: M. Heinzius Nachfolger, 1909. 139–143.

26 *Das das Prussische Mandat den XI. August dieses 55. Jahres ausgegeben Betreffend die Amnistia oder Vergessung der Osiandrischen Ketzerey mit gutem gewissen nicht kan angnommen werden etc. gründtliche ursachen. n. t. n. p. A v, A iij v. Fligge.* 281.

27 *Ein Sendtbrieff des ... Johann Albrechten.* 386.

1 *Cimelia Rhodostaurotica. Die Rosen-kreuzer im Spiegel der zwischen 1610 und 1660 entstandenen Handschriften und Drucke. Aus der Bibliotheca Philosophica Hermetica Amsterdam und der Herzog August Bibliothek Wolfenbüttel.* Amsterdam: In de Pelikaan, 1995.
2 *Vom Unterschayde des worts Gottes unnd der hayligen Schrifft auff Flacii Illyrici ander Schmachbüchlin: Antwort.* [Augsburg: Hans Gegler, 1554]. CS, XIII, 900–922.
3 *Ob Gott durch das Mündliche wortt khrefftigligk wirckhe zur Seligkaitt.* CS, XIII, 579–581.
4 CS, III, 28.
5 Review of Keller. 244.
6 Keller. 89–92.
7 *Von der heiligen Schrifft.* op. cit.

Luther's gospel and ministry are aimed only at destruction and not edification of the church. – Caspar von Schwenckfeld

Help, dear God; direct and restrain the godless Schwärmer, who darken, obscure and falsify the teaching of the law, of sin, of the gospel, of the forgiveness of sins and of Christ himself. – Flacius

The idea that human relationship to God can be direct and unmediated was identified by Luther as "the source, strength, and power of all heresy." He gave it a technical name: enthusiasm. A recent example of what he had in mind comes from a religious exhortation in an exhibition catalog of the Wolfenbüttel library: "Honored reader: from the brotherhood of life goes forth a personal mandate, which is as old as the world: strive for knowledge, beginning with knowing yourself, and achieve thereby a direct contemplation of the world of spiritual power." "Let one be conscious," it goes on, borrowing Christian terminology, "that the spiritual way which humanity has gone is the real meaning of the words, 'Jesus mihi omnia' [Jesus is all to me]." [1]

One man mentioned positively in the catalog is Caspar von Schwenckfeld. That he, too, recommended direct contemplation is easily apparent to browsers in the *Corpus Schwenckfeldianorum* – in his explanation of the liturgical words, "Lift up your hearts," for example, in his *Differentiation Between the Word of God and the Scriptures*[2] or his *Scriptural Evidence that the Spoken Word has no Saving Power*.[3] Schwenckfeld, that is to say, was an advocate of "spirituality," a religious tradition "as old as the world," as the catalog puts it, and a protean rival to Christianity. It surfaces in Hinduism, Buddhism, Gnosticism, Quakerism, Christian Science, and in New Age religion, for example, and (as in the Wolfenbüttel catalog) in Rosicrucianism. His spiritualist presupposition made Schwenckfeld an inevitable enemy of Luther. "Luther's gospel and ministry," he wrote, "are aimed only at the destruction and not the edification of the church."[4]

There was a shortage of troops to meet the challenge. "Flacius was almost the only theologian," Max Tratz writes, "who carried on the controversy after Luther's death."[5] When he read Schwenckfeld, Flacius was stirred to do more of his "sour work." By pressing him constantly to explain himself he was able to bring Schwenckfeld's teaching to full focus. According to Rudolf Keller, Flacius demonstrated how destructive "spirituality" is, and delivered weapons against it.[6]

When Schwenckfeld offered Jesus as an example of spirituality, Flacius took issue. "Spiritual exegesis," he wrote, fits scripture "like a fist fits into an eye." On the first page of his counter-attack, *On the Holy Scripture and its Effect*,[7] Flacius quoted Romans 10,17: "So faith comes from what is heard, and what is heard comes by the preaching of Christ." God takes account of man's physical nature. Enough to refute Schwenckfeld's theology was

Christ's Parable of the Sower (Mark 4), in which the seed of the Word of God enters the external ears of the hypocrites and proceeds thence to the heart. No special mystical sensory apparatus for receiving religious inspiration exists; even in the spiritual realm man is dependent on the normal physical senses. Citing Luther, he insisted that "we should and must constantly maintain that God will not deal with us except through his external Word and sacrament."[8]

> Unlike the angels, we have bodies, and God wills to deal with us in bodily ways – in teaching, by knowledge imparted through ears and eyes. He has given us, therefore, the Holy Scriptures, which can rightly be called his "rod." God's word addressed to us is his Word, whether it be written on stone, paper, pergament, the human memory, or spoken by a human voice. Absolution and preaching are effective whether the preacher is St. Paul, Christ, Augustine, or Judas.

Before Schwenckfeld had time to react to the first counter-attack, Flacius published a second, *On the Chief Parts, Points, or Articles of the Schwenckfeldian Schwärmerei.*[9] The Schwenckfeldians were saying that the Holy Spirit had not conceived Jesus by the Virgin Mary, but had somehow "overshadowed" her. Christ, thus, had always been merely a man. They were saying that Noah, Jeremiah, Elijah and Christ were not proper preachers. Schwenckfeld's spiritualizing, Flacius objected, takes scripture "by the hair"; it does violence to the plain sense.

In his *Confutation of Schwenckfeld's Short Answer* Flacius dealt with the attack on the Bible, the notion of a "Bible in the heart." "If God converts people completely without external means … what good or use are the Holy Scriptures, and what need do I have of the external Bible or those who write about it, its readers, the languages, the preachers and many labors of others, pains and vexations which I must have with the eternal teaching, if I want to understand? … Should I crawl into a corner and there study the Bible in my heart?"[10]

Schwenckfeld's third salvo against the Lutherans was *On the Word of God. Proof That there is no Word of God, Properly Speaking, Than the Son of God, Jesus Christ. So that the Derogatory Book of Matthias Flacius Illyricus Can be Answered As Well, With Exposure of its Manifold Errors.*[11]

No other Word of God than Jesus? Schwenckfeld's argument, it occurred to Flacius, sounded like what Melanchthon had written:

> The son is called Word by John, by Paul, the image of God [Colossians 1, Hebrews 17], the outpouring of his splendor, and the character of his substance. From which one can gather why John calls him Word; it is the word by which something is represented, and it is said that the Father himself conceived his image, which is called Word, and because it is a perfect image, the whole substance of the Father remains in it...[12]

But if Christ is the only Word of God, how could Schwenckfeld be refuted? Flacius decided to consult Melanchthon. He asked Pastor Werner Steinhaus, chaplain to the Count of Barby, to mediate. Apart from Revelation 19.13 which, being apocryphal, does not count, Steinhaus should remind Melanchthon, that Christ is called *logos* only once. If the Father produced the Son by the act of thinking, it follows that the Father ac-

8 Tappert. 313 = BSLK, 446.

9 *Vom furnehmsten Stücke*, op. cit., according to the Corpus Schwenckfeldianorum, the "second defamatory writing."

10 *Verlegung des kurtzen Antworts.* C iij v–f.

11 *Vom Worte Gottes. Das khein ander wort Gottes sei, aigentlich zureden, denn der Sun Gottes Jesus Christus Bewerung.* 1554. CS, XIII, 732–899.

12 *In Ioannis Evangelium Commentarii.* Basel: Adam Petri, 1523. 5.

13 CR, VIII, 922–924.

14 *Refutatio ... de Logo.* C ij r, Ciii; *Bericht*, 1559 [A iiij r].

15 *Verantwortung ... vom Logo* [B iv r].

16 *Gründliche Verlegung ... Menii.* G r.

17 CR, IX, 764.

18 Martin Schwarz Lausten. "König Christian III. von Dänemark und die deutsche Reformation. 32 Ungedruckte Briefe." ARG, LXVI (1975). 177.

19 *Epistola a Wernero Pastore Barbiensi scripta ex mandato Flacii Illyrici, et praescripta ab eo formula ad Phil. Melanchtonem, in qua quid sentiat Flacius Peri Logou seu de filio Dei Domino nostro Iesu Christo, qui est fundamentum fidei, & religionis nostrae, exponitur. Responsio D. Philippi Malanchtonis ad istam Epistolam.* [Wittenberg: Georg Rhau Erben, 1558]. A ij r.

20 "M. Tulli Ciceronis in L. Catilinam Oratio." Albertus Curtis Clark (ed.). *Marcus Tullius Cicero, Orationes.* Oxford: Clarendon Press, 1970. Part III, 2.

21 *Albini seu Caroli Magni Praeceptoris Confessio aut doctrina de Deo, compendio exposita, et nunquam antea impressa. Confessio M. Fla. Illyrici de sacrosancta Trinitate contra Servetianos, Stenckfeldianos, et alios seductores ac mendaces.* Magdeburg: [Ambrosius Kirchener], 1557.

22 Salig. III, 236, 156.

23 *Der Wittenbergischen und Leiptzischen Theologen Iudicium und zeügknus von den frommen manne Illyricus unnd seinem gesellen N. Gallus.* [Ulm: Hans Varnier d. J.], 1553.

24 *Auffdeckhung des letzten schmach und gräwliche Lügenbuchs so der grosse feind Jhesu Christi des eynigen lebendigen Worts Gottes Flacius Illyricus Anno 57. wider Herrn Casp. Schwenckfelden in Truck gegeben hat. Gründliche beweysung des Illyricus ein Arrianer ist. Mit einer Ableynung dergleichen unwarheyten unnd Calumnien Nicolai Galli Illyrici gesellens.* n. p. 1558. CS, XVI, 463.

complishes more through this Word than through the voice of a preacher. If, by contemplating Himself, the Father brought forth a person, why should the Son with the Holy Spirit, not also produce various persons...?

Steinhaus blundered. Instead of putting the questions to Melanchthon personally, he put them into a letter.

> Where in Holy Scripture was God's "word" the eternal Son of God, and when was it the external word or doctrine?
>
> Did the generation of God the Son take place through the Father's thinking?
>
> Does preaching the gospel include preaching repentance?[13]

The latter question had bothered Flacius since he had heard Melanchthon say that the gospel (not the law, as Luther had said) requires repentance, at the ceremonies for Isinder in the fall of 1548. When Steinhaus delivered his letter, Melanchthon angrily tore it up in the presence of students.

Flacius had to insist that he had not written the letter. "I did not ask him to write, but to ask orally, and he promised." But explanations were useless. Now Melanchthon had the proof he wanted that Flacius was a heretic; he persisted in treating Steinhaus' letter as Flacius'.[14] In all directions, to superintendents and princes,[15] he sent evidence of Flacius' heresy – that Flacius had failed to read the prologue of St. John's Gospel and chapter 1 of the First Epistle of St. John correctly.[16] In a letter to the Elector, he accused Flacius of unitarianism.[17] In another to the King of Denmark he accused him of wanting to alter the Nicene Creed.[18] Who did not know, he asked, the difference between the independent and the spoken word?

Schwenckfeld, he said, could be refuted without dragging in Paul of Samosata and the Servetians. Flacius might have countered that Melanchthon could have made his point without imitating Cicero.

> Melanchthon: Quo usque procedit tandem, Illyric Slave, rabies Tua? Quo effrenata sese efferent libido mentiendi?[19]
>
> Cicero: Quo usque tandem abutere, Catilina, patientia nostra? ...Quem ad finem sese effrenata iactabit audacia?[20]

Alarmed, Flacius attempted to establish his orthodoxy by publishing and standing by the confession, *On the Sacrosanct Trinity*, of Alcuin (c. 735–804), tutor of Emperor Charlemagne.[21] But in vain. And having strayed into the line of fire, Steinhaus was vilified as well. With great enthusiasm, like a buffoon, they said in Wittenberg, he proclaims his Flacius. Instead of preaching, he concerned himself with farming, and spent his time in drinking places and at crossroads.[22] Melanchthon's attack was usable for Schwenckfeldian propaganda. Schwenckfeld had already appropriated arguments in *The Judgment and Witness of the Wittenberg and Leipzig Theologians about the Pious Mann Illyricus and his Ally, N. Gallus* against Flacius.[23] Now "Theophilus Agricola" made use of Melanchthon's fresh accusations, and denounced Flacius as a "Wend," an Arian, and "the great enemy of Jesus Christ, the Living Word of God."[24]

Particularly irksome to Schwenckfeld was Flacius' emphasis on the importance of the sermon. Why, he asked, was a sermon not always effective? Flacius' answer: God must also give his blessing. He used an Aristotelian rule: the instrumental cause is not the only one: *Causa instrumentalis non est totalis. Posita causa instrumentali, non statim ponitur effectus.* "Trees do not fall over simply because there is an axe in the forest."[25] Flacius quoted St. Augustine's *De Bono Preservantiae*: "The holy men have well understood that it has been given to very few to receive the doctrine of salvation through the Lord himself without the preaching of men, or through angels of heaven. But it is given to many to believe God through men."

Schwenckfeld argued quite differently in *On the Teaching Office in the New Testament: That No Preacher Who is Not Pious and Who Does Not Live a God-Pleasing Life can Preach with Fruit.*[26] Now he had blundered into the Donatist heresy – the notion that sacraments are dependent on the moral character of the administrator. Flacius made the charge in *Thorough Confutation of Some New Donatist Writings of Stinkfield.*[27]

Pressing the attack, Flacius charged Schwenckfeld with agreeing with the teaching of the learned fantast, William Postel, self-proclaimed offspring of the mystical marriage of the world-soul and Johanna, the Venetian Virgin.[28] According to his cabbalist calculation, Postel predicted that the world would return to paradise in 1556, and that everyone would speak Hebrew.[29] As noted above, Flacius probably had encountered Postel's fanciful ideas in Venice during his schooldays. To prove the relationship between the two, he published a letter of August 17, 1553, from Postel to Schwenckfeld,[30] possibly intercepted by Wolfang Weissenburg, successor to Simon Grynaeus in the New Testament chair at Basel. "It is not really without reason," Flacius commented, "that in his book on the Venetian Virgin, the chief Schwärmer, William Postel, vigorously admonishes people to read Schwenckfeld's books."[31]

Postel concluded that Flacius was trying to have him murdered.[32] Jan Kvačala pronounced the charge "unbelievable," probably somebody's trick.[33] Postel biographer Marion Kuntz could not decide.[34] Postel identified the hit man, his former friend in Venice, Johann Schrötter,[35] and he went out of his way on a journey from Venice to Innsbruck to avoid Flacius' attack. Schwenckfeld did, in fact, admit that Postel had asked him to read about the Venetian Virgin. But, in spite of compelling evidence, he denied ever having received the letter Flacius published.[36] He had received only one letter from him, he insisted, in 1550. For his part, Postel denied sending the letter[37]; and denied even knowing Schwenckfeld until 1553. At least one of them was lying. "...it should not be forgotten," writes Carlos Gilly about the contradictory stories, "that ... both Schwenckfeld and Postel were more interested in concealing than revealing their mutual relationship beyond what had already been made public."[38]

Point-by-point replies to Flacius' first two "defamatory books" were prepared by Schwenckfeldians Georg Meyer and Adam Resner, but Flacius quickly produced a third and a fourth – *On the Chief parts, Points or*

25 *Vom fürnemlichen Stücke* [A iiij v].

26 *Vom Leerampt des neuen Testaments. Das khein Predicant der nicht fromm ist und gottselig lebt das Evangelium Christi vor Gott khan seliglich mit Frucht predigen.* [Ulm: Hans Varnier], 1555. CS, XIV, 460–491.

27 *Gründliche Verlegung etlicher newer Donatistischen Schrifften des Stenckfelds.* Nuremberg: Johann vom Berg und V. Newberg, 1555.

28 William Postel. *Le prime nove del altro mondo, cive, l'admirabile historici et non meno necessaria et utile da esser letta et intesa da ogniuo, che stupenda intitulata La Virgine.* [Venice], 1555. William J. Bouwsma. *Concordia Mundi: The Career and Thought of Guillaume Postel (1510–1581).* Cambridge, Mass.: Harvard University Press, 1957. 138. Marion Leathers Kuntz. "The Virgin of Venice and Concepts of the Millenium in Venice." *The Politics of Gender in Early Modern Europe.* Jean R. Brink, Allison P. Coudert and Maryanne C. Horowitz (eds.). Kirksville, MO: Sixteenth Century Journal Publishers, Inc. 1989. 111–130.

29 William J. Bouwsma. "Postel and the Significance of Renaissance Cabbalism." Paul Oskar Kristeller and Phillip P. Weiner. *Renaissance Essays.* New York: Harper and Row, 1968. 265.

30 *Epistola Guuilelmi Postelli ad C. Schwenckfeldium.* Jena: Christian Rhodius, 1556.

31 *Gründliche verlegung ... Donatischen Schrifften.* A viiij r.

32 "Ceterum apud eos gravissimum habuit hostem Flaccium Illyricum: iste 'nebulo Saxonicus,' sic Postello fides, qui velut papa novus in Germania dominabatur nec ipsi Melanchthonio parcebat. Nostrum interficere voluit..." Georges Weill. *De Guilelmi Postelli Vita et Indole.* Geneva: Slatkine Reprints, 1969. 61.

33 "Wilhelm Postel. Seine Geistesart und seine Reformgedanken." ARG, XV (1918). 178 f.

34 *Guillaume Postel*. The Hague, Boston, London: Martinus Nijhoff, 1981. 138n.

35 Kvačala. "Geistesart." 177.

36 CS, XIV, 1026–1031.

37 Guilaume Postel. *Apologies et Rétractiones. Manuscrits inédits publiés par François Secret*. Neiuwkoop: B. De Graaf, 1972. 234 f.

38 "Guillaume Postel et Bale." *Guillaume Postel 1581–1981. Actes du Colloque International d'Avranches 5–9 Septembre 1981*. Paris: Guy Trédaniel, 1985. 54n.

39 *Vom fürnemlichen Stücke*. UN, 1716. 771–774.

40 *Verlegung der Kurtzen Antwort*.

41 *Von der hailigen Schrifft*. CS, XII, 424 ff.

42 *Der 32. Sendbrief Geschrieben an alle die so sich an C. S. Leere halten*. CS, XIII, 521–543.

43 CS, XIII, 514.

44 *Fünfzig grobe Irthumer* [C iv v].

45 CS, XIII, 218, 221.

46 *Von der heiligen Schrifft*. C ij r.

47 *Gründliche Verlegung … Donatistischer Schrifften*. A iiiij v.

48 CS, XIII, 521–543.

49 *Juditium eines Predigers inn der Schlesien uber Matthie Flacii Illyric Schmachbuchlin, so er wider Caspar Schwenckfelden im Truck hat lassen ausgehen*. CS, XIII, 545–569. Flacius' reply: *Antwort auff das stenckfeldische Büchlein Judicium etc. genannt. Mit einem nötingen unnd schönen untgerricht, was der recte trost und wirckung der heyligen Schrifft bey allen glaubigen sey*. Nuremberg: Johannes vom Berg und Ulrich Newber, 1555.

50 CS, XIII, 545.

51 Ibid. 716.

52 *Kurtze und gründliche widderlegung der vier Schlussreden, die Johan Sigmund Werner etwa Pfarherr zu Lignitz aus Schwenckfeld's Bücher gezogen gestalt, und gericht hat wider die Christliche lere vom dienst des Göttlichen worts und der hochwirdigen Sakrament Jesu Christi des Sons Gottes*. Magdeburg: Hieronymus Wittich, 1555.

Articles of the Schwendkfeldian Schwärmerei,[39] and *Refutation of the Brief Answer of Schwenckfeld*.[40]

Flacius did not deny the importance of the Holy Spirit in creating faith, or with Schwenckfeld's statement that the Bible "cannot be rightly handled or used without the master through whom it was written, that is, without the Holy Spirit, just as it cannot be explained, translated, or understood without him, even when Hebrew, Greek, and all the arts are available."[41] But Flacius denied that the Holy Spirit was available through mystical means. Instead, God uses the Word, in the words of the Augsburg Confession, "when and where it pleases God." The Word is not in itself divine, as if it were a part of God. It is, rather, a teaching spoken or revealed by God from the whole Godhead and divine will. It has no power or effectiveness in itself, but only in that the one who speaks it wills to be powerful through it."

Flacius was a "letter theologian," the enraged Schwenckfeld wrote, who wanted to keep poor illiterates from salvation[42]; a philosopher who knew only the natural man but did not consider what Paul says: that the natural man does not understand the things of the spirit; an Aristotelian unable to distinguish between *signum* and *res*, a Thomist, a Hebrew Rabbi, a hypocrite. And now he could quote Johannes Pfeffinger's charge that Flacius was possessed by the devil.[43]

External man, Schwenckfeld said, was no more able to receive Luther's doctrine than a goose.[44] "All of Lutheranism," he wrote, "consists in that its adherents fight for the letter and the external word." The ten commandments were not God's word because they were carved in stone.[45] But the word is God's, Flacius returned, "whether it is on stone, tablets, paper, pergament, or the human memory, registered, composed, written, or spoken by the human voice.[46]

> ...when one says, "the Holy Scriptures, one does not mean the letters, a,b,c,d, or the syllables, ba, be, bi, bo, bu, or the row of the lines on the paper, ink, or the book in which it is published and recorded with letters, syllables and words in the Bible. Not only can the same meaning be written or thought, but it can also be said, sung, painted, carved, explained. It is called God's Word because God has said it, not only one time in the past, but he speaks it to us all every day and every year.[47]

In the beginning of December 1553, in answer to *On the Holy Scripture*, Schwenckfeld issued a circular letter[48] and followed it with The *Judgment of a Preacher in Silesia on the Little Book Matthias Flacius Illyricus Published against Caspar Schwenckfeld*,[49] which he sent to a "Junker," probably Flacius' friend, Sebastian von Zedlitz zu Neukirch.[50] On April 7, 1554, Schwenckfeld reported that Lutheran pastors in Silesia were levying taxes on their parishes to pay Flacius for writing against him.[51] Zedlitz saw to the publication of a *Short and Thorough Refutation of Four Farewell Speeches of J. S. Werner, Taken from Schwenckfeld's Books* by Hieronymus Wittich (Aegidius Faber of Leignitz?) and appended Flacius' "Refutation of the Book on the Word of God and of All Enthusiastic Books of Schwenckfeld," in which he included a selection of quotations from St. Augustine.[52]

Meanwhile, on September 19th, the Elector Palatine, engaged that year in introducing the Reformation, wrote Flacius that he needed learned men for the renewal of his university and church, and invited him to Heidelberg. Friedemann Merkel suggests that by calling Flacius the Elector had in mind to influence him to take a milder position and thus to further unity in the princes' Evangelical front.[53] There is, however, no evidence for such a plan. Serving as go-between, Gallus answered on October 16th that Flacius was needed in Saxony, and that he had certain difficulties with the Church Order of the Palatinate.[54] In his return letter, the Elector appears to have accepted Flacius' position.

After Johann Friedrich's death at Pentecost, 1556, *Hofmeister* Mylich asked Amsdorf if he wanted to proceed with calling Flacius. Amsdorf promptly wrote to Flacius, asking his salary requirement, and whether he could accept a call immediately in order to assist the Saxon Duke at the Diet of Regensburg.[55] On June 29 another letter arrived, inquiring about his health, and asking under what circumstances he would come.

Since the foundation of the new school at Jena, Flacius had been under consideration as professor, but Melanchthon's friends had been able to prevent the issuing of a call. Viktorin Strigel had brought with him an aristotelianizing Wittenberg curriculum, making Melanchthon the "spiritual founder" of the university.[56] He did not give up his opposition; he prohibited a student from agitating for Flacius' call,[57] and sent a letter to him, asking him not to accept the call, threatening that if he did and attempted reforms, he would not fight a "peasants' war," but would appeal to the court.[58] Flacius nevertheless accepted the call. "For the sake of Philipp the savants among us have to now been able to hinder it," he was told, "because they cannot tolerate it that anyone writes against him. But this is true: Philipp is a learned man, but Christ is much greater and higher than he."[59]

Before taking up duties in Jena, however, he had unfinished work to do – on the *Catalogus*, the church history, and the controversy with Schwenckfeld.[60] And he soldiered on. He could hardly stand reading Schwenckfeld, he said, because of the sophistries. But as *Some Contradictions or Contrary Doctrines*[61] shows, he still read him carefully. It was curious, he wrote, that Schwenckfeld, who crusaded against external doctrines and against books, produced so many of them. Flacius' latest was answered the same year by Schwenckfeld,[62] and by Georg Mayer of Leder in Swabia under the pseudonym, "Theophilus Agricola."[63] But Flacius continued with a *Thorough Refutation of All Harmful Schwärmerei*.[64] And for the first time, he printed Luther's formal curse on Schwenckfeld.

> The Lord rebuke you, Satan, and may your spirit, which has called you and your course in which you run, and all those who participate with you, Sacramentarians and Eutychians, be with you and with your blasphemies to destruction, as it is written, 'I did not send, yet they ran; I did not speak to them, yet they prophesied [Jeremiah 23.21.][65]

Schwenckfeld was eager to end the controversy; his *Conclusion and Farewell* was meant to be his last word.[66] He charged Flacius, "this slave," with

53 *Geschichte des evangelischen Bekenntnisses in Baden von der Reformation bis zur Union.* Karlsuhe: Verlag Evangelischer Presseverband, 1960. 51.

54 The letter of call and Gallus' reply are printed in Schottenloher. *Ottheinrich.* 168–170. Cf. p. 48.

55 Cod. Guelf. 79 Helmst. f. 123.

56 Wundt. 31.

57 MBW, 5760.

58 Johann Georg Walch. *Historische und Theologische Einleitung in die Religionsstreitigkeiten der evangelischen Lutherschen Kirchen* I. Jena, 1730. 70.

59 Hartmann. 94.

60 Ibid. 98.

61 *Ettliche Contradictiones, oder widerwertige Lehr des Stenckfelts, Daraus sein Geist leichtlich kan geprüfet und geurtheylet werden. Item Beweysung, das Stenckfeld die heylige Schrifft verwirffet, und in die höchste Verachtung bringet. Item, ein klares gezeugnus Hieremie Das die von Gott geoffenbarte, und nu beschribne Lere, ein warhafftiges wort Gottes sey und billig genant werde.* Nuremberg: Johann vom Berg und Ulrich Newber, 1556.

62 *Defension auff Flacij Illyrici Buchlin, Contradiction genandt.* [Augsburg: Hans Gegler], 1556. CS, XIV, 981–1031.

63 *Kurtze antwort auf das Büchlein so Matthias Flacius Illyricus wider Caspar Schwenckfeldt hat inn Druck lassen Ausgehen, das er nennet Etliche Contradictiones,* 1552. CS, XIV, 957–980; Salig. III, 1065 f.

64 *Gründliche Verlegung ... Stenckfelds.*

65 Pronounced December 6th, 1543, and printed for the first time by Flacius: *Antwort auf das Stenckfeldische Büchlein* etc. Schwenckfeld replied with *Ableinung D. Luthers Malediction, so erst durch Flacium Illyricum wider mich im truck ist publicirt worden. Item, vom rechten grund und verstande dess H. Sacraments des Herrn Nachtmals.* Ulm: Hans Varnier, 1555. CS, IX, 29–84; CS, XIV, 507–513; Williams and Mergal.

163–181. On the charge that Flacius falsified the text, cf. Enders. XV, 176; WA. *Tischreden* V. 300, 19.

66 *Beschluss unnds Valete. Auff Flacij Illyrici letste zwai schmachbüchlen, antwurt und gruntliche verlegung genant. Und das Caspar Schwenckfeld kain Donatist sey.* Ulm: Hans Varnier, 1555. CS, XIV, 514–595.

67 *Iuditium auff Flaccij Illyrici letztes Buchlin so im 1557 Jar wider C. Schwenckfelt an die von Strassburg ist Aussgangen.* n. p. 1558.

68 Keller. 26.

69 Ibid. 94 f.

70 Salig. III, 497–501.

71 *Fünffzig grobe Irthumer.* Op. cit.

72 *Ableynung und Verantwortung der fünfftzig Lügen oder Calumnien Flacii Illyrici so er felschlich auss meinen Buechern gezogen, jüngst in truck hat lassen aussgehen.* n. p. 1559. CS, XVI, 1052–1061.

73 *Urtheil von den Schwenckfeldischen Schwermerey. Von dem grewlichen irthumen der newen Schwenckfeldischen Postill unter dem namen des Johans Woermers newlich ausgangen.* Jena: Thomas Rebart, 1559.

74 [Civilius, pseudonym]. *Beweisung das auch die unwirdigen den Leib und Blut Iesu Christi im Abendmal empfahen, wieder ein Schwenckfeldisch Büchlein, so newlich ohne Namen durch den Druck ausgestrewet worden.* Ursel: Nicolas Henricus [1564].

75 CS, XV, 297.

having learned his grammar and Hebrew more in the school of the Jews than of the Holy Spirit, and admonished Lutheran preachers to "improve themselves, forsake their error, and give place in their hearts to truth." And in a two-page pamphlet, *Judgment on Flacus' latest Booklet* of 1557[67] he called Flacius Satan. "What have I to do with you?" he asks. "The truth of Schwenckfeld's writing is too searching for Flacius' unclean spirit."

People were recognizing Flacius as Luther's disciple. One heard quoted 2 Kings 2.25: "the Spirit of Elijah rests on Elisha." According to Keller, Flacius explicated what Luther wrote about the external word, *verbum externum*,[68] and the living voice of the gospel, *viva vox evangelii*.[69] By continuing Luther's polemics against Schwenckfeld, and in the process, developing further Luther's doctrine of the sacraments and of the ministerial office, Flacius can be thought of as a kind of Elisha. Schwenckfeld sourly agreed that a new Elisha was at work – one who was the equal of his mentor at producing polemics.

In 1558 Flacius charged Schwenckfeld with *Fifty Gross Errors*. Forty-two from his list made their way into a confession of the church of Mansfeld.[70] He appended the 1540 repudiation of Schwenckfeld by the Smalcaldic League.[71] Schwenckfeld undertook to answer all of the charges, but managed to reply to only one.[72] Flacius persisted in the attack. In 1559 he published a pamphlet against a much-used Schwenckfeldian postil,[73] and in 1564 against a Schwenckfeldian book on communion.[74]

His polemics contributed a great deal to the diminution, even the defeat, of Schwenckfeldianism. According to the editor of the *Corpus Schwenckfeldianorum*, Flacius' campaign was disastrous. "The persecutions of the Schwenckfelders in the villages and community surrounding Löwenberg [Silesia] in the last decades of the sixteenth century until their migration to America in 1734 are plainly traceable to the influence of such provocative writings as those of [Caspar] Radecker and his colleague, Musaeus of Breslau, who received inspiration and instruction thereto at Wittenberg and were spurred on by the garrulous Matthias Flacius Illyricus of Magdeburg."[75]

Facing Disunity

A FAILED HANSEATIC CONCORD

> I truly and ardently want to be one ... with all men, but in Christ. – Flacius

> Accusing Flacius of having caused division is like Ahab to Elijah: "Is it you, you troubler of Israel?" – Amsdorf

Like two tectonic plates, two Lutheran traditions confronted each other, the South and the North. In the South, as it had for a thousand years, feudal order prevailed. In the Hanseatic cities of the North, there was a semi-democracy. In the South, the *jus episcopale* was exercized by the princes, to whom it had been assigned at the 1526 Diet of Speyer. In the North, that right was exercised in a congregational (*gemeindekirchlich*) fashion, and the burghers participated in both secular and religious matters.[1]

After the Anabaptist Incident in Münster in 1534, Hamburg, Lübeck, Rostock and Stralsund acted together to ban preachers who rejected the Augsburg confession. "I discern," Flacius wrote, "that up to now God has willed to gather to himself a church, and to preserve true doctrine in those Saxon cities."[2] The same confessional unity continued during the Interim crisis. Although Hamburg Superintendent Johannes Aepinus was unable to organize common resistance at a *Hansetag*, he was able to lead the *Ministerium Tripolitanum*, Lübeck, Hamburg, and Lüneberg, to a common anti-Interim confession.[3] Their alliance was "the guarantor of Protestantism all over north and northwest Germany."[4]

In 1556, the summons to a Diet at Regensburg was cause for alarm. The end of effective imperial power over the Evangelical churches by the Princes' Revolt in 1552, the Treaty of Passau, and the Augsburg Diet of 1555, might have been expected to result in Evangelical unity. But the disarray the Interim law had produced continued. Flacius and Gallus denied that it was their fault.[5] Amsdorf agreed: "Accusing Flacius of having caused division is like Ahab to Elijah: 'Is it you, you troubler of Israel?'"[6]

Since the problem of religious unity was also the problem of political unity, it was not surprising that the princes intervened, and that their solution was compromise. Duke Christoph of Württemberg accordingly sent envoys to Weimar in January, 1556, to work out some common position. Although Flacius did not take part in their conference with the Ernestine theologians, it was nevertheless called the "Flacian Synod." Weimar theologians Stolz, Aurifaber, Schnepf and Strigel, unwilling to break faith with Johann Friedrich, announced their conditions for agreement: fidelity on the Lord's Supper, a return to the Augsburg Confession, condemnation of

1 Heinz Schilling makes a distinction between the Burgher church on one side, and the territorial, authoritarian system, with a bureacratic church under control of the prince and his central administration on the other. "The Reformation in the Hanseatic Cities." *Sixteenth Century Journal* XIV (1983). 453 ff.
2 *Catalogus*, 1562. A 3 r.
3 *Bekentnuß unnd Erklerung*. A ij v.
4 Ibid. 447.
5 *Provocation oder Erbieten*. Op. cit.
6 *Ein kurtzer Unterricht*. A iij r.

7 Ibid. 217.

8 *Bericht*, 1559. M i v.

9 Salig. III, 217.

10 Visser. 234.

11 *Von der Einigkeit. Op. cit.*
Flacius' 21 steps to unity are summarized by Diener, 144: (1) No one
admits to error for allowing the
Interim for four years, only
self-justification. (2) Philipp even
said for a public sin there should be
a public penance – for an acciden-
tal death. How much more so in the
case of the Interim? (3) When one
has committed a scandal, the first
responsibility is to undo the wrong.
(4) One is duty-bound to honor
God rather than men in times of
crisis, rebuilding the church (not as
though what happened was but a
slight perturbation!). (5) Stop the
false teaching; stop turning priorities around. (6) Where there had
been false teaching, a clear refutation and damnation are in order.
(7) Do the proper penance: to allow Adiaphorists peace and quiet is
to allow them to entrench themselves even deeper. (8) A proper
punishment for open wrong-doing
is in order. (9) Evil examples are to
be uprooted, not treated to amnesty. (10) Ingratitude is being cited:
how is gratitude shown by praising
evil, by commending what is wrong,
by flattering? (11) Those who fall
must be restored and forgiven, but
they must admit their wrong. For
eight years they prosper, not suffer;
they continue unchanged. Remember the story of Marcellinus and
three kernels of incense: he was
damned by a church council and
deposed. (12) The Adiaphorists
help turn over church properties to
anxious princes to rule, and cater to
the forms of protocol of Antichrist.
(13) Now the lay officers want the
power of the keys [in the consisto-
ries] to dictate what gets preached,
taught, prayed, sung, and how the
church is ruled, linking secular
powers and religious powers, politics and personalities. (14) The

Zwingli, Schwenckfeld, Major, and of the Wittenberg notions about the adiaphora and free will.

There was great concern for unity elsewhere as well. Superintendent Tilemann Heshusius of Goslar favored negotiating.[7] Prince Wolf of Anhalt and Baron Hans Ungnad recommended that Elector August take the Wittenberg theologians to court, or that they be induced in some way to come to a peaceful agreement.[8] Even his schoolboys at Meissen were concerned, Rector George Fabricius reported, observing that both Melanchthon and Flacius took more time for prayer than for study.[9]

Melanchthon preferred confidential theological talks out of the public eye,[10] but Flacius argued for "public unity" based on open debate. That was a thousand times better, he said, than "private unity." He contrasted the two methods in *On the Unity of Those, Who in the Years Past, Have Contended For and Against the Adiaphora.*[11] The pamphlet was part of his following Jesus' advice from St. Matthew 18.15: "... if he refuses to listen to them, tell it to the church."

He offered a plan: "Gentle Proposals to Bring About a Godly, Needful and Peaceful Reconciliation Between the Theologians of Wittenberg and Leipzig and Others Who have Written Against Them,"[12] which is notable for recognizing the Smalcald Articles for the first time as a confessional document. Flacius suggested that the two sides prepare written statements. They should agree on restoration of the Augsburg Confession, condemna-tion of the Council of Trent, the Augsburg Interim, Zwingli, Osiander, Schwenckfeld, and the Anabaptists. And, since he had concluded that the papal curia had finally prevailed over the Hussite movement by the tactic of "divide and conquer," curial influence should be avoided by an agreement that the pope was Antichrist.

His statement is also notable for recognizing the difference between politics and theology: politics demands compromise, but theology demands truth. "All intelligent, pious, earnest people must understand that it is necessary to act otherwise in matters of faith than in civil affairs, where amnesty is conceded, that is, errors are passed over in silence." And he repeated his essential argument in the adiaphora controversy, "We declare that it is not proper for the civil government to make any changes in good and tolerable ceremonies without the knowledge and consent of the churches..."

A meeting with Melanchthon in the interest of a common theological agreement was not easy to arrange. On July 13 in a letter to Languet, Fla-cius volunteered to come to a meeting at the small town of Coswig with two witnesses, and Melanchthon should do the same. "I will bring one or, at the most, two witnesses to the colloquy ... Philipp can do the same. In the word-ing I promise the highest restraint and mildness, but out of conscience I can forgive nothing of the matter itself."[13] Melanchthon emphatically re-fused. Someone had told him it would be dangerous. "What profit would there be," he asked, "in a meeting with uneducated, rabid, mad, parasitical or tribunicial courtiers [*aulicis gnathonibus at tribuniciis*], which the Proud

One is, and I see Gallus and Aurifaber are?"[14] Flacius observed that expressions like "unlearned, rabid, mad with hate" hardly made for peace.[15]

Melanchthon was convinced that Flacius was plotting to murder him. The Duke of Mecklenberg had asked Chytraeus whether anything could be done to restore peace, and Chytraeus had replied, "As long as Melanchthon is alive no unity will be restored." Caspar Peucer edited the story a bit, and had reported that "In order to make peace, Melanchthon should be removed."[16] "A sweet friendship and intimacy existed between Flacius and myself," Melanchthon had written once, but now meeting with him was not safe.

> I should like to discuss the whole system of doctrine with him. But he has circulated things about me which I have never uttered, and which never entered into my thoughts. Therefore, I fear treacherous intentions in all this. Oh! that he would act toward me with the same sincerity with which I should wish to approach him! But not one of my friends is willing to be present at such an interview and they are of the opinion that it is not safe for me to meet him alone, I am not concerned if others are pleased to seek power and influence. The Son of God will judge the life and sentiments of everyone, and he knows that I am only anxious to glorify the truth, to add to God's honor and to promote the good of the church.[17]

When Melanchthon complained of "oppression," Flacius remarked that he should recall who it was who had oppressed David of Freyberg and Pastor Martin Wolf of Colditz. On September 1, 1556, in another letter he summarized the situation, and asked Melanchthon to recant. Achieving unity would be simple, Flacius explained, if only Melanchthon and his friends were to confess and renounce their error publicly – to sing the dear *peccavi*, as he put it: "I have sinned." David had done it after his involvement with Bathsheba. After sacrificing three grains of incense to the emperor, Pope Marcellinus had done it. In his *Retractions*, St. Augustine had done it. Regretting his early writings on indulgences, Luther had done it.[18] In a letter of September 5, Melanchthon recanted:

> Conquer! I yield. I will not contend about these rites. I greatly desire that the church should have peace. I confess that in this matter I made a mistake, and I ask pardon from God that I did not fly far from those treacherous deliberations.[19]

It was his peccavi, *but not a public peccavi*. For Flacius, Melanchthon's simple admission was not enough. In private confession to Pastor Bugenhagen, he observed, he had already confessed that he had sinned in the question of adiaphora, and had been absolved.[20] But what he had confessed privately, Flacius observed, he had not admitted publicly.[21]

> It may have been sufficient for Ajax, who fought for his own glory and that of others that his proud opponent gave was before him in the presence of both armies. But for me, who do not seek glory or triumph, but only the continuation of truth and the destruction of error – for me and my conscience the retreat, couched and hidden in a few words, is not sufficient, when a threat is made at the same time of new writings, and it does not remove an error which has been defended violently.

> Nowhere is it demanded that you or another participant condemn yourself even with a single stroke of the pen, or that you give in to me like Hector or Ajax, or admit

godless bishops return for their jurisdictions and rules, also to the Evangelical preachers and churches. (15) Osiander is to be treated to amnesty, even though he is an open heretic, leading many people astray. (16) Those who were persecuted and driven off by the Adiaphorists are still out; the persecutors are still on top. (17) No attempt is made to undo the basic evils of the Interim, where people were forced to comply and are still forced against their wills. (18) Those who bore false witness should confess to the earlier character assassinations. (19) Those who refuse to damn the heretics and show what is wrong and right are also deniers of the truth. (20) Do not teach contrary to the truth. (21) Help lead the fallen back to confess, be absolved and live in God's grace again.

12 "Linde Vorschläge, dadurch man gottselige und notwendige friedliche Vergleichung machen könnte zwischen den Wittenbergischen und Leipzigischen theologen und den andern, so gegen sie gechrieben." Cod. Guelf. 11.13 Aug. 2° 115 f. Translation from Georg J. Fritschl. *The Formula of Concord: Its Origin and Contents*. Philadelphia: The Lutheran Publications Society, 1916. 69 f.

13 CR, VIII, 794 f.

14 Ibid. 798.

15 Ibid. 803.

16 Chytraeus: "nullam, dum viveret Philippus, concordiam in Ecclesia futuram esse." Peucer: "nullam in ecclesiae concordiam, nisi extincto Philippo sperandum esse; tollendum et opprimendum esse Praeceptorum." Otto Frid. Schütz. *De Vita Davidis Chytraei Commentorium Libri Duo ultimi*. Hamburg: Christian Guilielmo Brancitius, 1728. I, 147 f.

17 CR, VIII, 798 f.

18 *Epistola ad Phil. Melanchthonem missa d. 1. Sept. 1556 per quendam Scholasticum*. Bindseil. 573–589.

19 CR, VIII, 841 f.

20 *Auf das Auschreiben der zweien Universiteten.* C iij.

21 Ibid. C iiij v.

22 Preger. II, 29 f.

23 Schilling. "Hanseatic Cities." 443, 445.

24 Bernd Moeller. *Reichstadt und Reformation.* Gütersloh: Mohn, 1962. 62.

25 Salig. III, 239.

26 Wartenberg. "Nachwirkungen." 243.

27 "Marian exiles were drawing on a well-established Lutheran tradition when they propounded the theory of the right of inferior magistrates to resist their superiors." Cargill Thompson. 200, 202.

28 Oliver K. Olson. "Theology of Revolution: Magdeburg 1550–1551." *Sixteenth Century Journal* III (1967). 45–69.

29 *The Rise and Fall of the Third Reich.* New York: Simon & Schuster, 1960.

30 Sillem. II, 678.

31 Georg Theodor Strobel. "Nachricht von Michael Stiefels Leben und Schriften." *Neue Beiträge zur Litteratur besonders des sechzehnten Jahrhunderts.* Bd. I, Stück I. 73.

that you have erred. We only desire to acknowledge and indicate that peace has been reestablished among us on the basis of the articles submitted.[22]

The confrontation with Melanchthon would be historic. Flacius kept pressing for the public disavowal, and now matters were approaching a climax. To make his point, Flacius enlisted the complete leadership of the Hanseatic Reformation, the "bright light of the non-authoritarian elements of the Reformation."[23] Bernd Moeller has observed that the Northwest German towns never produced a "great and independent Protestant theologian,"[24] but in 1557 they adopted one: Flacius was accepted as the spokesman for Hanseatic Lutheranism. Representatives of North German churches gathered in Magdeburg, the Mediators, Superintendent Paul von Eitzen and Pastor Joachim Westphal of Hamburg; Superintendent Valentin Curtius (Korte) and Pastor Dionysius Schünemann of Lübeck; Superintendent Joachim Mörlin and Pastor Martin Chemnitz of Braunschweig; Superintendent Friedrich Henninges and Pastor Anton Wippermann of Lüneburg. Johann Wigand, Johann Baumgartner, Matthaeus Judex and Flacius represented the Magdeburg church.

The basis of the negotiations, the Mediators decided, would be Flacius' "Gentle Proposals," and they would not accept any agreement which deviated from his *On the Unity.* Martin Chemnitz announced that the mediators were not neutral, but in solidarity with Magdeburg. The representatives of the Hanseatic churches then formally accepted the 1550 *Confession and Apology of the Pastors and Other Ministers of the Church of Magdeburg.*[25]

The confession is the source of a doctrine of armed resistance to tyranny: the duty of inferior magistrates under certain circumstances to take up arms against superior magistrates. It was influential in stimulating the Princes' Revolution of 1552,[26] the Huguenot wars (via Theodore Beza), and the revolts of England,[27] Scotland and the Netherlands.[28] William Shirer over-simplifies the course of German political history in a fashion which makes him suspect of the logical fallacy, *post hoc ergo propter hoc.* Drawing a direct line from Luther to Hitler,[29] he makes reference neither to those unaware of the Confession of Magdeburg and its influence nor to the politically conservative influence of Melanchthon.

The next station of the mediators was at an inn at Coswig, thirteen kilometers from Wittenberg. It was crowded; Anton Otto of Nordhausen had to share a bed with Westphal.[30] Albert Christian, now Superintendent of Cothen, was there, sent by Prince Wolfgang of Anhalt, together with Pastor Peter Arbiter of Münchenwurmburg, and Henrich Brentius, pastor of Calbe. Luther's old friend, the mathematician and Pastor of Brück, Michael Stifel, appeared. He described his difficulties controlling his emotions when he saw Flacius for the first time. "It seemed to me," he wrote, "that I was seeing a second Luther."[31]

Flacius asked the mediators to set aside personal ambition and to conduct themselves manfully, insisting he was acting not from love of controversy, but for love of truth. They should tear the fig leaf from their body, remove the devilish poison planted in their beards, resist the Wittenbergers just as bravely as once Nathan had resisted King David, Elijah had resisted King Ahab, and Paul had resisted Peter. "Oral and written utterances of Flacius," Hans-Werner Gensichen concluded, "as well as his entire behavior, show that he was honestly striving for a settlement with Melanchthon. Untiringly he began new approaches to mediation as often as the previous attempt failed." Since Wittenberg was dangerous – unfriendly students might attack them – with Judex and Baumgärtner he stayed behind at Coswig. Caspar Peucer called it "Flacius' acropolis."[32]

Friedrich Loofs called the controversies of the post-Lutheran generation "pathological."[33] Otto Ritschl, in contrast, called them "a church-historical event of the first rank."[34] For one thing, Loofs did not consider the *political* implications of the adiaphora controversy. Joachim Westphal understood the problem:

> Ministers of the church and secular authorities have different callings. The secular rulers exercise their rule in the marketplace and in secular matters. In religious and spiritual matters, however, authority and subjects are equal. And both are responsible for obedience to their pastors, who rule with God's word. One should not be obedient to the government in that which is against God.[35]

Unlike the mediators of 1557, who spoke primarily in the name of the church, the formulators of the Concord of 1577 were also in the employ of autocratic princes. It was a circumstance that effected the softened wording of some parts of Article X of the Formula of Concord. To understand the significance of confrontation in 1557,[36] we should consider the description of the controversy in the 1577 Formula of Concord.

> The chief question has been, in times of persecution, when a confession is called for, and when the enemies of the Gospel have not come to an agreement with us in doctrine, may we with an inviolate conscience yield to their pressure and demands, reintroduce some ceremonies that have fallen into disuse and that in themselves are indifferent things and are neither commanded nor forbidden by God, and thus come to an understanding with them in such ceremonies and indifferent things?[37]

The statement is not innacurate, but it would have been understood more clearly as a controversy about the relationship of church and state had it been written thus:

> The chief question has been, whether secular government has the authority to regulate indifferent matters, and thus to assume the government of the church.

Saying farewell to the mediators, Flacius fairly trembled at the thought that they might decide to call off the negotiations prematurely.[38] The mediators met with Melanchthon at 6.00 a.m. on June 21. Mörlin, acting as spokeman, reviewed the history of the controversy. They offered to negotiate on the basis of Flacius' *On the Unity*. Chemnitz reported that they were not neutral, but agreed with *On the Unity* and the Magdeburg Confession of 1550.

32 "Peuceri Brieff vom Flacischen Vergleich." FS, 1726. 361–63. Here, 361.
33 Op. cit. 897.
34 Op. cit. II, 328.
35 *Gründliche verlegung des Gründlichen Berichts der Adiaphoristen.* D iv r.
36 Documents in Johann Bacmeister. *Acta Philippica. Sive: Theologorum Sachsonicorum & Legatorum megapolensium frustra tentata pacificatio inter Philippum Melanchthonem & Matthiam Flacium Illyricum.* Tübingen: Hiobus Franckus, 1716.
37 BSELK, 314; Tappert. 492 f.
38 Gensichen. 129.

39 "Philipp Melanchthon, der bedeutenste Sohn der Stadt Bretten." Alfons Schäfer. *Geschichte der Stadt Bretten von den Anfängen bis zur Zerstörung 1689.* Bretten, 1977. 273.

40 Salig. III, 343.

41 *Historische Nachricht von einem zu Coswig im Jahr 1557 im Jan. angestellten Convent.* Wolfenbüttel: Joh. Christoph Meisner, 1737. 100.

42 CR, IX, 38.

43 Ibid. 53–55.

44 Ibid. 55–57.

45 "Martin Luther, die Diaspora, Österreich und der Südosten-Reformation: Epoche oder Episode?" *Lutherische Kirche in der Welt. Jahrbuch des Martin Luther-Bundes* XXXII (1985). 150.

Had Melanchthon accepted the mediation, the Magdeburg Confession (with its resistance doctrine!), would have been the lasting Formula of Concord, and the difficult negotiations leading to the agreement of 1577 would not have been necessary.

Heinz Scheible calls the mediators "fanatical," bent on humiliating Melanchthon.[39] The record suggests something quite different. When they read their proposals, Melanchthon flew into a rage,[40] and shouted, "you have come to crush me! Take me away, make me a martyr, crucify me, strangle me! The courts and the common people are stirred up against me with cunning tricks!" So angry was he that the mediators, all of them his former students, feared he would become ill. They called in Paul Eber to assure him that they were not partisan. Eber finally succeeded in calming him down. Hardly a demonstration, Johann Marcus observed, of the famous *lenitas Philippica*.[41]

The next day, having regained his composure, Melanchthon made a speech.

> For thirty years I have labored not a little in these churches, in teaching, developing truths, in daily arguments, conferences, and in treacherous conflicts. And it would have been very becoming in you to spare and pity me. But now, that which the worthy Jacob Sturm prophesied to me has come to pass; for when he, together with some other friends, accompanied me a part of the way when I left Regensburg, and I said to him that we would not see each other again in this world, he replied, "We shall still come to you some day to crucify you."[42]

He refused to negotiate on the basis of Flacius "Gentle Proposals." He suggested that the mediators formulate their own articles. If the mediators would do so, he would consider them. They replied that that was precisely their task. Melanchthon addressed them formally in a speech in which he accused Flacius and Gallus of slander. The presupposition of unity was agreement on all of doctrine, and Flacius had expressed himself only on some matters. Melanchthon's practice, he said, to avoid increasing the controversy, was to remain silent. He was glad he would soon die.[43]

When the mediators presented their eight articles,[44] Melanchthon responded.

> Articles are laid before me, in which I am not only required to strangle myself, but very many of my friends. You spare Flacius. You know yourselves what intimate friendship subsisted between some of you and myself. And on this account, I am so much the more surprised to see you treat me so harshly. If I do not agree to your articles, you will excite your party against me; but if I do agree, many in our churches will complain of me that I have given them cause for offense. There is, consequently, danger on both sides, and it would have been better to negotiate with many concerning this."

As his reaction to the mediators' articles shows, Melanchthon was firm on two fateful matters: the freedom of the will, and the right of the secular government to determine adiaphora.

Resistance doctrine thus, as Peter Barton notes, was effectively neutralized in the Melanchthon school.[45] Hans Iwand compares Melanchthon's conservatism to Hegel's: "...thanks to the theological grounding of governmental authority by Melanchthon, the right of resistance against the government totally disappears, not otherwise as with Hegel in his *Staatslehre*, published three hundred years later."[46]

> Where Lutheranism succeeded, the church came to be conceived as invisible, apolitical, alegal, and the only sovereignty, the only law (in the political sense), was that of the secular kingdom as principality.[47]

> German Protestantism became an instrument of royal and princely absolutism from the sixteenth century until the kings and princes were dethroned in 1918.[48]

During the negotiations, reports were sent back to Coswig. In the presence of Melanchthon, Deacon Johan Curio denounced the mediators as heretics by name, calling Flacius "a cheater and rascal." "I hear you were sent by Flacius," thundered Bugenhagen. "Go and restrain the anger and madness of this fellow, so that he stops lying and abusing!"[49] The hostile atmosphere in those days is reflected by the charge in a Wittenberg poem announcing that the mediators came out of Illyricus' anus.

> Qui huc venistis, legati
> Illyrici permerdati,
> Ab illo concaccati,
> Polypragmones inflati,
> Illius natibus nati,
> Quae communio veritati
> Mendacio & vanitati?
> Nulla vmquam sit compositis
> Veritati cum mendacio,
> Viro bono cum fallaci,
> Viro candido cum mendaci.[50]

> Legates of Illyricus
> who have come here,
> covered with dung, defiled by him,
> puffed-up meddlers,
> born from his rump,
> what does truth have in common
> with falsehood and deceit?
> Let there be no connection, ever,
> between a good man and a deceitful one,
> between a pure man and a liar.

On June 27, Melanchthon refused to pursue the talks.

Disappointed, Flacius tried yet another means, and appealed for help to Duke Johann Albrecht of Mecklenburg, who had assisted in the matter of Osiandrism.[51] Four weeks later, George Venetus, professor at Rostock, and the councilor, Andreas Mylius, were in Wittenberg to lay new articles before Melanchthon.[52] Their articles on the sacrament and the place of the will in conversion had a Melanchthonian cast, but took a critical stance in the articles on justification, good works and the adiaphora. Among other matters, they contained a condemnation of Peter Canisius, who in a sermon

46 "Das Widerstandsrecht der Christen nach der Lehre der Reformatoren." *Nachgelassene Werke* II. ed. by H. Gollwitzer et al. Munich: Kaiser, 1966. 199f.

47 Herold Berman. *Law and Revolution.* Cambridge, MA: Harvard University Press, 1983. 29.

48 William Shirer. *The Nightmare Years, 1938–1940* II. Toronto et al.: Bantam Books, 1984, 188.

49 Heppe. *Geschichte* I. 129.

50 CR, IX, 50, cf. 65.

51 Marcus. 98.

52 CR, IX, 92–103.

53 *Beati Petri Canisii S. J. Epistulae et Acta* I. 1541–1546. Ed. Otto Braunsberger. Freiburg im Breisgau: Herder, 1896. 769, cf. 768; II, 83.

54 Strobel. *Ratzebergs ... Geschichte.* 120.

55 Döllinger. II, 240.

56 *Geschichte.* 34.

57 O. Ritschl. II, 361.

58 Diener. 191, 194.

59 *Omnia Latina Scripta* I. vij v.

60 Fligge, 1972. 376.

at Prague, had criticized the prayer, *Christe, ora pro nobis,* and attempted to establish rather the invocation of the saints. Sitting at the right hand of the Father, Canisius argued, Christ is the mediator between God and men only because of his merits, not by his intercession.[53] The Mecklenburgers said Canisius' doctrine was in contradiction to Hebrews 7.

Reacting to the new initiative, Melanchthon flew into a rage once again, and refused to listen. He shouted invectives against Illyricus and others, even the Prince and the envoys. They were asking him to strangle himself. The Mecklenburgers had all kinds of dangerous plots against him; to prove Illyricus right they would rob him of honor, body and possessions and make him an object of shame and scorn.[54] He brought up the old charges – Flacius denied Christ's divinity, and objected to using the word "gospel" to mean preaching repentance.[55]

The talks failed, Heussi thought, because of Flacius' intractability.[56] Otto Ritschl, on the other hand, blames the failure on Melanchthon's hatred.[57] In the end, in his *Testament,* and in the revised edition of the *Chronicle of Carion,* pointedly dedicated to Flacius' arch-enemy, Archbishop Sigismund, Margrave of Brandenburg,[58] Melanchthon repudiated even his small concessions. "I truly and ardently want to be one ..." Flacius insisted in his own defense, "with all men, but in Christ."[59] According to Jörg-Rainer Fligge, the records show "that Flacius was serious about the negotiations."[60] In his review of the controversy, Gensichen agrees.

> True, he was not ready to make any kind of substantive concessions to Melanchthon. The agreement he wanted would have resulted in a one-sided capitulation on the part of Melanchthon. But did he perhaps wish only to experience the personal triumph of seeing the celebrated teacher of the church come over to his side by an act of penitent recantation? Of this, too, there is no indication. The continued emphasis of his interest in the issues and the explicit repudiation of all purely personal motives may not be brushed aside as hypocrisy and deceit, as the Wittenbergers did. Now as during the Interim, Flacius was manifestly of the sincere conviction "that in an emergency one must for the sake of love pull his teacher out of the water, even if that required pulling his beard."

> Thus, the conclusion is inescapable that Flacius was entirely serious both in his demands for condemnation and in his will to union. It is evident that he did not regard these two aspects as being mutually exclusive. He sought an understanding on the basis of a joint condemnation, a condemnation which expected of one of the parties a repudiation of a cause he had hitherto espoused, even though, technically, he was not asked to condemn himself.

> It is quite understandable that Melanchthon could not agree to this proposal. Yet it does remain significant that Flacius could in all seriousness pursue such a goal until the end. If he had merely demanded the conversion of the "heretic" and had declared his willingness thereafter to sit at the same table, this would not yet have been anything unusual. However, his behavior would not be adequately explained in this way.

> The essential feature is that he simultaneously demanded condemnation and evinced the desire for conciliation. Apparently the condemnation did not imply for him a definitive suspension of fellowship. Rather he strove to go through and beyond the condemnation for each new accord and fellowship. It lost none of the rigor that the situation demanded. Yet it did not wish to slam the door for good or to block definitively

the way to fellowship, as this was clearly evidenced in Luther's last dealings with the Swiss.

On the contrary, the condemnation as Flacius saw it pointed beyond itself to a new fellowship that was to draw its strength from the feeling of joint responsibility for the integrity of the evangelical teaching.[61]

THE SYNOD OF THE BIRDS

> ... the swan of Wittenberg, Melanchthon as Philomela, the sweet nightingale, and Flacius the wendish cuckoo, were universally recognized. – F. J. Stopp

Melanchthon, Gottfried Arnold reported, was "so firmly-seated in his own opinions, that when anyone does not immediately accept them as authentic, he immediately calls him a bean [*Beanen*], a bachant, or a loutish ass [*tölpischer Tummelesel*]."[1] When Flacius dared the unthinkable, questioning the authority of the Preceptor, volunteers appeared to fight a guerilla war against him. They were recruits from Melanchthon's "humanistic, nepotistic clique," his poets' circle.[2] Only neo-Latin poet Peter Lotichius, unwilling to prostrate his trade, refused to participate.[3] Johann Stigel, whom Melanchthon called "the darling of my heart,"[4] and who followed Melanchthon "like a god,"[5] volunteered. He was joined by Georg Sabinus, "the German Ovid," bearer of a laureate title granted by Pope Clement VII, and Johan Major, bearer of another, given by the imperial family.

Melanchthon's poetical troops were concerned with the Preceptor's reputation, not with theological issues. Indeed, Melanchthon was known to disdain reading anyone else's writing, usually glancing only at the beginning and the end.[6] His indifference was shared by Stigel:

> Spare me, pure priest; I did not press eagerly into your controversies, and have no taste for the all-too-high. I do not want to disturb you, who shake the heavens with wrangling, and with bickering the stars.[7]

Flacius' carefully-prepared reactions, thus, were pointless. A controversy about important theological matters had been transformed into an *ad hominem* shouting match.

"It often happens," Melanchthon had observed in an "Oration on the Ingratitude of the Cuckoo," against Jakob Schenk, "that someone educated and instructed with great conscientiousness, forgetting all kindnesses, and roused by ambition or natural malice, or envy, mounts an attack against his preceptors, not only to harm them, but by his hate of them, attempts to crush out and destroy good qualities. Does not this kind of cuckoo seem worthy of hate?"[8] In a verse "On the Cuckoo and the Nightingale,"[9] Stigel identified the ungrateful bird as Flacius.

The Vergilian and Horatian verses of Johan Major, it was said, were "pearl strings of puns made to dance to the music of the meters."[10] But

61 Gensichen. 129.

1 *Unparteyische Kirchen- und Ketzer Historie.* Frankfurt am Main: Thomas Trische, 1700. II, 109.

2 Heinrich Hermelink. *Reformation und Gegenreformation.* Tübingen: J. C. B. Mohr (Paul Siebeck), 1931. 139; Ellinger. *Literatur* II, distinguishes two circles, an older circle consisting of Melanchthon, Sabinus and Stigel, 65–120, and a younger circle, 120–149.

3 Coppel. 428.

4 Wiessenborn. 7.

5 Hans-Henning Pflanz. *Johann Stigel als Theologe (1515–1562).* Ohlau in Schlesien: Dr. Hermann Eschenhagen, 1936. 34 f.; cf. the chapter, "Stigel und Flacius." 105–112.

6 Ritschl. II, 362.

7 Georg Ellinger. *Geschichte der neulateinischen Literatur Deutschlands im sechzehnten Jahrhundert.* Berlin: Walter de Gruyter, 1929–1933. II, 85.

8 *Selectarum Declamationum Philippi Melanchtonis, quas conscripsit, & partim ipse in schola Witebergensi recitavit, partim aliis recitandas exhibuit* I. Strassburg, 1569. 569; CR, XI, 509–30.

9 "De Cuculo et Philomela." *Poematum Io. Stigelii Gothuni.* Adam Silber (ed.). Jena: Donatus Richtzehan (1577). 258v.

10 Manfred P. Fleischer. "Melanchthon as Praeceptor of Late-Humanist Poetry." *Sixteenth Century Journal* XX (1989). 569.

11 Georg Loesche. "Ein ungedrucktes Gedicht von Joh. Major." JGGPO, XV (1894). 154.

12 Ellinger. *Literatur* II. 121.

13 Gustav Frank. *Johann Major der Wittenberger Poet.* Halle: C. E. M. Pfeffer, 1863. 4 f., 25 f.; ADB, XX, II.

14 Johannes Major. *Parentalia Decimum Facta D. Philippo Melancthoni, viro clarissimo, et praeceptori communis in Academia Witebergensi.* Wittenberg: Haeredas Laurentii Schurenck, 1575. C ij r.

15 Feller. *Hortus Libani.* Johannes Henricus Seelenius. *Philocalia Epistola s. Centuria Epistolae.* Lübeck: Böckmann, 1728. 66.

16 "Idyllion de Philomela." CR, XX, 776 f.; Clemen. KS, VI, 243.

17 Bindseil. 587.

18 Köstlin. *Baccalaurei.* 1538–1546. 18n.

19 August 20th. CR, IX, 235; "Philolelam quidam persuadebant nobis ipso [Melanchthon] invito aut nescio editam esse, sed iam tertio recusa et aucta est, ut audio ..." Cf. CR, XX, 776 f.; KS, IV, 243.

20 *Synodus Avium Depingens Miserum Faciem Ecclesiae propter Certamina Quorundam, Qui de Primatu contendunt, cum oppressione recta meritorum.* n. p. 1557.

21 Not the colloquy at Worms (Pflug. *Correspondance.* V/2, 253), or the conference at Frankfurt am Main (Salig. III, 257, CR, XX, 767). The latter was *another* "synod of the birds" – "Est igitur *altera* haec ornithosynodus." CR, IX, 178.

22 "Quam Dominum Philippum sua manu correxisse mihi constant." Clemen. KS, VI, 243.

23 CXX, 767, attributes the poem, a "camen acutoris nomine non adscripta" to Melanchthon.

24 "Pauli ab Eitzen Brief an Volquard Jonae." 1558. DB, IV (1743). 195 f.

25 Ritter. 88; Döllinger. II, 240.

among Flacius' supporters he was known as the "slander poet"[11]; he served as "Melanchthon's poetic shield-bearer against Flacius and his associates."[12] "Glorification of Melanchthon, which he overdid, even according to Wittenberg standards," writes his biographer, "and vilification of Flacius henceforth would be the prevailing theme of his life."[13]

Both themes are evident in the following:

> O fugite hos fumos, et lumen amate Philippi
> Quod praefert vobis quaerenda ad limina coeli,
> Oppositaque manu nocua defendite ab aura,
> Sive Caci, sive Illyria spiravit ab antro.[14]

> O flee these vapors, and love the light of Philipp
> That conveys that you should seek the gates of heaven,
> And with your hand, drive from the air the opposite poison.
> It blows from a cave of a rascal, or from Illyria.

In his "Garden of Lebanon," Flacius appeared as a noxious weed.[15] Filled at first by God at the foot of Lebanon (Wittenberg=White Mountain) with medicinal herbs, the garden had been like the original paradise that perished in the flood. The honey-flower, *Melissa* (Melanchthon), was able to heal the bite of scorpions, rabid dogs and unnumbered other illnesses. The lord of hell looked on the garden, but was not able to despoil it with storms from the North [the Lower Saxon theologians]. So he sowed weeds, including *Wolfwurz* (Flacius). From those poisonous plants, Circe prepared a sap that turned men into beasts and the garden into a wilderness.

Major, too, took up the cuckoo theme. Well-known was John Huss the goose ("Huss" in Czech is "Goose"), who, about to be burned at the stake, said he was only a goose, but that after him a swan would come. That swan, it was said, was Luther. And now another bird flew in – Flacius, the cuckoo. In his "Idyll of the Nightingale," Major describes "a hideous fowl ... A vagrant cuckoo (who) sensessly attacks Philomela."[16] When the poem was published a second time, Flacius objected. "About the 'philomela' I was persuaded by certain people, that it had been published against your will, but now, with a second printing in the volume of intimations, I do not believe you any more."[17] But the appellation stuck: in the faculty matriculation register in the margin next to his name, somebody explained that Flacius was a "cuckoo and zoilus [censorious person] and vicious persecutor of the school and the preceptors": *Cuculus et Zoilus deinde factus et scholae et praeceptorum sceleratus insectator.*[18] Then, the idyll of the Nightingale was published yet a third time.[19]

The most famous use of the theme was a poem of late July, 1557, "The Synod of the Birds."[20] It is a satire on the negotiations with the Hanseatic churches[21] in 367 hexameters, written by either by Johan Major with Melanchthon's assistance,[22] or by Melanchthon himself.[23] The poem, published three times, was recognized as the insult it was. "I know," wrote Paul Eitzen, the Hamburg Superintendent, "that that pasquinade offended many unjustly."[24]

Poet Johann Major. FS, 1738, 253.
The main theme of Major's poetical career was vilification of Flacius.

26 Böhl. 188.

27 F. J. Stopp. "Reformation Satire in Germany." *Oxford German Studies* 3. Oxford: Clarendon Press, 1968. 64; Burkhard Gotthelf Struve. *Acta Literaria* IV. Jena: Johannes Bielckius, 1706. Reprint 1806. 44.

28 Sillem. I, 287.

29 Seelenius. 65 ff. Another edition, 1729. 66; Other guesses in other copies, Wolfenbüttel signatures 125.3 Quod (13); P, 1514.8° Helmst. 152v ff.; CR, XX, 776.

30 Clemen. KS, I, 419n.

31 *Apologia ... Menij.* C r.

32 "In Synodum Avium Joh. Majoris in quibus Flacii innocentiam Fellerus contra calumnia Majoris defendit." Struve. 15–80.

33 "Flaciana und die Synode der Vögel." *Zeitschrift für die unierte evangelische Kirche* XV, 1853. 13, 225–239; XVI, 275–290; XVII, 297–308; and XVIII, 314–339.

34 "Deplumata et pudenda argumenta ex synodo avium nuper Wittebergae per maledicum [sic] poetam, Johannem Maiorem Ecelbolum, edita, simpliciter exerpta." Mentioned in "Pauli ab Eitzen Brief." DB, IV (1743). 195 ff.

35 "Elegia in calumniatorem Jo. Majorem." 1557. Mentioned by Schöttgen. *Leben M. Wagners.* 67.

36 *Dialogus oder ein Gespräch eines Esels und Bergknechts Jhesu Christo, unserm einigen Erlöser und seiner göttlichen Wahrheit zu Ehren, seiner christlichen Gemeinde in diesen betrübten Zeiten zu Trost und dem Synodo Avium zu lieb geschrieben.* [Lübeck: Georg Richholff d. J.], 1557; Mentioned in "Pauli ab Eitzen Brief." *loc. cit.*

37 *Ein newes lied von zweien Eseltreibern, Johan Ritzenbergen und Joach. Magdeburgio. Gestellet auff das Gesprech Joach. Magdeburgii, eines Esels und Matthei Berkgknechts.* [Wittenberg: Georg Rhau Erben], 1558; Cf. *Ein new Gedicht wider die Chammisten auff zwey newe Liedlein eines Eseltribers J. M. B. gemacht in Thon. Petransivit Clerus,* 1559. Böhl. 249n.

When the swan (Luther) died, the birds had a synod to choose a new master, and some favored the cuckoo (= Flacius, who also appeared as a Raabe = crow).[25] Ridiculing what must have been Flacius' lecture style, the poem reports that when the cuckoo made a speech he was so intense that his voice failed. Still, the "beastly [unflätig] sing-song" continued. "Always, eternally, the cuckoo makes his only call heard. He belongs to no place and obeys no laws; if he is some place, he does not remain. Hardly does he light on a branch, but with the speed of the storm wind he hurries away ..."

Who were the birds? Some were easy: Flacius was the cuckoo, Gallus, *turbatrix placidae nempe quietis avis*;[26] was the cock [Hahn = cock]. Amsdorf was the blackbird. "...the Swan of Wittenberg, Melanchthon as Philomele, the sweet nightingale, and Flacius, the Wendish cuckoo, were universally recognized shorthand descriptions of protagonists on the Protestant side."[27] The North German mediators were the bird choir, and that the heavens were black when the North wind blew, meant that Flacius had written enough to block out the sunlight. The hedge-sparrow was the University of Wittenberg, who accused the cuckoo of murdering her children. The more intelligent birds, such as the Goldfinch (Stieglitz = Stigel) supported the Nightingale. But who were the others? It was a game anyone could play. John Freder identified some of them, the *bubo, merops, merula, pica, fulica, fringilla, acanthiis, alauda, volucer* – but not the *osnyna*, the *ipsis* and the *trochius*.[28] Other solutions can still be consulted, scribbled in the margins of copies of the poem,[29] and, in one of them, Major's own solution.[30] Flacius, too, was drawn into the game. He observed that that the *columba* (dove) must be Justus Menius because he had "peculiar doves and crickets in his head." Looking back, he recalled ruefully that when the situation had turned dangerous, "the beautiful birds in the *Synodus Avium* did not dare hiss."[31]

The poem was republished in the eighteenth century, with an accompanying essay "Against The Synod of the Birds of Johan Major, in which Leipzig Professor Joachim Feller defends the innocence of Flacius against the calumnies of Major,"[32] and in the nineteenth by Eduard Schwarz,[33] when it played a role in the controversy on ecclesiastical Unionism.

Nor were defenders lacking in the sixteenth century; Flacius' friends counter-attacked with their own verses: Johan Wigand's "Defeathered and Disgraceful Arguments from the Synod of the Birds Newly Published at Wittenberg by the Scurrilous Poet, Johann Major,"[34] Marcus Wagner's "Elegy Against the Calumniator, Johann Major,"[35] Amsdorf's "Conversation between a Dove and A Raven," and Joachim Magdeburgius' "Dialogue between a Donkey and a Miner for the Honor of Jesus Christ our Only Savior and his Divine Truth, for the Comfort of his Christian Congregation und Written for the Sake of the Synod of Birds."[36] "A New Song about Donkey Drivers," complete with musical notation,[37] was suppressed by Paul Eitzen, and censored by the Hamburg senate. Melanchthon sent a note of thanks.

PART FOUR: JENA

Preventing a Political Solution

PROFESSOR AND PRIMATE

Christians who want to transmit our religion pure and unadulterated to our descendants must take pains to ensure that in the churches, Lutheran, that is, steadfast theologians, and not philosophical theologians are trained. – Flacius

[Flacius made] two suggestions worthy of consideration: the emphasis on the category of relationship, and the combining of theology with a philosophy abstinent in metaphysical questions. – Jörg Baur

1 J. C. E. Schwarz. *Das erste Jahrzehnd der Universität Jena.* Jena: Friedrich Frommann, 1868. 68.
2 Lietzmann. 153.
3 Oratio Illyrici Ihenae Recitata. Cod. Guelf. 79 Helmst. fol. 2–23.
4 Döllinger. I, 297.
5 Cf. his critique of Melanchthon's *Loci: Clavis* II. 37, 122.

The announcement that Matthias Flacius would join the faculty at Jena sent enrollment up – 111 in 1556 to 133 in 1557.[1] One measure of his reputation was the unusual call – a professor of the Greek New Testament was now to become Professor of Hebrew Old Testament. "There is no doubt," observed Hans Lietzmann, "that Flacius was by far the most important personality who, in its first period of existence, Jena could call its own."[2] He arrived on April 27 at the high point of political and scholarly success. There were high expectations for his May 17 inaugural lecture.[3]

His lecture reveals humanist themes. He shared the humanist distrust of the scholastics: in the Middle Ages students had been bedazzled by the secondary sources written by professors they called *doctor angelicus, doctor seraphicus* and *doctor subtilis.* He shared the humanist passion for leading students *ad fontes* – to original sources. The most important source was the Holy Scriptures. He quoted Horace: "You should not let the holy models out of your heads by day or by night." He challenged the Melanchthonian curriculum,[4] cautioning against a new intrusion of secondary sources into the curriculum – postills, institutes, enchiridia, catechisms, methods, compendia, and *loci communes.*[5]

And he pointed beyond humanism. The highest goal of the university, he told the crowded hall, was not erudition as Erasmus understood it, but certainty. The proper role of the professor of scripture, he said, was not to teach what we call systematic theology, but to assist the student in his own study of the biblical text.

The Augsburg Interim, he said, was like the seven-headed beast of Revelation 13.1; the Leipzig Interim was like the second, only apparently milder, beast. The beast's two horns were the concessions – marriage for priests and the chalice for laymen. The milder-seeming beast, nevertheless, like the dragon, breathed death on everyone who talked or wrote against it. Between the promulgation of the Augsburg Interim in mid-1548

6 On Flacius' part in solidifying Luther's authority, cf. Zeeden, op. cit. 47–51.

7 Moldaenke. 333 f.; note 50 thought Flacius was the first to call Luther the Third Elijah. But in *Recitationes Aliquid 1. De Concilia Scriti Libri Concordiae et Modo Agendi* etc. Leipzig: Georg Defner, 1581. 264; Nicolaus Selnecker wrote, "Philippus Lutherum agnovit et nominavit patrem, praeceptorem, postremae aetatis Eliam ..."; On Luther as Third Elijah in Flacius' circle, cf. Volz. *Lutherpredigten.* 67. Schönstedt. 298. Preger. II, 188 ff.; Böhl. 7.; A. Ritschl. "Entstehung." 103n.

8 The term was originated in the upper Rheinland and Switzerland and was used by Zasius and especially Zwingli. Heinrich Bornkamm. *Luther im Spiegel der deutschen Geistesgeschichte.* Heidelberg: Quelle & Meyer, 1965, ll; Wilhelm Gussmann. *Quellen & Forschungen zur Geschichte des Augsburgischen Glaubensbekenntnisses* II. Kassel: Edmund Pillardy, 1930. 233.

9 Zeeden. I, 49.

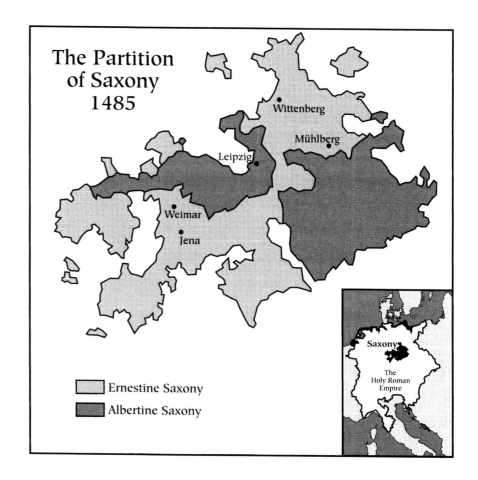

The Partition of Saxony 1485

Ernestine Saxony
Albertine Saxony

and 1551 when it ended, he added significantly, was the apocalyptic *limited* period of "a time, times and half a time," or forty-two months. But now the power of darkness was having its hour. Threatened with death, the church had an opportunity, which might involve shedding blood, to make a confession, since the only safety for the church was in God. Luther's role was apocalyptic.[6]

Luther was the the angel of Revelation 14.6: "Then I saw another angel flying in mid heaven, with an eternal gospel to proclaim to those who dwell on earth, to every nation and tribe and tongue and people..." He was the second Elijah of Malachi 4.5: "Behold, I will send you Elijah the prophet before the great and terrible day of the Lord comes." Following Melanchthon,[7] Flacius talked about Luther as the Elijah of the End time.[8] "In this view of history, Luther's appearance took on an entirely supernatural character. His coming was like the flash of divine truth in the midst of chaotic darkness..."[9] Luther had brought pure doctrine; he was the forerunner of Christ's second coming, the one (Malachi 3.23, Luke 1.17) who before the last judgment will accomplish the conversion of God's people, and who by his appearance held back the evil events of the world's last days.

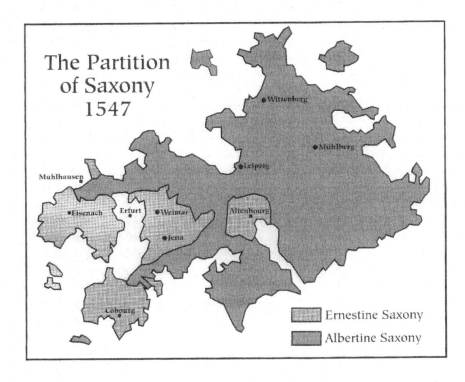

The Partition
of Saxony
1547

Ernestine Saxony
Albertine Saxony

10 "Das Augsburger Interim als apo-kalyptisches Geschehnis nach den Königsberger Schriften Andreas Osianders." ARG, XLIV (1973). 226n.

11 *Christoph Pezel (1539–1604) und der Calvinismus in Bremen.* Bremen: Verlag Einkehr, 1958. 137.

12 Karl Mollenhauer. "Eine Berufung Georgs von Venediger nach Jena." Sonderdruck. *Altpreussiche Forschungen* VIII (1931). 129–132.

13 Mentz. *Handschriften.* No. 176.

Martin Stupperich sees Flacius as the high-point of the apocalyptic thought stimulated by the Interim.[10] According to Jürgen Moltmann, "The apocalyptic background is the actual root of Lutheran early orthodoxy." It was not "rational penetration" and not "deification by the epigones," but in comparison with Luther himself, "a new apocalyptic understanding of the Reformation, that breaks out since 1549 in Flacian Lutheranism cannot hide its parallels to certain Anabaptist sentiments."[11]

Flacius began to construct a theological faculty. When Erhard Schnepf died, once Reformer in Nassau and Württemberg, Flacius attempted vainly to call George Venetus, the Superintendent of Pomerania.[12] In Magdeburg, the aged leader of the Magdeburg resistance, Levin von Emden, had died. Nobody could fill his shoes as diplomat-politican and lay spiritual leader. Wigand had attempted to carry out the ideas of the von Embden party, represented by some members of the prestigious Alemann family and the physician, Martin Copus. As a result of his efforts, several canons of the cathedral chapter "converted to the truth of the gospel and later instituted and conducted their rites and preaching in accord with the Augsburg Confession." By 1560, in the face of steadily weakening political support in the city council and betrayal by former allies, Wigand's position deteriorated, and he was willing, together with Judex, to move to Jena.

Flacius notified students of the scheduled time of his lectures by affixing a note on a bulletin board; a photograph of one of those notes appeared in a book illustrating sixteenth century handwriting.[13] Besides lectures, there were prescribed public disputations, which often lasted an entire day. Flacius gave to understand that he intended nothing less than shifting the

14 J. Hartmann. 102.

15 Heussi. *Geschichte*. 98.

16 *Clavis*. II, 670.

17 *De Materiis metisque scientarum et erroribus philosophiae in rebus divinis*. Basel: Oporinus, 1561. A summary in Moldaenke. 93 ff., 538 ff. Cf. Preger. II, 112. Haikola's *Gesetz und Evangelium* is based on *De Materiis*. See. 16n.

18 Moldaenke. 96. Cf. *Clavis*. II, 650. "Haec ... respondisse nunc sufficiat: quandoquidem de erroribus Philosophiae in rebus divinis et quod solum verbum Dei rerum eius cognitionem doceat, in oratione initio prioris Epistolae ad Corinthos habita, quae jam, sub titulo De metis Scientarum, edita est, abunde actum dictumque est."

19 Moldaenke. 541–49.

20 "Matthias Flacius Illyricus." 288.

21 "... hier die Wurzeln der besonders von Flacius ausgebildeten Geschichtsanschauung protestantischer Polemik liegen." Op. cit. 193.

22 Op. cit. 45.

23 Richard and Robert Keil. *Geschichte des Jenaischen Studentenlebens von der Gründung der Universität bis zur Gegenwart (1548–1858). Eine Festgabe zum 300. Jubiläums der Universität Jena*. Leipzig: F. A. Brockhaus, 1858. 51, 87.

24 Ibid. 48 ff.

25 Schwarz. *Jahrzehn*. 94–102.

26 *Ein Buch von ... Mitteldingen*. S ij r.

27 Appendix to *Clavis*. Tractate. VI, 667–79. Moldaenke. 179–190.

28 Ernst-Emil Klotz. "über die Herkunft der Jenaer Studenten im ersten Jahrhundert des Bestehens der Universität." *Geistliche Landeskunde und Universalgeschichte. Festschrift Hermann Aubin*. Hamburg, 1956. 107.

curriculum to a biblical basis.[14] His plan was to lecture on all of St. Paul's epistles.[15] In 1560, he lectured at 1.00 p.m., Monday through Friday, on I Corinthians, the basis for his plan for the university curriculum, and an alternative to Melanchthon's humanistic model. Whereas the first eight chapters of Romans treated faith and justification, I Corinthians treated faith in its relationship to wisdom, the business of the university.

> For since, in the wisdom of God, the world did not know God through wisdom, it pleased God through the folly of what we preach to save those who believe. For Jews demanded signs and Greeks seek wisdom, but we preach Christ crucified, a stumbling block to Jews and folly to Gentiles, but to those who are called, Jews and Greeks, Christ the power of God and the wisdom of God.

In the first of his Corinthian lectures,[16] *On the Materials and Limits of the Sciences and the Errors of Philosophy in Divine Matters*,[17] he offered his basic statement on the relationship of theology and philosophy.[18] If St. Paul was right, the most important questions – of ultimate truth and of being, of the relationship of man to God – cannot be dealt with by philosophy.[19] "If in the 'Flacian controversy later," comments Peter Barton, "he was guilty of using mere abstractions, here he carefully maintained the (non-philosophical) importance of the religious relationship between God and man."[20]

The questions of the origin and destiny of man – his *causa efficiens* and *causa finalis* – matters of relationship, are to be referred not to philosophy, but to theology. Tracing Flacius' historical perspective from Melanchthon's "first Reformation writing," *Didymi Faventi adversus Thomam Placentinum Oratio pro Martino Luthero Theologo*, Friedrich Lauchert calls attention to Melanchthon's notion that theology should take the place of philosophy.[21] Man is not a neutral thinking-machine; his own troubles with God cannot help affecting his judgment. Philosophical principles are valid in terms of evidence only in the realm of mathematics. It follows that in questions of life itself, philosophical speculation cannot be trusted. "Philosophy necessarily becomes the voice of the scepticism of the sinner," Jörg Baur continues, discussing Flacius' position, "for whom the order of the universe dissolves in his own experience." "Whoever contradicts Flacius here," he comments, "as I also would do, must at least give his reasons."[22]

A consciously modern foundation, Jena University, now housed in the abandoned Paulinist monastery, made little effort to organize, as the older, quasi-monastic *Bursen*, or dormitories had done.[23] In the interest of recruiting, enforcement was lax.[24] And so, from the beginning, Jena students were hard drinkers and the university eventually reaped the consequences – burglary, sexual misconduct, student rebellions, arson and even murder. In July of 1561, during a brawl in the streets between students and bakers' apprentices, the rector himself was wounded. One of the sixteen rules of 1558[25] prohibited weapons, which were forbidden in any case to the Burgher and workers. Now that the invention of gunpowder had made swords old-fashioned, young aristocrats swaggered around with *recontre* daggers, perfect for cut and thrust. Forbidden as well were *Pluderhosen* – baggy, puffed-out trousers, decorated with ribbons in the Spanish fashion, and provided with a codpiece and slits with colored lining, or open to reveal bare flesh.

Students nevertheless were also required to "hold to God's pure word, as it is explained in the Augsburg Confession, in the Apology following and in the Smalcaldic Articles." Flacius was concerned that from Wittenberg, "such students come, who out of fear of danger, or because of their own advantage, color over papal abuses and learn to direct the Christian religion according to the desires of the powerful." Already, Luther was being rejected. "...they say that Dr. Luther was all too violent, that he was fallible, and that he was a man, that one should serve the times..."[26] Jena, in contrast, should be faithful.

In his "Adhortation to the Study of Sacred Scriptures"[27] Flacius argues that the students' reading should be intensive, rather than extensive, and quotes Pliny the Younger: *Non multa sed multum esse legendum.* "Christians," he wrote, "who want to transmit our religion pure and unadulterated to our descendants must take pains to ensure that in the churches, Lutheran, that is, steadfast theologians and not philosophical theologians are trained." Nicolas Gallus agreed; his backing was evident in the 186 students from Regensburg in the first century and the 306 students from Austria, especially from Graz.[28] Those students who lived at Flacius' house on the corner of Collegiengasse and Rinnenstrasse (now number 6, opposite the Zeiss factory site),[29] one assumes, were among those who took the religious standards seriously.

Among them were Franz Alard, of the noble de Cantier family of Belgium, later Flacius' colleague in Antwerp, and Tobias Rupp, scholarship student from Lindau.[30] Flacius' linguistic preparation of students who became important figures in the beginnings of South Slavic literature that paralleled the Reformation is a promising theme for a specialist. One of his students, Adam Bohorić, became famous as the first Slovenian grammarian. Sebastian Krelj from Vipava (Wippach), later at the center of the springtime of Slovenian literature learned the Cyrillic and Glagolitic literature from Flacius,[31] and served him as an amanuensis.[32] When Krelj decided to use the Latin alphabet, rather than Cyrillic and Glagolitic letters to write slavonic, he explained that "we have carefully presented this Slovenian orthography this way, with good counsel of well-informed brothers"; he did not mention Flacius specifically, according to Jakob Rigler, but he had him in mind.[33] Another of Flacius' students, Bienemann, was good enough at Greek to be sent by Emperor Maximilian II to Greece as translator.[34]

In addition to his professorship, Flacius was called to be *Obersuperintendent*, with duties described by Amsdorf:

> ... he, together with the honorable and learned Erhard Schnepf, should be a General Superintendent and should exercize supervision over all superintendents, pastors and church employees of all the churches in the principality, that no one should introduce

29 Mirković, 1960. 198.

30 Sillem. II, 496; Johannes Wigand. *De Manichaeismo Renovato.* Leipzig: Henning Grasse, 1587. "Et Tobias quidem in Academia Ienensi Thuringia, Illyrico commendatos studuit ubi & in aedibus Illyrici vivens." 640.

31 "Über die Sprache der Slovenischen Protestantischen Schriftsteller des 16. Jahrhunderts." *Abhandlungen über die Slowenische Reformation.* Munich: Rudolf Trofenik, 1968. 82.

32 Günther Stökl. *Die deutsch-slavische Südostgrenze des Reiches im 16. Jahrhundert.* Breslau: Priebatsch's Buchhandlung, 1940, 128. Cf. Theodor Elze. "Die evangelischen Prediger Krains im XVI. Jahrhundert." JGGPO, XXI (1900). 176 ff.

33 "Ueber die Sprache der Slovenischen Protestantischen Schriftsteller des 16. Jahrhunderts." *Abhandlungen über die Slowenische Reformation.* Munich: Rudolf Trofenik, 1968. 83.

34 Gebhardt. 215.

35 Quoted by Preger. II, 106.

36 Johannes Günther. *Lebensskizzen der Professoren der Universität Jena seit 1558 bis 1858*. Jena: Druck und Verlag von Friedrich Mauke, 1858, 116. Reprint, Aalen: Scientia Verlag, 1979. 117.

37 Friedrich Lütge. *Geschichte des Jenaer Buchhandels, einschliesslich der Buchdruckerverein*. Jena: G. Fischer, 1929. 17.

38 Hülsse. "Beiträge." 359.

39 J. Hartmann. 97.

40 Döllinger. II, 242.

new doctrines and ceremonies, and that each pastor persevere in the religion established in the land. Beyond that, he should lecture one hour each day – three days a week in Greek on the New Testament and on the other days in Latin on a Gospel or an epistle of St. Paul.[35]

Since the superintendencies of Jena and Weimar were occupied by his supporters, his prospects were promising. Responsible for doctrinal matters, in 1557 Flacius demanded and obtained the dismissal of Luther's own son, Dr. Paul Luther, professor of medicine, whose orthodoxy was suspect.[36] When he noticed that the elderly women who came to St. Michael's daily to pray addressed their prayers to what remained of a carvings of the Flight into Egypt – St. Joseph and an ass – he asked the Duke Johann Friedrich II to have the figures removed. In 1559, at 72, Luther's friend, Michael Stifel, took up residence in Jena as a professor of mathematics. He was known for having prophesied that the world would end on October 19, 1533. Luther had tolerated his apocalyptic foolishness, in spite of Stifel's demonstrative resignation from his parish in Brück as a Flacian, he was denounced by the theology faculty as an antinomian.

Flacius also kept his hand in the book business; there is evidence of an order, for instance, for copies of volumes in the Jena edition of Luther's Works from the firm of Konrad König, which he offered for sale in Nuremberg, Lübeck, Straßburg and other cities.[37] When the printing firm of König became involved in a scandal because of over-billing, he was instrumental in having the Luther edition transferred on March 8, 1559, to Thomas Rebart, son-in-law of Christian Rödinger, the Magdeburg publisher.[38]

As Mirković noted with approval, Flacius was no sycophant. Somehow, the wit that enlivens his polemics was not always apparent, perhaps because of his imperfect mastery of German. Whereas Luther was able to win over a courtier or a German prince with a joke, from Flacius the government learned to expect only sober, rational arguments, long, systematic, written Latin memoranda. He was seldom invited to court, and never socially. The duke, ominously, had heard a rumor "that perhaps the learned of the place, especially Dr. Schnepf, Victorinus and other prominent persons, would not remain united with M. Illyricus very long..."[39] Nevertheless, at the beginning, Flacius had the full backing of the duke. "One should not vex Illyricus," the word went out, "because he has letters."[40]

> After the first attack on the Evangelical Faith with the sword, followed the second attack – with unity. – Flacius

> Not much different, our church and religion also began to change for the worse after the death of Luther of pious memory. May God prevent a similar end and ruin like that of the Bohemians! – Flacius

Until the recent publication of the critical edition by the Czechoslovakian Academy of Science, the standard text of the works of John Huss was the *editio princeps* edited by Matthias Flacius.[1] In collecting the manuscripts he was assisted at the highest level by Caspar von Nidbruck. Concentrating on Huss, Flacius was struck with the parallels between the Bohemian and German reform movements. What, then could be learned about the Bohemian reform to help the German reform? More specifically, what could be learned from the history of the Hussites after the death of Huss for the benefit of the Lutherans after the death of Luther?

Like opposition to the Hussites, opposition to the Lutherans was often justified by an appeal to the unity of Christendom. And who could not be moved by such an appeal? But what was the nature of that unity? Should it be based on military supremacy, as the emperor attempted in the siege of Magdeburg? Should unity in the evangelical camp be built on the shaky basis of amnesty, simply pardoning those who had yielded to the Interim law? And what kind of God-pleasing unity could be expected from the colloquium planned for Worms in 1557?

Since the 1555 Peace of Augsburg, the Holy Roman Empire had recognized as legitimate adherence to the Augsburg Confession. It would be important at Worms that the evangelicals be unified. Whatever their motives, Melanchthon and his followers insisted that evangelical unity included the position of George Major (together with Johann Brenz) of Andreas Osiander, and (for the sake of Protestant solidarity) of Ulrich Zwingli. Flacius and his allies, on the other hand, insisted on a distinction between those who followed the Augsburg Confession and those who did not. He wanted the deviants named by name. Like Melanchthon, Duke Christopher of Württemberg was concerned to present the appearance of unity at Worms in the Evangelical ranks. He issued a formal Opinion opposing naming the names of deviants,[2] and instructed the delegates from Württemberg not to allow the Weimar delegation any opportunity to register their condemnations.

Flacius had renewed evidence of Melanchthon's bitterness against him and his associates in a letter from Law Professor Basilius Monner, who described the Preceptor's August 28 arrival for the talks in Worms.

> All our theologians here received him in the most honorable manner, and adore him like a deity. When we came out of Church three days ago, everyone greeted him as his preceptor, but I stood aloof. When he saw me, he said, rather coldly, "doctor!" and touched my hand slightly. He turned away from me immediately, and departed to his

1 *Mag. Joannis Hus et Hironymi Pragensis Confessorum Christi Historia et Monumenta.* 2 vols. Nuremberg; Johannes Berg & Ulrich Neuberg, 1558. On Flacius' use of Huss, Hölzel. 130–137.

2 Gustav Wolf. *Zur Geschichte der deutschen Protestanten 1555–1559.* Berlin: Oswald Seehagen, 1888. 295–299.

3 CR, IX, 246.

4 Brodrick. 388.

5 *Confessio Waldensium de plerisque nunc controversis Dogmatibus ante cxxxiv. annos contra claudicantes* [claudico=I lame]. *Hussitas scripta, nostrisq[ue] temporibus statui, ac rebus pulchre correspondens.* Basel: Oporinus, 1568. On its use by the Waldensians, Amadeo Molnar. "Bekenntnisse der böhmischen Reformation." JGGPO, XCVI (1980). 319.

6 Balthasar Lydius. *Waldensia id est conservatio verae ecclesiae Demonstrata ex confessionibus, cum Taboritarum, ante CC fere annos, tum Bohemorum, circa tempora Reformationis, scriptis.* Rotterdam: Ioannes Londardus Berewout, 1616. Lydius followed Flacius in attributing the confession to the Waldensians. Bernard Czerwenka. *Geschichte der Evangelischen Kirche in Böhmen* II. Bielefeld and Leipzig: Velhage & Klasing, 1870. 30f. A modern edition: *Confessio Taboritarum.* Amedeo Molnar and Romolo Cegna (eds.). Rome: Nella Sede Dell' Istituto Palazzo Borromini, 1983.

lodgings, accompanied by a large number of persons. Martin Stössel and I went immediately to our own.

His heart seems to be entirely estranged from me. But I do not mind in the least, and I believe that we should not seek the friendship of persons who muddy pure doctrine, Indeed, I believe rather that we should flee from them, in obedience to the passage, "if there come any unto you and bring not this doctrine, receive him not into your house, neither bid him Godspeed."[3]

Since decisions of the Council of Trent were already in place, the Roman Catholic delegates would not negotiate seriously. Thus, as an instrument for reuniting the Western church, the colloquy was an empty exercise. If they were naive and took the negotiations seriously, the Lutherans could fall into a trap. "The image of the sad ruin of the church," he wrote, "and the religion of the Hussites, which is similar to ours, always stays before my eyes." It was dangerous for the evangelicals, who, following the failure to achieve unity with Melanchthon, to go to Worms divided.

No sympathy was to be expected from Roman Catholic delegates Julius Pflug, named president, and Michael Helding. Nor from Inquisitor General Iodocus Ravestyn, responsible for terrifying persecutions in the Netherlands, or from Strassburg Suffragan Bishop Johannes Delphius, Louvain Professor Martinus Rittonius, ex-Lutheran Friedrich Staphylus, or Peter Canisius – the Jesuit organizing the struggle against the Reformation. He wondered if he should have any contact at all with people he had no hope of converting.[4]

The tactic used against the Hussites, Flacius discerned, had been to divide and conquer. First, the Taborites were isolated. They were excluded from the Council of Basel, and then, in the battle of Lepany in 1434, deprived of political power militarily. In negotiations, the remaining Hussites were brought to heel. The four Prague Articles, a monument of the Hussite reform, were neutralized in an agreement called the *Compactata*: lay persons were allowed to drink from the chalice (a crucial Hussite demand) – but it was to be understood that Christ was entirely present in the bread alone. Free preaching was permitted – but priests had to be approved by their superiors, and the power of the bishops had to be recognized. An article prohibiting use of secular power by the clergy was reversed. Then, in 1462, Pope Pius II pronounced even the *Compactata* null and void. He prohibited communion in both kinds, and recognized the Bohemian King only under the condition that he agreed with the Roman Church.

Would the German reform be subverted as the Bohemian reform was? To avoid it, Flacius focused attention on 1431, a point in the Bohemian reform before the movement began to disintegrate. He published a text produced that year by the Taborites, whom he thought resembled Christ's Exiles in Magdeburg: the *Confession of the Waldensians Written 134 Years Ago about Dogmas now in Dispute, against the Laming Hussites, Which Corresponds Beautifully to the Situation and Issues of Our Times.*[5] Since the edition of 1616 it has been called the "Confession of the Taborites."[6] But Flacius' appellation, "confession" (a term the Taborites did not use), has stuck. He was able, writes Amedeo Molnar, "to draw the tense line of development from ... the 'stoic austerity of Huss' to the engagement within the Hussite era in the struggle for freedom of the Taborite confession, which was a true antitype of the freedom of the Christian man in the Reformation sense."[7] The main assertions of the confession were the following:

7 Molnar. "Bekentnisse." 310 ff.

8 Wolf. *Geschichte*. 300 f.

1. The basis of Christian thought and behavior is the law-giving sovereignty of Jesus Christ.
2. The law of Christ is completely sufficient, and superior to the Old Testament and all other laws.
3. The church is obligated to the truths of the Scriptural canon.
4. It is not obligated to the post-apostolic tradition.
5. A critique of symbols (as elements of the imperfect religion and the old law).
6. Certain symbolic actions (the liturgy) are non-biblical
7. Priests who reject such non-biblical rites are to be defended.

The text voiced the faith of the Lutherans as well. "Besides the Holy Scripture," it reads, "no other can be recognized as binding authority, and it is not allowable to oppose it with the authority of any human reasoning." In his introduction, Flacius described Huss's appeal of October 18, 1412, from the authority of the pope to that of Jesus, as "the expression of a congregation that knew it was addressed by the word proclaimed by Huss." He seconded the demands for reform of growing sacramentalism, of the liturgy, of the belief in purgatory, and the practice of praying to saints.

In his instructions to the delegates, August 9, 1557, Flacius urged that the basis of the negotiations should be the Augsburg Confession, the Apology and the Smalcald Articles. Further, the Anabaptists, Zwinglians, Osiandrians, Majorists, Schwenkfeldians and Servetians should be rejected in advance.[8] And he appealed for steadfastness, insisting that the defeat of the Hussites did not have to be repeated.

> ...the sad example of the extinct doctrine of the Hussite churches, similar to our situation, also really frightens me. It was not erudition, not even the strength of the enemies that was able to destroy them, since the Lord was mercifully protecting them, but their own inconstancy and faithless domestic vanity. For not so long after the death of Huss the University of Prague and the church, among whom was Prince Kokenzana, seeking the bishopric by evil means, the whole flower of the Bohemian estates and the greater part of the people, drew closer and closer to the papacy.
>
> For by that time they had been divided partly by long wars and unparalleled destruction, and partly they were weary of truth and because of the controversies about it that had arisen. Nor were there few, the lowest, who whispered together secretly with the enemies, hoping or seeking something different.
>
> Opposed to them was a certain city of the Hussites, Tabor by name, not so great or flourishing, which retreated even more from the pope and his errors than even Huss himself. For they refuted many abuses and abominations more passionately and clearly than he did. Then arose a regrettable separation or schism among the Hussites, which lasted many years. and sharp conflicts among them in print and in public disputes.

9 Edmund Basil Francis D'Auvergne. *The Coburgs: The Story of the Rise of a Great Royal House.* New York: J. Pott & Company, 1911. 22.

10 August Beck. *Johann Friedrich der Mittlere, Herzog zu Sachsen. Ein Beitrag zur Geschichte des sechzehnten Jahrhunderts* I. Weimar: Böhlau, 1858. 296; CR, IX, 213–214.

11 *Leben des Jakob Andreae, Doktor der Theologie, von ihm selbst mit grosser Treue und Aufrightigkeit beschrieben bis auf das Jahr 1562.* Ed. Herman Ehmer. Stuttgart: Calwer Verlag, 1991. 75.

I have an erudite and lengthy confession of the Taborites against the party in Prague and the papists. agreeing completely with our convictions on many articles which now are all controversial.

Finally those in Prague and the greatest and principal part of the Bohemians left the poor, despised Taborites, and with the Antichrist in the Council of Basel again the yoke of the pope and the bishops, retaining only a small part of the truer teaching, and having again accepted the yoke of the pope and the bishops, who afterwards saved almost nothing, as Sylvius himself says. And so finally, little by little, all Hussites, their religion and church were oppressed or destroyed.

Not much different, our church and religion also began to change for the worse after the death of Luther of pious memory. May God prevent a similar end and ruin as the Bohemians! Certainly for our disgraceful ingratitude and enthusiasm for colluding with the Babylonian Thaide we are worthy of this or even a greater evil, if there is any other evil worse than hunger and poverty of the Word of God, or annihilation or the pure and saving religion of Jesus Christ.

Like the Taborites, Flacius recognized, his Magdeburg party was vulnerable to the tactic of "divide and conquer." Fortunately, that was legally impossible in imperial law as long as he had the backing of Duke Johann Friedrich II. It would not be long until the duke would abandon him and favor the Melanchthonians. But, for the moment, the duke took Flacius' advice: "I feel with all my heart and soul that your first duty is to work with the greatest possible ardor for the utter rejection from the Church of God and everlasting damnation of the impious Interim with its allied corruptions of compromise, understandings, and bargainings with our adversaries." Although by now, the duke was being dismissed as a fool because of repeated official blunders,[9] he gave the Weimar delegation Johann Friedrich's full support. Flacius' request coincided for the moment with his passion for reclaiming the electoral title for himself, for a reversal of the Wittenberg Capitulation, and, without doubt, a lingering loyalty toward his father.

The duke instructed his delegates to stand fast.

> They should persist unshaken with the Augsburg Confession, the Apology, and the Smalcald Articles, to which Electors Johann and Johann Friedrich bound land and people. If the other counsellors and theologians of the Augsburg Confession say that they remained with the Augsburg Confession as well, but did not want to oppose the sects that have crept in explicitly, they should have no fellowship with them, but, before entering into discussion with the papists, first have the following sects condemned by all those related to the Augsburg Confession: the Anabaptists, the Zwinglians and the Sacrament enthusiasts, Osiander with his error about essential righteousness, Major with his new corruption about the necessity of good works for salvation, the horrible errors of Caspar Schwenckfeld, all Servetians, who are renewing the horrible old heresies against the person and divinity of Christ, and, finally, all who still struggle and defend, and will not abandon some godless ceremonies, because the Augsburg Imperial Recess and the established peace attack and exclude such sects by name.[10]

In his memoirs, Jakob Andreae remembered that during the colloquy Flacius had been somewhere in the vicinity.[11] His report cannot be dismissed – Flacius' reputation for gliding like a wraith over the German landscape is not wholly without foundation. If there were more evidence, our story would be more dramatic. Lacking that evidence, however, we must think of a nervous Flacius in Jena awaiting the outcome. *Would the German reform, like the Bohemian reform, be neutralized by negotiations?*

Finally, the news came. The Weimar delegation had avoided the fate of the Hussite reform by closing down the colloquy,[12] the last peaceful attempt to achieve imperial unity at the expense of the reform. In the fierce cross-fire the Weimar delegation had concluded that a Time of Confession had arrived. Accordingly, they registered a formal protest and followed it on October 1st by a walkout: the unity of Christendom would not be preserved at the price of religious compromise. Both Helding and Canisius, Flacius learned, had seen through Melanchthon's pretense; the doctrinal variations he sheltered were clear deviations from the Augsburg Confession, just as Flacius had said they were. Now, in the absence of the delegates from Ernestine Saxony, no compromises could be made with the remaining Protestants. Among other things, that was a kind of latter-day vindication for the Taborites. It was also crucial for the Lutherans: in 1557, once again – thanks in large part to Matthias Flacius – Luther's reform had survived.

12 CR, IX, 314 ff.

BIBLIOGRAPHY

FLACIUS' PRINTED WORKS

Albini seu Alcuini Caroli Magni praeceptoris confessio aut doctrina de Deo, compendio exposita, et nunquam antea impressa. Confessio M. Flac. Illyrici de sacrosancta Trinitate contra Servetianos, Stencfeldianos, et alios seductores ac mendaces. [Magdeburg: Ambrosius Kirchner] 1557.

Antidotum auff Osiandri gifftiges Schmeckbier, Durch Matt. Fla. Illyri. und Nico. Gallum. Magdeburg: Christian Rödinger [ca. 1552].

Antilogia papae: Hoc est, de corrupto ecclesiae statu, & totius cleri papistici perversitate, scripta aliquot veterum authorum, ante annos plus minus, & interea: nunc primum in lucem eruta et ab interitu vindicata: quorum catalogum proxima post praefationem pagina reperies: cum praefatione D. Wolfgangi Wissenburgij. Basel: Johannes Oporinus, 1555.

Antwort der Predicanten in Hessen auff die schrifft des Bischoffs von Meintz oder Rabsackesbrieff De abrogatione matrimonii der Prediger und von der Dispensation mit dem Babst zu halten vom brauch des Sacraments sub utraque specie, welche ihnen von Fürstlichen Rethen zu Cassel für gelesen, den fünfften tag Augusti diss XLIX. Jars. Magdeburg: Christian Rödinger [1549].

Antwort Matthiae Flacii Illirici, auff das Stenckfeldische Büchlein Iudicium &c. genant. Mit einem nötigen unnd schönen unterricht, Was der rechte trost und wirckung der heyligen Schrifft bey allen glaubigen sey. Nürnberg: Johann vom Berg; Ulrich Neuber, 1555.

Antwort Matth. Fl. Illyr. auff etliche Beschüldigung D. Gei. Maiores und D. Pommers. [Magdeburg: Christian Rödinger, ca. 1551].

Antwort M. Nicolai Galli und M Fla. Illyrici auff den brieff etlicher Prediger in Meissen, von der frage, Ob sie lieber weichen denn den Chorrock anzihen sollen. Magdeburg: Christian Rödinger [1550].

Apologia (...) auff zwo unchristliche Schrifften Justi Menij, Darinnen von den grewlichen Verfelschungen der Adiaphoristerey und Maioristerey allerley nützlichs angezeigt wird. Jena: Christian Rödinger der Ältere Erben, 1558.

Ein Artglichs new Lied, von der zart schönen Frawen Interim, Auch von zucht, ehr und lob irer Schöpffern. [Bern: Mathias Aparius], 1552.

Argumenta Psalmorum sexaginta, distributis ordine versuum sententiis, dictata a Matthia Flacio Illyrico, in Academia Witebergensi. Frankfurt/M.: Peter Braubach, 1550.

Aristotelous hapanta. Aristotelis opera quaecunque. hactenus extiterunt omnia quae quidem ut antea integris aliquot libris supra priores aeditiones omnes a nobis aucta prodierunt. Basel: Johann Bebel und Michael Isengrin, 1550.

Auff das ausschreiben der zweien Vniversiteten, und die Invectivam scholasticorum, Antwort (...), darin die Adiaphoristen aus iren eigen Schrifften und zeugnissen, irer grewlichen Bulerey mit der Babylonischen Bestien uberwiesen werden (...) Jena: Thomas Rebart, 1558.

[Joannes N., pseudonym]. Auff die unterredung, so (nach ubergebung der Schrifften)die newe Kirchenordnung belangend zu Torgaw geschehen, Freitags nach Judica M.D. XLIX. Durch Joannem. N. Pfarherr zu N. [Magdeburg: Christian Rödinger], 1549.

Auff die Vermanung Julij des Bepstlichen Bischoffs, darin er die Evangelischen vermanet, das sie sich wider zur Bepstischen Synagoga bekeren wolten. Antwort M. Flacij Illyrici. Aus des Bapsts Recht, dist. 40. Si papa. Jena: Christian Rödinger, 1554.

Der Ausszug des beschlusses oder der vorleuffer des Leipsischen Interims, Aus einem gedruckten Exemplar gedruckt. Magdeburg: Christian Rödinger, 1550.

Auszug etlicher alten Reformation der Kirchen, in den handlungen mit dem Geistlichen sehr nützlich zu wissen. Item eine uberaus feine History von Bepstlicher gewalt, die sich zur zeit Cypriani, ungefehr 250 Jar nach Christo zugetragen. n. p., 1556.

Bedencken auffs Interim des Ehrwirdigen und Hochgelarten Herrn Philippi Melanthonis. [Magdeburg: Hans Walther], 1548.

Bedencken Doctoris Martini Lutheri Auff dem Reichstag zu Augspurgk im XXX. yare gestellet. Item ein ander Bedencken auff den tag zu Schmalkalden den Ersten Martii, des 40. yars. Der Theologen So zu solcher zeit daselbst gewesen, welcher namen zu rücke verzeichnet. Zu diesen ferlichen zeiten nützlich und von nöten zu lesen. Damit yederman bericht werde, Was in Religionssachen nachzugeben oder nicht könne nachgegeben werden. [Magdeburg: Michael Lotter], 1548.

Bekentnus M. Flac. Illyrici von etlichen irthumen Maioris. Item etliche spruche Menij. n. p. 1557.

Bericht vom Interim der Theologen zu Meissen versamlet. Anno M. D. xlviij. [Magdeburg: Christian Rödinger], 1548.

Trewe Warnung und Vermanung, das man das heilige Testament des... Nachtmals... Jesu Christi unverfelscht... behalten sol... Item, Widerlegung vier Predigten eines Sacramentirers, mit zunamen Olevianus. Item, Beweisung, Das auch die unwirdigen den Leib und Blut Jesu Christi im Abendmahl empfahen, Wider ein Schwenckfeldisch Büchlein, so... newlich ohne Namen durch den Druck ausgestrewet worden. Ursel: Nicolas Henricus [1565].

Beweisung das nicht die unsere Christi, Sonder die papistische Religion, new und auffrürisch, und ein ursach alles unglücks sey. Wider das Gotteslesterisch buch Marani, oder des schwartzen Munchs zu Augspurg, von dem itzigen krieg geschrieben. [Magdeburg: Christian Rödinger], 1553.

Beweisung, da Osiander helt und leret, das die Gottheit eben also in den rechtgleubigen wone, wie in der menscheit Christi selbst. Und das weiter daraus folge, das die Christen eben also ware Götter sein, und angebetet müssen werden, als der mensch Jhesus selbst. Magdeburg: Christian Rödinger, 1553.

Brentij und Osiandri meinung, vom ampt Christi, und rechtfertigung des Sünders. Mit einer Vorrede M. Flac. Illyr. Magdeburg: Michael Lotter, 1553.

Ein buch, von waren und falschen Mitteldingen, Darin fast der gantze handel von Mitteldingen erkleret wird, widder die schedliche Rotte der Adiaphoristen. Item ein brieff des ehrwirdigen Herrn D. Joannis Epini superintendenten zu Hamburg, auch von diesem handel an Illyricum geschrieben. Magdeburg: Christian Rödinger, 1550. See Liber de Veris et Falsis.

Bulla Antichristi de retrahendo populo Dei in ferream Aegiptiacae servitutis fornacem, Maguntini Rabsaces blasphemis literis consona. Ex qua facile animadverti potest, quid Satan per untranque suam virtutem, scilicet, per patricidiale bellum contra Ecclesiam Dei susceptum, & per mendacia concilium, Interim, Adiaphora & Chorrock efficere conetur. [Magdeburg: Michael Lotter], 1549.

Bulla des Antichrists, dadurch er das volck Gottes widderumb inn den eisern ofen der Egiptischen gefengknis denckt zuziehen, gleichstimmig mit des Meintzischen Rabsakes briefe. Daraus wol zuvernemen, was der Teufel durch seine beide tugent, das ist, durch den Mörderischen krieg widder die Kirche Gottes, und durch seine lügen, als da sind, Concilium, Interim, Mittelding, Chorrock, denckt auszurichten. Magdeburg: Christian Rödinger, 1550.

Buspredigt für die öffentlichen Sünden jtziger zeit, die falschen Brüder, Nemlich für die Verlasser, Verleugker, Abtrünnige und Verfolger jhrer eignen Religion, an jrhen Brüdern. Durch Nicol: Gallum, und Matth: Fla: Illyr: [Magdeburg]: [Christian Rödinger] [1551]

Cantio de Papa Romanaque Ecclesia, per Boemum quendam ante annos circiter 100 composita, secundum ordinem alphabeti. n. p. [1548].

Carmina vetusta ante trecentos annos scripta, quae deplorant inscitiam Evangelii, et taxant abusus ceremoniarum, ac quae ostendunt doctrinam huius temporis non esse novam. fulsit enim semper et fulgebit in aliquibus vera Ecclesiae doctrina. Wittenberg: Georg Rau, 1548.

Catalogus testium Veritatis. Historia der Zeugen, Bekenner und Märterer, so Christum und die evangelische warheit hierher, auch etwa im Reich der Finsternus warhafftig erkennet ... erstlich widersprochen. Tr. Conrad Lautenbach. Frankfurt: Johann Schmidt, 1573.

Catalogus Testium Veritatis, qui ante nostram aetatem reclamarunt Papae. Basel: Johann Oporin, 1556.

Catalogus Testium Veritatis, qui ante nostram aetatem Pontifici Romano, eiusque erroribus reclamarunt: iam denuo longe quam antea, & emendatior & auctior editus. Strassburg: Paul Messerschmidt, 1562.

Ein Christliche vermanung zur bestendigkeit, inn der waren reinen Religion Jhesu Christi, unnd inn der Augspurgischen bekentnis. Geschrieben an die Meissnische Kirche, unnd andere, so das lauttere Evangelium Jhesu Christi erkant haben. Magdeburg: Michael Lotter, 1550.

Christlich warnunge und vermanunge an die Kirche Christi in Preussen den nechsten Abschied belangende. Magdeburg: Michael Lotter, 1555.

Clavis Scripturae sacrae: seu, De sermone sacrarum literarum, in duas partes divisae, quarum prior singularum vocum, atque locutionum sacrae scripturae usum ac rationem ordine alphabetico explicat: posterior de sermone sacrarum literarum plurimas generales regulas tradit. Authore Matthia Flacio Illyrico. Editio Nova Johannes Musaeus. Jena: Samuel Krebs for Johannes Ludovicus Neuenhahn, 1674.

Cleri Fletus. Est deploratio perditae maliciae Clericorum seu Spiritualium Antichristi, olim ante annos 100, vel amplius ab aliquo pio, templi Domini repurgatinem [sic] videre cupiente, conscripta. Magdeburg: Michael Lotter, 1550.

Confessio Waldensium... de plerisque nunc controversis dogmatibus ante 134. annos contra claudicantes Hussitas scripta, nostris que temporibus statui, ac rebus pulchre correspondens. Basel: Johann Oporin, 1568.

Confessionis An. Osiandri de iustificatione, in qua acerbe et impie insectatur adflictas Ecclesias, earumque ministros, qui hactenus doctinam in Augustana confessione compraehensam sonuerunt, Refutatio erudia & pia, scripta Magdeburgi. Frankfurt: Peter Braubach, 1552.

Contra quaedam interimistica et adiaphoristica scripta, quae a multis Gasparo Huberino tribuuntur. Item locus Brentii, praesentibus Christi & Belial conciliationibus admodum conveniens. Magdeburg: Christian Rödinger [ca. 1550].

Das alle Verfolger der Kirchen Christi zu Magdeburgk, Christi des Herrn selbs verfolger sindt. Geschrieben zur warnung an alle Christen, und sonderlich an das Kriegsvolch der Feinde. Magdeburg: Michael Lotter, 1551.

Das das Preusische Mandat den XI. Augusti dieses 55. Jahrs ausgegeben Betreffende die Amnestia oder Vergessung der Osiandrischen Ketzerey mit gutem Gewissen nicht kan angenomen werden, etc. grüntliche ursachen. Item vom weichen oder fliehen der Prediger in verfolgung. n. t. n. p.

Das das thewre Bludt oder gehorsamlich leiden Christi die ware, rechte, und einige Gerechtigkeit sey, dadurch wir für Gott gerecht, jm wolfgefellig und selig werden. Geschrieben an F. D. in Preussen, durch Matth. Flacium Illyricum. [Nüberg: Johann vom Berg und Ulrich Neuber], 1554.

Das der Bapst mit seinem hoffe das rechte Babylon und Babylonische Hure sey. Durch den hochgelarten Franciscum Petrarchum einen Welscher, der für 150. jarn gelebt hat. [Magdeburg: Christian Rödinger, 1550].

Das man in diesen geschwinden leufften, dem Teuffel und Antichrist zugefallen, nichts in den Kirchen Gottes vorendern soll. Durch Johannem Hermannum. [Magdeburg: Michael Lotter], 1548.

De Jesu, nomine Christi servatoris nostri proprio, contra Osiandrum. De Jehova nomine veri Dei proprio. Wittenberg: Hans Krafft der ältere, 1552.

De Materiis scientiarum, et erroribus Philosophiae, in rebus divinis. Basel: Johann Oporin, 1561.

De sectis, dissensionibus, contradictionibus et confusionibus doctrinae, religionis, scriptorum et doctorum Pontificorum Liber. Testimonia Recentissimorum Scholasticorum, Sophistarum, et Monachorum, contra Manichaeam Papistarum communionem sub una specie ... Appendix: Centum Gravamina Germanicae Nationis. Basel: Paul Queck, 1565.

De vocabulo fidei et aliis quibusdam vocabulis, explicatio vera et utilis, sumta ex fontibus Ebraicis. Cum praefatione Phil. Mel. Wittenberg: Veit Kreutzer, 1549.

De voce et re fidei, quod que sola fide iustificemur, contra pharisaicum hypocritarum fermentum, liber. Basel: [Johannes Oporin], 1563.

Declaratio Tabulae Trium methodorum Theologiae. [Jena: Donat Richttenhan, ca. 1560].

Demonstrationes evidentissimae doctrinae de essentia imaginis Dei et Diaboli, iustitiaeque ac iniustitae originalis una cum testimoniis veterum ac recentium theologorum... Basel: Peter Perna, 1570.

Duae veteres prophetiae de pia Ecclesiae Dei instauratione, ad nostra tempora pertinentes n. t. n. p.

Entschuldigung Matthiae Flacij Illyrici, geschrieben an die Universitet zu Wittemberg der Mittelding halben. Item sein brief an Philip. Melanthonem sampt etlichen andern schrifften dieselbige sach belangend. Verdeudscht. [Magdeburg: Christian Rödinger], 1549.

Eine Entschuldigung Matthiae Flacij Illyrici, an einen Pfarher. Item daeselben, was da sey die Kirchen verlassen odder nicht verlassen. It. zween Trewme Philippi. [Magdeburg: Christian Rödinger], 1549.

Epistola de Morte Pauli III Pontificis Maximi déque iis quae ei post mortem eius acciderunt. Piacenza [Basel: Oporinus], 1549.

Epistola Guuilelmi Postelli ad C. Schvvenckfeldium. Jena: Christian Rhodius, 1556.

Epistola Luciferi ad Spirituales circiter ante annos centum: ut ex codicis vetustate apparet, descripta, Auctore Nicola Oren. Magdeburg: Michael Lotter, 1549.

Epistola S. Hulrici episcopi Augustani, circiter ante sexcentos et 50 annos, ad Pontificem Nicolaum primum, pro defensione coniugii Sacerdotum, scripta, ex qua apparet, quam impudenter Papistae S. Patres jactent, cum et vita et doctrina cum S. Patribus plane ex Diametra pugnent. Magdeburg: Michael Lotter [1549].

Erklerung der schendlichen Sünde der jenigen, die durch das Concilium, Interim und Adiaphora, von Christo zum Antichrist fallen, aus diesem Prophetischen gemelde, des 3. Eliae seliger gedechtnis, D. M. Luth. genomen. [Magdeburg: Christian Rödinger, 1550].

Ermanung an alle Stende der Christlichen kirchen in Preussen Osianders lere halben. Magdeburg: Christian Rödinger, 1552.

Eine Erschreckliche Historia von einem, den die feinde des Evanglii inn welsch Land gezwungen haben, den erkanten Christum zuvorleugnen. [Magdeburg: Michael Lotter], 1549.

Etliche Brieffe, des Ehrwirdigen Herrn D. Martini Luthers seliger gedechtnis, an die Theologos auff den Reichtag zu Augspurg geschrieben, Anno M.D.XXX. Von der vereinigung Chirsti [sic] und Belials. Auss welchen man viel nützlicher lehr in gegenwertiger gefahr der Kirchen nemen kann, Verdeutscht. Item, etliche andere Shriefften [sic] nützlich und tröstlich zu lesen. Item zwo schriffte der Theologen zu Wittemberg, Eine an die Prediger zu Nürnberg, Die ander an den Churfürsten zu Sachsen, auch von voreinigung Christi und Belial, Anno XL. geschieben. Item eine schrifft der Prediger von Hamburg an die Theologen zu Wittemberg. Item sonst etliche brieff D. M. L. Magdeburg: Christian Rödinger, 1549.

Ettliche Contradictiones, oder widerwertige Lehr des Stenckfelts, Daraus sein Geist leichtlich kan geprüfet und geurtheylet werden. Item, Beweysung das Stenckfeld die heylige Schrifft verwirffet und in die höchste Verachtung bringet. Item, ein klares gezeugnuß Hieremie, Das die von Gott geoffenbarte und nu beschribne Lere, ein warhafftiges wort Gottes sey und billich genant werde. Nürnberg: Johann vom Berg und Ulrich Neuber, 1556.

Etliche greiffliche gewisse und scheinbarliche warzeichen, Daraus ein jeder wie gerinnges verstands er sey, Wo er nur zu erforschung der warheit geneiget ist, vormercken kan, das die Lehre der Evangelischen des Herrn Christi Lerer [sie] selbst ist, und das der Papisten Lehr falsch, Gottloss und vom Antichrist erfunden ist. Magdeburg: Christian Rödinger, 1549.

Etliche greiffliche gewisse und scheinbarliche warzeichen: Daraus ein jeder, wie gerinnges verstands er auch sey, Wo er nur zu erforschung der warheit geneigt isti [sie] vermercken kan, das die Lehre der Evangelichen des Herrn Christi Lehre selbs ist, und das der Papisten Lehr falsch, Gottlos, und vom Antichrist erfunden ist. Magdeburg: Christian Rödinger, 1550.

Etliche tröstliche vermanungen in sachen das heilige Gottliche Wort betreffend, zu dieser betrübten zeit sehr nützlich und tröstlich zu lesen. D. Martinus Luther Anno M.D.XXX. Preface by Flacius. Magdeburg: Christian Rödinger, 1550.

Explicatio loci Sancti Pauli Rom. 3. Nunc autem revelata est Iusticia Dei sine lege etc. In quo tum propositio ac scopus Epistolae ad Romanos continetur, tum tota ratio Iusticiae ac Iustificationis exponitur. Contra Osiandrum. Wittenberg: Joannes Lufft, 1553.

Fons atque origo purgatorii. n. p. 1555.

Form und weiss einer Bisschofflichen, ja Ertzbischoflichen Visitation am Rein, in welcher zu besehen ist, wie es kunfftig umb die Kirche wird gelegen sein, wenn die Bischoff ihre alte Jurisdiction wider bekommen werden. [Magdeburg: Christian Rödinger], 1549.

Forma inquisitionis Hispanicae instituta in inferiori Germania Anno 1550. Magdeburg: Michael Lotter, 1550.

Fragestücke unde Artikel, Auff welche die Pristerschafft im Stifft Meintz zuforderung des Teufflischen Pabsthumbs itzto Examiniert werden. [Magdeburg, 1548?].

Eine freuntliche, demütige und andechtige erinnerung an das heilige Volck, und Küniglliche priesterthumb des Antichrists, von der besserung des heiligen Canons oder Stilmessen. Magdeburg: Michael Lotter, 1550.

Eine freidige vermanung, zu klarem und öffentlichem bekentnis Ihesu Christi, wider die Adiaphoristische, Davidianische und Epicurische klugheit, des heuchelns und meuchelns, sehr nützlich zu lesen. Gestelt durch Civilium einen Italiener. Verdeudscht auss dem welschen. Magdeburg: Michael Lotter, 1550.

Fuünffzig grobe Irthumen der Stenckfeldischen Schwermerey, aus seinen eigen Büchern trewlich zusamen gelesen und verzeichnet, damit sich die einfeltigen Christen desto fleissiger für seinem Gifft schewen vnd hüten. Jena: Thomas Rebart, 1558.

Die Fürnemesten und gröbsten irthumb Osiandri, fein kurtz und klar jedermann zur warnung aus seinen eigenen Büchern gezogen und erzelet. Eisleben: Urban Gaubisch, 1555.

Ein geistlicher trost dieser betrübten Magdeburigschen Kirchen Christi, das sie diese Verfolgung umb Gottes worts, und keiner andern ursach halben, leidet. [Magdeburg: Michael Lotter, 1551].

Ein gemeine protestation und Klagschrifft aller frommen Christen wieder das Interim unnd andere geschwinde anschlege unnd grausame verfolgung der wiedersacher des

Evangelij, allen Gotfürchtigen gewissen, zu dieser betrübten zeit, überaus sehr nützlich unnd tröstlich zu lesen. Durch Joannem waremundum. [Magdeburg: Michael Lotter], 1549.

Ein grausam Meerwunder, den Bapst bedeutende, zu Rom gefunden, und zu Wittemberg erstlich Anno 23 und darnach abermal Anno 46. mit der auslegung Philippi gedruckt. Magdeburg: Christian Rödinger, [1550].

Gründliche Endtscheidung deß langwirigen und ergerlichen streits von der Erbsünde. n. p. 1578.

Gründliche Verlegung aller schedlichen Schwermereyen des Stenckfelds, zur unterricht und warnung der einfeltigen Christen. [Nürnberg: Johann vom Berg und Ulrich Neuber, 1557].

Gründliche verlegung aller Sophisterey, so D. Pfeffinger mit den andern Adiaphoristen, das Leiptzigsche Interim zubeschönen, gebraucht. Magdeburg: Christian Rödinger, 1551.

Gründliche verlegung aller Sophisterey, so Juncker Issleb, D. Interim, Morus, Pfeffinger, D. Geitz in seinem gründlichen bericht und jhre gesellen, die andere Adiaphoristen, das Leipsische Interim zu beschönen, gebrauchen. [Magdeburg: Christian Rödinger, 1551].

Gründliche Verlegung des langen Comments der Adiaphoristen, oder der verzelung jrer handlungen, Zu gründlicher erforschung der warheit in dieser sache sehr nützlich zu lesen. Jena: Donat Richtzenhan, 1560.

Gründliche verlegung etlicher newer Donatistischen schrifften des Stenckfelds. Nürnberg: Johann vom Berg & Ulrich Neuber, 1555.

Des h. Hulrichs etwa vor sechshundert jaren Bischoffs zu Augspurg schrifft wider das ehelos Leben der Priester, jtzt sehr nützlich zu lesen. Mit einer vorrede M. Fl. Illyrici, wider den Münch zu Augspurg. Magdeburg: Michael Lotter, 1553.

Des h. Merterers Christi, Georgen Scherers letzte bekentnis, Welcher umb der warheit Christi willen, von dem Antichristischen Wolffe zu Saltzburgk, grawsamlich ist ermordet worden. Mit einer Vorrede Matth. Facil. Illyri. An die verfolgete Christen im Bistumb Saltzburg, und Beiern. [Magdeburg: Michael Lotter], 1554.

Des Herrn Johan Brentii und anderer Wirtenbergischen Theologen, Declaration uber Osianders Disputation von der Rechtfertigung, sampt ihres glaubens bekentnis. Mit einer Vorrede Matth. Fla. Illyrici und Nicolai Galli, an die Preussischen Kirchen. Magdeburg: Michael Lotter, 1553.

Hertzogs Moritzen zu Sachsen, und des Marggrafen zu Brandenburg, bey der Churfürsten vereinigung, des Interims halben. n. p. [1549].

Historia certaminum inter Romanos episcopos et sextam Carthaginensem synodum, Africanasque ecclesias, de primatu seu potestate Papae, bona fide ex authenticis monumentis collecta. Quaedam vetusta monumenta, unde potissimum praedicta Historia desumpta est. Item Contra primatum seu tyrannidem papae. Basel: [Johann Oporin], 1554.

Des Interims und Interimisten warhafftige abgemalte figur und gestalt daraus yderman sonderlich bey dem Bretspiel, und der großen Kannen mit Bier, yhr andacht und messig leben erkennen kan. Broadsheet.

Julij Firmici Materni v. c. de errore profanarum religionum ad Constantium et Constantem Augustos liber. Strassburg: Paul Messerschmidt für Johann Oporin in Basel, 1562.

Klerliche beweisung, das alle die jenige, welche die schrifften widder das Interim und Mittelding feil zuhaben und zu lesen verbieten, Item, die zu dieser zeit, die von Magdeburg (auff waserley weise solchs geschehen mag) verfolgen oder verfolgen helffen, Christum den Son Gottes warhafftiglich selbs verfolgen. Geschrieben zur warnung an alle Christen, auff das sie sich für dieser grawsamen, Teufflischen wüterey fleissig hüten. Magdeburg: Christian Rödinger, 1550.

Eine köstliche Osterpredigt, zu Andtorff vor kurtzer zeit von einem Münch gehalten, das mann den Ketzern nicht leichtlich gleuben soll. [Magdeburg: Christian Rödinger, 1550].

Eine kurtze Antwort auff das lange Comment D. Ge. von guten wercken. Magdeburg: Christian Rödinger [ca. 1553].

Eine kurtze Tafel wider Osiandrum auf einem gantzen aussgeschlagenen Boten. n. t. n. p.

Kurtze und klare erzelung der argument Osiandri mit jhrer verlegung, und unserer beweisung wider ihn, von der gerechtigkeit des glaubens. Magdeburg: Christian Rödinger, 1552.

Ein kurtzer bericht vom Interim, darauß man leichtlich kan die leer unnd Geist desselbigen Buchs erkennen, Durch Theodorum Henetum allen frommen Christen zu dieser zeit nützlich unnd tröstlich. [Magdeburg: Michael Lotter], 1548.

Liber de veris et falsis adiaphoris, in quo integre propemodum Adiaphorica controversia explicatur. Magdeburg, 1549. See Ein Buch von waren und falschen Mitteldingen.

Joannis Hus et Hieronymi Pragensis Confessorum Christi historia et monumenta. 2. vols. Nürnberg: Johann vom Berg und Ulrich Neuber. 1558.

Missa latina, quae olim ante Romanam circa 700. Domini annum in usu fuit, bona fide ex vetusto authenticoque codice descripta. Item quaedam de vetustatibus Missae scitu valde digna. Adiuncta est Beati Rhenani Praefatio in missam Chrysostomi a Leone Tusco, Anno Domini 1070. versam. Strassburg: Christian Mylius, 1557.

Necessaria defensio contra famosam chartam, titulo, Wittebergensium scholasticorum, editam. Jena: Christian Rödinger der Ältere. 1558.

Newe Zeytung, Und Warhafftige Geschicht, die sich des vergangenen M.D.L. jars den 11. Februa. in der Löblichen Freyen Stadt Strassburg, in unser Frauwen Thumbstifft dz Münster genant an wiraufrichtung der Grausamen und abschühelichen Gotslesterung Böpstlicher Messen, so man der Pfaffn Interim nennet, hat beygeben vnd zugetragen, Hievor niemals, yetzund aber durch Blasium Argen von Magdeburg in den Truck gegeben Anno domini M.D. Lj. Gantz lustig und lieblich zu singen in der Narren Kappen oder Stoltzen Müllerin weiss. Magdeburg: Michael Lotter, 1551.

Neilou tou tón Thessalinikón Archiespiskopou peri tés tou Papa archés. Nili Thessalonicensis libellus de primatu Romani pontificis a Matthia Flacio Illyrico in Latinum sermonem conversus. Frankfurt: David Zäpfel, 1555.

Ein newer Antichristischer radtschlag oder bedencken, des Saltzbürgischen Bischoffs und anderer verfolger Christi, wie sie die Warheit des heiligen Evangelii auszurotten gedencken. Magdeburg: Michael Lotter, 1554.

Omnia latina scripta hactenus sparsim contra Adiaphoricas fraudes & errores aedita, & quaedam prius non excusa, catalogum versa pagina indicabit. Omnia correcta & aucta. [Magdeburg: Michael Lotter], 1550.

Ordenung und Mandat Keiser Caroli V. vernewert im April Anno 1550. Zu aussrotten und zu vertilgen, die Secten und spaltung, Welche enstanden sind, widder unsern heiligen Christlichen glauben, Und wider die ordenung unser Mutter der heiligen Christlichen Kirchen. Item ein Register der verworffenen und verbottenen Büchern, Auch von guten Büchern, welche man inn der Schulen lesen mag. Item eine vermanung des Rectors der Universitet zu Löven. Item ein ander Keisers Mandat, von dem selbigen handel im 40. jar ausgangen. Transferirt aus einem gedruckten Brabendischen Exemplar. Preface by Flacius. [Magdeburg: Michael Lotter, 1550].

Paralipomena Dialectices. Libellus lectu dignissimus, & ad Dialecticam Demonstrationem certius cognoscendam, cuius etiam in Prefatione prima quaedam principia proponuntur, apprime utilis. Basel: Iacobus Parcus, 1558.

Pia quaedam vetustissimaque poemata, partim Antichristum, eiusque spirituales filiolos insectantia, partim etiam Christum, eiusque beneficium mira spiritus alacritate celebrantia. Magdeburg: Michael Lotter, 1552.

Proba des geists Osiandri von der rechtfertigung durch die eingegossne wesentliche Gerechtigkeit Gottes. Nikolaus Gallus. Magdeburg: Michael Lotter, 1552.

Ein Procession, so die Hispanier am tage Mariae scheidung, welcher ist gewest der 15. Augustii, Anno 1554 zu Wien bey den Barfusern München gehalten haben, Darumb gedruckt, das alle Christliche hertzen deste klerer bebstliche Abgötterey in diesem Heidnischen Spectakel erkennen, Und dagegen Christliche lere suchen und annemen. Preface by Flacius. n. p. 1554.

Eine prophetische abconterfeihung des Tridentischen Conciliabuli. Durch D. Martinum Lutherum. Mit einer erklerung M. Fl. Illyr. Magdeburg: Christian Rödinger, 1551.

Ein Prophetische Buspredigt für die jenigen, So den erkanten und bekanten Christum mit dem Antichrist und seinem hauffen verfolget haben, oder noch verfolgen. [Magdeburg: Michael Lotter, 1547].

Protestatio con cinonatorium aliquot Augustanae confessionis, adversus conventum Tridentinum... Acc. norma simul et praxis constituendae religionis... iam pontifici et synodo recepta ac usitata. n. p. 1563.

Provocation oder erbieten der Adiaphorischen sachen halben, auff erkentnis und urteil der Kirchen. Magdeburg: Michael Lotter, 1553.

Quod hoc tempore nulla penitus mutatio in religione sit in gratiam impiorum facienda. Contra quoddam scriptum incerti autoris [Melanchthon] in quo suadetur mutatio piarum caeremoniarum in Papisticas per Hermannum Primatem. [Magdeburg: Michael Lotter], 1549.

Ein rechter lesteriger Rabsakes brieff, geschrieben von einem Bischoff an einen Christlichen Fürsten, in welchem er ihn vermanet das er sol von der erkanten warheit

Christi zu dem Antichrist abfallen, Daraus man sehr woll kan mercken wie gut es die Antichristische Wolffe mit den armen Schefflein Christi meinen. [Magdeburg: Christian Rödinger], 1549.

Recusationschrifft der Christlichen Augspurgischen Confessionsverwandten Stende, wider das vermeint, von Bapst Paulo dem dritten, weilandt zu Trient indicirt und angefangen Concilium, sampt einer gebürlichen provocation unnd erbietung, auff ein allgemein oder National, frey, Christlich und unparteisch Concilium inn Deudtschen Landen. Magdeburg: Michael Lotter, 1551.

Refutatio invectivae Bruni contra centurias Historiae Ecclesiasticae: in qua simul recitantur amplius 100 historica, maximique momenti Papistarum mendacia; accesserunt & alij libelli diversorum scriptorum, tum ad confirmationem illarum narrationum, tum alioqui ad praesens institutum cumprimis facientes. Basel: Johannes Oporinus, 1566.

Refutatio Missae. Widerlegung des Sophistischen Buchs des Schwartzen Münchs von der Opffer Mess, Anno 1555. außgangen Item die beschreibung der Meß oder Communion dreyer alten vätter, als Justini, welcher zu Rom ungefähr 150 Jar nach Christo gelebt, Clementis, welcher 200 unnd Dionisij, den 300 jar nach Christi geburt gewesen ist. [Strassburg: Samuel Emmel?], 1557.

Refutatio vanissimi Adiaphoristarum commenti de Logo, Verbo. Jena [Christian Rödinger der Ältere], 1558.

Ein register der hundert beschwerungen, damit Deudschland von dem Bapst und den seinen jemmerlich beschwert, und uberladen, ja gentzlich verterbt wird, auffm Reichstage zu Nürnberg Anno 1523. von dem Reich dem Bapst ubersendet. Magdeburg: Christian Rödinger, [1550?]

Regulae et tractatus quidam de sermone sacrarum literarum, ad genuinam multorum difficilium locorum explicationem perutiles. Magdeburg: Michael Lotter, 1551.

Responsio ad epistolam Philippi Melanthonis. Magdeburg: [Michael Lotter], 1549.

Ein schöne Historia von der standhaftigkeit des heiligen mans Basilij, beschrieben in der Tripartita Historia, und ander schöne Exempel mehr itzt zu dieser zeit sehr tröstlich und nützlich zu lesen. Magdeburg: Christian Rödinger, 1549.

Eine schrifft der Theologen zu Wittenberg an die Prediger von Nürnberg anno 1540. Von der vereinigung der Evangelischen mit den Papisten, daraus man sehr wol mercken kan, was von der jtzigen vereinigung Christi und Belials, der wolffe und der schaffe, zuhalten sey. Liß diesen brief Christlicher Leser, du wirst schweren, er sey widder die Adiaphoristen geschrieben. Item eine schrifft Lutheri und Pomerani, an Johan Friedrich Churfürsten, geschrieben anno 1541. Magdeburg: Christian Rödinger, 1549.

Ein Schrifft des Achtbarn und Ehrwirdigen Herren seliger gedechtnis, Doctoris Martini Lutheri, wider den Eisleben, kurtz vor seinem end geschrieben, vormals aber nie im Druck aussgangen. [Magdeburg: Christian Rödinger], 1549.

Ein schrifft, eines fromen Predigers aus der Türckey an Illyricum geschrieben, Darinnen angezeiget wird, wie es dort mit der Kirche und dem Evangelio zugehet. Magdeburg: Michael Lotter, 1550.

Eine schrifft widder ein recht Heidnisch ja Epicurisch Buch der Adiaphoristen, darin das Leiptzische Interim verteidiget wird, sich zu hüten für den jtzigen Verfelschern der waren Religion, sehr nützlich zu Lesen. Magdeburg: Christian Rödinger, 1549.

Eine Schrifft, wie die Pfarherrn an den örtern, da man die Papisterey widerumb auffricht, die Evangelisch lehr, welche sie Lutherisch nennen, verloben und verschweren müssen. [Magdeburg: Christian Rödinger], 1548.

Scripta quaedam Papae et Monarcharum, de concilio Tridentino, ad cognoscendam veritatem admodum lectu utilia, nunc primum in publicum edita Cum praefatione Matthiae Flacii Illyrici. Basel [ca. 1550].

Scriptum contra primatum Papae, ante annos 100 compositum. Item, Matthiae Flacii Illyrici de eadem materia. Magdeburg: Christian Rödinger, 1550.

Ein sehr schöne histori von der standhafftigkeit, in Bekentnis und leiden, des heiligen manns Simeonis, welcher ein öberster Superintendent gewesen ist in Persia, und von seinem gesellen, aus dem andern buch Sozomenis. Magdeburg: Christian Rödinger, n. t.

Ein Sendbrieff, P. Aesquillii von dem tode Pauli des dritten Babsts dieses namen. Item Was ihm nach seinem tode begegnet ist. [Magdeburg: Christian Rödinger], 1549.

Ein Sendtbrieff des Durchleuchtigsten, Hochgebornen Fürsten, und Herrn, Herrn Johann Albrechten von Mechelburg an Illyricum geschriben, von der Osiandrischen Ketzerey, wie die ist durch sondere Gottes gnade in Preussen gestillet worden. Nuremberg: Georg Merkel, n. t.

Sommighe troostelijke vermaninge, in saken die dat heylighe Godtlijcke Woort aengaen, in diese betroefden tijds seer hyttelyken ende troostlychen te lesen dor M. Lutherus. MDXXX. Wesel, 1567.

Sulpitii Severi Sacrae Historiae a mundi exordio ad sua usque tempora deductae, libri II. nunc primum in lucem editi. Item aliae quaedam Historicae appendices, lectu dignissimae. Basel: Johannes Oporinus, 1556.

Ein Supplication und demütige bitt einer Christlichen Gemein in Schwaben, an ihren Rath, Darinne sie bittet, das man ihn wolle die Tauffe lassen, nach Christi einsetzung, wie sie es zuvor gehabt haben. Magdeburg: Michael Lotter, 1550.

Sylva quaedam Testimoniorum ex propriis Papistarum, atque S. Patrum, atque Ecclesiasticorum Scriptorum libris collecta, qua meridiana luce clarium indicatur, probatur, & concvincitur: quod coram divino iudicio, sola fiducia gratiae & misericordiae Dei propter Christum sine ullis nostris meritis iustificemur & salvemur. Autore Ioanne Freyesleben. Nuremberg: Gabriel Heyn, 1556.

Sylvula carminum aliquot a diversis, piis, et eruditis viris conscriptorum; quibus variae de religione sententiae & controversiae brevissime explicantur. n. p. 1553. In: Naogeorgus, Thomas: Regnum papisticum.

Der Theologen bedencken, odder (wie es durch die ihren inn offentlichem Drück genennet wirdt) Beschluss des Landtages zu Leiptzig, so im December des 48. Jars, von wegen des Auspurgischen [sic] Interims gehalten ist. Welchs bedencken odder beschluss wir, so da widder geschrieben, das Leiptzigsche Interim genennet haben. Mit einer Vorrede und Scholien, was und warumb jedes stück bisher fur unchristlich darin gestraffet ist. Magdeburg: Michael Lotter, 1550.

Widerlegung der Opinion oder bekentnus, Osiandri, welches er nennet Von dem einigen mitler Jhesu Christo, und der rechtfertigung des glaubens, von F. G. Marggraff Johansen zu Brandenburgk etc. Theologen, in gehaltenem Synodo zu Custrin vorsamlett ausgangen. In massen solchs Marggraff Albrechten dem eltern, Hertzogen in Preussen, auff seiner F. D. selbst schreiben und begeren zugeschickt worden. Frankfurt/Od.: Johann Einhorn, 1552.

Trattato nel quale con certissimi ragioni nella Sacra Scrittura, si manifesta, come Pietro Apostolo non mai fu a Roma, ne anco pati in quella il Martirio: La onde si vede quanto debolmente il Romano pontefice si vanta di esser successore di Pietro. Regensburg: Johann Burger, 1566/67.

Tröstliche Gegensprüch des Ernwirdigen Herren Doctoris Martini Lutheri und Matthie Illyrici, wider des Rabe Osiandri Primarii spruch. n. p. 1552.

Der unschüldigen Adiaphoristen Chorrock, darüber sich die unrugige und Störrische Stoici mit ihnen zancken. Broadsheet.

Unterscheid zwischen der waren Religion Christi, und falschen Abgöttischen lehr des Antichrists, in den fürnembsten stücken. Broadsheet.

Urtheil von den Schwenckfeldischen Schwermerey. Von dem grewlichen irthumen der newen Schwenckfeldischen Postill unter dem namen des Johans Woermers newlich ausgangen. Jena: Thomas Rebart, 1559.

Varia doctorum piorumque virorum, de corrupto ecclesiae statu, poemata, ante nostram aetatem conscripta: ex quibus multa historica quoque utiliter, ac summa cum voluptate cognosci possunt. Magdeburg: Michael Lotter, 1554.

Verantwortung vom Logo von dem Wort, oder Son Gottes und etlichen andern aufflagen. [Jena: Thomas Rebart], 1561.

Verlegung der Apologiae Sydonii, damit er seinen Catechismum verteidinget. [Magdeburg: Christian Rödinger], 1553.

Verlegung der kurtzen antwort des Schwenckfeldts. Magdeburg: Michael Lotter, 1554.

Verlegung des Bekentnis Osiandri von der Rechtfertigung der armen sünder durch die wesentliche Gerechtigkeit der Hohen Maiestet Gottes allein. Durch Matth. Fla. Illyr. Mit unterschreibung Nicola. Gali [sic], darin der grund des irthums Osiandri sampt seiner verlegung auffs kürzest verfast ist. Magdeburg: Christian Rödinger, 1552.

Verlegung des unwarhafftigen ungegründten berichts Hansen Funckens, von der Osiandrischen Schwermerey. Die grewliche unerhorte schweremerey der Osiandrischen Götter inn Preussen so im neuen jarstag dieses 1554. jars ist offentlich vom Eichhorn gepredigt worden. n. t. n. p.

Verlegung des unwarhafftigen ungegründten berichts Hansen Funckens, von der Osiandrischen schwermerey. [Magdeburg: Christian Rödinger, 1554].

Verlegung zweier schrifften, eines Augspurgischen Münchs, mit namen Joannes Fabri, von des Babsts Primat und von Beicht. Item achtzehen beweisungen, das S. Petrus zu Rom nicht gewesen sey. Item ein trostbrieff D. Lutheri an die kirche zu Augspurg, itzt widder die Interimisten und Adiaphoristen, welche einen Christum one Schwerd, Fewr und Creutz zimmern, nützlich zu lesen. Item eine schrifft widder die vermeinte gewalt des Babsts, vor 100 jarn, zur zeit des Concilii zu Basel, von einem D. Georgius Hembergensis genant geschrieben. Magdeburg: Christian Rödinger, 1550.

Ein vermanung zur bestendigkeit, in bekentnis der warheit, Creutz, und Gebett, in dieser betrübten zeit sehr nützlich und tröstlich. Magdeburg: Michael Lotter [1549].

Vermanung zur gedult und glauben zu Gott, im Creutz dieser verfolgung Geschrieben an die Kirche Christi zu Magdeburg. Magdeburg: Christian Rödinger, 1551.

Vermanungk an die verfolgete Christen in Bistumb Saltzburgk unnd Beierlandt. [Magdeburg: Michael Lotter, 1554.]

Vom fürnemlichen stücke, punct, oder artickel der Schwenckfeldischen schwermerey. [Magdeburg: Michael Lotter, 1553].

Von der einigkeit derer, so für und wider die Adiaphora in vorgangenen Jaren gestritten haben, Christlicher einfeltiger bericht, sehr nützlich zu lesen. [Oberursel: Nicolaus Henricus], 1556.

Von der Gerechtigkeit wider Osiandrum, nützlich zu lesen. Magdeburg: Christian Rödinger, 1552.

Von der grewlichen Uneinigkeit, Zwitracht, Secten und Rotten der Bepstischen Religion und Kirchen. Itziger zeit sehr nützlich zu lesen. Jena: Thomas Rebart, 1559.

Von der h. Schrifft und irer wirckung, widder Caspar Schwenckfeld. Mit einer vermanung Nicolai Galli das ampt Gottlichs worts in ehren zuhaben. Magdeburg: Michael Lotter, 1553.

Von der Messe und ihrem Canone Magistri Johannis Agricolae Eyssleben, Lhere und schrifft, Welche er auff dem Reychstag zu Speyer in der Epistel zu den Colossern geprediget, und folgend Anno. M.D. XXVII. zu Wittenbergk im Druck offentlich hat ausgehen lassen, Dem Jnterim so er ytzt hat helffen stellen gantz entegegen Daraus sein geyst zuvermercken. [Magdeburg: Christian Rödinger, 1549].

Von der Papisten Tauff, und andern Caeremonien oder Kirchendiensten. ob die nach erkanter und angenomener Wahrheit, durch jemand Christlich zu besuchen und zu gebrauchen sein. Durch einen Prediger in Oberdeudschland gestellet. Magdeburg: Christian Rödinger, [1549].

Eine Vorrede Philippi Melanthon, auff das fürgelegte Buch zu Regensburg. Deudsch ausgangen zu Wittenberg, Darin er unterrichtet, Was man von aller Reformation und vergleichungen, so in der Religion mit den Papisten fürgenomen wird, halten sol, Not und nützlich zu lesen. Magdeburg: Christian Rödinger, 1549.

[Sigismund Cephalus, Pseud.?] Warer Grundt unnd beweisung das die unrecht handlen die jren Predigern verbieten, das Antichristisch Bapstumb mit seinen grewlen zustraffen. Magdeburg: Christian Rödinger, 1551.

Was vnnd wie man sich zu dem künfftigen Concilium zu Trydent versähen möge. Auch was gutts davon zu verhoffen. Bern: Matthias Apiarius, [1551].

Was von dem jetzt ausgeschriebenen Tridentischen Concilio zu halten sey, Drey gesprech. [Magdeburg: Michael Lotter], 1552.

Widder den ausszug des Leipsischen Interims, oder das kleine Interim. Magdeburg: Christian Rödinger, 1549.

Widder die newe Reformation D. Pfeffingers, des Meisnischen Thumbherrn. Magdeburg: Christian Rödinger, 1550.

Widder die newen Detzel, oder aussrüffer der Ablas Bullen, und Antichristischen Jubil yars. Item drey Bullen vom Jubel yar. Magdeburg: Michael Lotter, 1550.

Widder die unchristliche Vermanungschrifft, des Bisthumbs zu Naumburg. Magdeburg: Christian Rödinger, 1550.

Widder die vermeinte gewalt, und Primat des Bapstes, zu dieser zeit, da die gantze welt sich befleisset, den ausgetriebenen Antichrist, widderumb in den tempel Christi zu setzen, nützlich zu lesen. Magdeburg: Christian Rödinger, [1550]

Widder drei Gottislesterische unnd Sophistische Argumenta des Funckens, welche er newlich in Preussen widder das tewre blut Christi unter die Leute gestrewet hat. n. t. n. p.

Widderlegung der Predigten von der allerheiligsten Antichristischen Missa des frembden Bischoffs von Sydon, Meintzischen Weihbischoff. Magdeburg: Christian Rödinger, 1550.

Widderlegung des Catechismi des Larven Bischoffes von Sidon. Magdeburg: [Michael Lotter], 1550.

Wider das Interim, Papistische Mess, Canonem, unnd Meister Eissleuben, durch Christianum lauterwar, zu dieser zeit nützlich zu lesen. [Magdeburg: Michael Lotter], 1549.

Wider den Evangelisten des heiligen Chorrocks, D. Geitz Maior. Basel: [Magdeburg: Michael Lotter], 1552.

Wider den Schnöden Teuffel, der sich jtzt abermals in einen Engel des liechtes verkleidet hat, das ist wider das newe Interim, Durch Carolum Azariam Gotsburgensem. [Magdeburg: Christian Rödinger], 1549.

Wider die Götter in Preussen. Das nur eine einige wesentliche gerechtigkeit Gottes sey, die nemlich, so inn den Zehen gebotten offenbaret ist. Ein kurtzer, heller unnd klarer bericht von verdienst und gerechtigkeit Christi. [Magdeburg: Christian Rödinger 1552].

Wider die newe ketzerey der Dikaeusisten, vom spruch Christi Joan. am XVI. Der heilig Geist wird die Welt straffen umb die Gerechtigkeit, das ich zum Vater gehe. Magdeburg: Christian Rödinger [1551].

Wie iemmerlich und schendtlich der Babst sampt seinen Bischoven und geistlichen, die arme Scheflein Christi durch die Officialen schindet. Durch den Hochgelarten und grossen praelaten Petrum Blesensem, welcher für jaren gelebt hat. Magdeburg: Christian Rödinger, n. t.

Wonderfull newes of the death of Paule the III. last byshop of Rome, where is truly set out the abominable acts of his most mischevous life and of diverse thynges that after his death have happened. Written in Latin by P. Esquillus, and Englyshed by W. B. London: T. Gaultier, n. t.

Ein wunderlich gesicht newlich bey Braunschweig am hiemel gesehen, beschriben durch den hochgelerten hern Doctorem Nicolaum Medlerum superattendentem zu Braunschweig. [Magdeburg: Pankraz Kempf, 1549.]

Das ii. Capit. Syrach, Der xij. und xciiij. Psalm mit kurtzen Ausslegungen. n. p. 1551.

Zwei Capitel Polydori Virgilii vom Namen und Stifftern der Meß, ausgangen zu einem anfang widder des Sydonij predigten. Daraus erscheinet, wie er in seinen predigten öffentlich leugt, da er sagt, das die gantze Christenheit von 1500. Jaren her die Papistische Meß allezeit eintrechtiglich gehalten habe. Und das der Canon in allen seinen stücken von der Apostel zeit her im brauch gewesen sey. Item, Widderlegung D. Mart. Luth. des grewels der Stillmesse, so man den Canon nennet. Magdeburg: Christian Rödinger, 1550.

Zwey schriffte zweier gelerten und frommer menner, Widder die Adiaphoristische verfelschung. Gestelt zu Leiptzig, gantz nützlich zu lesen. Magdeburg: Michael Lotter, 1550.

Zwo fürnemliche gründe Osiandri verlegt, zu einem Schmeckbier. Magdeburg: Christian Rödinger [1552].

Sixteenth-Century Prints

Albrecht, Duke of Prussia. Ausschreiben an unsere alle liebe getrewen und Landschafften... wie sich die ergerliche zwispalt uber dem Artickel von unswer armen Sünder Rechtfertigung... erhaben. Königsberg: Hans Lufft, 1553.

– Mandat An ihr... Underthanen außgangen den 11 Augusti, Anno M.D.L.V. Königsberg: Johann Daubmann, 1555.

Alciatus, Andreas. Andree Alciati. De formula Romani Imperii Libellus. Accesserunt non dissimilis argumenti, Dantis Florentini de Monarchia libri tres. Radolphi Carnotensis De translatione Imperii libellus. Chronica M. Jordanis, Qualiter Romanum Imperium translatum sit at Germanos. Omnia nunc primum in lucem edita. Basel: Johannes Oporinus, 1559.

Amsdorf, Nicolaus von. Antwort, Glaub und Bekentnis auff das schöne und liebliche Interim. [Magdeburg: Michael Lotter], 1548.

– Auff die künstliche Spöttische und Bitterhönische Oration So D. Ziegler zu Leiptzig am Ostermontag widder die bestendigen Lutherischen recitiert hat. Beurische und einfeltige antwort. Magdeburg: Michael Lotter, 1549.

– Das die zu Wittenberg im andern teil der bucher Doctoris Martini im buch, "Das diese wort Christi 'Das ist mein Leib etc.' noch feststehen," mehr denn ein blat vier gantzer Paragraphos vorsetzlich aussgelassen haben wie folget. [Magdeburg: Michael Lotter], 1949.

– Das Doctor Pomer und Doctor Maior mit iren Adiaphoristen ergernis unnd zurtrennung angericht, unnd den Kirchen Christi unüberwintlichen schaden gethan haben. Derhalben sie und nicht wir zu Magdeburg vom Teuffel erwegt seint, wie sie uns schmehen und lestern. [Magdeburg: Michael Lotter], 1551.

– Das itzund die rechte zeit sey, Christum und sein Wort zu bekennen, und auff keine andere zu warten sey. Etliche sprüche, das man den Adiaphoristen nicht trawen noch gleuben sol. [Magdeburg: Christian Rödinger], 1551.

– Eine erinnerung an die Deudschen, das die einfeltigen ihre Sünde, so sie diese Fünff jar her gethan haben, erkennen, und bekennen sollen, sich bekeren und bessern, Auff das sie selig, und mit dem hauffen nicht verdampt werden. [Magdeburg: Christian Rödinger]. n. t.

– Des Gefangnen Christlichen Churfürsten, rechter Titel, so ihn yetziger zeit, von allen Gotseligen waren Christen, bilich gegeben wird zu Latein und Deudsch in ein Lied verfasset. [Magdeburg: Hans Walter]. n. t.

– Ein kuurtzer unterricht auff D. Georgen Majors Antwort, das er nit unnschüldig sey, wie er sich tragice rhümet. Das gute werck zu seligkeit nit von nöten sind. Das gute werck zu eim Christlichen leben hie auff erden nötig sind. Basel [Magdeburg: Michael Lotter], 1552.

– Wie sichs mit des Durchleuchtigsten Hochgebornen Fürsten und Herrn, Herrn
  Johans Friderich, des Eldern, weiland Hertzogen zu Sachssen, und gebornem Chur-
  fürsten, Landgraven in Düringen, und Marggraven zu Meissen, meines gnedigsten
  Herrn, Christlichem abschied zugetragen hat. Jena: Christian Rödinger, 1554.

Anonymous. De Locorum Theologicorum D. Philippi Melanthonis orthodoxa puritate et utilitate, adsertio & subscriptio praecipuorum aliquot doctorum. Frankfurt am
  Main: [Paul Reffeler], 1579.

– Ein newes Lied von zweien Eseltreibern, Johan Ritzenbergen, und Joachimo
  Magdeburgio. Gestellet Auff das Gesprech Joachimi Magdeburgii, eines Esels, und
  Matthei Berkgknechts. [Wittenberg: Georg Rhau Erben], 1558.

– Ein new Gedicht wider die Chammisten auff zwei newe Liedlein eines Eseltribers.
  J. M. B. gemacht im Thon Pertransivit Clericu. 1559.

– Praecationes Miserae & afflictae Ecclesiae quae est in Belgico, quae in hisce
  praesentibus periculis a solo Christo tota pendet. [Hamburg: Joachim Löw, ca.
  1566].

Aquinas, Dominicus. Ein seer Schön Christlich bedencken auff das Schendlich Interim.
  Mit antzeigung der zeichen, so für dem Jüngsten Tage her komen, und den itzigen
  Interimistischen Abfal mit sich bringen sollen. n. p. 1549.

Bale, John. Rhithmi Vetustissimi de Corrupto Ecclesiae Statu. Antwerp, 1546.

– Scriptorum illustrium Maioris Brytanniae quam nunc Angliam & Scotiam vocant:
  Catalogus. 2. vols. Basel: Johannes Oporinus, 1557–1559.

Bellarmine, Robert. Disputationes de controversiis Christianae fidei adversus huius
  temporis hereticos. 1586.

Bernat of Lublin. Raj Duszny. Cracow, 1513.

Besselmeyer, Sebastian. Gründtlicher Bericht, des Magdeburgischenn Kriegs, Schlacht,
  Belagerung, und fürnemsten Scharmützeln, und alles was sich von beyden teylen,
  innen und ausserhalb der Stadt, Vom Anfang bis zum ende, zugetragen hat. Auffs
  kürtzste, warhafftiger verfasset, denn zuvor mit unfleiß im Druck zu Basell, ausgangen ist. [Magdeburg: Christian Rödinger, ca. 1552.]

Blahoslav, Jan. Summa quaedam brevissime collecta ex variis scriptis Fratrum, qui falso
  Waldenses vel Piccardi vocantur, et eorundem Fratrum origine et actis. 1556.

Buchholzer, Noah. Carmen de natalibus, parentibus, vita, moribus, rebus gestis eiusdem
  Flacii. 1558. See Jacobus Diassorinus.

Camerarius, Joachim. De Philippi Melanchthonis Ortu, Totius Vitae Curriculo et
  Morte ... narratio. Leipzig: Ernst Vögelin, 1566.

Charles V, Emperor. Sacrae Caesareae Maiestatis Declaratio, Quomodo in Negocio
  Religionis per imperium usque ad definitionem Concilii generalis vivendum sit, in
  Comitiis Augustanis, XV. Mai, Anno 1548, proposita & publicata, & ab omnibus
  imperii ordinibus recepta. Augsburg: Philipp Ulhart, 1548.

Christianus, Albertus. Admonitio M. Alberti Christiani ad primarium nostri temporis
  Ecebolum Eislebium scripta, Anno M.D. XLIX. [Magdeburg: Michael Lotter], 1551.

Chytraeus, David. Saxonia, ab Anno Christi 1500. usque ad M.D.XCIX. Leipzig:
  Henning Grosse, 1599.

Diassorinus, Jacobus. Encomium Mataei Flacii Illyrici, scriptum Graecis versibus a Viro Illustri, Iacobo Diassorino, Domino Doridos, eiecto a Turcis patria & ditione, qui multis annis fuit ductor equitum Graecorum in exercitu Caroli V. Imperatoris in Italia & Gallia ... Item Carmen de natalibus, parentibus, vita, moribus, rebus gestis eiusdem Flacii. Autore Noah Bucholcero. [Wittenberg: Georg Rhau Erben], 1558.

Di Montalboddo, Francan. Paesi uovamente ritrovati. Venice, 1517.

Egnatius, Johannes Baptista. Ad Franciscum huius nominis Primum: De eius in Italiam ... Adventu... Panegyricus. Mediolani, 1515.

– De Exemplis Illustrium Virorum Venetae Civitatis atque Aliarum Gentium. Venice: N. Tridentinus, 1554.

Eisengrein, Wilhelm. Catalogus testium veritatis locupletissimus, omnium orthodoxae matris Ecclesiae doctorum, extantium et non extantium, publicatorum et in bibliothecis latentium, qui adulterina Ecclesiae dogmata, impuram impudentem & impiam haeresum vaniloquentiam, in hunc usque diem firmissimis demonstrationum rationibus impugnarunt, variaque scriptorum monumenta reliquerunt, seriem complectens. Dillingen: Sebald Mayer, 1565.

Epitimus, Andreas [Justus Jonas]. Pro ficticio missae sacrificio argumenta erronea sophistarum pontificiorum, cum refutationibus eorundem. Argumenta vera, firma & perspicua, contra sacrificium missae papisticae. Magdeburg: Christian Rödinger, 1550.

Erastus, Thomas. De Astrologia divinatrice epistolae ... in lucem aeditae, opera et studio Ioannis Iacobi Grynaei. Basel: Peter Perna, 1580.

Fabri, Johann. Antwort, auff das unnütz, unrain, irrig geschwetz Mathie Flacij Illyrici, so er geschriben wider das büchlein, genant Rechter weg. Und auff seine dreyundzwaintzig sectische Argument, so er geschriben an Osterreich unnd Bayern, wider die Evangeliche Meß. Mit einer vorgehenden Epistel darinn die unainigkait der secten under ainander, und verainigung derselben wider die hailige Catholische kirchen, mit warhafftem grund ausgeführt würdt. Dillingen: Sebald Mayer, 1558.

– Ein nutzlich Beychtbüchlin, wie der Mensch sich seiner Sünd erinnern unnd die bekennen soll. Augsburg: Philip Ulhart, n. t.

– Quod Petrus Romae fuerit, et ibidem Primus Episcopatum gesserit, atque sub Nerone martyrium passus fuerit: Et an fundamentum Ecclesiae dici possit. Dillingen: Sebald Mayer [1552].

– Der recht Weg: Welche weg oder strasz, der glaubig wandeln oder gehn soll, das er komme zu der ewigen rug und friden. Dillingen: Sebald Mayer, 1553.

– Testimonium Scripturae et patrum Petrum, Apostolum Romae fuisse: primumque ibidem Episcopum: et sub Nerone martyrium passum: ac fundamentum Ecclesiae dici. Cum Epistola Mamerani praefixa eiusdem argumenti. [Dillingen], 1553.

– Von Ankunfft und herkommen der römischen Bischöff, von Petro biß auf Julium den Dritten, Und die Namen aller Cardinäl, so yetzund Anno Domini M.D.L. bey Leben seind. Auch von des Römischen Reichs Monarchey, und ordenlichen Succession, oder volgung der Römischen Kaiser, von Julio Cesare, biß auf den großmächtigsten Kaiser Carolum den fünfften. Augsburg: Phillip Ulhart [1551].

- Was die Evangelich Meß sey, Grundtliche unnd Christenliche anzaigung auß der hailigen geschrifft, unnd auß den alten hayligen Kirchenlerern, zu trost und sterckung der Glaubigen. Dillingen: Sebald Mayer, 1555.

The Fortresse of Fathers, ernestlie defending the puritie of Religion and Ceremonies, by the trewe exposition of certaine places of Scripture: against such as wold bring in an Abuse of idol Stouff, and of thinges indifferent and do appoinct th' authority of Princes and Prelates larger than the trueth is. Translated out of Latine into English for there sakes that understand no Latin by I. B. 1566.

Foxe, John. The Ecclesiasticall History, contaynyng the Actes & Monumentes of Thynges passed in euery Kynges tyme in this Realme especially in the church of England principally to be noted ... from the primitive tyme till the reigne of K. Henry VIII. 2nd ed 2 vols. London: John Daye, 1570.

Funck, Johannes. Wider des unverschempten holhipplers unnd Auffrührischen Lugners Mats Flax Eillirrn ... Nottwendige gegenwehr, Schutzrede unnd widerlegung bis auff besere gelegenheit. 1555.

Gallus, Nicholas. Auff des Herrn D. Majors veranwortung und Declaration der Leiptzigischen Proposition, wie gute werk zur seligkeit nötig sind, zum zeugnis seiner unschult, das er mit der Leiptzigischen handlung nichts zu thun habe. Antwort. Basel [Magdeburg: Michael Lotter], 1552.

- Ein Christlich Gebet der Kirchen und Kriegsleute zu Magdeburgk, sonderlich in treffender not, wider ihre Feinde, durch die Prediger daselbs gestellet. Magdeburg: Michael Lotter, 1551.

- Einer Christlichen Stad unthertenigk antwort, auff das von Key. Ma. uberschickt Interim. Unnd ein Radtschlag der Predicanten der selbigen Stadt, n. p. 1548.

- Christliche vermanung etlicher Theologen zu Wittebergk an alle Christen, sonderlich an die Deudtschen Kriegsleut, nechst verschienener Jare und itzt schwebende Kriegshandlung wider die Christen betreffend, auffs newe wider im druck ausgangen. Mit einer Vorrede unnd Scholien M. Nicolai Galli, Pfarrhern der alten stadt Magdeburgk. Magdeburg: Michael Lotter, 1551.

- Disputatio de adiaphoris, & mutatione praesentis status pie constitutarum ecclesiarum. Magdeburg: Michael Lotter, 1551.

- Eine Disputation von Mitteldingen, und von den itzigen verenderungen in kirchen, die Christlich und wol geordent sind aus dem Latein verdeudscht. Magdeburg: Christian Rödinger, 1550.

- Der Prediger zu Magdeburgk ware, gegründte Antwort, auff das rhümen irer Feinde, das sie auch Gottes Wort reine, inhalts der Augspurgischen Confession, so wol als die zu Magdeburgk haben, Und was sie daraus mehr wider die Stadt einführen unnd fürgeben dürffen. Magdeburg: Michael Lotter, 1551.

- Ein sendbrieff Nicolai Galli Pfarherrn zu S. Ulrich der alten Stadt Magdeburgk an einen andern Pfarrhern ausserhalb, zum bericht gegen etlicher leichtfertigen Leut schmehung, als ob keine zucht noch Erbarkeit inn dieser belagerung mher bey uns fürhanden. Magdeburg: Michael Lotter [1551].

– Warer bericht und trost aus dem sechsten Capitel des propheten Baruchs, allen betrübten gewissen, so in diesen kümmerlichen zeiten des Interims und Adiaphora halben, nicht wissen, wie sie sich halten sollen. Nützlich und tröstlich zu lesen. Durch Thomam Rörer, prediger zu Chamb in Beiern. Preface by Gallus. Magdeburg: Christian Rödinger, 1550.

Goldast, Melchior. Monarchia S. Romani Imperii. 3 vols. Hanau, Frankfurt/M. 1611–14.

Hamburg clergy. Ein Brieff der Prediger zu Hamburg, an die Theologen zu Wittembergk, in welchem gehandelt wirt von Mitteldingen, zu dieser zeit sehr nützlich zu lesen. Magdeburg: Christian Rödinger, 1549. CR, VII, *367–382*.

Heinrich, Duke of Saxony. Kirchenordnunge zum anfang, fur die Pfarher in Hertzog Heinrichs zu Sachsen v. g. h. Fürstenthumb. Wittenberg: Hans Lufft, 1539.

Heldelin, Caspar. Eine Christliche predigt uber der Leiche des Ehrnwürdigen und hochgelerten Herrn M. Matthiae Flacii Illyrici, Weiland getrewen Dieners und bestendigen Merterers Jesu Christi Fromen Hertzen zu gut gestellet. [Oberursel: Nicolaus Henricus] 1575.

Helding, Michael. Brevis institutio ad christianam pietatem, secundum doctrinam catholicam ... Mainz, Ivo Schöffer, 1549.

– Institutio ad pietatem Christianem, secundum doctrinam Catholicam, complectens Explicationem Symboli Apostolici, Orationis Dominicae, Angelicae Salutationis, Decalogi & septem sacramentorum. In: Constitutiones concilii provincialis Moguntini sub ... Sebastiano Archiepiscopo Moguntino ... sexta Maii, Anno Domini M.D. XLIX celebrati. Mainz: Behem, 1549.

– Sacri Canonis Missae Paraphrastica Explicatio, cum Declaratione Ceremoniarum. Et brevi ad populum exhortatione, inter ipsum Sacrum habenda. Augsburg: Philipp Ulhart [1548].

– Von der Hailigisten Messe. Fünffzehen Predige, zu Augspurg auff dem Reichsztag im Jar M.D.XLVIII. gepredigt. Durch Michaeln Bischoff zu Sidonien, Meintzischen Suffraganeen. Ingolstadt: Alexander Weissenhorn, 1548.

Herold, Johann. Orthodoxographa Theologiae Sacrosanctae ac syncerioris fidei Doctores Numero LXXVI ... Basel: Heinrich Petri, 1555.

Holzmann, Ulrich. Ein new Lied, Wie die Predicanten der stat Augspurg geurlaubt und abgeschafft seind, den XXVI. Augusti, Anno Domini M.D.LI. geschehen. n. p., 1551.

Johann Friedrich, Duke of Saxony. Confession: H. Johann Friderich des Eltern, vor Kayserlicher Mayestat gethan zu Augspurg, Anno M.D.XLIX. do im auffgelegt von Kay: May: ins Interim zu willigen. n. p. [1549?].

Judex, Mattheus and Johann Wigand. Syntagma, seu Corpus doctrinae Christi, ex Novo Testamento tantum, methodica ratione, singulari fide et diligentia congestum. 2. vols. Basel: Johannes Oporinus, 1558.

Krenzheim, Leonard. Coniecturae. Christliche vermutungen, von künfftiger Zeit, Zustandt, in Kirchen und Regimenten ... Sampt den Weissagungen des Hocherleuchten Cardinals Nicolai Cusani; Görlitz: Ambrosius Fritsch, 1583.

Krowicki, Marcin. Chrzesczianskye, a zalobliwe napominanye... Magdeburg: Michael Lotter, 1554.

Leipzig University Faculty. Endlicher Bericht und Erklerung der Theologen beider Universiteten, Leipzig und Wittemberg ... belangend die Lere... Wittenberg: Hans Lufft, 1570.

Lindt, Wilhelm van der. Missa Apostolica. Antwerp: Christopher Platin, 1589.

– Panoplia evangelica, sive de verbo dei evangelico libri quinque. Cologne: Maternus Cholins, 1559.

Lübeck Pastors et al. Bekentnuß unnd Erklerung auffs Interim durch der Erbarn Stedte, Hamburg, Lüneberg, etc. Superintendenten, Pastorn unnd Predigern zu Christlicher und notwendiger unterrichtung gestellet. Magdeburg: Michael Lotter, 1549.

Luther, Martin. Der ander Psalm Davids, durch D. Martinum Luther heiliger gedechtnis ausgelegt. Darin auff die leuffte und hendel der Weltgelerten jtziger zeit so meisterlich geantwortt, und den armen betrübten Christen so reicher trost, Lehr und unterweisung vorgelegt wird, gleich als hette der heilige Geist sonderlich mit fingern auf diese zeit und tage weisen wollen. Magdeburg: Christian Rödinger, 1550.

– Enarratio 53. Capitis Esaiae prophetae ex praelectionibus Reverendi patris D. Martini Lutheri, summa fide & diligentia collecta, Anno 1544. & nunc hoc 1550. anno primum in lucem aedita. Magdeburg: Michael Lotter, 1550.

– Die letzte Predigt Doctoris Martini Lutheri heiliger gedechtnis, geschehen zu Wittenberg, am andern Sontag nach Epiphanias Domini, den xvij. Januarij, Im M.D. xlvj. Ihar. [Magdeburg: Michael Lotter], 1549.

– D. Martini Luthers auslegung, uber den 129. Psalm Verdeutscht, zu diesen betrübten zeiten fast nützlich zu lesen. Auch desselbigen, etliche Trostbrieff an betrübte Personen. Magdeburg: Michael Lotter, 1550.

– Parvus Catechismus, pro pueris in schola nuper auctus per Mart. Luth. [Magdeburg: Michael Lotter, ca. 1550].

– Der Spruch Esaie am XXXV. Ausgelegt aus den schrifften D. Martini Luth. seliger gedechtnis. Per N. E. E. N. 1548.

– Von der entheubtung Johannis des Teuffers, durch der Fuchs-König Herodem. [Magdeburg: Michael Lotter, ca. 1550].

Magdeburg Centuriators. Ecclesiastica Historia, integram Ecclesiae Christi ideam, quantum ad Locum, Propagationem, Persecutionem, Tranquillitatem, Doctrinam, Hereses, Ceremonias, Gubernationem, Schismata, Synodos, Personas. Miracula, Martyria, Religiones extra Ecclesiam, et statum Imperii Politicum attinet, secundum singulas Centurias perspicuo ordine complectens; singulari diligentia & fide ex vetustissimis & optimis historicis, patribus, & aliis scriptoribus congesta: per aliquot studios & pios viros in urbe Magdeburgica. Basel: Johannes Oporinus, 1559 etc.

Magdeburg City Council. Der von Magdeburgk Ausschreiben an alle Christen. Magdeburg: Michael Lotter, 1550.

– Der von Magdeburgk Entschüldigung, Bit, unnd gemeine Christliche erinnerunge. Magdeburg: Michael Lotter, 1549.

- Der von Magdeburg verantwortung alles unglimpffs, so ihnen in ihrer Belagerung von den Magdeburgischen Baals Pfaffen, und andern ihren unnd der Christen Feinden begegenet. Magdeburg: Michael Lotter, 1550.

- Confessio et Apologia pastorum & reliquorum ministrorum ecclesiae Magdeburgensis. Magdeburg: Michael Lotter, 1550.

- Geistlich Ringeltänze. Aus der Heiligen Schrift. Vor die Jugend. Magdeburg: Hans Walther, 1551.

- Deren zu Magdeburgk, so widder die Adiaphora geschrieben haben, ihres vorigen schreibens beschlus, auff der Adiaphoristen beschüldigung und lesterung, die zeit ihrer belagerung, und itzt zum teil newlich unter diesen friedshandlungen wider sie ausgangen. [Magdeburg: Michael Lotter], 1551.

- Ein Form zu Beten und Gott anzuruffen in dieser gegenwertigen not und trübsal. [Magdeburg: Michael Lotter, 1551].

- Grüntdlicher bericht aus heiliger schrifft, wie ferne man den Oberherrn, gehorsam schuldig, auch wer, wie, unnd in welcherley fellen, man den verderblichen Tyrannen, möge widerstand thun. Allen Christen, sonderlich den Kriegsleuten nützlich unnd tröstlich zuwissen. [Magdeburg: Michael Lotter], 1552.

- Der Prediger zu Magdeburgk ware, gegründte Antwort, auff das rhümen irer Feinde, das sie auch Gottes Wort reine, inhalts der Augspurgischen Confession, so wol als die zu Magdeburgk haben, Und was sie daraus mehr wider die Stadt einführen unnd fürgeben dürffen. Magdeburg: Michael Lotter, 1551.

Magdeburg, Joachim. Dialogus Oder Ein Gespreche eines Esels und Bergknechts. Jhesu Christo unserm einigen erlöser, und seiner Göttlichen Warheit zun ehren, seiner Christlichen Gemein in diesen betrübten zeiten zu troste und dem Synodo Avium zu lieb geschrieben. [Lübeck: Georg Richholf d. J.], 1557.

Major, Georg. Auff des Ehrenwirdigen Herren Niclas von Ambsdorff schrifft, so itzundt neulich Mense Novembri Anno 1551. wider Georgen Major öffentlich im Druck ausgegangen. Antwort. Wittenberg: Rhau, 1552.

- Ewiger: Göttlicher, Allmechtiger Maiestat Declaration. Wider Kaiser Carl, König zu Hispanien etc. Und Bapst Paulum den dritten. [Wittenberg: Hans Lufft], 1546.

- Ein Sermon von S. Pauli und aller Gottfürchtigen menschen bekerung zu Gott. Leipzig: Wolfgang Günther, 1553.

Major, Johannes. Parentalia Decimum Facta D. Philippo Melanthoni, viro clarissimo, et praeceptori communi: in Academia Witebergensi. Wittenberg: Lorenz Schwenck Erben, 1575.

- Synodus Avium depingens Miseram Faciem Ecclesiae propter Certamina Quorundam, Qui de Primatu contendunt, cum oppressione recte meritorum. n. p. 1557.

Mameranus, Nikolaus. Von anrichtung des newen Evangelii, und der alten Libertet oder Freyheit Teutscher Nation, An die Römisch Kayser. Mayestat geschriben. Cologne: Heinrich Mameranus, 1552.

Mansfeld Clergy. Bedencken, das diese Proposition oder Lere, nicht nütz, not, noch war sey, unnd ohne ergernis in der Kirchen nicht möge geleret werden. Das gute werck zur seligkeit nötig sind. Und unmöglich sey, one gute werck selig werden. Gestellet durch die Prediger zu Mansfelt, Unnd unterschrieben von andern Predigern derselben Herrschafft. Magdeburg: Michael Lotter, 1553.

Maurice, Elector of Saxony. Auszug aus dem Beschlusse jüngst gehaltenen landtags zu Leipzigk in Weynachten des neunundvierzigsten Jahrs. Dresden, 1549.

Medler, Nicolaus. Ratio instituendi juventutem christianum in scholis particularibus. Wittemberg: Peter Seitz, 1550.

Melanchthon, Philipp. Bedencken auffs Interim Des Ehrwirdigen und Hochgelarten Herrn Philippi Melanthonis. [Magdeburg: Michael Lotter], 1548.

— Confessio doctrinae Saxonicarum ecclesiarum synodo Tridentinae oblata, Anno Domini MDLI. Basel: Johann Oporin, 1552.

— Confession. Das ist, ain Bekandtnuß der Sächsischen Kirchen leer, welliche dem Concilio zu Triendt in dem MDLI. Jar ist überantwort worden. Darinnen ain yeder Christenlicher Leser sehen kan, wer von der allgemainen Christenlichen Kirchen abgetretten sey. Und an wem es ligt, das kein Gotsälige ainheligkeit in der Kirchen auffgericht wird. Durch M. Johann Matsperger von Augsburg verteütscht. Augspurg: Philipp Ulhart, 1552.

— Corpus Doctrinae Christianae. Wittenberg: Hans Krafft, 1576.

— Disputatio Theologica de poenitentia, respondente M. Melchior Isindero Suidnicensi. Wittenberg: Hans Lufft, 1548.

— In Ioannis Evangelium Commentarii. Basel: Adam Petri, 1523.

— Epistola a Wernero Pastore Barbiensi scripta ex mandato Flacii Illyrici, et praescripta ab eo formula, Ad Philippum Melanthonem. In qua quid sentiat Flacius Peri Logou seu de filio Dei Domino nostro Iesu Christo, qui est fundamentum fidei, & religionis nostrae, exponitur. Responsio D. Philippi Melanthonis ad istam Epistolam. [Wittenberg: Georg Rhau Erben], 1558.

— Epistola ad lectorem in qua respondetur Flacio Illyrico. Wittenberg: Josef Klug, 1549. In: Melanchthon: Doctrina de poenitentia...

— Oratio Recitata in Renunciatione gradus Theologici clarissimi viri Melchioris Isinderi Suidnicensis. n. p. 1548.

— Psalterium Davidis integrum, in quo psalmi 83 illustrati sunt argumentis et ennaratione Philippi Melanthonis. Wittenberg: Hans Krafft, 1561.

— Selectarum declamationum Philippi Melanthonis, quas conscripsit, & partim ipse in schola Witebergensi recitavit, partim aliis recitandas exhibuit. Tomus 1. Strassburg: Samuel Emmel u. Theobald Dietrich, 1569.

— A Waying and Considering of the Interim by the honourworthy and highly learned Philip Melanchthon. Translated into Englysh by John Roger. [London], 1549.

Menius, Justus. Verantwortung Justi Menii Auff Matth. Flacii Illyrici gifftige und unwahrhafftige verleumbdung und lesterung. [Wittenberg: Georg Rhau's Erben], 1557.

Merkel, Heinrich. Wahrhafftiger, aussfürlicher und gründlicher Bericht, von der Altenstadt Magdeburgk Belagerung, so die Röm: Key: May: Carolus Quintus, sampt Churfürsten, Fürsten und Stenden des Heiligen Römischen Reichs etc. Anno 50 am 16. Septembris angefangen, und bis auff den 9. Novembris Anno 51 continuirt: Und wie endlich die Stadt vortragen und zur Aussönung wieder kommen. Magdeburg: Paul Donat, 1587.

Mörlin, Joachim and Georg von Venediger. Von der Rechtfertigung des glaubens, gründtlicher warhafftiger bericht, auss Gottes Wort, etlicher Theologen zu Künigsberg in Preussen. Wider die newe verfürische und Antichristische Lehr Andreae Osiandri, Darinnen der leugnet das Christus in seinem unschüldigen Leiden und sterben unser Gerechtigkeit sey. Königsberg: [Hans Lufft], 1552.

Monner, Basilius. [Christian Aleman, pseudonym] Bedencken vonn dem Kriege, der Anno sechs, siben, und viertzig im land zu Meissen und Sachsen gefürt ist... Durch Christian Aleman, mit einer kurtzen vorrede Christoff Cunrads. Basel: Bartholomäus Stähelin, 1557.

Morata, Olympia Fulvia. Opera omnia, quae hactenus inveniri potuerunt. Basel: Peter Perna, 1570.

Naogeorgos, Thomas. [Kirchmeyer] Regnum Papisticum. Basel: Johannes Oporinus, 1559.

Niger, Antonius. Exhortatio ad liberalium artium studia, solidam erudiendae adolescentiae rationem complectens. Magdeburg: Michael Lotter, 1550.

Niger, Franciscus. De Fanini Faventini, ac Dominici Bassanensis morte, Qui nuper ob Christum in Italia Ro. Pon. iussu impie occisi sunt, Brevis Historia. n. p. 1550.

Osiander, Andreas. Schmeckbier. Aus D. Joachim Mörleins Buch. Aus M. Michael Rötings Buch. Aus des Nürmbergischen Uhu Buch. Aus Justi Menii Buch. Aus Mathiae Illyrici, und Nicolai Galli Buch. Aus Johannis Policarii Buch. Aus Alexandri Halesii Buch. Aus Nicolai Amsdorffs Buch. Aus Johannis Knipstro Buch. Das sein kurtze Anzaigung etlicher ... Stuck und Artickeln, Die in Iren Buchern wider mich begriffen sein... Königsberg: Hans Weinreich, 1552.

– Von dem Einigen Mitler Jhesu Christo und Rechtfertigung des Glaubens. Bekantnus. Königsberg: [Hans Lufft], 1551.

Palladius, Petrus und Johan Machabaeus. Brevis Censura impiarum aliquot concionum Illius Suffraganaei. Copenhagen, 1548.

Pantaleon, Heinricus. "Matthias Flaccius Illyricus Theologus." In: Prosopographiae Heroum atque Illustrium Virorum Totius Germaniae Partes III. Basel: Nicolaus Brylinger, 1565–1566. Ps. 3, 438–440.

Pfeffinger, Johannes. Gründtlicher und Warhafftiger Bericht der vorigen und jetzigen, für und nach dem Kriege ergangen Handlungen, von den Adiaphoris oder Mitteldingem. Leipzig: Valentin Bapst, 1550.

– Von den Traditionibus, Ceremoniis, Oder Mitteldingen, Christlicher warer bericht, allen lieben Christen in disen letzten und gefehrlichen zeitten, nützlich zu wissen. Leipzig: Nicolaus Wolrab, 1550.

Pflug, Julius. Christliche Ermanungenn, Welche die Seelsorgere des Stiffts Naumburg Bey dem Sacrament der Tauffe: Bey dem Sacrament des Altars: Bey der Verehlichung: Bey den Kranken: gebrauchen sollen und mögen. Erfurt: Melchior Sachse, 1550.

– Vermanung an die umbstehenden bey dem heiligen Ampt der Messe. [Leipzig: Nikolaus Wolrab, ca. 1545].

Pomarius, Johannes. Beschreibung des Newen S. Jacob Thorms. Magdeburg: Paul Donat, 1584.

Possevino, Antonio. Bibliotheca selecta. 2 vols. Cologne, 1607.

Porthaise, Jean. De verbis domini, hoc facite, pro Oecumenico Concilio Tridentino, adversus Sophistias nebulas Matthiae Flaccii Illyrici. Antwerp: Emanuel Philip Tronaesius, 1567.

Postel, Guillaume. Le prime nove del altro mondo, cioè, l'admirabile historia et non meno necessaria et utile da esser letta et intesa da ogni uno, che stupenda, intitulata La Vergine venetiana. [Venice], 1555.

Rabe, Ludwig. Historien der Martyrer. 2 vols. Strassburg: Josias Rihel, 1571–1572.

Rhenanus, Beatus. Missa D. Ioannis Chrysostomi secundum veterem usum Ecclesiae Constantinopolitanae, a forma illa quam Magnus Dionysius depingit, non ita multum evarians, insigne prorsus publici sacrificii specimen, digna planè quam docti piique cognitam ac perspectam habeant, à Leone Tusco Emanuelis Imperatoris Constantinopolitani Joannis F. Latinarum epistolarum magistro, iam olim conversa, regnante videlicet Friderico Aug. huius nominis primo. Colmar: Bartholomäus Grüninger, 1540.

Rhodius, W. Das die Magdeburger nicht umb Weltliche sachen oder Pfaffengüter, sonder im grunde, umb Gottes Worts, und des Bekentnis willen, verfolget werden. Magdeburg: Christian Rödinger, 1551.

Sanders, Nicholas. De Visibili Monarchia Ecclesiae Libri Octo. Louvain: J. Foulerus, 1571.

Saxon [Ernestine] Theologians. Der Prediger der Jungen Herrn, Johans Friderichen Hertzogen zu Sachssen etc. Sönen, Christlich Bedencken auff das Interim. n. p. 1548.

Schard, Simon. De jurisdictione, autoritate, et praeeminentia imperiali, ac potestate ecclesiastica, deque juribus regni & imperii, variorum authorum, qui ante haec tempora vixerunt, sripta. Basel: Johannes Oporinus, 1566.

Schwäbisch Hall Pastors. Bedencken Etlicher Predicanten, Als der zu Schwebischen Hall, Der in Hessen Und der Stadt N. N. auffs Interim Ihrer Oberkeit uberreicht. [Magdeburg: Michael Lotter], 1548.

Schwenckfeld, Kaspar von. Ableynung und verantwortung der fünfftzig Lügen oder Calumnien Flacii Illyrici, so er felschlich auß meinen Büchern gezogen, jüngst in Truck hat lassen außgehen. n. p. 1559.

– Ableinung D. Luthers Malediction, so erst durch Flacium Illyricum wider mich im truck ist publicirt worden. Item Vom rechten grund und verstande dess H. Sacraments des Herren Nachtmals. [Ulm: Hans Varnier d. J.], 1555.

– Auffdeckhung Des letsten schmach und gräwlichen Lügenbuchs, so der grosse feind Jhesu Christi des eynigen lebendigen Worts Gottes Flacius Illyricus Anno etc. 57. wider Herrn Casp. Schwenckfelden in Truck gegeben hat. Und: Gründtliche beweysung, das Illyricus ein Arrianer ist. Mit einer Ableynung dergleichen unwarheyten unnd Calumnien Nicolai Galli Illyrici gesellens. n. p. 1558

– Beschluss unnds Valete. Auff Flaccij Illyrici letste zwai schmachbüchlen, antwurt und gruntliche verlegung gennant. Und Das Caspar Schwenckfeld kain Donatist sey. [Ulm: Hans Varnier d. J.], 1555.

- Defension Auff Flacij Illyrici Büchlin, Contradiction genandt, oder widerwertige lehre, die er Herr Caspar Schwenckfeldt zumisset, Gründtlicher Bericht, das es lauter unwarheit unnd Calumnien seindt. [Augsburg: Hans Gegler], 1556.

- Iudicium Auff Flaccij Illyrici letzt Büchlin, so im 1557. Jar wider C. Schwenckfeldt an die von Strassburg, ist außgangen. n. p. 1558.

- Iuditium, eines Predigers inn der Schlesien: Uber Mathie Flacii Illyrici büchlin, so er wider Chaspar Schwenckfelden im Truck hat lassen außgehen. [Ulm: Hans Varnier d. J.], 1553.

- Kurtze antwurt auff das Büchlein, so Matthias Flacius Illyricus wider Caspar Schwenckfeldt hat inn Druckh lassen außgehen, das er nennet, Etliche Contradictiones. 1556.

- Ob Gott durch das Mündliche wortt khrefftig würckhe zur Seligkait. CS, XIII, 579–581. Manuscript.

- Vom Evangelio Christi und vom Missbrauch des Evangelii. n.p. 1552.

- Vom leerampt des newen Testaments. Das khein predicant der nicht fromm ist und Gottselig lebt, das Evangelium Christi vor Gott khan seliglich mit frucht predigen. [Ulm: Hans Varnier d. J.], 1555.

- Vom worte Gottes. Das khein ander wort Gottes sei, aigentlich zureden, denn der Sun Gottes Jesus Christus, Bewerung. Damit auch auff Matthie Flacij Illyrici schmachbüchlen, mit auffdeckung seiner vilfaltigen Irrthumb wirt geantwurt. Item, Iudicium uber Osianders leere von der Iustification. [Augsburg: Hans Gegler, 1554.] CS, XIII, 732–899. Therein: Von Osianders Meinung bei der Justification C. S. bedencken und Judicium. CS, XIII, 872–879.

- Der Wittenbergischen und Leiptzischen Theologen udicium und zeügknus von dem frommen manne Illyricus unnd seinem gesellen N. Gallus. [Ulm: Hans Varnier d. J.], 1553.

- Der 32. Sendbrief Geschrieben an alle Die, So sich an C. S. leer halten. CS, XIII, 521–545. Manuscript.

Selnecker, Nicolaus. Christliche unnd notwendige verantwortung auff der Flaccianer Lesterung, so sie auff sein und etliche andere unschüldige Personen in jhren verdechtigen Actis des Colloquii zu Aldenburg, unverschembter weise ausgesprenget haben. Item, Kurtze Antwort auff des Celestini schmehcharten. Leipzig: Jakob Bärwald, 1570.

- Recitationes Aliquot 1. De Consilio Scripti Libri Concordiae, et Modo Agendi... Leipzig: Georg Defner, 1581.

Spangenberg, Cyriacus. Adels Spiegel. Schmalkalden: Michael Schmuck, 1591.

Staphylus, Friedrich: Theologiae Martini Lutheri trimembris epitome... n. p. 1558.

Stigel, Johannes. Poematum Io. Stigeli Gothani vol. 1.2. Ed. Adam Silber. Jena: Donat Richtzenhan, 1577.

Trubar, Primus. [Philopatridus Illyricus, Pseudonym]. Catechismus in der Windischenn Sprach, sambt einer kürtzen Ausslegung in gesang weiss. Item die Litanai und ein predig vom rechten Glauben. Sybenburgen: Jernei Skuryaniz [Tübingen: Ulrich Morhart, 1550] Facsimile edition, Laibach [Ljubljana], 1935.

– Katehismus. Edna ma lahna kniga, ukoi esu vele potribni i prudni nauki i Artikuli prave Krštianske Vere, s kratkim istomačenem, za mlade i priproste liudi. I edna predika, od kriposti i ploda prave karštianske vere, Krozi Stipana Istrianina, s pomoštu dobri Hrvatov, sad naiprvo istomačena. Tübingen [Ulrich Morhart d. ä. Witwe, 1561].

– Ta Pervi dejl Tiga Noviga Testamenta. Tübingen: [Ulrich Morhart], 1557.

Ulrich, Bishop of Augsburg [Presumed Author]. Epistola Divi Hulderichi Augustensis Episcopi adversus constitutionem de cleri coelibatu, plane referens apostolicum spiritum. Wittenberg, [1521].

Virgile Urbinas, Polydore. Adagiorum Liber. Eiusdem de inventoribus rerum libri octo, ex accurata autoris castigatione, locupletationeque non vulgari, adeo ut maxima fere pars primae ante hanc utriusque voluminis aeditioni accesserit. Basel: Johann Froben, 1521.

Walther, Christoph. Antwort Auff der Flacianisten Lügen und falschen Bericht wider die Hauspostill Doctoris Martini Lutheri. Wittenberg: Hans Lufft, 1559.

– Bericht von den Wittenbergischen Tomis der Bücher des Ehrnwirdigen Herrn Doctoris Martini Lutheri. Wider Matthes Flacium Illyricum. Wittenberg: Hans Lufft, 1558.

– Register aller Bücher und Schrifften des Ehrnwirdigen Herrn Doctoris Martini Lutheri seliger gedechtnis, welche in die Eilff Deudsche Teil, und in die sieben Latinische Tomos, zu Wittemberg gedruckt sind. Item. Etliche Bücher und Schrifften welche in den zwelfften Teil, wils Gott, in kurtz gedruckt sollen werden, nach diesem Register verzeichnet. Wittenberg: Hans Lufft, 1558.

Westphal, Joachim. Des Ehrwirdigen und tewren Mans Doct. Marti. Luthers seliger gedechtnis meinung, von den Mitteldingen, durch M. Joachimum Westphalum Pfarhern zu Hamburgk zusamen gelesen. Magdeburg: Michael Lotter, 1550.

– Verlegung des Gründlichen Berichts der Adiaphoristen, zu diesen bösen zeiten, sehr nützlich zu lesen. [Magdeburg: Christian Rödinger], 1551.

Wigand, Johann. De Manichaeismo Renovato. Leipzig: Henning Grosse, 1587.

Wittenberg University "Students." Scholasticorum Academiae Witebergensis Epistolae. Editae contra Mathiam Flaciùm Illyricùm Anno M.D.LVIII...; Wittenberg: Johann Schwertel, 1571.

Wittenberg University Faculty. Ex Actis Synodicis et aliis diligenter et fideliter collecta expositio eorum, quae Theologi Academiae Wittebergensis et harum regionum alii, qui his adiuncti fuerunt, in deliberationibus provincialibus et alioquin extra has, de rebus ad religionem pertinentibus, monuerint... Wittenberg: Georg Rhaus Erben, 1559.

– Gründlicher und warhafftiger Bericht aller Rathschleg und antwort, so die Theologen zu Wittemberg, und andere darzu erforderte, auff den Landtegen, und andern Versammlungen, nach dem Krieg, wider die dazumal newen Reformation des Augspurgischen Buchs Interim genant, zur widerlegung desselbigen, gestelt. Auch was sie nachmals in Mitteldingen und aus was ursachen gerahten, verwilligt und nachgegeben haben, getrewlich und vleissig aus allen Actis und derselbigen Originalen zusammen gezogen. Daraus der Christliche Leser befinden wird, das gemelte Theologen sampt der Herrschafft, von etlichen unbedachtsamen und unruigen Leuten diese zehen Jar her derselbigen Handlungen halben one grund und billiche ursach mit unwarheit gelestert und gechmehet worden seien. Von den Professorn in der Universitet zu Wittemberg in druck verordnet. Wittenberg: Georg Rhau seligen Erben, 1559.

– Scriptorum publice propositorum a gubernatoribus studiorum in Academia Witebergensi tomus 1–7. Wittenberg 1562–Several ed.

Wittich, Hieronymus. Kurtze unnd gründtliche widderlegung der vier Schlusreden die Johan Sigmund, Werner, etwa Pfarherr zu Lignitz aus Schwenckfeldts Büchern gezogen, gestalt, und gericht hat wider die Christliche lehre vom dienst des Göttlichen worts und der hochwirdigen Sakrament Jesu Christi des Sons Gottes. Item... Flacij Illyrici Verlegung des Buchs vom wortt Gottis und aller Schwermerischen Bucher des Stenckfelts. Magdeburg: [Michael Lotter], 1555.

Witzel, Georg. Publicum ecclesiae sacrum. Von der Warheit der Altkyrchischen Liturgy und Opfferung, das ist, Catholischer Missen. Antwort Georgii Wicelii Orthodoxi, wider den Matthis Illyric. zu Magdenburg. Cologne: Johann Quentel, 1551.

Ziegler, Bernhard. De sacramento altaris seu Coena Dominica et Missa disputatio et capita proposita. n. p. 1548.

– Oratio de coniunctione et unitate Christianorum, contra non necessarias separationes, et aemulationes perversas, recitata in templo collegii Paulini, a Bernhardo Ziglero S. Theologiae Doctore, feriis secundis Paschalibus. Leipzig: Valentin Bapst, 1549.

Publications Since 1600

Ascham, Roger. *The Whole Works of Roger Ascham.* Ed. J. A. Giles. London: J. R. Smith, 1864.

Adam, Melchior. *Vitae Germanorum Theologorum, qui superiori seculo ecclesiam Christi voce scriptisque propagarunt et propugnarunt, congestae et ad annum 1618 deductae.* Heidelberg: Jona Rosa, 1620. Frankfurt: Johannes Georgius Geyder, 1653.

Albert, Peter Paul. *Matthias Döring, ein deutscher Minorit des 15. Jahrhunderts.* Stuttgart: Süddeutsche Verlagsburchhandlung (D. Ochs), 1892.

– "Die Confutatio Primatus Papae, ihre Quelle und ihr Verfasser." *Historisches Jahrbuch der Görres-Gesellschaft* XI (1890). 439–490.

Alberus, Erasmus. *Lob der Wetterau: enthaltend die "Kurze Beschreibung der Wetterau" (1552), zwölf auserlesene Fabeln aus Wetterau und Hessenland sowie als Anh. 5 geistl. Lieder.* Ed. Helmut Bode. Frankfurt am Main: Kramer, 1978. 7–83.

Alemann, Eberhard von. *Geschichte des Geschlechts von Alemann.* Magdeburg, 1911.

Alexander of Roes. *Alexander von Roes De Translatione Imperii und Jordanus von Osnabrück de Prerogative Romani Imperii.* [Veröffentlichungen des Forschungsinstituts an der Universität Leipzig. Institut für Kultur- und Universitätsgeschichte]. Leipzig: B. G. Tuebner, 1930.

Althaus, Horst. "Marginalien zu Lessings Wolfenbütteler Berengarforschung." *Zeitschrift für Kirchengeschichte* LXXII (1961). 336–344.

Andel, C. K. von. *The Christian Concept of History in the Chronical of Sulpicius Severus.* Amsterdam: Adolf N. Hakkert, 1976.

Anderson, Gordon Athol. *The Latin Compositions in Fascicules VII and VIII of the Notre Dame Manuscript Wolfenbüttel Helmstadt [sic] 1099 (1209). Part I: Critical Commentary, Translation of the Texts and Historical Observations.* Brooklyn: the Institute of Medieval Music, 1968.

Andreis, Josip. *Music in Croatia.* Ed. Stanley Sadie. Zagreb: Institute of Muscology, 1974; London: MacMillan, 1980.

Andrén, Carl-Gustaf. "Die Konfirmationsfrage in der Reformationszeit." *Zur Geschichte und Ordnung der Konfirmation in den lutherischen Kirchen. Aus den Verhandlungen des Internationalen Seminars des Lutherischen Weltbundes in Loccum 1961 über Fragen der Konfirmation.* Ed. Kurt Frör. Munich: Claudius, 1962. 36–57.

Andrieu, Michael. *Les ordines romani du haut moyen age. I: Les Monuments.* Louvain: Spicilegium Sacrum Lovaniense, 1931.

Anonymus. "Ein Beitrag zur Lebens Geschichte des Vlacich oder Flacius Illyricus," in *Allgemeiner literarischer Anzeiger.* July 10th, 1798. 1102.

– Review of Wilhelm Preger. *Matthias Flacius Illyricus und seine Zeit. Zeitschrift für die gesamte lutherische Theologie und Kirche* II (1865). 324–334.

– "Johannes Paul II: Vorblick auf das Jubiläumsjahr 2000." *Herder-Korrespondenz* XLVIII (1994). 604.

– "Notes and Documents." *Bibliothèque d'humanisme et renaissance* XI (1978). 538.

Arnauld, Antoine. *La perpetuité de la foy de l'eglise catholique touchant l'eucharistie, deffendue contre le livre du Sieur Claude Ministre de Charenton.* Paris, 1669.

Arnold, Gottfried. *Unpartheyische Kirchen- und Ketzer-Historie.* Frankfurt am Main: Thomas Trische, 1700. Thomas Trisches Erbe, 1729.

Arntzen, Door Marinus Johan. *Mystieke rechvaardignigsleer. Een bijdrage ter beoordeling van de theologie van Andreas Osiander.* Diss., Kampen, 1956.

Augustine, Saint. *The City of God.* New York: Modern Library, 1950.

Aulén, Gustav. *Christus Victor: An Historical Study of the Three Main Types of the Idea of the Atonement.* Tr. A. G. Herbert. New York: Macmillan, 1951.

Bacmeister, Johann. *Acta Philippica. Sive: Theologorum Saxonicorum & legatorum Megapolensium, frustra tentata pacificato inter Philippum Melanchthonem et Matthiam Flacium Illyricum.* Tübingen: Hiobus Francius, 1719.

Baldwin, William. *Beware the Cat by William Baldwin. The First English Novel.* ed. William A. Ringler, Jr. and Richard Flachmann. San Marino, California: Huntington Library, 1988.

– *Beware the Cat.* New London: Connecticut College, 1963.

Balla, Sándor. "Značenje Flaciusove Povijesti Kršćanstva (Magdeburske Centurije)." *Susreti* III (1971); Miroslav Bertoša (ed.). *Znanstevni Skup Posvećen Miji Mirkoviću.* Pula, 1978. 44–53.

Ballenstedt, Arnold. *Vitae Gregorii de Heimburg brevis narratio.* Helmstedt: Drimborn, 1737.

Baltzer, Rebecca. "Wolfenbüttel Helmstedt Ms 628 (St. Andrews MS)." *Dicitionary of the Middle Ages* XII. 670–672.

Barnard, Francis Pierrepont. *Satirical and Controversial Medals of the Reformation: The Biceps or double-headed Series.* Oxford: Clarendon Press, 1927.

Barton, Peter. "Martin Luther, die Diaspora, Österreich und der Südosten – Reformation: Epoche oder Episode?" *Lutherische Kirche in der Welt. Jahrbuch des Martin-Luther-Bundes* XXXII (1985). 132–166.

– "Matthias Flacius Illyricus." *Gestalten der Kirchengeschichte* VI. Stuttgart et al.: Kohlhammer, 1981. 277–293.

– *Um Luthers Erbe. Studien und Texte zur Spätreformation. Tilemann Heshusius (1527–1559).* Witten: Luther Verlag, 1972.

Bartos, Frantisek Michalek. "Zapadle dilko bratrske vedy" [A Forgotten work from the Science of the (Bohemian) Brethren]. *Vestnicka Kralovslé spolecnosti Nauk*, 1925.

Battaglia, Felice. *Marsilio da Padova e la filosofia politica del medioevo.* Florence, 1928.

Bauch, Gustav. "Das Leben des Humanisten Antonius Niger." *Zeitschrift des Vereins für Geschichte und Alterthum Schlesiens* XVI (1882). 204 ff.

Baumgarten, Hans. *Moritz von Sachsen der Gegenspieler Karls V.* Berlin: Paul Neff, 1941.

Baur, Ferdinand Christian. *Ferdinand Christian Baur on the Writing of Church History.* Peter C. Hodgson (ed.). New York: Oxford University Press, 1969.

– *Lehrbuch der christlichen Dogmengeschichte.* 3rd ed. Tübingen: Fues, 1867.

– *Paulus der Apostel Jesu Christi.* Stuttgart: Becher & Müller, 1845. 2. ed. Leipzig: Fues (L. W. Keisland), 1866.

Baur, Jörg. "Flacius – Radikale Theologie." *Matthias Flacius Illyricus, 1575–1975* [Schriftenreihe des Regensburger Osteuropainstituts 2]. Regensburg: Lassleben, 1975, 37–49; Reprinted, *Zeitschrift für Theologie und Kirche* LXXII (1975). 375–380.

Baxter, James Houston (ed.). *Copiale Prioratus Sanctiandree: The Letter-Book of James Haldenstone. Prior of St. Andrews (1418–1443).* London, etc.: Oxford University Press, 1930.

– *An old St. Andrews Music-book* (Cod. Helmst. 628) [St. Andrews Publications XXX]. London: Oxford University Press and Paris: H. Champion, 1931.

Bayle, Pierre. "Matthias Flacius Illyricus." *The Dictionary Historical and Critical of Mr. Peter Bayle.* Second ed. Vol. III. London: J. J. and P. Knapton, 1736. Reprint, New York: Garland, 1984. 557–563.

Beck, August. *Johann Friedrich der Mittlere, Herzog zu Sachsen. Ein Beitrag zur Geschichte des sechzehnten Jahrhunderts.* 2 vols. Weimar: Böhlaus, 1858.

Becker, Karl Josef. *Die Rechtfertigungslehre nach Domingo de Soto* [Analecta Gregoriana 158]. Rome: Verlagsbuchhandlung der Päpstlichen Universität Gregoriana, 1967.

Belkin, Johanna and Jürgen Meier. *Bibliographie zu Otfrid von Weißenburg und zur altsächsischen Bibeldichtung (Heliand und Genesis).* [Bibliographien zur deutschen Literatur des Mittelalters 7]. Berlin: E. Schmidt, 1975.

Bellarmine, Robert. *De Scriptoribus ecclesiasticis.* Rome, 1619.

– *Opera Omnia* IV. Naples: Joseph Giuliano, 1858.

Benrath, Karl. "Italien, reformatorische Bewegungen im XVI. Jahrhundert." RE3 9 530.

Benson, Heinrich Wilhelm. *Das Verhängnis Magdeburgs.* Schaffhausen: Hurter, 1858.

Bente, Gerhard Friedrich (ed.). *Triglot Concordia: The Symbolical Books of the Ev. Lutheran Church.* St. Louis: Concordia Publishing House, 1921.

Beringerius of Tours. *Beringerius Turonensis Rescriptum contra Lanfrannum.* Ed. Robert Burchard Constantyn Hygens [Corpus Christianorum, Continuatio Mediaevalis 84]. Turnhout: Brepols, 1988.

– *Berengarius Turonensis Rescriptum contra Lanfrannum. Faksimileausgabe der Handschrift Wolfenbüttel, Herzog August Bibliothek Cod. Guelf 101 Weissenburg.* Introduction by Wolfgang Milde [Corpus Christianorum, Continuatio Mediaevalis 84a]. Turnhout: Brepols, 1988.

Berger, Heinrich. *Calvins Geschichtsauffassung* [Studien zur Dogmengeschichte und systematischen Theologie Bd. 6]. Zürich: Zwingli-Verlag, 1955.

Berman, Herold. *Law and Revolution*. Cambridge, Mass.: Harvard University Press, 1983.

Bernays, Jacob. *Gesammelte Abhandlungen*. H. Usener (ed.). Bd. II. Berlin: Verlag von Wilhelm Herzt, 1885.

Bertoša, Miroslav. "Etnički Sastav Pučanstva Labina u XVI. Stoljeću." Istra VIII (1975). 42–46.

Bess, Bernhard. "Die Entwicklung der hessischen Kirche unter Philipp dem Großmütigen." ZKG, XXXIII (1912). 309–345.

Beutel, Georg. *Über den Ursprung des Augsburger Interims*. Dresden: J. Passler, 1888.

Beyer, Eduard. *Das Cistercienser-Stift und Kloster Alte-Zelle in dem Bisthum Meissen*. Dresden: In Commission von F. G. Janssen, 1855.

Beyreuther, Erich. "Die Kirche in der Neuzeit." Hans Patze & Walter Schlesinger (eds.). *Geschichte Thüringens* IV. Cologne and Vienna: Bölau, 1972. 1–52.

Bezold, Friedrich von. *Geschichte der deutschen Reformation*. Berlin: G. Grote'sche Verlagsbuchhandlung, 1890.

Bibl, Viktor. "Nidbruck und Tanner. Ein Beitrag zur Entstehungsgeschichte der Magdeburger Centurien und zur Charakteristik König Maximilian II." *Archiv für österreichische Geschichte* LXXXV (1898). 379–430.

Biographische Woordenboek van Protestantische Godgelaerden in Nederland. The Hauge: Martinus Nijoff, 1959.

Bieck, Johann Erdmann. *Das Dreyfache Interim*. Leipzig: John Christoph Cörner, 1721.

Bilokapić, Ante. Attività letteraria di Matthia Flacio Illyrico. Pars dissertationis, Antonianum, Rome, 1981.

Binke, Karl. "Zu Johann Walters Stellung als Hofkappelmeister in Dresden." *Jahrbuch für Liturgik und Hymnologie* V (1960. 235–243.

Bischoff, Bernhard. "über mittelalterliche Handschriften in Wolfenbüttel." Paul Raabe (ed.). *400 Jahre Bibliothek zu Wolfenbüttel, Reden-Vorträge-Berichte aus dem Festjahr 1972* [Wolfenbütteler Beiträge 2]. Frankfurt am Main: Klostermann, 1973. 96–109. Reprint, *Mittelalterliche Studien* II. Stuttgart: Anton Hiersemann, 1981.

Bishop, Edmund. "The Litany of Saints in the Stowe Missal." *Journal of Theological Studies* VII (1906). 122–136. Reprint, *Liturgica Historica*. Oxford: Clarendon Press, 1918. 137–164.

Biundo, Georg. "Aquila und das Interim." *Theologische Literaturzeitung* LXXIV (1949). 587–592.

– *Kaspar Aquila. Ein Kämpfer für das Evangelium, in Schwaben und in der Pfalz, in Sachsen und Thüringen*. Grünstadt/Pfalz: Verlag des Vereins für Pfälzische Kirchengeschichte, 1963.

Bizer, Ernst. "Analecta Brentiana." *Blätter für württemburgische Kirchengeschichte* LVII/LVIII (1957–58). 253–373.

Böhl, Eduard. *Beiträge zur Geschichte der Reformation in Österreich*. Jena: Gustav Fischer, 1902.

Böhme, Franz M. *Altdeutsches Liederbuch*. Hildesheim: Georg Olm & Wiesbaden: Briefkopf & Härtel, 1966.

Boghardt, Martin. "Partial Duplicate Setting: Means of Rationalization or Complication Factor in Textual Transmissen?" *The Library*, Sixth Series XV (1993). 306–331.

Bona, Giovanni. *Rerum Liturgicarum Libri Duo*. Rome, 1671.

Bonet, Jules. "La Reforme à Venise: Les Martyres." *Bulletin historique et littéraire de la Société de l'Histoire du Protestantisme Français*. 1870/1871. 145–157.

Bonhoeffer, Dietrich. *Gesammelte Schriften*. Hrsg. von Eberhard Bethge. 4 vols. Munich: Christian Kaiser, 1965.

Boniface, Saint. *Epistolae S. Banifaci Martyris, Primi Moguntini Archiepiscopi, Germanorum Apostoli; Pluriumque Pontificum, Regum & aliorum, nunc primum e Caesarae maiestatis Viennensi Bibliotheca luce, notisque donatae*. Ed. Nicolaus Serarius. Mainz: Michael Demen, 1629.

– *Sancti Bonifactii Epistolae, Codex Vindobonensis 751 der österreichischen Nationalbibliothek, Faksimile-Ausgabe der Wiener Handschrift der Briefe des heiligen Bonifacius* [Codices Selecti 24]. Einführung von Franz Unterkrichner. Graz: Akademische Druck- und Verlagsastalt, 1971.

Born, Karl Erich. "Moritz von Sachsen und die Fürstenverschwörung gegen Karl V." *Historische Zeitschrift* CXCI 1960. 18–66. Reprint, Darmstadt: Wissenschaftliche Buchgesellschaft, 1972.

Bornkamm, Heinrich. *Luther im Spiegel der deutschen Geistesgeschichte*. Heidelberg: Quelle & Meyer, 1965.

Bossert, Gustav. "Brenz und der Streit um den Chorrock." *Blätter für Württembergische Kirchengeschichte*. N. F. XXX (1926). 114–155.

Boucat, Antoine. *Theologia Patrum Scholatico-Dogmatica Sacramentis, tum in Genere, tum in particularis ... Tomus Quintus. Quarta Pars, seu Praxis Sacramentorum*. Rouen: Claudius Jove, 1725.

Bouwsma, William James. *Concordia Mundi: The Career and Thought of Guillaume Postel (1510–1581)*. Cambridge, Mass.: Harvard University Press, 1957.

– "Postel and the Significance of Renaissance Cabbalism." Paul Oskar Kristeller and Philipp P. Weiner. *Renaissance Essays*. New York: Harper & Row, 1968.

Bozemann, Theodore Dwigth. *To Live Ancient Lives. The Primitivist Dimension in New England Puritanism*. Chapel Hill: University of North Carolina Press, 1988.

Brady, Thomas J. "Luther and the State: The Reformer's Teaching in its Social Setting." James D. Tracy (ed.). *Luther and the Modern State in Germany* [Sixteenth Century Essays and Studies VII]. Kirksville, MO: Sixteenth Century Publishers, 1986.

Brandi, Karl. *Gegenreformation und Religionskriege*. Leipzig: Quelle & Meyer, 1930.

Braun, Josef. "Alter und Herkunft der sog. 'Missa Illyrica.'" *Stimmen aus Maria Laach* LXIX (1905). 143–155.

Bray, Gerald (ed.). *Documents of the English Reformation*. Minneapolis: Fortress, 1994.

Breest, Ernst. "Der Heinrich Toke, Domherr zu Magdeburg." *Geschichtsblätter für Stadt und Land Magdeburg* XVIII (1883). 43–72, 97–145.

Breyer, Mirko. "O Istrianu Fra Baldu Lupetini (1502–1556)." *Istra* II (1972). 35–42.

Brieger, Theodor. "Ein Brief Maximilians II. an Melanchthon." *Theologische Studien und Kritiken* XLVI (1873). 721–727.

– "Zu Jakob von Jüterbok." ZKG, XXIV (1903). 136–150.

Brock, Peter. *The Political and Social Doctrine of the Unity of the Czech Brethren in the Fifteenth and Early Sixteenth Centuries.* The Hague: Mouton, 1957.

Brodrick, James. *Petrus Canisius, 1521–1597.* Tr. from German by Karl Telch. New York: Sheed and Ward, 1935.

Brower, Christopher. *Fuldensium Antiquitatum Libri IIII.* Antwerp, 1612.

Brown, F. *Appendix ad Fasciculum rerum expetendarum et fugiendarum.* London, 1690.

Brown, George Kenneth. *Italy and the Reformation to 1550.* Oxford: Blackwell, 1933. Reprint, New York: Russel and Russel, 1971.

Brunner, Peter. *Nikolaus von Amsdorf als Bischof von Naumburg. Eine Untersuchung zur Gestalt des evangelischen Bischofsamt in der Reformationszeit* [Schriften des Vereins für Reformationsgeschichte 179]. Gütersloh: G. Mohn, 1961.

Bucholzer, Abraham. *Index Chronologicus cura secunda Gottfridi Bucholzeri ... locupuletus ... et ad finem 1589 continuatus.* Gorlitz: J. Ramba, 1599.

Bandschuh, Benno von. *Das Wormser Religionsgespräch von 1557 unter besonderer Berücksichtigung der kaiserlichen Religionspolitik* [Reformationsgeschichte Studien und Texte 124]. Münster: Aschendorff, 1988.

Burckhardt, Andreas. *Johannes Basilius Herold: Kaiser und Reich im protestantischen Schrifttum des Basler Buchdruckes um die Mitte des sechzehnten Jahrhunderts* [Basler Beiträge zur Geschichtswissenschaft 104]. Basel and Stuttgart: Helbing und Lichtenhahn, 1967.

Burckhardt, Johannes. *Die Entstehung der modernen Jahrhundertrechnung: Ursprung und Ausbildung einer historiographischen Technik von Flacius bis Ranke* [Göppinger akademische Beiträge 43]. Göppingen: Alfred Krümmerle, 1971.

Burdach, Konrad. "Einführende Worte nebst einer Abhandlung über die Nationale Aneignung der Bibel und die Anfänge der Germanischen Philologie." *Festschrift Eugen Mook.* Halle an der Saale: Max Niemeyer, 1924. I, 1014; II, 231–334.

– and Paul Piur. *Briefwechsel des Cola di Rienzo.* Berlin: Weidmansche Buchhandlung, 1928.

Burman, Edward. *The Inquisition, the Hammer of Heresy.* Wellingborough, Northamptonshire: The Aquarian Press, 1984.

Bursian, Conrad. *Iulii Firmici Materni de Errore Profanarum Religionum Libellus.* Leipzig: Breitkopf und Härtel, 1856.

Buscher, Hans. *Heinrich Pantaleon und sein Heldenbuch* [Basler Beiträge zur Geschichtswissenschaft 26]. Basel: Helbing & Lichtenhahn, 1946.

Buschbell, Gottfried. *Reformation und Inquisition in Italien um die Mitte des XVI. Jahrhundert*. Paderborn: Ferdinand Schönigh, 1910.

Butzmann, Hans. "Die Missa Illyrica und die Adoratio Crucis von Minden." *Wolfenbütteler Beiträge* III (1978). 35–42.

– "Einige Fragen zu Mindener Kreuz und die Adoratio Crucis des Bischofs Sigebert." Hans Nordsied (ed.). *Zwischen Dom und Rathaus* [Beiträge zur Kunst- und Kulturgeschichte der Stadt Minden]. Minden, 1977. 61–79.

Buxbaum, Engelbert M. "'Von der Priesterehe.' Die sogenannte Ulrichsepistel – Ihre Verbreitung, Bekämpfung und zeitliche Einordnung." Walter Brandmüller, Herbert Immerkötter und Erwin Iserloh (eds.). *Ecclesia Militans. Studien zur Konzilien- und Reformationsgeschichte Remigius Bäumer zum 70. Geburtstag gewidmet.* Paderborn et al.: Ferdinand Schönigh, 1988. 407–415.

Cabrol, Fernand. "La Messe Latine des Flacius Illyricus." *Revue Bénédictine* XXII (1905). 151–164.

– "La Messe Latine de Flacius Illyricus." *Dictionnaire d'Archéologie chrétienne et de Liturgie* 5 (1923). 1625–1635.

Caesar, Michael. *Dante. The Critical Heritage.* London: Rutledge, 1989.

Cale, Farno. *Dante i Slavenski Svijet/ Dante e il Mondo Slavo.* Zagreb: Jugoslavenska Akademija Znanosti i Umjetnosti, 1984.

Cameron, Evan. *The Reformation of the Heretics. The Waldensians of the Alps 1480–1580.* Oxford: Clarendon Press, 1984.

Canisius, Peter. *Beati Petri Canisii S. J. Epistolae et Acta.* Ed. Otto Braunsberger. 2 vols. Freiburg im Breisgau: Herder, 1896–1898.

Cargill Thompson, W. D. "Luther and the Right of Resistance to the Emperor." *Church, Society and Politics.* Ed. Derek Baker. Oxfort: Blackwell, 1979. 159–202.

Creva, Seraphimus. "Matthias Flaccus" [sic]. *Bibliotheca Ragusina* II. Zagreb, 1977. 425–443.

Chalybaeus, Albert. *Die Durchführung des Leipziger Interims.* Chemnitz: Oehme, 1905.

– "Sind 'Alba' und Krause durch das Leipziger Interim in Sachsen eingeführt worden?" *Beiträge zur Sächsischen Kirchengeschichte* XX (1906). 214–241.

Chiminelli, Piero. *La Fortuna di Dante nella Christianita Riformata.* Rome: "Bilychnis", 1921.

Christ, Karl. *Die Bibliothek des Klosters Fulda im 16. Jahrhundert. Die Handschriften Verzeichnisse.* Leipzig: Otto Harrassowitz, 1933.

– "Zur Geschichte der griechischen Handschriften der Palatina." *Zentralblatt für Bibliothekswesen* XXXVI (1919). 3–34, 49–66.

Christmann, Curt. *Melanchthons Haltung im Schmalkaldischen Kriege* [Historische Studien XXXI]. Berlin, 1902. Reprint, Vaduz: Kraus, 1965.

Cicero, Marcus Tullius. *De Finibus Bonorum et Malorum, with an English Translation by H. Rackham* [Loeb Classical Library]. Cambridge, MA: Harvard University Press; London: William Heineman Ltd., 1951.

    – *Orationes.* Oxford: Clarendon Press, 1970.

Cimelia Rhodostaurotica. Die Rosenkreuzer im Spiegel der zwischen 1610 und 1660 entstandenen Handschriften und Drucke. Aus der Bibliotheca Philosophica Hermetica Amsterdam und der Herzog August Bibliothek Wolfenbüttel. Amsterdam: in de Pelikaan, 1995.

Clemen, Otto. "Alte Einblattdrücke." Clemen. KS, VII, 97 f.

    – "Andreas Epitimus = Hartmann Bayer?" Clemen. KS, II, 338–342.

    – *Beiträge zur Reformationsgeschichte aus Büchern und Handschriften der Zwickauer Ratschulbibliothek.* 2. Heft. Berlin: C. A. Schwetschke und Sohn, 1902.

    – "Briefe Sächsischer Staats- und Schulmänner an Melanchthon." Clemen. KS, VI, 542–556.

    – "Eine Heliandhandschrift in Luthers Besitz." *Zentralblatt für Bibliothekswesen* XXXVI (1919). 256–258.

    – *Handschriftenproben aus der Reformationszeit.* Zwickau: Verlag von F. Ullmann, 1911.

    – "Kaspar von Niedbruck als Büchersammler." *Zentralblatt für Bibliothekswesen* LIX (1942). 168–169. Clemen. KS, VI, 514 f.

    – "Ein öffentlicher Anschlag gegen Matthias Flacius." *Zeitschrift für Systematische Theologie* XIX (1942). 334–351. Clemen. KS, VI, 558–575.

    – "Sechs Briefe aus Braunschweig an Melanchthon." *Zeitschrift der Gesellschaft für niedersächsische Kirchengeschichte* XLIII (1938). 110–116. Clemen. KS, VI, 262–268.

    – *Studien zu Melanchthons Reden und Gedichten.* Leipzig: M. Heinsius Nachfolger, 1913.

Clement, David. *Bibliothèque curieuse Historique et Critique ou Catalogue Raisonné des Livres Difficultes à Trouver.* Leipzig, 1759.

Colomiés, Paul. *Bibliothèque Choisie.* La Rochelle: Pierre Savouret, 1682.

Comba, Emilio. "Baldo Lupetina." *Revista Christiana* III (1875). 5–20, 49–70.

Communications of the Cambridge Antiquarian Society III, 1864–1876. Cambridge: Cambridge Antiquarian Society, 1879.

Congar, Y. M.-J. "Aspects ecclésiologiques de la querelle entre mendiants et séculiers dans la seconde moitié du XIIIe Siècle et le debut du XIVe." *Archives d'histoire Doctrinale et Literaire du Moyen Age* XXXVI (1961). 35–151.

Coppel, Bernhard. "Philomela in Bologna und Wittenberg. Die Nachtigall als Topos, Epigrammstoff und Vogelmaske in der propagandistischen Reformationsdichtung." *Acta Conventus Neo-Latini Bononiensis, Proceedings of the Fourth International Congress of Neo-Latin Studies.* Ed. Richard Joseph Schroek [Medieval and Renaissance Texts and Studies 37]. Binghamton, N. Y., 1985. 420–429.

Cornelius, A. "Kurfürst Moritz gegenüber der Fürstenverschwörung in den Jahren 1550–1551." *Abhandlung der Historischen Klasse der Königlicher Bayerischen Akademie der Wissenschaften* X, Abt. III (1968). 635–697.

Coulton, George Gordon. *Medieval Panorama: the English Scene from the Conquest to the Reformation.* Cambridge: Cambridge University Press; New York: Macmillan, 1944.

Cowell, Alan. "Pope Bids Church See Old Errors." *New York Times*. Novemberg 15th, 1944.

Cox, Francis Augusts. *The Life of Philip Melanchthon*. 2nd ed., London: Gale & Fenner; Edinburgh: Oliphant Waugh and Innes, 1817.

Cullman, Oscar. *Peter: Disciple-Apostle-Martyr*. Philadelphia: Westminster Press, 1953.

Curtius, Ernst Robert. *European Literature and the Latin Middle Age*. Tr. Willard R. Trask [Bollingen Series XXXVI]. Princeton: Princeton University Press, 1953.

Curtze, M. "Bemerkung zu dem Aufsatze: 'Geistliche Scherze des Mittelalters.'" *Anzeiger für Kunde der deutschen Vorzeit* XVI (1896). 9 f.

Cyprian, D. "Extract aus der Historia ecclesiastica manuscripta des Gothaischen Consistoria-Raths D. Cyprian, darinnen die Historia Tomorum Lutheri, aus denen Original-Acten des Waymarischen Gothaischen Archiv abgehandelt wird." FS, 1726. 735–766.

Cyprianus, Ernst. *Tabularium Ecclesiae Romanae Seculi Decimi in qua Monumenta restituti Calicis Ecclesiastici ... Continentur*. Frankfurt and Leipzig: Wolfgang Ludwig Spring, 1742.

Czerwenka, Bernard. *Geschichte der Evangelischen Kirche in Böhmen* II. Bielefeld and Leipzig: Velhagen & Klasing, 1870.

Dante Alighieri. *Il Convivio*. G. Busnelli and G. Vandelli (eds.). Florence: Felice le Monnier, 1964.

– *Dante. The Banquet*. Tr. Christopher Ryan. Saratoga, PA.: Anma Libri, 1989.

– *Monarchy and Three Political Letters*. Tr. Donald Nichol and Colin Hardie. London: Weidenfeld and Nicolson, 1954.

Davies, C. W. T. "A Bibliography of John Bale." *Oxford Bibliographical Society, Proceedings and Papers* V. Oxford: Oxford University Press, 1940. 203–279.

D'Auvergne, Edmund Basil Francis. *The Coburgs: the Story of the Rise of a Great Royal House*. New York: J. Pott & Company, 1911.

Dawson, James. "William of Saint-Amour and the Apostolic Tradition." *Medieval Studies* XL (1978). 223–228.

Deanović, Mirko. "Dante interpretato da Mattia Flacio Illirico (Vlačić)." *Studia Romanica et Anglica Zagrabiensis* XIX–XX (1965). 161–170.

De Bart, Pierre (ed.). *Illustrium et Clarorum virorum Epistolae Selectiores Superiore saeclo scriptae vel a Belgia vel ad Belgos in Centurias* II. Lugduni Batavorum: Ludovicus Elzevirius, 1617.

De Bujanda, J.-M. (ed.). *Index des livres interdits* III: *Index de Venise, 1549 et de Venise et de Milan, 1554*. Sherbrooke, Quebec: Centre d'Etudes de la Renaissance; Paris: Droz, 1987.

De Bure, Guillaume-François. *Bibliographie Instructive ou Traité de la Conoissance aux Livres Rares et Singuliers*. Paris: Guillaume François de Bure le Jeune, 1763.

De Clémages, Nicolas. *Traité de la Ruine de l'église de Nicolas de Clamanges.* Ed. A. Coville. Paris: Droz, 1936.

De Coussemacher, Charles Edmond Henri. *Scriptorum de Musica Medii Aevi Nova Series* I. Paris, 1864.

De Franceschi, C. *L'Istria. Note Storicha Parenzo,* 1879.

De Groot, Aart. "The Radical Reformation Revisited." *Nederlands Archief voor Kerkgeschiedenis* 73 (1993). 199–207.

De Lagarde, Georges. *La Naissance de l'Esprit Laique au Déclin de Moyen Age. III: Le Defensor Pacis.* Louvain and Paris: Editions Nauwelaerts, 1970.

Delehaye, Hippolyte. *Les Légends Hagiographiques.* Brussels: Societé des Bollandistes, 1905. 4th ed.: Brussels: Societé des Bollandistes, 1955.

– *Les Passions des Martyrs et les Genres littéraires.* Brussels: Societé des Bollandistes, 1921.

Della Casa, Giovanni. *Fifteen Fourteeners [Sonnets] from Giovanni della Casa.* Tr. Rudolf B. Gottfried. Bloomington, Indiana: Published by Rudolf B. Gottfried, 1979.

– *Galateo.* Tr. and ed. by Konrad Eisenbichler and Kenneth Bartlett [Center for Reformation and Renaissance Studies, Series 2]. Toronto: Dovehouse Editions, 1985.

De Maio, Romeo. "Savonarola, Alesandro VI ed il mito dell' Antichristo." *Riforme ed miti nella Chiese del Cinquecento.* Naples: Guida, 1973. 33–64.

De Mornay, Philippe. *Mysterium Iniquitatis, seu Historia Papatus.* Salmurii: Porthaeus, 1612.

De Orella y Unzue, Jose L. *Repuestas Católicas a Las Centarias de Magdeburgo (1559–1588).* Madrid: Fundacion Universitaria Espanolga. Seminaro "Suarez," 1976.

De Schweinitz, Edmond. *The History of the Church Known as the Unitas Fratrum or the Unity of Brethren.* 2nd. ed. Bethlehem, PA.: The Moravian Publishing Concern, 1901.

Devčić, Natko. *Labinska Vještica.* Zagreb: Union of Yugoslavian Composers, 1960.

De Vocht, Henry. *History of the Foundation and Rise of the Collegium Trilingue Lovansiense 1517–1550.* Louvain: Libraire Universitaire, 1951–1955.

Dickens, A. G. *Contemporary Historians of the German Reformation.* London: Institute of German Studies, 1978.

– and John Tonkin. *The Reformation in Historical Thought.* Cambridge, Mass.; Harvard University Press, 1985.

Dieckhoff, August Wilhelm. *Die Waldenser in Mittelalter.* Göttingen: Vandenhoeck & Ruprecht, 1851.

Diener, Ronald. *The Magdeburg Centuries: A Bibliothecal and Historiographical Analysis.* Diss., Harvard Divinity School, 1978.

Dietzfelbinger, Hermann. "Matthias Flacius–Ein Zeuge evangelischer Wahrheit." *Matthias Flacius Illyricus 1575–1975* [Schriftenreihe des Regensburger Osteuropainstituts 2]. Regensburg: Lassleben, 1975. 13–18.

Dilthey, Wilhelm. *Gesammelte Aufsätze.* Leipzig and Berlin: Tuebner, 1924–1936.

– *Weltanschauung und Analyze des Menschen.* 9. Aufl. Göttingen: Vandenhoeck und Ruprecht, 1970.

Dittmer, Luther A. (ed.). *Facsimile Reproduction of the Manuscript Wolfenbüttel 1099. Helmstadiensis 1206, W2 with an Introduction by Luther A. Dittmer.* Brooklyn: Institute of Medieval Music, 1960.

Dittrich, Ottmar. *Geschichte der Ethik* IV. Leipzig: Felix Meiner, 1932.

Dobiache-Rojdestvensky, Olga. *Les Poésies des Goliards.* Paris: Éditions Reider, 1931.

Doell, Ernst E. *Die Kollegiatstifte St. Blasius und St. Cyriacus zu Braunschweig.* Braunschweig: Waisenhaus, 1967.

Döllinger, Johann Joseph Ignaz von. *Die Reformation, ihre innere Entwicklung und ihre Wirkungen im Umfange des Lutherischen Bekenntnisses.* 3 vols. Arnheim: Josue Witz, 1853–4.

Döllinger, Robert. *Das Evangelium in Regensburg.* Regensburg: Evangelische Lutherische Gesamtkirchengemeinde Regensburg, 1959.

Doering, Oscar. "Reste der ehemaligen Ilsenburger Klosterbibliothek." *Zeitschrift für Bücherfreunde* I (1897/1898). 629–630.

Dörner, Isaak August. *Geschichte der protestantischen Theologie.* 2nd printing. Munich: F. G. Cotta, 1867.

– *History of Protestant Theology, particularly in Germany.* Tr. by George Robson and Sophia Taylor. 2 vols. Edinburg: T. and T. Clark, 1871.

Dörries, Hermann. "Von Boniface zu Luther." *Materialdienst des Konfessions-kundlichen Instituts (Bensheim).* 22 Jg. No. 4, July–August, 1960. 42–45.

Dopsch, Alfons. *Die Wirtschaftsentwicklung der Karolingerzeit vornemlich in Deutchland* I. Weimar: Hermann Böhlaus, 1912.

Drews, Paul. *Petrus Canisius, der erste deutsche Jesuit.* Halle: Verein für Reformationsgeschichte, 1892.

Drogman, Willy. "Die Praefatio in librum antiquum Lingua Saxonia conscriptum." *Jahrbuch des Vereins für niederdeutsche Sprachforschung* XLVIII–LXX (1943–47). 242–263.

Dronke, Peter. *Die Lyrik des Mittelalters: Eine Einführung.* Munich: C. H. Beck, 1968. Translation of *The Medieval Lyric.* London: Hutchinson University Library, 1968.

Druffel, August von. *Briefe und Acten zur Geschichte des sechszehnten Jahrhunderts mit besonderer Rücksicht auf Bayerns Fürstenhaus.* 5 vols. Munich: M. Rieger, 1873–1898.

– "Nachträgliche Bemerkungen über den Augustiner Johann Hoffmeister." ZKG, III (1879). 485–491.

Duch, Arno. "Eine verlorene Handschrift der Schriften Bernos von Reichenau in den Magdeburger Centurien." ZKG, LIII (1934). 417–435.

Dümmler, Ernst. "Über eine verschollene Fuldische Briefsammlung des neunten Jahrhunderts." *Forschungen zur Deutschen Geschichte* V. Göttingen: Dieterich, 1865. 369–395.

Dufeil, Michel-Marie. *Guillaume de Saint-Amour et la Polémique Universitaire Parisienne 1250–1259*. Paris: A. et J. Picard, 1972.

Du Peyrat, Guillaume. *L'Histoire ecclésiastique de la cour ou les antiquités et recherches de la chapelle et oratoire du Roy de France*. Paris, 1645.

Ebel, Jobst Christian. *Wort und Geist bei den Verfassern der Konkordienformel*. Munich: Christian Kaiser Verlag, 1981.

Ebner, Adalbert. *Quellen und Forschungen zur Geschichte und Kunstgeschichte des Missale Romanum im Mittelalter. Iter Italicum*. Freiburg im Breisgau: Herder, 1896. Reprint, Graz: Akademischer Druck und Verlagsansstalt, 1957.

Ehmer, Herman (ed.). *Leben des Jakob Andreae, Doktor der Theologie, von ihm selbst mit großer Treue und Aufrichtigkeit geschrieben bis auf das Jahr 1562*. Stuttgart: Calwer Verlag, 1991.

Ehrendenkmal treuer Zeugen Christi III. Zwickau: Johannes Hermann, 1879.

Elert, Werner. *Morphologie des Luthertums*. 2 vols. Munich: Beck, 1931–32. Munich: Beck, 1953–53, 1958, 1965.

Ellinger, Georg. *Geschichte der neulateinischen Literatur Deutschlands im sechszehnten Jahrhundert*. 3 vols. Berlin: Walter de Gruyter, 1929–1933. Reprint, Berlin, 1969.

– *Philipp Melanchthon. Ein Lebensbild*. Berlin: Gaertner, 1902.

Eltz-Hoffmann, Lieselotte von. *Protestantismus im Haus Hapsburg* [Studien und Dokumente 31/32, ed. Erik Turnwald]. Band Rappenau-Obergrimpern: Johannes-Mathesius Verlag, 1978.

Elze, Theodor. *Geschichte der Protestantischen Bewegungen und der deutschen evangelischen Gemeinde in Venedig*. Bielefeld: Velhagen & Klasing, 1883. New edition: Florence: Im Selbstverlag des Herausgebers und in Commission bei B. Coppini, 1941.

Enders, Ernst Ludwig (ed.). *Dr. Martin Luther's Briefwechsel*. Calw and Stuttgart: Verlag der Vereinsbuchandlung, 1898.

Erasmus, Desiderius of Rotterdam. *Opus Epistolarum Desiderii Erasmi Roterodami*. 12 vols. Ed. P. S. Allen, H. M. Allen and H. W. Garrod. Oxford: Clarendon Press, 1906–1958.

Erbe, Michael. *Françhois Bauduin (1520–1573). Biographie eines Humanisten*.Gütersloh: Gütersloher Verlagshaus Gerd Mohn, 1978.

Erbkam, Heinrich Wilhelm. *Geschichte der protestantischen Sekten im Zeitalter der Reformation*. Hamburg and Gotha: Dr. Martin Sändig, 1848.

Fabricius, Johann Andreas. *Abriß einer allgemeinen Historie der Gelehrsamkeit* III. Leipzig: Wiedmann, 1754.

Fairfield, Leslie P. *John Bale, Mythmaker of the English Reformation*. West Lafayette, Indiana: Purdue University Press, 1976.

Falk, Franz. *Beiträge zur Rekonstruktion der alter Bibliotheca Fuldensis und Bibliotheca Laureshamensis* [Beihefte zum Centralblatt für Bibliothekswesen 26]. Leipzig: Harrassowitz, 1902.

Farel, Edmond. *Les Arts Poétiques du XVe et du XVIe Siècle.* Geneva: Slatkine and Paris: Champion, 1982.

Fecht, Ioannes. *De Origine et Superstitione Missarum.* Rostock and Leipzig, 1725.

Fedderson, Ernst. "Philippismus und Luthertum in Dänemark und Schleswig-Holstein." Otto Scheel (ed.). *Festschrift für Hans von Schubert* [ARG Texte und Untersuchungen. Ergänzungsband V.]. Leipzig: M. Heinsius Nachfolger, Eger & Sievers, 1929. 92–114.

Feifel, Erich. *Grundzüge einer Theologie des Gottesdienstes. Motive und Konzeption der Glaubensverkündigung Michael Heldings (1506–1561) als Ausdruck einer "Katholischen Reformation."* Freiburg, et al.: Herder, 1960.

Feller, Joachim (ed.). *Hortus Libani.* Leipzig, 1687.

— "In Synodum Avium Joh. Majoris in quibus Flacii innocentiam Fellerus contra calumnia Majoris defendit." Burckard Gotthilf Struve. *Acta Literaria* IV. Jena: Johannes Bielckius, 1706. 15–80.

Feuerlein, Emil. "Dante unter den 'Warheitszeugen.'" *Literarische Beilage des Staats-Anzeigers für Württemberg,* 1881. 10–14.

Feuter, Eduard. *Geschichte der Neueren Historiographie.* 3rd. ed. Munich and Berlin: R. Oldenbourg, 1936. Reprint, New York et al.: Johnson [1968].

Ficker, Johannes and Otto Winckelmann. "Matthias Flacius Illyricus." *Handschriftenproben des sechszehnten Jahrhunderts* II. Straßburg: Karl J. Tuebner, 1905. No. 95.

Filipović, Vladimir. "Aktuelni Vlačić." *Dometi* [Rijeka], (1970). Unpaginated.

Fine, John van Antwerp. *The Late Medieval Balkans. A Critical Survey from the Late Twelfth Century to the Ottoman Conquest.* Ann Arbor: Unversity of Michigan Press, 1978.

Firmin-Didot, Ambroise. *Alde Manue et l'Hellénismse à Venise.* Paris: Typographie d'Ambroise Firmin-Didot, 1875.

Flacius, Matthias. *Alte Gedichte gegen das Jahr 1250 geschrieben welche die Unwissenheit des Evangelii beweinen, den Misbrauch der Ceremonien tadeln und zeigen, dass die Lehre dieser Zeit der Reformation Lutheri nicht new sey, Ehedem von Matthias Flaccius [sic] Illyricus als ein Beitrag zur Reformationsgeschichte der neueren Zeit aus dem lateinischen prosaisch übersetzt, und hier und da umschrieben.* Mühlhausen: Johann Daniel Müller, 1791.

— *Matthias Flacius Illyricus: De Ratione cognoscendi Sacras Literas.* Ed. Lutz Geldsetzer [Instrumenta Philosophica, Series Hermeneutica III]. Düsseldorf: Stern-Verlag Janssen & Co., 1968.

— *Dr. Matthias Flacius Illyricus: Eine christliche Vermahunung zur Beständigkeit in der wahren Religion Jesu Christi. Mit einem Vorwort wider den Byzantinismus, Opportunismus und Unionismus unswerer Tage von Dietrich Schwertfeger.* Eberfeld: Verlag des Lutherischen Büchervereins, 1906.

Fleischer, Manfred P. "Melanchthon as Praeceptor of Late-Humanist Poetry." *Sixteenth Century Journal* XX (1989). 559–580.

Fligge, Jörg Rainer. "Herzog Albrecht von Preussen und der Osiandrismus 1522–1568." Diss., Bonn, 1972.

– "Zur Interpretation der osiandrischen Theologie Herzog Albrechts v. Preussen." ARG, LXIV (1973). 245–280.

Florey, Gerhard. *Bischöfe, Ketzer, Emigranten: Der Protestantismus im Lande Salzburg von seinen Anfängen bis zur Gegenwart.* Graz, Vienna and Cologne: Hermann Böhlaus, 1967.

Flotzinger, Rudolf. *Beobachtungen zur Notre-Dame-Handschrift W1 und ihrem II. Fasikel* [Sonderdruck aus dem Anzeiger der phil.-hist. Klasse der österreichischen Akademie der Wissenschaft 105], 1968.

Förstemann, Carolus Eduardus. *Album Academiae Vitebergensis* I. Leipzig: Tauchnitz, 1841. Reprint, Aalen: Scientia Verlag, 1976.

Fontana, Bartolomeo. "Documenti Vaticani inediti Contro l'eresia lutherana in Italia." *Archivio della R. Società Romana di Storia Patria* XV (1892). 71–165, 365–474.

Fordun, Johann. *Johannes de Fordun Chronica Gentis Scotorum.* ed. William F. Skene. 2 vols. Edinburgh: Edmonston & Douglas, 1871–1872.

Foxe, John. *The acts and monuments of John Foxe: a new and complete edition: with a preliminary dissertation by the Rev. George Townsend.* London: R. B. Seeley and W. Burnside, 1837.

– *The Acts and Monuments of John Foxe.* ed. George Townsend. London: Burnside and Seeley, 1853.

– *The acts and monuments of John Foxe.* 4th ed., rev. and corr., with appendices, glossary, and indices, by Josiah Pratt. Introduction by John Stoughton. London: The Religious Tract Society, 1877.

Fraenkel, Peter. "Une Lettre Oubliée de Beatus Rhenanus: sa Préface à la Liturgie de S. Jean Chrysostome Dédiée à Johannes Hoffmeister 24 Janvier 1540." *Bibliothèque d'Humanisme et Renaissance* XLVIII (1986). 387–404.

– Review of Heinz Scheible. *Die Entstehung der Magdeburger Centurien. Bibliothèque d'Humanisme et Renaissance* XXIX (1967). 266–268.

– *Testimonium Patrum. The Function of the Patristic Argument in the Theology of Philipp Melanchthon* [Travaux d'Humanisme et Renaissance 46]. Geneva: Droz, 1961.

Fragnito, Gigliola. "Cultura umanistica e riforma religiosa: il 'De officio Boni viri ac Probi Epicopi' di Gasparo Contarini." *Studi Veneziani* XI (1969). 75–189.

Frank, Christiana Beatrice Melanie. "Untersuchungen zum Catalogus testium veritatis des Matthias Flacius Illyricus." Diss.: Tübingen, 1989.

Frank, Gustav. *Johann Major, der Wittenberger Poet.* Halle: C. E. M. Pfeffer, 1863.

– "Matthias Flacius Illyricus und seine Zeit" [Review of Preger]. *Protestantische Kirchenzeitung für das Evangelische Deutschland* XXVI (1859). 771–776; XXIX (1862). 738–742.

Fraustadt, Albert. *Die Einführung der Reform im Hochstift Merseberg.* Leipzig: Friedlein & Hirsch, 1843.

Friedberg, Emil. *Agenda, wie es in des Churfürsten zu Sachsen Landen in den Kirchen gehalten wirdt.* Halle: Verlag der Buchhandlung des Waisenhauses, 1869.

– "Zur Geschichte des Interims und der Agenda, wie es in des Churfürsten zu Sachsen Landen gehalten wird. 1549." *Zeitschrift für Historische Theologie* XL (1871). 36–41.

Friedensburg, Walter. "Die Anstellung des Flacius Illyricus an der Universität Wittenberg." ARG, XI (1914). 302–309.

– "Ein Brief Aurifabers an Flacius (1549)." ARG, XX (1923). 62–65.

– *Geschichte der Universität Wittenberg.* Halle: Max Niemeyer, 1917.

– "Zwei Briefe Michael Stifels an Flacius (1554 und 1555)." ARG, LXIII/LXIV (1919). 247–251.

Frischeisen-Köhler, Max and Willy Moog. *Die Philosophie der Neuzeit bis zum Ende des XVIII. Jahrhunderts [Friedrich überwegs Grundriß der Geschichte der Philosophie III].* 13. Auflage. Basel: Benno Schwalbe, 1953.

Fritschl, George J. *The Formula of Concord: Its Origin and Contents.* Philadelphia: The Lutheran Publisching Society, 1916.

Fuhrmann, Horst. *Einfluss und Verbreitung der pseudoisidorischen Fälschungen* I. Stuttgart: Anton Hiersemann, 1972.

Fumaroli, Marc. "Aux origines de la conaissance historique du Moyen Age: Humanisme, Réforme et Gallicanisme au XVIe siècle." *XVII Siècle*, CXIV/CXV (1977). 5–29.

Fürstenwerth, Ludwig. *Die Verfassungsänderungen in den oberdeutschen Reichsstädten zur Zeit Karls V.* Göttingen: Dietrichsche Universitäts Buchdruckerei (W. F. Kästner), 1893.

Gass, Wilhelm. *Georg Calixt und der Syncretismus.* Breslau: Gosohorsky, 1846.

Gauss, Karl. "Der Basler Reformationspfarrer Wolfgang Weissenburg." *Christlicher Volksfreund* LI (1925). 487.

Gebhardt, Hermann. *Thüringische Kirchengeschichte.* Zweite Hälfte: *Vom Beginn der Reformation bis zur neueren Zeit.* Gotha: Friedrich Andreas Pustet, 1881.

Gebhart, Bruno. "Matthias Döring der Minorit." *Historische Zeitschrift* LIX (1888). 248–294.

– "Die Confutatio Primatus Papae." *Neues Archiv der Gesellschaft für ältere deutsche Geschichtskunde* XII (1887). 517–529.

Geisberg, Max. *Der deutsche Einblatt-Holzschnitt in der ersten Hälfte des XVI. Jahrhunderts.* Munich: H. Schmidt [1923–1929].

– *The German Single-Leaf Woodcut: 1500–1550.* Revised and edited by Walter L. Strauss. 4 vols. New York: Hacker Art Books, Inc. 1974. 2 vols. New York: Abaris Books, 1975.

Gensichen, Hans-Werner. *We Condemn. How Luther and 16th-Century Lutheranism Condemned False Doctrine.* St. Louis: Concordia, 1967. Translation by Herbert J. A. Bauman of *Damnamus: die Verwerfung von Irrlehre bei Luther und im Luthertum des 16. Jahrhunderts.* AGTL, 1. Berlin: Lutherisches Verlagshaus, 1955.

Gerdes, Daniel. *Scrinium Antiquarium sive Miscellanea Groningana Nova* V. Gröningen and Bremen: Spandau & G. W. Rupp, 1756; VI, Groningen and Bremen, 1760.

Gerhard, Johann. *Confessio Catholica in qua doctrina catholica et evangelica, quam Ecclesiae Augustanae Confessionis addictae profitentur, ex Romano-Catholicorum Scriptorum suffragiis confirmatur, in quatuor tomes distributa.* Jena, 1634–1637.

Gesamtkatalog der preussischen Bibliotheken. Herausgegeben von der preussischen Staatsbibliothek VI. Berlin: Preussiche Druckerei- und Verlags-Aktiengesellschaft, 1934.

Geyer, Hans-Georg. "Welt und Mensch. Zur Frage des Aristotelismus bei Melanchthon." Diss.: Bonn, 1959.

Géza, Kathona. *Fejezetek a török hódoltsági reformáció törtenetéböl* [Contribution to the History of the Reformation in the Territory Occupied by the Turks]. Budapest, 1964. 19–22.

Gilbert, Felix. "Biondo, Sabellico and the Beginnings of Venetian Official Historiography." John Gordon Rowe and W. H. Stockdale (eds.). *Florilegium Historiale: Historical Essays Presented to Wallace K. Ferguson.* Toronto: University of Toronto Press [1971].

Gilbert, Neil W. *Renaissance Concepts of Method.* New York: Columbia University Press, 1960.

Gilly, Carlos. "Guillaume Postel et Bale." Carlos Gilly (ed.). *Guillaume Postel 1581–1981. Actes du Colloque International d'Avranches, 5–9 September 1981* [Ouvrage publié avec le concours du Centre National de la Recherche Scientifique d'Avranges]. Paris: Guy Trédaniel, 1985. 41–77.

– *Spanien und der Basler Buchdruck bis 1600* [Basler Beiträge zur Geschichtswissenschaft 151]. Basel and Frankfurt a. M.: Helbing & Lichtenhahn, 1985.

Gilmont, Jean-François. "Flacius Illyricus." *Dictionnaire d'Histoire et de Géographie Ecclésiastiques* 17 (1971). 311–316.

– *Les Martyrologes Protestants du XVIe Siècle: Essai de Présentation Générale.* Diss., Louvain, 1966.

Gindely, Anton. *Geschichte der Böhmischen Brüder.* Herrnhut: Verlag der Missionsbuchhandlung, 1931.

– *Quellen zur Geschichte der Böhmischen Brüder.* Vienna: Kaiserlich-königlicher Hof- und Staatsdruckerei, 1859.

Ginsburg, Christian David (ed.). *The Massoreth Ha-Massoreth of Elias Levita.* London: Longmanns, Green, Reader & Dyer, 1867. Reprint: *Introduction to the Rabbinic Bible, Hebrew and English ... and the Massoreth Ha-Massoreth of Elias Levita.* New York, KTAV, 1968.

Glass, Solomon. *Christliche Anfechtungs-Schul.* Nuremberg: Johann Andreae Etners, 1669.

Gönna, Sigfrid von der. "Beatus Rhenanus und Otfrid von Weissenburg. Zur Otfrid-Überlieferung im 16. Jahrhundert." *Zeitschrift für Deutsches Altertum und Deutsche Literatur* CVII (1978). 248–257.

Götze, [Ludwig]. "Die Magdeburger Presse zur Zeit der Reichsacht und der Belagerung durch den Kurfürsten Moritz von Sachsen, 1947 bis 1551." *Blätter für Handel, Gewer-*

be und sociales Leben [Beiblatt zur Magdeburgischen Zeitung 1876. No. 21, 22 Mai, 161–3; No. 22, 171–173; No. 23, 177–179].

Goez, Werner. *Translatio Imperii.* Tübingen: J. C. B. Mohr (Paul Siebeck), 1958.

Goldschmidt, Ernst Philip. *Medieval Texts and Their First Appearance in Print.* London: Oxford University Press, 1943.

Goll, Jaroslav. *Quellen und Untersuchungen zur Geschichte der Böhmischen Brüder.* Prague: J. Otto, 1878–1882.

Gortan, Veljko and Vladimir Vratović. "The Basic Characteristics of Croatian Latinity." *Humanistica Lovaniensia* XX (1971). 37–68.

Gose, Walther (ed.). *Reformationsdrucke von den Anfängen Luthers bis zum Ende des sechzehnten Jahrhunderts.* Nuremberg: Edelmann, 1972.

Gothein, Eberhard. "Die kulturellen Grundlagen der Gegenreformation." *Internationale Wochenschrift für Wissenschaft, Kunst und Technik* (10 August, 1907). 583–594.

– *Reformation und Gegenreformation.* Munich and Leipzig: Duncker & Humblot, 1924.

Gottlieb, Theodor. "Zwei Schriften über die Magdeburger Centuriatores" [Review]. *Göttingsche Gelehrte Anzeigen* CLXIV (1902). 444–465.

Graff, Paul. *Geschichte der Auflösung der alten gottesdienstlichen Formen in der evangelischen Kirche Deutschlands* I. Göttingen: Vandenoeck & Ruprecht, 1937.

Grauert, Hermann. "Dante in Deutschland." *Historisch-politische Blätter für das katholische Deutschland* CXX (1879). 81–100, 173–179, 321–356, 512–536, 633–652, 789–822.

– "Magister Heinrich der Poet in Würzburg und die römische Kurie." *Abhandlungen der Bayerischen Akademie der Wissenschaften, Philosophish-historische Klasse* XVII (1912). 1–528.

Grendler, Paul F. *The Roman Inquisition and the Venetian Press, 1540–1605.* Princeton: Princeton University Press, 1977.

Grescham, Stephen. "William Baldwin: Literary Voice of the Reign of Edward VI." *The Huntington Library Quarterly* XLIV, 1981. 101–116.

Gretzer, Jakob. *Epistolarum Quas Romani Pontifices ... miserunt ad Principes et Reges Francorum.* Ingolstadt: Andreas Angermanrius, 1613.

Grimm, Jakob. *Reinhart Fuchs.* Berlin: Reimer, 1834.

Gross, Reiner, Manfred Kobuch and Ernst Müller (eds.). *Martin Luther 1482–1546: Dokumente seines Lebens und Wirkens.* Weimar: Hermann Böhlaus Nachf., 1983.

Grützmacher, Richard H. *Wort und Geist: Eine historische und dogmatische Untersuchung zum Gnadenmittel des Wortes.* Leipzig: A. Deichert, 1902.

– "Schwenckfeld." RE3, 18. 76, 57–58.

Günther, Johann. *Lebenskizzen der Professoren der Universität Jena seit 1558 bis 1858.* Jena: Friederich Mauke, 1858; Reprint, Aalen: Scientia Verlag, 1979.

Gussmann, Wilhelm. *Quellen und Forschungen zur Geschichte des Augsburgischen Glaubensbekenntnisses* II: D. Johann Ecks Vierhundertundvier Artikel zum Reichstag von Augsburg 1530. Kassel: Edmund Pillardy, 1930.

Häberlin, Franz Dominicus. *Neuste Teutsche Reichs-Geschichte* III. Halle: Gebauers Witwe und Jacob Gebauer, 1770.

Häuser, Helmut. *Gibt es eine Gemeinsame Quelle zum Faustbuch von 1587 und zu Goethe's Faust?* Wiesbaden: Guido Preston Verlag, 1973.

– "Zur Verfasserfrage des Faustbuchs von 1587: Konrad Lautenbach." *Euphorion* LXVI (1972). 151–173.

Hafner, Stanislaus. "Südslawische Rara und Rarissima in der österreichischen Nationalbibliothek." *Festschrift Josef Stummvoll.* ed. Josef Mayerhöfer & Walter Ritzer. I. Vienna: Brüder Hollinek in Komm. 1970. 164–176.

Haikola, Lauri. *Gesetz und Evangelium bei Matthias Flacius Illyricus. Eine Untersuchung zur lutherichen Theologie vor dem Konkordienformel* [Studia Theologica Lundensia 1] Lund: C. W. K. Gleerup, 1952.

– "Melanchthon's und Luther's Lehre von der Rechtfertigung, ein Vergleich." *Luther und Melanchthon.* Vilmos Vajta (ed.). Göttingen: Vandenhoeck und Ruprecht, 1961. 89–103.

– "Die Reformatorische Anthropologie." *Studien zu Luther und Luthertum* [Uppsala Universitets Aarskrift 1952 2]. Uppsala: Lundequistska Bokhandeln und Wiesbaden: Otto Harrassowitz, 1958.

Haller, William. *Foxe's Book of Martyrs and the Elect Nation. The Meaning and Relevance of Foxe's Book of Martyrs.* London: Jonathan Cape [1963].

Halm, []. "Ueber die handschriftliche Ueberlieferung der Chronik des Sulpitius Severus." *Sitzungsbericht der königlichen Bayerischen Akademie der Wissenschaft. Philosophisch-historisch Classe* II. 1865. 37–64.

Hannemann, Kurt. "Der Humanist Georg Fabricius in Meissen, das Luthermonotessaron in Wittenberg und Leipzig und der Heliandpraefatiokodex aus Naumburg a. d. Saale." *Filologia Germanica* XVII (1974). 7–109.

– "Die Lösung des Rätsels der Heiliandpraefatio." *Forschungen und Fortschriftte* XV (1939). 327–329. Reprint: *Der Heliand* [Wege der Forschungen CCXXI]. Darmstadt: Wissenschaftliche Buchgesellschaft, 1973. 8–13.

Hareide, Bjarne. *Die Konfirmation in der Reformationszeit: Eine Untersuchung der lutherischen Konfirmation in Deutschland 1520–1585.* Tr. from Norwegian by Karin Kvideland. Göttingen: Vandenhoeck und Ruprecht [1971].

Harms, Wolfgang. *Deutsche Illustrierte Flugblätter des 16. und 17. Jahrhunderts* II. Munich: Kraus International Publications, 1980.

Harnack, Adolf von. *Lehrbuch der Dogmengeschichte.* 3. Aufl. Freiburg i. B. and Leipzig: J. C. B. Mohr (Paul Siebeck), 1894–1897.

Harris, Jesse W. *John Bale: A Study in the Minor Literature of the Reformation* [Studies in Language and Literature XXV]. Urbana: The University of Illinois Press, 1940.

Hartmann, Julius. *Erhard Schnepf, der Reformator in Schwaben, Nassau, Hessen und Thüringen.* Tübingen: Osiander, 1870.

Hase, Hans Christoph von. *Die Gestalt der Kirche Luthers. Der casus confessionis im Kampf des Matthias Flacius gegen das Interim von 1548.* Göttingen: Vandenhoeck & Ruprecht, 1940.

Hase, Karl Alfred von. *Herzog Albrecht von Preussen und sein Hofprediger. Eine Königsberger Tragödie aus dem Zeitalter der Reformation.* Leipzig: Breitkopf und Härtel, 1879.

Hase, Karl August von. *Kirchengeschichte auf der Grundlage akademischer Vorlesungen* III. Leipzig: Breitkopf & Härtel, 1891.

Hasslinger, Christina. "Die religiöse Propaganda des Matthias Flacius Illyricus und seiner Epigonen. Ein Beitrag zur Flugschriftliteratur der Reformationszeit." Diss., Vienna, 1970.

Hauke, Rainer. "Sola dei justitia. Die theozentrische Rechtfertigungslehre des Andreas Osiander (1498–1552): Eine mißlungene Belehrung der forensischen Rechtfertigungslehre?" *Belehrter Glaube: Festschrift für Johannes Wirsching zum 65. Geburtstag.* Ed. Elke Axmacher and Klaus Schwarzwäller. Frankfurt a. M.: Peter Lang, 1994. 101–132.

Hauréau, Jean-Barthélemy. *Notice sur Les Mélanges Poétiques d'Hildebert de Lavardin* [Extrait des Notices et extraits des Manuscrits de Bibliothèque Nationale, Tome XXXVII]. Paris: G. Pedone-Laureriel, 1882.

Hauschild, Wolf-Dieter. "Zum Kampf gegen das Augsburger Interim in norddeutschen Hansestädten." ZKG, LXXXIV (1973). 60–81.

Hausen, Karl Renatus. *Pragmatische Geschichte der Protestanten in Deutschland.* Halle: Curtius, 1767.

Haussleiter, Johannes. "Matthias Flacius als Herausgeber von Luthers Koburger Briefen und Trostsprüchen 1530." *Neue Kirchliche Zeitschrift* XXVIII (1917). 149–187.

Haye, Thomas. "Der 'Catalogus Testium Veritatis' des Matthias Flacius Illyricus zur Auswahl, Verarbeitung und kritische Bewertung seiner Quellen." Unpublished Examination paper. Seminar für Lateinische Philologie des Mittelalters, University of Göttingen, 1990.

– "Der Catalogus testium veritatis des Matthias Flacius Illyricus – eine Einführung in die Literatur des Mittelalters?" ARG, LXXXIII (1992). 31–48.

Heer, Friedrich. *The Holy Roman Empire.* London: Widdenfeld & Nicholson, 1968.

– *The Medieval World. Europe from 1110 to 1350.* Tr. Janet Sondheimer. New York and Washington: Praeger, 1969.

Heimpel, Hermann. "Habent sua fata libelli. Wolfenbüttel. Herzog August Bibliothek. Cod. 32.10, Aug. fol." *Wolfenbütteler Beiträge* III (1978). 59–63.

Hein, Lorenz. *Die Reformation und ihr Weg in die Republik Venedig.* Venice: [Centro di Meditazione Tra Oriente e occidente]. Florence: Leo S. Olscki Editione, 1827.

Heinemann, Otto von. *Die Herzogliche Bibliothek zu Wolfenbüttel, 1550–1893.* 2. Aufl. Wolfenbüttel: Zwissler, 1894. Reprint, Amsterdam: van Heusden, 1969.

Heinrich, Duke of Saxony. *Agenda. Das ist Kyrchenordnung wie sich die Pfarrherrn und Seelsorger ... Hertzog Heinrich zu Sachsen V. G. H. Furstenthump gestellet.* Leipzig, Nicolaus Wolrab, 1880.

Heppe, Heinrich.

– *Die Entstehung und Fortbildung des Luthertums und die kirchlichen Bekenntnisschriften desselben von 1548–1576.* Cassel: J. G. Krieger, 1863.

– *Geschichte des deutschen Protestantismus in den Jahren 1555–1581.* 4 vols. Frankfurt a. M.: Karl Theodor Volcker, 1852–1859.

– *Philipp Melanchthon, der Lehrer Deutschlands.* Nuremberg: Joh. Aug. Koch, 1860.

Herbers, Klaus. "Die Päpstin Johanna. Ein kritischer Forschungsbericht." *Historisches Jahrbuch* CVIII (1988). 174–194.

Hering, Hermann. *Doktor Pomeranus, Johannes Bugenhagen. Ein Lebensbild aus der Zeit der Reformation.* Halle: Verein für Reformationsgeschichte, 1888.

Hermelink, Heinrich and W. Maurer (eds.). *Reformation und Gegenreformation* [Handbuch der Kirchengeschichte für Studierende III]. Tübingen: J. C. B. Mohr (Paul Siebeck), 1931.

Herrmann, Fritz. *Das Interim in Hessen. Ein Beitrag zur Reformationsgeschichte.* Marburg: N. G. Elwert'sche Verlagsbuchhandlung, 1888.

– *Die evangelische Bewegung in Mainz im Reformationszeitalter.* Mainz: In Kommission bei Hermann Quasthof, 1907.

Herrmann, Johannes. "Augsburg-Leipzig-Passau. Das Leipziger Interim nach Akten des Landeshauptarchiv Dresden 1547–1552." Diss., Karl-Marx University, Leipzig, 1962.

Herte, Adolf. "Matthias Flacius." *Lexikon für Theologie und Kirche.* 2nd. ed. Freiburg: Herder, 1932. IV, 27–28.

Hertel, G. "Kleine Mitteilungen 3: Zur Geschichte der Gegenreformation." *Geschichts-Blätter für Stadt und Land Magdeburg* XXXIII (1898). 407–409.

Herzberg, Adalbert Joseph. *Der heilige Mauritius: Ein Beitrag zur Geschichte der deutschen Mauritiusverehrung.* Düsseldorf: Schwann, 1936.

Heussi, Karl. *Altertum, Mittelalter und Neuzeit in der Kirchengeschichte. Ein Beitrag zum problem der historischen Periodizierung.* Tübingen: J. C. Hinrichs, 1921.

– "Centuriae." *Harnack-Ehrung: Beiträge zur Kirchengeschichte ihrem Lehrer Adolf von Harnack zu seinem 70. Geburtstage (7. Mai 1921), dargebracht von einer Reihe seiner Schüler.* Leipzig: J. C. Hinrichs, 1921. 328–334.

– *Geschichte der theologischen Fakultät zu Jena.* Weimar: Hermann Böhlaus Nachfolger, 1954.

Heyne, M. "Über den Heliand." *Zeitschrift für die deutsche Philologie* I (1869). 275–290.

Hilka, Alfons and Otto Schumann (eds.). *Carmina Burana.* Band I: *Text.* Heidelberg: Carl Winter, 1930.

Hill, Charles L. "Some Theses of Philip Melanchthon." *Lutheran Quarterly* VI (1954). 245–248.

Hillinger, Johann Gottlieb. *Beytrag zur Kirchen-historie des Ertz-Bischofftums Saltzburg.* Saalfeld: C. M. Köhlern, 1732.

– *Memoria Schaereriana, das gute Andencken des Evangelischen Märtyrers Georg Schärer.* Saalfeld, 1732. Frankfurt and Leipzig, 1732.

Hirsch, Emanuel. *Die Theologie des Andreas Osiander und ihre geschichtlichen Voraussetzungen.* Göttingen: Vandenhoeck & Ruprecht, 1919.

– *Hilfsbuch zum Studium der Dogmatik der Reformatoren und der altevangelischen Lehrer quellenmässig belegt und verdeutscht.* 4th ed. Berlin: de Gruyter. 1964.

– "Melanchthon und das Interim." ARG, XVII (1920). 62–66.

Hölzel, Hildegund. "Heinrich Toke und der Wolfenbüttler 'Rapularius.'" Diss.: Göttingen, 1994.

Hoffmann, Friedrich Wilhelm. *Geschichte der Stadt Magdeburg.* 2 vols. Neu bearb. von Gustav Hertel und Friedrich Hülsse. Magdeburg: Albert Rathke, 1855.

Hoffmann, Georg. "Luther und Melanchthon. Melanchthons Stellung in der Theologie des Luthertums." *Zeitschrift für Systematische Theologie* XV (1938). 81–135.

Holstern, Friedrich Wilhelm Heinrich. *German Engravings. Etchings and Woodcuts, ca 1400–1700.* Amsterdam, 1954 ff.

Holtzmann, Robert. *Kaiser Maximilian II. bis zu seiner Thronbesteigung (1527–1564).* Berlin: C. A. Schwetschke und Sohn, 1903.

Holzmann, W. "Propter Sion non tacebo. Zur Erklärung von Carmina Burana 41." *Deutsches Archiv für Erforschung des Mittealters* X (1953). 170–175.

Honselmann, Klemens. *Das Rationale der Bischöfe.* Paderborn: Selbstverlag des Vereins für Geschichte und Altertum, 1975.

Hoornbeck, Johannes. *Summa Controversiarum Religionis* Editio secunda. Trajecti ad Rhenum: Joannis a Waesberge, 1568.

Hopp, E. "Zur Geschichte des Liedes 'Erhalt uns Herr bei deinem Wort.'" *Beiträge zur bayerischen Kirchengeschichte* VIII (1902). 79–87.

Hoppe, Willy. "Matthias Flacius." *Biographisches Wörterbuch zur deutschen Geschichte.* Munich: R. Oldenbourg, 1952.

Horawitz, Adalbert. "Beiträge zu den Sammlungen von Briefen Philipp Melanchthons." *Sitzungsberichte der kaiserlichen Akademie der Wissenschaften. Philosophisch-historische Classe* LXXVI (1874). 299–24.

Hortleder, Friedrich. *Der Römischen Keyser- und Königlichen Majesteten, auch des heiligen Römischen Reichs geistlicher unnd weltlicher Stände Handlungen und Ausschreibungen ... von Rechtmässigkeit. Anfang, Fort- und endlichen Ausgang dess Teutschen Kriegs Kaiser Carls des Fünfften wider die Schmalkaldische Bundts Oberste Chur- und Fürsten Sachsen und Hessen 1546 und 47 an den Tag gegeben.* 2. Aufl. Gotha: Wolfgang Endtes, 1645.

Hoskier, H. C. *De Contemptu Mundi; A Bitter Satirical Poem of 3000 Lines upon the Morals of the XIIth Century by Bernard of Morval, Monk of Cluny.* London: Bernard Quartitsch, 1929.

Hotchkiss, Valerie. "The Legend of the Female Pope in the Reformation." *Acta Conventus Neo-Latini Hafniensis.* Ed. Rhoda Schur. Binghamton, N. Y.: Center for Medieval and Renaissance Studies, State University of New York at Binghamgton, 1994. 495–505.

Hroch, Miroslav & Anna Skybova. *Ecclesia Militans. Inquisition im Zeitalter der Gegen-reformation.* Leipzig: Edition Leipzig, 1985.

Hubatsch, Oscar. *Die lateinischen Vagantenlieder des Mittelalters.* Osnabrück: Zeller, 1976.

Hülsse, Friedrich. "Beiträge zur Geschichte der Buchdruckerkunst in Magdeburg." *Geschichtsblätter für Stadt und Land Magdeburg* XV (1880), XVI (1881), XVII (1882), [= *Bibliographiae Reconditae* I. Amsterdam: Schuppers, 1966. 635–738].

– *Die Stadt Magdeburg im Kampfe für den Protestantismus während der Jahre 1547–1551* [Schriften für das deutsche Volk 17]. Halle: Verein für Reformationsgeschichte, 1892.

Husman, Heinrich. "The Origin and Destination of the Magnus Liber Organi." *The Musical Quarterly* XLIX (1963). 311–330.

Huygens, Robert. "A propos de Bérengar et son Traité de l'Eucharistie." *Revue Bénédictine* LXXVI (1966). 133–139.

Issleib, Simon. *Aufsätze und Beiträge zu Kurfürst Moritz von Sachsen (1877–1907).* Leipzig, DDR: Zentralantiquariat, 1988.

Iserloh, Erwin (ed.). *Katholische Theologen der Reformationszeit* II. Münster: Aschendorf, 1985.

– & Konrad Repgen (eds.). *Reformata Reformanda* II. Münster in Westphalia: Aschendorf, 1965.

Ittig, Thomas. *De Bibliothecis et Catenis Patrum ... Tractatus.* Leipzig: Hered. Friderici Lankisii, 1707.

Iwand, Hans. "Das Widerstandsrecht der Christen nach der Lehre der Reformation." *Nachgelassene Werke* II. Ed. H. Gollwitzer et al. Munich: Christian Kaiser Verlag, 1966. 193–229.

Jacobs, Eduard. "Ein Bisher ungekanntes, während der Belagerung von Magdeburg im Jahre 1550–1551 gedrucktes niederdeutsches Gesamgbuch nebst einer Übersicht über die geistig-literarischen Schutz- und Trutzwaffen der Belagerten." *Geschichtsblätter für Stadt und Land Magdeburg* VI (1871). Reprint, *Bibliographiae Reconditae* I. Amsterdam: P. Schippers, 1966. 757–797.

– "Bruder Henning von Himmelpforten, sein Zeugnis von Andreas Proles und der von demselben als nahe bevorstehend bestimmt geahnten Kirchenerneuerung." *Zeitschrift des Vereins für Kirchengeschichte der Provinz Sachsen* XIV (1917). 101–110.

Jacobs, Henry E. (ed.). *The Book of Concord, or the Symbolical Books of the Evangelical Lutheran Church with Historical Introduction, Notes, Appendixes and Indexes. Vol. II: Historical Introductions, Appendixes and Indexes.* Philadelphia: G. W. Frederick, 1883.

Jacobs de Voragine. *The Golden Legend of Jacobus de Voragine*. Tr. Granger Ryan and Helmut Ripperger. New York: Arno Press, 1969.

Jaffé, Philipp. *Monumenta Moguntina* [Bibliotheca Rerum Germanicarum III]. Berlin: Weidmann, 1866.

Jansen, Albert. "Julius Pflug. Ein Beitrag zur Geschichte der Kirchen und Politik Deutschlands im sechzehnten Jahrhundert." *Neue Mitteilungen aus dem Gebiet historischer-antiquarischer Forschungen des thüringischen-sächsischen Vereins zur Erforschung des vaterländischen Altertums* X (1863–64). Erste Abteilung 1–110. Zweite Abteilung 1–212.

Jasnowski, J. *Nikolaj Czarny Radziwill*. Warsau, 1939.

Jauering, Reinhold. "Die Konkurenz der Jenaer mit der Wittenberger Ausgabe von Martin Luthers Werke." *Luther Jahrbuch* XXVI (1959). 75–94.

– "Zur Jenaer Lutherausgabe." *Theologische Literaturzeitung* LXXVII (1952). 747–762.

Jeep, Ludovicus. *Quaestiones criticae ad emendationem Claudiani Panegyricorum Spectantes*. Nuremburg: Paetzius, 1869.

Jewel, John. *The Works of John Jewel, Bishop of Salisbury*. 4 vols. Ed. John Ayre. Cambridge: Cambridge University Press, 1845–1850; Reprint, New York: Johnston Reprint Corp., 1968.

Joel, F. "Herzog August von Sachsen bis zu Erlangung der Kurwürde. Schluß." *Neues Archiv für Sächsische Geschichte und Altertumskunde* XIX (1898). 116–153.

John Paul II [Pope]. "Science, Academic Research and the Church." *Origins* XII. Nr. 23 (Novemberg 18th, 1982). 369–371.

Jungmann, Joseph Andreas. *Missarum Sollemnia*. 5. Aufl. Vienna, Freiburg and Basel: Herder, 1962.

Kassel, Rudolf. *Der Text der Aristotelischen Rhetorik. Prolegomena zu einer Kritischen Ausgabe*. Berlin and New York: De Gruyter, 1971.

Kausler, Eduard von and Theodor Schott (eds.). *Briefwechsel zwischen Christoph Herzog von Württemberg und Petrus Paulus Vergerius*. Stuttgart: Litterarischer Verein, 1875.

Kawerau, Gustav. "Eine Episode aus dem Kampfe der Flacianer mit den Melanchthonianern." *Theologische Studien und Kritiken* LV (1882). 324–343.

– "Gutachten Joh. Agricolas für Christoph von Carlowitz über die Annahme des Augsburger Interims." *Neues Archiv für Sächsische Geschichte und Alterthumskunde* I (1880). 267–280.

– *Jahresberichte über neuere deutsche Literaturgeschichte* XXV (1894).

– *Johann Agricola von Eisleben. Ein Beitrag zur Reformationsgeschichte*. Berlin: Wilhelm Hertz, 1881.

– "Matthias Falcius." *The New Schaff-Herzog Encyclopedia of Religious Knowledge*. New York and London: Funk and Wagnalls Co., 1809. IV, 321–324.

– "Matthias Flacius." RE3, VI, 1899. 82 ff. and XXIII, 448.

– "Die 'Trostschriften' als eine der ältesten Quellen für Briefe Luthers." ARG XIV (917). 187–204.

Kawerau, Waldemar. "Erasmus Alberus in Magdeburg." *Geschichtsblätter für Stadt und Land Magdeburg* XXVIII (1893). 1–62.

Keil, Richard and Robert Keil. *Geschichte des Jenaischen Studentenlebens von der Gründung der Universität bis zur Gegenwart (1548–1858): Eine Festgabe zum 300. Jubiläums der Universität Jena.* Leipzig: Brockhaus, 1858.

Keim, Theodor. *Reformationsgeschichte der Reichsstadt Ulm.* Stuttgart: C. Belser, 1851.

Kelle, Johann Nepomuk. *Otfrids von Weissenburg Evangelienbuch: Text, Einleitung, Grammatik.* Regensburg: G. J. Manz, 1856–81.

Keller, Rudolf. *Der Schlüssel zur Schrift: Die Lehre vom Wort Gottes bei Matthias Flacius Illyricus* [Arbeiten zur Geschichte und Theologie des Luthertums N. F. 5]. Hannover: Lutherisches Verlagshaus, 1984.

Kelley, Donald R. "The Theory of History." *Cambridge History of Renaissance Philosophy.* Cambridge and New York: Cambridge University Press, 1988. 746–761.

Kettner, Friedrich Gottlieb. *Clerus Magdeburgensis. Clerus Ulrico-Levinianus.* Magdeburg: Christian Leberecht Faber, 1728.

– *Clerus Petrinus.* Magdeburg: Johan Siegelers Witwe, 1731.

Kidd, B. J. *Documents Illustrative of the Continental Reformation.* Oxford: Clarendon Press, 1911.

King, John N. *English Reformation Literature: The Tudor Origins of the Protestant Tradition.* Princeton: Princeton University Press, 1982.

Kinney, Arthur F. Review, "Beware the Cat by William Baldwin: the First English Novel." *Modern Philology* LXXXVII (1990). 396–399.

Kirchhoff, Albrecht. "Beiträge zur Geschichte der Pressmassregelung und des Verkehrs auf den Büchermessen im 16. und 17. Jahrhundert." *Archiv für Geschichte des Deutschen Buchhandels* II (1879). 33–67.

– "Die 'Famoss' Schriften." *Archiv für Geschichte des Deutschen Buchhandels.* N. F. V. (1880). 156–165.

Klopsch, Paul. *Lateinische Lyrik des Mittelalters.* Stuttgart: Philipp Reclam, 1985.

Klotz, Ernst-Emil. "Über die Herkunft der jenaer Studenten im ersten Jahrhundert des Bestehens der Universität." *Geschichtliche Landeskunde und Universalgeschichte. Festschrift Hermann Aubin.* Hamburg, 1950.

Kluge, F. "Zur Herkunft der Heliand-Praefatio." *Korrespondenzblatt des Vereins für niederdeutsche Sprachforschung* XXXVII (1919/21). 7.

Knaustius, Heinrich. *Fünf Bücher von der Göttlichen und Edlen Gabe der Philosophischen hochtheweren undwunderbaren Kunst, Bier zubrawen.* Erfurt: Nicolaus Schmach, 1614.

Kniewald, Carolus. "Ordo et Canon Missae e Missali S. Sabinae MR 166 Saec. XI." *Ephemerides Liturgicae* LXX (1956). 325–337.

Knöpfler, Alois. *Die Kelchbewegung im Bayern unter Herzog Albrecht V.* Munich: E. Stahl Sen. (Julius Stahl), 1891.

Koch, D. "Georg Schwerer, ein evangelischer Märtyer." *Die Wartburg* XXIX (1930). 93–95.

Koch, Franz. "Fünf Briefe des Professors der Theologie Franziscus Stancarus aus den Jahren 1551, 1552 und 1553." ARG, III (1905/6). 403–410.

Köhler, H. O. "Flacius und Dante." *Zeitschrift für die gesamte lutherische Theologie und Kirche* XXVIII (1867). 684–704.

Koehler, Walther. *Dogmengeschichte als Geschichte des Christlichen Selbstbewustseins.* Zurich: Max Niehans, 1951.

– Walter Sohm, Theodor Suppel & Friedrich Wihlem Schoff. *Urkundliche Quellen zur hessischen Reformationsgeschichte* III. Bearb. von Günter Franz & Eckhart G. Franz. Marburg: N. G. Elwert Verlag, 1955.

König, Georg Matthias. *Bibliotheca vetus atque Nova.* Altdorf: Heinrich Meyer, 1678.

Könneritz, Julius von. "Weigerung der Leipziger Ritterschaft, gegen Magdeburg zu zieh, und das hierauf von Kurfürst Moritz gegen dieselbe, so wie gegen deren Führer, den Oberhauptmann von Könneritz eingeleitete Verfahren, 1550 ff." *Archiv für die Sächsische Geschichte* IV (1886). 123–166

Körner, Emil. *Erasmus Alber. Das Kämpferleben eines Gottesgelehrten aus Luthers Schule.* Leipzig: M. Heinsius Nachfolger, 1910.

Köstlin, Julius. *Die Baccalaurei und Magistri der Wittenberger Philosophischen Fakultät 1503–1517* [Osterprogramm der Universität Halle-Wittenberg 1887]. Halle: Max Niemeyer, 1887; *1518–1537 ... und die ordentlichen Disputationen 1536–1537.* Halle: Max Niemeyer, 1888; *1538–1546 ... und die öffentliche Disputationen derselben Jahre.* Halle: Max Niemeyer, 1890; *1548–1560.* Halle: Max Niemeyer, 1891.

– *Martin Luther, sein Leben, und seine Schriften.* 5. Aufl. nach des Verfassers Tode fortgesetzt von Gustav Kawerau. Berlin: A. Dunker, 1903.

Kolb, Robert. "Georg Major as Controversialist: Polemics in the Late Reformation." *Church History* XLV (1976). 455–468.

– "The German Lutheran Reaction to the Third Period of the Council of Trent, 1563." *Lutherjahrbuch* LI (1984). 63–95.

Kolbert, Elizabeth. "For the Most Negative Ads, Turn on the Nearest Radio." *New York Times.* October 20th, 1992.

Kolde, Theordor. *Analecta Lutherana.* Gotha: Friedrich Andreas Perthes, 1883.

Koldewey, Friedrich. *Braunschweigische Schulordnungen von den älteren Zeiten bis zum Jahre 1828* [Monumenta Germaniae Paedagogica I]. Berlin: A. Hofmann & Co., 1886.

– *Geschichte des Schulwesens in Herzogtum Braunschweig.* Wolfenbüttel: Julius Zwissler, 1891.

- "Gesetze und Lehrpläne des Paedagogiums in Brundernkloster, 1547." *Schulordnung der Stadt Braunschweig* [Monumenta Germanaie Paedagogica I]. Berlin: H. Hotmann & Co., 1886.

Kot, Stanislav. "Odnosaji Matije Flacija Illirika prema reformaciji u Poljskoj" [Relationships of Matthias Flacius Illyricus to the Reformation in Poland]. *Šišćev Zbornik*. Zagreb, 1929. 149–154.

- "Opposition to the Pope by the Polish Bishops, 1557–1560. Three Unique Polish Reformation Pamphlets." *Oxford Slavonic Papers* IV (953). 38–70.

Krimm-Beumann, Jutta. "Der Traktat 'De Investitura episcoporum' von 1109." *Deutsches Archiv für Erforschung des Mittelalters* XXXIII (1977). 37–83.

Krizman, Mate. "O Nekim Izvorima Vlačićeve Jezikoslovne Naobrazbe" [On some sources of Flacius' linguistic education]. *Istra* XIV (1976), N. 6–7, 16–34.

Krones, Franz von. Review of Viktor Bibl., "Nidbruck und Tanner." *Mitteilungen des Instituts für österreichische Geschichtsforschung* XXI (1900). 697–700.

Krüger, Ingeborg. "Reformationszeitliche Bildpolemik auf rheinischen Steinzeug." *Bonner Jahrbücher* CLXXIX. Cologne: Rheinland Verlag, 1979. 259–295.

Kruse, Martin. *Spener's Kritik am Landesherrlichen Kirchenregiment und ihre Vorgeschichte.* Witten: Luther-Verlag, 1971.

Küng, Hans. *On Being a Christian.* Tr. by Edward Quinn. Garden City, N. Y.: Doubelday, 1976.

Kuntz, Marion Leathers. *Guillaume Postel.* The Hague, Boston and London: Martinus Nijhoff, 1981.

- "The Virgin of Venice and Concepts of the Millenium in Venice." *The Politics of Gender in Early Modern Europe.* Jean R. Brink, Allison P. Coudert, and Maryanne C. Horowitz (eds.), [Sixteenth Century Essays and Studies XII]. Kirksville, Missouri: Sixteenth Century Journal Publishers, Ind., 1989. 111–120.

Kurze, Dietrich. *Quellen zur Ketzergeschichte Brandenburgs und Pommerns.* Berlin and New York: de Gruyter, 1975.

Kusukawa, Sachiko. "Providence Made Visible: The Creation and Establishment of Lutheran Natural Philosophy." Diss., Cambridge University, 1991.

- "Law and Gospel: The Importance of Philosophy at Reformation Wittenberg." *History of Universities* XI. Oxford: Oxford University Press, 1992. 33–57.

Kvačala, Jan. "Die Beziehungen der Unität zu Flacius und Laski." I, JGGPO, XXX (1909). 138–156; II, JGGPO, XXXI (1910). 82–105.

- "Wilhelm Postel. Seine Geistesart und seine Reformgedanken." ARG, IX, 285–330; XI, 200–227; XV (1918). 157–203.

Labowsky, Lotte. *Bessarion's Library and the Biblioteca Marciana: Six Early Inventories.* Rome: Edizioni dei Storia e Letteratura, 1979.

Lamping, Antoine Jan. *Ulrichus Velenus (Oldřich Velenský) and His Treatise Against the Papacy.* Leiden: E. J. Brill, 1976.

Lau, Franz. "Adiaphora." RGG3, I, 93–96.

– "Melanchthon und die Ordnung der Kirche." Walter Elliger (ed.). *Philipp Melanchthon: Forschungsbeiträge zur vierhundertsten Wiederkehr seines Todestages dargeboten in Wittenberg 1960*. Göttingen: Vandenhoeck & Ruprecht, 1961. 98–115.

Lauchert, Friedrich. *Die Italienischen Literarischen Gegner Luthers* [Erläuterungen und Ergänzungen zu Janssens Geschichte des Deutschen Volkes VIII]. Freiburg i. B.: Herder, 1912; Reprint, Nieuwkoop: B. De Graaf, 1972.

LeCointe, Charles. *Annales Ecclesiae Francorum.* Paris: Typographie Regis, 1666.

Leder, Hans-Günter (ed.). Johannes Bugenhagen. Gestalt und Wirkung. Berlin: Evangelische Verlagsanstalt, 1984.

Lee, Sydney. "John Foxe (1516–1587)." *Dictionary of National Biography* XX. London: Smith, Elder & Co., 1889. 141–150.

Lehmann, Paul. *Franciscus Modius als Handschriftenforscher.* Munich: C. H. Beck, 1908.

– "Geisteswissenschaftliche Gemeinschafts- und Kollektivunternehmungen in der geschichtlichen Entwicklung." *Sitzungsberichte der Bayerischen Akademie der Wissenschaften, Phil.- Historische Klasse*, 1956. Heft 5. 39 ff.; Reprint, *Erforschung des Mittelalters: Ausgewählte Abhandlungen und Aufsätze* IV. Stuttgart: Anton Hiersemann, 1959–62. 353–385.

– *Eine Geschichte der alten Fuggerbibliotheken.* Tubingen: J. C. B. Mohr (Paul Siebeck). 2 vols, 1956–1962.

– *Mitteilungen aus Handschriften* [Sitzungsberichte der Bayrischen Akademie der Wissenschaften, Phil.-Historische Klasse 9]. Munich: Drei Masken Verlag, 1922; Munich: Verlag der Bayerischen Akademie der Wissenschaften, 1951.

– *Johannes Sichardus und die von ihm benutzten Bibliotheken und Handschriften* [Quellen und Untersuchungen zur lateinischen Philologie des Mittelalters IV, Heft 1]. Munich: C. H. Beck, 1911.

Le Plat, Josse. *Monumentorum ad Historiam Concilii Tridentini Potissimum Illustrandam. Spectantium Amplissima Collectio. III: Complectens Monumenta ab anno MDXLI. ad Februarii MDXLVIII.* Louvain: Ex typographica academia, 1783.

Lepori, Fernando. "La Scuola di Rialto dalla Fondazione alla metà del Cinquicento." *Storia Della Cultura Veneta* 3/II. Vicenza: Neri Possa Editore, 1980.

Lessing, Gotthold Ephraim. *Bergengarius Turonensis: oder Ankündigung eines wichtigen Werkes desselben in der Herzoglichen Bibliothek in Wolfenbüttel befindlich, welche bisher völlig unerkannt geblieben.* Braunschweig: Waisenhaus, 1770.

– *Sämtliche Schriften.* 3rd ed. Karl Lachmann and Franz Muncker (eds.). Stuttgart: G. J. Göschen, 1895.

Levison, Wilhelm. *England and the Continent in the Eighth Century.* Oxford: Clarendon Press, 1950.

Levy, F. J. *Tudor Historical Thought.* San Marino, California: The Huntington Library, 1967.

Lewis, C. S. *English Literature in the Sixteenth Century Excluding Drama.* New York: Oxford University Press, 1954.

Leyser, Polycarp. *Historia poetarum et poematum medii aevi decem post annum a nato Christo CCCC, seculorum, centum et amplius codicum.* Halle/Saale: sumptu novi bibliopoli, 1721. 34–41.

Libby, Lester J. Jr. "Venetian History and Political Thought After 1509." *Studies in the Renaissance* XX. New York: Renaissance Society of America, 1973.

Lietzmann, Hans. *Die Reformation und ihre Wirkungen in der Theologischen Fakultät der Universität Jena.* Leipzig: A. Diechert'sche Verlagsbuchhandlung Werner School, 1917.

Liliencron, Rochus von (ed.). *Die historischen Volkslieder der Deutschen vom 13. bis 16. Jahrhundert.* Leipzig: F. C. W. Vogel, 1865–1869. Reprint, Hildesheim: Georg Olms, 1966.

– "Dichtung über das Interim (1548–1552)." *Mitteilungen aus dem Gebiete der öffentlichen Meinung in Deutschland während der zweiten Hälfte des 16. Jahrhunderts* [Abhandlung der historischen Klasse der königlichen bayerischen Akademie der Wissenschaft XII, III]. Munich: Verlag der königlichen Akademie, 1874. 140–170.

Limbeck, Meinrad. "Die Klage–eine verschwundene Gebetsgattung." *Theologische Quartalschrift* CLVII (1977). 3–16.

Löbel, Hansgeorg. "Die Reformtraktate des Magdeburger Domherrn Heinrich Toke." Diss., Göttingen, 1040.

Loefgren, David. "Verschiedene Tendenzen in der neueren Lutherforschung." *Kerygma und Dogma* V (1959). 146–164.

Loesche, Georg. "Der Briefwechsel Mathesius." JGGPO, XI (1890). 1–38.

– "Ein ungedrucktes Gedicht von Joh. Major." JGGPO, XV (1894). 154–156.

– "Zur Melanchthon's vierter Säkularfeier. Melanthon's [sic] Beziehungen zu Österreich." JGGPO, XVIII (1897). 1–33.

Loewenich, Walter von. "Das Interim von 1548." Walter von Loewenich (ed.). *Von Augustin zu Luther.* Witten, 1959. 391–406.

Lohse, Bernard. "Lehrentscheidung ohne Lehramt." *Kerygma und Dogma* XXVI (1980). 174–184.

Loofs, Friedrich. *Leitfaden zum Studium der Dogmengeschichte.* IV. Aufl. Halle: Max Niemeyer, 1906.

Lorenz, Ottokar. *Deutschlands Geschichtsquelle im Mittelalter seit der Mitte des 13. Jahrhunderts* III. Berlin: Hertz, 1887.

Lortz, Joseph. *Die Reformation in Deutschland.* 3. Aufl. Freibug i. B.: Herder, 1949.

Lotichius, Petrus. *De Obsidione Urbis Magdeburgensis.* n. p. [1631].

Lowry, Martin. "The 'New Academy' of Aldus Manutius: A Renaissance Dream." *Bulletin of the John Rylands Library* LVIII (1975/76). 378–420.

– *The World of Aldus Manutius: Business and Scholarship in Renaissance Venice.* Ithaca, New York: Cornell University Press, 1979.

Luciani, Tomaso. *Matthia Flacio Istriano de Albona, Notizie e Documenti*. Pula: G. Seraschen, 1896.

Ludwig, Friedrich. *Repertorium Organorum Recentioris et Motetorum Vetustissimi Stili*. 2. erweiterte Auflage herausgegeben von Luther A. Ditmer and I: *Catalogue Raisonée der Quellen. Abteilung I: Handschriften in Quadrat Notation I*. Halle, 1910. New York: Institute of Medieval Music and Hildesheim, Georg Olms, 1964.

– "Über den Entstehungsort der grossen 'Notre Dame-Handschriften.'" *Studien zur Musikgeschichte: Festschrift Guido Adler zum 75. Geburtstag*. Vienna and Leipzig: Universal-Edition A. G., 1930. 45–90.

Lütge, Friedrich. *Geschichte des Jenaer Buchhandels, einschliesslich der Buchdruckereien*. Jena: Gustav Fischer, 1929.

Lutz, Heinrich. *Das römisch-deutsche Reich im politischen System Karls V*. Munich and Vienna: Oldenbourg, 1982.

Luykx, Boniface. "Essai sur les Sources de l'Ordo Missae Premontré." *Analecta Praemonstratensis* XXII–XXIII (1947). 35–90.

Mabillon, Jean. *De Liturgia Gallicana*. Paris, 1685.

M'Crie, Thomas. *History of the Progress and Suppression of the Reformation in Spain in the Sixteenth Century*. Edinburg: William Blackwood and London: T. Cadell, 1827.

McCulloch, Robert. "Gregorian Adaptation to the Augustine Mission in England." *Missiology* VI (1978). 323–334.

McLaughlin, E. Emmet. "Spiritualism and the Bible: The Case of Caspar Schwenckfeld 1498–1561." *The Mennonite Quarterly Review* LIII (1979). 282–298.

McNair, Philip M. J. "The Reformation of the Sixteenth Century in Renaissance Italy." *Religion and Humanism*. Keith Robbins (ed.). Oxford: Basil Blackwell, 1981. 149–166.

McNeill, John T. "John Foxe: Historiographer, Disciplinarian, Tolerationist." *Church History* XLIII (1974). 216–229.

Mager, Inge. "'Gott erhalte uns Philippum…' Antonius Corvin's Mahnbrief an Philipp Melanchthon wegen des Leipziger Interims." *Jahrbuch der Gesellschaft für Niedersächsische Kirchengeschichte* LXXXIV (1991). 89–103.

Maitland, Samuel. *A Review of Fox the Martyrologist's History of the Waldenses*. London: Printed for J. G. and J. Rivington, 1837.

Mancusi-Ungaro, Donna. *Dante and the Empire*. New York et al.: Peter Lang, 1987.

Mandić, Dominik. "Postanak Vlaha Nova Povijesna Istraživanja." *Rasprave i Prilozi iz Stare Hrvatscke Povijesti*. Rome: Hrvatski Povijesni Institut, 1963. 515–567.

Mangold, Wilhelm. "Luther und Melanchthon. Ein Vortrag aus dem Lutherjahr in dem Bonner Bürgerverein zur Eintracht gehalten." *Theologische Arbeiten aus dem rheinischen wissenschaftlichen Predigerverein* VII. 37–56.

Mangold, Wilhelm Julius. *Andreae Hyperii De Methodo in Conscribenda Historia Ecclesiastica Consilium*. Marburg: Typis Academicis Elwerti, 1866.

Manschrek, Clyde Leonhard. "A Critical Examination and Appraisal of the Adiaphoristic Controversy in the Life of Philipp Melanchthon." Diss., Yale University, 1948.

– "The Role of Melanchthon in the Adiaphora Controversy." ARG, XLVIII (1957). 165–182.

Marsilius of Padua. *Marsile de Padoue, Oevres Mineures, Defensor Minor, De Translatione Imperii*. Ed. Judy Collete & Jeannine Qullet [Sources d'Histoire Médiévale]. Paris: Centre National de la Recherche Scientifique, 1979.

Marcus, Johann Rudolf. *Historische Nachricht von einem zu Coswig im Jahr 1557 im Jan. angestellten Convent*. Wolfenbüttel: Joh. Christoph Meisner, 1737.

Maron, Gottfried. *Individualismus und Gemeinschaft bei Caspar von Schwenckfeld* [Beiheft zum Jahrbuch "Kirche in Osten" II]. Stuttgart: Evangelisches Verlagswerk, 1961.

Marsch, Angelika. *Bilder zur Augsburger Konfession und ihren Jubiläen* [Weißenhorn]: Anton H. Konrad Verlag [1980].

Martène, Edmond. *De Antiquis Ecclesiae Ritibus libri tres, ex variis insigniorum ecclesiarum pontificalibus, sacramentariis, missalibus, breviariis, ritualibus, seu manualibus, ordinariis seu consuetudinariis ... collecti atque exornate ... Edito seconda ... tertim ultra partem acuta, etc.* [Tomus quartus, continens libros quinque de monarchorum ribitus]. 4 Tom. Rouen, 1700–1702; Antwerp, 1736–1738; Basano, 1788; Hildesheim: G. Olms, 1967.

Martin, John. *Venice's Hidden Enemies. Italian Heretics in a Renaissance City*. Berkeley, Los Angeles and London: University of California Press, 1993.

Martini, Johann. *Die Waldenser und die hussistische Reformation*. Vienna and Leipzig: Heinrich Kirsch, 1910.

Massner, Joachim. *Kirchliche Überlieferung und Autorität im Flaciuskreis* [Arbeiten zur Geschichte und Theologie des Luthertums 14]. Berlin and Hamburg: Lutherisches Verlagshaus, 1964.

Matešić, Josip (ed.). *Matthias Flacius Illyricus – Leben & Werk. Internationales Symposium, Mannheim, Febrar 1991* [Südosteuropa-Studien 53]. Munich: Südosteruopa-Gesellschaft, 1993.

Matthes, Karl. *Philipp Melanchthon. Sein Leben und Wirken aus den Quellen dragestellt*. Altenburg: Julius Helbig, 1841. Zweite vermehrte Ausgabe. Altenburg: Helbig, 1846.

Maurenbrecher, Wilhelm. "Kurfürst Moritz von Sachsen." *Studien und Skizzen zur Geschichte der Reformation*. Leipzig: Wilhelm Grunow, 1874.

Maurer, Wilhelm. Review of Haikola, *Gesetz und Evangelium*. ARG, XLV (1954). 121–123.

– "Melanchthon als Humanist." Walter Ellinger (ed.). *Philipp Melanchthon. Forschungsbericht von Vierhunderten Widerkehr seines Todestages dargeboten in Wittenberg, 1560*. Göttingen: Vandenhoeck & Ruprecht, 1961. 116–132.

May, Clifford D. "Biden and the Annals..." *New York Times*. September 21th, 1987.

Mayer, Thomas F. "Starkey and Melanchthon on Adiaphora: A Critique of W. Gordon Zeeveld." *Sixteenth Century Journal* XI (1980). 39–49.

   – *Thomas Starkey and the Commonweal: Humanist Politics and Religion in the Reign of Henry VIII.* Cambridge et al.: Cambridge University Press, 1989.

Mecenseffy, Grete. *Evangelische Lehrer an der Universität Wien.* Graz, Vienna and Cologne: Hermann Böhlaus Nachfolger, 1967.

Meier, Ludger. "Zur Frage nach dem Verfasser der Confutatio Primatus Papae." *Scholastik, Vierteljahrschrift für Theologie und Philosophie* XI (1936). 539–562.

Meister, Aloys. *Gebhardts Handbuch der Deutschen Geschichte.* 6. Aufl. 2. Bd. Stuttgart, Berlin and Leipzig: Union Deutscher Verlagsgesellschaft, 1923.

Meinhold, Peter. *Geschichte der Kirchlichen Historiographie* I. Munich: Karl Albert, 1967.

   – *Philip Melanchthon, Lehrer der Kirche.* Berlin: Lutherisches Verlagshaus, 1960.

Meissburger, Gerard. *Grundlagen zu Verständnis der deutschen Mönchsdichtung im 11. und 12. Jahrhundert.* Munich: Wilhelm Fink Verlag, 1970.

Melanchton, Philipp. *Melanchthon in English.* Ed. Lowell C. Green. St. Louis: Center for Reformation Research, 1982.

   – *A Melanchthon Reader.* Ed. Ralph Keen. New York et al.: Peter Lang, 1988.

Melhausen, Joachim (ed.). *Das Augsburger Interim von 1548* [Texte zur Geschichte der evanglischen Theologie 3]. Neukirchen-Vluyn: Neukirchener Verlag, 1970.

Menagé, Gilles. *Anti-Baillet ou Critique du Livre de M. Baillet Intitulé Jugement des Savans* II. The Hague: Estinenne Foulque and Louis van Dole, 1688.

Mencik, Ferdinand. "Caspar Nydbruck's Verhältnis zu den Calixtern in Böhmen." JGGPO, XVIII (1897). 48–55

Mentz, Georg. *Handschriften der Reformationszeit.* Bonn: A. Marcus and E. Weber, 1912.

   – *Johann Friedrich der Großmütige (1503–1554)* III. Jena: Gustav Fischer, 1908.

Merkel, Friedemann. *Geschichte der evanglischen Bekenntnisses in Baden von der Reformation bis zur Union.* Karlsruhe: Verlag Evangelischer Presseverband, 1960.

Meunier, F. M. *Essai sur la vie et les ouvrages de Nicole Oresme.* Paris, 1557.

Meyer, Otto. "Reims und Rom unter Gregory VII (Analecta Centuriatoria I)." *Zeitschrift der Savigny-Stiftung für Rechtsgeschichte, Kanonistische Abteilung* XXVIII (1939). 135–143.

Milchsack, Gustav. "Faustbuch und Faustsage." *Gesammelte Aufsätze über Buchkunst und Buchdrucke, Doppeldrucke, Faustbuch und Faustsage, sowie über neue Handschriften von Tischreden Luthers und Dicta Melanchthonis.* Wolfenbüttel: In Kommission bei Julius Zwißlers Verlag, 1922. 114–152.

   – *Hymni et Sequentiae cum Compluris aliis et Latinis et Gallicis necnon Theotiscis carminibus medio aevo compositis Quae ex libris Impressis et ex codicibus manuscriptis Saeculorum a IX usque ad XVI partim post M. Flacii Illyrici curas congessit variisque lectionibus illustravit, et nunc primum in lucem proditi, parts prior.* [all]. Hallis Saxonum: Maximilian Niemaher, 1888.

Milde, Wolfgang. "The Library at Wolfenbüttel from 1550 to 1618." *Modern Language Review* LXVI (1971). 101–112.

Milosz, Czeslow. *The History of Polish Literatur*. London: Macmillan, 1969.

Mirbt, Carl. *Quellen zur Geschichte des Papsttums und des römischen Katholizismus* I. 6th ed. rev. by Kurt Aland. Tübingen: J. C. B. Mohr (Paul Siebeck), 1967.

Mirković, Mijo. *Flacius*. Zagreb: Hrvatska naklada, 1938.

– *Matija Vlačić*. Belgrade: Nolit, 1957.

– *Matija Vlačić Ilirik*. Zagreb: Jugoslavenska Akademija znanosti i umjetnosti, 1960. Revised edition in 2 volumes, Josip Bratulić (ed.): Paula and Rijeka, 1980.

Mittler, Elmar (ed.). *Bibliotheca Palatina. Katalog zur Ausstellung*. Heidelberg: Braus (1986).

Mix, Gustav. "Luther und Melanchton in ihrer gegenseitigen Beurteilung." *Theologische Studien und Kritiken* I (1901). 459–521.

Modrzewski, Andrzej [Andreas Fricius Modrevius]. *Opera Omnia*. Ed. Casimirus Kumaniecki. Warsaw: Pastwowy Instytut Waydawiczy [Academia Scientarum Polona], 1955.

Moeller, Bernd. *Reichsstadt und Reformation* [Schriften des Vereins für Reformationsgeschichte 100]. Gütersloh: Mohn, 1962.

Möller, Wilhelm. *Andreas Osiander, Leben und ausgewählte Schriften* [Leben und ausgewählte Schriften der Väter und Begründer der Lutherischen Kirche V]. Elberfeld: R. L. Friderich, 1870.

Moldaenke, Günter. *Schriftverständnis und Schriftdeutung im Zeitalter der Reformation. Teil I. Matthias Flacius Illyricus*. Stuttgart: W. Kohlhammer, 1936.

Mollenhauer, Karl. "Eine Berufung Georgs von Venedig nach Jena." Sonderdruck. *Altpreussische Forschungen* VIII (1931). 129–132.

Molnar, Amedeo. "Bekenntnisse der böhmischen Reformation." JGGPO, XCVI (1980). 310–332; Reprint, Martin Stohr (ed.). *Die erste Reformation* [Arnoldshainer Texte 36]. Frankfurt am Main: Haag & Herchen, 1987. 35–57.

– and Romolo Cagna (eds.). *Confessio Taboritarum*. Rome: Nella Sede Dell' Istituto Palazzo Borromini, 1983.

Moltmann, Jürgen, *Christoph Pezel (1539–1604) und der Calvinismus in Bremen*. Bremen: Verlag Einkehr, 1958.

Mosellanus, Petrus. *Epistolae Petri Mosellani ... aliorumque virorum doctorum seculi XVI pleramque partem ad Julium Plugium, ipsiusque Julii Pflugi nondum editae*. Ed. Christian G. Müller. Leipzig: Barth, 1802.

Mozley, James Frederic. *John Foxe and His Book*. London: SPCK and New York: Macmillan, 1948. Reprint, New York: Octagon Books, 1970.

Müller, Georg. "Quellenstudien zur Geschichte der sächsischen Hofprediger." III: Daniel Greiser, Superintendent zu Dresden und Hofprediger des Kurfürsten August." *Zeitschrift für Kirchliche Wissenschaft und Kirchliches Leben* VIII (1887). 180–197.

Müller, Gerhard. "Zum Verständnis Schwenckfelds." *Festgabe Karl Müller*. Tübingen: J. C. B. Mohr (Paul Siebeck), 1922. 145–170.

Mueller, Joseph T. *Geschichte der böhmischen Brüder*. 3 vols. Herrnhut: Verlag der Missionsbuchhandlung, 1922–1931.

— "Zur Geschichte des Interims." *Jahrbuch für Brandenburgischen Kirchengeschichte* V (1908). 51–171.

Müller, Otfried. "Schriften von und gegen Julius Pflug bis zu seiner Reise nach Trient 1554." Erwin Iserloh und Konrad Repgen (eds.). *Reformata Reformanda* II. Münster in Westphalia. Aschendorf, 1965. 29–69.

Munier, Charles. *Concilia Africae a. 345 – a.525* [Corpus Christianorum, Series Latina CCLIX]. Turnholt: Brepol, 1974.

Murko, Matthias. *Die Bedeutung der Reformation und Gegenreformation für das geistige Leben der Südslaven*. Prague: Ceska Grafica and Heidelberg: Winter, 1927.

Nacinovich, Ermano (Istriano). *Flacio. Studio Biografico Storico*. Fiume [Rijeka]: Emidio Mohovich, 1866.

Nardi, Bruno. *Saggi sulla Cultura Veneta del Quattro e cinquecento a cura di Paulo Muzzantini* [Medioevo e umanesimo 12]. Padua: Editorice Antenore, 1971.

Nauert, Charles G. Jr. "Humanists, Scientists and Pliny: Changing Approaches to a Classical Author." *American Historical Review* LXXXIV (1979). 72–85.

Naujoks, Eberhard (ed.). *Kaiser Karl und die Zunftverfassung. Ausgewählte Aktenstücke zu den Verfassungsänderungen in den Oberdeutschen Reichsstädten (1547–1556)*. Stuttgart: W. Kohlhammer, 1985.

Neudecker, Christian Gotthold. *Die handschriftliche Geschichte Ratzeberger's über Luther und seine Zeit*. Jena: Friedrich Mauke, 1850.

— *Neue Beiträge zur Geschichte der Reformation*. 2. vols. in 1. Leipzig, 1841.

Neuser, W. H. *Luther und Melanchthon; Einheit im Gegensatz*. Munich: Christian Kaiser, 1961.

— Review of Scheible, *Entstehung. Theologische Literaturzeitung* XCIII (1968). 126.

Neuss, Elmar and J. V. Pollet. *Pflugiana. Studien über Julius Pflug (1499–1564)*. Münster: Aschendorf, 1990.

New, John F. H. "The Whitgift-Cartwright Controversy." ARG, LIX (1968). 203–211.

Niceron, Jean Pierre. *Mémoires pour servir a l'histoire des hommes illustres dans la république des lettres* XXIV. Paris: Briasson, 1733. 1–25.

Nickson, Margaret. "The 'Pseudo-Reinerus' Treatise. The Final Stage of a Thirteenth Century Work on Heresy from the Diocese of Passau." *Archives d'histoire doctrinale et littéraire du Moyen Age* XLII (1967). 255–314.

Niemöller, Joseph. "Matthias Flacius und der Flacianische Geist in der älteren protestantischen Kirchenhistorie." *Zeitschrift für katholische Theologie* XII (1888). 75–115.

Nigg, Walter. *Die Kirchengeschichtsschreibung. Grundzüge ihrer historischen Entwicklung*. Munich: Beck, 1934.

Nürenberger, A. "Die Bonifatiuslitteratur der Magdeburger Centuriatoren." *Neues Archiv der Gesellschaft für ältere deutsche Geschichtskunde* XI (1886). 9–41.

O'Day, Rosemary. *The Debate on the English Reformation*. London and New York: Methuen, 1986.

Odenthal, Andreas. "Ein Formular des 'Rheinischen Messordo' aus St. Aposteln in Köln." *Archiv für Liturgiewissenschaft* XXXIV (1992). 333–344.

Odložlik, Otakar. "Two Reformation Leaders of the Unitas Fratrum." *Church History* IX (1940). 253–263.

Oelke, Harry. *Die Konfessionsbildung des 16. Jahrhunderts im Spiegel Illustrierter Flugblätter*. Berlin and New York: de Gruyter, 1992.

Offele, Wolfgang. *Ein Katechismus im Dienste der Glaubenseinheit. Julius Pflugs "Institutio Christiani Hominis" als katechetischer Beitrag zur Interkonfessionellen Begegnung*. Essen: Ludgerus-Verlag Hubert Wingen, 1965.

Oliphant, Margaret. *The Makers of Venice*. London: MacMillan and Co., 1888. Reprint, New York: AMS Press, 1972.

Olson, Oliver K. "Der Bücherdieb Flacius. Geschichte eines Rufmords." *Wolfenbütteler Beiträge* IV (1981). 111–145.

– "Flacius Illyricus als Liturgiker." *Jahrbuch für Liturgik und Hymonologie* XII (1967). 45–69.

– *The "Missa Illyrica" and the Liturgical Thought of Flacius Illyricus*. Diss., Hamburg, 1966.

– "Theology of Revolution: Magdeburg 1550–1551." *Sixteenth Century Journal* III (1972). 56–74.

Orelli, Conrad von. "Johann Pfeffinger." RE3, 15, 153.

Ortner, Franz. *Reformation, katholische Reformation und Gegenreformation im Erzstift Salzburg*. Salzburg: Pustet, 1981.

Ostermann, Theodor. *Dante in Deutschland: Bibliographie der Deutschen Dante-Literatur 1416–1927*. Heidelberg: Carl Winter, 1919.

Oswald, Stefan. *Die Inquisition, die Lebenden und die Toten. Venedigs Deutsche Protestanten*. Sigmaringen: Thorbecker Verlag, 1989.

Ovid Naso, Publius. *Metamorphoses*. With an English translation by Frank Justus Miller. Cambridge, Mass: Harvard University Press, 1966–1969.

Parks, George B. "The Pier Luigi Farnese Scandal: An English Report." *Renaissance News* XV (1962). 193–200.

– "William Barker, Tudor Translator." *Papers of the Bibliographical Society of America* LI (1957). 126–140.

Partner, Peter. *Renaissance Rome 1550–1559*. Berkeley: University of California Press, 1976.

Paschini, Pio. *Eresia e riforma cattolica al confine orientale dell' Italia*. Rome: Lateranum, 1951.

– *Pier Paulo Vergerio il giovane e la sua Apostasia: un Episodio della lotte religiose nel cinquecento*. Rome: Scuola typografica Pio X, 1925.

– *Venezia e l'inquisitione romana da Giulio III a Pio IV*. Padua: Editrice Antenore, 1959.

Passavant, Johann David. *Le Pientre-Graveur*. 6 vols. Leipzig, 1860–1864.

Pastor, Ludwig von. *Geschichte Pauls III (1534–1549)*. Freiburg i. B.: Herder, 1928.

– *Die Kirchliche Reunionsbestrebungen während der Regierung Karls V aus den Quellen dargestellt*. Freiburg: Herder, 1879.

Patschovsky, Alexander (ed.). *Der Passauer Anonymus. Ein Sammelwerk über Ketzer, Juden, Antichrist aus der Mitte des 13. Jahrhunderts* [Schriften der Monumenta Germanicae Historica 22]. Stuttgart: Hiersemann, 1968.

– *Die Anfänge einer ständigen Inquisition in Böhmen. Ein Prager Inquisitoren-Handbuch aus der ersten Hälfte des 14. Jahrhunderts* [Beiträge zur Geschichte und Quellenkunde des Mittelalters 3]. Berlin and New York: de Gruyter, 1975.

Pattison, Mark. *Isaac Casaubon, 1559–1614*. 2nd ed. Oxford: Clarendon Press, 1892.

Patze, Hans and Walter Schlesinger (eds.). *Geschichte Thüringens. III: Das Zeitalter des Humanismus und der Reformation*. Cologne: Böhlau Veralg, 1967.

– Patze, Hans. "Landesgeschichtsschreibung in Thüringen." *Jahrbuch für die Geschichte Mittel- und Ostdeutschlands* XVI/XVII (1968). 95–168.

Paul, Hermann. *Grundriß der Germanischen Philologie*. Straßburg: Karl J. Tuebner, 1893.

Paullinus, Christian Franziscus. *Historia Isenacensis, variis litteris et bullis Caesarum, Pontificum, Principum, Aliorumque, nunquam antea visis, Illustrata et confirmata, necnon multis memorabilis gratisque curiositatibus congressa*. Frankfurt a. M.: Bauer, 1698.

Paulus, Nikolaus. *Die deutschen Dominikaner im Kampf gegen Luther (1518–1563)* [Erläuterungen und Ergänzungen zu Janssens Geschichte des deutschen Volkes IV]. Freiburg i. B.: Herder, 1903.

– "Konrad Kling, ein Erfurter Domprediger des 16. Jahrhunderts." *Der Katholik. Zeitschrift für katholische Wissenschaft und Kirchliches Leben* IX (1894). 146 ff.

– "Michael Helding, Ein Prediger und Bischoff des 16. Jahrhunderts." *Der Katholik* LXXIV (1894). 410–430, 481–502.

Perels, Ernst. "Ein erhaltener Brief aus der verschollenen Fuldaer Briefsammlung." Neues Archiv der Gesellschaft für ältere deutsche Geschichtskunde XXX (1905). 145–147.

Pertusi, Agostino. "Giovanni Battista Egnacio (Cipelli) e Ludovico tuberone (Crijeva) tra i primi Storici occidentali del Populo Turko (vi assunto)." *Venezia e Ungheria nel Rinascimento*. Ed. Vittore Branca. Florence: Leo B. Olschoki, 1973, 479–487.

Peter, Hermann (ed.). *Jahresbericht der Fürsten- und Landesschule St. Afra in Meissen*, 1892.

Petersen, Peter. *Geschichte der aristotelischen Philosophie im Protestantischen Deutschland*. Leipzig: Felix Meiner, 1921. Reprint, Stuttgart and Bad Cannstatt: Fromman, 1964.

Petrarch, Francesco. *Petrach's Book Without a Name: A Translation of the Liber Sine Nomine*. Tr. Norman P. Zacour. Toronto: the Pontifical Institute of Medieval Studies, 1973.

Peucer, Casper. "Peuceri Brieff vom Flacischen Vergleich." FS, 1726. 361–363.

Pfeiffer, David. *Lipsia, seu Originum Lipsiensium Libri IV*. Leipzig and Martisburg, 1689; Frankfurt, 1750.

Pflanz, Hans-Henning. *Johan Stigel als Theologe (1515–1562)*. Ohlau in Schlesien: Dr. Hermann Schreiber, 1848; Eschenhagen, 1936.

– Review of Hans Christoph von Hase. *Die Gestalt der Kirche Luthers*. *Theologische Literaturzeitung* LXVI (1941). 109–111.

Pfeilschifter, Georg (ed.). *Acta Reformationis Catholicae Ecclesiam Germaniae concernantia saeculi XVI. Die Reformverhandlungen des deutschen Episkopats von 1520 bis 1570* V. 1538–1548. Regensburg: Verlag Friedrich Pustet, 1973.

Pfleger, Luzian. "Wilhelm Eisengrein, ein Gegner des Flacius Illyricus." *Historisches Jahrbuch der Görres-Gesellschaft* XXV (1904). 774–792.

Pflug, Julius. *Julius Pflug: Correspondance*. Ed. Jaques V. Pollet. 5 vols. Leiden: E. J. Brill, 1969–1982.

Piccolomini, Paolo (ed.). "Due Lettere inedite di Bernardino Ochino." *Archivio della Società Romana di Storia Patria* XXVIII (1905). 210–207.

Piepho, Lee. "Mantuan's Ecologues in the English Reformation." *Sixteenth Century Journal* XXV (1994). 623–632.

Pierce, Joanne. "Sacerdotal Spirituality at Mass: Text and Study of the Prayerbook of Sigbert of Minden (1022–1036)." Diss.: University of Notre Dame, 1988.

Piper, Ferdinand. *Einleitung in die Monumentale Theologie*. Gotha: Rud. Basser, 1876.

Piper, Paul. *Otfrids Evangelienbuch*. Paderborn: Ferdinand Schoenigh, 1878.

Pistorius, Johannes. *Rerum Germanicarum Veteres iam primum publicati Scriptores VI*. Frankfurt: Clausius Marinus & haeredes Iohannis Aubrii, 1607.

Piur, Paul. *Petrarcas "Buch Ohne Name" und die päpstliche Kurie: ein Beitrag zur Geistesgeschichte der frühen Renaissance*. Halle/Saale: Max Niemeyer, 1925.

Planck, Gottlieb Jakob. *Geschichte der Entstehung, der Veränderung, und der Bildung unsers protestantischen Lehrbegriffs von Anfang der Reformation bis zu der Einführung der Concordienformel*. 6 vols. in 8. Leipzig: S. L. Crusius, 1791–1800.

Plitt, G. "Matthias Flacius." RE2, Bd. IV, 1897. 563–567.

Plitt, Hermann. "Über die Lehreweise der böhmischen Brüder in Betriff der Rechtfertigung durch den Glauben und der Werke des Glaubens." *Theologische Studien und Kritiken* XLI (1868). 581–629.

Polenz, Gottlob von. *Geschichte des französischen Calvinismus* III. Gotha: Friedrich Andreas Perthes, 1860

Pollet, J. V. "La Diète d'Augsbourg 1547/48 et L'Intérim d'Après les Publications Récents." *Bibliothèque d'Humanisme et Renaissance* XXXVI (1974). 637–653.

Polmann Pontien. *L'Élément historique dans la controverse religieuse du XVIe Siècle* [Universitas Catholica Lovaniensis: Dissertationes ad gradum magistri in Facultate theologica consequendum conscriptqe, Series II, Tomus 23]. Gembloux: J. Duculot, 1932 [=Nova Antologia LV, fasc. 1182. 16 June 1921. 297–319].

– "Flacius Illyricus, Historien de l'Église." *Revue d'histoire Ecclésiastique* XXVII (1931). 27–73.

Pomarius, Elias. *Warhafftige, Grundtliche unnd Eygentliche Beschreibung der uberjähren Belagerung der kayserlichen freyen Reichstadt Magdeburgk.* Magdeburg: Johann Frankken, 1622.

Postel, Guillaume. *Apologies et Rétractiones. Manuscripts inédits publiés avec une introduction et notes par François Secret* [Bibliotheca humanistica et reformatorica 9]. Nieuwkoop: de Graaf, 1972.

Possevino, Antonio. *Bibliotheca Selecta.* Cologne, 1607.

Potthast, August. *Wegweiser durch die Geschichtswerke des Europäischen Mittelalters bis 1500.* 2. Aufl. Bd. II. Berlin: W. Weber, 1896.

Preger, Wilhelm. "Flacius von den kirchlichen Mitteldingen." *Zeitschrift für Protestantismus und Kirche* XXXV (1858). 165–186.

– *Matthias Flacius Illyricus und seine Zeit.* 2 vols. Erlangen: Theodor Blässing, 1859–61. = Hildesheim: Georg Olms & Nieukoop: B. de Graaf, 1964.

Preuss, Hans. *Luther der Prophet.* Gütersloh: Bertelsmann, 1933.

Primus, John Henry. *The Vestments Controversy. A Study of the Earliest Tensions within the Church of England in the Reigns of Edward VI and Elizabeth.* Kampen: J. H. Kok, 1960.

Raabe, Wilhelm. *Unseres Herrgotts Kanzlei: Eine Erzählung* [Sämtliche Werke IV]. Göttingen: Vandenhoeck und Ruprecht, 1969.

Rabe, Horst. *Reichsbund und Interim. Die Verfassungs- und Religionspolitik Karls V. und der Reichstag von Augsburg 1547/48.* Cologne and Vienna: Böhlaus, 1971.

Rabil, Albert Jr. *Renaissance Humanism. Foundations, Forms and Legacy.* Philadelphia: University of Pennsylvania Press, 1988.

Radtke, W. "Das Lüneburger Bekenntnis (1549) gegen das Augsburger Interim." *Zeitschrift der Gesellschaft für niedersächsische Kirchengeschichte* XLIV (1939). 40–63.

Rambach, Friedrich Eberhard. *Johan Peter Niceron's Nachrichten* 21. Halle: Christoph Peter Frankens, 1761. 153.

Ranke, Leopold von. *Deutsche Geschichte im Zeitalter der Reformation.* 7. Aufl. Wiesbaden and Berlin: Emil Vollmer, 1857. Cologne: Phaidon, 1970.

– *The Popes of Rome.* 4th ed. Vol. I. London: John Murray, 1866.

Rashdall, Hastings. *The Universities of Europe in the Middle Ages.* New ed. F. H. Powicke and A. B. Meden. I. Oxford: Clarendon, 1936.

Ratschow, C. H. *Lutherische Dogmatik zwischen Reformation und Aufklärung* I. Gütersloh: Gütersloher Verlagshaus Gerd Mohn, 1964.

Rechow, Fritz. *die Musiktraktate des Anonymus* IV [Beihefte zum Archiv für Musikwissenschaft, Bd. IV–V]. 2 vols. Wiesbaden: Steiner, 1967.

Reeves, Marjorie. *The Influence of Prophecy in the later Middle Ages: A Study of Joachimism.* Oxford: Clarendon Press, 1969.

Rehtmayer, Philip Julius. *Der berühmte Stadt Braunschweig Kirchen-Historie* III. Braunschweig: Johann Georg Zillingern, 1710.

Reichert, Ernst Otto. "Amsdorff und das Interim: Erstausgabe seiner Schriften zum Interim mit Kommentar und historischer Einleitung." Diss., Halle/Saale, 1955.

– "'In Tante Ecclesiarum Mestitia...' Eine Antwort Niklaus von Amsdorffs an Philip Melanchthon." ZKG, LXXVIII (1967). 253–270.

Ressor, Margaret. "The 'Indifferents' in the Old and Middle Stoa." *Transactions and Proceedings of the American Philosophical Association* (1951). 102–111.

Reusch, Fr. Heinrich. *Der Index der verbotenen Bücher* I. Bonn: Max Cohen & Sohn, 1883.

– *Die Indices Librorum Prohibitorum des sechzehnten Jahrhunderts.* Tübingen, 1886; Reprint, Nieuwkoop: de Graaf, 1961.

Rhenanus, Beatus. *Beati Rhenani Praefatio in Missam Chrysostomi à Leone Tusco, anno Domini 1070 versam, ad Joannem Hoffmeister, Priorem Augustinensem.* Graz: Akademische Druck- und Verlagsanstalt, 1957.

Richard, James William. *Philipp Melanchthon. The Protestant Preceptor of Germany 1497– 1560.* New York: Putnam, 1898. Reprint, New York: Bert Franklin Reprints, 1902.

Richter, Aemelius Ludwig. *Die Evangelischen Kirchenordnungen des 16. Jahrhunderts.* 2 vols. Weimar: Verlag des Landes-Industriecomptoirs, 1846.

Rigler, Jakob. "Über die Sprache der Slovenischen Protestantischen Schriftsteller des 16. Jahrhunderts." *Abhandlungen über die Slowenische Reformation.* Munich: Rudolf Trofenik, 1968. 65–89.

Ringler, William A. Jr. "Beware the Cat and the Beginnings of English Fiction." *Novel* XII (1979). 113–126.

Ritschl, Albrecht. *A Critial History of the Doctrine of Justification and Reconciliation.* Edinburgh: Edmonston & Douglas, 1872.

– "Die Entstehung der lutherischen Kirche." ZKG (1877). 51–110 [= Gesammelte Aufsätze, 1898. 170 ff.].

– *Theology and Metaphysik. Zur Verständigung und Abwehr.* Bonn: Adolph Marcus, 1881. 52 ff.

Ritschl, Otto. *Dogmengeschichte des Protestantismus.* 4 vols. I & II. Leipzig: Hinrichs, 1908–1927; II & V. Göttingen: Vandenhoeck und Rupreccht, 1924–1927.

Ritter, Johann Balthasar. *M. Matthiae Flacii, Illyrici, Ehemahls berümt- und gelährten Theologi in Teutschland Leben und Tod: Aus theils bekannt – theils unbekannten Urkunden, Schrifften und Brieffen anderer und seiner selbst, zur Erläuterung der Kirchen-Historie des XVI. Seculi mit sonderbarem Fleiß beschrieben von Johann Balthasar Ritter. 2. vermehret und verbesserte Auflage.* Frankfurt and Leipzig: Joh. Conrad Maximilian Ziegler, 1725.

Robertson, William. *The History of the Reign of the Emperor Charles V*, III. London: George Routledge, 1857. Philadelphia: Lippincott, 1763.

Robinson, Hastings (ed.). *Original Letters Relative to the English Reformation.* Cambridge: Cambridge University Press, 1847.

Rockinger, Ludwig. *Die Pflege der Geschichte durch die Wittelsbacher.* Munich: Im Verlage der Königlichen Akademie, 1880.

Roddewig, Marcella. "Flacius, Vergerius, Foxe, Wolfius, Mornay und der erste Übersetzungsversuch aus dem Paradiso vom Jahre 1573." *Deutsches Dante Jahrbuch* XLIV/XLV (1957). 100 – 149.

— "Matthia Flacio Illirico: Fortuna d'un Interprete Dantesco nei Paesi del Nord." *Dante i Slavenski Svijet.* Frano Cale (ed.). Zagreb: Jugoslavenska Akademija Znanosti i Umjetnosti, 1984. 553–559.

— "Matija Vlačići Illirik i Petar Pavao Vergerije i Recapzije Dantea u Sjevernoj Evropi." *Dometi*, 1984. 57–61.

Roesner, Edward H. "The Origins of W1." *Journal of the American Musicological Society* XXIX (1976). 337–380.

— "Magnus Liber Organi." *Dictionary of the Middle Ages* VIII. New York: Joseph Strayer, 1987. 42–45.

— "The Manuscript Wolfenbüttel, Herzog August Bibliothek, 628 Helmstadiensis. A Study of its Origins and of its Eleventh Fascicle." Diss., New York Uniersity, 1974.

Rössler, Helmut & Gunther Franz. Biographisches Wörterbuch zur deutschen Geschichte. Munich: R. Oldenbourg, 1952.

Romano, Ruggerio. "Intorno a talune opere di Monsignor Giovanni Della Casa." *Tra due crisi: L'Italia del Rinascimento.* Turin: Einaudi, 1971. 169–186.

Rome, Church of. *Corpus Juris Canonici.* Editio Lipsiensis secunda; post E. A. Richteri curas ... recognovit et adnotatione critica instruxit A. Friedverg. 2 pt. Leipzig: Bernard Tauchniz, 1879–81.

– *Index Librorum Prohibitorum Innoc. XI. P.M. Jussu Editus Usque ad Annum 1681.* Prague, 1726.

Roscher, W. H. *Ausführliches Lexikon der griechischen und römischen Mythologie.* Leipzig: B. G. Teubner, 1884–1937.

Rosenstock-Heusy, Eugene. *Die europäischen Revolutionen und der Charakter der Nationen.* Stuttgart & Cologne: W. Kohlhammer, 1951.

Ross, James Bruce. "Venetian Schools and Teachers, Fourteenth to Early Sixteenth Century: A Survey and Study of Giovanni Battista Egnazio." *Renaissance Quarterly* XXIX (976). 521–566.

Roth, Friedrich W. E. *Augsburg Reformationsgeschichte IV, 1547–1555.* Munich: Theodor Ackermann, 1911.

Roth, []. "Ein Braunschweiger Theologe des 16. Jahrhunderts: Mörlin und seine Rechtfertigungslehre." *Jahrbuch der Gesellschaft für niedersächsische Kirchengeschichte* L (1951). 59–81.

Roth, William H. *Martyrs of the Reformation.* London: John Mason, 1851.

Rupp, Heinz. "Forschungen zur althochdeutschen Literatur 1945–1962." *Deutsche Vierteljahrsschrift für Literaturwissenschaft und Geistesgeschichte.* Jahrgang XXXVIII, Sonderheft. Stuttgart: J. B. Metzler, 1964. 1–67.

Rupp, Gordon. Review of Bernard J. Verkamp. *The Indifferent Mean: Adiaphorism in the English Reformation to 1554. American Historical Review* LXXXIV (1970). 1361 ff.

– "Luther and the Castle Coburg, 1530." *Bulletin of the John Rylands Library of Manchester* XLI (1978). 182–205.

Sakrausky, Oskar. "Theologische Strömungen in der Reformatorischen Literatur der Slowenen und Kroaten." *Abhandlungen über die Slowenische Reformation.* Munich: Rudolf Trofenik, 1968. 135–151.

Salig, Christian. *Vollständige Historie des Augsburgischen Confession und derselben Apologie.* 3 vols. Halle: Rengerische Buchhandlung, 1730–1735.

Sander, Hjalmar. "Zur Identifizierung Zweier Bildnisse von Lucas Cranach d. Ä." *Zeitschrift für Kunstwissenschaft* IV (1950). 35–48.

Sandor, Payr. *Fláciánus Lelkészek Magyarországban.* Pozsony, 1916.

Santosuosso, Antonio. "Books, Readers and Critics. The Case of Giovanni Della Casa, 1537–1575." *La Bibliofila* LXXIX (1977). 101–186.

– "Giovanni Della Casa and the Galateo. On Life and Success in the Late Renaissance." *Renaissance and Reformation* XI (1975). 1–13.

– "The Moderate Inquisition–Giovanni Della Casa's Venetian Nunciature, 1554–1559." *Studi Veneziani.* N. S. II (1978). 119–210.

– *Vita di Giovanni Della Casa.* Rome: Bulzoni, 1979.

Scartazzini, Giovanni Andrea. *Dante in Germania.* 2 Bde. Milan & Pisa: G. Hoepli, 1883.

Schade, Oskar. *Satiren und Pasquille aus der Reformationszeit.* Hanover: Carl Rümper, 1863.

Schäfer, Rudolf. *Philipp Melanchthons Leben aus den Quellen dargestellt.* Gütersloh: Bertelsmann, 1894.

Schamelius, Joannes Martinus. *Numburgum Literatum.* Leipzig: Lankisch Erben, 1727.

Schatzmayr, E. "Beiträge zur Geschichte des Protestantismus in Istrien und Triest II." JGGPO, XV (1894). 58–77.

Schaumkell, Ernst. *Beitrag zur Entstehungsgeschichte der Magdeburger Centurien.* Ludwigslust: Hinstorff'sche Hofbuchhandlung (Carl Kober), 1898.

Scheible, Heinz. "Der Plan der Magdeburger Zenturien und ihre ungedruckte Reformationsgeschichte." Diss., Heidelberg, 1960.

– *Die Enstehung der Magdeburger Zenturien. Ein Beitrag zur Geschichte der Methode* [Schriften des Vereins für Reformationsgeschichte 183]. Gütersloh: Gütersloher Verlagshaus, Gerd Mohn, 1966.

– "Melanchthons Auseinandersetzung mit dem Reformcatholicismus." Rolf Decot (ed.). *Vermittlungsversuche auf dem Augsburger Reichstag 1530.* Stuttgart: Franz Steiner Verlag, 1989. 68–90.

– "Philipp Melanchthon, der bedeutenste Sohn der Stadt Bretten." Alfons Schäfer. *Geschichte der Stadt Bretten von den Anfängen bis zur Zerstörung 1689.* Bretten, 1977. 257–282.

– "Melanchthons Brief an Carlowitz." ARG, LVII (1966). 102–130.

– "Philipp Melanchthon (1497–1560)." TRE, 22, 371–410.

Schelhorn, Johann Georg. *Apologia pro Pietro Paulo Vergero Episcopo Justinopolitano adversus Joannem Casam Archiepiscopum Benevantanum.* Ulm & Memmingen: Gaumiano, 1754.

– *Historische Nachricht vom Ursprung, Fortgang und Schicksale der Evangelischen Religion in den Salzburgischen Landen.* Leipzig: Berhard Christoph Breitkopf, 1732.

Schelven, A. A. van. "Die Maagdeburgse Centurien als Getuigenes van Reformatorische Samenwerking." *Niederlands Archief voor Kerkgeschiedenis.* N. S. XXXIX (1952). 1 – 18.

Schelwig, Samuel. "Concentrirte Untersuchung wegen Hulderici, Episc. August. Brieff an den Papst Nicolaum I. von verbothener Priester-Ehe." UN, 1710. 137 – 41.

Schiess, Traugott (ed.). *Heinrich Bullingers Korrespondenz mit den Graubündern* I. Nieuwkoop: B. de Graaf, 1968.

Schilling, Heinz. "The Reformation in the Hanseatic Cities." *Sixteenth Century Journal* XIV (1983). 443–456.

Schloemann, Martin. "The Special Case for Confession: Reflections on the Casus Confessionis (Dar Es Salaam 1977) in the Light of History and Systematic Theology." *The Debate on Status Confessionis. Studies in Christian Political Theology.* Geneva: Department of Studies, Lutheran World Federation, 1983. "Der besondere Bekenntnisfall. Begriffsgeschichtliche und systematische Beobachtungen zum casus confessionis vor, in und nach Daresaalam 1977." Eckehart Lorenz (ed.). *Politik als Glaubenssache?* Erlangen: Martin Luther Verlag, 1983. 48–98.

Schlüsselburg, Konrad. *Haereticorum Catalogus.* 13 vols in 10. Frankfurt am Main: Excusis typis I. Saurius: Impensis P. Kopfii, 1597–1601.

Schmaltz, Karl. *Kirchengeschichte Mecklenburgs.* 3 vols. Schwerin: Verlag Friedrich Bahn, 1935–1952. Vol. II, Berlin: Ev. Verlags Anstalt.

Schmeller, J. A. *Heliand oder die altsächsische Evangelien-Harmonie. Erste Lieferung: Text.* Munich, Stuttgart and Tübingen, 1839.

Schmid, Eduard. "Des Flacius Erbsünde-Streit." *Zeitschrift für Historische Theologie* XIX (1899). 3–78, 218–279.

Schmid, Josef. "Des Cardinals und Erzbischofs von Salzburg Matthäus Lang Verhalten zur Reformation." JGGPO, XXI (1900). 1–41, 138–158.

Schmidt, Carl. *Philipp Melanchthon: Leben und Ausgewählte Schriften.* Elberfeld: R. L. Friderichs, 1861.

Schmidt, Johann Andreas (ed.). *Introductio Sagittarianae [Caspar Sagittarius] in Historiam Ecclesiasticam.* Jena: Io. Felix Bielck, 1718.

Schmidt, Ludwig Erich. *Kurzer Grundriß der germanischen Philologie bis 1500.* II: *Literaturgeschichte.* Berlin: de Gruyter, 1971.

Schmidt, Martin. *Evangelische Kirchengeschichte Deutschlands von der Reformation bis zur Gegenwart.* Berlin, Bielefeld and Munich: Erich Schmidt, n. t.

Schmidt, Oswald Gottlob. *Georg von Anhalt des Gottseligen Leben.* Leipzig & Dresden: Justus Raumann, 1864.

Schmitthenner, Adolf. "Dante in der konfessioneller Politik des sechzehnten und siebzehnten Jahrhunderts." *Die Grenzboten* LXIII (1904). Nr. 2. 87–98.

Schneider, Friedrich. "Melanchthon's Entscheidung nach der Katastrophe von Mühlberg." *Festschrift der Universität Halle und Wittenberg,* 1952. 313–322.

Schneider, Heinrich. *Beiträge zur Geschichte der Universitätsbibliothek Helmstedt.* Helmstedt: J. C. Schmidt, 1934. 29–38.

– "Die Bibliotheksreisen des Marcus Wagner." *Zentralblatt für Bibliothekswesen* L (1933). 678–682.

Schneider, Martin. *Europäisches Waldensertum im 13. und 14. Jahrhundert.* Berin and New York: de Gruyter, 1981.

Schnorr von Carolsfeld, Franz. *Erasmus Alberus.* Dresden: L. Ehlermann, 1897.

Schönemann, C. P. C. "Umrisse zur Geschichte und Beschreibung der Wolfenbüttler Bibliothek [I]." *Serapeum* IV (1843). 81–94.

Schönstädt, Hans-Jürgen. *Antichrist, Weltheilsgeschehen und Gottes Werkzeug.* Wiesbaden: Franz Steiner Verlag, 1978.

Schöttgen, Christoph. "Das Leben Marcus Wagners, eines bekannten Thüringischen Historici und Pfarrers zu Bussleben." Johann Georg Brückner. *Sammlung verschiedener Nachrichten zu einer Beschreibung des Kirchen- und Schulenstaats im Herzogthum Gotha* I. 12. Stück. Gotha: Christian Mevius, 1757. 56–91.

Schott, Theodore (ed.). Briefwechsel zwischen Christoph, Herzog von Württemberg und Petrus Paulus Vergerius. Stuttgart: Literarischer Verein, 1875.

Schottenloher, Karl. *Flugblatt und Zeitung.* Berlin: R. C. Schmidt, 1922.

– "Handschriftenforschung und Buchdruck im XV. und XVI. Jahrhundert." *Gutenberg Jahrbuch* (1931). 73–106.

– "Handschriftenschätze zu Regensburg im Dienste der Zenturiatoren (1554–1562)." *Zentralblatt für Bibliothekswesen* XXXIV (1917). 65–82.

– *Pfalzgraf Ottheinrich und das Buch: Ein Beitrag zur Geschichte der Evangelischen Publizistik, mit Anhang: Das Reformationsschrifttum in der Palatina* [Reformationsgeschichtliche Studien und Texte 50/51]. Münster in Westphalen: Aschendorff, 1927.

– "Reichenbacher Handschriften in der Flaciusbibliothek." *Zentralblatt für Bibliothekswesen* XXXIV (1917). 71–82.

Schulte, Johann Wilhelm. *Beiträge zur Entstehungsgeschichte der Magdeburger Centurien* [Jahres-Berichte der Philomathie (Niesse) XIX]. Niesse: Graveur G. Neumann, 1877. 50–148, 224–229.

– "Zur Heliandsfrage." *Zeitschrift für deutsche Philologie* IV (1873). 49–67.

Schultz, Selina Gerhard. *Caspar von Schwenckfeld von Ossig (1489–1561).* Pennsburg, Pennsylvania: The Board of Publication of the Schwenckfelder Church, 1977.

Schumacher, Andreas. *Gelehrter Männer Briefe an die Könige in Dänemark vom Jahr 1522 bis 1633.* 3 vols. Copenhagen and Leipzig: L. H. Lillie, 1758–1759.

Schutte, Anne Jacobson. *Pier Paolo Vergerio: The Making of an Italian Reformer.* Geneva: Droz, 1977.

Schütz, Otto Frid. *De Vita Davidis Chytraei Commentorum Libri Duo Ultimi.* Hamburg: Christian Guilielmo Brancitius, 1728.

Schwarz, Eduard. "Flaciana und die Synode der Vögel." *Zeitschrift für die unierte Evangelische Kirche* (1853). 225–239, 275–290, 297–308, 314–329.

Schwarz, J. C. E. *Das erste Jahrzehnd der Universität Jena.* Jena: Friedrich Frommann, 1858.

Schwarz, Rudolf. *Johannes Calvin's Lebenswerk in Seinen Briefen* II. Tübingen: J. C. B. Mohr (Paul Siebek), 1909.

Schwartz Lausten, Martin. *Biskop Peder Palladius og Kirken (1537–1560)* [Studier i den danske reformationskirke 2]. Copenhagen: Akademisk Forlag, 1987.

– "König Christian III. von Dänemark und die deutsche Reformation. 32 Ungedruckte Briefe." ARG, LXVI (1975). 151–181.

Scott, Mariana (ed.). *The Heliand Translated from the Old Saxon* [Studies in the Germanic Language and Literature 53]. Chapel Hill: The University of North Carolina Press, 1966. Reprint, New York: AMS Press, 1979.

Scriver, Christian. *Seelen-Schatz.* Leipzig: Andreas Zeidler, 1698.

Seebaß, Gottfried. "Antichrist." IV, TRE, III, 32.

– *Das reformatorische Werk des Andreas Osiander.* Nuremberg: Verein für Bayerische Kirchengeschichte, 1976.

Seehawer, Johannes. *Zur Lehre vom Brauch des Gesetzes und zur Geschichte des späteren Antinomismus.* Rostock: Carl Bolet, 1887.

Seelenius, Johannes Henricus. *Philocalia Epistolica s. Centuria Epistolae.* Lübeck: Böckmann, 1728; Ratzeburg: Andreas Harzius, 1729.

Segl, Peter. "Die Feindbilder in der politischen Propaganda Friedrichs II. und seiner Gegner." Franz Bosbach. *Feindbilder. Die Darstellung des Gegners in der politischen Publizistik des Mittelalters und der Neuzeit* [Bayreuther Historische Kolloquien 6]. Cologne, Wiemar and Vienna: Böhlau, 1992. 41–71.

Sehling, Emil (ed.). . 1. Abt.: *Sachsen und Thüringen nebst angrenzenden Gebieten.* 1. Halbband. 1. Bd. Leipzig: O. R. Reisland, 1902. Reprint, Aalen: Scientia Verlag, 1979.

– *Die Kirchengesetzgebung unter Moritz von Sachsen (1544–1549) und Georg III. von Anhalt.* Leipzig: Deichert, 1899.

Selge, Kurt Viktor. "Ein Magdeburger Flugblatt: Flacius Illyricus und die franziskanische Sonderfrömmigkeit im Streit um das Interim." *Communio Viatorum* XXV (1932). 219–226.

Selle, Götz von. *Geschichte der Albert-Universität zu Königsberg in Preussen.* 2. Aufl. Würzburg: Holzner Verlag, 1956.

Severus, Sulpicius. *Sulpicii Severi Libri qui Supersunt* I. Ed. Carolus Halm. Vienna: apud C. Geroldi Filium Bibliopolam Academiae, 1866.

Shannat, Johannes Fridericus. *Historia Fuldensis.* Frankfurt am Main: Johann Beniamin & Andreas Henr. Hort, 1729.

Shirer, William. *The Nightmare Years, 1930–1940.* II. Toronto et al.: Bantam Books, 1984.

– *The Rise and Fall of the Third Reich.* New York: Simon & Schuster, 1960.

Shuger, Deborah. *Sacred Rhetoric. The Christian Style in the English Renaissance.* Princeton: Princeton University Press, 1988.

Sicherl, Martin. "Handschriftliche Vorlagen der Editio Princeps des Aristoteles." *Abhandlungen der Geistes- und Sozialwissenschaftlichen Reihe, Akademie der Wissenschaften und der Literatur, Mainz.* Wiesbaden: Steiner, (1976).

Siemon-Netto, Uwe. *Luther als Wegbereiter Hitlers? Zur Geschichte eines Vorurteils.* Gütersloh: Gütersloher Verlagshuas, 1993; English translation: *The Fabricated Luther. The Rise and Fall of the Shirer Myth.* St. Louis: Concordia, 1995.

Sillem, Carl Hieronymus Wilhelm (ed.). *Briefsammlung des Hamburgischen Superintendenten Joachim Westphal aus den Jahren 1530 bis 1575.* Hamburg: Lucas Gräfe & Sillem, 2 vols. 1903.

Simon, Matthias. *Evangelische Kirchengeschichte Bayerns.* Nuremberg: Selbstverlag des Vefassers, 1952.

Sinapius, Johannes *Schlesischer Curiositäten* I. Leipzig: Auf Verlag des Authoris, gedruckt in der Fleischerischen Druckerey, 1720.

Skalweit, Stephan (ed.). "'Die Affaire des Placards' und ihr reformationsgeschichtlicher Hintergrund." Stephan Skalweit. *Gestalten und Probleme der frühen Neuzeit. Ausgewählte Aufsätze.* Berlin: Duncker & Humblot, 1987. 44–63.

– *Reich und Reformation.* Berlin: Propylaen, 1967.

Skinner, Quentin. "The Origins of the Calvinist Theory of Revolution." Barbara C. Malument (ed.). *After the Reformation. Essays in Honor of J. H. Hexter.* Manchester: Manchester University Press, 1980. 309–330

Smolinsky, Heribert. "Michael Helding." Erwin Iserloh (ed.). *Katholische Theologen der Reformationszeit* II [Katholisches Leben und Kirchenreform im Zeitalter der Glaubensspaltung, Heft 45]. Münster: Aschendorf, 1985. 124–136.

Spangenberg, Cyriakus. *Der Briefwechsel des M. Cyriacus Spangenberg. Briefe von 1550–1584.* Ed. Heinrich Rembe. Dresden: Heinrich J. Naumann, 1887.

– *Hennebergische Chronika d. uralten Grafen zu Henneberg.* Meinigen: Griesbach, 1768.

Spieker, Christian Wilhelm. "Beiträge zur Geschichte des Augsburger Interims, meistens aus dem Königlichen geheimen Staats- und Kabinetts-Archiv zu Berlin." *Zeitschrift für Historische Theologie* XXI (1851). 345–397.

Spieß, Werner. *Geschichte der Stadt Braunschweig im Nachmittelalter, von Ausgang des Mittelatlers bis zum Ende der Stadtfreiheit (1491–1671).* I. Braunschweig: Waisenhaus, 1966.

Spitta, Friedrich. *Bekenntnisschriften des Herzogs Albrecht von Preussen.* Leipzig: M. Heinsius Nachfolger, 1903.

Stancovich, Pietro. *Biografia degli Uomini Distinti dell' Istria* I. Trieste: Gio. Marenigh, 1828.

Steiger, Johann Anselm. "Das *verbum externum* in der Seelsorge-Theologie des Spiritualisten Caspar Schwenckfeld von Ossig." *Neue Zeitschrift für Systematischen Theologie und Religionsphilsophie* XXXV (1993). 133–149.

Steinlein, [|]. "Kritische Bemerkungen zur neuesten katholischen Lutherbiographien (Schluß)." *Neue Kirchliche Zeitschrift* XII (1911). 503–549.

Steinmann, Martin. *Johannes Oporinus.* Basel and Stuttgart: Helbing & Lichtenhahn, 1967.

Stella, Aldo. "Utopie e velleità insurrezionali dei filoprotestanti italiani (1545–1547)." *Bibliothèque d'Humanisme et Renaissance* XXVII (1965). 132–182.

Stephan, Horst. *Luther in den Wandlungen seiner Kirche* [Studien zur Geschichte des neueren Protestantismus I]. Giessen: Töpelmann, 1907.

Stöckl, Günter. *Die deutsch-slavische Südostgrenze des Reiches im 16. Jahrhundert.* Breslau: Priebatschs Buchhandlung, 1940.

Stopp, F. J. "The Early German Broadsheet and Related Ephemera: A Bibliographic Survey." *The Transactions of the Cambridge Bibliographical Society* V, 1970. 81–89.

– "Reformation Satire in Germany." *Oxford German Studies* 3. Oxford: Clarendon Press, 1968. 53–68.

Strauß, Walter Leopold. *The German Single-Leaf Woodcut, 1500–1600.* 3 vols. New York: Abaris Books Inc. 1975.

Strecker, Karl. *Die Apokalypse des Golias* [Texte zur Kulturgeschichte des Mittelalters 5]. Rome: W. Regensburg, 1928.

– "Quellen des Flacius Illyricus." *Zeitchrift für deutsches Altertum und deutsche Literatur* LXVI (1929). 65–67.

Strobel, Georg Theodor. *D. Matthaei Ratzebergers geheime Geschichte von den Chur- und Sächsische Höfen und den Religions-Streitigkeiten seiner Zeit.* Altdorf: Lorenz Schüpfel, 1774

– *Die Ehre Melanchthons gerettet wider die ungegründete Beschuldigungen Herrn Prof. Hausens.* Altdorf: John Paul Meyer, 1775.

– *Miscellaneen Literarischen Inhalts.* Sammlung 1–6. Nuremberg: Johann Jakob Bauer, 1778–1782.

– "Nachricht von Michael Stiefels Leben und Schriften." *Neue Beiträge zur Literatur besonders des sechzehnten Jahrhunderts.* Bd. I. Stück I. 73.

– *Neue Beiträge zur Literatur besonders des sechzehnten Jahrhunderts.* Bde. 1–5. Nuremberg and Altdorf: Monath & Kußler, 1790–1794.

Struve, Burckard Gotthilf. *Acta Literaria.* Jena: Johannes Bielckius, 1706. Reprint, 1806.

Stübler, Eberhard. *Leonhart Fuchs Leben und Werk.* Munich: Verlag der Münchner Drukke, 1928.

Stummvoll, Josef Leopold. "Die Praefekten der Bibliotheca Palatina Vindobonensis." *Die österreichische Nationalbibliothek Festschrift.* Vienna: H. Bauer, 1948. 67–71.

– *Geschichte der österreichischen Nationalbibliothek I. Die Hofbibliothek (1368–1922).* Vienna: Georg Prachner Verlag, 1968.

Stupperich, Martin. "Das Augsburger Interim als apokalyptisches Geschehnis nach den Königsberger Schriften Andreas Osianders." ARG, XLIV (1973). 225–245.

– *Osiander in Preussen, 1549–1552* [Arbeiten zur Kirchengeschichte 44]. Berlin and New York: de Gruyter, 1973.

Stupperich, Robert. "Melanchthons Gedanken zur Kirchenpolitik des Herzogs Mortiz von Sachsen." *Reformatio und Confessio. Festschrift für D. Wilhelm Maurer zum 65. Geburtstag am 7. Mai 1965.* Ed. Friedrich Wilhelm Kantzenbach and Gerhard Müller. Berlin and Hamburg: Lutherisches Verlagshaus, 1965. 84–97.

– *Der Unbekannte Melanchthon.* Stuttgart: W. Kohlhammer, 1961.

Suckale-Redlefsen, Gude. *The Black Saint Maurice.* Houston: Menil Foundation; Munich and Zurich: Verlag Schnell & Steiner, 1987.

Sulger-Gebing, Emil. "Dante in der deutschen Literatur bis zum Erscheinen der ersten vollständigen Übersetzung der Divina Commedia (1767/69)." *Zeitschrift für die vergleichende Literaturgeschichte.* N. F. VIII (1895). 221–253, 453–479.

Swift, Jonathan. *A Tale of a Tub with Other Early Works 1696–1707.* Ed. Herbert Davis. Oxford: Basel Blackwell, 1939.

Szöverffy, Josef. *Die Annalen der lateinischen Hymnendichtung. Ein Handbuch* I. Berlin: Erich Schmidt Verlag, 1964.

Talanga, Josip. "Paralipomena dialectices des Matthias Illyricus." Josip Matešić (ed.). *Matthias Flacius Illyricus–Leben & Werk. Internationales Symposium, Mannheim, Februar 1991.* Munich: Südosteuropa-Gesellschaft, 1993. 111–138.

Tangl, Michael. *Epistolae Bonifacii* [MGH Epistolae Selectae I]. Berlin: Weidmann, 1916.

– "Studien zur Neuausgabe der Bonifatius-Briefe I." *Neues Archiv für ältere deutsche Geschichtskunde* XL (1916). 639–790.

Tedeschi, John. "Toward a Statistical Profile of the Italian Inquisition, Sixteenth to Eighteenth Centuries." John Tedeschi, and William Monte (eds.). *The Persecution of Heresy: Collected Studies on the Inquisition in Early Modern Italy* [Medieval and Renaissance Texts and Studies 78]. Binghamton, N.Y.: Center for Medieval and Early Renaissance Studies, State University of New York, 1991.

Thalhofer, Valentin. *Handbuch der katholischen Liturgik*. Freiburg i. Br.: Herder. 1. Aufl. 1890–94.

Theobald, Hermann. *Beiträge zur Geschichte Ludwigs der Baiern*. Mannheim: Walter, 1897.

Theobald, Leonhard. *Die Reformationsgeschichte der Reichstadt Regensburg* II. Nuremberg: "Die Egge," 1951.

Thomas, Alan G. *Great Books and Book Collectors*. London: Weidenfeld and Nicolson, 1975.

Thorndike, Lynn. *A History of Magic and Experimental Science* V. New York and London: Columbia University Press, 1941.

Thouzellier, Christine. "La Place du De Periculis de Guillaume de Saint-Amour dans les Polémiques Universitaires du XIIIe Siècle." *Revue Historique* CLVI (1927). 69–83.

Thurston, Ethel (ed.). *The Conductus Collections of ms Wolfenbüttel W1099* [Recent Researches in the Music of the Middle Ages and Early Renaissance XI]. Madison: A–R Editions, 1980.

Tiraboschi, Girolamo. *Storia della Letteratura Italiana* VII. Milan: Società Tipografica dei Classici Italiana, 1824.

Toynbee, Paget. "John Foxe and the 'Editio Princeps' of Dante's Monarchia." *Dante Studies*. Oxford: Clarendon Press, 1921. 109–110.

– *Britain's Tribute to Dante in Literature and Art*. London: Publ. for the British Academy by H. Milford, Oxford University Press, 1921.

Tratz, Max. "Matthias Flacius Illyricus." *Lutherische Kirchen in der Welt: Jahrbuch des Martin Luther Bundes* XXII (1975). 9–42.

– Review of Rudolf Keller. *Der Schlüssel zur Schrift. Zeitschrift für bayrische Kirchengeschichte* LIV (1985). 243 f.

Trillhaas, Wolfgang. "Adiaphoron. Erneute Erwägung eines alten Begriffs." *Theologische Literaturzeitung* LXXIX (1954). 457–62.

Trinterud, Leonard J. *Elizabethan Puritanism*. New York: Oxford University Press, 1971.

Tschackert, Paul. *Die Entstehung der lutherischen und der reformierten Kirchenlehre samt ihren innerprotestantischen Gegensätzen*. Göttingen: Vandenhoeck und Ruprecht, 1910. Reprint, Göttingen: Vandenhoeck und Ruprecht, 1979.

Turner, Cuthbert Hamilton (ed.). *Ecclesiae occidentalis monumenta juris. antiquissimae. Canonum et conciliorum Graecorum interpretationes Latinae*. Oxford: Clarendon, 1899–1913.

Twesten, August Detlev. *Matthias Flacius Illyricus, eine Vorlesung. Mit autobiographischen Beilagen und einer Abhandlung über Melanchthons Verhalten zum Interim von Hermann Rössel*. Berlin: G. Bethge, 1844.

Ulenberg, Kaspar. "Vita et res gestae Matthiae Flacii Illyrici, ab Ortu ad Obitum usque." *Historia de vita, moribus, rebus gestis, studiis ac denique morte praedicantium Luther-*

anorum Philippi Melanchthonis, Matthiae Flacii Illyrici, Georgii Maioris, et Andreae Osiandri. Cologne: Bernardus Gualterus, 1622. 372–452.

Ullmann, Walter. "This Realm of England is an Empire." *Journal of Ecclesiastical History* XXX (1979). 175–203. Reprint, *Jurisprudence in the Middle Ages. Collected Studies.* London: Variorum Reprints, 1980.

Unterkircher, Franz. *Codex epistolaris Carolinus: Österreichische Nationalbibliothek Codex 449.* Einleitung und Beschreibung, Franz Unterkircher. Graz: Akademische Druck- und Verlagsanstalt, 1962.

– *Die datierten Handschriften in Wien ausserhalb der Österreichischen Nationalbibliothek bis zum Jahr 1600.* Vienna: Verlag der Österreichischen Akademie der Wissenschaften, 1981.

Vasoli, Cesare. "A Proposito di Francesco Patrizi, Gian Giorgo Patrizi, Baldo Lupatino e Flacio Illrico. Alcune Precisioni." *L'Umanesimo in Istria a cura di Vittore Branca e Sante Graciotti.* Florence: Olschoki, 1983. 37–61.

Veesenmeyer, Georg. "Von des Ulrich Velenus Schrifft, daß Petrus nie nach Rom gekommen sey, und die Schrifften dagegen." *Sammlung von Aufsätzen zur Erläuterung der Kirchen-, Literatur-, Münz-, und Sittengeschichte.* Ulm: In der Stettinschen Buchhandlung, 1827. 138–149.

Vergerio, Giovanni. *Von der wunderbaren Bekehrung Petri Pauli Vergerii Justinopolitanischen Bischoff, erwehlten Päpstl. Kardinals und Gesandtens in Teutschland wider D. Luther.* n. p. 1699.

Verheus, Simon. *Zeugnis und Gericht: Kirchengeschichtliche Betrachtungen bei Sebastian Franck und Matthias Flacius.* Tr. Ellen Vogelsang and R. Lamotte [Bibliotheca Humanistica et Reformatorica I]. Nieuwkoop: B. de Graaf, 1971.

Verkamp, Bernard J. *The Indifferent Mean: Adiaphorism in the English Reformation to 1554.* Athens, Ohio: Ohio University Press & Detroit: Wayne State University Press, 1977.

– "The Zwinglians and Adiaphorism." *Church History* XL (1973). 486 ff.

Verzeichnis der im deutschen Sprachgebiet erschienenen Drucke des XVI. Jahrhunderts (VD16). Ed. by the Bavarian State Library in Munich with the Herzog August Library in Wolfenbüttel. Stuttgart: Hiersemann, 1983.

Vetter, Theodor. *Englische Flüchtlinge in Zürich während der ersten Hälfte des Sechzehnten Jahrhunderts.* Zurich: Druck des art. Institut O. Füsli, 1893.

Visser, Derk. *Zacharius Ursinus the Reluctant Reformer.* New York: United Church Press, 1983.

Vogel, Cyrille. *Medieval Liturgy: An Introduction to the Sources.* Revised and translated by William B. Storey and Niels Krogh Rasmussen. Washington: Pastoral Press, 1986.

Vogt, Otto (ed.). *Dr. Johan Bugenhagens Briefwechsel.* Stettin: In Kommission bei Leon Saunien, 1888–89.

– "Melanchthon's und Bugenhagen's Stellung zum Interim und die Rechtfertigung des letztern in seinem Jonascommentar." *Jahrbuch für Protestantische Theologie* XIII (1887). 1–38.

Voigt, Johannes. *Briefwechsel der berühmten Gelehrten des Zeitalters der Reformation mit Herzog Albrecht von Preussen.* Königsberg: Bornträger, 1841.

– "Über Pasquille, Spottlieder und Schmähschriften aus der ersten Hälfte des 16. Jahrhunderts." *Raumers Taschenbuch* IX (1838). 321–524.

Voit, Hartmut. "Gallus und das Interim. Eine anonyme Druckschrift aus dem Jahr 1548." ARG, LXV (1974). 277–285.

– *Nikolaus Gallus: Ein Beitrag zur Reformationsgeschichte der nachlutherischen Zeit* [Einzelarbeiten aus der Kirchengeschichte Bayerns 54]. Neustadt a. d. Aisch: In Kommission bei Verlag Degener & Co., Inh. Gerhard Gessner, 1977.

Vollmer, Hans Arthur (ed.). *Bibel und deutsche Kultur* X. Potsdam: Athenaion, 1940.

Volz, Hans. *Die Frequenz der deutschen Universitäten in der Reformationszeit* [Deutscher Kulturatlas III]. Ed. Gerhard Lüdtke und Lute Mackensen. Berlin and Leipzig: de Gruyter, 1928.

– *Die Lutherpredigten des Johannes Mathesius.* Leipzig: M. Heinsius Nachfolger Eger & Sievers, 1930.

– *Martin Luthers Deutsche Bibel.* Hamburg: Friedrich Wittig, 1978.

Wackernagel, Hans Georg (ed.). *Die Matrikel der Universität.* 3 vols. *Basel.* Basel: Verlag der Universitätsbibliothek, 1951–1962.

Waddell, Helen. *The Wandering Scholars.* London: Constable, 1927.

Wagner, A. "Die Heliand Vorreden." *Zeitschrift für deutsches Altertum* XXV (1881). 173–181.

Wagner, Friedrich. "Dante in Deutschland: Sein staatlich-kirchliches Bild von 1417–1699." *Deutsches Dante-Jahrbuch* XVI (1934). 1–86.

Wagner, Harald. *An den Ursprüngen des Frükatholischen Problems. Die Ortbestimmung des Katholizismus im älteren Luthertum.* Frankfurt am Main: Josef Knecht, 1973.

Waitz, Georg (ed.). *Des Jordanus von Osnabrück Buch über den Römischen Reich* [Abhandlungen der historisch- philologischen Classe der königlichen Gesellschaft der Wissenschaften zu Göttingen]. Göttingen: Dieterische Buchhandlung, 1868.

Walch, Johannes Georg. *Historische und Theologische Einleitung in die Religionsstreitigkeiten der evangelischen Lutherischen Kirche.* 4 vols. Jena: Meyer, 1733–1739.

Waltz, Otto. "Epistolae Reformatorum I." ZKG, II (1878). 117–188.

Warmbrunn, Paul. *Zwei Konfessionen in einer Stadt. Das Zusammenleben von Katholiken und Protestanten in der Paritätischen Reichsstädten Augsburg, Biberach, Ravensburg und Dinkelsbühl von 1548 bis 1648.* Wiesbaden: Franz Steiner Verlag, 1983.

Wartenberg, Günther. "Nachwirkungen des Bauernkrieges in der albertinischen Politik unter Moritz von Sachsen (1547–1551)." *Jahrbuch für Regionalgeschichte* XVII (1979). 243–251

– "Philipp Melanchthon und die sächsische-albertinische Interimspolitik." *Lutherjahrbuch* LV (1988). 60–82.

Wattenbach, Wilhelm. *Deutschlands Geschichtsquellen im Mittelalter. Deutsche Kaiserzeit.* Hrsg. von Robert Holtzmann. Berlin: E. Ebering, 1938–43. Reprint, Darmstadt: Wissenschaftliche Buchgesellschaft, 1978.

– "Über Erfundene Briefe in Handschriften des Mittelalters, besonders Teufelsbriefe." *Sitzungsberichte der königlichen Preussischen Akademie der Wissenschaften zu Berlin* I, 1822. 91 ff.

Weber, Hans Emil. *Der Einfluss der protestantischen Schulphilosophie auf die orthodoxe lutherische Dogmatik.* Leipzig: Deichert, 1908. Reprint, Darmstadt: Wissenschaftliche Buchgesellschaft, 1969.

– *Reformation, Orthodoxie und Rationalismus.* 2 vols. Gütersloh.: C. Bertelsmann Verlag, 1937–1951. Reprint, Darmstadt: Wissenschaftliche Buchgesellschaft, 1966.

Wedel, Erwin. "Matthias Flacius, ein bedeutender kroatischer Humanist." *Matthias Flacius Illyricus 1575–1975* [Schriftenreihe des Regensburger Osteuropainstituts 2]. Regensburg: Lassleben, 1975. 23–35.

Wegele, Franz Xaver von. *Geschichte der deutschen Historiographie seit dem Auftreten des Humanismus* [Geschichte der Wissenschaft in Deutschland XX]. Munich and Leipzig: R. Oldenbourg, 1885.

Wegg, Jervis. *Antwerp 1477–1559.* London: Methuen & Co., 1916.

Weigel, Maximilian. "Michael Katzbeck, der letzte Abt des Klosters Reichenbach." *Zeitschrift für Bayrische Kirchengeschichte* XVIII (1949). 11–16.

Weigelt, Horst. *Spiritualistische Tradition im Protestantismus: die Geschichte des Schwenckfeldertums in Schlesien* [Arbeiten zur Kirchengeschichte 48]. Berlin: de Gruyter, 1973.

Weiland, J. Sperna and W. Th. M. Frijhoff. *Erasmus of Rotterdam: The Man and the Scholar.* Leiden et al.: E. J. Brill, 1988.

Weill, Georges. *De Guilelmi Postelli Vita et Indole.* Paris, 1892; Geneva: Slatkine Reprints, 1969.

Weiler, A. G. "The Turkish Argument and Christian Piety in Desiderius Erasmus' 'Consultatio de Bello Turcis Inferendo' (1530)." J. Sperna Weiland & W. Th. M. Frijhoff (eds.). *Erasmus of Rotterdam: The Man and the Scholar.* Leiden et al.: E. J. Brill, 1988. 30–39.

Weissenborn, Hermann. *Philipp Melanthons Briefwechsel über die Gründung der Universität Jena und seine Berufung an dieselbe aus zum Theil noch ungedruckten Briefen.* Jena: J. G. Schreiber, 1848.

Weller, Emil. "Die Lieder gegen das Interim." *Serapaeum* XXIII (1862). 289–297.

Weller, Johann Gottfried. *Altes aus allen Teilen der Geschichte* I. Chemnitz: Johann Christoph Stössel, 1762.

Welti, Manfred Edwin. *Der Basler Buchdruck und Britannien.* Basel: Helbing und Lichtenhahn, 1964.

Wendler, Johannes Christopherus. *De Praecipuorum Quorundam Sec. XVI et XVII Theologicorum Lutheranorum Martini Lutheri, Philippi Melanchthonis ... eruditae in ecclesiam meritis et scriptis.* Theological disputation, Altdorf: Cyril Osterlandus. Typis Kohlesii Acad. Typogr., 1710.

Werner, K. *Geschichte der Apologischen und Polemischen Literatur der Christlichen Theologie* IV. Schaffhausen: Hurter, 1865.

Westphal, F. *Zur Erinnerung an Fürst Georg den Gottseligen zu Anhalt* [Schriften des Vereins für Reformationsgeschichte 95]. Leipzig: In Kommissions Verlag von Rudolph Haupt, 1907.

Whitgift, John. *The Works of John Whitgift, Bishop of Salisbury.* ed. John Ayer. 3 vols. ed. Parker Society. Cambridge, 1851.

Widman, Simon. *Eine Mainzer Presse der Reformationszeit im Dienste der Katholischen Litteratur.* Paderborn: Ferdinand Schönigh, 1889.

Wiggers, Julius. *Kirchengeschichte Mecklenburgs.* Parchim and Ludwigslust: Hirstorff'sche Hofbuchhandlung, 1840.

Wilhelm, Friedrich. "Eine deutsche übersetzung der Praefatio." *Münchner Museum für Philologie des Mittelalters und der Renaissance* I (1911/12). 362–365.

Williams, George Huntston. "Joseph Priestly on Luther." Jaroslav Pelikan (ed.). *Interpreters of Luther. Essays in Honor of Wilhelm Pauck.* Philadelphia: Fortress, 1968. 121–158.

– *The Radical Reformation.* 3rd rev. ed. [Sixteenth Century Essays and Studies XV]. Kirksville, MO: Sixteenth Century Publishers, Inc. 1992.

– and Angel M. Mergal (eds.). *Spiritual and Anabaptist Writers. Documents Illustrative of the Radical Reformation* [The Library of Christian Classics 25]. London: SCM, 1957; Philadelphia: Westminster, 1957.

Williams, N. P. *The Grace of God.* London: Longmans, Green and Co., 1930.

Willkomm, Bernhard. "Beiträge zur Reformationsgeschichte aus Drucken und Handschriften der Universitätsbibliothek zu Jena." ARG, IX (1911–1912). 240–273.

Wilmart, André. "Poèmes de Gautier de Châtillon dans un Manuscrit de Charleville (Suite)." *Revue Bénédictine* XLIX (1937). 121–169, 322–365.

Wjtowytsch, Myron. *Papsttum und Konzile von den Anfängen bis zu Leo (440–461)* [Studien zur Entstehung der Überordnung des Papstes über Konzile]. Stuttgart: Anton Hiersemann, 1981.

Wolf, Gustav. *Quellenkunde der deutschen Reformationsgeschichte.* 2 Bde. Gotha, 1915–1922.

– *Zur Geschichte der deutschen Protestanten 1555–59.* Berlin: Oswald Seehagen, 1888. 304 ff.

Wolf, Johannes. "Ein bisher unbekannter Spottdruck auf das Augsburger Interim." *Zentralblatt für Bibliothekswesen* XLII. (1925). 9–19.

Wolf, Johannes. *Omnia Opera.* Frankfurt am Main: Hered. Henninigi Grossi, 1671.

Wolgast, Eike. "Bugenhagen in den politischen Krisen seiner Zeit." Hans-Günter Leder (ed.). *Johannes Bugenhagen, Gestalt und Wirkung.* Berlin: Evangelische Verlagsanstalt, 1989.

– "Der Streit um die Werke Luthers im 16. Jahrhundert." ARG, LIX (1968). 177–202.

– *Die Wittenberger Luther-Ausgabe* [Sonderdruck aus dem Archiv für Geschichte des Buchwesens XL, Lieferung 1–2]. Frankfurt a. M.: Buchhandler der Vereinigung, 1970.

Wollgast, Siegfried. [Sitzungsbericht der sächsischen Akademie der Wissenschaft Leipzig, Phil.-hist. Klasse. Bd. 122. Heft 6]. Berlin: Akademie Verlag, 1982.

Wolter, Michael. "Der Gegner als endzeitlicher Widersacher–Die Darstellung des Feinds in der jüdischen und christlicher Apokalyptik." Franz Bosbach (ed.). *Feindbilder. Die Darstellung des Gegners in der politischen Publizistik des Mittelalters und der Neuzeit.* Cologne, Weimar and Vienna: Böhlau, 1992. 23–40.

Wotschke, Theodor. "Francesco Stancaro." *Altpreussische Monatschrift* XLVII (1910). 496 ff.

Wright, Thomas. *The Latin Poems commonly Attributed to Walter Mapes.* London: Printed for the Camden Society. John Bowyer Nichols and Son, 1841.

Wrightman, William. "Quid sit Methodus? 'Method' in Sixteenth Century Medical teaching and 'Discovery'." *Journal of the History of Medicine* XIX (1964). 360–376.

Wundt, Max. *Die Geschichte der Philosophie an der Universität Jena.* Jena: Gustav Fischer, 1932.

Yates, Frances. *Astraea: The Imperial "Theme" in the Sixteenth Century.* London and Boston: Routledge and Kegan Paul, 1975.

– "Queen Elizabeth as Astraea." *Journal of the Warburg and Courtauld Institutes* X (1947). 27–82.

Zeeden, Ernst Walter. *Martin Luther und die Reformation im Urteil des deutschen Luthertums. Studien zum Selbstverständnis des lutherischen Protestantismus von Luthers Tode bis zum Beginn der Goethezeit.* 2 vols. Freiburg: Herder, 1952. Translation: *The Legacy of Luther.* Westminster, Maryland: The Newman Press, 1954.

Zeeveld, W. Gordon. *Foundations of Tudor Policy.* Cambridge, Mass: Harvard University Press, 1948.

Zeiblich, Christian Heinrich. *Historische Lebens-Beschreibung der Stiffts-Superintendenten in Merseberg von der Reformation an biß zu unseren Tagen.* Leipzig: Braun, 1752.

– *Zeichen um Himmel. Flugblätter des 16. Jahrhundert.* Catalog 15. Nuremberg: Germanisches Nationalmuseum. 1982.

Zeltner, Gustav Georg. *Kurtz-gefaßte Historie der gedruckten Bibel-Version und andrer Schriften D. Mart. Lutheri.* Nurenberg and Altdorf: Joh. Dan. Tanberg Erben, 1727.

Zenko, Franjo. "Flacius-Rezeption in Kroatien als ideologisierende Vermittlung mit dem gegenwärtigen Leben." Josip Matešić (ed.). *Matthias Flacius – Leben und Werk Internationales Symposium. Mannheim, Februar 1991.* Munich: Südosteuropa-Gesellschaft, 1993. 157–176.

Zeumer, K. *Quellensammlung zur Geschichte der deutschen Reichsverfassung im Mittelalter und Neuzeit.* 2. Aufl. Tübingen: Mohr, 1913.

Ziegler, Konrat (ed.). *Juli Firmici Materni V. C. De Errore Profanarum Religionum.* Leipzig: B. G. Teubner, 1907; Munich: Max Hueber, 1953.

– "Zur Überlieferungsgeschichte des Firmicus Maternus de Errore." *Rheinisches Museum für Philologie.* N. F. LX (1905). 417–424.

Zimmermann, Harald. *Ecclesia als Objekt der Historiographie* [Siztungsberichte der österreichischen Akademie der Wissenschaften, Philosophische- Historische Klasse 235, 4]. Graz, Cologne, Vienna: Hermann Böhlaus Nachf. 1960. 62–80.

– "Über das Anfangsdatum der Kirchengeschichte." *Archiv für Kulturgeschichte* XLI (1959). 1–34.

Zimmermann, Hildegard. "Von deutschen Holzschnitt der Reformationszeit." ARG, XXIII (1926). 101–112

Zorzi, Marino. *La Libreria di San Marco: Libri, Lettori. Società nella Venezia dei Dogi.* Milan: Arnoldo Mondadori, 1987.

MANUSCRIPTS MENTIONED

INDEX